Trade, Investment and Economic Growth

Pooja Lakhanpal · Jaydeep Mukherjee ·
Biswajit Nag · Divya Tuteja
Editors

Trade, Investment and Economic Growth

Issues for India and Emerging Economies

Springer

Editors
Pooja Lakhanpal
Department of Management
Indian Institute of Foreign Trade
New Delhi, Delhi, India

Jaydeep Mukherjee
Department of Economics
Indian Institute of Foreign Trade
New Delhi, Delhi, India

Biswajit Nag
Department of Economics
Indian Institute of Foreign Trade
New Delhi, Delhi, India

Divya Tuteja
Department of Economics
Indian Institute of Foreign Trade
New Delhi, Delhi, India

ISBN 978-981-33-6972-6 ISBN 978-981-33-6973-3 (eBook)
https://doi.org/10.1007/978-981-33-6973-3

This Springer imprint is published by the registered company Springer Nature Singapore Pte Ltd.
The registered company address is: 152 Beach Road, #21-01/04 Gateway East, Singapore 189721, Singapore

Foreword

The Indian Institute of Foreign Trade (IIFT) has established itself as an Academic Centre of Excellence in International Business. It is committed to high standards of teaching in international business as well as a centre for pioneering research and knowledge dissemination in the arena of foreign trade and policy issues. IIFT has been organizing the Empirical Issues in International Trade and Finance (EIITF) Research Conference series since 2008. From the beginning, the conference has brought to the fore academic discussions and discourse on contemporary issues relevant to international trade, finance and business as a whole. The themes of the conference series have reflected the rapid changes around the world, particularly contemporary themes which have been of interest to researchers in associated fields as well. The institute organized the Sixth EIITF on 18 and 19 December 2018 at its New Delhi Campus. In keeping with the latest developments, the themes of the conference were technology disruptions, global capital flows and international trade-drivers for economic development. The conference was attended by academicians, policy researchers, multilateral agencies, industry bodies and policymaking communities from across the globe.

The release of the current volume could not have been at a more appropriate time. International trade and capital flows, since the turn of the century, have been in a state of flux. In particular, international trade patterns have been marked by rising uncertainty, since the global financial crisis of 2008–2009 and the eurozone crisis of 2011–12. The world economy is currently reeling under an unprecedented health crisis due to spread of the COVID-19 pandemic which is expected to severely affect global economic activity. As a result, compared to the last year, growth in the global economy is expected to fall by as much as 3 per cent in the current year. IMF's *World Economic Outlook (WEO) Update (April 2020)* reports this to be much more severe than the growth contraction resulting from the financial crisis of 2008–09. Assuming that the pandemic is contained in the second half of 2020 and in view of the expansionary policy measures, *WEO (April 2020)* projects that a bounce back is expected in 2021, wherein the global economy is expected to expand by 5.8 per cent.

A key challenge for the global economy at the current juncture relates to the uncertainty regarding the time it would take for the pandemic to fade away and for economic activity to normalize. In the aftermath of the pandemic, consumer demand is expected to remain weak and employment in the informal sector is likely to remain stagnant. This is notwithstanding the bleak global growth prospects due to rising trade disputes and geopolitical tensions in 2018–19. The advanced economies have had a choppy and long road to recovery post the global financial crisis of 2008–09 (*Trade and Development Report 2019* (UNCTAD)).

While there is an urgent need for monetary as well as fiscal expansion, there may be limitations to the policy headroom. Another crucial aspect is the anchoring of inflationary expectations through communication by the monetary authorities. There is a risk of a debt-deflation spiral which may be abated by a strong government policy stance. In order to facilitate recovery, regulatory foresight in the form of strong insolvency and debt enforcement frameworks is required. Finally, multilateral cooperation is the need of the hour, especially in the economic as well as medical arena. This would mean the removal of tariff and non-tariff barriers to allow international trade and functioning of global supply chains along with measures to boost the global financial sentiment. Nations would need to work side by side to share information about the virus crucial for containment and development of the vaccine.

The present volume has been contributed by scholars who participated at the EIITF 2018 Conference and intends to make a significant contribution to the existing literature by including selected empirical works on critical policy issues in the spheres of international trade and foreign capital flows and their role in fostering economic growth and development in the context of India and several emerging market economies. Twenty papers included in the volume are classified appropriately under four broad themes, namely: (1) International Trade: Empirical and Policy Issues, (2) Foreign Capital Flows and Issues in Finance, (3) Trade and Development Interface: Implications for India and Emerging Economies and (4) Analysis of Sector-level Growth and Development in India, all of which are extremely relevant in the current context. The chapters in the volume have been contributed by leading academicians and researchers involved in the applied area of economics. I am confident that the empirical works presented in this comprehensive volume could serve as ready reference for academicians, researchers and policymakers, particularly in emerging economies facing similar challenges.

Prof. Manoj Pant
Director and Vice Chancellor
Indian Institute of Foreign Trade (IIFT)
New Delhi, India

Acknowledgements

All of the chapters included in this volume were originally presented in the 6th Conference on Empirical Issues in International Trade and Finance (EIITF) organized by the Indian Institute of Foreign Trade (IIFT) Delhi on 13 and 14 December 2018. The conference focused on technology disruptions, global capital flows and international trade-drivers for economic development.

Professor Manoj Pant, Director, IIFT, was a guiding light and extended his unconditional support. We are obligated to Springer for making this collection of papers accessible to students and researchers working in related fields in the form of a book. We are grateful to Nupoor Singh, Editor, Springer, and Daniel Joseph G. for their constant support in this endeavour. The authors are also grateful to two anonymous referees for constructive suggestions and comments.

We are thankful to all the authors who contributed their research work for the volume. We also gratefully acknowledge competent and diligent support from Ashima Puniani and Saloni Khurana, for compiling and editing the chapters in the volume. Research support from Tanya Dawar is also gratefully acknowledged. Lastly, we thank our families for facilitating us in countless ways.

Introduction[1]

This chapter introduces the background, recent developments, themes and the papers contained in this conference volume titled *Trade, Investment and Economic Growth: Issues for India and Emerging Economies*. The first section presents the background to the key issues covered in the volume. Subsequently, we discuss the recent developments and performance of emerging economies in the second and third sections. The last section discusses the themes which form the focal point of the papers and briefly outlines papers included in the present volume.

Background

The twenty-first century is being shaped by changing views on international trade in both goods and services along with global capital flows and their role in affecting the economic outcomes of various countries. Lately, the global economy has been under a lot of strain and is facing sluggish economic growth. This may be attributed to the dawdling trade along with mounting tariffs, unstable financial flows, decreased business confidence and rising policy uncertainty among others. Climate change, divergent public views on critical issues and an increasing distrust of political parties are also risking the medium- and long-term growth. In view of changes in volume as well as pattern of trade and investment flows, there is an urgent need to study the established paradigms of economics through a new lens with advances in theoretical and empirical models.

To add to the fire, the intensified trade tensions among the USA and China, Brexit negotiations, the shutdown of the US federal government, US-Iran trade rifts, Italy's conflict with EU regarding public debt and uncertainty in Mexico's policy direction under the new government are some of the many upsetting policy news from all around the world. China, one of the largest economies in the world, has been experiencing a decline in its growth due to policy pressures in the face of a debt overhang,

[1]Diligent research work by Tanya Dawar is gratefully acknowledged.

slower infrastructural investment and decline in exports as a result of the US tariffs. This has badly affected the imports in the economy and exports of its trade partners in Asia and Europe. India too is also slowing down, and its exports to the world are experiencing a secular decline.

With this backdrop, Indian Institute of Foreign Trade organized its 6th Conference on Empirical Issues in International Trade and Finance during 13–14 December 2018 at its New Delhi Campus. The editors of this volume have selected some of the best papers presented at the conference. The distinctive aspects of the volume are that it covers topical issues pertaining to international trade, capital flows and finance, development and sector-level growth in India with a focus on the policy point of view. Secondly, the discourse focuses mainly on empirical work and econometric aspects. Finally, the overall focus is on the lessons learnt from the trade–capital flows–growth experience of emerging economies.

Recent Developments

The global economy has been in a lot of flux lately; the paradigms for achieving a healthy and steady economic growth are continuously getting redefined. The world is currently staring at an unprecedented health crisis presented by the outbreak of the COVID-19 pandemic. The global economy, currently grappling with a health crisis resulting from the spread of COVID-19, is likely to witness a contraction in the economic activity. However, it is not possible to stray away from the existing theory, literature and evidence on the pillars of achievement of robust growth.

It is notable that the health crisis due to spread of COVID-19 is associated with a huge output loss. The growth in the global economy, year on year, is expected to fall by as much as 3 per cent. IMF's World Economic Outlook (WEO) Update (April 2020) reports this to be much more severe than the growth contraction resulting from the financial crisis of 2008–09. There is considerable ambiguity regarding the duration and intensity of this surprise. Clearly, innovative policy, both medical and economic, is the need of the hour to counter the effects of the crisis.

Assuming that the pandemic is contained in the second half of 2020, and in view of the expansionary policy measures, WEO (April 2020) projects that a bounce back is expected in 2021, wherein the world economy is expected to expand by 5.8 per cent. The recovery in global economic activity in 2021 is marked by enormous uncertainty. The implementation of effective policies is central to a gradual normalization of economic activity and a recovery in 2021 (WEO Update, April 2020). Cross-country cooperation on medical supplies, vaccines, therapies and other interventions is critical to slow down the transmission of the COVID-19 pandemic. However, countries should refrain from the imposition of additional trade restrictions and resort external funding wherever required. Apart from cooperation on healthcare systems, targeted policies, at both the local and national levels, are imperative at the current point in time.

The articles included in this volume provide contemporary dynamics of the pre-COVID period which will probably remain important in the post-COVID world also as globalization has made a tectonic shift to economic management. Perhaps, the post-COVID world will try to align the new reality with some of the fundamental aspects of the twenty-first-century world which are expressed through the papers. In particular, issues related to the development of emerging economies through the trade and finance channels are at the heart of the economic growth literature. Therefore, the papers in the volume bring to the fore critical issues which merit the attention of the policymakers and growth enthusiasts and these experiences will serve as lessons for the way forward in the post-COVID 'normal'.

Performance of Emerging Economies

The critical role played by investment and trade in the context of engendering economic growth cannot be emphasized enough. Truth be told, a vast majority of advanced economies have been able to sustain the growth momentum in view of conducive conditions for investment and trade. This is particularly true of the emerging and developing economies (EMDEs) which have struggled with the 'twin deficits' of trade deficit and budget deficit in the past. Before we delve further into the role played by investment and trade in economic growth of a nation, we define EMDEs and discuss their key economic performance measures.

As of June 2020, the World Bank has classified the countries given in Table 1 as emerging and developing economies (EMDEs) which include some of the largest and most populous economies of the world such as China, India and Brazil.

Table 1 Emerging market and developing economies (World Bank)

Country	Continent group
China	East Asia and Pacific
Indonesia	
Thailand	
Russia	Europe and Central Asia
Turkey	
Poland	
Brazil	Latin America and the Caribbean
Mexico	
Argentina	
Saudi Arabia	Middle East and North Africa
Iran	
Egypt	

(continued)

Table 1 (continued)

Country	Continent group
India	South Asia
Pakistan	
Bangladesh	
Nigeria	Sub-Saharan Africa
South Africa	
Angola	

Source Global Economic Prospects, World Bank, June 2020

Table 2 presents the rate of growth of real GDP for the advanced and emerging market and developing economies (EMDEs) in 2015–21. Clearly, the EMDEs have been growing at a much faster rate than the advanced economies over the period 2015–21. In particular, China and India have been the fastest growing and largest EMDEs during the last few years.

Table 2 Annual estimates and forecasts (f) of real GDP (World Bank)

	2015	2016	2017	2018e	2019f	2020f	2021f
World	**2.9**	**2.6**	**3.1**	**3.0**	**2.6**	**2.7**	**2.8**
Advanced economies	**2.3**	**1.7**	**2.3**	**2.1**	**1.7**	**1.5**	**1.5**
USA	2.9	1.6	2.2	2.9	2.5	1.7	1.6
Euro area	2.1	2.0	2.4	1.8	1.2	1.4	1.3
Japan	1.2	0.6	1.9	0.8	0.8	0.7	0.6
Emerging market and developing economies (EMDEs)	**3.8**	**4.1**	**4.5**	**4.3**	**4.0**	**4.6**	**4.6**
Commodity-exporting EMDE	0.8	1.5	2.1	2.2	2.1	3.1	3.0
Other EMDE	6.1	6.0	6.1	5.8	5.2	5.5	5.5
Other EMDE excluding China	5.2	5.1	5.4	4.9	4.2	4.8	5.0
East Asia and Pacific	6.5	6.3	6.5	6.3	5.9	5.9	5.8
China	6.9	6.7	6.8	6.6	6.2	6.1	6.0
Indonesia	4.9	5.0	5.1	5.2	5.2	5.3	5.3
Thailand	3.1	3.4	4.0	4.1	3.5	3.6	3.7
Europe and Central Asia	1.1	1.9	4.1	3.1	1.6	2.7	2.9
Russia	−2.5	0.3	1.6	2.3	1.2	1.8	1.8
Turkey	6.1	3.2	7.4	2.6	−1.0	3.0	4.0
Poland	3.8	3.1	4.8	5.1	4.0	3.6	3.3
Latin America and the Caribbean	0.1	−0.3	1.7	1.6	1.7	2.5	2.7
Brazil	−3.5	−3.3	1.1	1.1	1.5	2.5	2.3
Mexico	3.3	2.9	2.1	2.0	1.7	2.0	2.4
Argentina	2.7	−2.1	2.7	−2.5	−1.2	2.2	3.2

(continued)

Table 2 (continued)

Middle East and North Africa	2.9	5.1	1.2	1.4	1.3	3.2	2.7
Saudi Arabia	4.1	1.7	−0.7	2.2	1.7	3.1	2.3
Iran	−1.3	13.4	3.8	−1.9	−4.5	0.9	1.0
Egypt	4.4	4.3	4.2	5.3	5.5	5.8	6.0
South Asia	7.1	8.1	6.7	7.0	6.9	7.0	7.1
India	8.0	8.2	7.2	7.2	7.5	7.5	7.5
Pakistan	4.1	4.6	5.4	5.8	3.4	2.7	4.0
Bangladesh	6.6	7.1	7.3	7.9	7.3	7.4	7.3
Sub-Saharan Africa	3.0	1.3	2.6	2.5	2.9	3.3	3.5
Nigeria	2.7	−1.6	0.8	1.9	2.1	2.2	2.4
South Africa	1.3	0.6	1.4	0.8	1.1	1.5	1.7
Angola	0.9	−2.6	−0.1	−1.7	1.0	2.9	2.8

Source Global Economic Prospects, World Bank, June 2020

Table 3 Annual estimates and forecasts (f) of fixed investment rates in EMDEs (World Bank)

	2015	2016	2017	2018e	2019f	2020f	2021f
East Asia and Pacific	6.5	6.6	5.3	5.3	5.1	5.1	4.9
Europe and Central Asia	0.4	−0.1	6.3	2.5	−0.9	3.3	3.6
Latin America and the Caribbean	−4.5	−5.3	−0.2	2.2	1.3	3.1	4.4
Middle East and North Africa	1.6	−0.3	2.4	3.7	4.4	5.7	6.4
South Asia	3.5	7.7	7.0	10.5	8.3	7.8	7.9
Sub-Saharan Africa	3.7	−0.6	4.7	5.8	5.9	6.1	6.7

Source Global Economic Prospects, World Bank, June 2020

Table 3 depicts the fixed investment rates for EMDEs by region during 2015–21. We notice that the EMDEs located in Europe and Central Asia have had a relatively low rate of fixed investment in the recent past. However, the South Asian EMDEs have displayed a relatively consistent and higher rate of fixed investment along with those in East Asia and Pacific. EMDEs in Middle East and North Africa as well as those in sub-Saharan Africa are showing much promise and have an upward trend in the investment rates. Finally, the EMDEs located in Latin America and the Caribbean have a very volatile performance over the period 2015–21.

Table 4 focuses on the contribution of net exports or trade balance to GDP in case of EMDEs. We find that, in majority of the cases, the net exports' contribution to GDP growth has been negative or at best low. In case of Europe and Central Asia as well as Middle East and North Africa, the contribution has been consistently decreasing over 2015–21.

Figure 1 shows that general government gross debt levels of emerging economies reduced sharply post 2008 due to the global financial crisis. It was also adversely

Table 4 Annual estimates and forecasts (f) of net exports' contribution to growth in EMDEs (World Bank)

	2015	2016	2017	2018e	2019f	2020f	2021f
East Asia and Pacific	−0.1	−0.8	0.4	−0.9	−0.4	−0.4	−0.5
Europe and Central Asia	3.0	0.3	−0.7	1.0	0.5	−0.1	−0.4
Latin America and the Caribbean	1.2	0.8	−0.4	−0.3	0.2	−0.2	−0.2
Middle East and North Africa	2.0	4.8	−0.2	1.4	−0.5	0.8	0.4
South Asia	−0.2	−0.3	−2.0	−2.1	−0.6	−0.6	−0.6
Sub-Saharan Africa	0.0	1.6	1.2	−0.6	−0.2	−0.1	−0.2

Source Global Economic Prospects, World Bank, June 2020

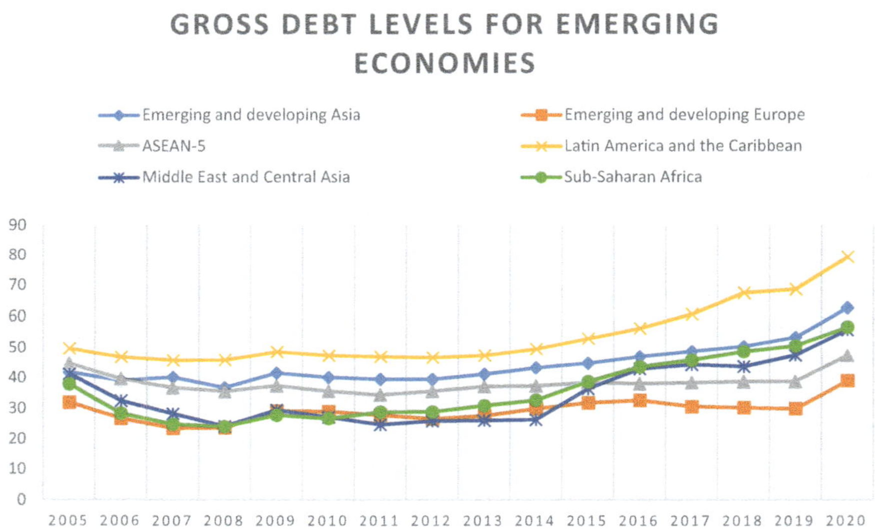

Fig. 1 General government gross debt of emerging economies between 2005 and 2020 as percentage of GDP (IMF). *Source* IMF World Economic Outlook Data (October 2020)

affected between 2014 and 2016 as a result of the collapse of commodity prices worldwide. Finally, it has further deteriorated in 2020 due to the ongoing COVID-19 pandemic.

Themes and Papers in the Current Volume

The current volume intends to contribute to the existing literature by covering select works on crucial policy issues in the international trade and financial flows and their role in fostering economic development in the context of India and several other emerging economies. In line with the research areas, twenty-one papers included in the volume are classified under four broad areas, namely:

(1) International Trade: Empirical and Policy Issues,
(2) Foreign Capital Flows and Issues in Finance,
(3) Trade and Development Interface: Implications for India and Emerging Economies and
(4) Analysis of Sector-level Growth and Development in India.

The papers included in this volume have dealt with emerging research questions on these broad themes empirically. In addition, detailed literature survey, discussions on data availability and issues relating to statistical estimation techniques in theoretical background ensure that each paper significantly contributes to the ever-growing literature on international trade and capital flows. The chapters in the current volume are contributed by leading academicians and researchers involved in the applied area of economics. The empirical evidences provided here could serve as ready reference for academicians, researchers and policymakers, particularly in emerging economies facing similar challenges.

The first part concerns empirical and policy issues relevant to international trade and includes six chapters, and it will be interesting to see how trade relations among economies shape up in the post-COVID world. The coverage of different papers in the volume is as follows. Chapter 1 of the volume is by Kanika Pathania, and it offers an understanding of the effective rate of protection by empirically estimating the inverted duty structure for 14 industries in India for the period 2000–2014. The study utilizes a modified version of Corden's measure of effective rate of protection. The paper finds that the higher the extent of positive protection, the lesser is the chance of duty inversion. Inverse duty structure is found for the Indian industry segments, viz. electronics and optical products, paper and paper products, computer, pharmaceuticals, machinery and equipment, and other transport equipment. The paper assumes significance as there is a suspected resurgence of 'protectionism' in recent times. The following chapter by Priyanta Ghosh and Aparna Sawhney focuses on whether a firm's home market performance plays a role in its decision to participate in exports for Indian manufacturing firms for the period 2000–2014. The study utilizes micro-level panel data to estimate a random effects Probit model and discern the export behaviour of new exporters vs. non-exporters basis their performance in the home market. The paper finds the interesting conclusion that firms which perform better in the home market are more likely to enter the export market in future. The third paper in the section by Vaishnavi Sharma and Akhilesh Mishra discusses the Indo-African trade with a focus on the post global financial crisis period. They utilize a generalized gravity model for overall trade, imports and exports over the period 1991–2014. The estimation results suggest that income levels of the trading partners, openness of the African nation, GDP of the African trade partner, inflation in India and the exchange rate are the key determinants of trade between India and African economies. The next chapter by Ganapati Mendali tests for the validity of the J-curve for India vis-à-vis BRICS nations using monthly data from 2011 to 2017 using panel co-integration methodology. The findings of the paper suggest that there does not exist a J-curve for the Indian economy. This chapter indicates that policies related to currency management merit further empirical attention. Chapter 5 by Divya Nagraj and Ishita Ghosh examines the challenges for trade between India and ASEAN economies with an emphasis on factors that contribute to trade costs. The authors employ the Novy approach to the gravity model of trade and discover that shipping connectivity and distance are major factors that contribute to rising trade costs. There are other costs such as those of sanitization which have increased in the current circumstances. The last chapter in the part by Areej Aftab Siddiqui and Parul Singh studies the relationship between information and communications technology (ICT) penetration and exports, imports and trade openness for major trading economies over the period 2001–2018. The authors construct an ICT penetration index using principal component analysis based on data for the trade of ICT goods and services, Internet use, mobile and broadband subscriptions. The authors utilize other control variables such as financial development index, domestic investment, foreign direct investment, exchange rate and growth and investigate the relationship between trade and ICT penetration while controlling cross-country effects. The chapter finds that there exists a significant link between ICT penetration and exports, imports and trade openness for the sampled countries. It is notable that the role of ICT in the post-COVID world cannot be emphasized enough.

The second part focuses on international capital flows as well as issues in finance and consists of six chapters, and these must be kept in mind while analysing the behaviour of FDI flows in the post-COVID scenario. The first chapter in part two by Ishita Ghoshal, Saylee Jog, Uday Sinha and Ishita Ghosh discusses the macroeconomic factors that impact foreign direct investment (FDI) inflows into emerging economies. The panel data under consideration comprises 17 emerging economies between 2000 and 2017. The findings suggest that capital formation, GDP growth rate, size of the economy, labour force participation rate, foreign exchange reserves and savings lead to higher FDI inflows into emerging economies. The subsequent chapter by Aparna Sawhney and Rashmi Rastogi studies the pattern of inward FDI to India and assesses the factors affecting the FDI into Indian industries. The chapter examines the composition of the FDI inflow by industry-specific characteristics (at disaggregated 3-digit industry classification) for Indian manufacturing firms and evaluates the characteristics of high-income source nations determining FDI in different Indian industries, over the period 2000 to 2014. The findings suggest that capital-intensive industries have attracted significant FDI inflows. Further, the source-country analysis shows FDI from capital-abundant, large nations, and especially those with stringent environmental regulations has been flowing to polluting industries. Chapter 9 by Aneesha Chitgupi inspects the current account sustainability and intertemporal budget constraint for India using the autoregressive distributed lag (ARDL) methodology for quarterly data from 2000 to 2017. The analysis reveals that exports and imports are co-integrated in the long run and the intertemporal budget constraint validity cannot be rejected for India. The next chapter by Saswata Chaudhury, Nitya Nanda and Bhawna Tyagi focuses on the role played by FDI in economic growth of South Asia with a special emphasis on greenfield versus merger and acquisition. The results indicate that the strength and pattern of impact of FDI depend on the nature of FDI (greenfield vs. M&A) as well as country-specific issues (such as domestic investment, inflation, infrastructure, external trade, among others). The fifth chapter in the part by P. K. Das discusses risk modelling by coherent measure using a family of generalized hyperbolic distributions. The study identifies the appropriate probability distribution for describing the return of BSE SENSEX to be the generalized hyperbolic family of distributions. The validity of the family of distributions was found to be adequate for describing the probability density based on AIC and likelihood function. The last chapter in the part by Kanika Dhingra and Sheeba Kapil analyses the impact of macroeconomic variables on stock market using co-integration analysis for monthly data from 1993 to 2019. The factors included in the analysis include wholesale price index (WPI), money supply (M3), consumer price index (CPI), index of industrial production (IIP), trade balance (TB), gold price (GP), call money rate (CMR), exchange rate (ER) and foreign portfolio investment (FPI).

Trade and development interface with a focus on implications for India and other emerging economies with five chapters is the next part of the volume. Trade has served as an engine of economic growth and development in the past. These chapters are a key reminder during the 'new normal' of the manner in which development outcomes may be achieved. The first paper in the part by Biswajit Nag and Saloni Khurana conducts a firm-level analysis to examine the relationship between employment generation and trade for India. The study employs Annual Survey of Industries data from 2008–09 to 2015–16 and finds that exporting industries' overall growth in employment is higher than the manufacturing sector as a whole for India. The next chapter by O. Olaiya and A. Bello assesses the complementary role of institutions to study the relationship between trade liberalization and poverty alleviation in Nigeria. The paper uses the time-varying parameter (TVP) approach of state-space model and fully modified ordinary least squares and shows that improvement in macroeconomic policies, indicators and institutions was on an average a declining function of poverty. Interestingly, policy inconsistencies have led to a sharp upward and downward movement in poverty rate for Nigeria. The third chapter in this part by Manoj Pant and Nidhi Dhamija focuses on the interface between trade liberalization, growth and poverty in India. The chapter uses panel data techniques on the data collected from NSSO's thick survey rounds (1993–94, 2004–05, 2009–10 and 2011–12) for 21 major states of India. The study concludes that trade liberalization process has helped in raising the per capita income levels in the Indian economy. The next chapter in the part by Vijaya Katti analyses India's labour-intensive exports (textile and clothing, leather products, gems and jewellery and electronic goods) and recommended policies to enhance exports to the USA. The paper also focuses on the competitors for India in the US market for these products and the reasons for India's poor performance in the US market relative to its competitions. The final chapter in the part by Debashis Chakraborty and Biswajit Nag presents empirical evidence and policy suggestions in the context of United Nations Economic Commission for Europe (UNECE) Agreements on harmonization of vehicle standards in India. Using WITS-SMART simulation, the authors suggest that there could be a degree of divergence in the pure tariff reduction outcomes in Indo-EU sectoral export and imports.

The last part deals with an analysis of trends in sectoral growth and development for India and includes four chapters. With an enhanced focus on 'Vocal for Local' by the Indian government, a sectoral perspective on growth and development makes for a fascinating exploration. The first chapter by Sanchita Roy Chowdhury and Siddhartha K. Rastogi evaluates the success of the 'Make in India' launched scheme by the Government of India in 2014. The study focuses on the electronics sector and chooses 46 items of six-digit HS code under the broad category of 'electrical and electronics goods'. The results show incongruent trends in terms of exports and imports for different products. The scheme is extremely important in the post-COVID times where looking inwards is the way forward in economic growth. The second chapter in the part by Taufeeque Ahmad Siddiqui and Kashif Iqbal Siddiqui utilizes the structural equation modelling framework to investigate the causal linkage between financial inclusion and telecommunication for the Indian states of Kerala and Bihar. The results suggest that despite the variation in the development of the two states, there exists a causality between telecommunication and financial inclusion variables in both states. The impact of telecom on financial inclusion is relatively higher, but the reverse causality is also found to be significant. The following chapter by Mousami Prasad and Trupti Mishra examines the relationship between environmental efficiency and trade theory and presents evidence from the metal sector for India. The authors utilize multiple output production technology in an output distance approach and stochastic frontier analysis to estimate the environmental efficiency. Findings of the study suggest that there exists a positive role of trade on environmental efficiency in case of metal firms. The last chapter of the part is by Anil K. Kanungo and Abhishek Jha and evaluates the prospects for air services in Indonesia under the Modified General Agreement on Trade in Services by focusing on the India–China dimension. The paper studies the future prospects in terms of providing air services to Indonesia by calculating the RCA index to arrive at export prospects. The research methodology includes World Input-Output Table and National Input-Output Table (NIOT) Database to evaluate Indonesia's outlook in air services.

Pooja Lakhanpal
Jaydeep Mukherjee
Biswajit Nag
Divya Tuteja

References

International Monetary Fund. (2020. April). *World Economic Outlook*. IMF WEO.
International Monetary Fund. (2020, October). *World Economic Outlook*. IMF WEO.
World Bank. (2020, June). *Global Economic Prospects*. World Bank.

Contents

Editors and Contributors

About the Editors

Pooja Lakhanpal is Professor and Head, Executive Management Programmes Division at Indian Institute of Foreign Trade, New Delhi. She obtained her Ph.D. in Humanities and Social Sciences from Indian Institute of Technology, Mumbai in 2000. Dr. Lakhanpal has more than 27 years of work experience in both industry and academics. She has worked in the corporate sector with reputed firms like Tata Consultancy Services, Drshti Strategic Research Services, AC Nielsen and Silverline Industries amongst others, in domain areas of Strategic Consulting and Business Research. She has also been associated with leading Indian corporates like Reliance Industries, Godrej, M&M and globally reputed firms like Unilever, P&G, Samsung, Toyota, Bayer, J&J, Kellogg's, BNP Paribas to name a few. Dr. Lakhanpal has also worked with various PSEs, Ministries, State Governments and Export Promotion Organisations. She was also a recipient of National Education Leadership Awards "Best Teacher in Human Resource Management" in July 2016 and was awarded "Best Professor in Human Resource Management" by World HRD Congress in February 2019. Her work was awarded "Best Paper" in the 5th International Conference on Social Sciences held in September 2018 at Colombo, Sri Lanka. Her research interests include sustainable business practices, business excellence and organisational transformation, corporate social responsibility, international business negotiations, human resource management etc.

Jaydeep Mukherjee is Associate Professor at Indian Institute of Foreign Trade, New Delhi. He was a Gold Medallist in Economics from Jadavpur University both at the undergraduate (Bachelors) and postgraduate (Masters) levels and was awarded Ph.D. from the same instiution in 2006. He has around 18 years of teaching and research experience and has completed more than 15 funded research projects sponsored by reputed organizations in India and abroad, namely, International Finance Corporation (IFC) under World Bank, DFID-UK, PwC, Reserve Bank of India, Ministry of External Affairs, Spices Board, Ministry of Statistics and Programme Implementation, Ministry of Commerce and Industry, Government of India, Indian

Embassy in Iran, etc. Dr. Mukherjee research papers are published in reputed peer-reviewed international journals namely, *Journal of Policy Modeling*, *Journal of Asian Economics*, *Management Research Review*, *South Asian Journal of Macroeconomics and Public Finance*, *Review of Market Integration*, *Journal of World Trade*, *Journal of World Investment and Trade*, *Global Business Review*, etc. He has also edited a book titled *Trade, Investment and Economic Development in Asia: Empirical and Policy Issues*. He is Associate Editor of *Foreign Trade Review*, quarterly journal of Indian Institute of Foreign Trade. His current areas of teaching and research interest include macroeconomic policy, open economy macroeconomy, international finance, time-series econometric applications in macroeconomics and finance, energy economics.

Biswajit Nag is Head of Economics Division and Professor of Economics at the Indian Institute of Foreign Trade (IIFT), New Delhi. He has been involved in empirical economic research for more than two decades in addition to have taught both in India and overseas. He has been a Visiting Research Fellow at the Institute of Developing Economies, Tokyo during 2018–19 and ICCR short term Chair Professor of India Studies at Ukraine in Feb, 2014. Earlier he was associated with Poverty and Development Division of UNESCAP, Bangkok in 2003–04. Dr. Nag has completed number of projects for Government of India and international agencies such as UN, World Bank, ADB, WTO, EU, DFID, JICA etc. He is also an advisor on Global Value Chain to Asia Pacific Research and Training Network on Trade (ARTNet) promoted by the UN-ESCAP. He is also a member of GERPISA, a European Consortium of Researchers on Automobile Sector. His current research interest covers areas of international production networks, global value chains, trade in services, regional trade agreements, trade and development. He has authored and edited number of books: *My World with Rafiki: An Economic Travelogue and Miscellany* (2014), *Business Innovation and ICT Strategies* (co-authored, 2018), and *India's Trade Analytics: Trends and Opportunities* (co-edited, 2019).

Prof. Divya Tuteja is Assistant Professor at the Indian Institute of Foreign Trade, Delhi since 2018. Earlier, she has also taught as Assistant Professor (Ad-hoc) at the Delhi School of Economics, University of Delhi from 2013 to 2018. She has also worked as a Manager in a reputed private bank for a year. She has taught courses at the Masters (MBA and MA Economics) and Ph.D. levels in the following areas, Business Economics, Econometrics (both introductory and advanced), Growth Theory (introductory) and Macroeconomics. She has also conducted training programmes for the Indian Economic Service (IES) officers. She received her doctoral degree from the Delhi School of Economics in 2015. She is recipient of the prestigious “Prof. M.J. Manohar Rao Award” bestowed to Young Economist for the year 2018.

Her research interests include macroeconomics, applications of time series and international financial markets where she has worked on inter-linkages across international asset markets, impact of financial crises and the possibility of ‘financial contagion’. She has published in international journals such as *World Development*, *Economic Modelling*, *Singapore Economic Review* and *Macroeconomics and*

Finance for Emerging Market Economies. She is currently involved in a government funded research project as well. She has presented papers in more than 20 national and international conferences.

Contributors

A. A. Bello Department of Economics, Faculty of Social Sciences, Usmanu Danfodiyo University, Sokoto, Nigeria

D. Chakraborty Indian Institute of Foreign Trade, Kolkata, India

S. Chaudhury The Energy and Resources Institute, New Delhi, India

Aneesha Chitgupi Fiscal Policy Institute (FPI), Government of Karnataka, Bengaluru, India

S. Roy Chowdhury IIM Indore, Indore, India

Prabir Kumar Das Indian Institute of Foreign Trade, Kolkata, India

N. Dhamija Hindu College, University of Delhi, Delhi, India

K. Dhingra IIFT, Delhi, New Delhi, India

I. Ghoshal Fergusson College (Autonomous), Pune, India

I. Ghosh Symbiosis School of Economics, Symbiosis International (Deemed University), Pune, Maharashtra, India

Priyanta Ghosh University of Gour Banga, Malda, India

Abhishek Jha Centre for the Study of Regional Development, Jawaharlal Nehru University, New Delhi, India

S. Jog Gokhale Institute of Politics and Economics, Pune, India

Anil K. Kanungo Lal Bahadur Shastri Institute of Management (LBSIM) Delhi, Dwarka, New Delhi, India

S. Kapil IIFT, Delhi, New Delhi, India

Vijaya Katti Indian Institute of Foreign Trade, New Delhi, India

S. Khurana Indian Institute of Foreign Trade, New Delhi, India

Ganapati Mendali Anchalik Kishan College, Bheden, Bargarh, Odisha, India

Akhilesh Mishra Department of Economics, SD (PG) College, Ghaziabad, India

T. Mishra India Institute of Technology, Bombay, India

B. Nag Indian Institute of Foreign Trade, New Delhi, India

D. Nagraj Symbiosis School of Economics, Symbiosis International (Deemed University), Pune, Maharashtra, India

N. Nanda Council for Social Development, New Delhi, India

Muftau Olaiya Olarinde Department of Economics, Faculty of Social Sciences, Usmanu Danfodiyo University, Sokoto, Nigeria

M. Pant Indian Institute of Foreign Trade (IIFT), Delhi, India

K. Pathania Department of Economics, Delhi School of Economics, Delhi, India

M. Prasad India Institute of Technology, Bombay, India

R. Rastogi Symbiosis Centre for Management Studies (Constituent of Symbiosis International (Deemed) University), Noida, India

S. Rastogi IIM Indore, Indore, India

Aparna Sawhney Centre for International Trade and Development, Jawaharlal Nehru University, New Delhi, India

Vaishnavi Sharma Indira Gandhi Institute of Development Research (IGIDR), Mumbai, India

Areej Aftab Siddiqui Indian Institute of Foreign Trade, New Delhi, India

Kashif Iqbal Siddiqui Centre for Management Studies, Jamia Millia Islamia, New Delhi, India

Taufeeque Ahmad Siddiqui Centre for Management Studies, Jamia Millia Islamia, New Delhi, India

Parul Singh Indian Institute of Foreign Trade, New Delhi, India

U. Sinha Fergusson College (Autonomous), Pune, India

B. Tyagi Alliance for an Energy Efficient Economy, New Delhi, India

Part I
International Trade: Empirical and Policy Issues

Chapter 1
Empirical Estimates of Inverted Duty Structure and Effective Rate of Protection—The Case of India

K. Pathania

1 Introduction

One of the major concerns with regard to the growth and development of the domestic industries is to analyse their tariff structure. In 1991, India's foreign exchange reserves had dropped significantly, putting pressure on its balance of payment. As mentioned by Singh (2017), "The 1991 Budget recognised the significance of trade-policy reform as part of overall reform programme, stating, 'The policies for industrial development are intimately related to policies of trade'".

The 1991 tariff reforms led to a reduction in the peak tariff rates applied to non-agricultural goods, mainly on industrial products (Singh, 2017). In fact, as shown in Table 1, on an average, the peak tariff rates imposed on imports of these products have experienced a decline since the year 1991–92. However, the country's tariffs on capital goods, chemicals, electronics, textiles and tyres, etc., have remained high, mainly due to significantly high tariff peaks on manufactured goods other than consumer goods (Rasheed, 2012; Singh, 2017).

The 2002–03 budget also expressed a vision that 'by the year 2004–05, there would be only two basic rates of custom duties—10% covering generally raw materials, intermediates and components and 20% covering generally final products' (Singh, 2017). Initially, it was expected that this tariff wall would give protection to final

This work is a part of my Ph.D. dissertation. Portions of this chapter have been adapted from the work Pathania and Bhattacharjea (2020). I would like to express my sincere gratitude to my supervisor, Prof. Aditya Bhattacharjea and co-supervisor, Prof. Uday Bhanu Sinha, for their invaluable suggestions and guidelines in bringing the chapter in its present shape. I would also like to thank my discussants and all the participants of the conferences held at the Indian Institute of Foreign Trade and Indian Statistical Institute, New Delhi, in the month of December 2018 for their useful suggestions. My sincere thanks are also due to Prof. Deb Kusum Das and all my professors at the Delhi School of Economics for their critical comments on empirical estimation.

K. Pathania (✉)
Department of Economics, Delhi School of Economics, Delhi 110007, India
e-mail: kanika@econdse.org

P. Lakhanpal et al. (eds.), *Trade, Investment and Economic Growth*,
https://doi.org/10.1007/978-981-33-6973-3_1

Table 1 India's peak tariff rates announced in the budget speech since 1991

Year	91–92	92–93	93–94	94–95	95–96	96–97	97–98	98–99	99–00	2000–01	2001–02	2002–03	2003–04	2004–05	2005–06	2006–07	2007–08
Peak rate (%)	150	110	85	65	50	52	45	45	40	38.5	35	30	25	20	15	12.5	10

Source Singh (2017)

Table 2 India simple average tariff by stage of processing in manufacturing 1990–91 to 2014–15

Category	1990–91	1993–94	1995–96	1996–97	1997–98	2010–11	2014–15
Unprocessed	107	50	27	25	25	22.5	23.5
Semi-processed	122	75	44	38	35	8.6	9
Processed	130	73	43	42	37	12.2	13.6

Source Singh (2017)

goods sector and, in turn, would improve the efficiency of the domestic supply chain by offering inputs at a lower tariff rate. However, with a rise in the number of India's regional trade engagements in the recent past, overall Most Favoured Nation (MFN) as well as the FTA tariff rates[1] have come down drastically across the sectors, which lead to the apprehension that large number of final goods would enter the country due to the significant tariff cuts under FTAs, as the duties on unprocessed goods remain relatively higher. Table 2 shows that during the years 1990–1991 to 2014–2015, tariff rates imposed on imports of processed, semi-processed and unprocessed goods fall significantly. If such a scenario remains, then it would negatively impact the final goods producers as they need to compete with cheaper foreign commodities especially from the East and South-East Asia. The technical term that describes this situation is referred to as the inverted duty structure (IDS). It implies that the tariff on import of intermediate inputs is more than tariff imposed on import of final output of goods produced with those inputs. On the contrary, tariff escalation implies that import duties on finished products are higher than on semi-processed products and the latter duties are higher than on raw materials. This practice protects domestic processing industries and inhibits the development of processing activities in the countries where raw materials originate.[2]

This issue of duty inversion has also been recognised by the Indian policy makers. In an interaction with the members of Economic Times, Finance Minister Arun Jaitley said (Seth, 2015 March 1),

> …I propose to reduce the rates of basic customs duty on certain inputs, raw materials, intermediates and components (in all 22 items) so as to minimize the impact of duty inversion and reduce the manufacturing cost in several sectors.

This is indeed required to promote domestic manufacturing as a part of its 'Make In India' campaign. In fact, in the past two years, various steps have been undertaken to rectify this problem in major sectors of the Indian economy; however, till now, no concrete study has been done to verify the existence of IDS in manufacturing production. Of crucial importance is another concern regarding the existence of negative protection in India's merchandise industries. If effective rate of protection

[1] 'FTAs are arrangements between two or more countries or trading blocs that primarily agree to reduce or eliminate customs tariff and non-tariff barriers on substantial trade between them. FTAs normally cover trade in goods or trade in services'. Source: Indian Trade Portal.

[2] https://www.wto.org/english/thewto_e/glossary_e/tariff_escalation_e.htm.

(ERP)[3] is positive in a sector which is characterised by duty inversion, then IDS may not affect the industry negatively, and there is some level of positive protection provided by the tariff structure. But if the opposite holds true, i.e. if ERP is negative in the presence of inverted duty structure, then the tariff structure may negatively impact the country's manufacturing sector. Hence, there is an emergent need to relook at the country's tariff structure and calculate the rate of effective protection accorded by India.

Thus, in this study, we empirically investigate the tariff structures characterising various Indian industries. We are particularly interested in analysing three rates of tariffs viz. nominal tariff (the duty imposed on imports of final goods, or NRP), input tariffs (duty imposed on imports of intermediate goods) and effective tariffs (based on input and output tariffs).

Subsequent sections of this chapter are structured as follows. Section 2 outlines the empirical methodology, followed by Sect. 3 explaining the data that we have utilised to compute different rates of protection. Section 4 discusses the empirical estimates of ERP, and the last section summarises the study.

2 Methodology

On the basis of the available data (World Input–Output Database), we modify the standard measure of ERP given by Corden. As defined in his study, for any sector j,

$$\mathrm{ERP}_j = \frac{\mathrm{VA}_{Tj} - \mathrm{VA}_{\mathrm{FT}_j}}{\mathrm{VA}_{\mathrm{FT}_j}} \times 100 \quad (1)$$

where VA_{Tj} refers to value added at basic price under restricted trade, and $\mathrm{VA}_{\mathrm{FT}j}$ represents the value added under free trade at basic prices. Based on Corden's methodology and given the properties of our data which entails information on actual trade (rather than free trade), we can algebraically represent the former as follows:

$$\mathrm{VA}_{Tj} = \mathrm{VO}_j - \sum\nolimits_i (\mathrm{IC}_{ij}) \quad (2)$$

where

VO_j represents sector j's value of output at basic prices.

IC_{ij} represents intermediate consumption of good i required to produce output of sector j at purchaser's price.[4]

[3]ERP is defined as the percentage excess of domestic value added due to imposition of tariff and non-tariff barriers over free trade value added.

[4]We have to calculate the value of intermediate consumption at purchasers' price as WIOD provides the same at basic price. Therefore, we add net indirect taxes (or NIT = taxes-subsidy) and international transport margin (ITM = lump sum international transport margins) to the value of IC at basic price and compute its value at purchaser's price.

Since we would be referring to each year's input–output table, whose values have been computed taking into account different rates of tariff imposed on imports of final output and intermediate input, therefore, in order to find value added under free trade, we will normalise the ex-post value of output by the amount of tariffs charged on each product, i.e. $\left(1+t_j\right)$ and ex-post intermediate consumption by $(1+t_i)$. Thus, we can write the value of $\mathrm{VA}_{\mathrm{FT}_j}$ as follows:

$$\mathrm{VA}_{\mathrm{FT}_j} = \frac{\mathrm{VO}_j}{\left(1+t_j\right)} - \sum_i \frac{\mathrm{IC}_{ij}}{(1+t_i)} \tag{3}$$

Here, t_j refers to ad valorem tariff on import of final output j, and t_i refers to ad valorem tariff on imports of intermediate consumption.

Substituting the values from Eqs. (2) and (3) in Eq. (1), we find

$$\mathrm{ERP}_j = \frac{\text{Eq. (2)} - \text{Eq. (2)}}{\text{Eq.(4)}} \times 100$$

$$\mathrm{ERP}_j = \frac{\frac{t_j \mathrm{VO}_j}{(1+t_j)} - \sum_i \frac{t_i \mathrm{IC}_{ij}}{(1+t_i)}}{\frac{\mathrm{VO}_j}{(1+t_j)} - \sum_i \frac{\mathrm{IC}_{ij}}{(1+t_i)}} \times 100 \tag{4}$$

Equation (4), therefore, becomes our final equation of interest, and we would now empirically estimate this equation. This Eq. (4) is actually a reformulation of Corden's measure based on the data that we use to compute the values of sectoral ERPs. It is crucial to note that since one product may employ more than one input in its production, we will first find out the import-weighted average tariff on intermediate imports (Avt_i) and then utilise it to compute ERP estimates.

The existing literature suggests two different possibilities about the treatment of non-traded inputs,[5] while calculating the measure of ERP—either to treat the non-traded inputs as part of value added (i.e. as primary factors as per Corden's 1971 study, or to consider them as traded inputs with zero tariff (Balassa, 1965). We have proceeded to compute effective rates for Indian industries using both the assumptions, and in accordance with Pathania and Bhattacharjea (2020), we assume that the true value of ERP lies within the bounds of these two assumptions defined by Corden and Balassa.[6]

---

[5]Non-traded: 'These are goods (and above all, services) where no significant part of domestic consumption is imported or of production is exported so that they do not have their prices set in the world market. They may be conceivably or physically tradeable, but because of transport costs or for other reasons are not actually traded'. Corden (1971).

[6]However, in such a case, even the value of non-traded inputs will get affected by exchange rate fluctuations. On the contrary, in case of Corden methodology, any change in the exchange rate will not impact the value of non-traded inputs. It is important to note that in the analysis that follows, we have not considered the effect of exchange rate fluctuations in impacting the rate of effective protection.

We also check if inverted duty structure exists in any of the selected industries for these two assumptions on the treatment of non-traded goods. If $\text{Avt}_i > t_j$, then it becomes the case of IDS.

3 Collection and Processing of Data

Unlike the existing studies on calculation of ERP for Indian manufacturing industries (e.g. Chand & Sen, 2002; Das, 2003; Nouroz, 2001; Das, 2012 among others), which use the National Input–Output tables for calculating sectoral value added, we propose to utilise the World Input–Output Database (WIOD) to compute data on value of output and intermediate consumption. Even though both are based on the Supply-Use tables (SUTs) of the Indian economy,[7] the problem with the former is that it is last available for the year 2007 and has not been formulated again afterwards. The advantage of the World Input–Output Database is that it consists of a time series data and covers 28 EU countries and 15 other major countries (total of 43 countries), including India, for the period 1995–2014. The second difference with the national tables is that the use of products is also broken down according to their origin.

Other than the data on value of output, we also require information on import tariffs. World Integrated Trade Solution or WITS is a World Bank database that provides commodity-wise data on import tariffs for all the economies around the globe. The advantage is that the data is also available in terms of ISIC rev. 3, which can be concorded with ISIC rev. 4. We would be referring to effectively applied tariff rates for import-weighted tariff.[8] We would refer to country-wise tariff lines to calculate ERP in any industry *j*. While calculating the component $\left(t_j\right)$ in Eq. (4), we will take the country's import-weighted tariffs.[9] In total, our analysis is based on 14 industries including agriculture and allied activities, mining, computer, etc. All the countries covered under WIOD are a part of our analysis.

[7] 'A supply table provides information on products produced by each domestic industry and a use table indicates the use of each product by an industry or final user'. (*Source*: WIOD).

[8] The World Bank's World Integrated Trading Solution (or WITS) entails information on effectively applied tariff rates, sourced from the UNCTAD TRAINS database or the WTO's IDB database. In the case when preferential tariff rates exist, they are used as the effectively applied tariffs. Otherwise, we use the MFN tariff rates.

[9] $t_j = \sum_k m_k * t_{kj}$. Here, *k* refers to countries, m_k represents the import weight of country *k* and is computed as $m_k = \frac{\text{import from country } k}{\text{total imports by India}}$. t_{kj} represents the tariff rate on final output '*j*' imposed by India on country *k*'s exports.

4 Sector-Wise Statistical Results and Analysis

This section will detail the results from our statistical analysis for 14 merchandise industries covered by WIOD. We use a graphical analysis to represent the trend in values of different rates of tariffs for these industries.

4.1 Crop and Animal Production, Hunting and Related Service Activities

As is evident from Fig. 1 and for the partners under consideration, the tariff on imports of this sector has increased steadily over time ranging from 11.53% in the year 2000 to reach as high as 30.90% in 2014, with an average tariff rate of about 30.25%.

The consequences of higher import tariffs are clearly reflected in the rates of effective protection—it has been positive throughout the 15 years long time period. This is true for both the Corden's and Balassa's measures. In fact, the extent of positive effective protection has increased from about 15.98% in the year 2000 to reach as high as 45.84% by the year 2014, only to experience a fall to about 24% in the year 2008. The estimates also suggest that the two rates of ERP almost coincide for the period under consideration, which may imply that this industry is characterised by very low amount of imports of non-traded intermediate inputs.

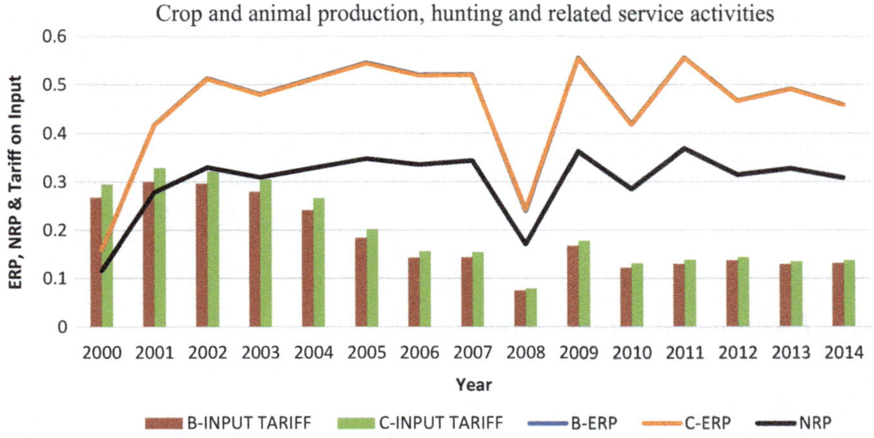

Fig. 1 Corden and Balassa ERP estimates of crop and animal production, hunting and related service activities. *Source* Author's own calculations

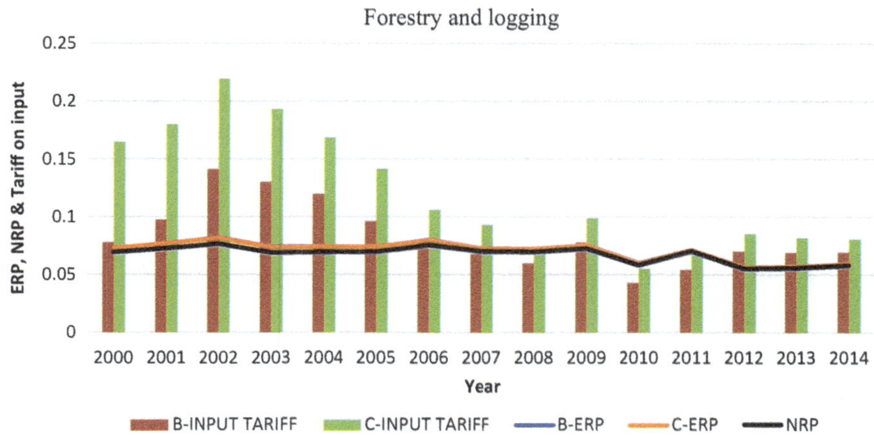

Fig. 2 Corden and Balassa ERP estimates of forestry and logging. *Source* Author's own calculations

4.2 Forestry and Logging

The import tariff on forestry and logging has remained relatively stable with an average tariff of 6.73% except with a maximum tariff of 7.66% in 2002, while the minimum tariff accorded in this sector is 5.55%.

As is evident from Fig. 2, Balassa's and Corden's measures have coincided with each other, with maximum protection of 8.2% and minimum protection of 5.6% and an average protection of approximately 7.1%. Also, the analysis demonstrates two points about the co-movement of the three rates of tariffs: One, both ERP and NRP have remained relatively stable throughout the period 2000–2014, while the rate of import tariffs on intermediate input initially increased and then started declining from the year 2003 onwards. This implies that in the case of this sector, tariffs imposed on import of inputs are quite high which lead to the lesser usage of foreign tradable input into its production. This is what commonly known as 'Water in tariff'.

4.3 Fishing and Aquaculture

As is evident from Fig. 3, the tariff on import of fishing and aquaculture has decreased from 38.5% in 2000 to 17.6% in 2014. The year 2010 experienced a steep decline to 5.88% in between; however, it was not so for the case of tariff on intermediate inputs in the industry.

What about the trend in ERP—has it increased or decreased over the years?—Overall the industry has experienced a fall in the rate of effective protection from about 41% in the year 2000 to approximately 17% by 2014. In fact, the rate has followed the trend of NRP over the 15 years' period. And this has happened despite

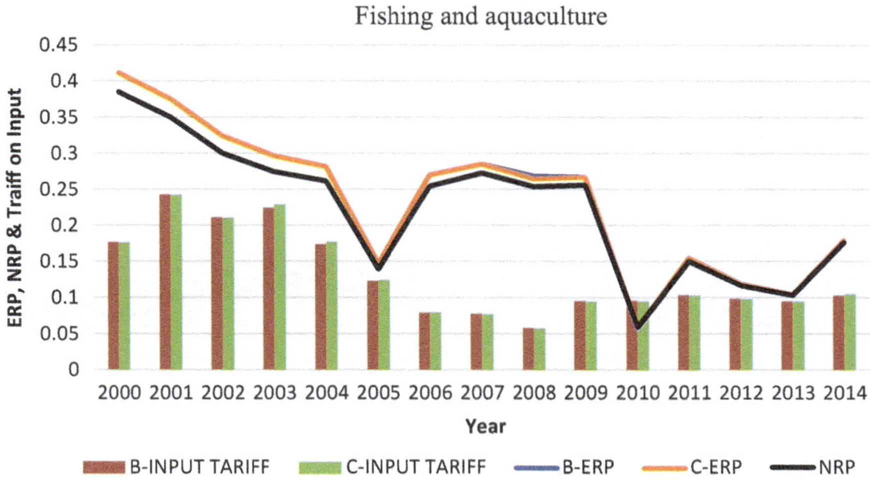

Fig. 3 Corden and Balassa ERP estimates of fishing and aquaculture. *Source* Author's own calculations

the initial fluctuation in the rate of import tariffs on intermediate inputs and existence of IDS in the year 2010. This implies that, in this specific case, the industry's imports of intermediate inputs are enough to sufficiently trigger the movement of ERP. As was true for crop and animal production, hunting and related activities, here also the value of NRP falls short of ERP for most of the years under consideration.

4.4 *Mining and Quarrying*

As is evident from Fig. 4, the tariff on import of mining and quarrying has decreased steadily from 20.37% in 2000 to 2.20% in 2014, and it reached as low as 1.7% in 2012.[10]

The consequence of lower import tariffs is clearly reflected in the rates of effective protection—though it has been positive throughout the time period under consideration but the extent of protection has been falling. This is true for both the Corden's and Balassa's measures. In fact, the extent of positive effective protection has decreased from about 27% in the year 2000 to reach 2.7 by the year 2014 and so is the case for tariff on imports of intermediate inputs. Thus, the co-movement of the three rates of tariffs (NRP, tariff on intermediate input and ERP) in addition to existence of IDS (as per Corden's measure) during all the 15 years clearly signifies that the movements in

[10]In an attempt to promote external liberalisation, in almost every budget speech starting from the year 2002 onwards, the Indian government has proposed to reduce the rates of import tariffs on all the non-agriculture and non-dairy products. This is also evident from our discussion on trends in import tariffs imposed on non-agricultural commodities.

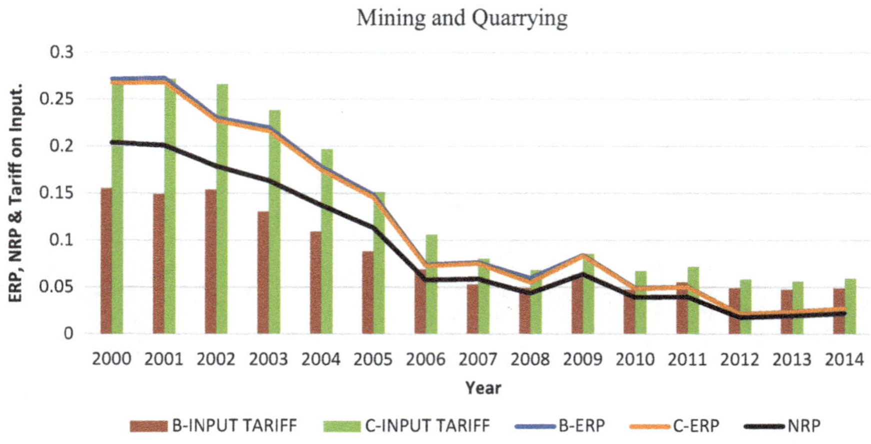

Fig. 4 Corden and Balassa ERP estimates of mining and quarrying. *Source* Author's own calculations

ERP are guided more by the value of output and tariff on final output than by tariff on intermediate input. As regards, the Balassa's measure, duty inversion is evident for most of the years starting from 2006 onwards.

4.5 Manufacture of Wood and of Products of Wood and Cork, Except Furniture; Manufacture of Articles of Straw and Plaiting Materials

Like in the case of item 4, here also, the co-movement between NRP and ERP (based on both Balassa's and Corden's estimates) is quite evident from Fig. 5. Even though both the rates have fallen over the years, with the rate of fall in ERP much greater than that of the NRP, the wood industry has always seemed to enjoy a relatively higher effective protection than what its nominal import tariff suggests—while, in nominal terms, the tariff rate is equivalent to about 9%, in effective terms, it equals approximately 25% as of 2014. The shortage of input tariff vis-à-vis that of output tariff obviously adds to the explanation as to why NRP must have fallen short of ERP in case of wood and products of wood and cork. Other than this, it could also be a possibility that the sector, at least during the initial years under coverage (from 2000 to 2005), received higher subsidies, which, in turn, would have added to their effective protection.

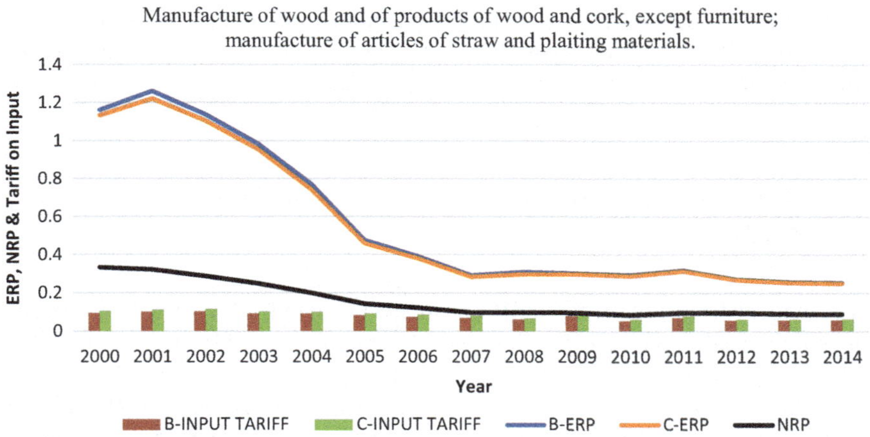

Fig. 5 Corden and Balassa ERP estimates of manufacture of wood and of products of wood and cork, except furniture; manufacture of articles of straw and plaiting materials. *Source* Author's own calculations

4.6 Manufacture of Paper and Paper Products

The tariff on manufacture of paper and paper products has decreased over time from 15.47% in 2000 to 8.82% in 2014. Similar is the case with input tariffs and rate of effective protection. In fact, as is evident from Fig. 6, ERP seems to follow the movement of both NRP and input tariffs, but the response is more than 1:1 for most of the years, meaning thereby if say, output tariff and input tariff are declining by

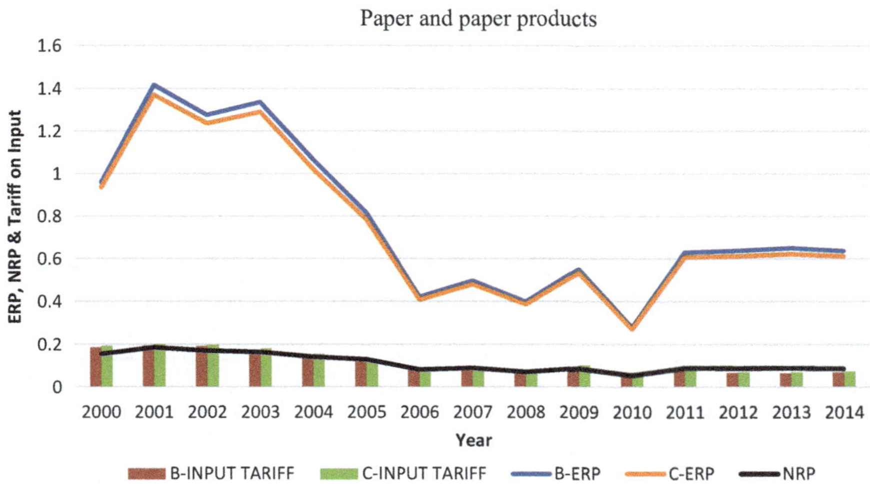

Fig. 6 Corden and Balassa ERP estimate of paper and paper products. *Source* Author's own calculations

1%, then ERP is declining by more than 1%. Another observation is that during the period 2000–2011, the industry is characterised by existence of duty inversion, post which the rates of ERP have remained relatively stable.

4.7 Manufacture of Textiles, Wearing Apparel and Leather Products

As is evident from Fig. 7, the tariff on import of manufacture of textile, wearing apparel and leather products has decreased steadily from 30.51% in 2000 to 9.85% in 2014 with a minimum tariff of 9% in 2011. The average tariff remained at 16.73%.

Unlike other cases discussed so far, not only Corden's and Balassa's ERP estimates are different, but also the two rates of input tariffs. In fact, higher the difference between the rates of input tariffs, higher is the difference between the corresponding ERP estimates, thus, highlighting the role of the former in defining the extent of protection in this industry. Also, overtime, with the decline in the gap between the two measures of input tariffs, the gap between the two measures of ERP has also fallen, thereby signifying the role of input tariffs in defining the extent of protection in this specific industry. And, what explains the decline in the two rates of input tariffs is nothing but the fall in the volume of non-traded (imports of service-inputs, in our case).

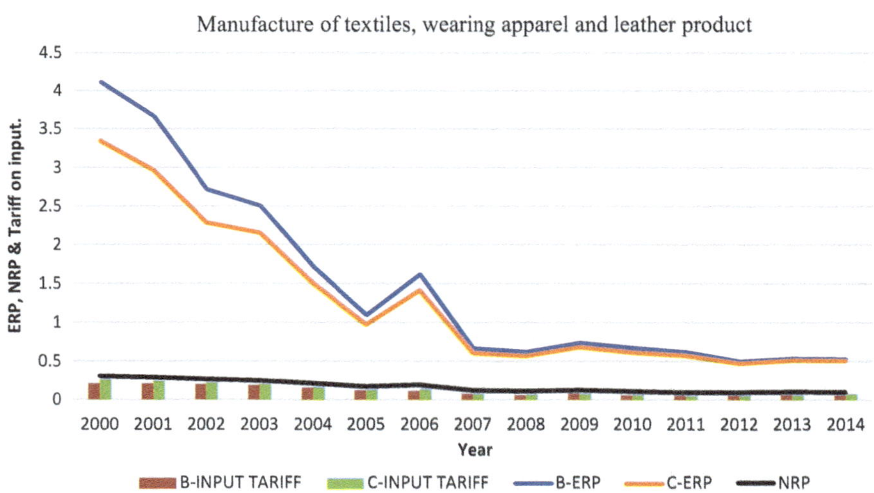

Fig. 7 Corden and Balassa ERP estimates of manufacture of textiles, wearing apparel and leather product. *Source* Author's own calculations

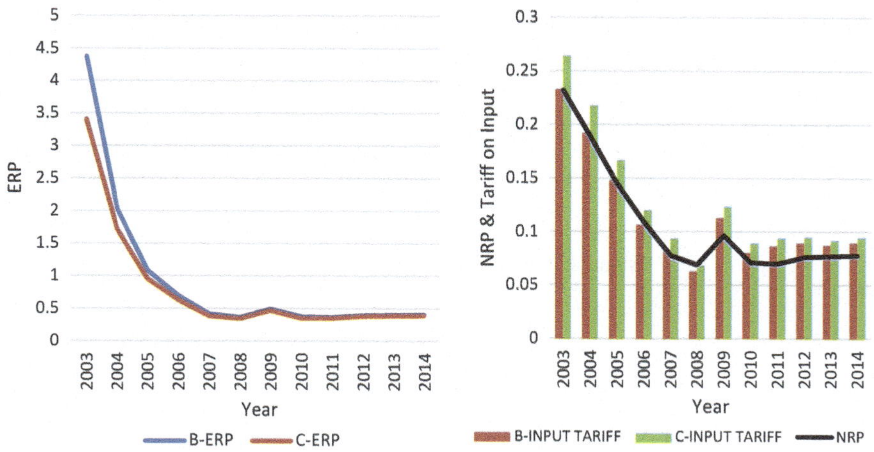

Fig. 8 Corden and Balassa ERP estimates of manufacture of basic pharmaceutical products and pharmaceutical preparation for 2003–2014. *Source* Author's own calculations

4.8 *Manufacture of Basic Pharmaceutical Products and Pharmaceutical Preparations*

This industry is also characterised by negative effective rate of protection as per Balassa's technique and positive ERP as per Corden's technique for the year 2001 because of the deduction of ITM and NIT from value of output under free trade. The industry seems to have experienced relaxations in terms of the reduction in both input and output tariffs, except for a rise in both in the year 2009, which is accompanied by a rise in the industry's ERP. This could be because of the higher proportionate increase in the input tariff vis-à-vis that of the rise in output tariff in the same year (Fig. 8).

4.9 *Manufacture of Computer, Electronic and Optical Products*

Here also, all the three rates of tariffs viz. nominal, import-weighted input tariffs and effective tariffs have fallen during the 15 years' period. Effective tariff is always greater than the rate of nominal tariffs and so are Corden's input tariff estimates thereby implying the existence of IDS in the computer, electronics and optical industry. During the initial 5 years, when both input and output tariffs were relatively higher in comparison with their rates in the last 10 years of the 15 years long period, ERP was high, and its responsiveness to the decline in input–output tariffs was also more. What does this imply? It seems reasonable to conclude here that the elasticity of ERP with respect to input and output tariffs is not constant and it depends on a lot of demand and supply side factors. The response of value of output/intermediate consumption to a change in rate of tariff be it input or output also plays a crucial role in determining the rates of effective tariff.

From 2005 onwards, however, the industry has experienced relatively stable and lower rates of all the three tariff rates, hence indicating the lower level of protection that is being accorded to its domestic firms (Fig. 9).

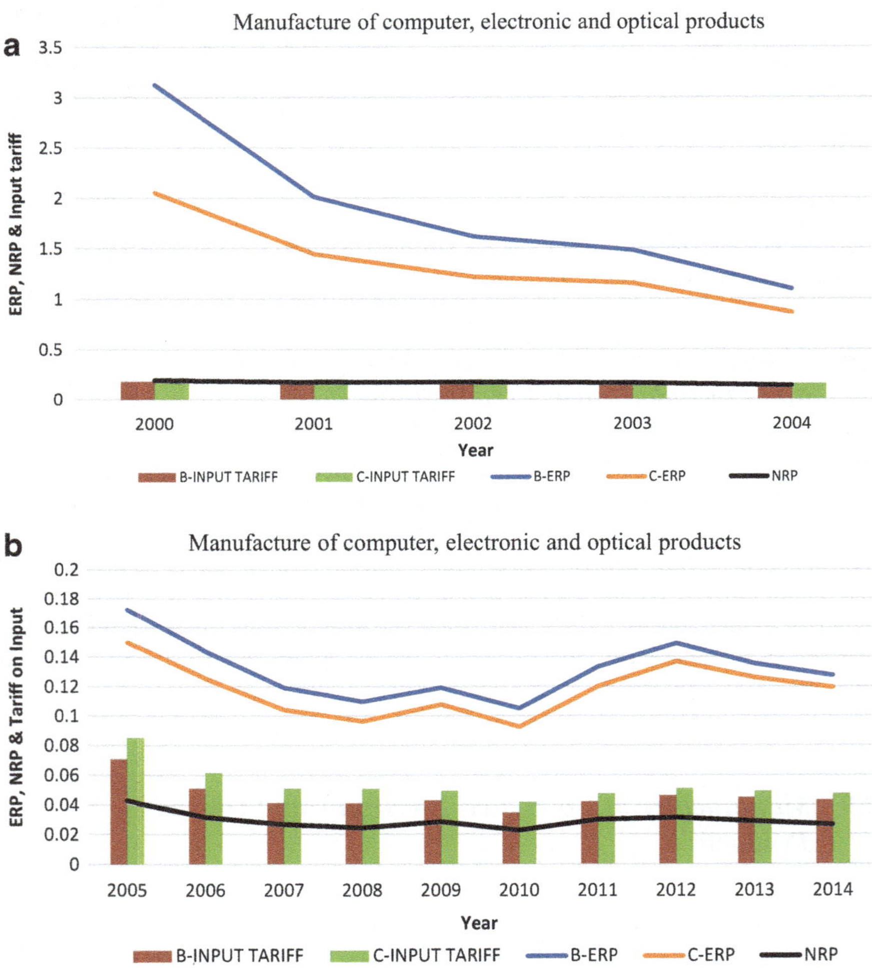

Fig. 9 A Corden and Balassa ERP estimates of manufacture of computer, electronic and optical products from 2000 to 2004. **b** Corden and Balassa ERP estimates of manufacture of computer, electronic and optical products from 2005 to 2014. *Source* Author's own calculations

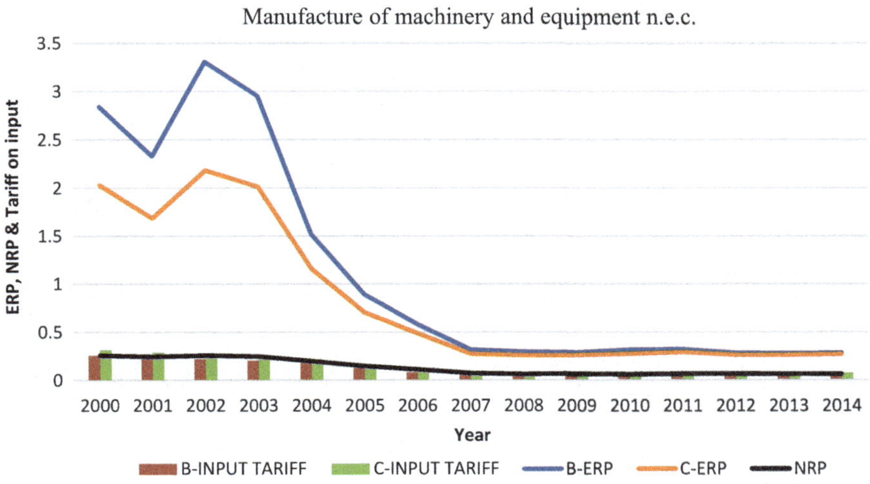

Fig. 10 Corden and Balassa ERP estimates of manufacture of machinery and equipment n.e.c. *Source* Author's own calculations

4.9.1 Manufacture of Machinery and Equipment N.E.C.

As is evident from Fig. 10, the industry has experienced a decline in the rate of import-weighted input, nominal and effective tariff over the 15 years' period, even though the last two experienced a rise during 2002. Post 2002, all the three rates start declining and became relatively stable from 2006 onwards. In fact, during the last few years, both B's and C's-based ERP estimates almost coincide and so do the corresponding input tariff rates.

It is worth mentioning here that since ERP, by its very definition, depends on the value added under free and restricted trade, a huge fall in its rate could also be explained by reasons other than change in nominal or input tariffs. For instance, a fall in subsidy or removal of any specialised treatment accorded to this industry (say, export promotion schemes) may have also reduced its ERP.

4.9.2 Manufacture of Motor Vehicles, Trailers and Semi-Trailers

Even though the industry is characterised by positive input and output tariffs (with former lesser than the latter during each year), yet it suffered from negative effective protection during the years 2000–2004 and 2011. In this case also, even though value added under restricted trade was positive but that under free trade, was negative, which guided the sign of ERP. A negative ERP may arise as a result of one of the following three possibilities:

1. If value added under free trade as well as under restricted trade are positive.

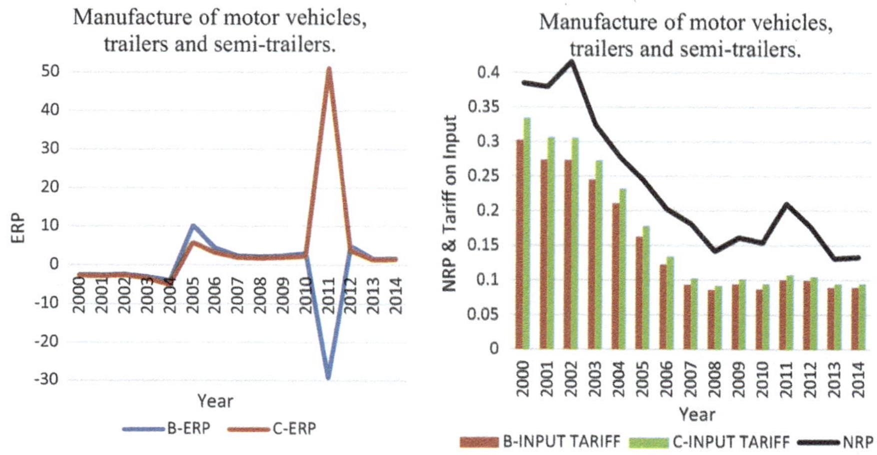

Fig. 11 Corden and Balassa ERP estimates of manufacture of motor vehicles, trailers and semi-trailers. *Source* Author's own calculations

2. If value added under free trade is negative and that under restricted trade is positive
3. If value added under restricted trade is negative while that under free trade is positive, and the magnitude of the former is more than that of the latter.

In the present case, however, the negative value of ERP is because of the existence of negative value added under free trade and existence of tariff escalation (Fig. 11).

For the year 2011, only Balassa's estimate is negative, while the other ERP is positive. This is because of the negative value under free trade for Balassa's estimate.

4.9.3 Printing and Reproduction of Recorded Media

Overall, comparing the two extreme time periods, all the three tariff rates have fallen—nominal tariff, two measures of input tariffs and the two measures of effective tariffs. However, ERP seems to be dependent upon the trend of nominal tariff more than that of input tariffs—every fall in the latter rate is accompanied with a fall in the former rate, and so does every rise. The response of ERP, however, is more than proportionate to the change in rate of nominal protection. This is more evident during the years 2005–06 when the gap between ERP and NRP reduced to the minimum, and this is because, in these two years, even though value of industrial output increased and the rate of import tariff fell. However, the proportionate rise in the former is much less than the proportionate fall in the latter, thus leading to a fall in the rate of effective protection (Fig. 12).

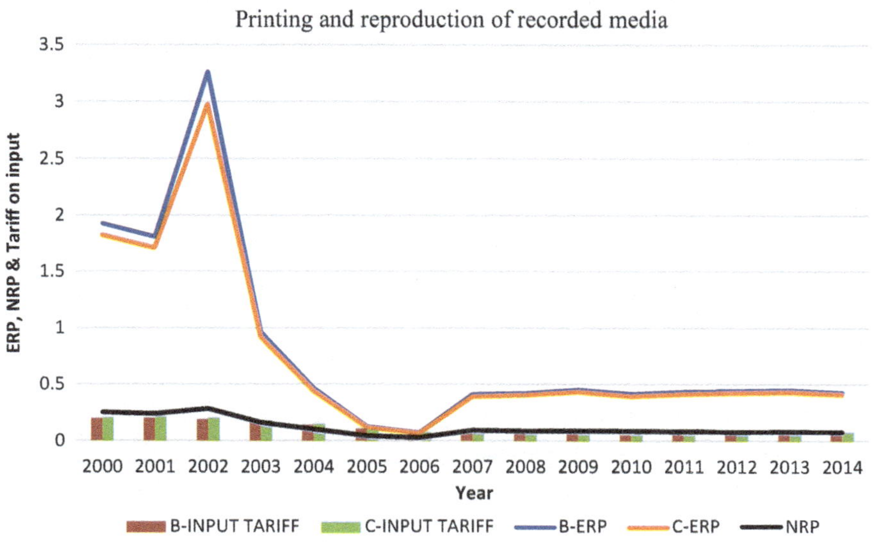

Fig. 12 Corden and Balassa ERP estimates of printing and reproduction of recorded media. *Source* Author's own calculations

4.9.4 Manufacture of Other Non-Metallic Mineral Products

The industry is characterised by a fall in the rate of nominal tariff from about 35% in the year 2000 to 8.9% by the year 2014. The rate of import-weighted input tariffs (measured according to Balassa's and Corden's technique) has also experienced a fall from an average of about 21.5% in 2000 to 3.3% in 2014 and so does the rate of effective protection. The latter fall at a higher rate during the first half of the last decade and then start rising gradually to reach 34.07% by the year 2014. In this case also, ERP is greater than NRP for all the years, thus signifying the role of factors other than tariffs in determining the former (Fig. 13).

4.9.5 Manufacture of Furniture; Other Manufacturing

As can be observed from Fig. 14, the industry's ERP seems to have followed the trend of the input and output tariff imposed on its imports. Started with a higher rate of effective protection of about 151% in the year 2000, the rate shot up further during the year 2001 followed by an 8-years' long period of decline. In the year 2009, ERP again increased, dropped to 2.9% in 2010 and has been increasing since then. However, the responsiveness of ERP to changes in the rate of tariffs differs in each year.

The industry also experienced IDS in the years 2008, 2010 and 2011, and this is true for both the rates of input tariffs.

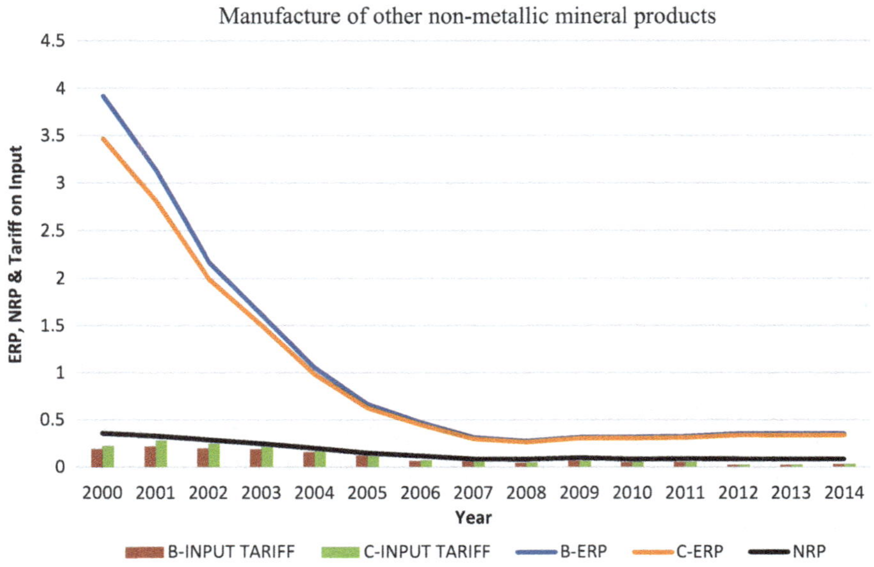

Fig. 13 Corden and Balassa ERP estimates of manufacture of other non-metallic mineral products. *Source* Author's own calculations

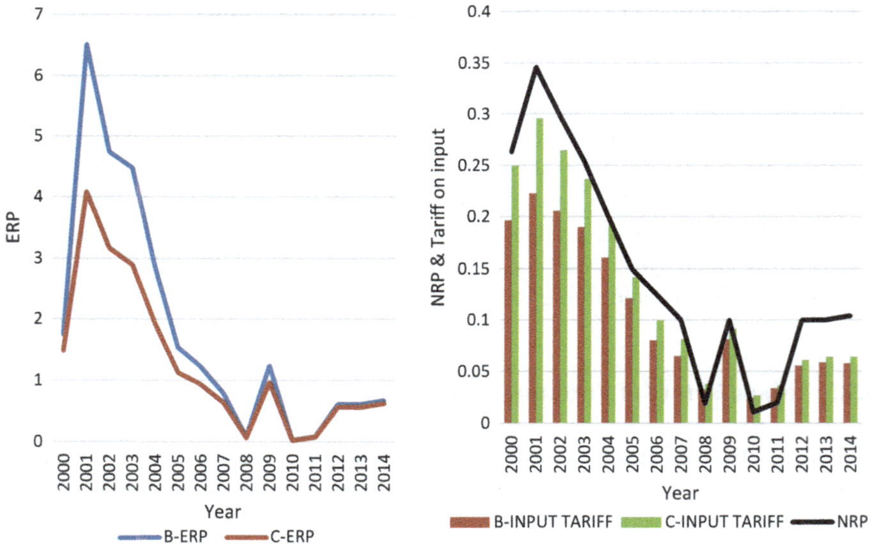

Fig. 14 Corden and Balassa ERP estimates of manufacture of furniture; other manufacturing. *Source* Author's own calculations

5 Concluding Remarks

Overall effective protection has declined, and so have the rates of nominal tariffs during the 15 years' period, thus highlighting the effect of trade liberalising policies being implemented by the government of India. These results are in line with the estimates of Das (2003 and 2012). In recent years, many PTAs and FTAs have been signed in which major relaxations have been given to non-agricultural products than on agricultural products. As a consequence, tariffs on non-agricultural products have fallen, while that on the agricultural and other allied activities have risen over time. Moreover, as recorded in the budget speeches, the peak tariff rates have fallen significantly in the past few years (Singh 2017).

It is well-known that apart from tariffs, imports of agriculture commodities are still restricted by high levels of non-tariff barriers (NTBs). However, in our calculation of ERP, we do not incorporate the role of NTBs. Hence, it is important to note that our measure of effective protection may not reflect the actual level of protection that is being accorded to firms in this sector, though it does indicate the association between existence of inverted duty structure and the level of effective protection (calculates using information on tariff barriers).

Our analysis shows that in most of the industries under consideration, the rates of effective protection have been quite high during the initial 3–4 years (starting 2000) and have experienced a decline thereafter. This is because initially the rates of tariff were quite high, thus leading to a higher value of effective tariff. Over the years, with fall in the rates of tariff, ERP also experienced a decline, though it still remained above nominal rates of tariffs in most of the cases. Further, we find that for most of the years under consideration, IDS exists in computer, paper and paper products, electronics and optical products, pharmaceuticals, machinery and equipment and other transport equipment. A study by FICCI (2016) also shows that machinery, electronics as well as capital goods suffer from duty inversion in the case of the Indian economy. Similarly, in another study, Hoda and Rai (2014) have highlighted the issue of IDS in commodities like ovens, refrigerators and the like.

Besides, we also find that the higher the extent of positive protection, the lesser is the chance of inverted duty structure in any industry. This is obvious because higher extent of positive protection means more tariff on output. More so, it is evident from our analysis that existence of IDS does not imply that ERP is negative. In all the cases discussed above, IDS is always accompanied with positive ERP though the magnitude of the two varies across different industries.

Overall, we do not have a case of negative ERP which arises in a situation where VA under restricted trade falls short of VA under free trade. Negative ERP exists only in manufacture of motor vehicles, trailers and semi-trailers in year 2000 for Balassa's estimate, and it exists only when there exists negative VA under free trade. This was also implied by Corden (1971) as one of the implications in his analysis.

References

Balassa, B. (1965). Tariff protection in industrial countries: An Evaluation. *Journal of Political Economy 73* (6), 573–594.

Chand, S., & Sen, K. (2002). Trade liberalization and productivity growth: Evidence from Indian manufacturing. *Review of Development Economics, 6*(1), 120–132.

Corden, W. M. (1971). *The theory of protection.* Oxford: Claredon Press.

Das, D. K. (2003). *Quantifying trade barriers: Has protection declined substantially in Indian manufacturing.* Economic and Political Weekly January 31st Issue.

FICCI. (2016). *FICCI survey on inverted duty structure in Indian manufacturing sector*. Retrieved from https://ficci.in/Sedocument/20375/FICCI-INVERTED-DUTY-Report-2016.pdf.

Hoda A, Rai D K (2014) *Trade and investment barriers affecting international production networks in India.* Working Paper 281 Indian Council for Research on International Economic Relations.

Nouroz, H. (2001). *Protection in Indian manufacturing: An empirical study.* Macmillan.

Pathania, K., & Bhattacharjea, A. (2020). Inverted duty structures and the paradox of negative effective protection in India, 2000–2014. *Foreign Trade Review, 55*(2), 139–167. https://doi.org/10.1177/0972266119894131.

Rasheed, T. (2012). *Implications of liberalizing trade and investment with India.* State Bank of Pakistan Karachi.

Seth, D. (2015, March 1). Budget 2015: FM Arun Jaitely proposes to rectify inverted duty structure for domestic units. *The Economic Times.* Retrieved from https://economictimes.indiatimes.com/news/economy/policy/budget-2015-fm-arun-jaitley-proposes-to-rectify-inverted-duty-structure-for-domestic-units/articleshow/46416455.cms.

Singh, H. V. (2017). *Trade-policy Reform in India Since 1991 In Rakesh Mohan Indian Transformed: 25 years of Economic Reforms* (pp. 110–161). India: Penguin Random House Private Limited.

World Input-Output Database. https://www.wiod.org/database/wiots16. Accessed on May 21, 2018.

World Integrated Trade Solution. https://wits.worldbank.org/. Accessed on May 21, 2018.

Chapter 2
Does the Past Performance in Home Market Affect Export Participation of New Exporters? Evidence from Indian Firms

Priyanta Ghosh and Aparna Sawhney

1 Introduction

The analysis of determinants of international competitiveness has been an important issue for both developed and developing countries and gained further attention with the increasing integration of countries in the global market. While early literature on comparative advantage focused on the macro-factors, such as inter-country differences in technology, factor endowment and exchange rates, more recent trade models have focused on micro-factors such as firm characteristics. Recognizing the firm as an active economic agent, the new trade theory emphasizes the role of firm heterogeneity in international trade. Using firm-level data, several studies have shown that only a small percentage of firms participate in cross-border exchange, particularly in export (Bernard and Jensen 1999). The characteristics of exporters differ substantially from non-exporters. Exporters are superior relative to non-exporters in terms of size, productivity, technology and factor payments (Bernard et al., 1995; Clerides et al., 1998; Bernard & Wagner, 2001; Wagner, 2012).

Exporting firms, however, are not a homogeneous category. Some are incumbent exporters, which have been in the export business for quite some time, while others are new exporters entering the export market for the first time. Exporting is a more risky and complex decision for new exporters, while less risky for incumbent exporters who benefit from their previous experience in the export market. Unlike incumbent exporters, new exporters face bigger hurdles in entering the export market. Although the literature on the role of sunk cost for export participation identified the differential nature of export decision of incumbent exporters and new exporters (Robert &

P. Ghosh (✉)
University of Gour Banga, Malda, India
e-mail: pgeconomics88@gmail.com

A. Sawhney
Centre for International Trade and Development, Jawaharlal Nehru University, New Delhi, India
e-mail: aparnasawhney@yahoo.com

P. Lakhanpal et al. (eds.), *Trade, Investment and Economic Growth*,
https://doi.org/10.1007/978-981-33-6973-3_2

Tybout, 1997; Campa, 2004; Sinani & Hobdari, 2010; Alvarez et al., 2013; Padmaja & Sashidharan, 2016), no previous study on export participation solely focused its attention on the new exporters.

There has been a lot of emphasis on the prior productivity difference between exporters and non-exporters, since prior productivity has been recognized as the key factor determining firm-level export participation decision (Melitz, 2003; Aw et al., 2007; Wagner, 2012; Temouri et al., 2013; Vu et al., 2016). However, none of the studies has identified the reasons for a priori difference in the productivity levels between exporters and non-exporters. The past experience in the home market could be one such reason. It is through its operation in the home market that firms may generate scale economies and become productive (Linder, 1961; Vernon, 1966; Basevi, 1970; Krugman, 1980; Porter, 1990). Firms that perform well in the home market are more likely to be the future exporters as they have better risk-taking abilities and resource base to undertake a risky activity like export.

Using the data on Indian manufacturing firms in this study, we analyse the determinants of export participation for new exporters with a particular focus on the role of firms' past performance in the home market. In our analysis, we consider a 15-year period from 2000 to 2014, a decade after India embarked on the path of liberalization. Many firms entered the export business as new exporters; they include young as well as the existing old firms, which earlier operated solely in the domestic market and then transited to the world market. The 15-year period allows us to observe their transition behaviour, as it is long enough to trace the behaviour of new exporters and non-exporters and examine the role of the past home market performance in the export entry decision of new firms.

The literature on the determinants of firm export participation is substantive, with several analyses focused on India. Many of these studies have dealt with the importance of technology investment in export participation (Kumar & Siddharthan, 1994; Aggarwal, 2002; Hasan & Raturi, 2003; Bhat & Narayanan, 2009, Chadha, 2009). Nagaraj (2014) examined the relation between financial health of a firm and its potential to export, while Aggarwal (2002) discussed the role of foreign ownership on export. More recent studies have dealt with export-productivity linkages in Indian context (Haidar, 2012; Pattnayak & Thangavelu, 2014; Sharma & Mishra, 2015; Thomas & Narayanan, 2016; Gupta et al., 2018). However, no study has explored the role of the home market performance as a determinant of export entry, for new exporters among Indian manufacturing firms. To the best of our knowledge, this is the first such study that attempts to contribute to this literature.

The paper is organized as follows. In Sect. 2, we briefly discuss the data, and in Sect. 3, we describe the classification of firms and compare different categories of firms. In Sect. 4, we lay out an analytical model to examine the determinants of firm export participation, including home market performance. Section 5 discusses the estimation results and Sect. 6 concludes.

2 Data

We use the Prowess database for information on the characteristics of Indian firms. Prowess provides longitudinal data on financial performance of Indian companies since 1989 where each company is tracked over the years through unique company code.[1] Based on the main product produced by the firm, the database provides the industry classification of the firms and covers companies from both manufacturing and service sectors. However, the present study includes only manufacturing firms. The database provides a good representation of the organized manufacturing sector covering around 80% of its total output as per the CMIE Report of 2009. We extracted data of 8260 manufacturing firms from Prowess for the period 2000–2014; however, after cleaning, we are left with a sample of 5334 firms.[2] Due to the irregular reporting of data by Indian firms, we have an unbalanced panel.[3]

3 Comparing New Exports to the Non-exports

3.1 Classification of Firms

In examining the determinants of export participation for new exporters, we clarify the following: Who are new exporters? How are they different from incumbent exporters and non-exporters? New exporters are defined as firms that did not export in the past but export in the present year. Incumbent exporters, on the other hand, are firms that had exported in some of the past years. Firms that are never observed to export in our sample are defined as non-exporters. It is evident that the classification of firms is conditional on our observation of export status in the past years. However, we cannot observe export status prior to 2000 since our sample covers period 2000–2014. As a result, export status in all the past years cannot be traced, especially, for the firms born prior to 2000 and such firms are majority in our sample.[4] In other words, for a large number of firms, full information of firm export status is not observable.

In the absence of the full information of firm export status, we classify firms based on an important feature of new exporters that distinguish them from incumbent exporters. Unlike incumbent exporters, export decisions of new exporters in the current year do not depend on the past exporting experience. Some studies, such

[1] All actively listed companies in the Bombay stock exchange and some unlisted companies are included in Prowess. The availability of the audited report is the basis for the inclusion of a company in this database. Apart from that, CMIE conducts its own surveys to collect information on small companies that do not prepare annual reports.

[2] While cleaning, we have dropped firms that did not have data on the key variables like sales, wages and salaries, gross fixed assets for at least five years.

[3] Only 25% firms have data for every year of the sample period.

[4] There are only 358 firms out of 5334 firms which incorporated post 2000.

as Robert and Tybout (1997), showed that after exiting from export market if a firm does not export for at least two consecutive years, then it behaves like a new exporter. The reason being during the non-exporting years, a firm loses its foreign networks and faces similar difficulties in reappearing in the export market as a new exporter does when entering for the first time. Therefore, even if we cannot observe the export status in all the past years, observing it for a few consecutive years is sufficient to identify the new exporters.

We consider firms that are observed for at least five consecutive years in the dataset. Assuming the fifth year as the current period, we classify firms in two broad categories—non-exporters and exporters, and the latter group is further categorized into new exporters and incumbent exporters. Firms which do not export in any of the five consecutive years (including the current period) are classified as non-exporters. Exporters are the firms that export in the current period, i.e. in the fifth year, but may or may not export in the past years. Among the exporters which export in at least one of the past four years are the incumbent exporters, while those that do not export in any of the past four years are new exporters.

3.2 *Differential Characteristics of Various Types of Firms*

After categorizing firms based on export status, we examine the characteristics of firms in each category. The characteristics considered are— size, productivity, technology and financial health. Here, our interest lies in understanding the nature of new exporters in comparison with the other two groups—non-exporters and incumbent exporters. In order to do so, we run the following regression equation.

$$Y_{it} = \alpha_0 + \alpha_1 \text{Exp}_{it} + \alpha_2 \text{Exp}_{it} * \text{New}_{it} + \alpha_4 Z_{it} + \delta_J + \omega_t + \varepsilon_{it} \quad (1)$$

The dependent variable Y_{it} denotes characteristic of the ith firm in tth year such as size. We identify exporters by the dummy variable, Exp_{it}, which takes value 1 if the firm is an exporter in tth year and 0 if it is a non-exporter. The dummy variable, New_{it}, differentiates exporters between new exporters and incumbent exporters. For new exporters, it takes value 1, while for incumbent exporters, it takes value 0. Note that non-exporters form the omitted category. The coefficient of the interaction term, α_2, compares between new exporters and incumbent exporters within the group of exporters. While the estimate of α_1 gives the difference in the characteristics of incumbent exporters from non-exporters, the sum of α_1 and α_2 gives the magnitude of the difference in the characteristics of new exporters from non-exporters. We report the exact percentage differences in firm characteristics between various types of exporters in Table 1, such as $(\exp(\alpha_1) - 1) * 100$, providing the percentage difference between incumbent exporters and non-exporters in the respective firm characteristics. The vector of control variables is denoted by $\boldsymbol{Z}_{it}$, and it constitutes of -log of age

Table 1 A comparison of firm characteristics across various categories of firms

	Dependent variables						
Variables	Sales	Capital stock	Total factor productivity	Capital intensity	R&D intensity	Technology import intensity	Liquidity
Exp	41.90*** (0.038)	21.95*** (0.020)	3.15** (0.013)	−4.45** (0.020)	0.08** (0.0002)	0.43*** (0.001)	0.03*** (0.010)
Exp*New	−19.22*** (0.042)	−8.42*** (0.015)	−1.19 (0.027)	10.48*** (0.031)	−0.06** (0.0002)	−0.41**** (0.001)	−0.03** (0.012)
N	22,747	22,747	22,747	22,747	22,747	22,747	22,747

Notes The reported values are the percentage difference in the respective firm characteristics between various categories of firms: incumbent exporters and new exporters, with non-exporters being the omitted category. Dependent variables are expressed in logs, except liquidity. Each regression includes ownership dummies, industry and year fixed effects. A (unbalanced) panel of 3888 firms is used. Robust standard errors are reported in parentheses. '***' and '**' refer 1% and 5% level of significance

Source Authors' own calculations

and ownership dummies. Industry and year differences are accounted by including industry fixed effects (δ_J) at NIC3-digit level and year fixed effects (ω_t).

Table 1 draws a comparison between new exporters, incumbent exporters and non-exporters. Within each industry and ownership category, incumbent exporters sell about 41.90% more than the non-exporters. Moreover, they possess 21.95% more stock of capital than non-exporters. Productivities of incumbent exporters are higher relative to non-exporters, and they are more labour-intensive than non-exporters. Furthermore, technology investment and liquidity are higher for incumbent exporters vis-à-vis non-exporters.

The interaction term compares between two types exporters—new exporters and incumbent exporters. The coefficient is positive and significant for capital intensity indicating new exporters as 10.48% more capital-intensive than incumbent exporters. In terms of productivity, new exporters are no different from incumbent exporters. However, new exporters are smaller in size with respect to incumbent exporters both in terms of sales and capital stock. Numerically, capital stock for new exporters is 8.42% lesser than incumbent exporters. The negative coefficient of the interaction term for R&D intensity and technology import intensity suggests that new exporters invest less on technology acquisition relative to incumbent exporters. Incumbent exporters are also financially healthier than new exporters; however, the difference is very small. Overall, new exporters are more capital-intensive but smaller, less technology-intensive and less liquid vis-à-vis incumbent exporters.

The coefficient in the first and second row can be added to compare new exporters from non-exporters. Our findings suggest that new exporters are bigger than non-exporters by 22.68% (13.53%) in terms of sales (capital stock). New exporters are also more productive and use a more capital-intensive production technology relative to the non-exporters. With respect to R&D investment, technology import and liquidity, however, the two categories of firms have no significant difference.

4 Role of Home Market Performance on Export Entry of Firms

In order to understand the role of home market performance on the export entry decision of a firm, we focus on firms that have never exported before, i.e. new exporters along with non-exporters.[5] To motivate our empirical exercise, we proceed by laying out an analytical model of export participation drawing from Robert and Tybout (1997), Arnold and Hussinger (2005) among others.

[5]Unlike new exporters, home market performance of the incumbent exporters is likely to be influenced by their past export performance and therefore may not truly reflect the feature of the home market.

4.1 Export Decision Model

Export is a costly activity, as entering the export market requires payment of sunk cost. Let N be the sunk export entry cost and $\hat{\pi}_{it}$ be the incremental profit of the ith representative firm from exporting in the tth time period. Suppose, to maximize profit, ith firm export q_{it} amount of good at price p_t where c_{it} is the production cost. Then, profit from exporting in tth period is

$$\hat{\pi}_{it} = p_t q_{it} - c_{it}(X_{it}, \omega_t) - N\left(1 - \text{Exp}_{it-1}\right) \tag{2}$$

where $\boldsymbol{X}_{it}$ and ω_t are the vector of firm characteristics and vector of time varying exogenous factors, respectively. Firm does not pay the sunk cost, if the previous period export is positive, i.e. if $\text{Exp}_{it-1} = 1$.

Since, in the present exercise, our sample consists of new exporters and non-exporters, we have no firm with non-zero export in either of the previous four years. Consequently, profit becomes a function of only $\boldsymbol{X}_{it}$ and ω_t.[6]

$$\hat{\pi}_{it} = \hat{\pi}_{it}(X_{it}, \omega_t) \tag{3}$$

In a multi-period model, a firm maximizes its composite profit which is the sum of current profit and the present values of the expected future profits. If Π^*_{it} is the composite profit, then, it can be expressed as

$$\Pi^*_{it} = \hat{\pi}_{it}(X_{it}, \omega_t) + E_t(\Pi^*_{it+1}|\text{Exp}_{it}) \tag{4}$$

Applying non-structural approach, we derive a reduced form expression of the composite profit as follows.

$$\Pi^*_{it} = \gamma_0 + \gamma_1 \text{HP}_{it_0} + \gamma_2 \boldsymbol{X}_{it_0} + \delta_J + \omega_t + \varepsilon_{it} \tag{5}$$

Here, HP_{it_0} is the indicator of a firm's past performance in the home market. This is the primary variable of interest. We call it home market performance and measure it by the average growth rate in the home market sales in the past years, specifically, in the past four years. Firm-level primitives such as, size, age, liquidity, R&D intensity, capital intensity, productivity, intensity of imported technology and ownership categories are taken as the control variables. They form the control vector $\boldsymbol{X}_{it_0}$. The suffix t_0 denotes realization in the past years. We take average of the past four years' values of these variables.

Since in our sample firms did not export in the past years, realizations of the variables are associated only with the home market. We use capital stock at replacement cost to represent firm size which we calculate using perpetual inventory method

[6]This is because q_{it} depends $\boldsymbol{X}_{it}$ and ω_t. We have assumed that price p_t is constant across firms. Price, although varies across time, is controlled in the empirical exercise by use of price deflators. N is constant and does not vary across firms.

following Balakrishnan et al. (2000). Following Levinsohn and Petrin (2003), we estimate total factor productivity. Capital intensity is measured as the ratio of stock of capital and compensation to employees, where both the numerator and the denominator are expressed in real terms. Control variables that capture technology are R&D intensity and technology import intensity, and the former is the ratio of expenditure on R&D activities to sales, while the latter is the ratio of import of capital goods to sales. The control variable liquidity is a measure of financial situation of the firm. The current liability is subtracted from current assets and normalized by current assets to obtain the measure of liquidity. We express all the control variables except liquidity in natural logarithm. There are many observations with zero values of the control variables. To avoid their exclusion, we add 1 to the value of the control variables, before taking log. To control the effect of ownership, we consider two ownership dummies—private and the interaction of private with business group affiliation. Private dummy distinguishes private firms from state-owned/public firms where the latter is the omitted category. The interaction term differentiates business group-affiliated private firms from other private firms. To account for industry and time effects, we include industry fixed effects (denoted by, δ_J) and time fixed effects (denoted by, ω_t).

The composite profit Π_{it}^* is a latent variable observed by the firm but not by us. However, exporting behaviour of firm is observable, and it is likely that the firm chooses to export when profit from export is positive and vice versa. Hence,

$$\text{Exp}_{it} = \begin{Bmatrix} 1 \text{ if } \Pi_{it}^* > 0 \\ 0 \text{ if } \Pi_{it}^* \leq 0 \end{Bmatrix} \tag{6}$$

5 Results and Discussions

Using Eqs. (5) and (6), we estimate the probit model to identify the factors that determine export entry for new exporters. Primarily, our objective is to gauge the effect of the past performance in the home market on export entry decision for a firm starting to export for the first time. We use random effect probit model to exploit the panel form of our data, and the estimated coefficients from various specifications are presented in a staggered manner in Table 2. We find home market performance, firm size, total factor productivity, import of foreign technology as well as liquidity to be significant determinants that aid in the export decision of a firm, and the staggered form suggests estimates are robust across specifications.

We find that home market performance is significant and positive across all specifications. The result implies that higher growth rate in the domestic market in the past years induces firms to enter the export market. While operating in the domestic market, some firms grow bigger than others. They gather essential resources through

Table 2 Determinants of export participation for new exporters, 2004–2014

Dependent variable: export status									
Independent variables	(1)	(2)	(3)	(4)	(5)	(6)	(7)	(8)	(9)
Home performance	0.047***	0.048***	0.046***	0.043***	0.045***	0.045***	0.041***	0.042***	0.040***
	(0.009)	(0.009)	(0.009)	(0.009)	(0.009)	(0.009)	(0.009)	(0.009)	(0.009)
Size		0.014***	0.015***	0.018***	0.020***	0.020***	0.020***	0.020***	0.025***
		(0.002)	(0.002)	(0.002)	(0.002)	(0.002)	(0.002)	(0.002)	(0.003)
Age			−0.008*	−0.006	−0.008*	−0.008*	−0.008*	−0.007	−0.006
			(0.004)	(0.004)	(0.005)	(0.005)	(0.005)	(0.005)	(0.005)
Productivity				0.025***	0.023***	0.023***	0.023***	0.018***	0.017***
				(0.006)	(0.006)	(0.006)	(0.006)	(0.006)	(0.006)
Capital intensity					−0.009***	−0.009***	−0.009***	−0.008**	−0.014***
					(0.003)	(0.003)	(0.003)	(0.003)	(0.004)
R&D intensity						0.024	−0.053	−0.057	−0.029
						(0.210)	(0.220)	(0.223)	(0.216)
Tech import intensity							0.206**	0.204**	0.195**
							(0.085)	(0.086)	(0.085)
Liquidity								0.037***	0.036***
								(0.011)	(0.011)
Private									0.088***
									(0.018)
Private*business group									−0.014**
									(0.007)

(continued)

Table 2 (continued)

Dependent variable: export status

Independent variables	(1)	(2)	(3)	(4)	(5)	(6)	(7)	(8)	(9)
Constant	−0.694	−0.675	−0.645	−0.654	−0.647	−0.647	−0.644	−0.628	−0.703
	(1401.83)	(284.33)	(248.76)	(231.16)	(369.15)	(369.23)	(368.21)	(203.72)	(356.29)
Likelihood value	−1652.43	−1627.74	−1626.14	−1616.97	−1613.32	−1613.32	−1610.38	−1604.01	−1588.21
Observations	8098	8098	8098	8098	8098	8098	8098	8098	8098
Number of firms	1961	1961	1961	1961	1961	1961	1961	1961	1961

Note The analysis pertains to the period 2004–2014, and the first three years, 2000–2003, are non-exporting years for both new exporters and non-exporters. The reported values are average partial effects. Standard errors are included in the parentheses. Industry and year dummies are included in all specifications. Private and the interaction of private with business group are the two ownership variables. While the former refers to all the private firms, the later refers to private firms those are affiliated to business groups. State-owned firms form the omitted category of ownership. Random effect probit model is employed in all the specifications. 1% (***), 5% (**) and 10% (*) significance level

Source Own calculation

their performance in the domestic market. Use of such resources increases the risk-taking capabilities of these firms enabling them to enter the export market. Coefficient of home market performance varies only marginally across the specifications.

Firm size is significant and positive, implying that scale advantage enables the large firms to enter the export market. Firm age is negative but insignificant. Age may affect export positively or negatively. Older firms are experienced and therefore are more likely to enter the foreign market. However, since their production technology is deeply rooted, they cannot easily shift to a new modern technology like younger firms. Our result seems to suggest that the export propensity of both experienced and young exporters in our sample is likely offsetting the two types of age effects.

We find a significant negative association between capital intensity and the propensity to export indicating greater likelihood of labour-intensive firms to start export compared to the capital-intensive firms. It corroborates the traditional comparative advantage theory of trade that suggests that a labour abundant country like India would export labour-intensive products. However, it is inconsistent with our finding in Table 1 that showed more intensive use of capital by new exporters compared to non-exporters. The difference in the finding is likely due to the different measure of the capital intensity variable used in the two regressions. Here, in the probit model, we use the past values of capital intensity, whereas in Table 1, capital intensity was a contemporaneous variable. It seems that following entry, capital-intensive technology is used by the new exporters.

Our result supports the self-selection hypothesis since we find that prior productivity increases the present probability of exporting. The result corroborates earlier studies (see, Haidar, 2012; Gupta et al., 2018). As, financially, healthy firms are more capable of paying the entry cost (Greenaway et al., 2007; Nagaraj, 2014), we find that probability of export entry is higher for financially healthy firms. We use two technology variables, namely R&D intensity and imported capital goods, while the former represents research and innovation activities within the firms, the latter represents use of foreign technologies embodied within imported machines and other capital goods. We find that import of capital goods is a positive and significant determinant of export entry. R&D intensity, however, is insignificant. This is not a surprising result as Indian firms do less of innovation and more of imitation.[7]

Probability of export is more for private firms than state-owned firms. This suggests lack of incentives among public firms to improve their size and efficiency that would help in improving productivity and likelihood of export. Business groups affiliated firms are more export oriented than other non-affiliated private firms since they have better business networks and technologies of the parent firm. However, we find the opposite. This could be because of our sample choice. In our sample, we did not consider the incumbent exporters, and this may have excluded many business group-affiliated firms.

---

[7]Innovation activities exclusively happen in pharmaceuticals and chemicals industries in India. Importance of R&D therefore may get reflected in some industry-specific analysis where R&D activities are prevalent. On the other hand, in almost every industry, machines are imported and adapted to the local conditions.

6 Conclusion

We have attempted to empirically investigate the role of the past performance in the home market on a firm's decision to enter the export market in the context of a developing country—India. We considered new exporters as a distinct category, different from incumbent exporters. For our analysis, we divided firms into three categories—incumbent exporters, non-exporters and new exporters—based on the export status of firms in a continuum of five years. We considered new exporters as firms that did not export in the past four years but enter the export market in the current year. Incumbent exporters being firms had exported at least for one year in the past. Firms that did not export in any of the five consecutive years were termed as non-exporters. Comparing between the three groups of firms, we found that both new exporters and incumbent exporters are larger, more productive and more technology-intensive than non-exporters. The comparison between a new exporter and an incumbent exporter revealed that the former is smaller in size relative to the latter, but similar in productivity.

Our analytical model examined the determinants of export entry for new exporters focusing on the role of the past performance in the home market. We measured the past home market performance by the average growth rates in home market sales during the four years prior to entry. Using random effect probit model, we found that the past performance in the home market has been a significant determinant of export entry, where firms that performed well in the domestic market prior to entry are more likely to venture into the export market. Among other factors, firm size, productivity, use of imported of technology and financial health are also confirmed to be important factors that enhance export entry.

References

Aggarwal, A. (2002). Liberalisation, multinational enterprises and export performance: Evidence from Indian manufacturing. *Journal of Development Studies, 38*(3), 119–137.

Alvarez, R., Faruq, H., & Lopez, R. A. (2013). Is previous export experience important for new exports. *Journal of Development Studies, 49*(3), 426–441.

Arnold, J. M., & Hussinger, K. (2005). Export behaviour and firm productivity in germen manufacturing: A firm-Level analysis. *Review of World Economics, 141*(2), 219–243.

Aw, B. Y., Roberts, M. J., & Winston, T. (2007). Export market participation, investments in R&D and worker training, and the evolution of firm productivity. *The World Economy, 30*(1), 83–104.

Balakrishnan, P., Pushpangadan, K., & Babu, M. S. (2000). Trade liberalization and productivity growth in manufactuirng: Evidence from firm-level panel data. *The Economic and Political Weekly, 353*(41), 3679–3682.

Basevi, G. (1970). Domestic demand and ability to export. *Journal of Political Economy, 78*(2), 330–337.

Bernard, A. B., & Jensen, J. B. (1999). Exceptional exporter performance: Cause, effect, or both? *The Journal of International Economics, 47*(1), 1–25.

Bernard, A. B., Jensen, J. B., & Lawrence, R. Z. (1995). Exporters, jobs and wages in U.S. manufacturing: 1976–1987. *Brooking papers Econ Act. Micro, 1995*, 67–112.

Bernard, A. B., & Wagner, J. (2001). Export entry and exit by German firms. *Weltwirtschaftliches Archiv, 137*(1), 105–123.

Bhat, S., & Narayanan, K. (2009). Technological efforts, firm size and exports in the basic chemical industry in India. *Oxford Development Studies, 37*(2), 145–169.

Campa, J. M. (2004). Exchange rates and trade: How important is hysteresis in trade? *The European Economic Review, 48,* 527–548.

Chadha, A. (2009). Product cycles, innovation, and exports: A study of Indian pharmaceuticals. *World Development, 37*(9), 1478–1483.

Clerides, S. K., Lach, S., & Tybout, J. R. (1998). Is learning by exporting important? micro-dynamic evidence from Colombia, Mexico, and Morocco. *Quarterly Journal of Economics, 113*(3), 903–947.

Greenaway, D., Guariglia, A., & Kneller, R. (2007). Financial factors and exporting decisions. *The Journal of International Economics, 73*(2), 377–395.

Gupta, A., Patnaik, I., & Shah, A. (2018). Exporting and firm performance: Evidence from India. *Indian Growth Dev Rev, 12*(1), 83–104.

Haidar, J. I. (2012). Trade and productivity: Self-selection or learning-by-exporting in India. *Economic Modelling, 29*(5), 1766–1773.

Hasan, R., & Raturi, M. (2003). Does investing in technology affect exports? evidence from Indian firms. *Rev Dev Econ, 7*(2), 279–293.

Krugman, P. (1980). Scale economies, product differentiation, and the pattern of trade. *American Economic Review, 70*(5), 950–959.

Kumar, N., & Siddharthan, N. S. (1994). Technology, firm size and export behaviour in developing countries: The case of Indian enterprises. *Journal of Development Studies, 31*(2), 289–309.

Levinsohn, J., & Petrin, A. (2003). Estimating production inputs to functions using control for unobservables. *Review of Economic Studies, 70,* 317–341.

Linder, S. B. (1961). *An essay on trade and transformation.* New York: John Wiley Sons.

Melitz, M. J. (2003). The impact of trade on intra-industry reallocations and aggregate industry productivity. *Econometrica, 71*(6), 1695–1725.

Nagaraj, P. (2014). Financial constraints and export participation. *International Economics, 140,* 19–35.

Padmaja, M., & Sashidharan, S. (2016). Sunk costs, firm heterogeneity, export market entry and exit: Evidence from India. *The Journal of Quantitative Economics, 15*(2), 367–393.

Pattnayak, S. S., & Thangavelu, S. M. (2014). Productivity and learning by exporting: A firm-level analysis of Indian manufacturing. *World Econ, 37*(7), 1016–1026.

Porter, M. E. (1990). *The competitive advantage of nations.* New York: Free Press.

Robert, M. J., & Tybout, J. R. (1997). The decision to export in Colombia: An empirical model of entry with sunk costs. *American Economic Review, 87*(4), 545–564.

Sharma, C., & Mishra, R. K. (2015). Intenational trade and performance of firms: Unravelling export, import and productivity puzzle. *The Quarterly Review of Economics and Finance, 57,* 61–74.

Sinani, E., & Hobdari, B. (2010). Export market participation with sunk costs and firm heterogeneity. *Applied Economics, 42*(25), 3195–3207.

Temouri, Y., Vogel, A., & Wagner, J. (2013). Self-selection into export markets by business services firms-evidence from France, Germany and the United Kingdom. *Struct Change Econ Dyn, 25,* 146–158.

Thomas, R., & Narayanan, K. (2016). Productivity heterogeneity and export market participation: A study of Indian manufacturing firms. In F. De Beule & K. Narayanan (Eds.), *Globalization of Indian industries: Productivity, exports and investment.* New York: Springer.

Vernon, R. (1966). International investment and international trade in the product cycle. *Quarterly Journal of Economics, 80*(2), 190–207.

Vu, H. V., Holmes, M., Tran, T. Q., et al. (2016). Firm exporting and productivity: What if productivity is no longer a black box. *Baltic Journal of Economics, 16*(2), 95–113.

Wagner, J. (2012). International trade and firm performance: A survey of empirical studies since 2006. *Review of World Economics, 148*(2), 235–267.

Chapter 3
Indo-African Trade: A Gravity Model Approach

Vaishnavi Sharma and Akhilesh Mishra

1 Introduction

Africa has been emerging as a promising trading partner of India in recent times. The overall trade between India and Africa has been on a consistent rise since the nineties. The African continent comprises fifty-four nations characterized by variations in physical, economic, political and social dimensions and displays diverse pattern in economic development (World Bank, 2017). Despite facing the world's most formidable development challenges, this region has emerged as an important destination of trade and investment, especially after the integration of the Sub-Saharan continent with the global economy. The competition between firms of India and China to hold significance in African market in recent pasts has renewed the interest of the long forgotten issues of international trade and economic development in general and south–south trade in particular.

The political, cultural and trade relationship between nations of the African subcontinent and India predates to ancient times. The merchants of both sides mutually gained through trade and exchange because of geographical proximity, easily navigable routes and strong complimentary of demand and supply of goods and services (Dubey & Biswas, 2016). The cultural and religious factors also played an important role in promotion and sustenance of the trade for long time specifically during the Sultanate and later Mughal periods of medieval India. It was during the colonial rule that the two subcontinents witnessed notable decline in volume of trade.

However, the recent decades have witnessed a drastic improvement in the socioeconomic relationship between India and Africa. Besides exchange of goods and

V. Sharma (✉)
Indira Gandhi Institute of Development Research (IGIDR), Mumbai, India
e-mail: vaishnavisharma.igidr@gmail.com

A. Mishra
Department of Economics, SD (PG) College, Ghaziabad, India
e-mail: mishraakh@gmail.com

P. Lakhanpal et al. (eds.), *Trade, Investment and Economic Growth*,
https://doi.org/10.1007/978-981-33-6973-3_3

services, there have been grants and issue-based support which has led the relationship (bilateral and multilateral) being scaled to new heights with greater focus on capacity building, development cooperation, economic and technological initiatives and cultural ties. The comprehensive sets of diplomatic mechanisms and summits such as India–Africa Forum Summit (IAFS), India Regional Economic Communities (RECs) meetings, annual India–Africa trade ministers meeting, regular meetings of joint working groups, intergovernmental joint commissions, foreign office consultations and business enclaves have helped in fostering and strengthening India's relation with Africa. The crucial 'Pan-African e-Network' project and interactions at various multilateral forums such as 'Indian Ocean Rim Association for Regional Cooperation' (IOR–ARC)' are opening opportunities for new vista of cooperation.

In the present paper, we focus on the determining factors of Indo-Africa trade using panel data estimation techniques. We have employed generalized gravity models to study our objective.

2 Literature Survey

The conventional trade theories had been interested in identifying the list of the products for trade between the nations that could enhance the welfare of the societies through the gain from the specialization and exchange. But, these theories were unsuccessful in explaining the precise reason behind the concentration of the trade flows across the nations or among the geographical regions over the time. The gravity model derives its name from Newton's theory of gravitation, which simply states that two planets are attracted to each other in proportion to their sizes and proximity to each other. Tinbergen (1962) using Newton's universal gravitation formula concluded that bilateral trade between two countries is directly proportional to their size and inversely proportional to their distance, where levels of income symbolize size and the physical distance characterizes proximity. Several other country-specific characteristics and trade costs[1] are roped into the gravity model to study their impact in later stage (Ranajoy & Tathagat, 2006). Anderson (1979) adopting a linear expenditure system explained the gravity model for aggregate-level parameters. He postulated that preferences for a variety are homothetic and uniform across importing countries. Bergstrand (1985, 1989) developed a microeconomic foundation to the gravity model. According to him, a gravity model is a reduced-form equation of a general equilibrium of demand and supply systems. Since the reduced form eliminates all endogenous variables out of the explanatory part of each equation and gives scope for inclusion of the income and prices as explanatory variables in bilateral trade. The

[1] Anderson and Wincoop (2003) define trade costs to include 'all costs incurred in getting a good to a final user other than the marginal cost of producing the good itself: transportation costs (both freight costs and time costs), policy barriers (tariffs and non-tariff barriers), information costs, contract enforcement costs, costs associated with the use of different currencies, legal and regulatory costs, and local distribution costs (wholesale and retail).'.

inclusion of the income and price in the model gave the foundation for the generalized gravity equation (Krishnakumar, 2002).

Evenett and Keller (2002) noted that the volume of trade is determined by the extent of product specialization, and argue that increasing returns to scale model rather than the perfect specialization version of the Heckscher–Ohlin model is more likely to be a candidate for explaining the success of the gravity equation. They further stipulated that models with imperfect product specialization are more likely to explain variations better in the volume of trade than that of the models with perfect product specialization.

Eaton and Kortum (2002) derived the gravity equation in Ricardian framework using cross-sectional data of nineteen Organisation for Economic Co-operation and Development (OECD) countries. Their model captures the competing forces of comparative advantages promoting trade and of geographic barriers and explored the gains from trade, the effects of tariff reduction, usefulness of technology use and so on.

In the present study, we take up three gravity models to estimate the trade relations between India and Africa. In the first model, we take up the estimation of overall trade, i.e., sum of total exports and imports between India and its African trading partner. In the second and third models, we take up exports of India to Africa and imports of India from Africa, respectively.

The estimation results of the overall trade model suggest that the income levels of both the trading partners (India and African nations) play an important (positive) role in determining the overall trade between them. The openness of the African nation also plays a positive and significant factor in this context. For the gravity model of exports from India to Africa, GDP of the African trading partner of India holds a positive and significant coefficient implying that as their economy grows, their demand for Indian goods (and services) increases. Interestingly, GNP per capita of India exhibits a negative and significant coefficient implying India's exports to Africa decrease on account of rise in its per capita GDP. This may be due to the absorption effect (the increase in income is absorbed due to either increase in imports or more consumption of the export items). The variable imports of Africa hold a positive and significant coefficient with the implication that exports from India to Africa hold a prominent share in African import portfolio. In both these models, the distance variable is associated with a negative and significant coefficient implying the gravity model's other important attribute to hold. The estimation results of the imports of India from Africa also suggest the importance of the income levels of the trading partners. The findings also suggest that when inflation rates in India are high, i.e., money supply growth rate is high, India's imports from Africa are on a rise. The exchange rate is associated with a negative and significant coefficient. This is indicative of the fact that as exchange rate increases, which means that as Indian currency depreciates with respect to African currencies, the imports of India from Africa deteriorate.

The rest of the paper is organized as follows: In Sect. 2, we present some stylized facts of the Indo-African trade. Section 3 presents the sources of the employed data, the variables undertaken and some descriptive statistics. In Sect. 4, we present the methodology, and empirical analysis is done in Sect. 5. Section 6 concludes.

3 Some Stylized Facts of Indo-African Trade

Table 1 shows a snapshot of change in GDP, population, export and import of India, Africa and world over between 1991 and 2014. As is evident from the table, about 32.2% of the world population resided in India and countries of the African continent in 2014 but had disproportionately low shares in world GDP (5.25%), export (4.10%) and import (4.48%). Nevertheless, their shares in aforementioned macro-indicators of the world have started improving with gradual integrations with the rest of the world.

Although nations of the African subcontinents were not privy to the financial and economic crisis of 2008, its impact is clearly visible on the growth of the macroeconomic indicators of these countries through the spread effect (please see Table 2).

Direction of Trade Statistics (DOTS) published the by International Monetary Fund (IMF) records notable progress in trade between India and African nations post-economic liberalizations. India's exports to African nations increased from 460.97 million US dollar (2.6% of the total export value of India) in 1991–92 to 30.85 billion US$ (9.7% of the total export value of India) in 2014–15. The export value increased almost 66.9 times between 1991 and 2014. Not only substantial increase was recorded in export, but import also increased from 909.6 million US $ in 1991(4.7% of the total import value of India) to 34.81 billion US in 2014–15 (8.3% of the total import of India). Despite slow increase in import from Africa (almost 42.2 times between 1991 and 2014), the trade balance remained negative throughout the period under analysis for India.

As is evident from this table, India and Africa witnessed significant improvement in GDP, export and import growth in current dollar terms during 2001–08, but observed notable decline in subsequent period particularly for Africa.

Figure 1 shows closer trade ties between India and African nations, especially in post-liberalization period (1991 onwards). It is also lucid that post the global financial crisis of 2008, the African market is of growing importance to India.

4 Data

4.1 Data Sources

Data sources are World Development Indicators (WDI) Database of the World Bank, United Nations Conference on Trade and Development (UNCTAD) Database of the

Table 1 Trends in GDP, export, import and population (1991–2014)

Year	GDP			Export			Import			Population		
	(Current billion US $)			(Current billion US $)			(Current billion US $)			(In millions)		
	India	Africa	World	India	Africa	World	India	Africa	World	India	Africa	World
1991	274.8	405	23,917	23	94	4483	27	68	4448	888.1	583	5375.5
	(1.15)	(1.69)	(100)	(0.51)	(2.1)	(100)	(0.61)	(1.53)	(100)	(16.5)	(10.8)	(100)
2001	494	453	33,367	62	116	7670	71	87	7621	1071.5	753	6201.3
	(1.48)	(1.36)	(100)	(0.81)	(1.51)	(100)	(0.94)	(1.14)	(100)	(17.3)	(12.1)	(100)
2011	1815.9	1854	73,297	446	572	22,473	553	444	21,271	1247.2	973	7015
	(2.48)	(2.53)	(100)	(1.99)	(2.55)	(100)	(2.6)	(2.09)	(100)	(17.8)	(13.9)	(100)
2014	2042.4	2113	79,131	486	491	23,865	553	443	22,726	1293.9	1048	7271.3
	(2.58)	(2.67)	(100)	(2.04)	(2.06)	(100)	(2.43)	(1.95)	(100)	(17.8)	(14.4)	(100)

Note Figure in brackets indicates share in percent. *Source* Authors' calculations from World Development Indicators (World Bank, 2018)

Table 2 Annual growth of GDP, export and import

Region	GDP			Export growth			Import growth		
	1991–00	2001–08	2009–14	1991–00	2001–08	2009–14	1991–00	2001–08	2009–14
India	6.9	15.5	6.7	11.1	26.9	12.1	12.2	28.7	10.2
Africa	2.1	17.7	9.7	3.2	26	5.3	3.5	24.4	6.5
World	3.8	10	5.5	6.3	15.3	8	6.3	14.9	7.9

Source Authors' calculations from World Development Indicators (World Bank, 2018)

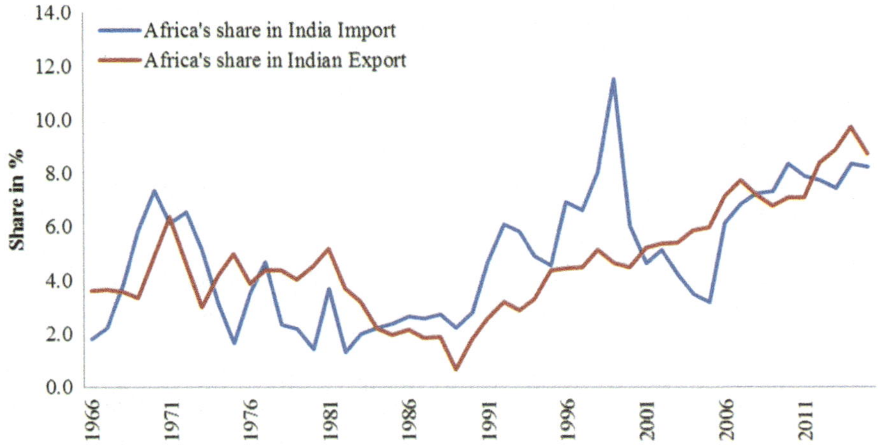

Fig. 1 Trends in share of African nations in export and import of India. *Source* Based on authors' calculation from DOTS (IMF) and UNCTAD

United Nations and RBI's Database on Indian Economy. For calculating the distance between two capital cities, we use the site https://www.distancecalculator.net/.

We have considered fifty African nations for our analysis based on data availability. We have taken annual data on import and export (trade) between an African nation and India from UNCTAD. All the other annual data come from WDI database. The time period of the study is 1991–2014.

4.2 Variables Employed

(i) Gross domestic product (GDP)[2]: It is a representative of any economy's overall size. With increase in the size of an economy, there is increase in likelihood of higher trade. And hence, a positive association between GDP and trade is expected. We have taken the log of the GDP for India and the African countries.

(ii) GDP per capita: An increase in GDP (or GNP) per capita is an indication of overall development of any economy. We can say this as developed economies of the world have GDP per capita way higher than that prevailing in developing or poor economies. Hence, a rise in GDP per capita would imply better economic prospects and hence better economies of scale and hence enhanced trade. So, we expect a positive relationship between GDP per capita and trade. On the other hand, if due to absorption effect, the country

[2]Alternatively, we also use gross national product (GNP).

produces less export than earlier then there would be a negative association between GDP per capita and trade. We have also used GDP per capita differential between India and African nations in our analyses.

(iii) Distance: This refers to the physical distance between India and an African nation. As per the basic premise of gravity model, an increase in the physical distance between two trading nations has an adverse impact on the trade between them as this increases the transportation costs. We have taken the log of distance for our analysis.

(iv) Trade tax: We have taken trade tax as taxes on international trade as percent of revenue. Any kind of tax on trade is expected to prevent free flow of trade. Hence, a negative association is expected between trade tax and trade.

(v) Inflation rate: An increase in inflation in a country would hurt exports but at the same time encourage imports. Hence, an increase in the inflation rate in India would imply an increase in overall imports of India and decrease in its overall exports (of which African imports or exports would also be a part).

(vi) Exchange rate: An increase in exchange rate of a country implies depreciation of the currency. Depreciation boosts exports while discourages imports. Hence, if Indian currency depreciates, Indian exports would be on a rise while imports would fall.

(vii) Trade/GDP: This would be an indicator of how open an economy is. With increase in this ratio, an increase in exports or imports (or both) of that particular country is expected. We have also used import–GDP ratio and export–GDP ratio for our different gravity models.

(viii) Export and import data: We have used total export and import data of India and African nations and also exports of India to African nations and imports of India from these nations to study different objectives.

Wherever applicable, we have employed current USD. For India, for total trade (sum of imports and exports) we have used the sum of exports of goods and services (current USD, BOP) and imports of goods and services (current USD, BOP) since data on imports based on current USD were unavailable.

Table 3 presents the various variables employed in our study, their descriptions and their sources.

4.3 Descriptive Statistics

Table 4 presents the summary statistics of the variables which we have used in our analysis. As is evident from the table, trade between India and the African nations varies significantly with each African nation. While the minimum value of trade between them is 0.19 (USD million per year), the maximum value is in the range of 19,000 USD million. Of the African nations, Nigeria, South Africa and Kenya are the highest importers of Indian goods and services in recent times; Nigeria and South Africa are also among the highest exporters to India.

Table 3 Variables employed

Variable	Unit	Description	Source(s)
Trade	In USD million	Sum of imports and exports of India from African nations	UNCTAD
Log (GDP_AN)	Logarithm	GDP of African nation	WDI
Log (GDP_IN)	Logarithm	GDP of India	WDI
GDP PC_AN	In USD	GDP per capita of African nation	WDI
GDP PC_IN	In USD	GDP per capita of India	WDI
Log (Distance)	Logarithm	Geographical distance between India and African nation	https://www.distancecalculator.net/
ExchRate	Per INR	Currency of African nation per INR	WDI, RBI
Inflation_AN	Percent	Inflation rate in African nation, CPI $q-q\%$ change	WDI
Inflation_IN	Percent	Inflation rate in India, CPI $q-q\%$ change	WDI
Trade/GDP_AN	Ratio	Trade as percent of GDP of African nation	WDI
Trade/GDP_IN	Ratio	Trade as percent of GDP of India	WDI
Import_IN_AN	In USD	Import to India from African nation	UNCTAD
Export_IN_AN	In USD	Export of India to African nation	UNCTAD
GNP PC_AN	In USD	GNP per capita of African nation	WDI
GNP PC_IN	In USD	GNP per capita of India	WDI
GNP PC_Diff	In USD	GNP per capita differential between India and African nation	WDI
Tradetax_AN*IN	Percent	Product of tax on trade in India and African nation	WDI
Log (GNP_AN*IN)	Logarithm	Product of GNP of India and African nation	WDI
Export_AN	Logarithm	Total exports of African nation	WDI
Export_IN	Logarithm	Total exports of India	WDI
Import_AN	Logarithm	Total imports of African nation	WDI
Import_IN	Logarithm	Total imports of India	WDI

Source Authors' calculations from World Development Indicators (World Bank, 2018)

Table 4 Summary statistics

Variable	Mean	Std. dev	Min	Max
Trade	455.16	1627.16	0.19	18,547.74
Log (GDP_AN)	22.31	1.59	18.10	27.07
Log (GDP_IN)	27.27	0.67	26.34	28.35
GDP PC_AN	1548.73	2630.80	64.81	23,347.66
GDP PC_IN	751.52	431.14	307.41	1576.82
Log (Distance)	8.87	0.23	8.30	9.18
ExchRate	13.45	36.16	0.00	404.55
Inflation_AN	76.95	1061.30	−35.84	24,411.03
Inflation_IN	7.65	2.98	3.68	13.23
Trade/GDP_AN	77.89	49.65	11.47	531.74
Trade/GDP_IN	34.72	12.99	18.21	56.10
Import_IN_AN	268.95	1248.35	0.00	15,674.13
Export_IN_AN	166.82	495.57	0.01	5614.39
GNP PC_AN	1407.82	2129.94	80	14,090
GNP PC_IN	745.00	423.51	330	1560
GNP PC_Diff	−660.82	2054.17	−12,530	1290
Tradetax_AN*IN	354.87	276.85	3.38	1411.36
Log (GNP_AN*IN)	13.01	1.38	10.65	16.91
Export_AN	21.05	1.77	16.22	25.70
Export_IN	25.35	1.03	23.86	26.91
Import_AN	21.41	1.47	17.86	25.54
Import_IN	25.54	1.04	24.02	27.09

Source Authors' calculations from World Development Indicators (World Bank, 2018)

If we look at the per capita income (per capita GDP/GNP) of the African nations, we find the standard deviation to be very high. This is so because while some of the African nations have their per capita incomes quite high (much higher than India), others have their per capita incomes very low. This points to the huge disparity in terms of income in the African nations. Even the inflation rate in Africa exhibits strikingly huge standard deviation.

5 Methodology

As per the generalized gravity model of trade, the volume of trade between two nations is a function of their income levels, populations in the two countries, the physical distance between them, some other country-specific factors and a set of dummy variables either facilitating or restricting trade between pairs of countries.

The econometric specification for gravity model can be presented as:

$$X_{ij} = \beta_0 Y_i^{B_1} Y_j^{\beta_2} N_i^{\beta_3} N_j^{\beta_4} D_{ij}^{\beta_5} A_{ij}^6 U_{ij} \tag{1}$$

where X_{ij} is the trade between the two nations i and j. Y is the national income of the nations (GDP/GNP). N is the population, and D_{ij} is the geographical distance between the capital cities of the two nations. A is the set of dummy variables, U is the error term, and $\beta's$ are parameters to be estimated.

Employing per capita income instead of population, the formulation in 1 can be rewritten as:

$$X_{ij} = \beta_0 Y_i^{B_1} Y_j^{\beta_2} y_i^{\beta_3} y_j^{\beta_4} D_{ij}^{\beta_5} A_{ij}^6 U_{ij} \tag{2}$$

where y is the per capita income.

Since the gravity model is formulated in multiplicative form, for simplification purposes (as we are interested in seeing the impact of each variable) we linearize the model by taking the natural logarithm of all variables. Hence, the gravity model in log-linear terms is given as:

$$\begin{aligned} \text{Log}X_{ij} &= \beta_0 + \beta_1 \text{Log}Y_i + \beta_2 \text{Log}Y_j + \beta_3 \text{Log}y_i \\ &\quad + \beta_4 \text{Log}y_j + \beta_5 \text{Log}D_{ij} + \beta_6 \text{Log}A_{ij} + U_{ij} \end{aligned} \tag{3}$$

We estimate the trade between India and Africa by employing three different gravity models which are as follows:

1. Total Indo-African trade (exports + imports)
2. India's exports to Africa
3. India's imports from Africa.

For the first model, we have followed Frankel (1997). The dependent variable in the gravity model is bilateral trade (sum of exports and imports) between India and African nation. The product of GNP/GDP and the product of per capita GNP/GDP have been used as independent variables. We have added some additional independent variables in our model. Thus, the gravity model of trade in this study is:

$$\begin{aligned} \text{Log}X_{ij} &= \alpha_1 + \alpha_2 \text{Log}(\text{GNP}_i * \text{GNP}_j) \\ &\quad + \alpha_3 \text{Log}(\text{GNPPC}_i * \text{GNPPC}_j) \\ &\quad + \alpha_4 \text{Log}(\text{TRADETAX}_i * \text{TRADETAX}_j) \\ &\quad + \alpha_5 \text{Log}(\text{DISTANCE}_{ij}) + \alpha_6 \text{Log}(\text{PCGNPDIFF}_{ij}) \\ &\quad + \alpha_7 (\text{TRADE/GDP})_i + \alpha_8 (\text{TRADE/GDP})_j + U_{ij} \end{aligned} \tag{4}$$

where

X_{ij}	is the total trade between India (country *i*) and an African country (country *j*).
$GNP_i(GNP_j)$	is the gross national product of country *i*(*j*).
$GNPPC_i(GNPPC_j)$	is the GNP per capita of country *i*(*j*).
$TRADETAX_i(TRADETAX_j)$	is the trade tax as percent of revenue of country *i*(*j*).
$DISTANCE_{ij}$	is the distance between country *i* and country *j*.
$PCGNPDIFF_{ij}$	is the per capital GNP differential between country *i* and country *j*.
$(TRADE/GDP)_i$	is the trade–GDP ratio of country *i*.
$(TRADE/GDP)_j$	is the trade–GDP ratio of country *j*.
U_{ij}	is the error term.
α's	are the parameters to be estimated.

In this gravity model of trade, a priori, we expect the coefficients of the products of GNP_s and $GNPPC_s$ to be positive, the coefficient of the product of $TRADETAX_s$ to be negative, the coefficient of DISTANCE to be negative and the coefficient of TRADE/GDP (for both *i* and *j*) to be positive for reasons explained in the 'variables employed' section. For the coefficient of PCGNPDIFF, two contradicting theories coexist. As per the Linder hypothesis which suggests that countries with similar per capita GNP would trade more, the coefficient of PCGNPDIFF should be negative (as larger the difference in per capita GNP of two countries, lesser would be the trade) while as per the Heckscher–Ohlin theory which suggests that countries with dissimilar incomes should trade more based on their respective favorable factors of production (which they can use the most intensely), the coefficient of PCGNPDIFF should be positive.

For exports from India to Africa, we consider the following gravity model:

$$\begin{aligned}\mathrm{Log}Y_{ij} = {} & \beta_1 + \beta_2\mathrm{Log}(\mathrm{GNP}_i) + \beta_3\mathrm{Log}(\mathrm{GNP}_j) \\ & + \beta_4\mathrm{Log}(\mathrm{GNPPC}_i) + \beta_5\mathrm{Log}(\mathrm{GNPPC}_j) \\ & + \beta_6\mathrm{Log}(\mathrm{DISTANCE}_{ij}) + \beta_7\mathrm{Log}(\mathrm{PCGNPDIFF}_{ij}) \\ & + \beta_8\mathrm{Log}(\mathrm{EXCHRATE}_{ij}) + \beta_9\mathrm{Log}(\mathrm{INFL}_i) \\ & + \beta_{10}\mathrm{Log}(\mathrm{INFL}_j) + \beta_{11}\mathrm{Log}(\mathrm{TOTEXP}_i) \\ & + \beta_{12}\mathrm{Log}(\mathrm{TOTIMP}_j) + \beta_{13}(\mathrm{TRADE/GDP})_i \\ & + \beta_{14}(\mathrm{TRADE/GDP})_j + U_{ij} \end{aligned} \tag{5}$$

where

Y_{ij}	is the total exports from India (*i*) to an African nation (*j*).
GNP	denotes gross national product and GNPPC stands for GNP per capita.
DISTANCE*ij*	is the physical distance between the two countries.

PCGNPDIFF is the difference between per capita GNP between the two countries.
EXCHRATE is the exchange rate prevailing between the two nations i and j.
INFL stands for inflation rate.
TOTEXP stands for total exports.
TOTIMP stands for total imports.
And (TRADE/GDP) is the trade–GDP ratio.

In this case of the gravity model of exports from India to Africa, a priori, we expect the coefficients of GNPs to be positive. We expect the coefficient of exchange rate to be positive as higher exchange rate (Indian rupee *vis-à-vis* African nation's currency) would imply cheaper exports for African nations. We also expect β_{10} to be positive as higher inflation rate in Africa would imply higher flow of money in their economy which would imply higher demand for imports. Further, we expect the coefficients of β_{11}, β_{12}, β_{13}, β_{14} and β_{15} to be positive. We expect negative signs for β_6 and β_9. β_4 and β_5 may be of wither sign depending upon how the increase in per capita income is put to use. If this leads to increase in economies of scale, the coefficients would be positive but if this leads to the absorption effect which would mean decrease in exports, then the coefficients would be negative. For reasons explained in the trade model, the sign of the coefficients of β_7 is also ambiguous.

For India's imports from Africa, we consider the following gravity model:

$$\begin{aligned}\text{Log}Z_{ij} = {} & \delta_1 + \delta_2\text{Log}(\text{GNP}_i) + \delta_3\text{Log}(\text{GNP}_j) \\ & + \delta_4\text{Log}(\text{GNPPC}_i) + \delta_5\text{Log}(\text{GNPPC}_j) \\ & + \delta_6\text{Log}(\text{DISTANCE}_{ij}) + \delta_7\text{Log}(\text{EXCHRATE}_{ij}) \\ & + \delta_8\text{Log}(\text{INFL}_i) + \delta_9\text{Log}(\text{INFL}_j) + \delta_{10}(\text{EXP/GDP})_j \\ & + \delta_{11}(\text{TRADE/GDP})_i + \delta_{12}(\text{TRADE/GDP})_j + U_{ij} \end{aligned} \tag{6}$$

Here,

Z_{ij} is the total imports of India from Africa.
(EXP/GDP) implies export–GDP ratio of African nation (j).

All the other variables are characterized in the same manner as in the export gravity model. We expect positive signs for δ_2, δ_3, δ_9, δ_{11}, δ_{12} and δ_{13} and negative signs for δ_6, δ_8 and δ_{10}. For δ_4, δ_5 and δ_7, the signs may be either positive or negative.

6 Empirical Analysis

First of all, we see if the data series employed to study our objectives are stationary or not. This is important since a non-stationary data series tends to give us spurious results. We conduct fisher-type tests for checking the stationarity of our data series.

Table 5 Presence of unit roots

Variables	Fisher-type	Integration order
GNP_AN*IN	Yes	I(1)
GNPPC_AN*IN	Yes	I(1)
Tradetax_AN*IN	No	I(0)
GNP PC_Diff	Yes	I(1)
Trade/GDP_IN	Yes	I(1)
Trade/GDP_AN	No	I(1)
Exports_IN_AN	Yes	I(1)
GDP_IN	Yes	I(1)
GDP_AN	Yes	I(1)
GDP PC_IN	Yes	I(1)
GDP PC_AN	Yes	I(1)
Exchrate	Yes	I(1)
Inflation_IN	No	I(0)
Inflation_AN	No	I(0)
Export_IN	Yes	I(1)
Import_AN	Yes	I(1)
Imports/GDP_AN	Yes	I(1)
Import_IN_AN	Yes	I(1)
Exports/GDP_IN	No	I(0)
Population	Yes	I(1)
Trade	Yes	I(1)

Source Authors' calculations from World Development Indicators (World Bank, 2018)

Table 5 presents the results of the unit root tests. Except for trade tax between India and Africa, trade–GDP ratio of Africa, export–GDP ratio of India and inflation rates, all the other series are found to be integrated of order one. We first difference the series to make them stationary.

6.1 The Gravity Model of Overall Trade Between India and Africa

In our estimation of the model, we have a strongly balanced dataset and individual effects are included in the model. These individual effects can be fixed as well as random. We present results for both country fixed effects (FE) and random effects (RE). We do this for two reasons. First, with FE estimation the unobserved heterogeneity among countries is taken into consideration which render us relatively unbiased estimates, while with RE estimation this unobserved heterogeneity is considered

Table 6 RE estimation results of trade between India and Africa

Log trade	Random effects			
	(1991–2014)			
Variables	Coefficient	Std. error	t ratio	P > |t|
Log (GNP_AN*IN)	**0.627**	0.230	2.730	0.006
Log (GNPPC_AN*IN)	0.070	0.311	0.220	0.823
Log (Tradetax_AN*IN)	0.358	0.144	2.480	0.659
Log (Distance)	**−0.155**	0.353	−0.440	0.013
Log (GNPPC_Diff)	−0.004	0.117	−0.030	0.973
Trade/GDP_AN	**0.012**	0.004	2.770	0.006
Trade/GDP_IN	0.013	0.013	0.950	0.341
Constant	**−30.587**	8.973	−3.410	0.001
R^2	0.556			
No. of observations	171			
No. of groups	21			

Source Authors' calculations from World Development Indicators (World Bank, 2018)

to be random which leads to biased estimates but then with RE estimation we get more efficient estimates of those variables that do not change much over time like in our case, distance is a fixed factor but is quite important in our analysis (Nier et al, 2014). Table 6 presents the results of the RE estimation of trade between India and Africa.

As is evident from the findings, the coefficient of the product of the GNPs of both the trading partners which is a representative of their size, i.e., India and African nation, is positive and significant implying growth of their economies leads to increase in trade between them. The coefficient of distance between India and its African trading partner is negative and significant proving the gravity theorem to hold place here. It is also found that as the total trade–GDP ratio (which shows how open a country is) of the African nation increases, its trade with India rises significantly. The other variables exhibit expected signs but do not emerge as significant. In Table 7, we take the country fixed effects into consideration. Here, we find only distance and trade–GDP ratio to be significant (with expected signs).

The country-specific effect comes significant for majority of the African nations of our sample. This implies that country-specific characteristics play an important role in determining the trade between them and India.

6.2 The Gravity Model of Exports from India to Africa

Table 8 presents the estimation results of the gravity model of exports from India to Africa.

Table 7 Country FE estimation results of trade between India and Africa

Log trade	Country fixed effects			
	(1991–2014)			
Variables	Coefficient	Std. error	t ratio	P > t
Log(GNP_AN*IN)	0.275	0.311	0.880	0.377
Log(GNPPC_AN*IN)	0.344	0.388	0.890	0.375
Log(Tradetax_AN*IN)	0.385	0.158	2.440	0.150
Log Distance	**−2.829**	1.604	−1.760	0.078
Log(GNPPC_Diff)	0.084	0.127	0.660	0.507
Trade/GDP_AN	**0.008**	0.005	1.700	0.090
Trade/GDP_IN	0.021	0.013	1.560	0.119
Country fixed effects				
Benin	**1.878**	1.065	1.760	0.078
Burkina Faso	0.462	1.123	0.410	0.681
Burundi	**−2.881**	0.571	−5.050	0.000
Central African Rep	**−3.784**	0.549	−6.900	0.000
Congo, Dem. Rep	**−1.117**	0.640	−1.740	0.081
Cote d'Ivoire	−0.130	0.537	−0.240	0.809
Ethiopia	**−4.218**	2.375	−1.780	0.076
Ghana	**2.161**	1.077	2.010	0.045
Guinea	0.439	1.497	0.290	0.769
Kenya	−1.883	1.799	−1.050	0.295
Madagascar	**−2.974**	0.755	−3.940	0.000
Mali	1.024	1.248	0.820	0.412
Mozambique	**1.548**	0.560	2.770	0.006
Rwanda	**−2.985**	0.839	−3.560	0.000
Senegal	**2.676**	1.482	1.810	0.071
Sudan	**−3.527**	1.979	−1.780	0.075
Tanzania	−0.155	1.096	−0.140	0.887
Togo	**1.913**	1.128	1.700	0.090
Zambia	**−2.637**	1.494	−1.770	0.077
R^2	0.896			
No. of observations	171			
No. of groups	21			

Source Authors' calculations from World Development Indicators (World Bank, 2018)

Table 8 RE estimation results of exports from India to Africa

Log exports from India to Africa	Random effects			
	(1991–2014)			
Variables	Coefficient	Std. err	t ratio	P > |t|
Log (GDP_IN)	1.539	1.305	1.180	0.238
Log (GDP_AN)	**0.396**	0.175	2.260	0.024
Log (GNP PC_IN)	**−1.387**	0.771	−1.800	0.072
Log (GNP PC_AN)	−0.277	0.106	−2.610	0.119
Log (Distance)	**−0.472**	0.181	−2.610	0.009
Log (ExchRate)	**−0.071**	0.020	−3.600	0.000
Log (Inflation_IN)	**−0.184**	0.105	−1.760	0.078
Log (Inflation_AN)	−0.026	0.028	−0.940	0.346
Log (Exports_IN)	0.595	0.834	0.710	0.476
Log (Imports_AN)	**0.373**	0.165	2.260	0.024
(Trade/GDP)_IN	0.008	0.021	0.380	0.704
(Trade/GDP)_AN	−0.005	0.002	−3.140	0.200
Constant	**−57.902**	13.983	−4.140	0.000
R^2	0.629			
No. of observations	898			
No. of groups	47			

Source Authors' calculations from World Development Indicators (World Bank, 2018)

In this case, we find the coefficients of the GDP of the African trading partner of India to hold a positive and significant coefficient implying that as their economy grows, their demand for Indian goods (and services) increases. Interestingly, GNP per capita of India exhibits a negative and significant coefficient implying India's exports to Africa decrease on account of rise in its per capita GDP. This may be due to the absorption effect (the increase in income is absorbed due to either increase in imports or more consumption of the export items). In this model too, the distance variable is associated with a negative and significant coefficient. The variable imports of Africa hold a positive and significant coefficient with the implication that exports from India to Africa hold a prominent share in African import portfolio.

6.3 *The Gravity Model of Imports of India from Africa*

Table 9 presents the estimation results of the gravity model of imports of India from Africa.

The estimation results suggest that with increase in the GDP of both India and its African exporter nation, the imports of India from Africa increase. This is also

Table 9 RE estimation results of imports of India from Africa

Log imports of India from Africa	Random effects			
	(1991–2014)			
Variables	Coefficient	Std. err	*t* ratio	$P > \|t\|$
Log (GDP_IN)	**1.827**	1.078	1.69	0.09
Log (GDP_AN)	**0.926**	0.179	5.16	0
Log (GNP PC_IN)	−0.957	1.446	−0.66	0.508
Log (GNP PC_AN)	−0.071	0.215	−0.33	0.742
Log (Distance)	0.463	0.336	1.38	0.168
Log (ExchRate)	**−0.151**	0.053	−2.85	0.004
Log (Inflation_IN)	**0.288**	0.156	1.84	0.065
Log (Inflation_AN)	0.002	0.057	0.04	0.97
(Exports/GDP)_AN	−1.274	0.991	−1.29	0.199
(Trade/GDP)_IN	0.019	0.016	1.2	0.232
(Trade/GDP)_AN	0.005	0.004	1.09	0.276
Constant	**−64.320**	20.787	−3.09	0.002
R^2	0.461			
No. of observations	822			
No. of groups	47			

symbolic of how individual African nations' growth in GDP boosts their exports to India. The inflation rate of India is associated with a positive and significant coefficient. This suggests that when inflation rates in India are high, i.e., money supply growth rate is high, India's imports from Africa are on a rise. The exchange rate is associated with a negative and significant coefficient. This is indicative of the fact that as exchange rate increases, which means that as Indian currency depreciates with respect to African currencies, the imports of India from Africa deteriorate.

7 Summary and Conclusion

There has been a considerable rise in the overall trade between India and Africa, particularly after the global financial crisis. The last decade has witnessed an unprecedented growing engagement of India with the African continent. Competition between Indian and Chinese firms to trade more with Africa only proves its hidden trading potential. The present study tries to understand the underlying determinants of trade between India and Africa. We employ generalized gravity models to study our objective. Gravity model has been used extensively in the economic literature to analyze the trade pattern between nations. In our analysis, we estimate the gravity models of overall trade and also of import and that of export between India and Africa.

The estimation results of the overall trade model suggest that the income levels of both the trading partners (India and African nations) play an important (positive) role in determining the overall trade between them. The openness of the African nation also plays a positive and significant factor in this context. For the gravity model of exports from India to Africa, GDP of the African trading partner of India holds a positive and significant coefficient implying that as their economy grows, their demand for Indian goods (and services) increases. Interestingly, GNP per capita of India exhibits a negative and significant coefficient implying India's exports to Africa decrease on account of rise in its per capita GDP. This may be due to the absorption effect (the increase in income is absorbed due to either increase in imports or more consumption of the export items). The variable imports of Africa hold a positive and significant coefficient with the implication that exports from India to Africa hold a prominent share in African import portfolio. In both these models, the distance variable is associated with a negative and significant coefficient implying the gravity model's other important attribute to hold. The estimation results of the imports of India from Africa also suggest the importance of the income levels of the trading partners. The findings also suggest that when inflation rates in India are high, i.e., money supply growth rate is high, India's imports from Africa are on a rise. The exchange rate is associated with a negative and significant coefficient. This is indicative of the fact that as exchange rate increases, which means that as Indian currency depreciates with respect to African currencies, the imports of India from Africa deteriorate. Overall, the findings suggest that this south–south cooperation of Indo-African trade has great potential benefits which if realized will lead to economic gains for both the trading partners.

References

Anderson, J. E., & van Wincoop, E. (2003). Gravity with Gravitas: A solution to the border puzzle. *American Economic Review, 93*(1), 170–192.

Anderson, J. E. (1979). A theoretical foundation for the gravity equation. *American Economic Review, 69*, 106–116.

Bergstrand, J. H. (1985). The gravity equation in international trade: Some microeconomic foundations and empirical evidence. *Review of Economics and Statistics, 67*(3), 474–481.

Bergstrand, J. H. (1989). The generalised gravity equation, monopolistic competition, and the factor proportion theory in international trade. *Review of Economics and Statistics, 71*(1), 143–153.

Dubey, A.K., & Biswas, A., (2016). India–Africa relations: historical goodwill and a vision for the future. India: Springer

Evenett, S. J., & Keller, W. (2002). On the theories explaining the success of the gravity equation. *Journal of Political Economy, 110*(2), 281–316.

Frankel, J. A. (1997). *Regional trading blocks in the World economy*. New York: Institute of International Economics.

Krishnakumar, J. (2002). *A SUR-EC-AR system gravity model of trade*. Working Paper. Geneva, Switzerland: University of Geneva, Department of Economics.

Nier, E., Sedik, T. S., & Mondino, T. (2014). *Gross private capital flows to emerging markets: can the global financial cycle be tamed?* (No. 14–196). International Monetary Fund.
Ranajoy, B., & Tathagat, B. (2006). *Does the gravity model explain India's direction of trade?* A Panel Data Approach W.P. No. 2006–09–01. IIM Ahmadabad
RBI's Database on Indian Economy
Tinbergen, J. (1962). *Shaping the world economy: Suggestions for an international economic policy.* New York, NY: The Twentieth Century Fund.
United Nations Conference on Trade and Development (UNCTAD) Database.
World Bank. (2018). World Bank Annual Report 2018.
World Development Indicators Database of the World Bank.

Chapter 4
The Validity of *J*-Curve: India Versus BRICS Countries: A Panel Cointegration Approach

Ganapati Mendali

1 Introduction

Devaluation[1] is a more effective macroeconomic policy which helps in the attainment of competitiveness in trade (Bahmani-Oskooee & Harvey, 2009). However, there is a diverse effect seen in the economy because of it. In the short run, there may be deterioration in trade balance, but it would improve over the long run. It is normally depicted as the *J*-curve phenomenon. It has achieved ample attention from scholars in international economics (Magee, 1973).

Magee argued that in the post-devaluation period, the country's (obliged) transactions made based on earlier contracts (i.e., before the declaration of devaluation) put pressure on the balance of trade (owing an increase in foreign currency) and influence the short-run situation. When time passes, a brand new agreement is completed at fresh prices resulting in the rise of elasticities that exert a favorable effect on the balance of trade. Junz and Rhomberg (1973) discovered five kinds of lags such as recognition, decision, delivery, replacement, and production lags, which delay favorable outcomes on the trade balance. Arndt and Dorrance (1987) believe that stickiness in domestic currency prices of exports is responsible for the occurrence of *J*-curve.

According to economic theory, the positive result of devaluation depends on the elasticities of exports as well as imports. If the sum of elasticities of exports and imports is larger than one (popularly recognized as Marshall–Lerner stipulation), there will be an improvement in the balance of trade after currency devaluation.

G. Mendali (✉)
Anchalik Kishan College, Bheden, Bargarh, Odisha 768104, India
e-mail: ganapatimendali@gmail.com

[1] Devaluation denotes decreasing the value of a country's currency with reference to other currencies officially, and depreciation shows decrease in the value of a country's currency concerning other currencies owing to market forces. However, in this study, these terms are used interchangeably.

P. Lakhanpal et al. (eds.), *Trade, Investment and Economic Growth*,
https://doi.org/10.1007/978-981-33-6973-3_4

However, Bahmani-Oskooee (1985) found the deterioration of trade balance even with the fulfilment of the Marshall–Lerner criterion.

It recommended that the focal point of trade ought to be on the short-run elements which could plot the post-devaluation conduct of trade balance. Bahmani-Oskooee and Harvey (2012) demonstrated that the short-run response of the balance of trade to currency devaluation does not adhere to a specific pattern. However, the exchange rate and trade balance are shown concrete evidence in the long run.

Devaluation of a currency is required to develop its trade balance by the way of impact on export (increase) and import (decline). But it takes some time to realize the full effect. Junz and Rhomberg (1973) stated that it takes three years for 50% of the final long-run quantity response and five years for 90% to occur. Often, the devaluating countrys may experience deterioration in its balance of trade in the short run before any improvement in its trade balance in the long run. This deterioration of trade balance initially and its expansion latter resembles letter J and known as the J-curve hypothesis. Since Magee introduced this phenomenon in 1973 (Brooking Papers on Economic Activity, 1, pp. 303–25), various endeavors are made to examine the occurrence of this.

Several studies established the reality of the *J*-curve. For example, Hacker and Hatemi (2004) for Czech Republic, Hungary, and Poland; Bahmani-Oskooee (1985) for Greece, India, Korea, and Thailand; Narayan and Narayan (2004) for Fiji, and Gomes and Paz (2005) for Brazil. There are also studies refuting this existence in the countries, like Australia (Bahmani-Oskooee et al., 2005), Brazil (Moura and Da Silva, 2005), China (Bahmani-Oskooee and Wang, 2006), Turkey (Halicioglu, 2008), and Pakistan (Bahmani-Oskooee and Cheema, 2009). Rose and Yellen (1989) examined the instance of America and found that the balance of trade was not responding to the real exchange rate both in the short and long run for neither the G-7 countries nor a group of developing countries. Similarly, Hsing (2005) discovered the non-occurrence of the *J*-curve of the USA concerning bilateral trade of Japan, Korea, and Taiwan. Using quarterly data, Halicioglu (2008) studied bilateral *J*-curve elements of Turkey with her 13 trading partners[2] and found that there is no occurrence of *J*-curve with any of the trading partners.

However, some studies report mixed results of the *J*-curve. Bahmani-Oskooee and Brooks (1999) established no hint of any short-run conduct of the *J*-curve experience. Anyway, over the long haul, a real depreciation of the dollar positively affects the balance of trade of the USA concerning her six trading partners.[3] By applying the cointegration techniques of the ARDL approach, Bahmani-Oskooee and Kantipong (2001) examined the *J*-curve trend of Thailand with her five biggest trading accomplices (Germany, Japan, Singapore, the UK, and the USA) from 1973:I to 1997:IV. It established that *J*-curve happened in the bilateral trade balance between Thailand and Japan and between Thailand and the USA. Bahmani-Oskooee and Ratha (2007)

[2]The data is from 1985Q1 to 2002Q1 for Austria, Belgium, France, Germany, Holland, and Italy, and for Canada, Denmark, Japan, Sweden, Switzerland, UK, and the USA, it is from 1985: I to 2005: IV.

[3]Canada, France, Germany, Italy, Japan, and the UK.

investigated the impact of real depreciation of Swedish Krona on her balance of trade both in the short and long run by utilizing quarterly bilateral information of Sweden and her 17 trading accomplices.[4] It discovered 14 out of 17 cases that there exists a short-run impact of the depreciation of krona on the balance of trade. The *J*-curve phenomenon for Sweden occurs just with five countries, i.e., the UK, Netherlands, Austria, Denmark, and Italy. Then again, the short-run impacts do not keep going into the long run. Bahmani-Oskooee and Harvey (2009) found a short-run impact of real depreciation of rupiah in most of the cases while analyzing bilateral trade balance between Indonesia and her 13 trading partners.[5] However, *J*-curve criteria are fulfilled only in five out of 13 trading partners such as Singapore, Canada, Malaysia, Japan, and the UK. Similarly, Bahmani-Oskooee and Harvey (2012) established support for *J*-curve in four of 13 cases.[6] The outcomes offer support for a *J*-curve between Singapore and the countries such as Saudi Arabia, the USA, Canada, and the Philippines. By using fully modified OLS for heterogeneous cointegrated panel (panel FMOLS) and panel error correction model (panel ECM), Wang et al. (2012) found the transformed *J*-curve hypothesis between China and its trading associates. It also established that the appreciation of renminbi does not affect the balance of trade of China in the long run.

It is also seen that there is a lot of advancement in the empirical literature in terms of the methodology used in the estimations of *J*-curve. Bahmani-Oskooee and Ratha (2004) have made a chronological survey of the empirical works related to *J*-curve. Most of the earlier papers used aggregate data[7] which may cover the authentic movement at the bilateral level (Bahmani-Oskooee and Brooks, 1999) and suffer from aggregation bias (Bahmani-Oskooee and Brooks, 1999; Halicioglu, 2008). Later on (especially, since the latter part of the 1980s), studies used data related to bilateral trade to examine the occurrence of *J*-curve. Both these categories have adopted different models (like VAR, ECM, VECM, ARDL) along with different concepts and variables but provide an overall conclusion of an inconclusive short-run trade balance outcome of currency depreciation. In the case of long-run outcomes, the models using bilateral data yield higher positive trade balance outcomes than the aggregate trade models. However, none of these two categories could highlight the sensitivity of specific export and import items (of comparative advantaged and disadvantaged ones) to exchange rate change. This requires analysis using disaggregated trade data (commodity/industry-specific) of a country with its single trade partner. Breuer and Clements (2003) studied the effect of taking 58 US commodities exports to Japan as well as 50 US commodities imports from Japan. This study is followed by several such industry-disaggregated investigations. Bahmani-Oskooee and Hegerty (2010)[8]

[4]The USA, France, Australia, Italy, New Zealand, Switzerland, Austria, Denmark, Japan, Norway, Canada, Finland, Germany, Netherlands, Portugal, Spain, and UK.

[5]The USA, Australia, Hong Kong, Malaysia, Singapore, the UK, Canada, Japan, New Zealand, Saudi Arabia, China, Korea, and the Philippines.

[6]13 main trading partners of Singapore.

[7]where trade flows of one nation with the rest of the world are considered.

[8]It has also reviewed the studies based on aggregate as well as bilateral trade data.

made a survey some of such studies. These studies using disaggregated data (industry level) reveal significant results that are not properly captured in the case of bilateral and aggregate data. Thus, more hold in favor of the *J*-curve is found from studies using disaggregated data (*ibid*).

Bahmani-Oskooee et al. (2011) investigated the bilateral trade connection between Canada and Mexico. It studied 27 industries from 1973 to 2006, using cointegration analysis. It found the *J*-curve experience for certain electrical and mechanical industries. Bahmani-Oskooee et al. (2014) examined the US trade balance of the USA in the company of Chile for 49 industries by employing the bounds testing ARDL cointegration methodology. There is a long-run improvement in the trade balance of 10 out of 40 cointegrated industries after dollar depreciation; however, the majority industries react negatively in the short run. Taking the disaggregated trade data between Indonesia and the USA in terms of the commodity (from 1973 to 2011) and using the bound testing approach, Bahmani-Oskooee and Harvey (2015) established the trade balances of nearly all industries which are influenced by the exchange rate changes although the *J*-curve experience is found in only nine industries. Jelassia et al. (2017) examined the reaction of the Tunisian trade balance due to changes in the exchange rate from 1993:01 to 2014:03 by using a state-space specification method. It found significant effect on Tunisia's trade balance due to real effective exchange rate. It demonstrated that an oscillating effect could be best portrayed as a "W-curve". Using a medium-scale dynamic stochastic general equilibrium (DSGE) open-economy model, Ali and Anwar (2018) explained that when terms of trade (ToT) upset has both predictable and unforeseen apparatus, *J*-curve happens when ToT shock (unexpected part) and time lag required for recognition of the predictable upset are small.

Largely, these (industry-specific) studies are based on data of either USA or a developed country. Even among the studies using bilateral or aggregate data, the majority of them take the developed countries, for example, the two review papers (i.e., Bahmani-Oskooee and Ratha, 2004; Bahmani-Oskooee and Hegerty, 2010). Not many investigations are found on the underdeveloped countries such as Aftab and Aurangzeb (2002) for Pakistan; De Silva and Zhu (2004) for Sri Lanka; Rahman and Islam (2006) for Bangladesh. Thus, there are fewer studies on the underdeveloped countries, and further no conclusive support for *J*-curve is found from these studies (of course, this is also true for the studies on developed countries). Hence, more studies are required to improve knowledge regarding its operation. As it has been noticed that model/data and the country characteristics influence the results, it is felt that more studies on under-developed countries (UDCs) are required. India is one such country whose case was examined by Bahmani-Oskooee (1985), Himarios (1989), and Bahmani-Oskooee and Malixi (1992).

Bahmani-Oskooee (1985) examined four developing countries (India, Greece, Thailand, and Korea) from 1973 to 1980, operating under different exchange rate regimes.[9] It used a different way of detecting the existence of the *J*-curve by imposing

[9]During the investigation time frame, Thailand and India are pegged their currency to the US dollar; Korea fixed its currency with the US dollar, and Greece adopted a managed float system.

an Almon lag structure on the exchange rate. It supports the presence of the *J*-curve phenomenon. Further extending the study to additional nine LDCs and period to 1985 (earlier one was to 1980), Bahmani-Oskooee and Malixi (1992) as well established support of the *J*-curve operation in the four earlier mentioned countries including India. However, this study also reports no standard pattern of short-run effect, i.e., occurrence of *N*, *M*, and *I* (shaped) curves in some cases. Favorable long-term effects are found in most cases. In the case of India, the long-run effect was not found to be favorable (i.e., devaluation was ineffective to improve trade balance). Taking a much larger and different period (1953–73 and 1975–84), one relating to IMF's pegged exchange rate and another post-IMF regime, Himarios (1989) studied the cases of 27 countries experiencing 60 devaluation episodes in total. It found an apparent confirmation of *J*-curve effects in four countries such as France, Greece, Zambia and Ecuador. It did not found *J*-curve consequence concerning India; however, it discovered that real depreciation of Indian rupee has favorable results on the trade balance in India.

The introduction of economic reforms and implementation of the floating exchange rate in the nineties brought substantial changes in India, in its domestic arena and external sector. Its position in the international market improved sharply, requiring further investigation of short- and long-term consequences of exchange rate fluctuation on the balance of trade. Very few attempts like Arora et al. (2003) and Bahmani-Oskooee and Mitra (2009) are found capturing some of these aspects. The former utilized segregated bilateral data of India's seven major trading partners to examine the short- as well as long-run reaction of trade balance to currency depreciation. Quarterly data over 1977: I-1998: IV are engaged to perform the empirical work by using the ARDL cointegration approach. The *J*-curve model is not happened according to the study. However, it found a long-term positive impact of real depreciation of Indian Rupee concerning the currencies of Italy, Japan, Germany, and Australia on trade balance of India with every single one of these nations. Bahmani-Oskooee and Mitra (2009) likewise attempted to examine the *J*-curve taking a very long period (i.e., the trade data from 1962 to 2006 of India with the USA) for as high as 38 industries. It employed the bounds testing method to cointegration and error correction modeling to check short-run effects (*J*-curve) of real depreciation of the rupee and long-run impact on the trade balance. It established the occurrence of *J*-curve in eight industries only.

Thus, findings relating to the occurrence of *J*-curve in India are not conclusive. The vast majority of the literature has concentrated on developed nations. As the significance of emerging markets increases worldwide, it is imperative to examine if there exists any *J*-curve effect for emerging economies. Along these lines, the principal point of the study is to explore the occurrence of *J*-curve on a bilateral basis for a growing emerging market, particularly India, for the period of 2011m1 to 2016m7. The data period is chosen as BRICS[10] formally came into effect at the end of 2010. It considers utilizing a panel cointegration procedure to examine trade dynamics of India with other BRICS nations such as Brazil, Russia, China, and

---

[10]Brazil, Russia, India, China, South Africa.

South Africa. It contributes to the relevant literature as it spotlights on the BRICS, not earlier examined in this circumstance of the relevance of the *J*-curve of India despite their growing importance.

1.1 Stylized Facts of BRICS

The BRICS came into force in the year 2010 although the BRIC emerges in the year 2006. The BRICS assumes an inexorably significant job in the world economy because of their quickly rising share in world trade. These countries are also identified as the fastest-growing economies in the world. These nations represent 26.46% of the world land region and 42.58% of the global population. As indicated by the IMF's assessments, BRICS nations made 22.53% of the world GDP in 2015. It has also added over half of world economic growth during the most recent 10 years.

India's trade share and trade balance with four BRICS trading partners are shown in Table 1.

India has a trade surplus with Brazil, while she has a trade deficit with Russia, China, and South Africa from 2011 to 2017.

The framework is as per the following. Section 2 states the econometric modeling technique. Section 3 depicts the data and shows the empirical discoveries. Section 4 sums up major findings and state final comments.

Table 1 India's trade with BRICS countries from 2011 to 2017 (in US $ Millions)

Trading partners	Exports	Exports/total world exports (%)	Imports	Imports/total world exports (%)	Trade balance (+/−)
World*	1,917,478.006	100	2,851,881.786	100	−934,403.78
Brazil	30,501.23351	1.59	28,712.37498	1.01	1788.858524
Russia	12,849.81846	0.67	30,306.13652	1.06	−17456.31806
China	86,263.46836	4.50	372,047.9467	13.05	−285784.4783
South Africa	29,352.44859	1.53	46,620.79507	1.63	−17268.34648

Source Author's calculation from Direction of Trade and Statistics CD-ROM 2016 and 2017, IMF)
*India's total export to the world

2 Econometric Modeling

2.1 The Bilateral Trade Balance Model

The reduced bilateral trade balance model of Bahmani-Oskooee et al. (2006) and Bahmani-Oskooee and Harvey (2015) is used which is expressed as follows:

$$\ln TB_{q,t} = \gamma_0 + \gamma_1 \ln \mathrm{RER}_{q,t} + \gamma_2 \ln YW_{q,t} + \gamma_3 \ln \mathrm{YIND}_{q,t} + u_t \quad (1)$$

$\mathrm{TB}_{q,t}$ implies trade balance; it is characterized as the proportion of India's export to country q over her imports from country q. The major advantage of this evaluation is that it is a unit of free estimation. It also can be construed as the balance of trade in real or nominal expression (Bahmani-Oskooee, 1991). It can also be articulated in log type. YIND denotes India's real income, which is also unit free. YWq is trading partner's q real income and RERq is the real bilateral exchange rate between ₹ and trading partner q's currency. It is defined in the way that the bilateral exchange rate ₹ concerning trading partner q's currency multiplied by the ratio of CPI of trading partner q's by CPI of India. Therefore, a rise in RER is stated as real depreciation of ₹. All series are converted into natural logarithms.[11]

To utilize panel cointegration and to include a cross-sectional variable; consequently, it is astute to consider the joint impact of real income by setting up the restriction $\gamma_3 = -\gamma_2$. Therefore, the reduced trade balance model is as per the following:

$$\ln \mathrm{TB}_{j,t} = \beta_0 + \beta_1 \ln RER_{j,t} + \beta_2 \ln X_{j,t} + u_t \quad (2)$$

where $X_{j,t} = \ln\left(\mathrm{YW}_{j,t}/\mathrm{YIND}_{j,t}\right)$

If the J-curve trend exists, it is anticipated that in the short run, the coefficient of the real exchange rate should be negative and afterward transform into positive in the long run due to real depreciation of the domestic currency.

3 Data and Empirical Findings

3.1 Data

Data on real income and trade balance are compiled from the International Financial Statistics (IFS) CD-ROM, 2016 and 2017, Direction of Trade Statistics (DOTS) CD-ROM, 2017, of International Monetary Fund (IMF) and data of exchange rate are collected from the Bloomberg database.

[11]The log-linear condition provides proficient outcomes in contrast to simple specifications.

Table 2 Panel unit root tests

	LLC	IPS	ADF-FC	LLC	IPS	ADF-FC
Variable	Level			First difference		
TB	−3.94 (0.00)	−3.91(0.00)	37.72 (0.00)	0.97(0.83)	−10.41(0.00)	93.14 (0.00)
RER	−0.75(0.22)	−0.55(0.29)	8.90(0.35)	−2.89(0.00)	−8.33(0.00)	73.67(0.00)
X	1.74(0.95)	−2.34(0.01)	37.15(0.00)	92.75(1.00)	−1.97(0.00)	42.75(0.00)

Source Author's calculation from Direction of Trade and Statistics CD-ROM 2016 and 2017, IMF and Bloomberg Database
Notes These three variables were brought together into one panel where sample $N = 4$, $T = 78$. The parenthesis values are the probability of rejection

3.2 Empirical Results

3.2.1 Panel Unit Root

Before employing panel cointegration tests, the unit root test of the series needs to be investigated by using panel unit root tests. Table 2 illustrates outcome of the three-panel unit root test so as to appear to be Levin, Lin, and Chu (LLC), Im, Pesaran, and Shin (IPS), and augmented Dickey–Fuller–Fisher chi-square (ADF-FC) tests. LLC is general, whereas IPS and ADF-FC are individual unit root tests. The consequences of all tests do not discard the null hypothesis of non-stationary at level with individual effect except TB. However, most of the tests discard the null hypothesis of nonstationarity at first difference. It indicates that these variables such as TB, RER, and X are integrated of order one, i.e., an I(1) procedure. Therefore, these variables could be cointegrated.

3.2.2 Cointegration

The panel cointegration test is done by employing Pedroni panel cointegration tests. The results of Pedroni cointegration test are given in Table 3. To test the null hypothesis of no cointegration in heterogeneous panels, Pedroni presents seven statistics. By means of this procedure, two representations are established, i.e., (1) with no deterministic trend and (2) with the deterministic trend. According to the outcomes, for both models, the null hypothesis of no cointegration is discarded for six tests out of seven tests at five percent level. This indicates that cointegration exists for the group as whole and individual countries of the panel.

Thus, utilizing Pedroni cointegration test, a dynamic alliance among real exchange rate and difference of real income and trade balance in the long run is found. This is because additional tests bring about the refutation of no cointegration.

Kao residual cointegration test is also employed to verify the existence of cointegration. The consequence of this is stated in Table 4.

Table 3 Pedroni panel cointegration tests

Test statistics	No deterministic trend				Deterministic trend			
	Statistics	Probability	Weighted statistics	Probability	Statistics	Probability	Weighted statistics	Probability
Panel cointegration statistics (within dimension)								
Panel v-statistics	−0.10	0.50	−0.56	0.71	−1.39	0.92	−1.90	0.97
Panel rho-statistics	−12.57*	0.00	−12.36*	0.00	−10.76*	0.00	−10.67*	0.00
Panel PP-statistics	−10.49*	0.00	−10.05*	0.00	−11.57*	0.00	−11.09*	0.00
Panel ADF-statistics	−8.35*	0.00	−8.22*	0.00	−8.37*	0.00	−7.59*	0.00
Group mean panel cointegration statistics(between-dimension)								
Group rho-statistics	−10.99*	0.00			−8.51*	0.00		
Group PP-statistics	− 10.64*	0.00			− 10.23*	0.00		
Group ADF-statistics	− 8.75*	0.00			− 7.54*	0.00		

Source Author's calculation from Direction of Trade and Statistics CD-ROM 2016 and 2017, IMF and Bloomberg Database
Note It describes Pedroni (2004) residual cointegration tests. The number of lag truncations employed in the calculation of statistics is 1. The estimated values are distributed N (0, 1)
*Significance at 5% level

Table 4 Kao residual cointegration Test

Model specification:	ADF t-statistics	Probability
No deterministic trend	2.96	0.00

Source Author's calculation from Direction of Trade and Statistics CD-ROM 2016 and 2017, IMF and Bloomberg Database
Note A maximum lag of 11 is used in the estimation which is based on the automatic lag selection, i.e., Schwarz information criterion (SIC). The null hypothesis is that there exists no cointegration. Asymptotic Chi-square distribution is used to calculate probability values

The Kao Residual Cointegration test illustrates that the value of ADF t-statistics is 2.96. Therefore, the null hypothesis of no cointegration is discarded at five percent level of significance. Hence, we can certainly say that there subsists a long-run relationship among real exchange rate differences of real income and trade balance for the panel of BRICS countries.

3.2.3 FMOLS Estimates

Pedroni (2001) Panel FMOLS technique is utilized to study individual coefficients which focused bilateral basis as well as the whole group. The assessed FM-OLS coefficients have appeared in Table 5.

The assessed long-run dynamics demonstrate that a real depreciation enhances India's trade balance with Brazil and China. Likewise, an expansion (decline) in real income of Brazil and China in comparison with the real income of India gets better (worsens) trade balance of India with those nations. For the entire group, the FMOLS coefficients confirm that a real depreciation does improve India's trade balance, whereas an increase in real income does not. This is exact proof against *J*-curve.

Table 5 FMOLS estimates

	Independent variable			
	RER	Prob.	X	Prob.
Countries				
Brazil	0.18*	0.00	3.15*	0.00
China	0.49*	0.00	−1.95*	0.00
Russia	−1.68*	0.00	1.30	0.44
South Africa	0.22*	0.00	1.28	0.23
Panel group	1.15*	0.00	−0.35	0.29

Source Author's calculation from Direction of Trade and Statistics CD-ROM 2016 and 2017, IMF and Bloomberg Database
*Significance at 5% level

The existence of *J*-curve is likewise analyzed by utilizing impulse response functions. The generalized impulse response functions are obtained from vector error correction model representations that are utilized to check the veracity of *J*-curve. The reaction of the trade balance to 1 SE depreciation in the real exchange rate is followed. On account of devaluation, if the *J*-curve effect is detected, trade balance initially gets worse and afterward recovers. Figures 1, 2, 3 and 4 show the generalized impulse response functions regarding all nations in the panel.

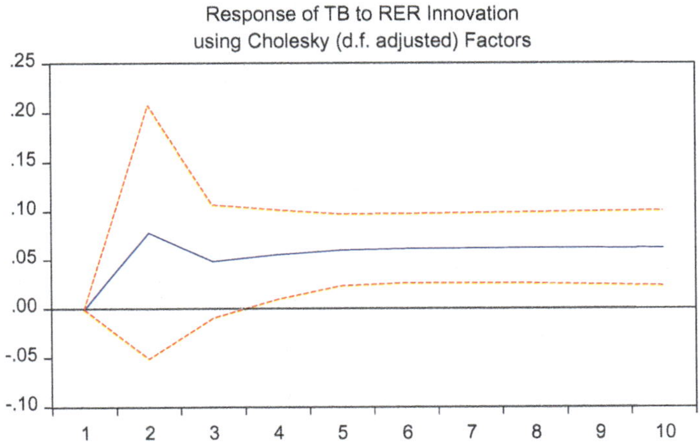

Fig. 1 Generalized impulse response function of Brazil *Source* Author's calculation from Direction of Trade and Statistics CD-ROM 2016 and 2017, IMF and Bloomberg Database

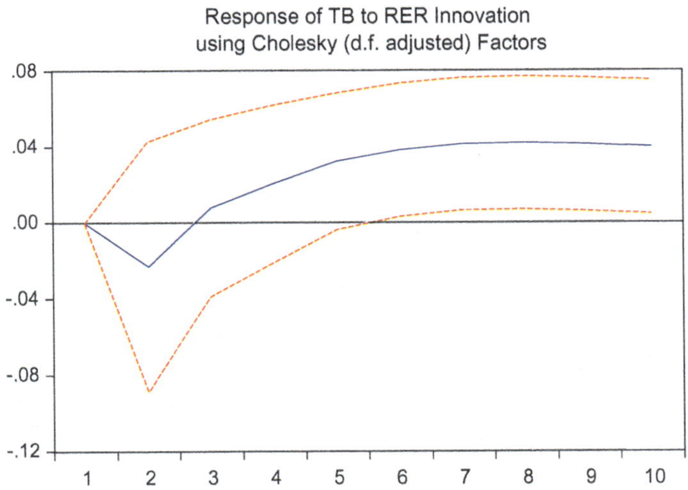

Fig. 2 Generalized impulse response function of Russia *Source* Author's calculation from Direction of Trade and Statistics CD-ROM 2016 and 2017, IMF and Bloomberg Database

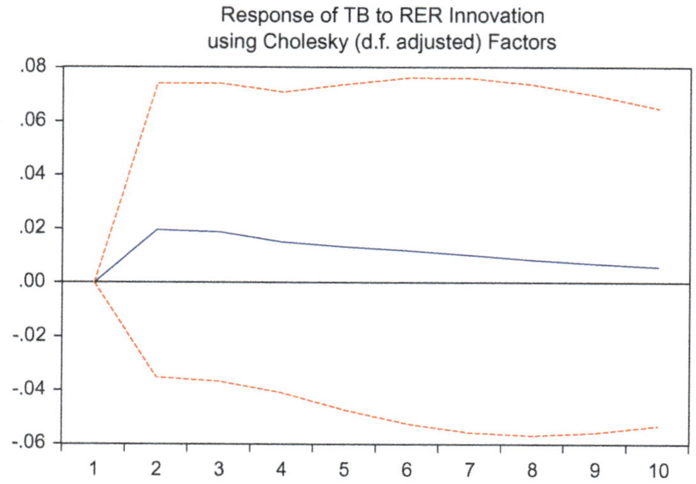

Fig. 3 Generalized impulse response of China *Source* Author's calculation from Direction of Trade and Statistics CD-ROM 2016 and 2017, IMF and Bloomberg Database

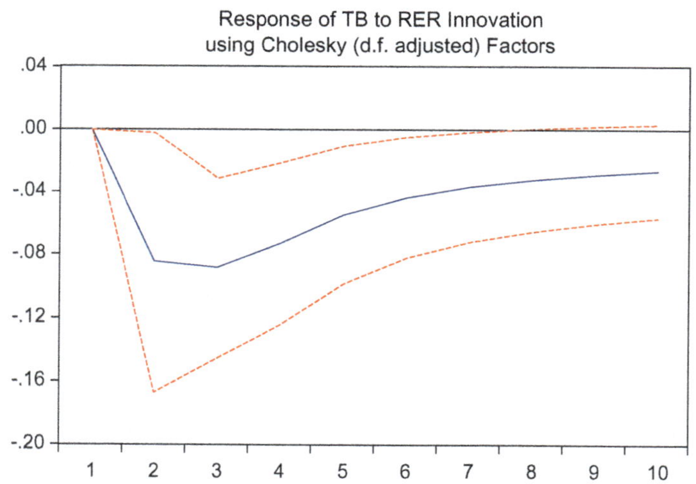

Fig. 4 Generalized impulse response of South Africa. *Source* Author's calculation from Direction of Trade and Statistics CD-ROM 2016 and 2017, IMF and Bloomberg Database

The generalized impulse response functions demonstrate that *J*-curve impact does not exist. Table 6 sums up the results of all impulse response functions.

Table 6 Effect of devaluation on the trade balance

Trading partner	The main impact of devaluation on the trade balance
Brazil	Trade balance first improves and then deteriorates, but remains in the positive zone
Russia	Trade balance initially worsens, after that improves and remains stagnant for some time
China	Trade balance initially gets better then deteriorate yet remains in the positive zone
South Africa	Trade balance initially worsens, after that improves but remains in the negative zone

4 Summary and Conclusion

This study examines the presence of *J*-curve by examining the dynamic relationship between real income, real exchange rates, and trade balance of India with BRICS countries by utilizing the panel study. Both panel cointegration methods identify a long-run association of real depreciation which leads to better trade balance with Brazil and China on a bilateral basis and also with the entire panel of nations. Derived generalized impulse response functions illustrate the absence of *J*-curve effect of India with BRICS countries. The consequences of this investigation are very much analogous to other studies. While the *J*-curve phenomenon is not apparent in India with BRICS trading partners, the monetary authority of the country would adopt ₹ depreciation to encourage exports to BRICS countries.

References

Ali, S. Z., & Anwar, S. (2018). Anticipated versus unanticipated terms of trade shocks and the J-curve phenomenon. *The Journal of International Money and Finance, 81,* 1–19.

Arndt, H. W., & Dorrance, G. (1987). The *J*-curve. Aust. *Economic Review, 20*(11), 9–19.

Aftab, A. Z., & Aurangzeb, (2002). The long-run and short-run impact of exchange rate devaluation on Pakistan's trade performance. *The Pakistan Development Review, 41*(3), 277–286.

Arora, S., Bahmani-Oskooee, M., & Goswami, G. (2003). Bilateral J-curve between India and her trading partners. *Applied Economics, 35*(9), 1037–1041.

Bahmani-Oskooee, M. (1985). Devaluation and the J-curve: Some evidence from LDCs. *The Review of Economics and Statistics, 67*(3), 500–504.

Bahmani-Oskooee, M. (1991). Is there a long-run relation between the trade balance and the real effective exchange rate of LDCs? *Economics Letters, 36*(4), 403–407.

Bahmani-Oskooee, M., & Malixi, M. (1992). More evidence on the J-curve from LDCs. *Journal of Policy Modeling, 14*(5), 641–653.

Bahmani-Oskooee M, Brooks TJ (1999) Bilateral J-curve between U.S. and her trading partners. *Welt Arch Bd. 135*(H1), 156–165

Bahmani-Oskooee, M., & Kantipong, T. (2001). Bilateral J-curve between Thailand and her trading partners. *The Journal of Development Economics, 26*(2), 107–117.

Bahmani-Oskooee, M., & Ratha, A. (2004). The J-curve: A literature review. *Applied Economics, 36*(13), 1377–1398.

Bahmani-Oskooee, M., & Wang, Y. (2006). The J-curve: China versus her trading partners. *Bulletin of Economic Research, 58*(4), 323–343.

Bahmani-Oskooee, M., & Ratha, A. (2007). The bilateral J-curve: Sweden versus her 17 major trading partners. *The International Journal of Applied Economics, 4*(1), 1–13.

Bahmani-Oskooee, M., & Cheema, J. (2009). Short-run and long-run effects of currency depreciation on the bilateral trade between Pakistan and her major trading partners. *The Journal of Development Economics, 34*(1), 19–46.

Bahmani-Oskooee, M., & Harvey, H. (2009). The J-curve: Malaysia vs her major trading partners. *Applied Economics, 42*(9), 1067–1076.

Bahmani-Oskooee, M., & Harvey, H. (2012). J-Curve: Singapore versus her major trading partners. *Economic Papers, 31*(4), 515–522.

Bahmani-Oskooee, M., & Harvey, H. (2015). The J-curve: Evidence from industry-level data between the U.S. and Indonesia. *International Journal* of *Translation*, 29(2), 103–114.

Bahmani-Oskooee, M., & Hegerty, S. W. (2010). The J- and S-curves: A survey of the recent literature. *Journal of Economic Studies, 37*(6), 580–596.

Bahmani-Oskooee, M., & Mitra, R. (2009). The J-curve at the industry level: Evidence from US-India trade. *Economics Bulletin, 29*(2), 1531–1540.

Bahmani-Oskooee, M., Goswami, G., & Talukdar, B. (2005). The bilateral J-curve: Australia versus her 23 trading partners. *Australian Economic Papers, 44*(2), 110–120.

Bahmani-Oskooee, M., Economidou, C., & Goswami, G. (2006). Bilateral J-curve between the UK vis-a -vis her major trading partners. *Applied Economics, 38*(8), 879–888.

Bahmani-Oskooee, M., Bolhassani, M., & Hegerty, S. W. (2011). Industry trade between Canada and Mexico: Will a weakening peso help Mexican manufacturing in the long run? *The North-American Journal of Economics and Finance, 22,* 89–101.

Bahmani-Oskooee, M., Harvey, H., & Hegerty, S. W. (2014). Industry trade and exchange-rate fluctuations: Evidence from the U.S. and Chile. *The International Review of Economics and Finance, 29,* 619–626.

Breuer, J. B., & Clements, L. A. (2003). The Commodity Composition of US-Japanese Trade and the Yen/Dollar Real Exchange Rate. *Japan and the World Economy, 15*(3), 307–330.

De Silva, D., & Zhu, Z. (2004). Sri Lanka's experiment with devaluation: VAR and ECM analysis of the exchange rate effects on trade balance and GDP. *International Journal of Translation, 18*(4), 269–301.

Gomes, F. A. R., & Paz, L. S. (2005). Can real exchange rate devaluation improve the trade balance? The 1990-1998 Brazilian case. *Applied Economics Letters, 12*(9), 525–528.

Hacker, R. S., & Hatemi, A. J. (2004). The effect of exchange rate changes on trade balances in the short and long run. *Econ Tran, 12*(4), 777–799.

Halicioglu, F. (2008). The bilateral J-curve: Turkey versus her 13 trading partners. *The Journal of Asian Economics, 19*(3), 236–243.

Himarios, D. (1989). Do devaluations improve the trade balance? The evidence revisited. *Economic Inquiry, 27,* 143–168.

Hsing, H. M. (2005). Re-examination of J-curve effect for Japan, Korea and Taiwan. *Japan and the World Economy, 17*(1), 43–58.

Jelassia, M. M., Trabelsia, J., & Turki, M. (2017). Does the J-curve hypothesis hold for a small open economy? *Evidence from time-varying coefficients of a distributed-lag model for Tunisia Int Econ.* https://doi.org/10.1016/j.inteco.2017.06.002.

Junz, H. B., & Rhomberg, R. R. (1973). Price-competitiveness in export trade among industrial countries. *The American Economic Review, 63*(2), 412–418.

Magee, S. P. (1973). Currency contracts, pass through and devaluation. *Bro Pap Econ Act, 4*(1), 303–325.

Moura, G., & Da Silva, S. (2005). Is there a Brazilian J-curve? *Economics Bulletin, 6*(10), 1–17.

Narayan, P. K., & Narayan, S. (2004). The J-curve: evidence from Fiji. *International Review of Applied Economics, 18*(3), 369–380.

Pedroni, P. (2001). Fully modified OLS for heterogeneous cointegrated panels. In B.H. Baltagi, T.B. Fomby, H.R. Carter (Eds.), *Nonstationary panels, panel cointegration, and dynamic panels* (Advances in Econometrics, Vol. 15, pp. 93–130), Bingley: Emerald Group Publishing Limited.

Pedroni, P. (2004). Panel cointegration: Asymptotic and finite sample properties of pooled time series tests with an application to the ppp hypothesis. *Theo-economics, 20,* 597–625.

Rahman, M., & Islam, A. (2006). Taka-dollar exchange rate and Bangladesh trade balance: Evidence on J-curve or S-curve? *International Journal of Economics and Business Research, 5*(2), 279–288.

Rose, A. K., & Yellen, J. L. (1989). Is there a J-curve? *J Mon Econ, 24*(1), 53–68.

Wang, C. H., Lin, C. H., & Yang, C. H. (2012). Short-run and long-run effects of exchange rate change on trade balance: Evidence from China and its trading partners. *Japan and the World Economy, 24,* 266–273.

Chapter 5
Trade Costs Between India and ASEAN: A Gravity Framework

D. Nagraj and I. Ghosh

1 Introduction

Trade costs have recently gained a lot of importance in policy-making and governance related to international trade. The difference between the final price paid by the consumer and the cost of the traded commodity is the cost of trading. In the globalized world, these trade costs determine the trends and pattern of bilateral trade and investment. Geographical distance, protection policies like import tariffs, poor governance and infrastructure, etc., affect trade costs. Miroudot and Shepherd (2015) describes that policy framework of each country has a significant contribution to trade costs. He explains these policy measures as: (a) policies at the border (tariffs, custom duty) (b) policies between the border (transportation) (c) policies behind the border (product standards, regulations). Higher trade costs can isolate countries from the global market, while production and trade patterns distort and countries cannot take full advantage of economic gains derived from specialization. As a result, trade flows are negatively impacted and thereby affecting the economic welfare and development of the country (World Trade Organization [WTO], 2015). Many countries in the recent past have lowered or removed various tariffs, but trade costs in terms of non-tariff barrier still remain high, especially in developing nations.

Anderson and Van Wincoop (2004) estimated that in the advanced economy, trade cost is as high as 170%. According to them, multilateral trade barriers affect international trade, that is, the multilateral resistance term embedded in the augmented gravity model of international trade.

D. Nagraj · I. Ghosh (✉)
Symbiosis School of Economics, Symbiosis International (Deemed University), Pune, Maharashtra, India
e-mail: ishita.ghosh@sse.ac.in

D. Nagraj
e-mail: divya.nagaraj.2016@sse.ac.in

P. Lakhanpal et al. (eds.), *Trade, Investment and Economic Growth*,
https://doi.org/10.1007/978-981-33-6973-3_5

Kee et al. (2009) mention that developing countries generally have higher trade costs than developed countries, originating from both, tariffs and non-tariff barriers. Therefore, trade costs affect policy decisions and global competitiveness, which are crucial for a country's ability to participate in cross-border trade. It is also necessary to recognize the sources of trade costs, and strategies, which could be adopted to diminish trade costs, for instance, trade facilitation, governance and bureaucracy systems, etc.

Tinbergen's (1962) gravity equation of international specifies that distance between the two trading partners acts as a proxy variable for measuring trade costs. However, many proxy variables such as tariffs, transportation costs, infrastructure, common languages and culture have been used in place of distance to evaluate trade costs.

Anderson (1979) reinforces the gravity literature with the estimation of bilateral trade flows by applying the concept of expenditure systems various countries. Assuming, distance and borders as proxy variables for trade costs, McCallum (1995) revealed that trade patterns between USA and Canada did not conform to the gravity model as expected. Trade between Canadian provinces was found to be 2200% times the trade between USA and Canada. He termed this outcome as the "border puzzle". This "puzzle" solved by Anderson and Van Wincoop (2003) by establishing trade costs exogenously to the model and introducing the multilateral resistance term—the resistance originating from various non-tariff barriers among trading partners.

Typically, the literature on trade costs focuses on the factors that affect such costs, as well its estimation by aggregating them (Arvis et al., 2011). Novy (2013) contributed to this literature by estimating trade costs using a "top-down" approach and examining the trends of trade across economies. The current study follows such an approach to estimate trade costs between India, Japan, China, South Korea and the ASEAN economies during 2006–2015. As a developing economy, India has taken several trade facilitation measures to increase its integration with the global economy. Regional studies pertaining to Asia suggests that India's inclusion in trade organizations will prove to be advantageous for Asia in meeting the continent's challenges in trade (Asher & Sen, 2005). Greenaway et al. (2009) mention that with the decreasing trends in tariff rates, studies are now concentrating on the impact of non-tariffs barriers among trading partners. The Indian government is also recognizing the importance of mitigating such barriers (Ghoshal, 2009).

The current study aims to analyse the trade relation between India and Association of Southeast Asian Nations (ASEAN)[1] by measuring the trade costs. India became a sectoral dialogue partner of ASEAN in the year 1992 after it saw a relative increase in trade with the ASEAN countries to the rest of the world. These countries entered into a free trade agreement (FTA) under the initial framework of ASEAN–India Free Trade Area (AIFTA) and gradually signed various other FTAs such as the Regional Comprehensive Economic Partnership (RCEP) and subsequently increased market accessibility by introducing new FTA partners like China, Japan, South Korea,

[1]ASEAN = Indonesia, Malaysia, Philippines, Singapore, Thailand, Brunei, Vietnam, Laos, Myanmar and Cambodia.

Australia and New Zealand. A key characteristic of an FTA is that they are intended to reduce the trade barriers between the two trading partners and enhance the trade volume. However, over time, the trade gap between India and ASEAN has been steadily increasing (Economic Times, 2018). Thus, this study investigates the factors responsible for the creation these trade gaps by analysing the trade costs in the goods market using gravity framework between India and ASEAN + 3 countries[2] by considering the total value of trade only (without any sectoral detail).

The paper is bifurcated into two parts: (a) understanding the challenges faced by India and ASEAN in trade that contribute to trade costs and (b) applying the gravity model (Novy's version) to measure the factors or variables that contribute to trade costs. In addition, only factors affecting the trade costs from the perspective of India have been considered here. Sectoral detailing can be considered for further research. The scope of this study can also be expanded to ASEAN + 6 region in the future.

2 Background

Free trade agreement between India and ASEAN is the result of common interests: to augment economic growth. The economies signed the goods FTA in 2009 and the agreement came into effect in 2010. Total trade volume between India and ASEAN in the year 2015–16 was 65 bn USD (around 10% of India's total trade). Bulk of the Indian trade was directed towards Singapore, Malaysia, Thailand, Indonesia and Vietnam (ASEAN Trade Statistics, 2015). India has strong market potential in ASEAN because of its superior R&D, knowledge base and human capital. India has received notable FDI inflows in real estate sector, constituting 27.9% of total the FDI inflows from ASEAN, followed by coal, oil and natural gas sector. India's outward FDI has been primarily directed towards coal, oil and natural gas and metals sectors, followed closely by the services sector such as IT services, financial services and business services (ASEAN Trade Statistics, 2015). However, India witnessed a surge in trade deficit with the ASEAN from USD 0.5 bn in 2005–06 to USD 14.6 bn in 2015–16. With respect to market share, India's aggregate share of imports from ASEAN increased from 7.3% in 2005–06 to 10.5% in 2015–16 and share of aggregate exports to ASEAN tumbled from 10.1 to 9.6% over the same period (ASEAN Trade Statistics, 2015).

ASSOCHAM (2016) reported that India had the highest trade deficit with Indonesia (USD 14.6 bn), followed by Malaysia (USD 5.4 bn) and then Thailand (USD 2.5 bn) in 2015. India enjoyed trade surplus with Vietnam (USD 2.7 bn), Philippines (USD 826 mn) and Singapore (USD 416 mn) in the year 2015. Economic Times (2018) mentions that India's trade deficit with China and South Korea rose up to USD 63.12 bn and USD 11.96 bn, respectively, in 2017–18 from USD 51.11 bn and USD 8.34 bn, respectively, in 2016–17. In contrast, India's trade deficit with Lao, Brunei and Cambodia dipped in 2017–18 (Table 1).

[2]ASEAN + 3 = ASEAN + Japan, China and South Korea.

Table 1 India's trade deficit with ASEAN countries ($ million)

Year	India export	India import	India share of total exports	India share of total imports	Trade balance	Total trade
I	II	III	IV	V	(II − III)	(II + III)
2006–07	12.61	18.11	10	9.7	−5.5	30.72
2007–08	16.41	22.67	10.1	9	−6.26	39.08
2008–09	19.14	26.2	10.3	8.6	−7.06	45.34
2009–10	18.11	25.8	10.1	8.9	−7.69	43.91
2010–11	25.63	30.61	10.3	8.3	−4.98	56.24
2011–12	36.74	42.16	12	8.6	−5.42	78.9
2012–13	33	42.87	11	8.7	−9.87	75.87
2013–14	33.13	41.28	10.5	9.2	−8.15	74.41
2014–15	31.81	44.71	10.2	10	−12.9	76.52
2015–16	25.2	39.84	9.6	10.5	−14.64	65.04

Source Ministry of Commerce (2016)

It was also observed that imports rose from the ASEAN countries significantly while exports to ASEAN did not show a similar pattern of increment. Lack of standardization in tariff reduction rules and product specification, absence of proper governance structure of customs, etc., are some of the major factors responsible for the increased trade gap between India and ASEAN. For instance, the tariff reduction structure under the ASEAN–India Free Trade Area (AIFTA) agreement mentions that tariffs over 4000 merchandize should be removed by 2016 and tariffs on sensitive products, reduced to 50% and 25% according to their respective category by 2019. Major resistance for lowering tariffs comes from Indonesia. Indonesia has committed to reduce tariffs only on 50% of its items (EXIM Bank, 2018).

3 Literature Review: Trade Cost Between India and ASEAN

3.1 *Tariff Barrier*

India and ASEAN have huge trade potential. However, it will require more effort in terms of building connectivity and institutional linkages with the ASEAN counterpart and it is crucial; to realize this prospect. Francis (2011) found that India's international trade is shifting towards developing countries from developed countries of Asia. He observed that the labour-intensive and natural resource-based sectors of export were diminishing in volume. The author also mentions about significant growth in bilateral trade in several other sectors, owing to the rapid increase in regional as well as global integration, particularly with the ASEAN. Currently, India's aggregate trade balance with ASEAN is negative. Tariff elimination and reduction structures in goods proposed under the AIFTA framework involve high tariff reductions that are way beyond the levels of the most-favoured-nations (MFN) arrangement. Therefore, farmers in India will face tremendous competition due to increased imports. Increase in agricultural production and distribution can be attributed to growing dominance of multinational corporations (MNCs). The factors responsible for this are technological change, trade liberalization and foreign investment. The author argues that the small and medium enterprises (SMEs) of India will not benefit much from this FTA but countries like Thailand, Indonesia and Malaysia will (Chanda and Gopalan, 2009).

Tariff levels in India are higher compared to the other ASEAN member nations. India's average agricultural tariff rate is above 34% vis-à-vis 13% in ASEAN. Similarly, MFN tariffs for manufacturing products are also greater than 10% as against 7.5% for ASEAN. Though India and ASEAN countries focus on liberalizing tariffs in order to increase trade between partners, it is also important to highlight that tariff liberalization is necessary but not sufficient for boosting trade and economic integration (Helble et al., 2007). Although many researchers were in the favour of trade liberalization through tariff reduction through the FTA route, Joseph (2009) opposed this view as this could disproportionately increase imports, especially in the plantation sector, resulting in the waning of prices and diminishing the security of domestic manufacturers. In his analysis, it was found that the imports are affected not only by the reduction in tariff but also by exchange rate, productivity and market structures.

Investigating the tariff structure, Pal and Dasgupta (2009) concluded that India has very little to gain in terms of market share from the India–ASEAN FTA. Given the fact that the ASEAN economies have a higher export to GDP ratio coupled with India's commitment for major tariff reduction shows that this FTA will provide ASEAN better access to Indian markets and not vice versa and might trigger trade deficit for India. This agreement would also lead to increase in competition for domestic players since ASEAN countries are competitive exporters of products like light manufacturing and agricultural items. However, India can gain through economies of scale via increased market access. Singapore and Thailand are the two major countries where India accounts for 60% of its export. Since India has a bilateral trade agreement with Myanmar, the India–ASEAN FTA will provide access to the remaining countries, like, Indonesia, Philippines, Malaysia and Vietnam. However, India could gain from the cheaper availability of intermediate goods from the ASEAN region. For some companies operating in India and ASEAN countries, this agreement could also lead to improvements in their intra-firm production networks.

The scope of the negative list was the main dispute in the trade in goods (TIG) understanding. After the initial hesitation, India included only five items in the sensitive list, that is, tea, coffee, pepper, crude palm oil and refined palm oil, and Pal and Dasgupta (2008) recognized that India has maintained a defensive stance during the negotiations because India faces a substantially large trade deficit with ASEAN and a further decline in tariff would only increase the deficit unless there was a boost in export.

The major drawback faced by India in trading with ASEAN countries is that different sets of countries have different timeline and percentages for reduction in tariffs. Least developed countries (LCDs) such as Vietnam, Myanmar, Cambodia, Indonesia and Lao impose high import tariffs and restriction measures which make trade costlier to India. For instance, in the case of coffee, tea, spices, vegetable fats and natural rubber, the number of tariff lines under the exclusion/sensitive lists was higher than the number of tariff lines that were offered full duty concessions—implying a limited reduction in tariffs from already existing levels. Therefore, despite India's increasing trade deficit with ASEAN, tariff reductions under AIFTA have not had a significant effect on import trends (Anderson and Neary, 2003; Batra, 2007).

According to the multi-country survey report presented by the Asian Development Bank (ADB), there are various reasons which restrict economies to participate in FTAs; one of the major reason is that the businesses consider rules of origin (RoO) as restrictive, followed by lack of information, administrative costs, non-tariff measures and small preference margins (Kawai and Wignaraja, 2011). The rationale behind (RoO) was to prevent trade deflection, but due to its complexity, it actually increases the costs of doing business, as well as, the burden on origin certifying institutions (Rajan and Sen, 2004).

There are a few drawbacks regarding the rules of origin (RoO) under the AIFTA framework. India is relatively flexible in applying the RoO which encourages the entry of non-member country products into India through the preferential route. With respect to the rules of origin, India has determined these in two categories; they are—change in tariff heading and value addition. Although only 35% of value addition is limited in the rules of origin criteria, this dilution is crucial with respect to the above-mentioned criteria, and also, the 40% value addition rule which is currently in existence for the India–Singapore and India–Thailand free trade agreements. Furthermore, the revision of tariff classification norms show that rules under the 6-digit classification in the ASEAN are less restrictive as compared to the 4-digit level tariff classification (ASSOCHAM, 2016).

3.2 Non-Tariff Barrier

Analysing the non-tariff measures through the surveys based on exporters' perceptions, Saqib and Taneja (2005) identified that 32.6% faced some kind of barrier for the firms trading with less than 20 million of exports. Their case study further indicated that exporters face difficulties to meet with multiple product standards set for each ASEAN member. Further, packaging, labelling, language, mark-up and environmental considerations create even more barriers. Other barriers faced by the exporters are lack of subsidies by domestic government and under invoicing demand by importers such as Sri Lanka.

One of the major barriers for movement of skilled professionals is lack of recognition of qualifications among nations. To avoid this problem, Pal and Dasgupta (2008) suggested having a mutual recognition agreement (MRA) among trading partners.

Thus, the Indo-ASEAN trade in goods agreement may not be beneficial for India in the short run, but it can be thought of as a part of a long-term strategy to improve India's economic and strategic presence in the neighbourhood. Negotiations between India and ASEAN on services trade liberalization have just started, and it will be up to the Indian negotiators to ensure that the lack of tangible benefits accruing to India in the goods sector is offset through an agreement on trade in services.

The United Nations Conference on Trade and Development (UNCTAD) created an Integrated Trade Intelligence Portal (I-TIP) that focuses on database which provides information on non-tariff barriers in the ASEAN region. According to I-TIP records, there are approximately 6000 non-tariff barriers. The results of I-TIP suggest that the majority of the existing non-tariff barrier is classified into two groups: (1) Sanitary and Phytosanitary (SPS) and (2) Technical Barriers to Trade (TBT).

Majority of the SPS measures are applied on food and drink items, while TBT measures are applied on chemical products and allied industries. The rationale behind the prohibition on import on some of these products may be valid for, for instance, in public safety or national security. However, these restrictive measures can also be misused, particularly for protecting the domestic players.

The Integrated Trade Intelligence Portal's results suggest that the country which has the maximum number of SPS and TBT measures among ASEAN countries is Thailand. For example, SPS measures in Thailand is 20 times than that adopted by Cambodia and Lao PDR and approximately 15 times the TBT measures as that in Myanmar. Thus, the differences cause hurdles to the growth of CLMV countries, who are the least developed ASEAN member nations. Furthermore, Thailand, at a global level, also imposes about 40% of the world's existing SPS measures and 20% of TBT measures. Rapid increase of non-tariff barriers has negative effect on inter, as well as, intra-ASEAN trade (ATC, 2016).

Mohanty (2007) analysed the then on-going negotiations between India and ASEAN to establish an FTA in merchandize by gradually removing the barriers, both, the tariff and non-tariff forms. He pointed out that the primary reason for hindrance was the list of items covered under the sensitive track. However, India's approach to these restrictions is more flexible as compared to ASEAN. India maintains a uniform list of 489 products as negative items, which constitute less than 5% of the ASEAN exports to India. In contrast, each country of ASEAN maintains a separate list of negative items. Further, India has offered to reduce customs duty on crude palm oil and refined palm oil by 2018, but Malaysia (largest producer of palm oil in the world) and Indonesia are pressurizing to further reduce it. Similar is the case for pepper and black tea. These are highly sensitive items, and if India reduces the tariffs further, then internally some lobbyists and political parties may raise objections. The author also noted that India has been comparatively more flexible and more receptive as compared to ASEAN. ASEAN must also show more appreciation and flexibility so as to close the deal soon (which has now been done).

Another aspect of trade cost explains that a country's cross-membership in multiple FTAs can lead to contradictions in obligations and can also create confusion for investors about rules, obligations and incentives corresponding to the partners.

Thus, wider gaps in trade and investment may be observed between rich and less well-off economies because of power asymmetry (Rajan and Sen, 2004).

The tariffs in India are comparatively higher than tariffs in ASEAN countries, and there is less scope of gains from trade for India in the goods agreement. Tariff rate in India for the agricultural sector is in excess of 34% as compared to 13% for ASEAN. Similarly, ASEAN has 7.5% MFN tariffs rates for manufacturing, which is lower as compared to the MFN tariffs prevalent in Indian manufactured goods—which is also in excess of 10%. Currently, around 75% of Indian goods are available to the ASEAN market at duty-free tariff rates. On the contrary, tariffs imposed by ASEAN countries have remained low for quite a while, and the modifications made to generate benefits from the FTA will not be so significant for India. The scope for gains to India from the FTA is smaller for merchandise trade as compared to trade in services and investment. Undoubtedly, the possibility for trade in services and investment opportunities is huge, and globally, India ranks within the top ten in exporting services globally, wherein the ASEAN constitutes a large share in the import of services from India (ASSOCHAM, 2016).

Karmakar (2005) has explained that India has large potential in the services market in ASEAN. ASEAN being a net importer of services, has service imports that are 2.8 times more than India's total service exports. Also, the demand for services in the ASEAN region is rising due to the shortage of skilled labour at cheaper costs in service sector, resulting in the ASEAN countries' rise in trade deficits in international services trades (unlike the favourable net merchandise trade balance). It has been suggested that given that ASEAN countries and India are relatively closed to foreign service providers (even the member countries) and that they have limited commitments under GATS, they can make use of the service market potential in the region. Negotiations should be based on market access and other consular cooperation. The countries can make use of India's low-cost skilled professionals, especially focusing the areas like education, IT, telecommunications, etc., to maintain aggregate economic growth in the FTA. India will benefit from the Comprehensive Economic Cooperation Agreement (CECA) as this will provide opportunities to access ASEAN markets.

4 Theoretical Framework for Trade Cost: Gravity Model

Trade costs constitute a significant part in describing the trends of bilateral trade and investment between two trading partners along with the distribution of production on the basis of geography. The main focus of the empirical literature on the theory of international trade has been on utilizing the gravity model to distinguish specific components, for example, distance between geographies.

A method to estimate the cross-border flows empirically in international trade was provided by Tinbergen (1962) in the form of the gravity equation. The reference of this equation has been taken from Newton's law of gravity. The analogy being that trade between two countries is directly proportional to their economic sizes and inversely proportional to the distance between them. Here, distance between the two trading partners acts as a proxy variable for measuring trade costs. As mentioned previously, Anderson (1979, 2003, 2004) and McCallum (1995) have made significant contributions in refining the applications of the gravity model of trade.

Anderson and Van Wincoop (2004) attempted to bring together the literature on different factors affecting trade costs. Their approach included a review of various available literature and adding the trade costs, such as tariffs, transportation costs and domestic distribution costs, to the existing models. Their results showed that 170% of trade costs for developed nations comprised of 55% wholesale and retail distribution costs, 44% cross-border trade barriers and 21% transportation costs.

Typically, the literature pertaining to trade costs focuses on the fundamental factors which affect these costs and then estimates the overall measure of the said trade costs, by summing them together (Arvis et al., 2011).

Arvis et al. (2011) argues that the development of assessing trade costs in the existing literature is rather weak, with each paper, managing the best-case scenario with a subset of variables that assumes to impact trade costs. This approach has two disadvantages:

1. It does not help in providing an overall estimate of the trade cost level between the trading partners, which is frequently used in theoretical models of trade.
2. Incorporation of fewer variables gives rise to an omitted variable bias, to the extent that the variables included in the model have a correlation with trade costs.

To cope with these challenges, Novy (2013) used the "top-down" approach to estimate trade costs by analysing the trends of trade across economies. Similar to Head and Ries (2001), Novy (2013) expressed his views differently for measuring the trade costs. He determined a comprehensive way to compute the trade costs which have been constructed by observing the trade patterns to eliminate the singular approach in his previous work. This new approach is straightforward and depends on the traditional gravity model. His analysis showed that factors contributing to the trade costs along with the traditional trade costs sources include, for example, tariffs and other external factors such as geographical distance and digital connectivity and an array of trade policy components.

This study focuses on the Novy (2008) "Gravity Redux" approach. Novy's derivation of trade costs is derived from Anderson and van Wincoop's (2003) model, where each country produces different goods, and consumers enjoy vast assortment of products. Utility maximization is characterized by identical preferences across countries with constant elasticity of substitution.

The principal component in this analysis is the exogenous bilateral trade costs (Anderson and van Wincoop, 2003). When the goods are delivered from country i to j, transportation costs and other various trade costs between the trading partners add up to the trade cost of each unit of goods delivered. Therefore, prices of goods differ in each country, that is, if p_i = net supply price of the goods originating from country i, then $p_{ij} = p_i t_{ij}$ is the cost of the goods in country j, where $t_{ij} \geq 1$ is the gross bilateral trade cost factor, that is, one plus tariff equivalent. According to this framework, Anderson and van Wincoop (2003) determined a micro-founded gravity equation with trade costs:

$$X_{ij} = \frac{y_i y_j}{y^W}\left(\frac{t_{ij}}{\pi_i P_j}\right)^{(1-\sigma)} \quad (1)$$

Here, X_{ij} represents nominal exports from country i to j, y_i is nominal income of country i and y^W is world income defined as $y^W = \sum_j y_j$. $\sigma > 1$ is the elasticity of substitution across goods. π_i and P_j are country i's and country j's price indices. The gravity equation infers that all things being constant, rich countries trade with each other. Bilateral trade declines in the presence of bilateral trade costs t_{ij} since they have to be calculated against π_i and P_j. These indices are referred to as multilateral resistance variable since it involves trade costs with all other trading partners and can be referred as average trade costs. π_i is outward multilateral resistance and P_j is inward multilateral resistance variable.

Anderson and van Wincoop (2003) assume that bilateral trade costs are a function of border barrier and geographical distance.

The above mentioned is represented as "$t_{ij} = b_{ij} d K_{ij}$", where b_{ij} is a border-related indicator variable, d_{ij} is bilateral distance and K is the distance elasticity.

Novy specifies that bilateral trade barrier not only affect international but also affect intra-national trade. This can be seen formally by using gravity Eq. (1):

$$\pi_i P_i = \left(\frac{\frac{x_{ii}}{y_i}}{\frac{y_i}{y^W}}\right)^{\frac{1}{1-\sigma}} t_{ii} \quad (2)$$

The above equation explains that for a given trade cost (t_{ij}), the change in the multilateral resistance over time is easy to measure as it does not depend on time-invariant trade cost proxies such as distance.

Equation (1) holds the product of the inward multilateral resistance of one country and outward multilateral resistance of another country. If Eq. (1) is multiplied for the trade flows in the opposite direction, i.e.X_{ji}, bidirectional gravity equation is obtained containing both countries outward and inward multilateral resistance variable.

$$X_{ij} X_{ji} = \left(\frac{y_i y_j}{y^W}\right)^2 \left(\frac{t_{ij} t_{ji}}{\pi_i P_i \pi_j P_j}\right)^{(1-\sigma)} \quad (3)$$

Substituting the values of $\pi_i P_i$ from Eq. (2) and rearranging yields, we get

$$\left(\frac{t_{ij} t_{ji}}{t_{ii} t_{jj}}\right) = \left(\frac{x_{ii} x_{jj}}{x_{ij} x_{ji}}\right)^{\left(\frac{1}{\sigma-1}\right)} \quad (4)$$

As shipping costs between i and j can be asymmetric, i.e. $(t_{ij}) \neq (t_{ji})$ and as domestic trade costs can differ across countries, i.e. $(t_{ii}) \neq (t_{jj})$, it is useful to take the geometric mean of the barriers in both directions.

Therefore, resulting trade cost measure (T_{ij}):

$$T_{ij} = (\frac{t_{ij}t_{ji}}{t_{ii}t_{jj}})^{\frac{1}{2}} - 1 = (\frac{x_{ii}x_{jj}}{x_{ij}x_{ji}})^{\frac{1}{2}(\sigma-1)} - 1 \quad (5)$$

By deducting one from the above Eq. (5), we get an expression for tariff equivalent. T_{ij} is the trade cost relative to domestic trade cost $t_{ii}t_{jj}$. The basis behind T_{ij} is fairly simple. If bilateral trade flows $x_{ij}x_{ji}$ rise with relation to domestic trade flows $x_{ii}x_{jj}$, it must be easier for the two countries to trade with each other versus trading domestically. This is captured by a fall in T_{ij}, and vice versa. The measure thus captures trade costs in an indirect way by inferring them from observable trade flows. Since these trade flows differ over time, trade costs T_{ij} can be calculated not only for cross-sectional data but also for time series and panel data. This is an advantage over the procedure adopted by Anderson and van Wincoop (2003) who only use cross-sectional data. It is important to stress that bilateral barriers might be asymmetric $(t_{ij}) \neq (t_{ji})$ and that bilateral trade flows might be unbalanced $x_{ij} \neq x_{ji}$. T_{ij} indicates the geometric average of relative bilateral trade barriers (Arvis et al., 2011).

The Novy (2013) method has been practically implemented in various published papers, although none of them have the geographical, sectoral or time-based scope of the present one. Jacks et al. (2008) use the Novy (2013) methodology to estimate trade costs in the first wave of globalization (1870–1914) through the help of data on GDP and total trade flows for major economies. Subsequently, the authors have applied the same technique to examine the role of fluctuations in trade costs as drivers of trade cycles in the long run. (Jacks et al., 2011). Correspondingly, Chen and Novy (2011) have examined trade costs among European countries by means of comprehensive trade and production data that differentiate between sectors and in addition offer an econometric decomposition of trade costs that highlights the part they play in that factors such as distance, non-tariff measures and memberships in certain European initiatives, such as the Schengen Agreement.

Although this paper considers only merchandise trade, Miroudot et al. (2013) apply the same methodology to services trade; however, their sample is much more restricted than this study due to the general lack of availability of high-quality data on services trade.

The technique portrayed above provides inferred estimates of bilateral trade costs, t_{ij}. With respect to policy decision making, it will be useful to sum up trade costs across partner countries in order to create a sole and reliable approach to calculate trade costs for each country. To construct such a measure, Arvis et al. (2011) augment the Novy (2013) approach by aggregating Eq. (5) which gives a symmetric gravity equation considering trade in both directions set to be equal to the geometric average of actual trade.

5 Data Treatment and Methodology

The study uses panel data, and the data are obtained for 12 countries in total—India is the reporter country and following are the partner countries—Brunei Darussalam, China, Indonesia, Japan, Cambodia, South Korea (Korea, Rep.), Lao PDR, Malaysia, Singapore, Thailand and Vietnam.

5.1 Limitations

ASEAN is an amalgamation of developed, developing and less developed countries; the paper faces data constraints especially for less developed countries. Countries like Myanmar and Philippines have been dropped due to lack data availability for majority of the variables considered for analysis. Similarly, the study is limited to 10 years. This study considers only total goods traded for the analysis and hence does not provide any detailed sectoral analysis.

Based on the above discussion, the Table 2 provides information about the data, definition of the variable, time period and source taken for analysis in this study.

5.2 Hypothesis

The ASEAN–India free trade agreement is expected to reduce the trade costs and thus support in increasing the trade flow between the two trading partners. Therefore, on the basis of this, the hypothesis for this study is presented as:

Set I:

H_0 The free trade agreement between India and ASEAN has helped in reducing trade costs.

Set II:

H_0 Distance between India and ASEAN affect trade costs
H_0 Entry costs affect trade costs
H_0 Liner Shipping Connectivity Index affect trade costs
H_0 Tariffs affect trade costs.
H_0 Nominal exchange rate affect trade costs
H_0 GDP per capita affect trade costs.

Table 2 Variable source, definition and time period considered

Variable	Definition	Year	Source
Trade costs	Geometric average trade costs in country *i* and *j*	2006–2015	UNESCAP
Liner shipping Connectivity index (LSCI)	Geometric average of country *i*'s and *j*'s score on liner shipping connectivity index	2006–2015	UNCTAD
Entry costs	Geometric average of the cost of starting a business in country *i* and *j*	2006–2015	World bank—world development indicators
Tariffs	Weighted mean based on applied rated weighted by the product import shares corresponding to each partner country. Data are classified using the HS codes at the six- or eight-digit level	2006–2015	World bank—world development indicators
Nominal exchange rate	Geometric average of the nominal exchange rate of country *i* and *j*	2006–2015	World bank—world development indicators
GDP per capita	Geometric average of gross domestic product per capita (PPP basis, constant terms) in country *i* and *j*	2006–2015	World bank—world development indicators
Distance	Weighted average distance between the country *i* and *j*	2006–2015	CEPII

5.3 Gravity Model Specification

The following equation is used to explain the determinants of trade cost level between India and ASEAN. This section follows the approach proposed by Chen and Novy (2011) by the way of regression analysis to investigate the factors contributing to bilateral trade costs. The focus here is on the factors that are principally the sources of international trade costs. It is important to note that the interpretation of the dependent variable—trade costs—in the regression analysis is the ratio of international to domestic trade costs, and also as is the case in Chen and Novy (2011), the interpretation of the independent variables is in terms of their effect on dependent variable—that is, trade costs.

Following is the gravity equation:

$$\begin{aligned}\log t_{ij} = \beta_0 + \beta_1 \log(entrycosts_{ij}) + \beta_2 \log(LSCI_{ij}) + \beta_3 \log(tariffs_{ij}) \\ + \beta_4 \log(ner_{ij}) + \beta_5 \log(gdppc_{ij}) + \beta_6 \log(dist_{ij}) + \varepsilon_{ij}\end{aligned}$$

where t_{ij} is the geometric trade costs between the two trading partners and also acting as dependent variable, $\log(entrycosts_{ij})$ are the cost of doing business taken from World Bank's Doing Business project, acting as a proxy variable for the cost of market entry, $\log(LSCI_{ij})$ represents as a proxy for international transport connectivity, $\log(tariffs_{ij})$ are the weighted mean applied rates between the exporting and importing countries explaining that higher the tariffs, higher the trade costs, $\log(ner_{ij})$ are the nominal exchange rates of two countries involved in bilateral trade representing the country's competitiveness, $\log(gdppc_{ij})$ are the per capita GDP explaining the country's level of development and welfare, and $\log(dist_{ij})$ is the weighted average of distance between two trading countries.

6 Results

The empirical analysis involves running the panel fixed effect model, then panel random effect model and finally the Hausman specification test which will help to determine to choose between random and fixed effect models. Hausman test conducted in this paper showed the value of Prob > chi2 greater than 0.05 (0.7747), which means that the random effect model will be accepted for analysis (Table 3).

The first variable under consideration is distance whose coefficient is positive at 0.44, indicating that 1% increase in distance will result in 44% increase in trade costs. Geographic distance represents transportation costs between the two trading partners. This is in line with the main idea of gravity model theory; as distance between the two trading partner increases, the trade costs also increase. Hence, distance plays a crucial role in the international trade. Though the ASEAN countries have close proximity to India, still there exists significant percentage of trade costs. The major factors

Table 3 Random effect model results

Independent variable	Coefficient values	P-value
Constant	0.31	0.00***
Distance (dij)	0.44	0.10*
Entry costs (entry costsij)	0.22	0.21
Liner shipping connectivity index (lsciij)	−0.91	0.01***
Tariffs (tariffsij)	0.12	0.00***
Nominal exchange rate (nerij)	−0.06	0.01***
GDP per capita (gdppcij)	−0.37	0.04**
R^2 0.82		

Source Author's calculations
*, ** and *** represents the coefficient is significant at 1%, 5% and 10% level of significance respectively

attributed to this are lack of infrastructure and proper road, rail and sea connectivity which are as proxy variables for distance.

Entry cost is the cost of starting a business in any foreign country. The World Bank says that "this indicator measures the procedures, time, cost and paid-in minimum capital required for a small or medium-size limited liability company to start up and formally operate." The second variable, "entry costs", shows the expected positive coefficient estimate and is insignificant. Although fixed costs of market entry contribute to aggregate trade costs, in this case, it is insignificant. As per the results, India has been a favourable destination, providing a supportive environment to set up multinational businesses on its home-turf.

The Liner Shipping Connectivity Index (LSCI) shows negative parameters that are significant at 1%, and the coefficient value is −0.90 which is quite high showing a strong correlation with the trade costs. LSCI variable is a proxy for international transport connectivity. In an international trade, shipping has a huge impact on the trade volume as well as on trade costs; better the port connectivity, better the trade volume and lesser the trade cost. Since the conditions of port infrastructure in India are non-supportive to the trade, it contributes 90% to the trade costs. In order to facilitate trade and economic growth, India should focus on improving port infrastructure.

The tariff variable is also positively correlated to the trade costs. Tariff is a result of a country's protection measures. If the levels of tariffs are more in a country, more will be the trade cost. Therefore, trade costs aggravate if India and its partner countries apply the tariff rates. India has almost eliminated the tariffs for ASEAN member nations except for the goods included under highly sensitive track.

Nominal exchange rate variable included in the study is defined in terms of local currency units to the US dollar. The nominal exchange rate depicts country's competitiveness and has a negative correlation with the trade costs. In viewing the exchange rate from India's perspective, it signifies that if exchange rate rises, it will result in depreciation in the Indian currency. If the Indian currency depreciates, exports will increase and imports may fall. Thus, aggregate trade volume rises, which also shows that trade costs are decreasing, at ceteris paribus.

The distance variable is positively affecting the trade costs which means that India is facing high trade costs from its far located trading partners.

The final variable considered under observation is per capita GDP. It shows an inverse relationship indicating that the 1% increase in GDP per capita will decrease the trade cost by 3.6%. Finally, the value of overall R^2 is 0.82 which means that the abovementioned factors of trade costs are explaining almost 80% of the calculated trade costs, and remaining 20% still remains unexplained. Hence, other variables such as logistics and transport costs (freight or iceberg) are also contributing to trade costs in India.

7 Conclusion

This study has attempted to examine the determinants of trade cost as well as assessing the challenges faced by India and ASEAN countries over the years, thereby contributing to trade costs. The estimates based on the empirical results showed that trade cost levels are significant, giving a broader picture about the factors affecting the trade cost.

From the policy perspective, the results were significant and indicated the level of decline of trade costs. In ASEAN countries, low-income countries face high levels of trade costs—Cambodia, Lao PDR, Myanmar and Vietnam are such instances. India can take advantage of low labour costs of production by investing in these countries and thus increasing the market access. Though India and ASEAN have taken many initiatives to improve their trade relations through agreements in goods and services for tariff reduction or elimination, there still remains a long path to achieve full integration.

The empirical results also show clearly that there are more non-tariff barriers than tariff barriers between India and ASEAN + 3 countries. The free movement of goods, services, labour, capital and investment within the ASEAN Economic Community (AEC) will be beneficial for countries like Cambodia, Laos, Myanmar and Vietnam. However, since India is not a part of the AEC, it will hamper India's prospects with respect to the movement of skilled labours. Also, ASEAN economies are a hub for global value chains (GVCs). India has immense opportunities to gain from by increasing its participation in these value chains. However, India's current approach towards the FTA with ASEAN will erase the opportunity of integrating with value chains.

One of the major obstacles in India's trade comes from the lack of proper infrastructure and connectivity. Various reasons such as finances, priorities of the ruling parties, political instability, etc., cause delay in completing the connectivity and logistics projects which are adding up to the trade costs. Furthermore, India has a comparative advantage in services sector, particularly in software. However, the service sector in ASEAN remains largely protected, due to which India is unable to explore the ASEAN market in the service sector.

The levels of reduction in trade costs have been low since the elimination of tariffs and some other non-tariff barriers have been planned in a slow and phased manner. India, in particular, is attempting to reduce the non-tariff barriers such as transport connectivity, cost of doing business and infrastructure. For instance, India has introduced the "Sagarmala Project" which looks into port development and modification. Given the fact that port infrastructure is at the crux of international trade and also that the current state of India's port system requires attention, these initiatives are imperative and should be implemented at the earliest.

The payoffs for ASEAN from the FTA with India are substantial. Benefits with respect to economic arising from fall in prices, larger variety of products being available through trade, increased efficiency of firms and more of foreign investments substantiates this fact. However, the FTA has also negatively impacted some industries. Redistribution of wealth to such industries will help. Besides, India can leverage its historical and cultural ties with the region to strengthen economic and political cooperation. Apart from the economic benefits, what the countries need to look for in regional associations is social and human development. This will ensure a wider and more sustainable development for every country.

In summary, the econometric results show that trade costs have significant impact on trade volumes and that the Indian and ASEAN economies should focus on boosting trade facilitation infrastructure to reduce some of these costs at the earliest.

References

Anderson, J., & Neary, P. (2003). The mercantilist index of trade policy. *International Economic Review, 44*(2), 627–649.

Anderson, J., & Van Wincoop, E. (2003). Gravity with gravitas: A solution to the border puzzle. *American Economic Review, 93*(1), 170–192.

Anderson, J., & Van Wincoop, E. (2004). Trade costs. *Journal of Economic Literature, 42*(3), 691–751.

Arvis, J. F. (2011). Transit regimes. In G. McLinden, E. Fanta, D. Widdowson, & T. Doyle (Eds.), *Border Management Modernization* (Chapter 17, pp. 279–296). Washington D.C. Available at: http://publications.worldbank.org/index.php?main_page=product_info&products_id=23919.

Asher, M. G., & Sen, R. (2005). India-East Asia integration: A win-win for Asia. *Economic and Political Weekly*, 3932–3940.

Batra, A. (2007). Asian economic integration: ASEAN + 3 + 1 or ASEAN + 1. *ASEAN Economic Bulletin*, 181–204.

Chanda, R., & Gopalan, S. (2009). Understanding India's regional initiatives with East and Southeast Asia. *Asian-Pacific Economic Literature, 23*(1), 66–78.

Chen, N., & Novy, D. (2011). Gravity, trade integration and heterogeneity across industries. *Journal of International Economics, 85*(2), 206–221.

Francis, S. (2011). A sectoral impact analysis of the ASEAN-India free trade agreement. *Economic and Political Weekly, 46*(2), 46–55.

Greenaway, D., McGowan, D., & Milner, C. (2009). *Country trade costs, comparative advantage and the pattern of trade: Multi-country and product panel evidence, GEP research paper: 2009/96*. GEP Leverhulme Centre: University of Nottingham.

Ghoshal, B. (2009). India, Southeast Asia and the FTA: Strengthening economic integration. Institute of Peace and Conflict Studies, Issue Brief (114).

Head, K., & Ries, J. (2001). Increasing returns versus national production differentiation as an explanation for the pattern of US-Canada trade. *American Economic Review, 91*(4), 858–876.

Helble, M., Shepherd, B., & Wilson, J. S. (2007). Transparency, trade costs, and regional integration in the Asia Pacific. *World Bank Policy Research Paper no: 4401*, World Bank.

Jacks, D., Meissner, C., & Novy, D. (2008). Trade costs 1870–2000. *American Economic Review, 98*(2), 529–534.

Jacks, D., Meissner, C., & Novy, D. (2011). Trade booms, trade busts, and trade costs. *Journal of International Economics, 83*(2), 185–201.

Joseph, K. J. (2009). ASEAN-India pact and plantations: Realities of the myths, *Economic and Political Weekly*, 14–18.

Karmakar, S. (2005), *India–ASEAN cooperation in services—An overview, Indian council for research on international economic relations (ICRIER)*. Working Paper (176).

Kawai, M., & Wignaraja, G. (2011). Asian FTAs: Trends, prospects and challenges. *Journal of Asian Economics, 22,* 1–22.

Kawai, M., & Wignaraja, G. (Ed.) (2011). Asia's free trade agreements: How is business responding? *Edward Elgar*. Available for free download at http://www.adbi.org/files/2011.01.31.book.asia.free.trade.agreements.pdf.

Kee, H.-L., Nicita, A., & Olarreaga, M. (2009). Estimating trade restrictiveness indices. *Economic Journal, 119*(534), 172–199.

McCallum, J. (1995). National borders matter: Canada-U.S. regional trade patterns. *The American Economic Review, 85*(3), 615–623. Retrieved February 22, 2021, from http://www.jstor.org/stable/2118191.

Miroudot, S., & Shepherd, B. (2015). Regional trade agreements and trade costs in services. *Robert Schuman Centre for Advanced Studies Research Paper No. RSCAS 2015/85, SSRN Electronic Journal*. https://doi.org/10.2139/ssrn.2691497.

Miroudot, S., Sauvage, J., & Shepherd, B. (2013). Measuring the costs of international trade in services. *World Trade Review, 12*(4), 719–735.

Mohanty, S. (2007). India-ASEAN FTA negotiations: The way forward. *India and World Articles*, 2434.

Novy, D. (2013). Gravity redux: Measuring international trade costs with panel data. *Economic Inquiry, 51*(1), 101–121.

Pal, P., & Dasgupta, M. (2008). Does a free trade agreement with ASEAN make sense? *Economic and Political Weekly*, 8–12.

Pal, P., & Dasgupta, M. (2009). The ASEAN-India free trade agreement: an assessment. *Economic and Political Weekly*, 11–15.

Rajan, R. S., & Sen, R. (2004, July). The new wave of FTAs in Asia: With particular reference to ASEAN, China and India.

High-level Conference on Asia's Economic Cooperation and Integration at the *Asian Development Bank* (pp. 1–2).

Saqib, M., & Taneja, N. (2005). Non-tariff barriers and India's exports: the case of ASEAN and Sri Lanka (No. 165). In *Indian Council for research on international economic relations*. New Delhi, India.

Shepherd, B., & Wilson, J. S. (2008). Trade facilitation in ASEAN member countries: Measuring progress and assessing priorities. *World Bank Policy Research Working Paper*: 4615, World Bank.

The role of non-tariff measures in achieving AEC blueprint (2025), *Asian Trade Centre (ATC)*, Policy Brief, Number 16-03, April, 2016.

Tinbergen, J. (1962). *Shaping the world economy*. New York: The Twentieth Century Fund.

Chapter 6
Dynamics of ICT Penetration and Trade: Evidence from Major Trading Nations

Areej Aftab Siddiqui and Parul Singh

1 Introduction

The world has seen notable changes in the past few years which have come with the proliferation of Information and Communication Technology (ICT) across countries, industries, sectors, and organizations. Information technology and the Internet technologies have been the key drivers for innovation, growth, research, and social change. Technology has thus become pervasive and has played a vital role in promoting exports, imports, and trade openness. These three indicators, i.e., export, import, and trade openness, contribute to the growth and development of a country primarily by capital formation. At the country level, ICT has played a tremendous role in expanding the growth of the nation. The literature demonstrates that investment in the development of ICT infrastructure and its penetration at various levels substantially benefit the country. Penetration rate of technology is determined by income, youth dependency ratio, human capital, legal quality, telephone density, and banking sector (Chinn & Fairlie, 2010). In case of developing countries, low rate of penetration of technology is mainly due to disparity in income, telephone density, legal quality, and human capital. ICT is no less than a transformation in relation to provide improved labor skills, consumer intellect, and education which in turn drives the growth of the country directly or indirectly (Quah, 2002). The foremost indicators of development of ICT have been recognized as investment in ICT (Sridhar & Sridhar, 2009; Waverman et al., 2005) and ICT penetration (Vu, 2011). Apart from these factors, there are certain specific indicators such as Internet use, mobile networks, access to computers, and ICT trade (Sassi & Goaied, 2013; Freund & Weinhold, 2002;

A. A. Siddiqui (✉) · P. Singh
Indian Institute of Foreign Trade, New Delhi, India
e-mail: areej@iift.edu

P. Singh
e-mail: parulsingh@iift.edu

P. Lakhanpal et al. (eds.), *Trade, Investment and Economic Growth*,
https://doi.org/10.1007/978-981-33-6973-3_6

Yushkova, 2014; Sridhar & Sridhar, 2009; Siddiqui and Singh, 2020). ICT penetration not only enhances economic growth of a country but also enhances productivity and trade openness (Sassi & Goaied, 2013; Hassan 2005). The improved ICT access and e-commerce applications' adoption accelerates bilateral trade flows at several levels. For developing and least developed nations, ICT, high-speed Internet and secured servers are important for exposing the e-trade potentials (Xing, 2018). The higher the level of ICT development in both the trading partner nations, the higher the bilateral services exports among them (Tee et al., 2020). Internet promotes international trade, especially in developing economies, and hence, trade positively boosts growth (Meijers, 2014). At the firm level, ICT has a vital role in its growth and development across various economic sectors as it shrinks the transaction costs and enhances production of the firms (Röller & Waverman, 2001).

This chapter further adds to the literature by creating an ICT index to assess the effect of ICT on trade and its subsets, i.e., exports and imports. Hence, the study provides new directions for future scope of research on the ICT-trade nexus in major trading nations from 2001 to 2018.

2 Linkage Between ICT and Trade: Review of Literature

Information and Communication Technology (ICT) can be understood as components and infrastructure that enables computing. It refers to the technologies that make available the access to the information using telecommunications. ICT has influenced growth and development at all the levels—country level, industry level, firm level, and individual level. At the same time, a country's trade openness and education can be deemed as a contributing factor of ICT innovation (Lee et al., 2016).

ICT impacts economic growth of the country through international trade. The usage of ICT increases foreign trade as trade of ICT goods and services upsurges in the international market. The increased flow of exports directs economic growth and development and creates opportunities for the employment (Yushkova, 2014). The deployment of ICT by the business sector decreases trade costs and facilitates trade relations between countries. It can act as a source of comparative advantage in trade as it fosters export more in industries using intensive ICT. If, in a country, ICT development index and industry's R&D intensity increases by 1 standard deviation each, then export in one industry increases 10% (Wang & Li, 2017). ICT development has positive impact to the international trade growth as studied on select service items; as in certain number of services, it is found to have more importance as that of access and skills for trade (Nath & Liu, 2017). The Internet technologies are imperative in placing contacts between international organizations by enabling fixed-line and mobile phones. There is evidence of causal effect from the Internet on trade in business services (Kneller & Timmis, 2016). In many nations, application of ICT for business process indicated by the amount of the Internet usage by the business signifies a significant linkage with the export. Hence, the Internet adopted by the business sector promotes exports. Internet is also linked to the growth of international trade in services sector. It is stated that 10% increase in Internet penetration in an overseas market country is related with 1.7 and 1.1% points increase in the growth of the export and import, respectively (controlling GDP and exchange rate). It has been established that the development of the facilities related to the Internet technologies increased services' export to the USA. It can be concluded that growth of trade in services has positive effects for the growth at the world level (Freund & Weinhold, 2002). The work of Freund and Weinhold (2004) yielded three predictions. Firstly, bilateral trade growth between two countries is facilitated by the growth in Internet connectedness between these two countries. Secondly, in case of more neighboring countries, Internet will offer advantage by greater import growth, consequently expanding the effect of distance on trade, and lastly, Internet advancement is expected to expand total trade.

Certain studies conducted at the country and/or regional level also suggest that investment in ICT is crucial for the growth and productivity. Findings also underline the significance of ICT in improving exports by boosting productivity (UNCTAD, 2008; Ahmed, 2008). This is evident in the case of 57 US industries (Stiroh, 2002). Another evidence comes from the study performed by Statistics Canada (2008) on ICT investment made by the provinces and established that investment in ICT is important for the productivity growth (Sharpe & Arsenault, 2008). In numerous European counties, there is a significant linkage between the use of ICT and firms exporting (Kotnik et al., 2013). It is also witnessed in the case of Turkey that ICT has placed more positive effect on Turkish imports as that of Turkish exports. Export volume increases with increased access levels of ICT and skills (Ozcan, 2018). The Internet technologies and increased Web connectivity promote trade in countries as witnessed in case of Bolivia and support the country to gain a significant economic benefit (Freund & Weinhold, 2004). In case of the effect of broadband on European trade union, it has been found that it exerts positive effect on trade. The proximity between countries also increases the outcome of ICT. This is because knowledge exchange takes place in activities related to the trade. The usage of ICT and proximity between regions brings in trade competitiveness (Ozcan, 2018). It is seen that ICT plays more important role in exports from developing economies. It helps in reducing sunk costs which results in more participation of developing countries in international trade. Hence, ICT plays a larger marginal impact on developing economies (Tee et al., 2020). The conclusion is coherent that states that the Internet enables trade for goods, thus decreasing exporting costs (Freund & Weinhold, 2004).

Enhanced access to ICT and related skills are crucial factors to enhance the volume of export. Also, increased level of ICT indices is crucial for an improved volume of import. In case of small- and medium-sized firms, there is a significant relationship between ICT capacities and the engagement in export-related activities. There are also signs that intensity of export is further strongly associated to improved capacities of ICT than the sheer choice to export (Hagsten & Kotnik, 2017). In terms of network effects, the Internet is the prime channel for both the manufacturing and service sectors (Lee, 2012). ICT reduces the trade costs (Yushkova, 2014) including market entry costs, transportation costs, and communication and information costs resulting in higher trade flows (Ozcan, 2018; Yushkova, 2014). Internet accelerates trade by reducing fixed cost of trade. This boosts export growth and increases the whole effect of distance on trade (Freund & Weinhold, 2004). There are ways by which ICT reduces the trade costs such as it brings in transparency and openness in the market which leads to decreased match cost, search cost, and communication cost. It also decreases monitoring and management cost of the organizations (Venables, 2001; Shemayev, 2014). Deployment of ICT creates organizational changes and digitization resulting in lowered shipping cost of an organization which incorporates transit time and further related costs (Venables, 2001). ICT also decreases information costs across international boundaries and hence affects trade positively (Mattes et al., 2012). It reduces inefficiencies by acting as a mediation between sellers and buyers and establishes an e-marketplace that reduces the buyer's costs for obtaining information related to the product offerings and prices by the seller (Shemayev, 2014). ICT offers better access to market information by the organizations which bring in economic growth as witnessed by the countries such as Japan and Hong Kong in the late twentieth century (Vu, 2011). It is an essential driver in offering access to information which accelerates faster growth because of improved investment (Levine & Zervos, 1993). It enables generation and diffusion of information around diverse territories. The usage of ICT infrastructure decreases fixed transaction costs for instance entry costs to foreign markets (Freund & Weinhold, 2004). It also plays a crucial role in overcoming trade costs associated with distance (Yushkova, 2014; Ahmed, 2008). Usage of ICT brings in digitization and organizational changes and hence reducing shipping costs (Yushkova, 2014). It also reduces the transit time and associated transport costs (Mattes et al., 2012; Yushkova, 2014).

Besides ICT and trade openness, financial development is also an important catalyst of growth. It holds an important role in shaping the performance of the export sector as exporters need external finance and also face limitations around credits. According to a study performed on cross-country analysis, export diversification is significantly impacted by access to the domestic financial services. This is because financial services relieve the credit constraints of the exporters. Financial development affects extensive and intensive margins of exports (Nieminen, 2020). It employs a significant causal effect on the level exports and also on the trade balance as seen in case of the manufactured goods. The sector having greater scale of economies benefits more for the higher level of financial development as that of the other sector. Therefore, countries with an improved and better financial development have a comparative advantage in sectors possessing high scale of economies. Also, economies with greater intensity of financial development have greater shares of industrial exports in GDP and have a better trade balance in manufactured goods. Hence, it can be established that financial development is important for economic expansion (Beck, 2002). It leads to larger value of exports among trade partners (Berthou, 2007). Increased financial development has a significant impact on the export value (Beck, 2002; Manova, 2005) among trading partners by growing the number of incumbent firms. It also has a constructive influence on the possibility that two countries are trade partners (Berthou, 2007). Improved availability of the financial resources for the exporters with larger export values may lead to vital economic policy implications at both regional and national level (Kadochnikov & Fedyunina, 2017). Financial development also plays an important role in economic growth of the developing countries (Nieminen, 2020). In case of China, in the period 1971–2011, financial development and international trade along with other variables were found to have significant effect on its economic growth (Shahbaz et al., 2013). Financial constraints limit an organization from entering the export market. Accordingly, government, while forming export promotion policy, should consider and address the problem of credit constraint met by the organizations (Nagaraj, 2014).

3 Framework and Methodology

To analyze the impact of ICT on exports and imports, an attempt is made to develop an ICT penetration index for the top trading nations for the time period 2001–2018. The index has been constructed using principal component analysis (PCA) on the components selected from the existing literature. As ICT penetration cannot be assessed by a single variable, PCA results in transforming a set of correlated variables into linearly uncorrelated factors by orthogonal transformation and explains maximum variability of data. Another index for explaining the financial development of the selected nations is also developed by applying PCA in a similar manner. The variables used for constructing the two indices are as listed in Table 1.

Once the ICT penetration and financial development index are developed, data analysis is carried out by first checking the stationarity, cointegration, regression, and finally causality test. To assess the objective of the paper, the relations which are examined are as depicted in Eqs. (5), (6) and (7)

$$\text{lnEx} = \beta_0 + \beta_1\text{lnICT} + \beta_2\text{lnGrowth} + \beta_3\text{lnDI} + \beta_4\text{lnFDI} + \beta_5\text{lnFD} + \beta_6\text{lnExR} + \varepsilon \quad (5)$$

$$\text{lnIm} = \beta_0 + \beta_1\text{lnICT} + \beta_2\text{lnGrowth} + \beta_3\text{lnDI} + \beta_4\text{lnFDI} + \beta_5\text{lnFD} + \beta_6\text{lnExR} + \varepsilon \quad (6)$$

$$\text{lnTr} = \beta_0 + \beta_1\text{lnICT} + \beta_2\text{lnGrowth} + \beta_3\text{lnDI} + \beta_4\text{lnFDI} + \beta_5\text{lnFD} + \beta_6\text{lnExR} + \varepsilon \quad (7)$$

where ICT is the ICT penetration index, Ex is the exports of goods and services, Im is the imports of goods and services, Tr is trade openness which is the ratio of sum of exports and imports to GDP, FD is financial development index, growth is per capita GDP at constant prices, DI refers to domestic investment and is the gross fixed capital formation at constant prices, FDI refers to the foreign direct investment as a percentage of GDP, ExR is the real effective exchange rate for each period and country. The data for the selected variables is accessed from World Development Indicators given by World Bank. Log values of the selected variables have been taken to check the data for heteroskedasticity.

If the series are non-stationary, the results from regression may be spurious and thus have no meaning. Hence, the panel data is first checked forstationarity through

Table 1 ICT penetration and financial development index

Variables	Definitions
ICT penetration index	
Fixed broadband subscriptions (per 100 people)	It refers to fixed subscriptions to high-speed access to the public internet. it excludes subscriptions that have access to data communications (including the internet) via mobile cellular networks
Fixed telephone subscriptions (per 100 people)	It refers to the sum of active number of analog fixed telephone lines, voice-over-IP (VoIP) subscriptions, fixed wireless local loop (WLL) subscriptions, ISDN voice-channel equivalents, and fixed public payphones
ICT trade (% of total trade)	Exports and imports of computers and peripheral equipment, communication equipment, consumer electronic equipment, electronic components, and other information and technology goods (miscellaneous)
Individuals using the internet (% of population)	Internet users are individuals who have used the internet (from any location) in the last 3 months
Mobile cellular subscriptions (per 100 people)	Mobile cellular telephone subscriptions are subscriptions to a public mobile telephone service that provide access to the PSTN using cellular technology
Financial development index	
Private sector credit to GDP	It indicates the financial resources provided to private sector by intermediaries other than central banks divided by GDP
Total assets held by deposit money banks as a share of GDP	It indicates the assets held by commercial banks and other financial institutions that accept transferable deposits, such as demand deposits
Central bank assets to GDP	Central bank assets are claims on domestic real nonfinancial sector by the Central Bank. It includes ratio of central bank assets to GDP
Liquid liabilities of the financial sector to GDP	It is a broad indicator comprising of the liquid liabilities of the financial system and is currency plus demand and interest-bearing liabilities of the financial sector as a percentage of GDP
Remittance inflows to GDP	It is the remittances and compensation of individuals working abroad

(continued)

Table 1 (continued)

Variables	Definitions
M2 (ratio to monetary GDP)	This is used as a primary indicator to forecast inflation as it includes currency in hand, savings, deposits, overnight repos at commercial banks, and non-institutional money market accounts
Financial system deposits to GDP	This parameter is a total of demand, time and saving deposits in deposit money banks, and other financial institutions as a share of GDP
Credit to government and state-owned enterprises to GDP	This parameter is the ratio between credit by domestic money banks to the government and state-owned enterprises and GDP
Gross domestic savings as a share of GDP	This parameter is derived by subtracting final consumption expenditure from GDP
The stock market capitalization to GDP ratio	This parameter indicates the value of listed shares divided by GDP. The market value also known as market capitalization is the product of share price and number of shares outstanding
Stock market total value traded to GDP	This parameter refers to the total value of shares traded during a period. It is used to verify market capitalization ratio, i.e., market size with trading
Total reserves to GDP (TR)	This indicator is the sum of monetary gold, special drawing rights, reserves of IMF members and holdings of foreign exchange as percentage of GDP

Source Authors Compilation from Definitions as given by World Development Indicators, World Bank, and International Financial Statistics (IFS), International Monetary Fund (IMF)

panel root tests.[1] As per practice, non-stationary series at level are transformed into stationary series by differencing and then checked for cointegration as per Engel and Granger. Long-run equilibrium may exist in non-stationary series of the series which are cointegrated as per various tests of cointegration like Kao and Pedroni. Regression is applied to the data series once checked for stationarity and cointegration. Within regression, a number of tests can be applied, and hence, the data set is checked for the applicability of fixed vs random effects by using Hausman specification test and pooled vs panel regression by using Breusch Pagan LM test. Primarily, pooled regression is applied to non-stationary series which are cointegrated and are effective if no cross-dependencies exist. While in case of panel ordinary least squares, cross-sectional dependencies with fixed effects can be tested.

[1] Levin, Li and Chu t test for common unit root, Im, Pearson and Shin W-test, ADF–Fisher chi-square and PP-Fisher chi-square.

4 Results and Discussions

To develop an index for ICT penetration, principal component analysis has been used, and similarly, financial development index has been constructed. PCA has been used as it resolves the problem of high correlation among the selected parameters and avoids the problem of multicollinearity and thus develops a single weighted index. KMO and Bartlett's tests for sampling adequacy for ICT penetration index are greater than 64.8%, while for financial development index, it is more than 75.4%. The weightage allocated to each of the variables for ICT index and financial development index is as indicated in Table 2 and Table 3 respectively.

The weights inferred through PCA find justification in the existing literature which indicate that Internet, broadband, and cellular network are more important as compared to trade in ICT (Sassi & Goaied, 2013, Sridhar & Sridhar 2009). ICT

Table 2 Component score coefficient matrix for ICT index

Components	Coefficients
Internet users	0.417
Broadband users	0.482
Fixed telephone users	−0.029
Mobile users	0.279
Total trade in ICT	−0.203

Table 3 Component score coefficient matrix for financial development index

Components	Coefficients
Broad money	0.045
Central bank assets to GDP (%)	−0.189
Credit to government and state-owned enterprises to GDP (%)	−0.030
Financial system deposits to GDP (%)	0.128
Liquid liabilities to GDP (%)	0.082
Private credit by deposit money banks and other financial institutions to GDP (%)	−0.041
Remittance inflows to GDP (%)	0.134
Stock market total value traded to GDP (%)	0.211
Gross domestic savings (% of GDP)	−0.093
Total reserves (% GDP)	0.214
Stock market capitalization to GDP (%)	0.276
Deposit money banks' assets to GDP (%)	0.006

Extraction Method: Principal Component Analysis. Rotation Method: Varimax with Kaiser Normalization
Source Authors Calculations

penetration index for the present study can be now treated as a dependent variable. The variables indicate low correlation as depicted in Table 4.

The log-transformed data for exports, imports, trade openness, growth, foreign direct investment, direct investment, and exchange rates was tested for stationarity; as if the panel data series are non-stationary, there is a risk of obtaining spurious results. The results are depicted in Table 5.

The results indicate that at the first difference level, none of the variables have a unit root and hence are stationary. As the data is stationary at first order of integration, Kao cointegration test is applied, and it is seen that the variables are cointegrated as depicted in Table 6.

Thus, in order to analyze the relationship between ICT penetration and exports, imports and trade, panel least squares or pooled regressions can be applied to Eqs. (5), (6), and (7). The present model is best suited for panel least squares with fixed effects with cross-sectional effects as indicated by Hausman specification test and Breusch and Pagan (1980) LM test as depicted in Table 7.

The results of the selected model to estimate the relationship of ICT penetration with the selected variables are presented in Table 8.

The results indicate that ICT penetration index constructed in the present study has a positive and significant relationship with various variants of international movement of goods like exports, imports, and trade openness. ICT penetration has a considerable impact on exports as compared to imports and trade. Thus, it can be said that if ICT penetration improves, then exports, imports, and trade all together will rise (Vemuri & Siddiqi, 2009). In terms of financial development, it is seen that there is no individual relationship between financial development and exports or imports but a significant relationship with trade openness though negative, pointing toward the fact that financial stimulus may favor domestic over international trade (Freund & Weinhold, 2002).

To examine the impact in each country, cross-sectional effect is seen in Table 9. The effect of ICT on exports, imports, and trade openness is primarily positive for Belgium, Germany, Hong Kong, Mexico, and Netherlands while negative for Canada, China, France, Italy, Japan, South Korea, Russia, Spain, United Kingdom, and Spain.

It has been seen that ICT adoption is used for promoting trade, and most of the countries are in the process of adopting ICT applications and further developing policies of digitalizing trade (Nath and Liu 2017, Thiemann et al., 2012). The results indicate that ICT penetration is favorable for encouraging trade whether exports or imports.

There exists unidirectional causality from ICT penetration to exports, imports, and trade openness, and the results are depicted in Table 10.

The present study indicates the relationship of penetration of ICT on various variants of international transactions like exports, imports, and trade openness for the selected nations, which has a significant and positive impact on international trade (Yushkova, 2014; Freund & Weinhold, 2002). On examining individual country effects, the results are mixed, but in totality, the ICT penetration index developed by the authors consisting of trade of ICT, broadband and cellular network penetration,

Table 4 Correlation between variables

	Exports	Imports	Trade	ICT	Fin Dev	FDI	Growth	Domestic investment	Exchange rates
Exports	1.000	0.976	−0.222	0.600	−0.095	0.367	0.686	0.755	0.119
Imports	0.976	1.000	−0.255	0.568	−0.080	0.395	0.706	0.783	0.169
Trade	−0.222	−0.255	1.000	0.440	0.761	0.101	−0.850	−0.770	0.267
ICT	0.600	0.568	0.440	1.000	0.397	0.200	−0.015	0.112	0.179
Financial development	−0.095	−0.080	0.761	0.397	1.000	0.188	−0.601	−0.525	0.282
FDI	0.367	0.395	0.101	0.200	0.188	1.000	0.149	0.135	0.084
Growth	0.686	0.706	−0.850	−0.015	−0.601	0.149	1.000	0.962	−0.134
Domestic investment	0.755	0.783	−0.770	0.112	−0.525	0.135	0.962	1.000	0.014
Exchange rates	0.119	0.169	0.267	0.179	0.282	0.084	-0.134	0.014	1.000

Table 5 Summary of panel root test

Variables	Level	Levin, Li and Chu t test for common unit root	Im, Pesaran and Shin W-test	ADF–Fisher chi-square	PP-Fisher chi-square
ICT penetration index	Level	−3.460*** (0.000)	−3.521*** (0.000)	60.274*** (0.000)	296.455*** (0.000)
	First diff	−7.722*** (0.000)	−9.722*** (0.000)	141.295*** (0.000)	50.586*** (0.010)
Financial development index	Level	1.028 (0.848)	−0.959 (0.168)	33.701 (0.292)	51.839*** (0.007)
	First diff	5.070*** (1.000)	−3.343***(0.000)	61.380*** (0.000)	132.185***(0.000)
Exports	Level	−8.105*** (0.000)	−4.303*** (0.000)	67.718*** (0.000)	178.776*** (0.000)
	First diff	−8.303*** (0.000)	−5.793*** (0.000)	86.775*** (0.000)	119.197*** (0.000)
Imports	Level	−7.656*** (0.000)	−4.075*** (0.000)	64.807*** (0.000)	148.581*** (0.000)
	First diff	−7.875*** (0.000)	−5.535*** (0.000)	82.815*** (0.000)	120.878*** (0.000)
Growth	Level	−3.62*** (0.000)	0.249 (0.598)	24.971 (0.726)	67.052*** (0.001)
	First diff	−7.848*** (0.0000)	−5.593*** (0.000)	86.236*** (0.000)	118.659*** (0.000)
Trade openness	Level	−4.18*** (0.000)	0.153 (0.561)	30.415 (0.343)	76.999*** (0.000)
	First diff	−9.244*** (0.0000)	−6.525*** (0.000)	93.365*** (0.000)	177.870*** (0.000)
FDI	Level	−10.020 *** (0.000)	−7.505*** (0.000)	106.788*** (0.000)	85.758*** (0.000)
	First diff	−8.523*** (0.000)	−7.593*** (0.000)	119.104*** (0.000)	344.270*** (0.000)
Exchange rates	Level	−2.748*** (0.000)	−1.544* (0.06)	39.514 (0.114)	30.764 (0.427)
	First diff	−7.843*** (0.000)	−5.498*** (0.000)	82.799*** (0.000)	93.961*** (0.000)
Domestic investment	Level	−4.376*** (0.000)	−3.418*** (0.000)	59.746*** (0.000)	69.098*** (0.000)
	First diff	−5.573*** (0.000)	−4.825*** (0.000)	74.310*** (0.000)	85.712*** (0.000)

*Significant at 10%, **Significant at 5%, ***Significant at 1% level of significance
Source Authors' Calculations

Table 6 Kao cointegration test

	t-statistic	Prob
ADF	−6.788	0.000
Residual variance	0.000	
HAC variance	0.000	

*Significant at 10%, **Significant at 5%, ***Significant at 1% level of significance
Source Authors' Calculations

Table 7 Robustness tests

Test summary	Hausman specification test (Prob)	Breusch–Pagan test (Prob)	Pesaran CD (Prob)
ICT penetration index and exports	0.000	0.000	0.000
ICT penetration index and imports	0.000	0.000	0.000
ICT penetration index and trade openness	0.000	0.000	0.000

Source Authors' Calculations

Table 8 Panel least squares with cross-sectional fixed effects

Independent variable	Model 1 (Exports)	Model 2 (Imports)	Model 3 (Trade openness)
ICT penetration index	0.000*** (0.103)	0.000*** (0.087)	0.000*** (0.04)
Financial development index	0.573 (−0.005)	0.996 (0.000)	0.001*** (−0.013)
Growth	0.000*** (0.396)	0.204 (0.107)	0.000*** (0.483)
Foreign direct investment	0.407 (0.009)	0.437 (0.006)	0.130 (0.008)
Domestic investment	0.000*** (0.447)	0.000*** (0.687)	0.132 (−0.045)
Exchange rates	0.010*** (−0.259)	0.000*** (−0.467)	0.094* (−0.085)
Constant	0.024 (2.138)	0.000 (3.341)	0.000 (−5.483)

Source Authors' Calculations

Internet usages, and mobile phone penetration indicates positive relationship with exports, imports, and trade openness.

Table 9 Cross-sectional effect of ICT penetration index

	Country	Exports effect	Imports effect	Trade openness effect
1	Belgium	0.246	0.215	0.293
2	Canada	−0.083	−0.073	−0.025
3	China	−0.031	−0.131	−0.013
4	France	−0.092	−0.055	−0.096
5	Germany	0.081	0.072	0.035
6	Hong Kong	0.518	0.476	0.702
7	Italy	−0.048	−0.029	−0.102
8	Japan	−0.341	−0.323	−0.348
9	Korea, Rep	−0.025	−0.075	0.093
10	Mexico	0.084	0.086	−0.044
11	Netherlands	0.203	0.169	0.240
12	Russian Federation	−0.013	−0.152	−0.186
13	Spain	−0.090	−0.070	−0.081
14	United Kingdom	−0.004	0.079	−0.063
15	United States	−0.347	−0.142	−0.403

Source Authors' Calculations

Table 10 Granger causality

Null hypothesis	F-Stat	Prob
ICT does not Granger cause exports	10.725	0.000***
Exports does not Granger cause ICT	0.864	0.423
ICT does not Granger cause imports	11.450	0.000***
Imports does not Granger cause ICT	1.591	0.206
ICT does not Granger cause trade openness	2.659	0.072*
Trade openness does not Granger cause ICT	2.331	0.100
Financial development does not Granger cause ICT	2.757	0.066*
ICT does not Granger cause financial development	0.456	0.634
Growth does not Granger cause ICT	0.824	0.440
ICT does not Granger cause growth	5.397	0.005***
Foreign direct investment does not Granger cause ICT	0.523	0.594
ICT does not Granger cause foreign direct investment	0.367	0.693
Domestic investment does not Granger cause ICT	2.441	0.089*
ICT does not Granger cause domestic investment	10.695	0.000***
Exchange rates does not Granger cause ICT	0.782	0.459
ICT does not Granger cause exchange rates	0.251	0.778

Source Authors Calculations

5 Conclusion

Thus, as compared to studies in the past on examining the relationship between ICT and trade, the present study draws a comparative examination between ICT penetration and exports, imports, and trade for the top trading nations of the world. It is seen that the results are consistent across all three models. Trade being a major determinant of growth as established in the literature, it becomes imperative to assess the role of ICT in enhancement of trade. The ICT penetration index developed using principal component analysis has variations in country effects of trade.

Though a number of studies have been conducted at the national, regional and global level for the role of ICT in trade, no specific study has been carried out for trading nations and the comparative role of ICT for export, import, and trade. The present study thus adds another dimension to the existing literature by developing a comprehensive ICT index incorporating the broad dimensions of reach, development, and applicability of ICT. The cross-country effect in each nation indicates the need of devising policies for developing further linkages between ICT penetration and trade across nations. The results indicate that advancements in ICT lead to increase in exports, imports, and trade, thus indicating that use of technology in trade facilitates it to a large extent. This is evident from the adoption of ICT in export and import clearances globally. Moving toward paperless trade has increased and will increase the ease of doing business which at present has been done to a large extent.

References

Ahmed, E. M. (2008). ICT and human capital intensities impact on ASEAN5 productivity. *The Journal of Knowledge Economy & Knowledge Management, 4.*

Beck, T. (2002). Financial development and international trade: Is there a link? *Journal of International Economics, 57*(1), 107–131.

Berthou, A. (2007, June). Credit constraints and zero trade flows: The role of financial development. In *Empirical investigations in international economics, 4th annual conference.*

Chinn, M. D., & Fairlie, R. W. (2010). ICT use in the developing world: An analysis of differences in computer and internet penetration. *Review of International Economics, 18*(1), 153–167.

Freund, C. L., & Weinhold, D. (2004). The effect of the internet on international trade. *Journal of International Economics, 62*(1), 171–189.

Freund, C., & Weinhold, D. (2002). The internet and international trade in services. *American Economic Review, 92*(2), 236–240.

Hagsten, E., & Kotnik, P. (2017). ICT as facilitator of internationalisation in small-and medium-sized firms. *Small Business Economics, 48*(2), 431–446.

Hassan, M. K. (2005). FDI, information technology and economic growth in the Mena region. 10th ERF paper.

International Financial Statistics (IFS), International Monetary Fund (IMF).

Kadochnikov, S. M., & Fedyunina, A. A. (2017). The impact of financial and human resources on the export performance of Russian firms. *Economic Systems, 41*(1), 41–51.

Kneller, R., & Timmis, J. (2016). Ict and exporting: The effects of broadband on the extensive margin of business service exports. *Review of International Economics, 24*(4), 757–796.

Kotnik, P., Hagsten, E., & Sweden, S. (2013). ICT as Enabler of Exports.

Lee, J. (2012). Network effects on international trade. *Economics Letters, 116*(2), 199–201.

Lee, S., Nam, Y., Lee, S., & Son, H. (2016). Determinants of ICT innovations: A cross-country empirical study. *Technological Forecasting and Social Change, 110,* 71–77.

Levine, R., & Zervos, S. J. (1993). What we have learned about policy and growth from cross-country regressions? *The American Economic Review, 83*(2), 426–430.

Manova, K. (2005). Credit constraints in trade: Financial development.

Mattes, A., Meinen, P., & Pavel, F. (2012). Goods follow bytes: The impact of ICT on EU trade.

Meijers, H. (2014). Does the internet generate economic growth, international trade, or both? *International Economics and Economic Policy, 11*(1–2), 137–163.

Nagaraj, P. (2014). Financial constraints and export participation in India. *International Economics, 140,* 19–35.

Nath, H. K., & Liu, L. (2017). Information and communications technology (ICT) and services trade. *Information Economics and Policy, 41,* 81–87.

Nieminen, M. (2020). Multidimensional financial development, exporter behavior and export diversification. *Economic Modelling, 93,* 1–12.

Ozcan, B. (2018). Information and communications technology (ICT) and international trade: Evidence from Turkey. *Eurasian Economic Review, 8*(1), 93–113.

Quah, D. (2002). Technology dissemination and economic growth: Some lessons for the new economy. *Technology and the New Economy, 3,* 95–156.

Roller, L. H., & Waverman, L. (2001). Telecommunications infrastructure and economic development: A simultaneous approach. *American Economic Review, 91*(4), 909–923.

Sassi, S., & Goaied, M. (2013). Financial development, ICT diffusion and economic growth: Lessons from MENA region. *Telecommunications Policy, 37*(4–5), 252–261.

Shahbaz, M., Khan, S., & Tahir, M. I. (2013). The dynamic links between energy consumption, economic growth, financial development and trade in China: Fresh evidence from multivariate framework analysis. *Energy Economics, 40,* 8–21.

Sharpe, A., & Arsenault, J. F. (2008). *ICT investment and productivity: A provincial perspective* (No. 2008-06). Centre for the Study of Living Standards.

Shemayev, V. (2014). An alloy of steel and information and communication technology (ICT): Does it facilitate trade?

Siddiqui, A. A., & Singh, P. (2020). ICT penetration and economic growth: An empirical analysis of major trading nations. *The Indian Economic Journal.* https://doi.org/10.1177/0019466220951787.

Sridhar, K. S., & Sridhar, V. (2009). Telecommunications infrastructure and economic growth: Evidence from developing countries.

Stiroh, K. J. (2002). Are ICT spillovers driving the new economy? *Review of Income and Wealth, 48*(1), 33–57.

Tee, B. A., Tham, S. Y., & Kam, A. J. Y. (2020). The role of ICT in ASEAN-5's services exports: A panel study. *Malaysian Journal of Economic Studies, 57*(1), 1–19.

Thiemann, F., Fleming, E., & Mueller, R. A. F. (2012). Impact of information and communication technology (ICT) on international trade in fruit and vegetables: A gravity model approach. Selected paper prepared for presentation at the International Association of Agricultural Economists (IAAE) Triennial Conference, Foz do Iguacu, Brazil, 18-24 August, 2012

United Nations Conference on Trade and Development (UNCTAD). (2008). Measuring the impact of ICT use in business: The case of manufacturing in Thailand. Geneva, Switzerland: Author.

Vemuri, V. K., & Siddiqi, S. (2009). Impact of commercialization of the internet on international trade: A panel study using the extended gravity model. *The International Trade Journal, 23*(4), 458–484.

Venables, A. J. (2001). Geography and international inequalities: The impact of new technologies. *Journal of Industry, Competition and Trade, 1*(2), 135–159.

Vu, K. M. (2011). ICT as a source of economic growth in the information age: Empirical evidence from the 1996–2005 period. *Telecommunications Policy, 35*(4), 357–372.

Wang, Y., & Li, J. (2017). ICT's effect on trade: Perspective of comparative advantage. *Economics Letters, 155,* 96–99.

Waverman, L., Meschi, M., & Fuss, M. (2005). The impact of telecoms on economic growth in developing countries. *The Vodafone Policy Paper Series,* 2(03), 10–24.

World Development Indicators, World Bank.

Xing, Z. (2018). The impacts of information and communications technology (ICT) and E-commerce on bilateral trade flows. *International Economics and Economic Policy, 15*(3), 565–586.

Yushkova, E. (2014). Impact of ICT on trade in different technology groups: Analysis and implications. *International Economics and Economic Policy, 11*(1–2), 165–177.

Part II
Foreign Capital Flows and Issues in Finance

Chapter 7
Macroeconomic Factors Affecting FDI Inflows into Emerging Economies—A Panel Study

I. Ghoshal, S. Jog, U. Sinha, and I. Ghosh

1 Introduction

Foreign capital inflow, particularly foreign direct investments (FDI), has been a focus of research in both the academic and corporate field over the past few decades. This is not surprising when one considers the power of FDI, and in the multinational corporations (MNC), it is so often associated with, to shape and transform the economic landscapes of nations, perhaps none more than emerging economies. Rapid increases in inflows of foreign capital to emerging economies have generally resulted in a far greater and speedy expansion in the global economy. This can be seen right from the early days of the modern economy when the period from about 1870s to the advent of World War I witnessed a huge increase in bond finance, largely to recently established European colonies which were labour-scarce and resource-abundant economies. Another surge was witnessed in the 1990s, with the development of better means of communications and processing information. This period witnessed a surge in both the amounts of foreign capital flows as well as the variety of financial tools utilized to enable such flows. Both these periods saw a rapid increase in international trade and levels of investment. However, these periods have often ended in serious global upheavals in the form of a financial crisis. After

I. Ghoshal · U. Sinha
Fergusson College (Autonomous), Pune, India
e-mail: ishita.ghoshal@fergusson.edu

U. Sinha
e-mail: udaysinha245@gmail.com

S. Jog
Gokhale Institute of Politics and Economics, Pune, India
e-mail: saylee91@gmail.com

I. Ghosh (✉)
Symbiosis School of Economics, Symbiosis International (Deemed University), Pune, India
e-mail: ishita.ghosh@sse.ac.in

P. Lakhanpal et al. (eds.), *Trade, Investment and Economic Growth*,
https://doi.org/10.1007/978-981-33-6973-3_7

the 2008 crisis, the world is now primed for the next surge in foreign capital flow, and emerging markets are going to be central players in this next act. With continued technological progress, general economic stability in the global economy and the demographic dividends available to the most emerging economies, the expansion in foreign capital flows is set to potentially surge for the coming years and expand the economies of these emerging markets very rapidly. However, recently, in 2017, there has been a sharp decline in global flows of FDI, with very minimal recovery expected for 2018 (UNCTAD, 2018). Such a decrease in the size of the FDI pie is a cause for alarm for a lot of countries, particularly to those with emerging economies. Various studies have found a strong causal relation between the increase in levels of inflows of FDI and growth of GDP (Hansen & Rand, 2006; Herzer et al., 2008; Hsiao & Hsiao, 2006; Nair-Reichert & Weinhold, 2001).

Under these circumstances, it becomes of utmost importance for emerging economies to try and win the biggest part of the pie that they can in order to better their own economic prospects. This can be done only by understanding the factors which drive the flow of capital into a nation.

This paper tries to empirically investigate the major determinants of the level of FDI in an economy with special attention to emerging economies. In order to achieve a better understanding of various macroeconomic factors determining the flow of FDI and the extent of the relationship, panel data analysis is employed across Argentina, Brazil, China, Egypt, India, Indonesia, Iran, Mexico, Nigeria, Pakistan, Poland, Russia, Saudi Arabia, South Africa, South Korea, Thailand and Turkey for the period between 2000 and 2017. The authors have utilized a generalized method of moments keeping in mind the similarity in the numbers of years (T) and the number of cross observations (N) as well as to capture any endogeneity inherent in the model. Identification of the nature of the determinants of FDI inflows will hopefully aid in both policy formulations and in decision-making of foreign investors.

This paper is organized as follows. Section 2 discusses the findings of empirical literature on the determinants of FDI, while Sect. 3 describes the variables and methodologies used in the paper. The empirical results and discussions are presented in Sect. 4, and finally, in Sect. 5 conclusions are drawn.

2 Review of Literature

The notable growth in capital flows to developing economies and emerging markets since the early 1990s has stirred an extensive debate in the literature on the determinants of these flows. Private capital flows to developing economies have increased dramatically, from around $44 billion in 1990 to $257 billion in 2000 (World Bank, 2005). This trend has been attributed to various factors such as changes in capital controls, exchange rates, global and country specific monetary shocks and inflationary pressures.

The literature highlights various effects and implications of foreign direct investment and portfolio investment both individually as well as in aggregated manner.

Igan, Ali and Mirzaei (2016) studied 22 emerging market economies from 1998 to 2010 and found that the private capital inflows were associated with higher output growth during the pre-crisis years in industries more dependent on external finance, which broke down during the crisis period. They further found that this association was significant only for debt inflows and not equity inflows, proving that composition of capital inflows matters for growth. The study further concluded that a more competitive banking sector is a catalyst in reaping the benefits of capital inflows by external finance-dependent firms, in the case for both equity and debt inflows. Yu and Walsh (2010) tried to see the determinants of FDI for primary, secondary and tertiary sectors for data drawn from a sample of 27 emerging and developed economies, for the period of 1985–2008 and found that exchange rate affected each sector differently. It hardly had any impact on the primary sector. However, a weaker real effective exchange rate increased the level of FDI in the secondary sector but in some cases reduced the flow of FDI into the tertiary sector.

De Vita and Kyaw (2008) employed quarterly data from 1976–2001 for Brazil, Mexico, Korea, South Africa and the Philippines and observed the range of variations in foreign direct investment and portfolio flows that are because of push and pull factors across time horizons. The reserach determined that the shocks to foreign output and domestic productivity clarify the majority of the variations in both foreign direct investment and portfolio flows, while the foreign interest rate shock and the domestic money shock are less responsible for various time horizons.

Conventional wisdom on the relationship between exchange rate and the foreign investment decision held that any change in the exchange rate would not affect the decision of investment made by the firms. However, Froot and Stein (1991), in their paper, considered capital markets to be imperfect and found that empirical evidence showed that currency depreciation led to an increase in inflows of FDI. Klein and Rosengren (1994) also managed to replicate this result by showing that US FDI increased due to depreciation in the exchange rate when he studied the source country wise disaggregated data for levels of US FDI. Blonigen (1997) studied data of Japanese acquisitions in the Unites States of America and found that the maximum-likelihood estimates from discrete-dependent variable models supported the supposition that as the Dollar depreciates in relation to the Yen, Japanese acquisitions of American industries become more and more likely.

Yang et al. (2013) used a panel data set covering six Asian countries and seven Latin American countries in the period from 1981 to 2011 and found that the general perception of GDP being an important determinant for any country to attract FDI inflows holds true only in case of the Asian economies, as GDP fails to be an important explanatory variable in the case of Latin American countries. Yang et al. (2013) found a positive impact for policy changes on FDI inflows for the Asian countries, while a negative impact is for the Latin American ones. Further, expectation factors were found to hold great importance with FDI and FPI in these regions, with FDI being more prone to be affected by economic expectation while FPI was linked to exchange rate expectation.

Ang (2008) additionally elaborated that the size of the market if given by the size of the real GDP of a country has a positive impact on the inflow of FDI in the case of

Malaysia in the period 1960–2005. The author also found evidence that the growth rate in GDP also provided a small positive boost to FDI inflows. The study also found that appreciation of the real exchange rate had a negative impact on the FDI inflow into Malaysia.

By studying 15 developing countries grouped as per their income groups, Yasmin et al. (2003) found that on application of panel data analysis techniques, it was revealed that urbanization, GDP per capita, standard of living, inflation, current account and wages were affecting FDI significantly in low-income groups, urbanization, labour force, domestic investment, trade openness, standard of living, current account, external debt and wages in lower middle-income groups while urbanization, labour force, GDP per capita, domestic investment, trade openness and external debt in the sample upper middle-income countries. Additionally, Vijaykumar et al. (2010) found that a panel data analysis of BRICS nations for the period of 1975–2007 revealed that for these countries the level of FDI inflows was determined primarily by the variables—gross capital formation, labour costs, market size value of the currency and levels of infrastructure. However, inflation rate and trade openness do not determine the levels of FDI inflows in any significant manner.

A more recent study by Saini & Singhania (2018) concluded on investigating 20 countries (11 developed and 9 developing) over a period of 2004–2013 using GMM and Hausman test that the FDI seeks policy-related determinants in developed countries, whereas it showed positive association for economic determinants (gross fixed capital formation, trade openness and efficiency variables) in the case of developing countries.

Natural resources of any economy are paramount to its economic development, especially the resource of productive human capital. Liu & Li (2005) found that FDI not only affects economic growth directly, but indirectly as well through its interactions with human capital. The study also found a negative coefficient for FDI when it is interacted with the technology gap between the source and host economies. Similarly, Noorbakhsh et al., (2001) find that the level of human capital in host countries may affect the distribution of foreign direct investment to developing countries. The study concluded that human capital is a statistically significant determinant of FDI inflows, whose importance is on the rise through time.

Belderbos and Sleuwaegen (1996) studied the decision-making criterion of Japanese firms to set up manufacturing plants in countries of South East Asia, Europe and North America by analysing micro data pertaining to the firms and found that the decisions to invest in countries of South East Asia were heavily influenced by labour costs.

Erdogan and Unver (2015) measured the determinants of FDI inflows for 88 countries during the period of 1985–2011, using both a static as well as dynamic panel data analysis method. The study showed that urbanization rate, the ratio of population over the age of 65, social security spending and health spending have a negative impact on FDI, while per capita GDP, GDP growth, market size, inflation rate, unemployment rate, labour force growth, credit to private sector and control of corruption have a positive impact on FDI inflows.

Based on the available literature, we can conclude that no specific research has been conducted on various variables responsible for the flow of capital towards emerging markets and developing economies, in particular for the top 17 emerging market economies as classified by the World Bank. This paper will look to establish the impact of macroeconomic variables such as savings, GDP, interest rate, trade openness and foreign exchange on the rate of capital inflows to the above-mentioned countries.

3 Data and Methods

Based on the above discussion, the study considers the ten big emerging markets (BEM) economies (Argentina, Brazil, China, India, Indonesia, Mexico, Poland, South Africa, South Korea and Turkey) and other major emerging markets (Egypt, Iran, Nigeria, Pakistan, Russia, Saudi Arabia, Taiwan and Thailand). Taiwan could not be included due to non-availability of data. The following variables are used in the study for the above-mentioned economies for the time period of 2000–2017:

- Annual foreign direct investment, net inflows to the 17 countries from all over the world
- Annual trade as a percentage of GDP of the home countries (to capture trade openness)
- Annual gross saving as a percentage of GDP (to capture future potential for capital formation)
- Annual gross capital formation as a percentage of GDP
- Annual GDP (to capture the market size of the home country)
- Annual GDP growth rate
- Annual GDP deflator (as a measure of inflation)
- Annual exchange rate (LCU per US$)
- Annual real interest rate
- Annual total reserves minus gold (to capture foreign exchange reserves)
- Annual undisbursed external debt
- Annual labour force participation rate.

The data for these variables were collected from the World Development Indicators provided by the World Bank. Panel data for the 17 countries for the 18 years under consideration have been used for the study.

The study checks whether the inflow of FDI into the emerging economies is affected by the selected variables and in which direction does the effect work (if there exists an effect). The analysis begins by checking for the presence of unit roots in the panel data using the methods suggested by Levin et al. (2002) and Im et al. (2003). The tests check for stationarity of the variables and dictate the order of integration to be considered for further analysis. Evidence from the unit root tests prompts whether the study should check for co-integrating relationships or not (if a pair of variables are found to be integrated of order 1, then they may be co-integrated).

Next, the authors check for causal relationships running from the selected variables to the FDI flows into the emerging economies with the method suggested by Hurlin and Venet (2001). The study goes on to estimate the relationships running from various selected variables to the inflow of FDI to the country. In the number of cross sections and time periods being very close to each other, the estimation method used is generalized method of moments (GMM) rather than the auto-regressive distributed lags (ARDL) model which otherwise would have been an appropriate choice given the orders of integration of the variables involved.

The equation that is to be estimated is as follows:

$$\begin{aligned}\text{FDI Inflow}_{it} &= a + b_1\text{Capital}_{it} + b_2\text{ER}_{it} + b_3\text{GDP Growth}_{it} \\ &\quad + b_4\text{GDP}_{it} + b_5\text{Inflation}_{it} + b_6\text{Interest Rate}_{it} + b_7\text{LFPR}_{it} \\ &\quad + b_8\text{Debt}_{it} + b_9\text{FOREX}_{it} + b_{10}\text{Savings}_{it} + b_{11}\text{Trade Openness}_{it} + \varepsilon_{it}\end{aligned} \tag{1}$$

However, the number of cross-sectional units being 17 and the number of time units being 18, the above-mentioned model could not be estimated. This is due the fact that the number of parameters, 12 in this case, was too many to be estimated given the numbers of cross-sectional and time units. Instead, the study clusters some variables together and estimates multiple equations. In one model, interest rate, LFPR, debt and savings are included as explanatory variables to capture the effect of core macroeconomic indicators on FDI inflows. In other model, inflation and GDP growth rate are included to see whether growth conditions of the economy affect FDI inflows. The rest of the variables are found to be statistically insignificant and are hence not included in the estimation process. Hence, the following two models are estimated:

Model 1:

$$\text{FDI Inflow}_{it} = a + b_1\text{Interest Rate}_{it} + b_2\text{LFPR}_{it} + b_3\text{Debt}_{it} + b_4\text{Savings}_{it} + \varepsilon_{it} \tag{2}$$

Model 2:

$$\text{FDI Inflow}_{it} = a + b_1\text{Inflation}_{it} + b_2\text{GDP Growth}_{it} + \varepsilon_{it} \tag{3}$$

4 Results and Discussion

The results show that FDI inflow, growth rate, inflation, interest rate, LFPR, debt, savings and trade openness variables are stationary in level, i.e. they are integrated of order zero I(0). However, capital formation, exchange rate, GDP and foreign

Table 1 Results for panel stationarity

Variable	Im-Pesaran-Shin		Levin-Lin-Chu	
	p-value			
	Level	1st diff	Level	1st diff
FDI inflow	0.0072		0.0000	
Capital	0.2466	0.0000	0.0458	0.0000
ER	1.000	0.0516	0.9998	0.0004
GDP growth	0.0000		0.0000	
GDP	1.0000	0.0000	0.9841	0.0000
Inflation	0.0000		0.0000	
Interest rate	0.0003		0.0000	
Lfpr	0.0348		0.0011	
Debt	0.0238		0.0593	
FOREX	0.9570	0.0000	0.3681	0.0000
Savings	0.3157		0.04	
Trade openness	0.0666		0.0005	

Source Authors' calculations

exchange reserves contain unit roots in level but they become stationary after taking first difference of the variables, i.e. they are integrated of order one I(1) (Table 1).

Since FDI inflow turn out to be stationary at level, there remains no possibility of suspecting long-run co-integrating relationships running from any of the I(1) variables to FDI inflow. Hence, the study moves on to check for causal relationships. The results for the panel causality test to check for causality running from the selected variables to FDI inflows into the emerging economies are reported in the Table 2.

The panel causality results show that capital, GDP growth rate, size of the economy, LFPR, foreign exchange reserves and savings cause FDI inflows into the emerging economies but exchange rate, inflation, interest rate, debt and trade openness do not have any causal effect.

Next, the study estimates the linear dependence of FDI inflows into the emerging economies on the selected macroeconomic indicators through the two models illustrated in Eqs. (1) and (2). The results are presented in the Table 3.

The results show that interest rate, LFPR, debt, savings and GDP growth rate have positive and statistically significant effect on the inflows of FDI into the emerging economies; inflation has a negative effect on the FDI inflow, and this effect is also statistically significant. Size of the economy, capital, trade openness, FOREX reserves and exchange rate does not have any significant effect on the FDI inflows to emerging economies, and hence they are not reported here.

Given the observations from this study, it would be prudent for emerging economies to invest in human capital along with hard and soft infrastructure. These factors will enable existing sectors in the economy to open up and create new markets,

Table 2 Results for panel causality

Causal Variable	F statistic	*p*-value
Capital	2.97	0.0534*
ER	1.46	0.2349
GDP growth	4.89	0.0083***
GDP	2.99	0.0517**
Inflation	0.24	0.7902
Interest rate	1.22	0.297
Lfpr	3.53	0.0308**
Debt	1.07	0.3433
FOREX	8.85	0.0002***
Savings	2.39	0.0939*
Trade openness	0.7	0.494

Source Authors' calculations
*, ** and *** represent the coefficient is significant at 10, 5 and 1%, respectively

Table 3 Estimates of linear dependence of FDI inflows into the emerging economies

Model 1	Variable	Coefficient	t-statistic
	Interest rate	0.02	2.5**
	LFPR	0.05	4.81***
	Debt	0.21	3.79***
	Savings	0.06	5.49***
Model 2	Inflation	−0.03	−2.92***
	GDP growth	0.06	2.72***

Source Authors' calculations
*, ** and *** represent the coefficient is significant at 10, 5 and 1%, respectively

as well. Employability will improve with augmented human capital and the appropriate infrastructure in place. Undoubtedly, monetary policies that encourage savings and investment will stimulate the economy to grow.

An inflated economy will take away from the FDI earnings and will clearly not be an attractive indicator in terms of inward flow of funds from a foreign nation. Therefore, it makes sense to keep a check on inflation—a situation that is frequently recorded in the case of many emerging economies either because of fuel or food-related factors, mostly; environmental disasters in smaller economies do trigger inflationary effects in the short and medium run, too.

The study has also indicated that debt is a positive and statistically significant factor in attracting inward FDI. This is possibly explained by the fact that emerging economies would be fuelled to grow with more consumption and expenditure. At the same time, external borrowings for development may bring about a debt burden. As long as the resources are being mobilized in the direction of building the economy, these debts will not affect the flow of inward FDI adversely.

Size of the economy, capital, trade openness, FOREX reserves and exchange rate for emerging economies are in many ways compromised because of the typical economic and market characteristics associated with such nations. However, as long as the inward flow of funds is being channelized into sectors that reap profits for the investing nations while benefitting the recipients, FDIs will typically continue to flow, keeping other factors constant.

The main restriction on the current study was posed by the availability of data for the economies under consideration. Data for saving and foreign exchange reserves were not available at all for Iran. Data for undisbursed debt were not available for South Korea, Poland and Saudi Arabia. Annual exchange rate was not available for certain years for many of the economies. Interest rate was not available for Russia, Saudi Arabia and Turkey for any of the years and for Poland since 2007. Due to this, the analysis had to rely on lesser number of observations than what was initially intended.

The study may be extended with FII as the dependent variable to capture the financial capital inflows instead of only FDI. A comparative analysis may be conducted to check the pattern of dependence of FDI and FII on macroeconomic and open economy factors for the emerging economies. Also, an extension to compare the current results with patterns and behaviours in the advanced economies may be useful in identifying idiosyncrasies in the emerging economies and advanced economies, if any.

5 Conclusion

Academic investigations of this nature have often clearly indicated the prescribed paths that emerging economies can take, spelling out each factor that may or may not affect the inward flow of FDIs. However, such policies take time to be formulated, implemented and eventually take effect. Enhancing human capital and infrastructure are long-term plans in most emerging economies. Also, not all sectors grow at the same pace—some sectors are dependent on other sectors to thrive on, especially in manufacturing that involve global value chains (GVCs). The economies under consideration have rampant socio-economic shortcomings in terms of corruption, institutional, legislative and governance strength and quality, over and above gross developmental issues that they are grappling with. In short, if the gaps between the demand and supply sides of the economy can be matched, then the success of attracting FDIs and actually translating emerging economies into global players may be fulfilled. However, this is a long and difficult path in spite of various recommended routes that have been empirically carved out for such nations.

References

Ang, J. B. (2008). Determinants of foreign direct investment in Malaysia. *Journal of Policy Modeling, 30*(1), 185–189. https://doi.org/10.1016/j.jpolmod.2007.06.014.

Belderbos, R., & Sleuwaegen, L. (1996). Japanese firms and the decision to invest abroad: Business groups and regional core networks. *The Review of Economics and Statistics, 78*(2), 214. https://doi.org/10.2307/2109923.

Bevan, A. A., & Estrin, S. (2004). The determinants of foreign direct investment into European transition economies. *Journal of Comparative Economics*. https://doi.org/10.1016/j.jce.2004.08.006.

Blonigen, B. A. (1997). Firm-specific assets and the link between exchange rates and foreign direct investment. *American Economic Review*.

De Vita, G., & Kyaw, S. (2008). Determinants of capital flows to developing countries: A structural VAR analysis. *Journal of Economic Studies, 35*(4), 304–322.

Erdogan, M., & Unver, M. (2015). Determinants of Foreign Direct Investments: Dynamic Panel Data Evidence. *International Journal of Economics and Finance, 7*(5), 82–95. https://doi.org/10.5539/ijef.v7n5p82.

Froot, K. A., & Stein, J. C. (1991). Exchange rates and foreign direct investment: An imperfect capital market approach. *Quarterly Journal of Economics*.

Igan, D., Ali, K. M., & Mirzaei, A. (2016). *Real effects of capital inflows in emerging markets*. International Monetary Fund.

Hansen, H., & Rand, J. (2006). On the causal links between FDI and growth in developing countries. *World Economy*. https://doi.org/10.1111/j.1467-9701.2006.00756.x.

Herzer, D., Klasen, S., & Nowak-Lehmann, D. (2008). In search of FDI-led growth in developing countries: The way forward. *Economic Modelling*. https://doi.org/10.1016/j.econmod.2007.11.005.

Hsiao, F. S. T., & Hsiao, M. C. W. (2006). FDI, exports, and GDP in East and Southeast Asia-panel data versus time-series causality analyses. *Journal of Asian Economics*. https://doi.org/10.1016/j.asieco.2006.09.011.

Hurlin, C., &Venet, B. (2001). Granger causality tests in panel data models with fixed coefficients. https://basepub.dauphine.fr/bitstream/handle/123456789/6159/3F117993d01.pdf?sequence=1

Hurlin, C., & Dumitrescu, E. (2012). Testing for Granger non-causality in heterogeneous panels. https://halshs.archives-ouvertes.fr/halshs-00224434/document

Im, K. S., Pesaran, M. H., & Shin, Y. (2003). Testing for unit roots in heterogenous panels. *Journal of Econometrics, 115*, 53–74.

Klein, M. W., & Rosengren, E. (1994). The real exchange rate and foreign direct investment in the United States. *Journal of International Economics, 36*(3), 373–389. https://doi.org/10.1016/0022-1996(94)90009-4.

Levin, A., Lin, C. F., & Chu, C.-S.J. (2002). Unit root tests in panel data: Asymptotic and finite sample properties. *Journal of Applied Econometrics, 108*, 1–22.

Liu, X., & Li, X. (2005). Foreign direct investment and economic growth: An increasingly endogenous relationship. *World Development, 33*(3), 393–407.

Nair-Reichert, U., & Weinhold, D. (2001). Causality tests for cross-country panels: A new look at FDI and economic growth in developing countries. *Oxford Bulletin of Economics and Statistics*. https://doi.org/10.1111/1468-0084.00214.

Noorbakhsh, F. F., Paloni, A., & Youssef, A. (2001). Human capital and FDI inflows to developing countries: New empirical evidence. *World Development, 29*(9), 1593–1610.

Saini, N., & Singhania, M. (2018). Determinants of FDI in developed and developing countries: A quantitative analysis using GMM. *Journal of Economic Studies, 45*, 348–382.

United Nations Conference on Trade and Development (UNCTAD). (2016). *World Investment Report 2016—Investor nationality: Policy challenges*. United Nations Publication, UNCTAD.

Vijayakumar, N., Sridharan, P., & Rao, K. C. S. (2010). Determinants of FDI in BRICS countries: A panel analysis. *International Journal of Business Science and Applied Management, 5*(3),

1–13. https://www.business-and-management.org/library/2010/5_3--1--13-Vijayakumar,Sridharan,Rao.pdf

Yang, H., Xiong, Y., & Ze, Y. (2013). A comparative study of determinants of international capital flows to Asian and Latin American emerging countries. *Procedia Computer Science*, 1258–1265. https://doi.org/10.1016/j.procs.2013.05.160

Yasmin, B., Hussain, A., & Chaudhary, M. A. (2003). Analysis of factors affecting foreign direct investment in developing countries. *Pakistan Economic and Social Review*.

Yu, J., & Walsh, J. P. (2010). *Determinants of Foreign Direct Investment: A Sectoral and Institutional Approach. IMF Working Papers*. https://doi.org/10.5089/9781455202218.001

Chapter 8
The Pattern of Inbound Foreign Direct Investment into India

A. Sawhney and R. Rastogi

1 Introduction

Foreign direct investment (FDI) is a catalyst for economic development and remains an important component of development strategies in a capital-scarce country like India. Over the last three decades, reforms and liberalization policies adopted in India, since 1991, attempted to boost FDI by expanding the list of high-priority manufacturing industries, increasing the foreign equity limit in manufacturing, allowing automatic approval in all industries, and opening up of new sectors (in infrastructure and services). This systematic liberalization has resulted in a significant increase in FDI inflows into India.

While the total FDI into India remains abysmally small (considering that it is a large emerging economy), the growth in FDI achieved is encouraging. For example, during 2000–2014, total FDI inflow increased more than sevenfold (at constant prices). In particular, the real FDI in manufacturing sector increased more than tenfold during this period. The increase in manufacturing FDI is important, since FDI stock and manufacturing in India have been found to be mutually reinforcing (Chakraborty & Nunnenkamp, 2008).

Manufacturing industries receiving the bulk of FDI inflows, however, are polluting in nature. These industries received around 60% in total FDI inflows in India during the period 2000–2014. The increasing FDI inflows in Indian manufacturing industries and particularly in polluting industries raise an important question as to what factors have been attracting FDI inflows in India.

A. Sawhney
Center of International Trade and Development, Jawaharlal Nehru University, New Delhi, India
e-mail: aparnasawhney@yahoo.com

R. Rastogi (✉)
Symbiosis Centre for Management Studies (Constituent of Symbiosis International (Deemed) University), Noida, India
e-mail: rash.rastogi@gmail.com

P. Lakhanpal et al. (eds.), *Trade, Investment and Economic Growth*,
https://doi.org/10.1007/978-981-33-6973-3_8

There are several country-level features including capital abundance, skilled labor abundance, and size of the economy (Chung, 2014; Waldkirch & Gopinath, 2008) and industry-level features such as factor intensity (Helpman, 1984), scale economies (Brainard, 1993; Markusen, 1998), and domestic market size (Markusen, 1998) that serve as key determinants of FDI flows across countries. The stringency of environmental regulations is considered to be a key determinant of FDI in polluting industries as the countries with more stringent environmental regulations may invest in pollution-intensive industries in developing countries with lax environmental regulations. The phenomenon is driven by comparative cost advantage enjoyed by developing countries which avoid pollution abatement cost. Polluting industries are typically capital-intensive in nature, and the literature on the flight of polluting industries from developed countries toward developing countries shows mixed results. An analysis of outbound FDI from USA into Mexico and Brazil found evidence of pollution offshoring (Cole & Elliott, 2005), while the outbound investment from developed countries like the USA, UK, and France toward developing countries has not found any evidence of migration of polluting industries (Eskeland & Harrison, 2003; Elliott & Shimamoto, 2008; Manderson & Kneller, 2012). Analyses of inbound FDI in polluting industries from the perspective of developing countries cover countries like China and Mexico. A study of inbound FDI into Mexico from high-income OECD countries (including the USA) also found evidence of pollution offshoring at disaggregated industry level (Waldkirch & Gopinath, 2008). Similarly, the studies for China have found evidence of migration of polluting industries in the country, and such firms, particularly, locate in provinces with relatively less stringent environmental regulations than source countries (Di, 2007; Dean et al., 2009).

While India has featured in some of the cross-country studies examining outbound investment of developed countries in polluting industries (Chung, 2014; Xing & Kolstad, 2002; Poelhekke & Ploeg, 2015; Mulatu, 2017), there is no study analyzing the inbound FDI into India at the disaggregated industry-level to find the determinants of FDI in manufacturing industries, specifically polluting industries, and to analyze the characteristics of top 10 investing countries that have been investing in India from a long time. This study tries to fill that gap in the literature.

This study first analyzes the role of industry-specific characteristics that have been attracting foreign investment into Indian manufacturing during the last one and half decade. The study considers FDI inflows in India from the top 10 investing countries, contributing around 85% of total FDI in the manufacturing sector. Our analysis covers a fifteen-year period from 2000 through 2014. Although systematic industrial pollution or abatement data is not available in India, we glean several industry characteristics (at disaggregated 3-digit industrial classification) from the Annual Survey of Industries and match them with the FDI sectors in the data from the Department of Industrial Policy and Promotion (DIPP) for our analysis. Since data on pollution load by industry is not available, we use the Central Pollution Control Board (CPCB) classification of polluting industries. Based on the pollution score, the CPCB of India categorizes industries into red, orange, green, and white, with red consisting of the most hazardous industries and white covering less-polluting industries.

As several polluting industries (like iron and steel, chemicals, etc.) fall in the category of basic industries, there is a large domestic market for their output in a developing economy like India. Indeed, the large domestic market for basic polluting industries such as chemicals, metal products, and transport equipment industries has been an attraction for foreign investors (Uchikawa, 1999; Nagaraj, 2003; Balasubramanyam & Sapsford, 2007; Wei, 2005; Chakraborty & Nunnenkamp, 2008). So, we expect that FDI in these industries in India would be market-seeking in nature rather than just resource-seeking, i.e., to avoid high labor costs or stringent environmental regulations.

Since the migration of polluting industries under the pollution haven effect can be in the nature of horizontal export-platform FDI (Tang, 2015), in order to serve markets other than the host country, we also control for export- orientation of the industries, among several other industry characteristics. We use the export data from UNCOMTRADE Stats defined by ISIC Rev. 3, in order to track the annual industry-level exports of India. We also analyze the source-country characteristics for the FDI inflows into India, in various industries during the period from 2000 to 2014. The rest of the paper is organized as follows: Sect. 2 discusses the pattern of FDI inflows in India; Sect. 3 discusses empirical model and data sources; Sect. 4 summarizes empirical results; Sect. 5 concludes the paper.

2 The Pattern of FDI Inflows in India

The pattern of FDI across manufacturing industries from top 10 investing countries has been explained earlier in Rastogi and Sawhney (2014) and Sawhney and Rastogi (2019). The set of top ten investing countries in Indian manufacturing have remained the same through the years and together have contributed about 85% of the total (cumulative) FDI received in manufacturing industries during 2000 through 2014 (see Table 1). The contribution of these ten countries in total FDI into polluting industries (red and orange CPCB category) is around 86%. It is important to note that although Mauritius appears to be the single largest source of FDI for India, it serves as a routing country for foreign investors due to tax benefits, and thus the FDI cannot be truly attributed to Mauritius completely.

Distinguishing between the FDI inflows into polluting industries (red and orange category of CPCB) versus the relatively cleaner industries (green and white category), these ten countries contributed to 87% of the FDI in polluting industries. Among the top investing countries, UK and Japan have been the most prominent investors in Indian manufacturing and, in particular, in polluting industries.

Considering the three-year moving average of FDI inflows (to smooth out the annual fluctuations) from the top 10 investing countries during 2000 through 2014, we observe that FDI increased sharply after 2004 (see Fig. 1). The initial decline in inflows during 2000–2004 may be seen as an aftermath of the Asian crisis (Baer & Sirohi, 2013), and the rise in foreign investment after 2004 may be credited to the simplified procedures for approvals and increase in private equity (Rao &

Table 1 Percentage share of top 10 countries in total FDI in India (Sawhney & Rastogi, 2019)

Source country	Manufacturing sector	Polluting industries#
Cyprus	1.6	1.5
France	2.3	2.9
Germany	4.3	4.2
Japan	11.8	14.4
Mauritius	25.2	14.2
Netherlands	7.2	9.2
Singapore	11.5	9.8
United Arab Emirates	0.9	0.9
UK	14.4	23.1
USA	5.5	5.4
Subtotal	84.7	85.6

Source Sawhney and Rastogi (2019)

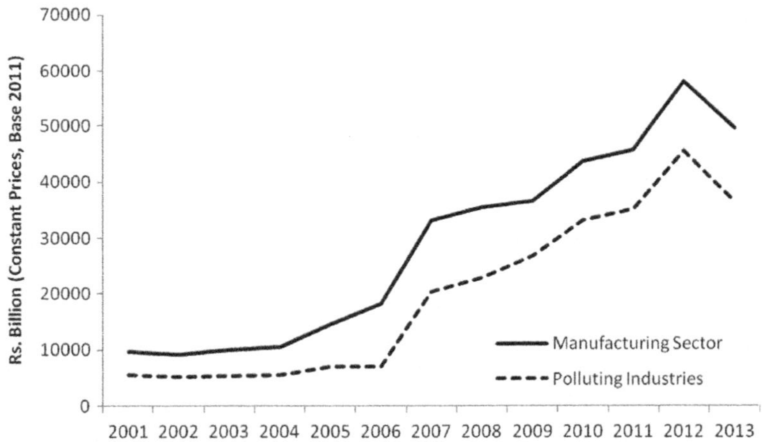

Fig. 1 FDI inflows in India from top 10 investing countries (in constant Rs. billion) (*Source* Sawhney & Rastogi, 2014)

Dhar, 2011). For instance, FDI in manufacturing sector rose sharply in 2006 when the limit of foreign equity increased from 51 to 100% through automatic route.[1] The industries that received the bulk of FDI inflows during the last one and half decades include computer hardware and software (15.09%); drugs and pharmaceuticals (14.6%); automobiles (12.0%); chemicals (other than fertilizers) (10.0%); petroleum and natural gas (7.4%); and metallurgical (6.4%). Some of these industries are polluting and come under the red and orange categories of CPCB.

[1]DIPP Press Note No. 4 (2006).

3 Empirical Model and Data

The pattern of inbound investment into India is analyzed by examining the characteristics of Indian manufacturing industries and the characteristics of source (home) countries, including their environmental regulatory stringency, since 2000. We use FDI inflows to capture the FDI behavior across industries and countries.

(a) Industry analysis

We examine the characteristics of manufacturing industries that have been attracting FDI inflows in India, and the differential impact of these industry characteristics on FDI inflows in polluting industries. While Rastogi and Sawhney (2014) had examined the determinants of inbound FDI in Indian manufacturing industries during 2000–10 and included several features of industries like capital intensity, scale economies, market size, industrial growth, and energy intensity,[2] here we extend the model by incorporating several other industry features and expand the period of analysis from 2000 to 2014. The FDI inflow in Indian manufacturing sector in industry *i* in year *t* is modeled as:

$$\begin{aligned}\log(FDI_{it}) = {} & \beta_0 + \phi_i + t_t + \beta_1 \log(K/L_{it-1}) + \beta_2\big[\log(K/L)^* \text{ Polluting }\big]_{it-1} \\ & + \beta_3 \ln\big(\text{ skill intensity }_{it-1}\big) + \beta_4\big[\ln(\text{skill intensity})^* \text{ Polluting }\big]_{it-1} \\ & \beta_5 \text{ Exportorientation }_{it-1} + \beta_6[\text{ Exportorientation } * \text{ Polluting }]_{it-1} \\ & + \beta_7 \text{ Industria } \lg r_{it-1} + \beta_8[\text{ Industria } \lg r * \text{ Polluting }]_{it-1} \\ & + \beta_9 \ln(\text{ Energy int}_{it-1}) + v_{it} \end{aligned} \quad (1)$$

"Equation 1"FDI_{it} is the natural logarithm of FDI inflow in industry *i* in year *t*, modeled on the industry characteristics in India (host country), including capital intensity of industries (K/L), export orientation of the industry, skill intensity, industrial growth, and energy intensity of production. Industry dummies (ϕ_i) and time dummies (t_t) are introduced to control for unobserved effects not varying across industries and years, respectively. We use two databases for industry-level analysis—DIPP data for FDI inflows and ASI data for industry characteristics. We matched DIPP industry classification with NIC classification followed in ASI data at the 3 digits to capture information at the disaggregated industry level.

We control for the polluting Indian industries by using a discrete variable, *Polluting*, that takes the value 1 for red and orange category industries, and 0 for the less-polluting industries.[3] Dummy variable for pollution-intensive industries is interacted with industry characteristics to distinguish the impact of industry characteristics on FDI inflows in pollution-intensive industries.

---

[2]Rastogi and Sawhney (2014) followed Cole and Elliott (2004) and Waldkirch and Gopinath (2008) to model the FDI inflows into Indian manufacturing sector at disaggregated industry level.

[3]The polluting industries include metallurgical; petroleum refineries; chemicals and chemical products; drugs; leather and leather products; cement; fermentation; paper and pulp; sugar; automobile; railway-related components; printing; glass; textiles; and food processing.

Alternatively, we control for energy intensity of the Indian industries, $Energy\,\mathrm{int}_{it-1}$, measured as the log of the ratio of value of fuels consumed in value of materials consumed in industry i in year $t-1$. Since industries with relatively large energy consumption are polluting in nature (Eskeland & Harrison, 2003), this variable provides us a continuous variable control for the polluting nature of industries. In case polluting industries in India are attracting more FDI inflows to save environmental cost, we would expect the coefficient β_9 to be positive.

In Eq. (1), we control for factor intensity of industries by incorporating the capital intensity of industries and the skill intensity of industries. The capital intensity of industries is measured by ratio of real net fixed assets to number of workers and expect both the coefficients (β_1 and β_2) to be positive for a capital-scarce country like India, where FDI is expected to help capital-intensive industries and the polluting industries are also capital-intensive in nature. Skill intensity of industries is represented by log of ratio of number of supervisors and managers to number of total persons engaged in industry. Skill labor-intensive production activities (namely "headquarter services") may locate in skill-abundant country, while production activities intensively using unskilled labor may locate to countries abundant in unskilled labor. India is a relatively unskilled labor-abundant country, so we expect β_3 and β_4 to be negative.

We control for the export orientation of Indian industries. The export orientation of industries is measured by ratio of exports of each industry to value of output of that industry. The definition of export orientation of industries is consistent with Sawhney and Rastogi (2019). Export-oriented industries attract foreign investment; therefore, we expect the coefficients β_5 and β_6 to be positive. The model also controls for growth in the output of each industry to capture the effect of fastest growing industries on FDI. Interaction term between industrial growth and dummy for polluting industries depicts industrial growth of polluting industries. The industries with high growth rate tend to attract more FDI; therefore, we expect the coefficient β_7 and β_8 to be positive.

Data on actual FDI inflows from the top 10 investing countries for the period from January 2000 to December 2014 has been obtained from Directorate of Industrial Policy and Promotion (DIPP), Ministry of Commerce, Government of India. The data on actual FDI inflows represents foreign equity inflows in various manufacturing industries, and these industries follow DIPP industrial classification based on the Industrial (Development and Regulation) Act, 1951. The top 10 investing countries include Mauritius, Singapore, UK, Germany, USA, France, Netherland, Cyprus, United Arab Emirates, and Japan.

Data on various characteristics of industries is obtained from Annual Survey of Industries (ASI) at 3-digit NIC 2004 and NIC 2008 classification. In order to get comprehensive dataset of FDI inflows and industry characteristics for each industry, the DIPP industry classification is concorded with the various versions of National Industrial Classification (NIC). Data on India's exports to rest of the world by industry is obtained from UNCOMTRADE stats, using the ISIC (Rev.3) 3-digit industry classification. Since the trade classification based on the ISIC Rev.3 matches with

3-digit NIC-04 classification, the three industry classifications (DIPP, NIC, and ISIC) are matched to get comprehensive dataset.

(b) Country analysis

To test the characteristics of source FDI countries that have been investing in Indian manufacturing industries, we follow an empirical model in Chung (2014), Waldkirch and Gopinath (2008) and Sawhney and Rastogi (2019). We examine the important characteristics of the source countries investing in the manufacturing industries and particularly in polluting industries. The FDI from source country *j* in year *t* is modeled as follows:

$$\begin{aligned}\ln(FDI)_{jt} &= \alpha_0 + \delta_j + t_t + \alpha_1 \ln(K/L)_{jt-1} + \alpha_2 \ln(\text{skill labor})_{jt-1} \\ &+ \alpha_3 \ln(\text{Carbon Intensity})_{jt-1} + \alpha_4 \ln(GDP)_{jt-1} \\ &+ \alpha_5 \ln(\text{Trade openness})_{jt-1} + \varepsilon_{jt} \qquad (2)\end{aligned}$$

Dependent variable in "Eq. 2" is log of real FDI inflow in Indian manufacturing from source country *j* in year *t*. The dependent variables represent two groups of manufacturing industries—aggregate FDI in all manufacturing industries and aggregate FDI in polluting industries.

The source-country characteristics include capital abundance, skilled labor, environmental stringency, domestic market size, and trade openness. Capital abundance is measured by ratio of real capital stock to total persons engaged in source country. Skilled labor abundance of home country is represented through log of the ratio of skilled labor to total workforce (wherein skilled labor is highly skilled labor working as managers, professionals, technicians, and kindred workers). Environmental stringency in the home country is measured through log of carbon emissions per GDP.[4] Size of the country is represented through real GDP. Openness of source country is measured as a ratio of total trade to GDP. We expect capital abundance (α_1), skilled labor abundance (α_2), size of the country (α_4), and openness (α_5) to be positive, and environmental stringency (α_3) to be negatively affecting FDI inflows in India.

Equation (2) also includes country dummies (δ_j) to control for unobserved heterogeneity across countries that impacts FDI inflows in India, and year dummies (t_t) to capture the time-varying economy-wide changes that affect decisions to invest in the Indian manufacturing sector.

4 Empirical Results

The results of Eqs. (1) and (2) are shown in Tables 2 and 3, respectively. We estimated Eq. (1) using fixed effects estimations, controlling for variations within the sector to estimate the effect of industry characteristics on FDI inflows in India.

[4]This is a proxy of stringency of environmental regulations. Countries with stringent regulations of environment have relatively lower emissions as compared to the countries with lax environment regulations.

Table 2 FE estimations of FDI inflow in India from top ten countries into Indian industries. Dependent variable is log (real aggregate FDI) in polluting industry in year *t*

Variables	All industries					Polluting industries	Less-polluting industries
	R1	R2	R3	R4	R5	R6	R7
Ln(K/L)	0.294*	0.295*	0.308*	0.456**	0.454**	−0.098	0.539***
	[0.157]	[0.158]	[0.158]	[0.189]	[0.189]	[0.299]	[0.188]
Export intensity	−0.002	−0.002	−0.001	−0.003*	−0.002*	0.039***	−0.002*
	[0.001]	[0.001]	[0.001]	[0.001]	[0.001]	[0.010]	[0.001]
Ln(energy intensity)			−0.197		−0.2	−0.576**	−0.11
			[0.140]		[0.149]	[0.258]	[0.168]
Industrial growth		−0.00007	-0.0004	0.0002	−0.0003	0.001	−0.001
		[0.001]	[0.001]	[0.002]	[0.002]	[0.002]	[0.002]
Ln(skill intensity)	−0.151	−0.151	−0.162	−0.032	−0.067	−0.529	−0.099
	[0.181]	[0.182]	[0.188]	[0.199]	[0.209]	[0.461]	[0.248]
Ln(K/L) * Poll				−0.225	−0.201		
				[0.254]	[0.252]		
Industrial Gr * Poll				0.001	0.002		
				[0.003]	[0.003]		
Export intensity * Poll				0.035***	0.036***		
				[0.010]	[0.009]		
Ln(Skill Int) * Poll				−0.799*	−0.729		
				[0.448]	[0.451]		
Time dummies	Yes	Yes	Yes	Yes	Yes	Yes	Yes
Industry dummies	Yes	Yes	Yes	Yes	Yes	Yes	Yes
Observations	378	378	378	378	378	210	168
Adjusted R-squared	0.696	0.695	0.696	0.706	0.707	0.686	0.749
F test	11.26	10.57	10.07	9.606	9.294	7.516	5.644
Prob > F	0	0	0	0	0	0	0

Robust standard errors in parentheses. ***$p < 0.01$, **$p < 0.05$, *$p < 0.1$
Note #Estimations are based on all 27 industries, *Source* Authors' own calculations

We stagger the full specification of the regression (R1−R5) in order to check the robustness of the coefficient estimates. We also estimate our model separately for the polluting and less-polluting industries (R6 and R7). We find that the coefficients of our control variables to be robust through the staggered specifications.

We find that FDI inflows in India are concentrated in capital-intensive industries (R1−R3). When the binary variable for polluting industries is interacted with industry

Table 3 FE estimations of FDI inflow in India from top ten countries. Dependent variable is log (real aggregate FDI) in manufacturing industry *i* in year *t*

Variables	All top 10 countries		Top 9 countries (excluding Mauritius)	
	All industries R1	Polluting# R2	All industries R3	Polluting# R4
lnKLhome	0.27	0.79	1.49*	2.09**
	[0.70]	[0.82]	[0.81]	[0.94]
Ln(gdp)	3.08***	4.52***	4.22***	5.37***
	[0.92]	[1.03]	[0.88]	[0.96]
Lnskillhome	−0.94	−0.38	0.96	2.04
	[1.27]	[1.42]	[1.63]	[1.79]
ln(Carbon Intensity)	−1.02**	−2.02***	−0.34	−1.41**
	[0.51]	[0.59]	[0.65]	[0.60]
Ln(TradeOpenness)	1.26	2.08**	0.97	1.89*
	[0.79]	[0.88]	[0.84]	[0.99]
Observations	150	148	135	133
R-squared	0.78	0.72	0.78	0.72
Adjusted R-squared	0.73	0.66	0.73	0.65
F test	12.68	14.15	14.46	24.2
Prob > F	0.00	0.00	0.00	0.00

Note All regressions contain country and year dummies. Robust standard errors are in brackets
includes FDI in all highly polluting industries taken together
Source Authors' own calculations

characteristics (R4–R5), we find that FDI in less-polluting industries is concentrated in capital-intensive, less export-oriented industries (indicating India's large market attracted these FDI). On the other hand, FDI in polluting industries is significant in capital-intensive, highly export-oriented, less skill-intensive industries.

Table 3 represents cross-country results of Eq. (2) for aggregate FDI in all industries and a group of highly polluting industries. We estimate Eq. (2) using fixed effect technique for the top 10 investing countries.

Considering the aggregate investment from the top 10 investing countries, the results indicate that FDI in manufacturing industries was sourced from large countries and those with relatively stringent environmental regulations. The results are similar for aggregate FDI in polluting industries, with trade openness of source country also being a significant determinant.

We check for robustness of our results by estimating Eq. (2) for a set of nine countries excluding Mauritius as the latter has been the route for many countries for tax benefits (R3–R4, Table 3). We expect that the exclusion of Mauritius from the group of top 10 investing countries would yield more meaningful results, with respect to the country characteristics analysis. Capital abundance and large size of source countries are two significant determinants of FDI into aggregate Indian manufacturing, as well as polluting manufacturing. Moreover, countries with stringent environmental standards are also found to be significant source of FDI in the polluting industries, reflecting a pollution haven effect (R6).

5 Conclusion

Following the liberalization of foreign direct investment policies in India, the FDI inflows in India have increased during the period 2000–2014. In particular, the manufacturing sector witnessed dramatic increase in FDI inflows during this period. However, FDI in polluting industries also increased substantially as compared to inflows in clean manufacturing industries. The increasing inflows in manufacturing sector and particularly in polluting industries raise the question as to what factors have been attracting FDI inflows in India, and whether there is a pollution haven effect. This question has been addressed at the disaggregated industry level and by source country of FDI flows in Indian manufacturing.

We find that aggregate FDI inflows in Indian manufacturing are concentrated in capital-intensive industries, while inflows in polluting industries are significant in export-intensive industries. We infer that FDI in polluting industries is driven by an export-platform motive (Tang, 2015). Our country-level analysis reveals that FDI inflows in India are sourced from large size countries. Polluting industries have been attracting foreign investment from capital-abundant, large size countries, and countries with stringent environmental regulations. We conclude that FDI in polluting industries in India is export-oriented and sourced from relatively large open countries with stringent environmental regulations and reflects the presence of a pollution haven effect.

References

Baer, W., & Sirohi, R. A. (2013). The role of foreign direct investments in the development of Brazil and India: A comparative analysis. *KYKLOS, 66,* 46–62.

Balasubramanyam, V. N., & Sapsford, D. (2007). Does India need a lot more FDI? *Economic and Political Weekly, 42,* 1549–1555.

Brainard, S. L. (1993). *A simple theory of multinational corporations and trade with a trade-off between proximity and concentration.* NBER Working Papers 4269, National Bureau of Economic Research, Inc.

Chakraborty, C., & Nunnenkamp, P. (2008). Economic reforms, FDI and economic growth in India: A sector level analysis. *World Development, 36,* 1192–1212.

Chung, S. (2014). Environmental regulation and foreign direct investment: Evidence from South Korea. *Journal of Development Economics, 108,* 222–236.

Cole, M. A., & Elliott, J. R. (2005). FDI and the capital intensity of "dirty" sectors: A missing piece of the pollution haven puzzle. *Review of Development Economics, 9,* 530–548.

Dean, J. M., et al. (2009). Are foreign investors attracted to weak environmental regulations? Evaluating the evidence from China. *Journal of Development Economics, 90,* 1–13.
Di, W. (2007). Pollution abatement cost savings and FDI inflows to polluting sectors in China. *Environment and Development Economics, 12,* 775–798.
Elliott, J. R., & Shimamoto, K. (2008). Are ASEAN countries havens for Japanese pollution-intensive industry? *The World Economy, 31,* 236–254.
Eskeland, G. S., & Harrison, A. E. (2003). Moving to greener pastures? Multinationals and the pollution haven hypothesis. *Journal of Development Economics, 70,* 1–23.
Globerman, S., & Shapiro, D. (2002). Global foreign direct investment flows: The role of governance infrastructure. *World Development, 30*(11), 1899–1919.
Hanna, R. (2010). US environmental regulations and FDI: Evidence from a panel of US-based multinational firms. *American Economic Journal: Applied Economics, 2*(3), 158–189.
Helpman, E. (1984). A simple theory of international trade with multinational corporations. *Journal of Political Economy, 92,* 451–471.
List, J. A., & Co, C. Y. (2000). The effects of environmental regulations on foreign direct investment. *Journal of Environmental Economics and Management, 40,* 1–20.
Manderson, E., & Kneller, R. (2012). Environmental regulations, outward FDI and heterogeneous firms: Are countries used as pollution havens. *Environmental and Resource Economics, 51,* 317–352.
Markusen, J. R. (1998). Multinational firms, location and trade. *The World Economy, 2*(16), 733–756.
Mulatu, A. (2017). The structure of UK outbound FDI and environmental regulations. *Environmental and Resource Economics.* https://doi.org/10.1007/s10640-017-0145-4.
Nagaraj, R. (2003). Foreign direct investment in India in the 1990s: Trends and issues. *Economic and Political Weekly, 38,* 1701–1712.
Poelhekke, S., & Ploeg, F. V. (2015). Green havens and pollution havens. *The World Economy.* https://doi.org/10.1111/twec.12219.
Rao, K. S. C., & Dhar, B. (2011). India's FDI inflows—trend and concepts. Institute for Studies in Industrial Development. Working Paper 01.
Rastogi, R., & Sawhney, A. (2014). *What attracts FDI in Indian manufacturing industries?* Berlin Working Papers on Money, Finance, Trade and Development 2.
Sawhney, A., & Rastogi, R. (2019). FDI in Indian manufacturing: Whither high-tech industries? *Economics Bulletin, 39*(3), 2192–2209.
Tang, J. (2015). Testing the pollution haven effect: Does the type of FDI? *Environmental and Resource Economics, 60,* 549–578.
Uchikawa, S. (1999). Economic reforms and foreign trade policies: Case study of apparel and machine tools industries. *Economic and Political Weekly* 138–148.
Waldkirch, A., & Munisamy, G. (2008). Pollution control and foreign direct investment in Mexico: An industry-level analysis. *Environmental and Resource Economics, 41,* 289–313.
Wei, W. (2005). China and India: Any difference in their FDI performances. *Journal of Asian Economics, 16,* 719–736.
Xing, Y., & Kolstad, C. D. (2002). Do lax environmental regulations attract foreign investment? *Environmental and Resource Economics, 21,* 1–22.

Chapter 9
Sustainability of India's Current Account Deficit: Role of Remittance Inflows and Software Services Exports

Aneesha Chitgupi

1 Introduction

Maintaining external stability and current account sustainability have been vital to India's macroeconomic policies. Except for a few years in the early 2000s, India experienced a perpetual current account deficit (CAD) due to large deficit in merchandise trade, whereas invisibles[1] component, which includes services trade, current transfers and current income, has contributed to lessen the CAD. In particular, exports of software services and private transfers (remittances) have been important positive contributors to India's current account balance (CAB). Net software services exports were 72.1%, and net private transfers (remittances) were 58.2% of total net invisibles in 2016–17. Together, the remittance inflows and software services exports were 56% of invisibles (credit) in 2016–17.

The policy changes in the developed world with respect to increasing anti-immigration sentiments leading to tightening of immigration policies by US and European countries are seen as a major challenge for India's services export industry (especially software services), and labour market adjustment and preference for local labour in Gulf Cooperation Council (GCC) countries are seen as new threat for aspiring Indian emigrants to these countries (GOI, 2018). Given that these adverse

This research work is an adaptation of the author's working paper (Chitgupi, 2019). The author is grateful to her Ph.D. supervisor, Prof. M. R. Narayana, for his guidance. Thanks are due to members of the Doctoral Committee and Bi-Annual Panel members at the Institute for Social and Economic Change (ISEC) for their suggestions on earlier versions of this work, and to participants' comments and suggestions at the 6th EIITF Conference, Indian Institute of Foreign Trade, New Delhi. However, the usual disclaimers apply.

A. Chitgupi (✉)
Fiscal Policy Institute (FPI), Government of Karnataka, Bengaluru, India
e-mail: aneeshachitgupi@gmail.com

[1]Invisibles as per RBI Balance of Payments Manual (2010) include services (such as travel, transportation, insurance, software services), transfers (public and private) and income (compensation of employees and investment income).

P. Lakhanpal et al. (eds.), *Trade, Investment and Economic Growth*,
https://doi.org/10.1007/978-981-33-6973-3_9

conditions of increasing nationalist agenda among countries are here to stay and a change towards progressive and conducive environment for migration and towards foreign workers seems uncertain in future, then the two main positive contributors towards India's current account, namely software services exports and remittances, may decline.

The paper investigates the sustainability of India's current account by analysing the relationship between imports and exports with and without key contributors (software services exports and remittances). How would a reduction in remittance inflows and software services exports affect the current account balance (CAB) for India? Does the absence of software services exports and remittances from the current account make it unsustainable? The analysis examines the individual and combined impact of these contributors on current account sustainability.

Rest of the paper is structured as follows: Sect. 2 discusses related literature; Sect. 3 presents some basic data on current account components. Section 4 discusses the methodology, conceptual framework and theoretical background. Empirical estimation and results are discussed in Sect. 5, and Sect. 6 concludes with implications and recommendations.

2 Review of Literature

Sustainability of current account assessed on the basis of inter-temporal budget constraint (IBC) was developed by Sachs (1981) where the current account movements were driven by two sets of motives, 'consumption tilting' (preference for present or future consumption based on subjective discount rate and world interest rate) and 'consumption smoothening' (smoothening consumption during shocks to output, investment and fiscal spending) (Callen & Cashin, 1999). The theoretical framework of IBC was further extended by Obstfeld and Rogoff (1996) under the assumption of perfect capital mobility and consumption smoothening behaviour. Using consumption smoothening approach, sustainability of India's current account has been analysed by restricting or stabilising the net external debt-to-GDP ratio by Callen and Cashin (1999), Goyal (2012), Phillips et al. (2013) and IMF' individual country-specific External Sector Reports.

Apart from viewing sustainability of the current account as a repayable level of external liabilities, it can also be viewed in terms of stationarity (mean-reverting property) of current account. Developed by Husted (1992), this approach to assess current account sustainability suggests that CADs are sustainable and IBC is valid for a country if the sum of discounted future values of current account surpluses is equal to the external borrowings. This implies that the current account is mean-reverting or stationary in nature and the exports/credit side of current account (exports of goods and inflow of invisibles) and imports/debit side (imports of goods and outflow of invisibles) are co-integrated by the presence of a long-run co-integrating vector.

Employing the methodology developed by Husted (1992), numerous country-specific and panel studies have analysed current account sustainability and validity of

IBC by examining the long-run relationship between exports and imports (including net invisibles). Country-specific studies include Husted (1992), Fountas and Wu (1999), Mann (2002), Christopoulos and León-Ledesma (2010) for the US current account, and Apergis et al. (2000) for Greece. Cross section and panel studies include Chen (2011) for a group of OECD countries, Baharumshah et al. (2005) for East Asian Countries and Sahoo et al. (2016a) for SAARC nations. In panel study, Shastri et al. (2018) on SAARC countries, including India, Pakistan, Bangladesh, Sri Lanka and Nepal, for the period 1985–2016 found weak sustainability primarily due to large deficits in the goods trade account and recommend stronger control over the increasing trade deficits in the face of fragility experienced in remittance inflows from US, EU and Middle Eastern countries.

Not all studies establish the validity of IBC and sustainability of CAD. In a study by Sahoo et al. (2016a) except Maldives and Sri Lanka, all other SAARC nations suffered from unsustainable current account deficits, and Gundlach and Sinn (1992) also find non-stationarity for major industrialised nations in a sample of 23 countries.

India-specific studies which examine the sustainability of current account through the existence of co-integration between exports and imports include Holmes et al. (2011), Singh (2015), Sahoo et al. (2016b). The study by Holmes et al. (2011) employs three tests to examine the presence of co-integration between exports and imports which include Johansen (1995), Saikonnen and Lütkepohl (2000) and Breitung (2002). Their results suggest against sustainability of current account prior to 1991 and in favour of sustainability towards the late 1990s. Singh (2015) employs the OLS-based two-step estimator of Gregory and Hansen (1996) and maximum likelihood system estimator of Johansen et al. (2000) to examine the long-run relationship between exports and imports for India. The OLSGH analysis does not yield any support for the presence of long-run co-integration, but MLE technique establishes sustainability of current account by providing evidence in support for long-run co-integration between exports and imports. Sahoo et al. (2016b) use Bayer and Hanck (2013) and ARDL (Pesaran et al. 2001) techniques to establish long-run co-integration between exports and imports for China and India and conclude that both the tests support sustainability of current account for China and unsustainability of current account for India. Thus, studies pertaining to India give a mixed account of sustainability of current account due to differing methodologies and varying estimation techniques using different time periods for the study.

Hassan and Holmes (2016) analyse the importance of invisibles, specifically, remittances in attaining current account sustainability for a panel of 47 emerging and developed economies over the period 1990–2011, and their study highlights the role of remittances in achieving current account sustainability. Their analysis estimates the presence of co-integration between exports and imports (with and without remittances). They define imports as a sum of imports of goods and services and net invisibles and subtract remittances (from net invisibles) to capture the co-integration between imports (without remittances) and exports. The results of panel co-integration test of Pedroni (2004) based on group Phillips–Perron and group augmented Dickey–Fuller statistics suggested that there existed weak sustainability (i.e. co-integrating coefficient less than unity for exports and imports) when imports included remittances and null of no co-integration could not be rejected when remittances were excluded.

3 Description of Basic Data

India is one of the leading exporters of software services in the world with 23.7% of total world software services in the year 2014 (IMF, 2017) and the largest recipient of remittance inflows which were US$ 72.7 billion for 2014 (World Bank, 2017). Software services exports and remittance inflows are important components of India's current account in the balance of payments. Table 1 presents the trends in the major components of current account from 2000–01 to 2016–17.

Table 1 Components of current account in BOP as a percentage of GDP, 2000–01 to 2016–17, India

Year	BOT	Invisibles[a] (net)	Remittances (net)	Software services exports (Net)	CAB
2000–01	−2.77	2.17	2.85	1.28	−0.59
2001–02	−2.47	3.20	3.29	1.47	0.73
2002–03	−2.07	3.30	3.17	1.71	1.23
2003–04	−2.19	4.44	3.45	1.97	2.25
2004–05	−4.55	4.22	2.77	2.28	−0.33
2005–06	−6.27	5.07	2.96	2.69	−1.20
2006–07	−6.27	5.30	3.03	2.95	−0.97
2007–08	−7.34	6.07	3.35	2.96	−1.26
2008–09	−10.81	8.28	4.03	3.95	−2.52
2009–10	−8.24	5.58	3.61	3.36	−2.66
2010–11	−7.29	4.54	3.04	2.91	−2.75
2011–12	−11.10	6.53	3.71	3.57	−4.57
2012–13	−10.71	5.88	3.52	3.47	−4.82
2013–14	−7.91	6.18	3.51	3.59	−1.73
2014–15	−7.30	5.95	3.34	3.54	−1.35
2015–16	−6.30	5.23	3.06	3.46	−1.07
2016–17	−4.81	4.16	2.42	3.00	−0.65

Source RBI (2018)
Note Data for the Financial Year beginning 1 April to 31 March
[a]The invisibles (net) as a percentage of GDP is for some years less than remittances (net) and software services exports (net) on account of larger outflows of other invisibles components such as interest income, G.N.I.E and official transfers.
BOT Balance of trade; *CAB* Current account balance

Table 1 highlights the positive contribution of invisibles in maintaining current account sustainability. The balance of trade (BOT), which is merchandise trade balance, has stayed in deficit for the entire period (2000–01 to 2016–17). The lowest deficit was 2.07% of GDP in 2002–03 and highest deficit of 11.1% in 2011–12 attributed to the escalation in crude oil prices and gold imports. In contrast, the CAB has always experienced lower deficits when compared to trade deficit, even in 2011–12 when BOT suffered a peak deficit, CAB was half of it at 4.57% of GDP. Thus, surpluses in the invisibles offset the large deficits experienced in BOT. The CAB moves in tandem with the merchandise trade deficit, but the deficit experienced is far less on account of invisibles' surpluses. Net invisibles grew steadily from 2.17% of GDP in 2000–01 to peak in 2008–09 at 8.28% of GDP. Remittance inflows and software services exports, the key contributors, peaked in 2008–09 with 4.03 and 3.95% of GDP, respectively. Since 2014–15, these key contributors have steadily declined as a share of GDP and because they contribute towards more than half of invisibles' surpluses, a decline is witnessed for net invisibles as well.

The other important aspect is that crude oil prices are closely linked to CAB by way of imports as well as through remittances. Nearly 55.6% of remittance inflows into India come from the Middle East countries whose economic activity depends on oil exports. Increased oil prices ratchet up economic activities in these countries, thus increasing demand for labour and wages. On the one hand, higher oil prices adversely affect BOT due to higher oil import bill but at the same time it increases remittance inflows. In the present scenario, with a tilt towards domestic labour and restrictions on immigrant workers in Gulf Cooperation Council (GCC) countries, an increase in oil prices may not culminate into higher remittances, whereas it will continue to increase BOT deficit as India is dependent on crude oil imports for its domestic energy requirements. At the same time, stringent immigration policy adopted by the USA, UK and other European countries may adversely affect remittance inflows. The share of USA and UK to total remittance inflows for India in 2016 was 17 and 5.7%, respectively (World Bank, 2016).

The impact of such nationalist, anti-immigrant policies may be felt not just on remittances but also on services exports, especially software services. For the year 2014–15 and 2015–16, India's software services exports witnessed a decline in mode 1 (cross-border sales) from 68.4 to 64.8% of total software services exports and mode 4 (presence of natural persons) from 17.1 to 16.1% whereas exports through mode 3 (commercial presence) increased from 14.4 to 18.9% (RBI, 2016). This underscores the competitive advantage that India had in providing cheap and skilled labour may be eroded as increased exports through commercial presence will require domestic hiring constraints and wages decided by the host/client market. Apart from changes in the foreign trade and migration policies, another key contributor to volatility in software services exports could be the advent of new disruptive technologies such as cloud computing, machine learning and artificial intelligence. India experienced a boom in its software exports on account of information technology (IT) services that were on the lower spectrum of the value chain such as website maintenance, data warehousing and other customised services. A shift towards automation of these services may render India's software industry obsolete.

Given the above facts and changes in world economy, the question that arises is that will India's current account be sustainable in the absence of its invisibles component (especially remittance inflows and software services exports)? How important are software services exports and remittances in contributing to India's current account sustainability?

4 Methodology

4.1 Conceptual Framework

Among the three definitions of CAB: (i) difference between imports and exports of goods and services; (ii) difference between national investments and savings; and (iii) change in international debt/investment position (Sachs, 1981), this chapter explains the concept of current account sustainability using the third definition of change in debt/investments of a country. Persistent deficits in the current account lead to accumulation of borrowing from international capital markets making the country an international debtor with foreign investors having a claim on the country's economic assets.

Thus, current account sustainability refers to a situation where a country is able to repay its external debts by generating current account surpluses in future. Using inter-temporal budget constraint of the economy, current account sustainability means that the present value of future current account surpluses is able to meet the existing external borrowings and interest payments. In practice, it refers to the solvency of a country and its ability to honour external debts (Melesi-Ferretti & Razin, 1996).

Further, CAB in essence is change in the international debt position for a country. One way to ensure its sustainability is to link the size of net borrowings to the size of the economy (GDP), thus restricting growth of liabilities to specified ratio of the GDP. External stabilisation, which is restricting or gradually reducing the CAD-to-GDP ratio and shifting towards surpluses over time, can be looked upon as reducing the level of what a country owes as a share of what it produces. Thus, current account sustainability, which in a nutshell is paying the present deficits through future surpluses, leads to external stabilisation as it ensures gradual reduction in CAD to GDP and reduced dependence on foreign borrowings.

4.2 Theoretical Background

Current account is defined as the change in net foreign assets or borrowings, or net international investment position.

$$CAB_t = B_{t-1} + rB_{t-1} - B_t \tag{1}$$

Table 2 Description of notations

	Notations	Description
1	CAB_t	Current account balance in time t
2	X_t	Merchandise/goods exports in time t
3	M_t	Merchandise/goods imports in time t
4	B_t	Borrowings in time t
5	R	Mean rate of interest
6	NI_t	Net invisibles
7	MM_t	Merchandise imports + net invisibles
8	λ_t	Discount rate at time t
9	r_o	Current rate of interest
10	Z_t	Merchandise imports + net invisibles + difference in interest payments between long-run mean interest rate r and current rate of interest r_0

Source Author

where CAB_t is the current account balance in time period t, which is equal to external borrowings in time period $t - 1$ plus interest payments ($rB_{t\text{-}1}$) minus any further borrowings made during period t. Equation (1) is rewritten as:

$$CAB_t = B_{t-1}(1 + r) - B_t \quad (2)$$

If borrowings in period t are greater than $t - 1$, then CAB would deteriorate by the difference between B_t and $B_{t\text{-}1}(1 + r)$ (Table 2).

Sustainability of current account requires establishing relationship between current account components. The methodology is co-integration of exports and imports to check for current account sustainability, originally developed by Husted (1992). It was modified by Hassan and Holmes (2016) to analyse the impact of remittances on current account sustainability by way of including and excluding it from total imports in a panel analysis. Analysis in this paper modifies and uses the methodology of Hassan and Holmes (2016) to include SSE and remittances under invisibles for India. In the first step towards analysing current account sustainability, the budget constraint for an economy is derived as follows:

$$Y_t = C_t + I_t + (X - M)_t + \mathrm{NI}_t \quad (3)$$

where Y is a measure of national income which includes consumption expenditure (C), investment (I), balance of trade ($X - M$) and net invisibles (NI). Together, $(X - M)_t + \mathrm{NI}_t$ constitute the CAB for time t.

Net invisibles include the following:

$$\mathrm{NI} = \mathrm{NST} + \mathrm{NCT} + \mathrm{NY} \quad (4)$$

where NST stands for net services trade, NCT is net current transfers and NY is net current income.

Substituting Eq. (2) in Eq. (3), one arrives at:

$$C_t = Y_t - I_t + B_t - B_{t-t}(1 + r) \tag{5}$$

where consumption is financed from income and external borrowings and rewritten as:

$$Y_t - C_t - I_t = (X - MM)_t \tag{6}$$

where $(X - MM)_t = CAB_t$ and $MM = M + N$; if NI is positive, then M will reduce by the same extent and vice versa as imports are negative or debit item in CAB.

Equations (5) and (6) are used to derive the inter-temporal budget constraint (IBC).

$$(X - MM)_t = B_{t-1}(1 + r_t) - B_t \tag{7}$$

IBC is obtained by solving forward (Appendix Equations A.1):

$$B_t = \sum_{i=1}^{\infty} \lambda_i (X - MM)_{t+i} + \lim_{n \to \infty} \lambda_n B_{t+n} \tag{8}$$

where $\lambda_i = \prod_{j=1}^{i} \frac{1}{1+r_{t+j}}$

where λ_i is discount rate and defined as product of i terms of $(1/1 + r_t)$. Thus, discounted future value of current account balances (CAB = $X - MM$) is difference between present borrowing and present value of future borrowings in international financial markets. Thus, the accumulated current account balances is equal to total change in foreign borrowings (or lending) for a given time period. The study by Husted (1992) derived the above equations to state that term $\lim_{n \to \infty} \lambda_n B_{t+n}$, if equal to zero, ensures that present value of future current account surpluses is able to repay the borrowings from international capital markets, whereas if positive it suggests that the country is 'bubble financing' its external borrowings, i.e. borrowing in the present for repaying past debts.

4.3 Formation of Testable Hypothesis

Testable equation to analyse current account sustainability by establishing co-integrating relationship between exports (X) and imports plus invisibles (MM) is derived as follows:

Equation (7) is expanded to include prevailing interest rate (r_t) in international financial markets, greater or less than long-run mean (r). The fluctuations in interest rate may affect interest burden of a country and thereby the CAB.

$$Z_t = MM_t + (r_t - r)B_{t-1} \tag{9}$$

$$Z_t + (1 + r)B_{t-1} = X_t + B_t \tag{10}$$

Rearranging Eq. (10)

$$B_t = Z_t - X_t + (1 + r)B_{t-1} \tag{11}$$

The forward iterations of foreign borrowings in Eq. (11) yield (Appendix Equations A.2):

$$rB_{t-1} + Z_t = X_t + \sum_{j=1}^{\infty} \lambda^j (\Delta X_{t+j} - \Delta Z_{t+j}) + r \lim_{n\to\infty} \lambda^{n+1} B_{t+n} \tag{12}$$

Substituting Eq. (9) in (12)

$$r_t B_{t-1} + MM_t = X_t + \sum_{j=1}^{\infty} \lambda^j (\Delta X_{t+j} - \Delta Z_{t+j}) + r \lim_{n\to\infty} \lambda^{n+1} B_{t+n} \tag{13}$$

The LHS of Eq. (13) is total imports plus invisibles including interest payments on external borrowings.

Assuming that exports of goods (X_t) and imports of goods plus net invisibles (Z_t, which includes net services exports, net current transfers and net current income) are non-stationary series, i.e. they are random walks with drift (intercept term) and follow auto-regression of order one AR(1) processes with representation as follows:

$$X_t = a_1 + X_{t-1} + e_{1t}$$

$$\Delta X_t = a_1 + e_{1t}$$

$$\Delta X_{t+j} = a_1 + e_{1t+j} \tag{14}$$

Similarly,

$$Z_t = a_2 + Z_{t-1} + e_{2t}$$

$$\Delta Z_t = a_2 + e_{2t}$$

$$\Delta Z_{t+j} = a_2 + e_{2t+j} \tag{15}$$

where a_1 and a_2 are drift parameters and e_{1t} and e_{2t} are error terms.

Substituting Eqs. (14) and (15) in Eq. (13), deterministic equation is transformed into stochastic form as follows:

$$r_t B_{t-1} + MM_t = X_t + \sum_{j=1}^{\infty} \lambda^j (a_1 + e_{it+j} - a_2 + e_{2t+j}) + r \lim_{n\to\infty} \lambda^{n+1} B_{t+n} \tag{16}$$

$$r_t B_{t-1} + MM_t = X_t + \left(\frac{a_1 - a_2}{r}\right) + \sum_{j=1}^{\infty} \lambda^j (e_{it+j} - e_{2t+j}) + r \lim_{n\to\infty} \lambda^{n+1} B_{t+n} \tag{17}$$

Because $\sum_{j=1}^{\infty} \lambda^j = \sum_{j=1}^{\infty} \frac{1}{(1+r)} = \frac{1}{r}$

$$X_t = MM_t + r_t B_{t-1} + \left(\frac{a_2 - a_1}{r}\right) + \sum_{j=1}^{\infty} \lambda^j (e_{2t+j} - e_{1t+j}) - r \lim_{n\to\infty} \lambda^{n+1} B_{t+n} \tag{18}$$

$$\sum_{j=1}^{\infty} \lambda^j (e_{2t+j} - e_{1t+j}) = u_t$$

And, $\left(\frac{a_2 - a_1}{r}\right) = a$

This can be rewritten as:

$$X_t = \alpha + \beta \bar{M}_t + u_t \tag{19}$$

where $MM_t + r_t B_{t-1} = \bar{M}_t$ and $\lim_{n\to\infty} \lambda^{n+1} B_{t+n} = 0$.

The following section presents the empirical framework to estimate Eq. (19).

4.4 Technique of Estimation

In Sect. 4.3, mathematical derivations emanating from theory yielded Eq. (19) as the testable equation, where stationarity of current account deficits is established by finding that exports and imports plus invisibles are co-integrated with a known long-run co-integrating vector β [1, −1].

If β equals 1, then one % increase in $\bar{M}_t$ leads to a percentage increase in X_t and CAB remains at the same level as before, but in a situation where β is less than one ($\beta < 1$) one % increase in $\bar{M}_t$ is accompanied by β% increase in X_t which is less than increase in $\bar{M}_t$ culminating into an increase in CAD by $(1 - \beta)$%.

If there exists a long-run equilibrium between X_t and $\bar{M}_t$, the current account is sustainable but in a weak sense, it settles at a higher deficit in the long run rather than return to its initial deficit level. As only a part of the increase in imports is met by increase in exports, the excess deficit needs to be financed through external borrowings at higher interest (Hassan & Holmes, 2016). Thus, a value of β closer to one gives stronger evidence of sustainability of current account.

Non-stationarity of current account indicates that discounted deficits do not converge asymptotically to zero, making the country a net debtor as exports are insufficient to pay for imports. The increased accumulation of foreign debt due to increasing divergence between exports and imports may precipitate into BOP instability.

Based on Eq. (19), to test for sustainability of current account, four alternatives of $\bar{M}$ are used. In Eq. (19), $\bar{M}$ includes imports and net invisibles (NI), and this is the first measurement of $\bar{M}$. The second measurement excludes only net remittances ($\bar{M} - q$), and other components of NI are included. The third measurement excludes only SSE ($\bar{M} - s$), and the last measurement excludes both remittances and SSE ($\bar{M} - q - s$). The aim of this analysis is to assess the sensitivity of co-integration for different measurements of $\bar{M}$.

In order to empirically estimate the testable hypothesis, the autoregressive distributed lag (ARDL) model is used. The model is specified as follows:

$$\Delta X_t = \alpha + \sum_{i=1}^{m} \lambda_i \Delta X_{t-i} + \sum_{i=0}^{n} \tau_i \Delta \bar{M}_{t-i} + \varphi X_{t-1} + \beta \bar{M}_{t-1} + \varepsilon_t \quad (20)$$

The bound-testing approach to ARDL model developed by Pesaran et al. (2001) is used to estimate the long-run relationship between (X) and different measurements of ($\bar{M}$). The ARDL method is known to incorporate differentiated lags for independent variables and includes lagged values of dependent variable presented in Eq. (20).

4.5 Variables and Data Description

The RBI's data on private transfers is similar to IMF's BPM6 definition of personal transfers. Items included in private transfers are workers' remittances for family maintenance, local withdrawals from Non-Resident Rupee Account (NRE/NRO), gold and silver brought in through passenger luggage and personal gifts, donations

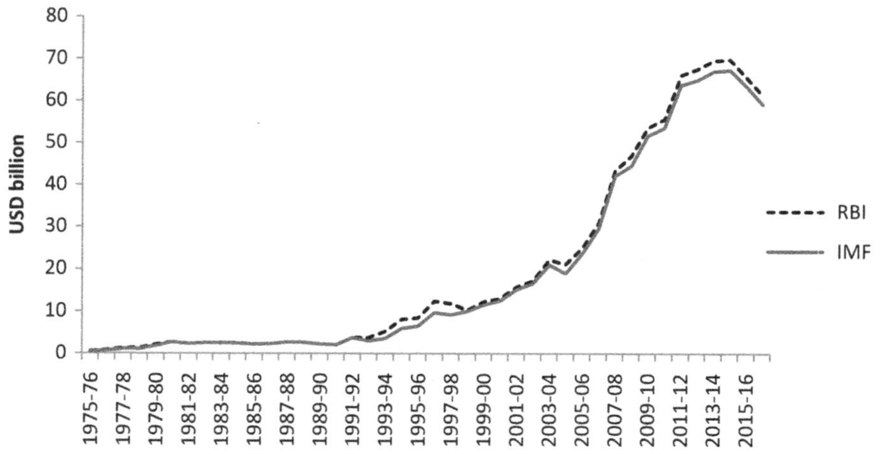

Fig. 1 Comparison between RBI and IMF databases on total remittance inflows, 1975–76 to 2016–17, India. *Source* RBI (2018) and IMF (2017)

to charitable/religious institutions. The only items not included in personal transfers according to BPM6, but included in private transfers by RBI, are donations to charitable/religious institutions. By definition, personal transfers are inter-household transfers, and gifts/donations to charitable/religious institutions are recorded in secondary income account under other current transfers and not personal transfers. Thus, the difference between IMF's personal transfers and RBI's private transfers is negligible as gifts/donations to charitable/religious institutions form a small part of total private transfer inflows (Fig. 1). This chapter uses the term remittances synonymous to private transfers.

Data on software services as a separate item on the services trade is available from 2000–01 and was included with miscellaneous services before 2000–01. As per RBI definition, software services exports include hardware consultancy and implementation, software consultancy and implementation, database and data processing charges, and repair and maintenance of computers which is synonymous to computer services exports as per IMF BPM6 (Tables 3 and 4).

5 Estimation Results

The sustainability of current account is tested using ARDL approach to co-integration (Eq. 20) and quarterly data from 2000–2001: Q1 to 2016–17: Q3. The analysis considers three cases, i.e. $\bar{M}$ without net remittances $(\bar{M} - q)$, $\bar{M}$ without net software services exports $(\bar{M} - s)$ and $\bar{M}$ without net remittances and net software services exports $(\bar{M} - q - s)$ to study whether net remittances and net SSE are vital

Table 3 Variables and data sources

	Variables	Measurement	Sources
1	Merchandise exports	Quarterly data, percentage of GDP at current (market prices)	RBI (2018)
2	Merchandise imports		
3	Private transfers/remittances		
4	Software services exports		
5	Net invisibles (net services, net transfer and net income)		
6	GDP at current (market prices)		RBI (2018)

Source Author

Table 4 Descriptive statistics

Statistics (1)	X (exports)	$\bar{M}$(imports plus net invisibles) (2)	$\bar{M}-\text{q}$ (without net remittances) (3)	$\bar{M}-\text{s}$ (without net SSE) (4)	$\bar{M}-\text{q}-\text{s}$ (without net remittances and net SSE) (5)
Mean	13.39	12.95	16.21	15.78	19.03
Median	13.15	12.98	16.10	16.10	19.00
Maximum	18.26	20.43	24.28	23.78	27.94
Minimum	8.44	5.42	8.79	7.17	10.17
Std. dev	2.57	4.14	4.29	4.77	4.92
Observations	67	67	67	67	67

Source Author's calculations

to ensure current account sustainability or whether their contributions are marginal with minimal impact.

5.1 *Test Results for Stationarity*

The prerequisite before undertaking time series econometric analysis is to establish the order of integration of the variables under study. Tables 5 and 6 present the unit root tests for exports of goods (X) and imports ($\bar{M}$), under the four specific measurements using the ADF and Phillips–Perron tests for stationarity. Results show that all the series are integrated of order one, I(1).

Table 5 Stationarity, augmented Dickey–Fuller test (Null hypothesis: series has unit root)

Variable	t statistic					
	At level			At first difference		
	None	Intercept	Intercept + Trend	None	Intercept	Intercept + Trend
X	0.16	– 2.02	– 1.12	– 4.09***	– 4.11***	– 4.48***
$\bar{M}$	– 0.19	– 1.51	– 0.89	– 4.28***	– 4.25***	– 4.43***
$\bar{M}$-q	– 0.21	– 1.54	– 0.87	– 4.13***	– 4.11***	– 4.42**
$\bar{M}$-s	0.00	– 1.67	– 0.66	– 4.18***	– 4.19***	– 4.51***
$\bar{M}$-q-s	– 0.05	– 1.69	– 0.73	– 4.06***	– 4.08***	– 4.57***

Note ***, ** denote significance at the 1 and 5% level, respectively
Source Author's estimation with maximum lag length equal to 4 and based on AIC

Table 6 Stationarity, Phillips–Perron test (Null hypothesis: series has unit root)

Variable	Adj. t statistic					
	At level			At first difference		
	None	Intercept	Intercept + Trend	None	Intercept	Intercept + Trend
X	0.13	−2.47	−2.53	−10.8***	−11.21***	−23.98***
$\bar{M}$	−0.24	−2.17	−2.26	−11.17***	−12.01***	−12.77***
$\bar{M}$-q	−0.16	−2.08	−2.13	−9.04***	−9.09***	−10.58**
$\bar{M}$-s	−0.06	−2.12	−2.15	−9.69***	−10.47***	−12.71***
$\bar{M}$-q-s	−0.00	−2.02	−2.02	−8.56***	−8.73***	−10.7***

Note ***, ** denote significance at the 1 and 5% level, respectively
Source Author's estimation based on Newey–West using Bartlett kernel

5.2 ARDL Estimation Results

The presence of co-integration between variables in the ARDL model specified in Eq. (20) is examined using F test. The F statistic is compared with two sets of critical values or bounds (upper bound and lower bound). If the value of calculated F statistic is greater than the upper bound, then the null of no co-integration can be rejected. However, if the computed F statistic is smaller than the lower bound, the null cannot be rejected. The test is inconclusive if the F statistic falls between the two bounds.

Table 7 presents the long-run co-integration coefficient for total exports (X) and total imports of goods (M) significant under all specifications. The error correction term (ECT), which tests whether the short-term deviations between exports and

Table 7 Co-integrating equations and error correction term, 2000–2001: Q1 to 2016–17: Q3, India (Dependent variable: X)

	M (total goods imports) (1)	$\bar{M}$(imports plus net invisibles) (2)	$\bar{M} - q$ (without net remittances) (3)	$\bar{M} - s$ (without net SSE) (4)	$\bar{M} - q - s$ (without net remittances and net SSE) (5)
Lag structure of ARDL	(2, 1)	(1, 3)	(2, 1)	(1, 2)	(2, 1)
Long-run coefficients					
Import variable (β)	**0.45***** (11.81)	**0.59***** (12.13)	**0.54***** (8.61)	**0.5***** (11.94)	**0.48***** (9.59)
Constant term	4.61*** (5.94)	5.75*** (8.71)	4.67*** (4.42)	5.55*** (8.1)	4.4*** (4.53)
Co-integrating form					
Error correction term	-0.56*** (−4.27)	−0.6*** (−5.58)	−0.43*** (−3.99)	−0.6*** (−5.28)	−0.47*** (−3.92)
D(X(−1))	−0.28*** (-2.88)		−0.27*** (−2.86)		−0.23** (−2.4)
D(Imports)	0.49*** (8.57)	0.38*** (6.19)	0.44*** (7.68)	0.39*** (7.03)	0.42*** (7.67)
D(Imports(−1))		−0.16*** (−2.85)		−0.11** (−2.02)	
D(Imports(−2))		−0.10* (−1.68)			
F statistic	5.88***	10.03***	5.15**	9.01***	4.97**
Critical value bounds					
Significance	Lower bound	Upper bound			
10%	3.02	3.51			
5%	3.62	4.16			
1%	4.94	5.58			

Note ***, **, * denote significance at 1, 5 and 10%, respectively
Source Author's calculations using Eq. (6.20)
Values in parenthesis are t statistic
Lag selection is based on AIC

imports return to the equilibrium path, is negative and highly significant indicating the presence of long-run relationship between the variables across all the measurements of imports (M). Also, the F statistic lies above the critical bounds at either 1% or 5% level of significance. Thus, the null of no co-integration is rejected for all the specifications estimated.

Column (1) shows the co-integrating coefficient for merchandise imports which is 0.45 and highly significant. This indicates that for every one percentage point increase in total imports of goods, exports of goods increase by 0.45 percentage point. Thus, there exists a 0.55 percentage point deficit in the balance of trade (BOT). In the short run, however, 0.56% of the deviations in X are adjusted per quarter towards long-run equilibrium level. As the long-run equilibrium coefficient under this specification is far less than one, India would suffer from weak sustainability of current account and larger deficits.

In the second specification, imports include merchandise, services, transfers and income ($\bar{M}$), thereby reducing the total imports as India enjoys surpluses in its invisibles component. The long-run coefficient of 0.59 in column (2) implies that when invisibles are included, higher sustainability is ensured for India's current account. The long-run coefficient improves from 0.45 to 0.59 when net invisibles are included. In order to calculate the specific component of net invisibles contributing to higher sustainability (higher β value), net remittances and net software services exports are subtracted from net invisibles in columns (3) and (4), respectively.

It is observed that when net remittances and net SSE are subtracted from net invisibles, the long-run coefficient reduces to 0.54 and 0.5, respectively, from 0.59 in column (2). This implies that individually net remittances and net software services exports make considerable contribution towards India's current account sustainability. If net remittances are excluded from net invisibles, then one percentage point increase in $\bar{M}$ is accompanied by 0.54 percentage point increase in X and in the case of exclusion of SSE, X would increase by 0.5 percentage point.

In column (5), net remittances and net SSE are subtracted from net invisibles which yields a long-run coefficient of value 0.48 which is closer to 0.45 in column (1) where net invisibles were excluded for estimation. This offers evidence for net remittances and net SSE as primary components of net invisibles, and their absence yield results similar to a situation when net invisibles are excluded.

Analysing the speed of adjustment parameter or the error correction term (ECT), as mentioned earlier, is negative and significant for all the specifications. This evidence can be used to justify the time taken to adjust towards long-run equilibrium after a short-run shock. In column (1) where co-integration between imports and exports of merchandise goods is estimated, 45% of the short-run disequilibrium of the previous quarter is corrected in the current quarter, indicating that it would take slightly over two quarters for short-run shock to be absorbed by the system. In the case where import component included net invisibles (column (2)), 60% of the short-run shocks of previous quarter is corrected in current period. In comparison with the ECT in column (1), the time taken to correct the short-run disequilibrium improved in column (2). Thus, inclusion of net invisibles reduces the time taken to adjust the system to the long-run path. In the absence of contributions from invisibles component, India's current account would have taken comparatively more time to correct the short-run disturbances. Comparison between the ECTs of column (3) and column (4) which excludes net remittances and net SSE, respectively, shows that while 43% of short-run disequilibrium is corrected in the absence of remittance, about 60% is corrected without SSE. This implies that contribution by remittances in ensuring current account sustainability is greater than SSE as it would take shorter time to adjust the disequilibrium in the presence of remittances rather than SSE.

The presence of co-integration between exports and imports for all specifications implies sustainability of India's current account with and without net invisibles. However, sustainability is weaker in the absence of net invisibles implying that India's dependence on foreign capital and external borrowings would be higher without the contributions of net invisibles. This has two implications on the external stabilisation: (a) a larger deficit in the absence of invisibles may increase dependence on foreign financing to bridge the gap, further widening the CAD due to increased interest payments and adversely affecting CAD/GDP ratio, and (b) increase in exposure to foreign capital and borrowings in the BOP may require larger surpluses to be generated in future to repay the increased accumulated debt. Weak sustainability observed in the absence of net invisibles, could lead to India increasing its dependence on external sources of finance which may percolate to higher interest rates in the domestic economy and increased vulnerability to external capital movements.

The necessary diagnostic tests presented in Table 8 indicate that the estimated ARDL model does not suffer from non-normality, serial correlation, heteroscedasticity or misspecification error. The table also provides the ARDL model representation across different measurements of imports used to calculate the long-run coefficients.

6 Conclusion and Policy Implications

The trends in foreign capital flows suggest high volatility, especially post 2008–09 GFC. This could lead to deterioration in quality of financing CAD with increase in external borrowings rather than non-debt capital flows. In the light of volatile movements of foreign capital on the one hand and increased global uncertainty with respect to trade and migration on the other, this paper attempts to provide a snapshot of the dependence of India's current account on its invisibles components (especially net remittances and net SSE).

Using time series data for India from 2000–01 to 2016–17, the analysis highlighted the magnitude of their contribution in reducing CAD by establishing a co-integrating relationship between exports and imports. The evidence supporting higher co-integrating coefficient in the presence of net invisibles highlights the importance of remittances and SSE in ensuring current account sustainability in the long run. In addition, it was observed that in the absence of net invisibles, speed of adjustment was longer and the short-run economic shocks continued to persist in India's current account for a longer duration. This further underlines the importance of net invisibles in arresting further deterioration in current account as the disequilibrium is adjusted swiftly in the presence of net invisibles. The analysis also probes into the individual contribution of remittances and SSE. In doing so, it was found that remittances assist more towards sustainability of India's current account as compared to SSE. Thus, reductions in remittances could deteriorate the current account more than reductions

Table 8 ARDL model representation, 2000–2001: Q1 to 2016–17: Q3, India (Dependent variable: *X*)

	M (total goods imports) (1)	$\bar{M}$(imports plus net invisibles) (2)	$\bar{M}-q$ (without net remittances) (3)	$\bar{M}-s$ (without net SSE) (4)	$\bar{M}-q-s$ (without net remittances and net SSE) (5)
Lag structure	(2, 1)	(1, 3)	(2, 1)	(1, 2)	(2, 1)
X(−1)	0.16 (1.25)	0.39*** (3.59)	0.3** (2.4)	0.39*** (3.42)	0.29** (2.36)
X(−2)	0.29*** (2.82)		0.27*** (2.79)		0.233** (2.36)
Imports	0.49*** (8.15)	0.38*** (5.96)	0.44*** (7.23)	0.39*** (6.65)	0.41*** (7.23)
Imports(−1)	−0.25*** (−3.12)	−0.18** (−2.07)	−0.21*** (−2.67)	−0.19** (−2.37)	−0.19** (−2.55)
Imports(−2)		0.06 (0.76)		0.11* (1.96)	
Imports(−3)		0.10 (1.64)			
C	2.56*** (3.75)	3.47*** (4.82)	2.02*** (3.09)	3.34*** (4.58)	2.09*** (3.10)
R sq	0.89	0.87	0.87	0.87	0.88
DW stat	1.93	2.17	1.99	2.16	1.98
Diagnostic tests					
Jarque–Bera: χ^2 (normality)	2.27 (0.32)	1.35 (0.21)	2.99 (0.31)	2.42 (0.74)	1.33 (0.54)
Breusch–Godfrey: χ^2 (no serial correlation)	0.34 (0.85)	2.63 (0.45)	0.24 (0.88)	2.13 (3.45)	0.04 (0.97)
Breusch–Pagan–Godfrey: χ^2 (homoskedasticity)	5.43 (0.25)	3.29 (0.65)	4.94 (0.29)	4.75 (0.31)	5.35 (2.53)
Ramsey RESET: F-stat (model specification)	0.44 (0.51)	0.48 (0.49)	0.19 (0.67)	0.69 (0.41)	0.72 (0.39)

Note ***, ** and * denote significance at 1, 5 and 10%, respectively
Values in parenthesis are t statistic
Source: Author's calculations

in SSE. Sustainability of the current account is analysed in the context of international debt position of a country. Exclusion of net remittances, specifically SSE and remittances, shows weakening of India's current account sustainability. Reductions in invisibles could enhance India's dependence on foreign debt in the absence of stable non-debt creating capital inflows. This may have detrimental impact on India's external stabilisation as increased debt requires generation of larger future surpluses in the current account and larger current CAD due to increased interest payments.

Increasing uncertainty with respect to immigration policies in developed countries such as the USA, UK, Europe and GCC due to rise in nationalist agenda and increased trade frictions, may have a detrimental impact on key contributors of invisibles. Thus, policies need to be focused on developing new avenues and markets for migration and services exports (specifically software services in which India holds comparative advantage). With the advent of disruptive technologies (artificial intelligence, cloud computing, machine learning etc.), a serious consideration in upgrading and enhancing the competiveness of India's software services is the need of the hour in order to maintain strong exports. In addition, there needs to be a thrust on exports in general to reduce India's dependence on foreign capital by bridging the gap between imports and exports.

Appendix

Equations A.1

Solving for IBC: Derivations for Eq. (8)

$$(X - MM)_t = B_{t-1}(1 + r_t) - B_t$$

$$B_t = -(X - MM)_t + B_{t-1}(1 + r_t) \tag{a.1}$$

$$B_{t+1} = -(X - MM)_{t+1} + B_t(1 + r_{t+1})$$

$$B_{t+2} = -(X - MM)_{t+2} + B_{t+1}(1 + r_{t+2})$$

which can be rewritten as

$$B_{t+2} = -(X - MM)_{t+2} - (X - MM)_{t+1}(1 + r_{t+2}) + B_t(1 + r_{t+1})(1 + r_{t+2})$$

$$B_{t+3} = -(X - MM)_{t+3} - (X - MM)_{t+2}(1 + r_{t+3}) - (X - MM)_{t+1}(1 + r_{t+2})(1 + r_{t+3}) + B_t(1 + r_{t+1})(1 + r_{t+2})(1 + r_{t+3})$$

$$B_{t+n} = -(X - MM)_{t+n} - (X - MM)_{t+n-1}(1 + r_{t+n}) - \cdots - (X - MM)_{t+1}(1 + r_{t+2}) \ldots (1 + r_{t+n-1})(1 + r_{t+n}) + B_t(1 + r_{t+1}) \cdots + (1 + r_{t+n-1})(1 + r_{t+n})$$

$$B_t = \frac{(X-MM)_{t+n}}{(1+r_{t+1})\cdots+(1+r_{t+n-1})(1+r_{t+n})} + \frac{(X-MM)_{t+n-1}}{(1+r_{t+1})\cdots+(1+r_{t+n-1})}\cdots$$
$$+\frac{(X-MM)_{t+1}}{(1+r_{t+1})} + \frac{B_{t+n}}{(1+r_{t+1})\cdots+(1+r_{t+n-1})(1+r_{t+n})}$$

$$B_t = \sum_{i=1}^{\infty} \lambda_i (X-MM)_{t+i} + \lim_{n\to\infty} \lambda_n B_{t+n} \tag{a.2}$$

where $\lambda_i = \prod_{j=1}^{i} \frac{1}{1+r_{t+j}}$

Equations A.2

Iterative Dynamics of Foreign Borrowings: Derivations for Eq. (18)

$$B_t = Z_t - X_t + (1+r)B_{t-1} \tag{b.1}$$

$$B_{t+1} = Z_{t+1} - X_{t+1} + (1+r)B_t$$

$$B_{t+2} = Z_{t+2} - X_{t+2} + (1+r)B_{t+1}$$

which can be rewritten as

$$B_{t+2} = Z_{t+2} - X_{t+2} + (1+r)(Z_{t+1} - X_{t+1}) + (1+r)^2 B_t$$

Expanding B_t further

$$B_{t+2} = Z_{t+2} - X_{t+2} + (1+r)(Z_{t+1} - X_{t+1}) + (1+r)^2(Z_t - X_t) + (1+r)^3 B_{t-1}$$

$$B_{t+3} = Z_{t+3} - X_{t+3} + (1+r)(Z_{t+2} - X_{t+2}) + (1+r)^2(Z_{t+1} - X_{t+1})$$
$$+ (1+r)^3\,(Z_t - X_t) + (1+r)^4 B_{t-1}$$

$$B_{t+n} = Z_{t+n} - X_{t+n} + (1+r)(Z_{t+n-1} - X_{t+n-1}) + (1+r)^2(Z_{t+n-2} - X_{t+n-2}) + \cdots + (1$$

$$B_{t+n} = \sum_{j=0}^{n} (1+r)^{n-j}\left(Z_{t+j} - X_{t+j}\right) + (1+r)^{n+1} B_{t-1}$$

$$B_{t-1} = \frac{B_{t+n}}{(1+r)^{n+1}} - \frac{\sum_{j=0}^{n} (1+r)^{n-j}(Z_{t+j} - X_{t+j})}{(1+r)^{n+1}}$$

$$B_{t-1} = \frac{B_{t+n}}{(1+r)^{n+1}} - \frac{\sum_{j=0}^{n}(Z_{t+j} - X_{t+j})}{(1+r)^{1+j}}$$

$$B_{t-1} = \sum_{j=0}^{n} \lambda^{1+j}\left(X_{t+j} - Z_{t+j}\right) + \lambda^{n+1} B_{t+n} \quad \text{(b.2)}$$

$$\text{where}\lambda = \frac{1}{(1+r)}$$

Solving the process till infinity yields

$$B_{t-1} = \sum_{j=0}^{\infty} \lambda^{1+j}\left(X_{t+j} - Z_{t+j}\right) + \lim_{n\to\infty} \lambda^{n+1} B_{t+n} \quad \text{(b.3)}$$

Expanding the above equation

$$B_{t-1} = \lambda(X_t - Z_t) + \lambda^2(\Delta X_{t+1} - \Delta Z_{t+1}) + \lambda^2(\Delta X_t - \Delta Z_t) \\ + \lambda^3(\Delta X_{t+2} - \Delta Z_{t+2}) + \lambda^3(\Delta X_{t+1} - \Delta Z_{t+1}) + \cdots + \lim_{n\to\infty} \lambda^{n+1} B_{t+n}$$

$$B_{t-1} = \lambda(X_t - Z_t) + \lambda \sum_{j=1}^{\infty} \lambda^j (\Delta X_{t+j} - \Delta Z_{t+j}) + \lambda \sum_{j=1}^{\infty} \lambda^{1+j}\left(\Delta X_{t+j} - \Delta Z_{t+j}\right) + \cdots + \\ \lim_{n\to\infty} \lambda^{n+1} B_{t+n} \quad \text{(b.4)}$$

Rearranging Equation (b.3)

$$\sum_{j=0}^{\infty} \lambda^{1+j}\left(X_{t+j} - Z_{t+j}\right) = B_{t-1} - \lim_{n\to\infty} \lambda^{n+1} B_{t+n} \quad \text{(b.5)}$$

Substituting (b.5) in (b.4)

$$B_{t-1} = \lambda(X_t - Z_t) + \lambda \sum_{j=1}^{\infty} \lambda^j (\Delta X_{t+j} - \Delta Z_{t+j}) + \lambda\left[B_{t-1} - \lim_{n\to\infty} \lambda^{n+1} B_{t+n}\right] + \cdots + \lim_{n\to\infty} \lambda^{n+}$$

$$B_{t-1} = \lambda(X_t - Z_t) + \lambda \sum_{j=1}^{\infty} \lambda^j (\Delta X_{t+j} - \Delta Z_{t+j}) + \lambda B_{t-1} + (1-\lambda) \lim_{n\to\infty} \lambda^{n+1} B_{t+n}$$

$$B_{t-1} - \lambda B_{t-1} = \lambda\left[(X_t - Z_t) + \sum_{j=1}^{\infty} \lambda^j (\Delta X_{t+j} - \Delta Z_{t+j}) + \frac{(1-\lambda)}{\lambda} \lim_{n\to\infty} \lambda^{n+1} B_{t+n}\right]$$

$$\frac{1-\lambda}{\lambda} B_{t-1} + Z_t = X_t + \sum_{j=1}^{\infty} \lambda^j (\Delta X_{t+j} - \Delta Z_{t+j}) + \frac{(1-\lambda)}{\lambda} \lim_{n\to\infty} \lambda^{n+1} B_{t+n}$$

As $\frac{1-\lambda}{\lambda} = r$

$$rB_{t-1} + Z_t = X_t + \sum_{j=1}^{\infty} \lambda^j (\Delta X_{t+j} - \Delta Z_{t+j}) + \frac{(1-\lambda)}{\lambda} + r \lim_{n\to\infty} \lambda^{n+1} B_{t+n} \quad \text{(b.6)}$$

References

Apergis, N., Katrakilidis, K. P., & Tabakis, N. M. (2000). Current account deficit sustainability: The case of Greece. *Applied Economic Letters, 7,* 599–603.

Baharumshah, A. Z., Lau, E., & Fountas, S. (2005). Current account deficit sustainability: A panel approach. *Journal of Economic Integration, 20*(3), 514–529.

Bayer, C., & Hanck, C. (2013). Combining non-cointegration tests. *Journal of Time Series Analysis, 34*(1), 83–95.

Breitung, J. (2002). Nonparametric tests for unit roots and cointegration. *Journal of Econometrics, 108,* 343–363.

Callen, T., & Cashin, P. (1999). *Assessing External Sustainability in India.* IMF Working Paper No. WP/99/181, International Monetary Fund, Washington DC.

Chen, S. W. (2011). Current account deficits and sustainability: Evidence from the OECD countries. *Economic Modelling, 28*(4), 1455–1464.

Chitgupi, A. (2019). *Sustainability of India's Current Account Deficit: Role of Remittance Inflows and Software Services Exports.* ISEC Working Paper No. 469. https://www.isec.ac.in/wp469.htm

Christopoulos, D., & León-Ledesma, M. A. (2010). Current account sustainability in the US: What did we really know about it? *Journal of International Money and Finance, 29*(3), 442–459.

Fountas, S., & Wu, J. L. (1999). Are the U.S. current account deficits really sustainable? *International Economic Journal, 13,* 51–58.

Gregory, A., & Hansen, B. E. (1996). Residual-based tests for cointegration in models with regime shifts. *Journal of Econometrics, 70,* 99–126.

GOI (2018) Economic Survey 2017–18. Department of Economic Affairs. New Delhi: Ministry of Finance. Retrieved on November 27, 2018, from https://mofapp.nic.in:8080/economicsurvey/

Goyal, R. (2012). *Sustainable Level of India's Current Account Deficit.* RBI Working Paper No. 16/2012. Retrieved on September 18, 2017, from https://rbidocs.rbi.org.in/rdocs/Publications/PDFs/WPSSLI070812.PDF

Gundlach, E., & Sinn, S. (1992). Unit root tests of the current account: Implications for international capital mobility. *Applied Economics, 24*(6), 617–620.

Hassan, G. M., & Holmes, M. J. (2016). Do remittances facilitate a sustainable current account? *The World Economy, 39*(11), 1834–1853.

Holmes, M. J., Panagiotidis, T., & Sharma, A. (2011). The sustainability of India's current account. *Applied Economics, 43,* 219–229.

Husted, S. (1992). The emerging US current account deficit in the 1980s: A cointegration analysis. *The Review of Economics and Statistics, 74*(1), 159–166.

IMF. (2013). IMF Multilateral Policy Issues Report: 2013 Pilot External Sector Report. Retrieved on November 22, 2017, from https://www.imf.org/external/np/pp/eng/2013/062013.pdf

IMF. (2016). Balance of Payments and International Investments Position. Retrieved on February 3, 2018, from https://data.imf.org/?sk=7A51304B-6426-40C0-83DD-CA473CA1FD52&sId=1390030341854

IMF. (2017). IMF Policy Paper 2017 External Sector Report. Retrieved on October 10, 2018, from https://www.imf.org/external/pp/ppindex.aspx

Johansen, S. (1995). *Likelihood-based inference in cointegrated vector autoregressive models.* Oxford: Oxford University Press.
Johansen, S., Mosconi, R., & Nielsen, B. (2000). Cointegration analysis in the presence of structural breaks in the deterministic trend. *The Econometrics Journal, 3*(2), 216–249.
Mann, C. L. (2002). Perspectives on the US current account deficit and sustainability. *The Journal of Economic Perspectives, 16*(3), 131–152.
Milesi-Ferretti, G. M., & Razin, A. (1996). *Current-account sustainability.* International Economics Section, Department of Economics: Princeton University, New Jersey.
Obstfeld, M., & Rogoff, K. (1996). *Foundations of international macroeconomics.* Cambridge: MIT Press.
Obstfeld, M., & Rogoff, K. (2007). The unsustainable U.S. current account position revisited. In R. H. Clarida (Ed.), *G7 current account imbalances: Sustainability and adjustment* (pp. 339–375). University of Chicago Press.
Pedroni, P. (2004). Panel cointegration: Asymptotic and finite sample properties of pooled time series tests with an application to the PPP hypothesis. *Econometric Theory, 20*(3), 597–625.
Pesaran, M. H., Shin, Y., & Smith, R. J. (2001). Bounds testing approaches to the analysis of level relationships. *Journal of Applied Econometrics, 16*(3), 289–326.
RBI. (2016). *Survey on computer software & information technology enabled services exports: 2015–16.* Retrieved on September 19, 2017, from https://rbidocs.rbi.org.in/rdocs/PressRelease/PDFs/PR981E3ABC6F678684C4AA9769D52B2BB9925.PDF
RBI. (2018). *Database on Indian economy.* RBI, Mumbai. Retrieved on May 19, 2019, from https://dbie.rbi.org.in/DBIE/dbie.rbi?site=publications
Sachs, J. D. (1981). The current account and macroeconomic adjustment in the 1970s. *Brookings Papers on Economic Activity, 12*(1), 201–282.
Saikkonen, P., & Lütkepohl, H. (2000). Testing for the cointegrating rank of a VAR process with an intercept. *Econometric Theory, 16,* 373–406.
Sahoo, M., Babu, S. M., & Dash, U. (2016). Current account sustainability in SAARC economies: Evidence from combined co-integration approach. *Theoretical and Applied Economics, 23*(4), 281–298.
Sahoo, M., Babu, S. M., & Dash, U. (2016). Long-Run Sustainability of current account balance of China and India: New evidence from combined cointegration test. *Intellectual Economics, 10*(2), 78–91.
Shastri, S., Giri, A. K., & Mohapatra, G. (2018). Testing the sustainability of current account for major south Asian economies: A panel data approach. *South Asia Economic Journal, 19*(1), 1–21.
Singh, T. (2015). Sustainability of current account deficits in India: An intertemporal perspective. *Applied Economics, 47*(46), 4934–4951.
World Bank. (2017). *World development indicators database.* Washington, DC: World Bank. Retrieved on July 20, 2018, from https://databank.worldbank.org/data/source/world-development-indicators

Chapter 10
Green-Field Versus Merger and Acquisition: Role of FDI in Economic Growth of South Asia

S. Chaudhury, N. Nanda, and B. Tyagi

1 Introduction

Economic liberalization has opened the door for flow of foreign capital investment in the majority of developing nations. Foreign investment, especially foreign direct investment (FDI), is a prime source of foreign exchange reserves which eases out the balance of payment constraint of economic growth. Additionally, it complements and/or substitutes domestic investment necessary for economic growth. In the last couple of decades, some of the developing countries including South-East Asian countries achieved significant economic growth by efficiently utilizing the large amount of FDI. However, South Asian nations primarily adopted restrictive policies post-independence. The success of other economies and persistence of low level of economic growth, high level of unemployment and infrastructure bottlenecks induced them to change their policy regime through economic reform. From the late 80s, most of the nations in the South Asian region adopted a market-oriented policy framework and opened their door to welcome foreign investors to integrate the domestic economy with other economies.

The unutilized potential of the huge consumer market, availability of skilled resources, strengthening financial systems, emerging but limited entrepreneurial class are some of the reasons making South Asian countries attractive destination for foreign investors. However, despite being the prime destination of investment,

S. Chaudhury (✉)
The Energy and Resources Institute, New Delhi, India
e-mail: saswatac@teri.res.in

N. Nanda
Council for Social Development, New Delhi, India
e-mail: nanda.nitya@gmail.com

B. Tyagi
Alliance for an Energy Efficient Economy, New Delhi, India
e-mail: bhawna.tyagi34@gmail.com

P. Lakhanpal et al. (eds.), *Trade, Investment and Economic Growth*,
https://doi.org/10.1007/978-981-33-6973-3_10

neither the investment pattern nor the economic growth experience is homogeneous across South Asian countries. Thus, it is interesting to analyse the differential impact of FDI inflows on the economic growth in these countries. This may help the policymakers to accommodate this differential aspect in the policy framework and focus on more sustainable and suitable strategy.

1.1 Trends in FDI—Global and South Asian Region

Global FDI inflows increased five folds in the last two decades and stood at USD 1.76 trillion in 2015. The relative share of developing countries increased up to 2014 in the total FDI inflows globally. In 2000–2014, the share of developing countries has increased from around 17% to 55%, while it has declined to 43% in 2015. During the 2010–15, the average growth rate of global FDI was 6.2%, while the growth rate for developed and developing countries was 12% and 4.2%, respectively. Post-1990s, Asian developing countries used to attract more than 50% of the FDI inflows among all developing countries. In the Asian region, South-East Asian region becomes the most preferred FDI destination. South Asian nations witnessed FDI inflows at the rate of 8.5% in this period.

Among South Asian countries, due to economic size and other factors such as infrastructure, India continues to be the 'most important' FDI hub followed by Bangladesh and Sri Lanka. Nearly 80% of South Asian FDI inflow destined towards India. The share (within South Asian FDI inflow) of Afghanistan, Bhutan, Nepal and Pakistan is less than 1%. Among other countries, Bangladesh (21%) witnessed the highest growth rate of FDI inflows followed by Maldives (19%) and India (13%) in the last five years.

Per capita FDI inflow was highest for developed countries at USD 474.4 in 2014 compared to USD 129.2 for developing countries while the global average was at USD 180.6. Among South Asian countries, it is the highest in Maldives at USD 1033.3 per capita. In case of India, per capita FDI inflow (USD 27.2) was slightly higher than that of South Asian Region (USD 23.2). In 2014, the contribution of FDI inflow in global GDP stood at 1.7% compared to 2.6% and 1.1%, respectively, for developing and developed countries. In the same year, FDI contributed approximately 1.4% to South Asian regional GDP while 12.2 and 1.7% to GDP of Maldives and India, respectively. Global FDI inflow was about 6.9% of global merchandise trade (in 2014). The corresponding figure was 8.6% for South Asia and 10.7% for India, while it was 111% for the Maldives. In gross capital formation, the contribution of FDI inflows was about 8–9% (average of 2010–14) at the global level, while it was approximately 4–5% for the South Asian region with an exceptional figure of more than 50% for the Maldives. The next section discusses some important and/or recent literature related to FDI-economic growth nexus.

2 Literature Review

Post-1990s, after the initiation of economic liberalization, the South Asian region witnessed significant growth in FDI inflows. However, FDI had a differential impact on individual countries depending on the domestic environment and the nature of FDI. Thus, it attracts the attention of researchers and policymakers and creates a demand for a proper and holistic analysis of FDI-economic growth dynamics.

Globally, viewpoints differ regarding the impact of FDI on economic growth and largely two schools of thoughts exist. First, the modernization theory argues that FDI contributes positively to economic growth through capital investment and knowledge transfer. The second school of thought is the dependency theory, which emphasizes the negative relationship between FDI and economic growth. As per this view, FDI creates a monopoly in the market and prevents full utilization of domestic resources and weakens the potential multiplier effect.

Many studies (e.g. Blomstrom et al. 1994 and Borenzstein et al. 1998) argued that FDI inflow stimulates the economic performance of the destination country through technology transfer and spillover effects. The spillover efficiency happens when local firms absorb the tangible and intangible assets embodied in FDI. In contrast, some studies (like Bloomstorm & Kokko, 2003) argued that FDI inflow does not necessarily ensure the knowledge spillover to the local industry. FDI benefit in terms of spillover effect can be only realized when domestic firms have the potential to absorb such spillovers.

However, there are studies (e.g. Singer, 1950 and Griffin, 1970) that indicate the existence of a negative relationship between FDI and economic growth, especially for developing nations. Saqib et al. (2013) observed the negative impact of foreign investment on the economic performance of Pakistan whereas the positive impact of domestic investment. Herzer (2012) studied the data for thirty-five years time period for developing countries and found a negative relationship between FDI and economic growth due to factors such as distortionary market policies, economic and political instability and lack of natural resources. However, Minhaj et al. (2007) concluded that both in the short and long run, FDI inflows have the potential to improve the socio-economic condition of an economy.

Some studies also indicated FDI has an insignificant effect on economic growth. Lund (2010) examined the relationship for both developed and developing countries but found an insignificant impact of FDI in developing countries. This study indicated that a minimum level of development is necessary to take full advantage of FDI. Similarly, Uwubanmwen and Ajao (2012) and Asheghian (2011) found an insignificant impact of FDI on the economic performance of Nigeria and Canada, respectively.

There are many studies which have identified some other factors which influence FDI-economic growth nexus. Trade openness has been identified by many studies (e.g. Iqbal et al. 2014; Agrawal, 2000 and Balasubramanyam et al. 1996) as a pre-requisite condition to utilize the potential benefits of FDI. Iram and Nishat (2009) found that factors such as macroeconomic stability, privatization and export-oriented policies are critical to realizing the positive impact of FDI on the economic growth of Pakistan. On the other hand, Asheghian (2011) identified total factor productivity and domestic investment are key factors in economic growth for Canada. However, Blomstrom et al. (1994) and Blomstrom and Kokko (2003) identified a significant role of the educated workforce to influence the impact of FDI through technology spillovers.

FDI inflow comes either via green-field mode (where the investment is utilized to build new facilities) or M&A route (where existing firms in the host country are acquired by the investor). But, it is well established (e.g. Blonigen (1997), Nocke and Yeaple (2004 and 2007)) that these modes are significantly different in nature. They are neither perfect substitute for each other nor have a similar impact on economic growth. While UNCTAD (2000) acknowledged that M&A FDI is less beneficial, there are studies which postulate that green-field FDI is less beneficial (Blonigen and Slaughter (2001)) or M&A is more beneficial (Bresman et al. (1999) and Conyon et al. (2002)). On the other hand, Liu and Zou (2008) found that positive contribution of green-field investment is more compared to M&A because the former induces both intra-industry and inter-industry spillovers while the latter one augments only inter-industry spillovers. But, their conclusion is based on a study of firm-level panel analysis for Chinese high-tech industries. However, Wang and Wong (2009) found that green-field investment has a significant positive impact on economic growth while the impact of M&A is negative using data for 84 countries over the period 1987–2001. On the other hand, using a cross-section analysis of 83 countries, Nanda (2009) concluded that not only M&A FDI is less beneficial for economic growth compared to green-field FDI, but M&A FDI may have an adverse impact on economic growth. Similarly, Neto et al. (2008) used panel data from 1996 to 2006 for 53 countries and concluded that green-field FDI has a significant positive impact both in developed and developing countries. They also found that M&A FDI has a significant negative effect on economic growth in developing countries but has an insignificant impact on developed countries.

Thus, there is no consensus in terms of the role of FDI and its composition (mode) in promoting economic growth in the existing literature. Moreover, there is a lack of recent data-based evidence especially in the context of South Asian countries. This study proposes to address this gap by conducting a holistic analysis of FDI-economic growth dynamics (role of FDI and its mode along with other factors) using the most recent data. The next section describes the methodology adopted to examine the FDI-economic growth nexus for South Asian countries.

3 Methodology

The paper has measured the contribution of FDI (overall and route-wise) to economic growth using panel data of eight South Asian countries for the period (1990–2014). We identified the factors which have significant potential to augment or retard the impact of FDI and analysed the role of those factors. However, 'labour' has been dropped from the list of explanatory variables considered in this study, because all South Asian countries are labour surplus economies. On the other hand, due to insufficient data on infrastructure (especially for Afghanistan and Bhutan), we have not considered 'infrastructure' as an independent variable and failed to measure its role. Since FDI like other investment requires a gestation period to contribute towards economic growth, we have considered the lagged values of FDI. Based on literature as well as statistical methods, the number of lags required has been identified. Moreover, the lagged FDI will also help to overcome the impact of economic growth on FDI. The next sections will describe the empirical model and the variables considered in the study.

3.1 Measure the Impact of Overall FDI

The study has used following empirical model to examine the nature and degree of FDI impact on economic growth:

$$Y_t^g = b_0 + b_1 * FDI_{t-m} + b_2 * K_{t-m} + b_3 * P_t + b_4 * ET_t + b_5 * CV_t + \varepsilon$$

where $b_i(i = 0, 1, 2 \ldots)$ refers to coefficients and measures the impact of independent variables on economic growth and direction of impact is shown by the sign.

t and m refer to time period and lag ($m = 1, 2, 3\ldots$), respectively

Y^g refers to the economic performance of the country measured, i.e. a growth rate of GDP.

FDI refers to net FDI inflow-GDP ratio used as a proxy for total FDI inflows.

K refers to the gross domestic capital formation which is a proxy for capital investment.

P refers to inflation and measured by GDP deflator/change in WPI (wholesale price index) or CPI (consumer price index).

ET refers to total export/total import/net export which is used as a proxy for external trade.

CV refers to other independent variables such as HDI (Human development index used as a proxy for livelihood status) or gross enrolment ratio/mean year of school/literacy rate (used as a proxy for the level of education or human capital factor) and/or any health indicator such asper capita health expenditure/health expenditure-GDP ratio/health output like maternal mortality rate/infant mortality rate.

And Ɛ refers to the error term and explains the impact not being captured by any of the explanatory variables.

3.2 Measure the Impact of Green-Field Versus M&A FDI

The study has used following empirical model to examine the differential impact of M&A and green-field FDI:

$$Y_t^g = b_0 + b_1 * \text{JFDI}_{t-m} + b_1 * K_{t-m} + b_3 * P_t + b_4 * ET_t + b_5 * CV_t + \varepsilon$$

where $b_i(i = 0, 1, 2 \ldots)$ refers to coefficients and measures the impact of independent variables on economic growth and direction of impact is shown by the sign.

t and m refer to time period and lag ($m = 1, 2, 3 \ldots$), respectively

Y^g refers to the economic performance of the country measured, i.e. a growth rate of GDP.

JFDI refers to net FDI inflow of specific routes to GDP ratio used as a proxy for different routes (green-field/M&A) of FDI inflow.

K refers to the gross domestic capital formation which is a proxy for capital investment.

P refers to inflation and measured by GDP deflator/change in WPI or CPI.

ET refers to total export/total import/net export which is used as a proxy for external trade.

CV refers to other independent variables such as HDI (used as a proxy for livelihood status) or gross enrolment ratio/mean year of school/literacy rate (used as a proxy for the level of education or human capital factor) and/or any health indicator such as per capita health expenditure/health expenditure-GDP ratio/health output like maternal mortality rate/infant mortality rate.

And $\mathcal{E}$ refers to the error term and explains the impact not being captured by any of the explanatory variables.

We have tested and rectified for the presence of any specification errors or if any occurred due to simple model specification. The results of the empirical analysis have been discussed in the next section.

3.3 Data Source and Data Period

The data is sourced from the database of World Economic Outlook spanning from 1990 to 2014 for variables such as GDP, inflation and exports. FDI flow data both overall, as well as route-wise (green-field and M&A), was retrieved from UNCTAD FDI statistics. Other data were collected from the database of World Development Indicators.

4 Empirical Results

STATA has been utilized to measure the impact of FDI using the panel data and model structure described in the previous sections. Regression results of FDI impact on economic growth for various combination of control variables were tabulated in the appendix section. This section will discuss the level and pattern of the impact of FDI and other determinants on economic growth. Prior to the regression analysis, the data was utilized to check for the presence of heteroscedasticity, auto-correlation and multi-collinearity using relevant statistical tests. Suitable statistical measures were applied on the data to get rid of any such issue if present.

4.1 Impact of Overall FDI

Previous year FDI (one year lagged) has a direct and significant effect on GDP growth of South Asian countries (as indicated in Appendix Table 1). The robustness of the finding confirmed by similarity in the nature of the impact even with several combinations of other control variables. Many other empirical studies (Germidis, 1977; Mansfield & Romeo, 1980 and Minhaj et al., 2007) found a similar positive significant effect of FDI on economic growth in the context of various developing countries. This study also found that domestic investment (measured by gross domestic capital formation) is another important determinant of economic growth in South Asian countries along with FDI. This study found that current year domestic investment has a consistent positive (but not statistically significant) impact on economic growth. Thus, it plays a complementary role of FDI in promoting economic growth. This study found that inflation has a significant inverse impact on economic growth in most cases. This finding indicates that the persistence of high inflation may harm economic growth and can even hinder the potential positive effect of FDI. Moreover, this study found a consistent positive (but not statistically significant) impact of HDI on the economic growth of South Asian countries. This indicates that improvement in HDI (in other words health and education) can promote economic growth and may induce a positive role of FDI. Finally, the role of export on economic growth is found to be ambiguous in the case of South Asian countries. The effect is mixed (positive and negative) across various cases. This indicates that the composition of exported items may determine economic growth.

4.2 Impact of M&A Versus Green-Field FDI

This study has found that previous year M&A FDI has an inverse effect on the economic growth of South Asian countries (as indicated in Appendix Table 2). The effect is not statistically significant but consistent across the choice of control variables. Based on a cross-country analysis, Nanda (2009) concluded that FDI inflow is not always beneficial for economic growth especially if FDI enters as M&A. The finding of the current study is not only in line with Nanda (2009), but a step forward to establish that in case of South Asian countries, FDI may even hinder economic growth when it flows as M&A. The study found that previous year domestic investment has neither significant nor unambiguous effect on economic growth in the context of South Asian countries. However, the current year domestic investment has a consistent significant positive effect on economic growth. The study found that in the South Asian context, domestic investment is relatively more important to promote economic growth when the nature of FDI flow is M&A. Thus, domestic investment has the potential to offset the detrimental effect of M&A FDI on economic growth. The influential role of domestic investment in economic growth was also highlighted by Saqib et al. (2013). This study failed to get any significant effect of inflation and HDI on the economic growth of the South Asian countries. However, the study found that, export (as a proxy of external trade) has a positive impact on economic growth, but not significant in all cases.

Previous year FDI flow in the form of green-field investment has a positive and consistent (but not significant in all cases) effect on the economic growth of South Asian countries (as indicated in Appendix Table 3). This result reveals that FDI inflows will augment economic growth when FDI flows in the form of green-field investment (new business set-up, new job creation). This finding confirms the Nanda (2009) conclusion that green-field FDI is more valuable as it results in knowledge transfer and hence favourable for economic growth. However, Nanda (2009) concluded the constructive role of green-field FDI with cross-country data, while this study concluded the same using panel data in the South Asian context. On the other hand, this study failed to reach any definite conclusion about the role of domestic investment when FDI inflows in the form of green-field investment. Similarly, the role of inflation and HDI on economic growth are also mixed and ambiguous. However, this study found that export has consistent and positive (significant in many cases) effect on economic growth.

5 Conclusion

Using panel data, this study has analysed the role of overall FDI inflow and its nature (M&A versus green-field) on the economic growth of South Asian countries. FDI needs some gestation period to influence economic growth, while economic growth may have some causal influence on current year FDI flow. Thus, this study has considered the lagged period (previous year) FDI to avoid both the issues. The study has also identified some other factors which have a significant role in determining economic growth and measured the level and extent of their impact. The study found that previous year FDI has a significant effect on economic growth in South Asia, but the nature of FDI flow also plays an important role. FDI inflow in the form of M&A may have a detrimental effect on economic growth and failed to serve the desired purpose. However, FDI as green-field investment is favourable for economic growth through new employment generation and knowledge transfer. Domestic investment also plays an important role in supplementing the impact of FDI. Thus, policymakers need to distinguish between the nature of FDI as well as to channelize the available investment (both FDI and domestic investment) in a proper direction to ensure desired economic growth. Unavailability of suitable data for the selected period in case of Afghanistan and Bhutan (Nepal and Maldives also in some cases) is a shortcoming of the study. The presence of missing data led to lesser degrees of freedom in few cases which might have reduced the significance level of some of the estimates.

Appendix

See Table 1, 2 and 3.

Table 1 Impact of overall FDI on growth

Dependent variable: Growth rate of GDP				
Overall FDI				
	b/se	b/se	b/se	b/se
FDI (lag 1)	366.152***	260.102***	266.385**	217.347**
	(85.48)	(72.23)	(100.74)	(76.89)
Inflation	−0.371*	−0.379*	−0.318	−0.331*
	(0.17)	(0.15)	(0.17)	(0.15)
Domestic investment (lag 1)	−0.103	−0.033		
	(0.10)	(0.08)		
HDI	14.085		15.091	
	(10.47)		(14.11)	
Export	−0.087	0.03	−0.209	−0.033
	(0.12)	(0.09)	(0.14)	(0.10)
Domestic investment			0.137	0.072
			(0.13)	(0.09)
Constant	5.201	9.476***	1.561	7.964**
	(4.67)	(2.36)	(6.65)	(2.75)
N	125	148	124	146

Note *Significant at 1% level, **Significant at 5% level and ***Significant at 10% level; *Source* Author's own calculations

Table 2 Impact of merger and acquisition FDI on Growth

Dependent variable: Growth rate of GDP						
M&A FDI						
	b/se	b/se	b/se	b/se	b/se	b/se
M&A FDI (lag 1)	−192.178	−183.996	−193.174	−261.209	−282.929	−268.612
	(240.66)	(237.33)	(239.76)	(232.72)	(230.41)	(225.33)
Inflation	-0.218	-0.178	0.289			
	(0.35)	(0.32)	(0.26)			
Domestic investment (lag 1)	0.188	0.181	0.137	0.125	0.131	0.123
	(0.26)	(0.26)	(0.25)	(0.25)	(0.25)	(0.24)
HDI	0.067		0.008	-0.174		-0.164
	(0.23)		(0.22)	(0.22)		(0.21)
Export	65.022*	63.849*		13.797	16.647	
	(29.19)	(28.70)		(28.51)	(28.20)	
Domestic investment				0.730*	0.633*	0.840**
				(0.33)	(0.30)	(0.25)
Constant	−24.356	−23.327	0.765	−14.168	−16.792	-9.363
	(13.27)	(12.70)	(6.35)	(12.81)	(12.34)	(6.08)
N	74	74	78	74	74	77

Note *Significant at 1% level, **Significant at 5% level and ***Significant at 10% level; *Source* Author's own calculations

Table 3 Impact of green-field FDI on Growth

Dependent variable: Growth rate of GDP						
Green-field FDI						
	b/se	b/se	b/se	b/se	b/se	b/se
Green-field FDI (lag 1)	371.258**	352.142**	168.408	257.939*	212.316	115.374
	(127.63)	(119.33)	(94.50)	(129.82)	(121.89)	(96.20)
Inflation	−0.391	−0.409	0.17			
	(0.22)	(0.22)	(0.13)			
Domestic investment (lag 1)	−0.299	−0.292	−0.339*	−0.342*	−0.328	−0.308*
	(0.17)	(0.17)	(0.15)	(0.17)	(0.17)	(0.15)
HDI	−0.07		0.083	−0.162		0.111
	(0.16)		(0.14)	(0.16)		(0.14)
Export	51.361*	52.982*		7.36	10.228	
	(21.29)	(20.88)		(20.70)	(20.51)	
Domestic Investment				0.434	0.406	0.343*
				(0.22)	(0.22)	(0.13)
Constant	−7.403	-9	3.607	−2.373	−5.924	−1.659
	(9.71)	(8.95)	(4.37)	(9.55)	(8.90)	(4.71)
N	125	125	148	124	124	146

Note *Significant at 1% level, **Significant at 5% level and ***Significant at 10% level; *Source* Author's own calculations

References

Agrawal, P. (2000). Economic impact of foreign direct investment in South Asia. In A. Mattoo & R. M. Stern (Eds.), *India and the WTO*. Washington: World Bank and Oxford University Press.

Asheghian, P. (2011). Economic growth determinants and foreign direct investment causality in Canada. *International Journal of Business and Social Science, 2*(11), 1–9.

Balasubramanyam, V. N., Salisu, M., & Dapsoford, D. (1996). Foreign direct investment and growth in EP and IS countries. *Economic Journal, 106,* 92–105.

Blomstrom, M., & Kokko, A. (2003) The. *Economics of foreign direct investment incentives.* National Bureau of Economic Research Working Paper 9489

Blomstrom, M., Lipsey, R., & Zejan, M. (1994). What explains growth in developing countries? *Convergence of productivity: Cross-national studies and historical evidence* (pp. 243–259)

Blonigen, B. (1997). Firm-specific assets and the link between exchange rates and foreign direct investment. *American Economic Review, 87,* 447–465.

Blonigen, B., & Slaughter, M. (2001). Foreign-affiliate activity and U.S. skill upgrading. *Review of Economics and Statistics, 83,* 362–376.

Bresman, H., Birkinshawand, J., & Nobel, R. (1999). Knowledge transfer in international acquisitions. *Journal of International Business Studies, 30,* 439–462.

Borenzstein, E., Gregorio, J. D. & Lee, J. W. (1998). How does Foreign direct investment affect economic growth? *Journal of International Economics, 45*, 115–35.

Conyon, M., Girma, S., Thompson, S., & Wright, P. (2002). The productivity and wage effect of foreign acquisition in the UnitedKingdom. *Journal of Industrial Economics, 50*, 85–102.

Germidis, D. (1977). *Transfer of technology by multinational corporations*. Paris: Development Centre of Organization for Economic Cooperation and Development.

Griffin, K. B. (1970). Foreign capital, domestic savings and development. *Oxford Bulletin of Economics and Statistics, 32*, 99–112.

Herzer, D. (2012) How does FDI really affects developing countries growth? *Review of International Economics, 20*(2), 396–414

Iqbal, N., Ahmad, N., Haider, Z., & Anwar, S. (2014). Impact of foreign direct investment (FDI) on GDP: A case study from Pakistan. *International Letters of Social and Humanistic Sciences, 16*, 73–80.

Iram and Nishat. (2009). Sector level analysis of fdi-growth nexus: a case study of Pakistan. *The Pakistan Development Review, 48*(4), 875–882.

Liu, X., & Zou, H. (2008). The impact of Greenfield FDI and mergers and acquisitions on innovation in Chinese high-tech industries. *Journal of World Business, 43*(3), 352–364

Lund, M. T. (2010). *Foreign direct investment: catalyst of economic growth*? Doctoral Dissertation, Department of Economics. The University of Utah

Mansfield, E., & Romeo, A. (1980). Technology transfers to overseas subsidiaries by US-based firms. *Quarterly Journal of Economics, 95*(4), 737–750

Minhaj, S. Q., Ahmed, R., & Hai, S. S. (2007). *Globalization, foreign direct investment and the human development index: The case of Pakistan*. Department of Economics, University of Karachi. Pakistan. Unpublished Paper

Nanda, N.(2009). Growth effects of FDI: Is green-field greener? *Perspectives on Global Development and Technology, 8*(1), 26–47

Neto, P., Brandão, A., & Cerqueira, A. (2008). The impact of FDI, cross border mergers and acquisitions and Greenfield investments on economic growth. *TheIUP Journal of Business Strategy*, 24–44

Nocke, V., & Yeaple, S. (2004). Mergers and the composition of international commerce (No. w10405). National Bureau of Economic Research.

Nocke, V., & Yeaple, S. (2007). Cross-border mergers and acquisitions vs. greenfield foreign direct investment: The role of firm heterogeneity. *Journal of International Economics, 72*(2), 336–365.

Saqib, N., Masnoon, M., & Rafique, N. (2013). Impact of foreign direct investment on economic growth of Pakistan. *Advances in Management & Applied Economics, 3*(1), 35–45.

Singer, H. W. (1950). The distribution of gains between investing and borrowing countries. *American Economic Review, 40*, 473–485.

The World Factbook CIA. https://www.cia.gov/llibrary/publications/the-world-factbook/fields/2012.html. Retrieved on December 12, 2016

The World Factbook CIA. https://www.cia.gov/Library/publications/the-world-factbook/fields/2048.html. Retrieved on December 12, 2016

Uwubanmwen, A. E., & Ajao, M. (2012). the determinants and impacts of foreign direct investment in Nigeria. *International Journal of Business and Management, 7*(24), 67–77.

UNCTAD FDI Statistics data base

Wang, M., & Sunny Wong, M. C. (2009). What drives economic growth? The case of cross-border M&A and Greenfield FDI activities. *Kyklos, 62*(2), 316–330

Chapter 11
Risk Modeling by Coherent Measure Using Family of Generalized Hyperbolic Distributions

Prabir Kumar Das

1 Introduction

The value at risk (VaR) is a comprehensive probabilistic measure of market risk. We apply it for assessing risk and selection of portfolios, among other applications (RiskMetrics Group, 1994; McNeil et al., 2005, Jorion, 2006). However, VaR estimates can be subjected to model risk arising due to incorrect model specification and the risk of error resulting from erroneous implementation. If a financial asset's risk behavior was not captured correctly, its price would be misleading and may result in inefficient allocation of funds. Under the occurrence of tail events, the loss can be more than the estimate of VaR (Grootveld & Hallerbach, 2004). It is a stylized fact that the Indian market volatility is high, resulting in more probability of higher loss. This study computes Sensex's market risk using the coherent risk measure, namely expected shortfall (ES). Coherent risk measure is theoretically more appealing than VaR due to its axioms. These axioms are translational invariance, monotonicity, subadditivity, and positive homogeneity (Artzner et al., 1996, 1997; Artzner, 1999). The risk measures viz., VaR, and ES are quantile values located in the tails of a distribution. The stylized fact of the fat tail distribution of return cannot be modeled using a normal probability distribution. The generalized hyperbolic family of distributions was reported to be appropriate for describing return series (Barndorff-Nielsen, 1998; Eberlein & Prause, 1998; Prause, 1999). A review of estimation methods of the expected shortfall was carried out by Nadarajah et al. (2014). Several studies were conducted on risk measures (VaR and ES) using Sensex (Jadhav et al., 2009; Chauhan, 2011; Roy, 2011; Karmakar, 2013). Jadhav et al.'s (2009) work was based on the nonparametric estimation method, which lacks statistical power. Roy (2011) used VaR and estimation method employed was a historical simulation. Extreme value theory was employed by Chauhan (2011) and Karmakar (2013). In recent work,

P. K. Das (✉)
Indian Institute of Foreign Trade, Kolkata, India
e-mail: pkdas@iift.edu

P. Lakhanpal et al. (eds.), *Trade, Investment and Economic Growth*,
https://doi.org/10.1007/978-981-33-6973-3_11

Burdorf and Vuuren (2018) compared VaR and ES using a normal distribution. To the best of this author's knowledge, no attempt was made to compute VaR and ES using a generalized hyperbolic family of distributions for Sensex. This study's objectives are as follows: (i) To identify the best-fit probability model for describing the return series of BSE Sensex (ii) To employ the best-fit probability model to compute coherent risk.

2 Methodology

The generalized hyperbolic distribution (GHD) and its variants, namely, the hyperbolic (HYP) and normal inverse Gaussian (NIG) distributions can be used to model return series. The probability density function of the GHD is given below:

$$gh(x; \lambda, \alpha, \beta, \delta, \mu) = A(\lambda, \alpha, \beta, \delta)(\delta^2 + (x-\mu)^2)^{(\lambda-\frac{1}{2})/2} * B_{\lambda-\frac{1}{2}}\left(\alpha\sqrt{\delta^2 + (x-\mu)^2} \exp(\beta(x-\mu)\right), \quad (1)$$

where $A(\lambda, \alpha, \beta, \delta)$ is given by

$$A(\lambda, \alpha, \beta, \delta) = \frac{(\alpha^2 - \beta^2)^{\lambda/2}}{\sqrt{2\pi}\alpha^{\lambda-1/2}\delta^{\lambda} B_{\lambda}(\delta\sqrt{\alpha^2 - \beta^2})},$$

furthermore, B_v is the modified third-order Bessel function with index value v.

Further details about the probability distribution are available in Barndorff–Nielsen (1997, 1998). The emerging markets' indices and the Bucharest stock exchange index were described using NIG and GHD, respectively (Cepni et al., 2013; Baciu, 2015). The HYP and NIG can be obtained by setting $\lambda = 1$ and $-1/2$, respectively. The parameters of the distribution are estimated using the maximum likelihood method. The log-likelihood (LL) function is maximized numerically. Coherent risk measures can be obtained from the best-fit model based on Akaike Information Criterion (AIC) and LL. AIC is a measure of the relative fit of the model to the sample data. The best model is the one with the smallest AIC. The AIC is defined as

$$\text{AIC} = 2k - 2\text{LL}, \quad (2)$$

where k is the number of parameters in the model, and LL is the maximum value of the likelihood function of the fitted model. The ES is the average of the worst $100(1-\alpha)\%$ of losses. For a continuous variable, it is defined as (Dowd 2005; Pfaff 2016):

$$ES_\alpha = \frac{1}{1-\alpha}\int_\alpha^1 q_p dp, \quad (3)$$

where α is the confidence level, $p = 1-\alpha$ and q_p is the p-quantile of a stock's profit/loss over some holding period. We define the VaR as

$$\text{VaR} = -q_p. \tag{4}$$

We employ the R software environment and IBM SPSS for carrying out the computation (R Core Team, 2016, IBM, 2017).

3 Results

We collected the daily adjusted closing values of BSE Sensex from Yahoo Finance (2018) https://in.finance.yahoo.com from November 6, 2013, to November 5, 2018. The missing observations were imputed using linear interpolation. The return series was obtained by

$$\text{bseret} = \frac{P_i - P_{i-1}}{P_{i-1}}, \tag{5}$$

where P_i and P_{i-1} are the ith and the $(i-1)$th values of the original prices, respectively. The return series is denoted by bseret. The summary statistics of the series are presented in Table 1.

The excess kurtosis and skewness were different from zero, indicating deviation from a normal distribution. The empirical distribution of the return series of BSE Sensex is depicted in Fig. 1. The density plot shows a fat tail on both ends, indicating the occurrence of extreme events. It depicts the deviation from the normal density. The QQ plot is drawn and is depicted in Fig. 2, to understand the extent of deviation

Table 1 Return of BSE sensex: summary statistics

Measure	bseret
Mean	0.000453
Standard Error	0.000238
Median	0.000590
Standard deviation	0.008364
Sample variance	0.000070
Kurtosis	5.782999
Skewness	−0.386318
Range	0.093157
Minimum	−0.059362
Maximum	0.033795
Observations	1232

Source Author

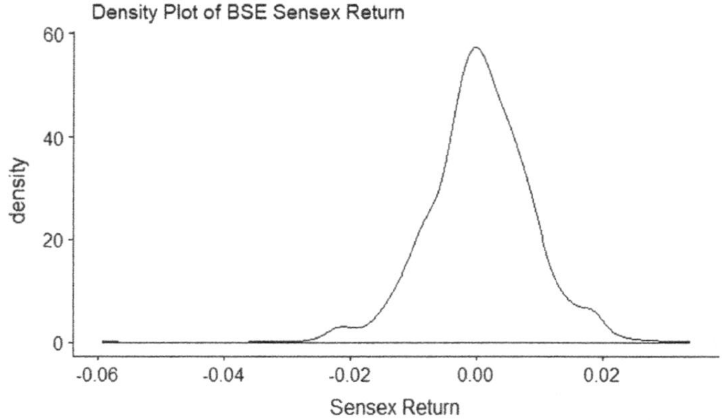

Fig. 1 Density plot of return series of BSE sensex. *Source* Author

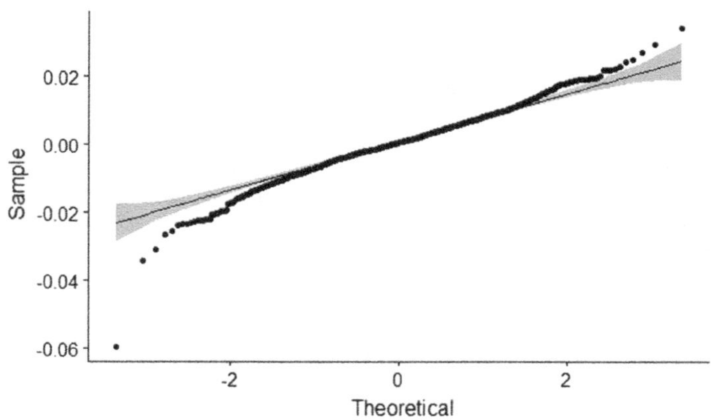

Fig. 2 QQ plot of sensex return. *Source* Author

from normality. It shows that the deviation from normality is mostly on the two ends of the distribution.

In Table 2, we present the results of the analytical tests. The four tests of normality,

Table 2 Tests of normality

	Statistic	*df*	*P*-Value
Kolmogorov–Smirnov[a]	0.047	1232	0.000
Shapiro–Wilk	0.979	1232	0.000
Anderson–Darling	3.899		0.000
Jarque–Bera	428.23	2	0.000

[a] Lilliefors Significance Correction
Source Author

viz Kolmogorov–Smirnov, Shapiro–Wilk, Anderson–Darling, and Jarque–Bera, were employed. The results clearly show that the return series is not normally distributed.

To obtain an appropriate probability distribution for the return series, probability distributions viz. GHD, HYP, NIG, and normal were fitted to the return series. In Fig. 3, we present the fitted densities superimposing on the empirical density.

The daily return of BSE Sensex fitted better with the GHD than with the HYP and NIG distributions, especially in the tail regions. In Fig. 4, we depict the plot of empirical density and the probability density function of GHD.

In Table 3, out of three models, the GHD model is found superior over NIG and HYP based on AIC and LL values. However, the difference between the GHD and NIG log-likelihood is minimal, and so is the GHD and HYP. To find out if there is any significant difference in the explanatory power of GHD to HYP, and GHD to NIG, hypothesis testing can be conducted. The null hypothesis of the two distributions' equal explanatory power, namely GHD and HYP, is tested using the likelihood ratio test (statistic $L = 0.8456$, p-value $= 0.56$). We cannot reject the null hypothesis with one df at 95% confidence level. The corresponding test statistic for GHD and NIG ($L = 0.9797$,p-value $= 0.84$) depicts that we cannot reject the null hypothesis of the equal explanatory power of GHD and NIG with one df at 95% confidence

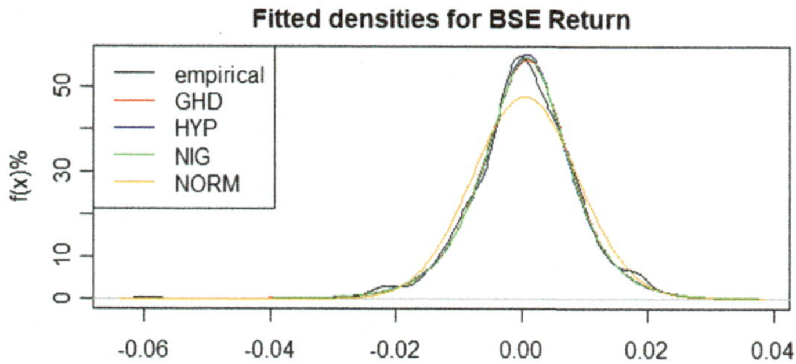

Fig. 3 Superimposed densities on empirical density. *Source* Author

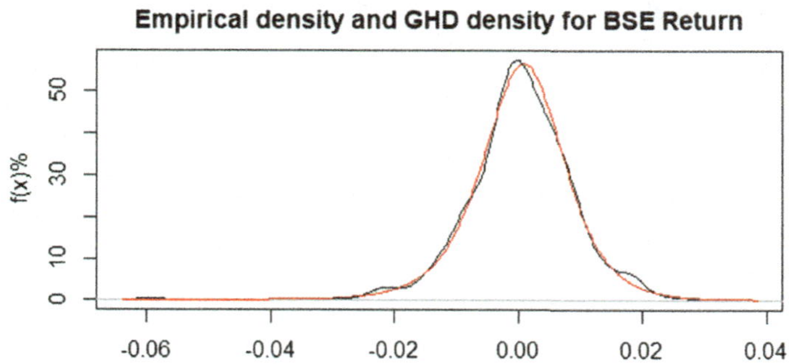

Fig. 4 Empirical and GHD densities. *Source* Author

Table 3 Results of distributions fitted to return series of BSE sensex

Distribution	AIC	LL	λ	$\overline{\alpha}$	μ	σ	γ
NIG	8353.35	4180.67	−0.5	1.7214	0.0012	0.0083	−0.0008
HYP	8353.05	4180.53	1.0	1.4000	0.0012	0.0083	−0.0007
GHD	8351.39	4180.69	−1.4528	1.6094	0.0012	0.0083	−0.0008

Source Author

level. Hence, we can consider the GHD and its two variants HYP and NIG, equally adequate in describing the return distribution of BSE Sensex. The VaR and ES are computed from GHD, HYP, and NIG probability distributions using Sensex's return data. The VaR of empirical and GHD, and the VaR of empirical, GHD, HYP, NIG, and normal are depicted in Figs. 5 and 6, respectively. These measures are computed over a range starting from 0.1 to 5%. The computed path of the VaR and ES is compared to their empirical counterparts. Normal VaR and GHD family-based VaR are similar up to 97%, whereas normal VaR provides a conservative estimate beyond 97%. However, ES's estimate is found to be different for all the models, even at the 95% level. The underestimation is less severe for the GHD family-based models than the normal distribution-based model for almost all the levels (Figs. 5, 6, and 7).

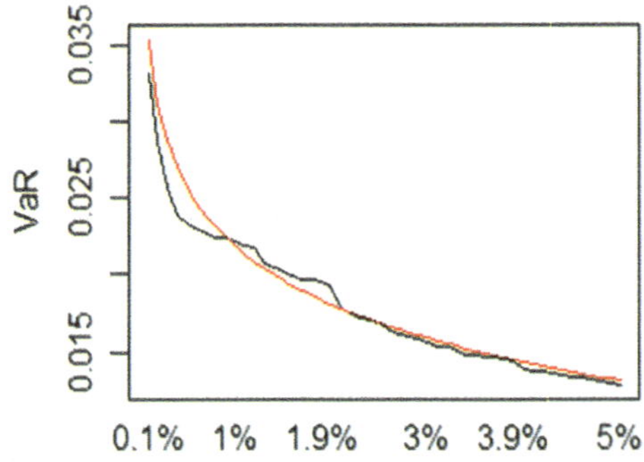

Fig. 5 VAR of empirical and GHD. *Source* Author

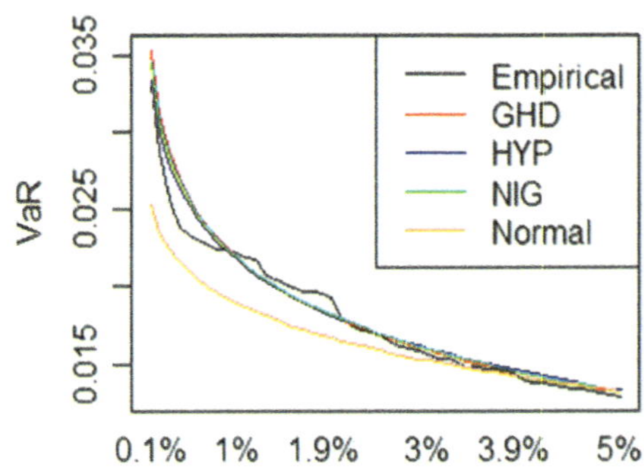

Fig. 6 VAR of empirical and fitted densities. *Source* Author

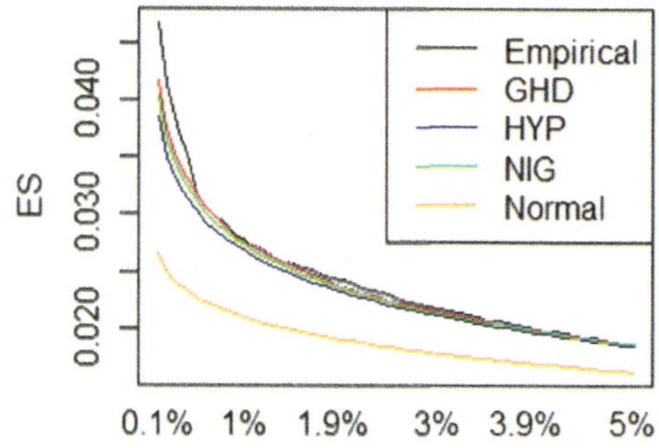

Fig. 7 ES of empirical and predicted densities. *Source* Author

4 Conclusions

The normal distribution fails to capture extreme risk events of Sensex. The risk measures, viz. VaR, and ES, which are computed using the normal distribution, are too conservative. It is imperative to identify suitable probability distribution for computation of risk measure, particularly the expected shortfall. The family of generalized hyperbolic distributions is more appropriate than the normal distribution for describing Sensex's return series. The coherent risk measure, viz. the expected shortfall, based on GHD, is found to adequately model the risk trajectory for levels of significance ranging from 95 to 99.9%. Extreme value distributions and conditional distributions can be considered to present a comparative assessment of risk.

References

Artzner, P., Delbaen, F., Eber, J., & Heath, D. (1996). *A characterization of measures of risk.* Technical Report 1186. Ithaca, NY: School of Operations Research and Industrial Engineering, College of Engineering, Cornell University.

Artzner, P., Delbaen, F., Eber, J. M., & Heath, D. (1997). Thinking coherently. *Risk, 10*(11), 68–71.

Artzner, P. (1999). Coherent measures of risk. *Mathematical Finance, 9,* 203–228.

Baciu, O. A. (2015). Generalized hyperbolic distributions: Empirical evidence on Bucharest stock exchange. *the Review of Finance and Banking, 7*(1), 7–18.

Barndorff Nielsen, O. (1997). Normal Gaussian distributions and stochastic volatility modelling. *Scandinavian Journal of Statistics, 24,* 1–13.

Barndorff-Nielsen, O. (1998). Processes of normal inverse Gaussian type. *Finance and Stochastics, 2,* 41–68.

Burdorf, T., & van Gay, V. (2018). An evaluation and comparison of value at risk and expected shortfall. *Investment Management and Financial Innovations, 15*(4), 17–34.

Cepni, O., Goncu, A., Karahan, M. O., & Kuzubas, T. U. (2013). *Goodness-of-fit of the Heston, Variance-Gamma and Normal-Inverse Gaussian models.* Working Papers 2013/16, Bogazici University, Department of Economics.

Chauhan, G. S. (2011). Modelling of extreme market risk using extreme value theory (EVT): An empirical exposition for Indian and global stock indices Indore. *Management Journal, 3*(1), 23–33.

Dowd, K. (2005). *Measuring Market Risk* (2nd ed.). New York: Wiley Finance, Wiley.

Eberlein, E., & Prause, K. (1998). *The generalized hyperbolic model: financial derivatives and risk measures*. FDM Preprint 56, University of Freiburg.
Grootveld, H., & Hallerbach, W. G. (2004). Upgrading value-at-risk from diagnostic metric to decision variables: A wise thing to do? In G. Szego (Ed.), *Risk Measures for the 21st Century* (pp. 33–50). Chichester: Wiley.
IBM SPSS. (2017). IBM Corp. Released 2017. *IBM SPSS Statistics for Windows*, Version 25.0. Armonk, NY: IBM Corp.
Jadhav Deepak, T. V., Ramanathan, U. V., & Nimbalkar, N. (2009). Modified estimators of the expected shortfall. *Journal of Emerging Market Finance, 8*(2), 87–107.
Jorian, P. (2006). *Value at risk, the new Benchmark for managing financial risk* (3rd edn.). McGraw Hill.
Karmakar, M. (2013). Estimation of tail-related risk measures in the Indian stock market: An extreme value approach. *Review of Financial Economics, 22*(3), 79–85.
McNeil, A., Frey, R., & Embrechts, P. (2005). *Quantitative risk management: Concepts techniques and tools*. Princeton, NJ: Princeton University Press.
Nadarajah, S., Bo, Z., Stephen, C. (2014). Estimation methods for expected shortfall. *Journal of Quantitative Finance, 14*(2), 271–291.
Pfaff Pfaff, B. (2016). *Financial risk modelling and portfolio optimization with R* (2nd ed.). Wiley.
Prause, K. (1999). *How to use NIG laws to measure market risk FDM Preprint 65*. University of Freiburg.
Roy, I. (2011). Estimating value at risk (VaR) using filtered historical simulation in the indian capital market. *Reserve Bank of India Occasional Papers, 32*(2), 1–18.
RiskMetrics Group. (1994). *RiskMetrics technical document Technical report, J.P.* New York: Morgan.
R Core Team. (2016). *R: A language and environment for statistical computing R foundation for statistical computing Vienna*. Austria.
Yahoo Finance. (2018). https://in.finance.yahoo.com.

Chapter 12
Impact of Macroeconomic Variables on Stock Market—An Empirical Study

K. Dhingra and S. Kapil

1 Introduction

One of the most important areas of finance is investigating the influence of economic factors on stock market returns. Since 1991 in Indian economy, under the changes brought by economic reforms, capital market in India has witnessed changes, on adoption of liberalization and globalization policies by the Government. By stabilizing the financial sector, a sound financial market induces growth in economy, which plays a significant part in the base of a firm and effectual fiscal system of an economy. Ray (2012) as well as Patel (2012) observed that stock markets replicate the health of the country's economy, which plays a critical part in the financial system of each nation. It plays a main role in intermediation of emerging nations. From aggregate economy point of view, the stock market is of prime importance. Presently, stock markets are an essential driving force of market-built nation as well as it is one of the chief elements of acquiring finances for Indian Companies, facilitating the economic development. Flannery and Protopapadakis (2002) said that directly or indirectly various national and international elements impact the performance of stock market. By utilizing investment towards the shareholders and the entrepreneurs, a vigorous and prosperous stock market can be taken as indicator of national economic growth.

Actually, Indian stock market is one the evolving markets in the sphere. In terms of volatility or unpredictability, the price range of securities changes in very short span of time. It has been observed that too much unpredictability proves to be a stumbling block in functioning of financial markets. Further, according to Ahmed (2008), the stock markets of evolving nations counting India are subtle to elements

K. Dhingra (✉) · S. Kapil
IIFT, Delhi, New Delhi, India
e-mail: kdhingra01@gmail.com

S. Kapil
e-mail: sheebakapil15@gmail.com

P. Lakhanpal et al. (eds.), *Trade, Investment and Economic Growth*,
https://doi.org/10.1007/978-981-33-6973-3_12

such as variations in the level of economic activities, alterations in political and international economic environment and also connected to the transformations in other macroeconomic elements. Occasionally, share prices can seem separated from economic factors, as movements in the stock market can be fairly unstable. Some fundamental causes have robust effect over the movement of share prices and the stock market in common. Gurloveleen (2015) explained that for any shareholder in the stock market, unpredictability is the foremost concern as their return is contingent on numerous tasks in the economy system. It is one of the utmost significant features of any stock market, which is also an imperative necessary statistical risk process. According to Kumar (2011), instability can be expended to measure the market peril of a specific tool or an all-inclusive portfolio of implements. This can be conveyed in distinctive modes, and statistically, unpredictability of an arbitrary variable is its standard deviation. Sireesha (2013) elaborated that in everyday real-world lifetime, it is computed for all types of casual financial variables such as stock returns, interest rates and the market value of a portfolio where stock return impulsiveness measures the random inconsistency of the stock returns. This is to take the average range for all period, from the low-price worth to the high price worth. This range is then stated as a percentage of the commencement of the era. Standard Deviation of stock prices explains variation between actual or closing price and average value or mean closing price. Higher the variation, more volatile the prices are in stock market.

The different school of thoughts like classical theory by Adam Smith, Theory by David Ricardo, Malthus, John Stuart emphasized the significance of macroeconomic factors under various assumptions in an economy. The economic environment composed of macroeconomic variables displays the trend in the economy. Also, according to Liu and Shrestha (2008), the economic policies of an economy impact the stock market. According to Hojatallah and Ramanarayana (2011), there was influence of FPI on volatility of Indian Stock Market during Financial Crisis. Hosseinin (2011) opined that there stands relationship between stock market prices and macroeconomic variables of India and China. In another study by Tripathi (2011) examining the weak form of market efficiency and cause and effect relationship was established between macroeconomic variables and Indian stock market. Mishra (2012) have justified the association between certain macroeconomic variables, namely, exchange rate, interest rate, FPI, industrial production with indices of stock exchange, i.e. Nifty and Sensex. As per some other scholars, Victor (1992), Peiro (1996), Srivastava (2010) and Humpe and Macmillan (2009), the stock market is efficient and could predict the changes in economic variables. On the other hand, authors like Rapach et al (2005), Schwert (1990) and Wasserfallen (1989) have analysed under different circumstances the factors impacting the national and international economics. Bhunia (2012) analysed that the growth rate of GDP was influenced by the stock prices, exchange rates and prices of oil. So, Indian stock market is subtle to factors like political environment, economic environment, financial environment, international environment. The study takes into consideration nine macroeconomic variables—foreign portfolio investment (FPI), inflation (WPI & CPI), index of industrial production (IIP), exchange rate, trade balance, call money rate and gold prices and indices of Indian stock market, Nifty and Sensex.

- Factors That Affect Volatility
  - Interest Rates (CMR)
    - Inflation (CPI & WPI)
    - Interest rates (CMR)
    - Exchange rate (Dollar Price)
    - Foreign portfolio investment (FPI)
    - Money supply (M3)
    - Trade balance (TB)
    - Gold price (GP)
    - Index of industrial production (IIP).

- Factors That Affect Volatility

The changes in economic factors such as tax and interest rate policy leads to unpredictability in the stock market. For example, the central bank arrays the short-term interest rates for overnight borrowing by banks. When they make modification the overnight rate, it may reason stock markets to counter, occasionally viciously. Variations in inflation movements affect the long-term stock market trends and unpredictability. Naka et al. (1999) explained that augmented stock market unpredictability can also be triggered by industry and sector elements. For example, in the oil sector, a chief weather storm in a vital generating region can instigate prices of oil to jolt up. As a consequence, the price of oil-related stocks will trail suit. Some stakeholders will get advantage from the higher prices of oil whereas other stakeholders will be upset due volatility of stock prices.

- Inflation (CPI & WPI)

Inflation is an upsurge in the overall level of prices, or, otherwise, it is a reduction in the worth of money. Inflation is one of those macroeconomic variables that disturb every Indian citizen, regardless of an investor, borrower or lender, practically every day. Inflation is seen as unconstructive news by the stock markets, because it inclines to restraint consumer expenditure and therefore corporate profits. It also disturbs the worth of the domestic currency unfavourably in the foreign exchange markets. The two recurrently used processes of inflation in India are built on the wholesale price index (WPI) and the consumer price index (CPI).The overnight call money or the inter-bank money market rate is seemingly the most thoroughly observed variable in everyday manner of monetary processes and often aids as a functioning object for policy reasons. This rate is entirely market-driven and reliant on the demand–supply equilibrium relationships. Variations in the CMR disturb the Indian stock markets by disturbing the corporate profits, general demand for goods and services in the economy.

- Exchange Rate (Dollar Price)

Apart from elements such as interest rates and inflation, the exchange rate is one of the utmost significant causes of a nation's relative level of economic health. Gay (2008) states that exchange rates show a dynamic part in a country's level of trade, which is analytical to each free market economy in the world. For this cause, exchange rates are amongst the most observed and governmentally deployed economic measures. A higher currency builds a country's exports more luxurious and imports inexpensive in foreign markets; a lower currency builds a country's exports inexpensive and its imports more luxurious in foreign markets. The stock market will get advantage when the domestic currency value is escalating.

- Foreign Portfolio Investment (FPI)

FPI comprises a shareholder or investment fund that is from or registered in a state outside of the one in which it is presently financing. Portfolio investors comprise hedge funds, insurance companies, pension funds and mutual funds. The period is used most ordinarily in India to mention to outside corporations financing in the financial markets of India. International institutional investors must register with the Securities and Exchange Board of India to partake in the market. FPI is permissible to arrive into our nation only through stock exchanges either in the form of equity or debt. Thus, it creates an influence on the increase or decrease of Sensex, since FPI is permitted to be purchased or sold daily. The everyday transaction of FPI is the object following the unpredictability in the stock markets undertaking to a larger level. It has been witnessed that Sensex upsurges when there are affirmative inflows of FPIs and decline when there are negative FPI inflows.

- Money supply (M3)

It is an imperative variable to steady the economy because it can be expended for instantaneous transactions. Monetary aggregates, known also as "money supply", are the quantity of currency obtainable within the economy to procurement of goods and services. M3 is a broad monetary aggregate that contains all physical currency flowing in the economy (banknotes and coins), operational deposits in central bank, money in current accounts, saving accounts, money market deposits, certificates of deposit and all other deposits.

- Trade balance (TB)

It displays the variance amongst the monetary value of imports and exports of a nation. It may be favourable or unfavourable for a state. It disturbs their currency relative value. The huge trade deficits are apparent as challenging for an economy, but not the smaller ones. If it is favourable, it will produce sureness amongst the stakeholders. They would like to participate or vice versa.

- Index of Industrial Production (IIP)

A measure of real output or real economic pursuit frequently cast-off is gross domestic product (GDP) or index of industrial production (IIP). Since, this analysis is grounded on monthly data and due to the accessibility of only quarterly, half yearly and yearly GDP data, IIP is selected as a measure of real output and a proxy to GDP. This IIP is the usual IIP figured as the weighted average of all routine-based IIP, by the Ministry of Statistics and Programme Implementation, Government of India. IIP statistics measures the manufacturing activity or industrial production in different economic sectors, it impacts stock prices by having effect on upcoming cash flows making it difficult for prediction.

- Gold Price (GP)

Gold is chiefly a monetary asset and moderately a commodity. Gold is the realm's aged worldwide currency. It is a significant component of global monetary reserves. Gold is a supernumerary investment opportunity for Indian investors. Kudal (2014) expresses, as the gold price increases, Indian investors incline to spend fewer in stocks, instigating stock prices to decrease. Therefore, an adverse association is predictable amongst gold price and stock price. Thus, this very significant macroeconomic variable has also been comprised in this analysis. The remainder of this paper is prearranged as tracks; section two analyses are examining the association between macroeconomic variables and stock market. Section three outlines the methodology, i.e. research variables, hypothesis and statistical techniques. Section four gives results of the paper, and lastly, section five concludes the study.

2 Literature Review

The conclusion given by Chandni Makan (2012) elaborated that out of seven variables impacting stock market, three variables are comparatively more significant. Those factors are FII, call rate and exchange rate. Sensex has positive association with FII and call rate. On the other hand, Sensex has negative association with exchange rate. According to the study of Singh (2014), the Indian stock market is being impacted by macroeconomic determinants. The factors impacting stock exchange were identified as gold, exchange rate, FII and money supply. The paper of Rakesh Kumar (2013) highlighted that favourable macroeconomic determinants of stock market improve the price earning ratio. According to author, stock market is impacted by real variables in the economy like growth of industry which is further impacted by macro-economic environment. Wycliffe Ouma and Muriu (2014) investigated that in Kenya the macroeconomic determinants of returns of NSE are inflation rate, money supply, exchange rate and interest rate. Sameer Yadav (2017) states that the stock market has different market cycles, the bull phase is analysed to have more volatility, gains and the bear phase has comparatively lesser gains or more of losses with low volatility in the market. M. Subramanian (2015) found that the macroeconomic variables, i.e. GDP, inflation, CRR, index on industrial production and USD (US dollars, Forex) are influencing the stock market index (Sensex). Venkatraja (2014) discovered that any difference in the value of WPI, IIP, FII and REER has sturdy positive encouragement on the BSE stock market performance. While an escalation in gold price is uncovered instigating smash in stock market and vice versa. Walia (2012) mentioned supplementary, of the five variables, the coefficients of all the variables excluding IIP are statistically substantial. This clues to the conclusion that inflation, inflow of foreign institutional investment; exchange rate and gold price influence the Indian stock market performance meaningfully. Kumuda and Verghese (2015) exposed that interest rate; unemployment rate, inflation rate and GDP have a connection with the stock index. It is discovered that inflation rate and unemployment rate are positively interrelated with Nifty while GDP and interest rate are negatively interconnected with Nifty. Kantesha Sanningammanavara et al. (2014) resolved that the depreciation in the rupee beside the Dollar has headed to reduction in the share prices. It has an adverse impression on the stock prices, and rise in the inflation rate has directed to reduction in the share prices. They also resolved that other than the exchange rate and inflation rate factors, there are other causes such as interest rate, global factors, performance of company, etc., which disturb the share prices of Indian stock market.

Lokeswar Reddy (2012) clarified that the explanatory variables accounted for 95.6% of the difference in stock prices, which is revealed by regression analysis. While a lessening in interest and inflation rate ensued in augmented stock prices, amplified RDGP has a positive influence. Parmar (2013) and Sangmi and Mubasher (2013) observed the influence of macroeconomic variables on the Indian stock prices. Sangmi (2013) also explained that six variables inflation, exchange rate, industrial production, money supply, gold price, interest rate were chosen to plaid its consequence on the performance of three indices Sensex, Nifty and BSE 100. Multiple regressions have been pertained on monthly data, which specified a noteworthy connexion amongst the dependent and independent variables, i.e. stock market prices and macroeconomic variables. Mohapatra and Panda (2012) correlated top ten escalations and top ten drops of Sensex with matching net flows of FIIs and also verified the influence of other macroeconomic factors alongside with FIIs disturbing Sensex for a 10 year period and establish that IIP and exchange rate (INR/USD) have a greater effect than FIIs on the stock markets. Naik and Padhi (2012) witnessed bidirectional connectedness amongst industrial production and stock prices, unidirectional causativeness from money supply to stock price, stock price to inflation and interest rates to stock prices. The authors Jha and Shing (2014) determine that macroeconomic variables and the stock market index are co-integrated, and hence, a long-run equilibrium association subsists amongst them. Kalra (2012) witnessed that Forex rate, whole sale price index, inflation rate and gold price were the most noteworthy variables. Kaur (2016), the researcher smeared multiple correlations, multiple regression and Anova test to report the influence of macroeconomic variables on Indian stock market. The monthly data of nominated variables like cash reserve ratio, reverse repo rate, gold price, silver price, inflation rate, whole sale price index, GDP and Forex rate were examined to attain the objectives.

3 Inferences and Research Gap

At final, it is to remark that from all those paper, which have been mentioned to in groundwork of this analysis, it has been decided that macroeconomic variables (foreign institutional investment, exchange rate, money supply, inflation and gold price) have influenced the Indian stock market performance suggestively. The literature is providing insights that the study is been conducted for macroeconomic variables only almost all the time instead of defining them different variables or factors names as such in specific.

4 Research Approach

In this exploration, quantitative research approach is expended. The mathematical and statistical grounded approaches and tools are cast off to gather the data and enumerate the outcomes, which aid the researcher to appeal conclusions.

5 Research Design

The co-relational research design is expended in this analysis. It is a design, which is expended to discover out the association amongst two variables of the alike group. In supplement, it examines either there is any impression of one variable on the other or not. In simple verses, variation in one variable (independent) carries variation in other variable (dependent) or not and to which degree this change occurs.

6 Sample Size and Period

In this analysis, the average closing monthly data of Sensex and Nifty, from the year April 1993–December 2019, are occupied. Likewise, for all macroeconomic variable, monthly data are acquired from April 1993—December 2019 accumulation of 312 months for every variable.

7 Data Source

Secondary data are the data that have been previously gathered by and freely obtainable from other sources. In this reading, the secondary data are extricated from the bona fide sources, which are the Websites of the RBI and TRADING ECONOMICS. Macroeconomic data such as exchange rate (Rs/USD), gold price, call money rate, money supply (M3), trade balance, foreign institutional investment were occupied from the official site of RBI's Database on Indian Economy (DBIE). BSE Sensex and Nifty monthly average value were also appropriated from the official site of RBI's Database on Indian Economy (DBIE). The monthly percentage change values for inflation rate (WPI), inflation rate (CPI), index of industrial production are gained from the "trading economics" Website.

Variables	Symbol	Proxy
Rate of interest	IR	Weighted average rates of call money
Rate of exchange	ER	Monthly average rupees (per $)
Inflation	IF	Consumer price index (CPI), wholesale price index (WPI)
Index of industrial production	IIP	General index of industrial production (%)
Foreign portfolio investors	FPI	Monthly net investments in Rs. Crores
Money supply	MS	M3(Rs. Billion)
Trade balance	TB	Monthly trade balance (Rs. Billion)
Gold price	GP	Average rupee price of Mumbai (per 10 gms)
Stock indices	BSE, Nifty	Sensex and nifty monthly average price

8 Objective

- To analyse whether macroeconomic variables chosen for study namely portfolio investment (FPI), inflation (WPI & CPI), industrial production index, exchange rate, money supply, call rate, gold price and trade balance have influence on the stock exchange indices. BSE Sensex and NSE Nifty are the indices taken as indicators of Indian stock market.
- To study the direction and degree of relationship between selected macroeconomic environment indicators and Indian stock market indices.

9 Need of the Study

The stock market being one of the leading opportunities for investments, it befits significant to comprehend the elements that disturb it and thereby prediction of the forthcoming trend of the same. The main purposefulness of the reading is to comprehend and discover association amongst stock market and macroeconomic variables and get visions of the movement in the index at a theoretical level. The analysis of macroeconomic variables is also vital as countless foreign investors formerly building any investment always examine the factors like inflation rate, interest rate, industrial production, GDP rate, etc., of the nation, so it is vital that this elements must be steady which will surge the foreign investment and it will upturn the progression of the nation.

10 Hypothesis

The subsequent hypothesis has been made:

Null Hypothesis

H0 There is no momentous relation amongst all these macroeconomic variables and Sensex.

H0 There is no noteworthy association amongst all these macroeconomic variables and Nifty.

Alternate Hypothesis

Ha There is a momentous relation amongst all these macroeconomic variables and Sensex.

Ha There is noteworthy association amongst all these macroeconomic variables and Nifty.

11 Data Analytical Tools and Techniques

Time series analysis, correlation analysis and multiple regression analysis were cast off over SPSS and E views to unravel the connexion amongst macroeconomic variables and stock market indices.

Time Series Analysis—Unit root test is used to check whether the time series data are stationary or non-stationary. Stationary refers to the movement of time series around a mean value. Augmented Dickey Fuller test has been applied to find out the stationary of time series data. After stationary of data has been confirmed, the analysis has proceeded to check the co-integration between the endogenous and exogenous variables. The study has used Johansen co-integration test to analyse the co-integrating relationship amongst the selected variables. Co-integration analysis validates the long-run relationship between endogenous and exogenous variables. Granger causality test was used to check the causality.

Correlation Analysis—In this analysis, it defines the connection amid stock market and macroeconomic variables, which have been explored using Pearson's correlation analysis.

Regression analysis—In this analysis, it is a statistical extent, which tries to establish association amongst a dependent variable and the other independent variables. The multiple linear regression models have been pertained to recognize the consequence of macroeconomic variables on stock market.

12 Data Analysis and Interpretation.

The results of stationarity tests are given in Table 1. It confirms non-stationarity

Table 1 Stationary tests of stock indices and macroeconomic variables using augmented dickey fuller test

Variables	Probabilities (at first difference)
Rate of interest	0.0906
Rate of exchange	0.0014
Inflation	0.0201
Index of industrial production	0.0215
Foreign portfolio investors	0.0436
Money supply	0.0034
Trade balance	0.0003
Gold price	0.0022
Stock index (BSE Sensex)	0.0551
Stock index (Nifty)	0.0810

of variables and indices, and hence, we repeat stationarity tests on return series (estimated as first difference) which are also provided in Table 1, they are stationary at first level of difference. The table describes the stock indices and macroeconomic variables that have been tested using Augmented Dickey Fuller (ADF) 1981.

Table 2 summarizes the consolidated output of Johansen co-integration test applied on stock indices and macroeconomic variables. After checking the time series of properties of variables through unit root test, the study is proceeded to test the co-integrating relationship between stock indices and macroeconomic variables. Johansen co-integration analysis helps to find out whether there exists a co-integrating relationship between the variables or not. It enables to identify more than one co-integration relationship between time series data. In order to accept the co-integrating relationship between variables, Trace and Max-Eigen Statistics value should be higher than the critical value at 5% significance level. The results exhibit that all the variables are co-integrated with BSE Sensex and Nifty at 5% level of significance. Further, the evaluation of co-integration is done by test for causality.

Causality is Explained by the Given Equation

$$X(t) = \sum_{j=1}^{P} A_{11,j} X(t-j) + \sum_{j=1}^{P} A_{12,j} Y(t-j) + \varepsilon_1(t)$$

$$Y(t) = \sum_{j=1}^{P} A_{21,j} X(t-j) + \sum_{j=1}^{P} A_{22,j} Y(t-j) + \varepsilon_2(t)$$

Table 3 signifies the outcomes of Granger causality test of stock indices and macroeconomic variables. Granger causality analysis is a statistical hypothesis test for defining whether one times series data are beneficial in forecasting one more. Granger causality test outcomes have revealed the unidirectional positive association amongst stock indices and macroeconomic variables.

Table 2 Co-integration test of stock indices and macroeconomic variables

Pairwise	Eigen value	Trace statistic	Critical value (5%)	Max-eigen value
Rate of interest-BSE Sensex	0.134842	20.98515	15.49471	18.111215
Rate of exchange-BSE Sensex	0.050026	4.873933	3.841466	5.873933
Inflation-BSE Sensex	0.268198	26.83926	25.87211	27.79800
Index of industrial production-BSE Sensex	0.068444	14.041255	12.51798	15.041255
Foreign portfolio investors-BSE Sensex	0.122849	16.35151	15.49471	16.471353
Money supply-BSE Sensex	0.098018	5.880153	3.841466	5.880153
Trade balance-BSE Sensex	0.094926	18.514226	15.49471	17.685082
Gold price-BSE Sensex	0.048422	4.829144	3.841466	5.829144
Rate of interest-Nifty	0.120202	16.24945	15.49471	18.299557
Rate of exchange-Nifty	0.027604	4.949897	3.841466	5.165643
Inflation-Nifty	0.345678	26.86758	25.87211	28.934856
Index of industrial production-Nifty	0.057896	13.987465	12.51798	15.675439
Foreign portfolio investors-Nifty	0.134563	16.988876	15.49471	18.965464
Money supply-Nifty	0.045674	6.768655	3.841466	4.876567
Trade balance-Nifty	0.087435	17.675433	15.49471	16.879877
Gold price-Nifty	0.043253	4.765543	3.841466	4.889908

12.1 Macroeconomic Variables and BSE Sensex

Correlation Analysis

This analysis is connected to influence of several macroeconomic variables on the stock market in India. Variables recognized to as macroeconomic variables in the study are anticipated to be correlated amongst themselves. Table 4 shows the correlation matrix of BSE Sensex with numerous macroeconomic variables.

The association amongst stock market and macroeconomic variables has been studied using Pearson's correlation analysis. The correlation outcomes during the entire phase of analysis disclose the constructive connotation of BSE Sensex with exchange rate, consumer price index, gold price, money supply and foreign portfolio investors while unconstructive with trade balance, industrial production, wholesale price index and interest rate. But meaningfully, affirmative association is for exchange rate, gold price, money supply and foreign portfolio investors with BSE Sensex. Thus, these variables have noteworthy connotation with stock index (Sensex). The exchange rate has substantial affirmative connotation with FPI (0.195). During the absolute

Table 3 Granger causality test of stock indices and macroeconomic variables

Null hypothesis Ho	*F*-statistic	*P*-value
Rate of interest does not granger cause BSE Sensex	0.21538	0.8069
Rate of exchange does not granger cause BSE Sensex	0.17607	0.8391
Inflation does not granger cause BSE Sensex	2.39301	0.1012
Index of industrial production does not granger cause BSE Sensex	0.59887	0.5531
Foreign portfolio investors does not granger cause BSE Sensex	0.38909	0.6796
Money supply does not granger cause BSE Sensex	0.34564	0.5678
Trade balance does not granger cause BSE Sensex	0.26789	0.6543
Gold price does not granger cause BSE Sensex	2.86756	0.5453
Rate of interest does not granger cause Nifty	0.45363	0.2335
Rate of exchange does not granger cause Nifty	3.32456	0.6543
Inflation does not granger cause Nifty	1.23462	0.5666
Index of industrial production does not granger cause Nifty	0.56765	0.5003
Foreign portfolio investors does not granger cause Nifty	3.33456	0.6544
Money supply does not granger cause Nifty	0.34522	0.5632
Trade balance does not granger cause Nifty	0.23345	0.8534
Gold price does not granger cause Nifty	2.34543	0.2453

phase of analysis, money supply has extremely substantial affirmative connotation with exchange rate (0.882) and also with gold prices (0.963) at 5% level of significance. Meaningfully, positive association also occurs amid money supply and foreign portfolio investors (0.279). Gold prices are another variable that displays positive connotation with foreign portfolio investors (0.326) at 5% level of significance. The IIP has noteworthy positive relationship with trade balance (0.303).

The exchange rate and gold has extremely noteworthy connotation, which is 0.800 at 5% level of significance. The escalation in the exchange rate clues to the degeneration in the value of Indian rupee with respect to US dollars. Thus, the currency converts weaker in the international market, which is optimistically interrelated to gold prices in India. As the second largest nation in the world in the utilization of gold after China, India has enormous requirement of gold in the countrywide market due to numerous causes. This product has arisen as protected investment chance for the shareholders because of its enormous return and high liquidity. Correlation coefficients are expended for observing short-run co-movements and multi-collinearity amid the variables. Some of the variables have correlation coefficient larger than 0.8. If correlation coefficient is larger than 0.8, it specifies that multi-collinearity subsists. To overcome the difficulty of multi-collinearity and have effectual outcomes, factor analysis approach of data reduction has been pertained.

Table 4 Correlation matrix

	BSE Sensex	Ex rate USD IND	FPI	IIP	Infl. CPI	Infl. WPI	Money Supply	Call money Rate	Trade balance	Gold price
BSE Sensex	1									
Ex rate USD IND	0.781 0.000	1								
FPI	0.328 0.000	0.195 0.001	1							
IIP	−0.208 0.000	−0.446 0.001	−0.025 0.671	1						
Infl. CPI	0.048 0.414	−0.236 0.000	0.068 0.242	−0.049 0.396	1					
Infl. WPI	−0.362 0.000	−0.568 0.000	−0.083 0.155	0.183 0.002	0.712 0.000	1				
Money supply	0.960 0.000	0.882 0.000	0.279 0.000	−0.380 0.000	0.016 0.786	−0.398 0.000	1			
Call money rate	−0.176 0.002	−0.253 0.000	−0.098 0.093	0.069 0.233	0.217 0.000	0.322 0.000	−0.174 0.003	1		
Trade balance	−0.873 0.000	−0.704 0.000	−0.316 0.000	0.303 0.000	−0.154 0.008	0.195 0.001	−0.879 0.000	0.137 0.018	1	
Gold price	0.917 0.000	0.800 0.000	0.326 0.000	−0.406 0.000	0.140 0.016	−0.246 0.000	0.963 0.000	−0.113 0.052	−0.919 0.000	1

12.2 Macroeconomic Variables and Nifty

Correlation Analysis
This analysis is connected to influence of numerous macroeconomic variables on the stock market in India. Variables recognized to as macroeconomic variables in the study are predictable to be correlated midst them. Table 5 demonstrates the correlation matrix of Nifty with several macroeconomic variables.

The association amongst stock market and macroeconomic variables has been examined exercising Pearson's correlation analysis. The correlation consequences throughout the all-inclusive period of analysis disclose the affirmative connotation of Nifty with exchange rate, consumer price index, gold price, money supply and foreign portfolio investors while adverse with trade balance, industrial production, wholesale price index and interest rate. But meaningfully, affirmative association for exchange rate, gold price, money supply and foreign portfolio investors with Nifty. Thus, these variables have noteworthy connotation with stock index (Nifty).

Throughout the intact phase of analysis, money supply has extremely momentous progressive connotation with exchange rate (0.882) and also with gold prices (0.963) at 5% level of significance. Meaningfully, affirmative association also occurs amongst money supply and foreign portfolio investors (0.279). Gold prices are additional variable that unveils constructive connotation with foreign portfolio investors (0.326) at 5% level of significance. The IIP has noteworthy affirmative connotation with trade balance (0.303). The exchange rate and gold has extremely momentous relationship, which is 0.800 at 5% level of significance. The increase in the exchange rate hints to the weakening in the value of Indian rupee with respect to US dollars. Thus, the currency develops fainter in the international market, which is confidently connected to gold prices in India. As the second largest nation in the world in the utilization of gold after china, India has enormous demand of gold in the nationwide market due to numerous purposes. This product has arisen as safe investment opportunity for the financiers because of its enormous return and excessive liquidity. Correlation coefficients are expended for probing short-run co-movements and multi-collinearity amongst the variables. Certain of the variables have correlation coefficient larger than 0.8. If correlation coefficient is larger than 0.8, it specifies that multi-collinearity occurs.

13 Limitations

- This analysis chiefly focuses on chosen nine independent variables, which may not totally epitomize the macroeconomic variables.
- The outcomes were sketched on the basis of time series analysis, correlation analysis and multiple regression. The distinctive statistical methods can be applied to do the similar analysis.

Table 5 Correlation matrixes

	Nifty	Ex rateUSD IND	FPI	IIP	Infl. CPI	Infl. WPI	Money Supply	Call Money Rate	Trade Balance	Gold Price
Nifty	1									
Ex rate USDIND	0.790 0.000	1								
FPI	0.325 0.000	0.195 0.001	1							
IIP	−0.218 0.000	−0.446 0.001	−0.025 0.671	1						
Infl. CPI	0.037 0.525	−0.236 0.000	0.068 0.242	−0.049 0.396	1					
Infl. WPI	−0.372 0.000	−0.568 0.000	−0.083 0.155	0.183 0.002	0.712 0.000	1				
Money supply	0.965 0.000	0.882 0.000	0.279 0.000	−0.380 0.000	0.016 0.786	−0.398 0.000	1			
Call money rate	−0.181 0.002	−0.253 0.000	−0.098 0.093	0.069 0.233	0.217 0.000	0.322 0.000	−0.174 0.003	1		
Trade balance	−0.872 0.000	−0.704 0.000	−0.316 0.000	0.303 0.000	−0.154 0.008	0.195 0.001	−0.879 0.000	0.137 0.018	1	
Gold price	0.920 0.000	0.800 0.000	0.326 0.000	−0.406 0.000	0.140 0.016	−0.246 0.000	0.963 0.000	−0.113 0.052	−0.919 0.000	1

14 Conclusion

This analysis assesses the association amongst the stock market and a set of macroeconomic variables by exercising monthly data for the phase April 1993 to December 2019. The time period includes years like 1999 and 2008 which are period of structural breaks in the economy leading to variations in data to a high or low which have been tried to be kept as constant to provide smooth data. The macroeconomic variables are characterized by the industrial production index, consumer price index, wholesale price index, interest rate (call money rate), exchange rate, gold price, trade balance, foreign portfolio investment and money supply. It is supposed that, the particular macroeconomic variables characterize the state of the economy. The BSE Sensex and Nifty is expended to signify the Indian stock market index. The paper used time series analysis, correlation analysis and multi-regression analysis to assess such associations. Outcomes specify that exchange rate, gold price, money supply, trade balance, wholesale price index, call money rate, IIP and foreign portfolio investors have noteworthy constructive association with Indian stock market.

It has been recognized that the numerous macrovariables are extremely correlated. From the results, it can be displayed that Indian stock market is exceedingly absolutely responsive to the macroenvironment, economy rates and foreign investment. Numerous other elements like government policies, political turbulence, investor confidence and social variables disturb variations in BSE Sensex and Nifty. The analysis approves the opinions that macroeconomic factors resume to disturb the Indian stock market. The outcome presented that all the data sets are stationary at first difference, grounded on this consequence, Johansen co-integration tests are directed. It is discovered that long-run associations occurs in amongst stock indices and macroeconomic variables. It means, in long run, every nation's stock exchanges are determined by nation explicit aspects. In order to quantify practicality of a time series in forecasting another in short run, the Granger causality is used. The outcomes of these tests propose that, the positive unidirectional association prevailing amongst stock indices and macroeconomic variables signifying that the macroeconomic variables when changing, it has a repelling impact in form of growth of stock markets with the overall growth of nations.

References

Ahmed, S. (2008). Aggregate economic variables and stock market in India. *International Research Journal of Finance and Economics, 14*, 141–165.

Bhunia, A. (2012). The shock of the shock of crude price, stock price and selected macroeconomic variables on the growth of Indian economy. *Sumedha Journal of Management, 1*, 82–89.

Chandni Makan, A. K. (2012). A *Study of the effect of macroeconomic variables on stock market: Indian perspective*. Munich Personal RePEc Archive.

Flannery, M. J., & Protopapadakis, A. A. (2002). Macroeconomic factors do influence aggregate stock returns. *Review of Financial Studies, 15*, 751–782.

Gay, R. D. (2008). Effect of macroeconomic variables on stock market returns for four emerging economies: Brazil, Russia, India and China. *International Business & Economics Research Journal, 7*(3), 1–8.

Gurloveleen, K. B. B. (2015). An impact of macroeconomic variables on the functioning of Indian Stock Market: A study of manufacturing firms of BSE 500. *Journal of Stock & Forex Trading, 5*(1), 1–7.

Hojatallah, G., & Ramanarayana, C. S. (2011). Empirical analysis of the impact of foreign institutional investment on the Indian stock market volatility during world financial crisis. *International Journal Economics of Finance, 3,* 214–226.

Hosseini, M. A. (2011). The role of macroeconomic variables on stock market index in China and India. *International Journal of Economics and Finance, 3,* 233–243.

Humpe, A., & Macmillan, P. (2009). Can macroeconomic variables explain long-term stock market movements? A comparison of the US and Japan. *Applied Financial Economics, 19,* 111–119.

Jha, A. K., & Shing, N. K. (2014). Predicting the volatility of stock markets and measuring its interaction with macroeconomic variables: Indian evidence, case study of NIFTY & SENSEX. *International Journal of Sciences: Basic & Applied Research, 13,* 371–393.

Kalra, R. (2012). Impact of macroeconomic variables on Indian stock market. *IUP Journal of Financial Risk Management, 9,* 43–54.

Kantesha Sanningammanavara, K. K. (2014). Macro-economic forces and Indian stock market: An empirical relation. *International Journal of Commerce, Business and Management, 3*(3), 457–465.

Kaur, H. J. S. (2016). Impact of macroeconomic variables on stock market: A review of literature. *International Journal of Applied Business and Economic Research, 14*(14), 9775–9804.

Kudal, P. (2014). Impact of macroeconomic variables on Indian stock market and strategies for investors—post global financial crisis. *Tirpude's National Journal of Business Research* , 39–55.

Kumar, A. (2011). An empirical analysis of causal relationship between stock market and macroeconomic variables in India. *International Journal of Computer Science and Management Studies, 11,* 8–14.

Kumar, R. (2013). The effect of macroeconomic factors on Indian stock market performance: A factor analysis approach. *IOSR Journal of Economics and Finance, 1*(3), 14–21.

Kumuda, P. R., & Verghese, S. S. (2015). Macro economic variables and stock prices—evidence from India. *International Journal of Current Engineering and Scientific Research, 2*(11), 15–19.

Mishra, S. (2012). Do macroeconomic variables explain stock market returns? Evidence using a semi-parametric approach. *Journal of Asset Management, 28,* 1–13.

Naik, K. P. (2012). The impact of macroeconomic fundamentals on stock price revisited: Evidence from Indian data. *Eurasian Journal of Business and Economics, 5,* 25–44.

Naka, A., Mukherjee, T., & Tufte, D. (1999). Macroeconomic variables and the performance of the Indian Stock Market. *Financial Management Association meeting.*

Ouma, W. N. (2014). The Impact of macroeconomic variables on stock market returns in Kenya. *International Journal of Business and Commerce, 3*(11), 1–31.

Padhi, P. K. (2012). The impact of macroeconomic fundamentals on stock prices revisited: evidence from Indian data. *Eurasian Journal of Business and Economics, 5*(10), 25–44.

Parmar, C. (2013). Empirical relationship among various macroeconomic variables and indian stock market. *International Journal of Advance Research in Computer Science and Management Studies, 1*(6), 2321–7782.

Patel, S. (2012). The effect of macroeconomic determinants on the performance of the Indian stock market. *NMIMS Management Review, 12,* 117–127.

Peiró, A. (1996). Stock prices, production and interest rates: Comparison of three European countries with the USA. *Empirical Economics, 21,* 221–234.

Rapach, D. E., Wohar, M. E., & Rangvid, J. (2005). Macro variables and international stock return predictability. *International Journal of Forecasting, 21,* 137–166.

Ray, S. (2012). Foreign exchange reserve and its impact on stock market capitalization: Evidence from India. *Research on Humanities and Social Sciences, 2,* 46–60.

Reddy, D. V. (2012). Impact of inflation and GDP on stock market returns in India. *International Journal of Advanced Research in Management and Social Sciences, 1*(6), 120–136.
Sangmi, M. D., & Mubasher, M. H. (2013). Macroeconomic variables on stock market interactions: The Indian experience. *Advances in Management, 6*(8), 39–51.
Schwert, G. W. (1990). Stock returns and real activity: A century of evidence. *the Journal of Finance, 45,* 1237–1257.
Singh, P. (2014). Indian Stock market and macroeconomic factors in current scenario. *International Journal of Research in Business Management, 2*(11), 43–54.
Sireesha, P. B. (2013). Effect of select macro economic variables on stock returns in India. *International Journal of Marketing, Financial Services & Management Research, 2*(6), 197–209.
Srivastava, A. (2010). Relevance of macro economic factors for the Indian stock market. *Decision, 37,* 69–89.
Subramanian, M. (2015). A study on impact of macroeconomic variables in the stock market. *SSRG International Journal of Economics and Management Studies, 2*(5), 25–33.
Tripathy, N. (2011). Causal relationship between macro-economic indicators and stock market in India. *Asian Journal of Finance & Accounting, 3,* 208–226.
Venkatraja, B. (2014). Impact of macroeconomic variables on stock market. *International Journal of Business Quantitative Economics and Applied Management Research, 1*(6), 71–85.
Victor, Z. (1992). Major macroeconomic variables and leading indexes. In Z. Victor (Ed,), *Business cycles: theory, history, indicators and forecasting* (pp. 357–382).
Walia, S. (2012). Impact of global economic crisis on Indian economy: An analysis. *International Journal of Latest Trends in Engineering and Technology, 1,* 31–36.
Wasserfallen, W. (1989). Macroeconomic news and the stock market: evidence from Europe. *Journal of Banking and Finance, 13,* 613–626.
Yadav, S. (2017). Stock market volatility—a study of Indian stock market. *Global Journal For Research Analyses, 6*(4), 629–632.

Part III
Trade and Development Interface: Implications for India and Emerging Economies

Chapter 13
India's Trade-Sensitive Employment: A Comprehensive Firm-Level Analysis

B. Nag and S. Khurana

1 Introduction

The relationship between international trade and employment growth is complex. Trade liberalisation in developing countries triggers a process of specialisation in favour of labour-intensive goods. Since labour is an abundant factor of production in most developing countries, it implies that openness to trade increases the demand for labour and hence has the potentiality to generate employment in large scale. However, the historical evidence shows mixed results. Many studies find that it is true mostly in East and South East Asia (Milner and Wright, 1998; Orbeta, 2002, etc.). On the contrary, African and Latin American economies have reported that trade integration has a negative impact on domestic employment (Mesquita and Najberg, 2000; Ravenga, 1999; Rattso and Torvik, 1998; etc.). The idea that specialisation in labour-intensive industries in labour-abundant developing countries will generate substantial employment comes from the theoretical background of Heckscher–Ohlin type models which have a strong assumption on identical technology across the countries. It is far from a realistic scenario. The new trade theories on the other hand with an assumption of technological differences among countries argue that trade liberalisation produces multiple equilibria (Grossman and Helpman, 1991) and countries may land up with different equilibrium situation in the post-liberalisation scenario. Vivarelli (2002) opines in reference to 'technological catch-up' hypothesis that trade openness may bring new technologies in developing countries which potentially affect employment adversely through an increase in total factor productivity. So, trade theories provide a conditional link between trade and employment, especially for developing countries. Trade openness could increase employment by increasing

B. Nag (✉) · S. Khurana
Indian Institute of Foreign Trade, New Delhi, India
e-mail: biswajit.nag@gmail.com

S. Khurana
e-mail: saloni.khurana471@gmail.com

P. Lakhanpal et al. (eds.), *Trade, Investment and Economic Growth*,
https://doi.org/10.1007/978-981-33-6973-3_13

output growth but it could hamper employment also by enhancing total factor productivity. The final outcome depends on the interaction between these two competing effects. According to Vivarelli (2002), the possibility of declining employment is high in countries those have significant supply-side constraints such as poor infrastructure and inefficient labour market. Aho and Orr (1981) published a paper in the Monthly Labour Review which analysed the trade-sensitive employment in the US economy. The paper argues that with the expansion of exports, significant job opportunities have been created in the USA. However, imports have also grown, slowing employment growth or displacing workers in import-competing industries. The net effect of the trade-related changes in employment opportunities is relatively small and is largely a function of the business cycle. But, the net effect masks the impact on workers because international trade theory predicts that workers in export- and import-competing sectors will possess different skills. Due to the rise of the global value chain and international production network, export-oriented sectors also outsource components and accessories internationally which rise the share of foreign value added in national exports. This also has a potential negative impact on domestic employment even when total export rises.

Kucera et al. (2012) estimate the effects of the 2008–09 trade contraction on employment in India and South Africa, using social accounting matrices (SAMs) in a Leontief multiplier model. The study finds that India and South Africa experienced substantial employment decline because of trade contraction with the European Union and the USA. Wagner (2002) has evaluated the regular performance of non-exporters and export starters using matching approach. He established the fact that exports will lead to the growth of employment and wages but weaker evidence for a positive impact on productivity. Hasan et al. (2012) studied the impact of trade liberalisation on employment in India using state and industry-level unemployment and trade protection data. The state-level analysis reveals that urban unemployment declines with trade liberalisation in states with flexible labour markets and larger employment shares in net exporter industries; and industry-level analysis indicates that workers in industries experiencing greater reductions in trade protection were less likely to become unemployed, especially in net export industries. Vashisht (2015) noted that the direct impact of trade on manufacturing jobs has been positive. However, trade-induced decrease in labour demand is significant which neutralised direct job gains to a great extent. Therefore, unlike other Asian economies, the overall employment gain from trade has been minimal in India. Veeramani (2016) also found that employment supported by Indian exports (both merchandise and services) increased at an annual growth rate of 3.4% from about 34 million in 1990–00 to 62.6 million in 2012–13, which is faster than that of country's total employment. However, while the export-led employment increased in absolute terms, jobs supported per million dollars of exports declined during the period. This can be attributed to change in the composition of exports in favour of more capital and import-intensive sectors.

Studies conducted on Indian data have also recognised the change in employment trend and structure. Several experts identified trade liberalisation as a major catalyst for this change. Mehrotra et al. (2014) noted that there has been a fall in demand for manufacturing exports and increasing capital intensity also resulted in a decline in manufacturing employment during 2004–05 to 2009–10. Kapoor (2016) also observed that with the growing capital intensity of production, the role of labour vis-à-vis capital has declined in the production process, and in India, we have observed declining share of labour payment as a percentage of gross value added. The share of skilled labour (non-production workers, i.e. supervisory and managerial staff) in the wage pie rose from 26.1 to 35.8%, while that of unskilled labour (production workers) fell from 57.6 to 48.8% of total wage bill during 2000/01–2011/12. However, we have observed the rise of unskilled and contractual workers in the production process.

The existing literature on India reveals that the employment structure has undergone a significant change in the last two decades. On the one hand, more jobs are created for unskilled workers but their share in factor payments is not increasing. Secondly, technology integration in the production system, rising import of parts and components, increase in productivity, etc., have a negative impact on the job growth. Jobs are created for more skilled workers in sectors which are embracing more capital-oriented production system. Overall, there has been job growth when export rises steadily and it slows down when export stabilises or declines. Most of the studies look at one or two issues in one go and do not provide a holistic view. In this paper, our main attempt is to see at sector and firm[1] level the relationship among major variables such as employment, export, productivity and wages together. The dynamics among the variables will help us to validate theoretical and empirical findings of earlier studies and let us know the extent of negative and positive forces to determine the relationship between employment and exports in the Indian context.

2 Trade and Employment Equilibrium Framework: Based on Substitution of Unskilled and Skilled Labour Force

The current section makes an attempt to discuss the above-mentioned issues through graphical exposition. Figure 1 below explains the stylised facts in a four-quadrant diagram where the trade-off between skilled and unskilled workers plays an important role with respect to rising wages, increasing labour supply, skill enhancement, changing export demand (effect of the business cycle), etc.

In the model, labour demand constitutes two types of labour: unskilled labour (L_u) and skilled labour (L_s). The demand of both types of labour depends on the wage rate, while it is also considered that pool of the unskilled workers is more than skilled workers and wages of unskilled workers are less than the wages of skilled workers. Total labour supply is $\overline{L} = L_S + L_U$. It is assumed that all these workers are absorbed, and hence, there is no unemployment. If $\overline{L}$ curve shifts out, it implies that economic system is able to absorb more workers, and if it shifts in, then there

[1]Firm is defined as per the size. Small firms are the firms which hires less than 50 people, medium firms hire more than 49 but less than 250, and large firms hire more than 249 people.

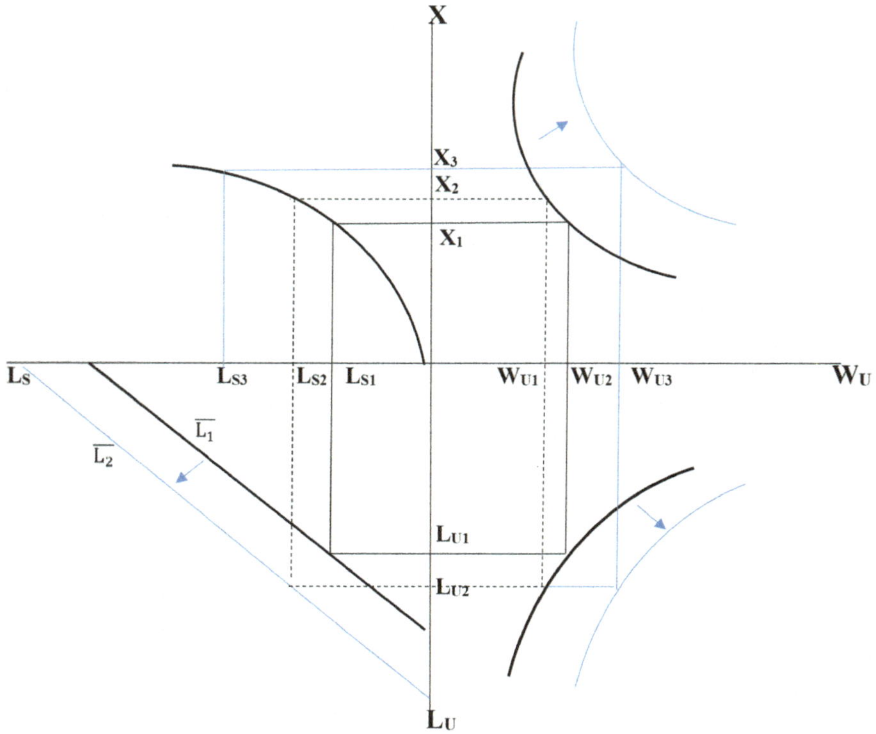

Fig. 1 Trade and employment equilibrium framework. *Source* Authors' output

is potential unemployment as labour demands drop. Unskilled labour demand is the negative function of wages while skilled labour is the positive function of exports. As wages of unskilled labour would increase, unskilled labour demand would decrease. In addition, as exports will increase, the demand for skilled labour would increase.

At the initial stage, export demand is X_1 which requires L_{S1} and L_{U1} skilled and unskilled workers. The wage rate for unskilled workers is W_{U1}. Total labour supply of $\overline{L}$ is matched with a demand for skilled and unskilled labour.

Suppose export demand rises (X_1–X_2) may be due to favourable business cycle, then it demands more increased skilled labour (L_{S2}). Keeping the labour supply constant at$\overline{L}_1$, this indicates a reduction in demand for unskilled workers which pushes the wage rate up for unskilled workers eventually. However, in developing countries, labour supply increases consistently and jobs can be created due to higher export demand. This can be explained by pushing $\overline{L}_1$ curve outwards to $\overline{L}_2$. Under such situation, higher exports can support more skilled as well as unskilled workers, and wage rate can also be kept under control.

The lower wage rate for unskilled workers is feasible under full employment assumption. However, the wage rate is not the only function of labour demand but it also depends on the bargaining power of workers, institutional policies on minimum wage rate, etc. It is natural that with the economic growth, wage rate will rise, and in such case, the industry will have a choice between skilled and unskilled workers.

If it pushes the wage rate of unskilled workers much, there will be some degree of negative impact on the export. The assumption of full employment is responsible for such a situation. Assuming the existence of unemployment, if more skilled labour is absorbed to sustain the export growth, they will substitute unskilled labour, thereby creating a potential situation of significant job loss at the level of unskilled workers particularly when wage rates for unskilled workers are sticky downwards.

To arrest such a situation, the government may take up skill development programme for unskilled workers. This will turn them to become semi-skilled workers in short to medium term and push the labour demand curve for unskilled workers outward along with a rise in wages of unskilled workers. Keeping everything constant, this will pull down the demand for skilled workers and have a negative impact on the exports.

To come out from such situation, more capital is required to be infused into the system so that demand for skilled labour increases along with the export productivity. Rising skill requires a matching capital for a balance in the job market so that overall economies of scale are maintained. This is reflected in by an outward shift of the X curve, which can sustain the higher supply of unskilled/semi-skilled and skilled workers. This process must continue with increasing labour supply. The model thus describes the virtuous cycle where higher export demand and productivity can generate employment for skilled and unskilled workers. This is important to note that if there is declining productivity, X curve can move backwards and improved skill may not create sufficient jobs in the export sector and higher wages will be responsible for the loss of comparative advantage eventually. Also, higher productivity along with declining export demand can create a similar situation.

Thus, the complex relationship between trade and employment depends on how the growth of labour supply is balanced through skill development and export productivity growth. Not all sectors or even firms can keep this balance and thereby bring up a potential loss in employment as well as competitiveness. This is also true for sectors with a significant presence of SMEs who are incapable of increasing capital significantly. With the increase in wages of unskilled workers, they slowly start substituting unskilled workers by skilled workers. Only bigger companies can move ahead and take the advantage of capital-driven productivity growth and provide ample employment opportunity especially when export demand rises, especially in the long run.

3 Industry's Outlook on Employment: An Empirical Model

Indian manufacturing sector has the advantage of the shifting labour supply. That implies India has the potential to increase employment by increasing exports specifically in the period of the favourable business cycle. But the employment of whom will increase skilled or unskilled workers, that is a question needs to be addressed.

As per the above model, if additional skilled labour is engaged to sustain the export growth, they will substitute unskilled labour that can result in significant job loss of unskilled workers. Imbibing skill in the system can help maintain the balance. But only skill could not work alone, needs capital also in the framework to match the demand for skilled labour that can together work on the export productivity.

Thus, to frame out this model, in our system we need to analyse the data points of Indian manufacturing industry as a whole and as well as with respect to their firm size. Vital variables through which exports affect the employment are total factor productivity, factor intensity, business cycle and firm size. Empirically, we will try to find the exact linkage between them. Four sets of regressions have been conducted to study the effect of exports on employment by taking controls. Following equation[2] is analysed using fixed effect:

$$(\text{“}x\text{”})_{\text{it}} = \alpha_0 + \alpha_1\left(\text{world}_{gdp}\right)_t + \alpha_2(\text{export})_{\text{it}} + \alpha_3(tfp\_\text{hat})_{it} + \alpha_4((\text{“}x\text{”})\text{wages})_{\text{it}} + \alpha_4 D_{L/K_{\text{it}}} + \alpha_5\left(\frac{L}{K} * \frac{D}{D_{\frac{L}{K}}}\right)_{it} + \epsilon_{\text{it}}$$

The list of dependent variables (“*x*” in the equation is used for):

- All employed = direct male and female workers + contractual workers + supervisors and managers + other employees + unpaid family members + proprietor + coop. members
- Workers employed through contractors
- Supervisory and managerial staff.

Independent variables used in the regressions.

- **$\textbf{World}_{\textbf{gdp}}$**: World per capita GDP at PPP
- **Export**: Exports by the industries
- **tfp_hat**: Estimated total factor productivity
- **‘*x*’_wages**: Average real wages and salaries of corresponding employee
- $D_{L/K}$**:** Dummy variable of labour-intensive industry
- $(L/K * D_{L/K})$**:** Interaction of dummy variable and corresponding labour by capital ratio.

Subscripts used in the regression equation:

- *i*: industries at NIC 3-digit
- *t*: time period, i.e. 2008/9–2015/16.

For this, we have used plant/firm level Annual Survey of Industries (ASI) database. Sample period considered for our empirical application is from 2008–09 to 2015–16 as the year 2008–09 in a way represents a period where India was not having many FTAs and 2015–16 is a representative year in post-FTA era. India signed number of FTAs with Asian countries during 2010–2011.

---

[2]Log of all variables are considered in the equation.

We estimated total factor productivity in our paper considering the Cobb–Douglas production function with three inputs: capital, labour and material (given in appendix).

3.1 Methodology Used

Factor Intensity

The vital task is to identify the industries/firms which are labour- or capital-intensive or changing behaviour with time in the manufacturing sector. Labour intensity is defined as the ratio of total workers over the capital. Here, workers include both directly employed and employed through contractors, employees other than workers (supervisory, managerial and other employees) and unpaid family members/proprietor, etc.

Das et al. (2009) and Radhicka Kapoor (2016) have also operated on same grounds to ascertain the labour- and capital-intensive industries. In our paper, we are using the relatively different definition of labour- and capital-intensive industries:

> An industry is classified as labour intensive if its labour intensity (identified using labour-capital ratio) is above the median value of all the industries given in a year. Similarly, an industry is classified as capital intensive if its capital intensity is below the median value.

Labour-intensive industries:

$$\left\{\begin{array}{c} \text{for } t \geq 6, \\ \text{if} \\ \left(\frac{L}{K}\right) \geq \text{median}\left(\frac{L}{K}\right) \\ \text{else,} \\ \left(\frac{L}{K}\right) \geq \text{mean}\left(\frac{L}{K}\right) \end{array}\right\}$$

Capital-intensive industries:

$$\left\{\begin{array}{c} \text{for } t \geq 6, \\ \text{if} \\ \left(\frac{L}{K}\right) < \text{median}\left(\frac{L}{K}\right) \\ \text{else,} \\ \left(\frac{L}{K}\right) < \text{mean}\left(\frac{L}{K}\right) \end{array}\right\}$$

For $t < 6$, industries are recorded as fluctuating.

3.2 Measuring Capital Stock

To get the value of capital–labour ratios, capital stock for that year is prerequisites. However, capital which is given in ASI database is based on the book value of the fixed assets at the end of the year. We calculated capital stock for period t using the perpetual inventory accumulation method, which is defined as.

$K_t = (1 - \delta)K_{t-1} + I_t$, where δ_{is} depreciation rate and I_t is investment in period t. Depreciation rate is determined endogenously following Srivastava (1996)

$$Dep_t = AD_{t+1} - AD_t$$

And $\delta_t = {}^{2}/_{L_t}$, where, $L_t = \frac{\text{GFA}_t}{\text{Dep}_t}$, Dep_t is the depreciation in year t and AD_i is the accumulated depreciation in year i.

Thus, we have calculated the unique depreciation rate of all firms in all years by taking mean of depreciation rate over all years. Now, capital stock can be determined easily, and to get K_{2008}, we have used the 'replacement value' considering the ratio of gross capital formation at national level at current and constant prices.

3.3 Measuring Total Factor Productivity

One of the most important variables that can affect the employment in the exporting sectors is the total factor productivity. Frontier production function[3] approach has been deliberated to estimate the total factor productivity both at industry and firm level using Cornwell et al. (1990). Here, dependent and independent variables are conveyed in terms of log. Functional form of the model is

$$y_{\text{it}} = \alpha_t + x'_{\text{it}}\beta + v_{\text{it}}$$

and

$$v_{it} \sim (0, \sigma_v^2) \;=\; 1, 2, \ldots, N, \quad t = 1, 2, \ldots, T$$

$$\alpha_i = \alpha_0 - u_i, \quad u_i \geq 0$$

To get the time-varying effect in the model, α_i is replaced by the quadratic function of time

$$\alpha_{\text{it}} = C_{i1} + C_{i2t} + C_{i3t2}$$

[3]We have considered a Cobb–Douglas production function with inputs (capital, labour and material) to estimate the productivity.

Or

$$W'_{\mathrm{it}} = [1, t, t^2]$$

And

$$\vartheta i = [Ci1, Ci2, Ci3]$$

Thus, the equation becomes

$$yit = x'it\beta + w'it\delta + vit$$

Here, δ_i can be estimated by regressing the residuals of $(y_{\mathrm{it}} - x^{'})$ for firm i on w'_{it}: that is on the quadratic function of time. Group OLS is used to get the estimated value of α_{it} which is consistent for all i and t as$T \rightarrow \infty$. Thus, productivity of each industry i at time t can be calculated as follows:

$$\mathrm{TFP}_{\mathrm{it}} = \exp(\hat{\alpha}_{\mathrm{it}})$$

4 Performance of Indian Industries

Indian manufacturing industries are producing the output to sell in the market but not all firms are able to enter the export market. In this section, we will tap the performance of Indian manufacturing sector and major exporting sector in terms of their firm size, employable capacity, factor intensity and productivity using the Annual Survey of Industries data set.

Table 1 provides a snapshot of the output and employment growth of overall manufacturing sector and export-oriented sector.[4] It explains that prima facie overall employment growth of exporting firms during the selected period is more than employment growth in the manufacturing sector as a whole but medium-sized exporting firms have lesser employment growth. It is the large and small size exporting firms which grew substantially both in terms of output and employment during the period. One of the things to contribute to the expansion of exportable industries is capital formation which is given in Table 2. Gross fixed capital formation as the percentage of output is decreasing and capital–labour ratio increased for the manufacturing and exporting sector as a whole implying capital deepening of Indian industry. Output growth in export-oriented industries is also significant which corroborates the finding in Table 1.

[4]If an industry is exporting more than 15% of its ex-factory output, we have considered it an exporting industry.

Table 1 Output and employment growth

	Output by ASI (in billion)			Employment by ASI (In million)		
	2008–09	2015–16	Growth (%)	2008–09	2015–16	Growth (%)
Manufacturing sector						
Overall	27,821.00	39,779.00	5.2	10.90	13.72	3.3
Large firms	23,400.00	32,500.00	4.8	8.45	10.70	3.4
Medium firms	4150.00	6680.00	7.0	2.26	2.72	2.7
Small firms	271.00	599.00	12.0	0.19	0.29	6.2
Exporting Sector						
Overall	1734.50	9312.80	27.1	1.67	2.83	7.8
Large firms	1410.00	8920.00	30.2	1.42	2.56	8.8
Medium firms	311.00	346.00	1.5	0.24	0.25	0.4
Small firms	13.50	46.80	19.4	0.01	0.02	12.0

Source Calculated from ASI firm-level data

Table 2 Important ratios in manufacturing and export-oriented sectors

	2008–09	2013–14	Growth (%)
Manufacturing Sector			
Gross fixed capital formation/output	0.09	0.08	−1.0
Capital/labour	1.35	1.42	1.1
Exporting Sector			
Gross fixed capital formation/output	0.12	0.07	−10.1
Capital/labour	0.34	1.10	26.4

Source Authors' calculations from ASI firm-level data

As discussed the factor intensity, it may be noted that employment growth has been 2.1% in labour-intensive industries but it was 6.5% in the case of capital-intensive sectors as given in Table 3. This corroborates with the idea articulated in the beginning that higher infusion of capital may increase productivity and in turn can also increase employment. It is also observed that wages and salaries growth also has been higher in capital-intensive sectors compared to labour-intensive sectors. However, the total people employed in the labour-intensive sector have been much higher than the capital-intensive sector. Interestingly, the textile industry alone has the potential to employ more than total workers in the capital-intensive sector. And overall employment of textile industry grew at 1.60%. The growth of supervisory and managerial staff and contractual workers in the capital-intensive sector has also superseded the labour-intensive sector.

Another important aspect to look at to complete the factors discussed in our model is productivity growth. It is interesting to observe that total factor productivity has increased for some of the labour-intensive exports and who are also export-oriented

Table 3 Employment and wages as per ASI sata

	Employment (in million)			Real wages and salaries (in Rs billion)		
	2008–09	2013–14	Growth (%)	2008–09	2013–14	Growth (%)
Labour-intensive sector						
Workers employed through contractors	0.79	0.87	1.4	27.5	39.5	5.3
Supervisory and managerial staff	0.17	0.22	3.8	51.6	80.2	6.5
Total employees	2.53	2.93	2.1	180.0	258.0	5.3
Capital-intensive sector						
Workers employed through contractors	0.25	0.48	9.9	14.80	32.60	11.9
Supervisory and managerial staff	0.10	0.14	5.8	42.20	79.80	9.5
Total employees	0.87	1.35	6.5	115.00	203.00	8.5
Textile sector						
Workers employed through contractors	0.18	0.22	2.4	9.44	13.20	4.9
Supervisory and managerial staff	0.09	0.11	1.5	22.20	32.60	5.6
Total employees	1.40	1.57	1.6	98.00	133.00	4.5

Source ASI satabase

sectors during the period 2008/09 and 2015/16. For example, wood products, textile and apparel, etc., have higher TFPG. However, the majority of the industries is lost in terms of productivity growth during this time. Table 4 arranges the industries in terms of productivity growth. In a dynamic sense, lower productivity has a negative impact on export competitiveness, and this gets accentuated in a situation with increasing wages. As a result, export-oriented sectors are unable to increase employment in the long run. However, in the short run, a country can sustain higher employment in the export-oriented industries in a situation with lower productivity if export demand is high. This may be analysed in Fig. 1.

Factors such as productivity growth, factor intensity and skill have a significant impact to make on the industry's output and employment. But as conversed in the model, these factors cannot help alone to accomplish the benefits of exports on employment growth. There exists a dependency on the factors that are not substitutable. Thus, in the next section, we have presented the empirical results of our model.

Table 4 Factor intensity and productivity growth

Industries	Intensive	TFPG
16 Manufacture of wood and products of wood and cork, except furniture; manufacture of articles of straw and plaiting materials	Labour intensive	6.65
13 Manufacture of textiles	Fluctuating	2.33
19 Manufacture of coke and refined petroleum products	Capital intensive	2.25
20 Manufacture of chemicals and chemical products	Capital intensive	1.50
14 Manufacture of wearing apparel	Labour intensive	1.29
30 Manufacture of other transport equipment	Fluctuating	−0.67
17 Manufacture of paper and paper products	Capital intensive	−2.11
10 Manufacture of food products	Labour intensive	−2.66
28 Manufacture of machinery and equipment n.e.c	Labour intensive	−3.06
31 Manufacture of furniture	Labour intensive	−4.29
15 Manufacture of leather and related products	Labour intensive	−4.41
22 Manufacture of rubber and plastics products	Capital intensive	−4.71
11 Manufacture of beverages	Capital intensive	−5.09
18 Printing and reproduction of recorded media	Labour intensive	−5.89
29 Manufacture of motor vehicles, trailers and semi-trailers	Capital intensive	−6.09
23 Manufacture of other non-metallic mineral products	Capital intensive	−6.26
21 Manufacture of pharmaceuticals, medicinal chemical and botanical products	Capital intensive	−6.29
25 Manufacture of fabricated metal products, except machinery and equipment	Labour intensive	−7.11
12 Manufacture of tobacco products	Labour intensive	−7.30
24 Manufacture of basic metals	Capital intensive	−7.60
26 Manufacture of computer, electronic and optical products	Fluctuating	−8.01
27 Manufacture of electrical equipment	Labour intensive	−12.16
32 Other manufacturing	Labour intensive	−21.50

*TFPG calculated for the period 2008/09–2013/14
Manufacture of textiles seems to be fluctuating behaviour between labour- and capital-intensive according to median of K/L. But as per mean, it is labour-intensive industry. Following NSSO data, in manufacturing sector, textile is among one of the sectors where the highest number of people is employed, and hence, we have considered it separately to understand its employment structure in organised sector

5 Estimation Results

Table 5 shows the impact of the factors that affect different kinds of employment together at various levels. We can learn from these results that labour-intensive industries have generated more employment significantly and have the potential to hire more workers. And wages play the significant positive role to increase the employment in the industry as well as at firm level. This accords with our equilibrium

Table 5 Regression results of employment at NIC 3 digit industry and firm level

	Industry			Small			Medium			Large		
	(1)	(2)	(3)	(4)	(5)	(6)	(7)	(8)	(9)	(10)	(11)	(12)
Variables	Contractual workers	Supervisory and managerial staff	All workers	Contractual workers	Supervisory and managerial staff	All workers	Contractual workers	Supervisory and managerial staff	All workers	Contractual workers	Supervisory and managerial staff	All workers
World_gdp	0.6394***	0.2677***	0.2796***	2.4640***	1.2428***	1.4676***	−0.6315***	−0.2482**	−0.4291***	−0.2938***	0.0164	−0.0053
	(0.1131)	(0.0791)	(0.0627)	(0.3180)	(0.1578)	(0.1525)	(0.0884)	(0.0972)	(0.0645)	(0.1076)	(0.1401)	(0.0880)
Deflated export	0.0152*	0.0174***	0.0101**	0.0186	0.0070	0.0063	0.0003	0.0109	0.0049	−0.0156	0.0396***	0.0187**
	(0.0080)	(0.0053)	(0.0042)	(0.0156)	(0.0071)	(0.0069)	(0.0075)	(0.0080)	(0.0050)	(0.0103)	(0.0133)	(0.0084)
tfp_hat	−0.0397**	−0.0373***	−0.0371***	−0.0494*	−0.0260*	−0.0312**	0.0297*	−0.0787***	−0.0532***	−0.0021	−0.0332	−0.0375**
	(0.0160)	(0.0104)	(0.0082)	(0.0293)	(0.0132)	(0.0127)	(0.0176)	(0.0183)	(0.0115)	(0.0224)	(0.0286)	(0.0181)
"x"_wages	0.5689***	0.4275***	0.4915***	0.3892***	0.3691***	0.3515***	0.8616***	0.4883***	0.6208***	0.7826***	0.4119***	0.5370***
	(0.0173)	−0.0176	(0.0171)	(0.0332)	(0.0276)	(0.0309)	(0.0161)	(0.0243)	(0.0216)	(0.0238)	(0.0347)	(0.0278)
D_L/K	4.5063***	5.0008***	4.5457***	4.7367***	3.3555***	3.7853***	1.7508***	3.8350***	3.5340***	3.1016***	13.0482***	8.5465***
	(0.5939)	(0.3839)	(0.3074)	(1.1465)	(0.5217)	(0.5047)	(0.5196)	(0.5316)	(0.3451)	(0.8913)	(1.0801)	(0.7080)
L/K*D_L/K	0.3254***	0.3627***	0.3267***	0.3354***	0.2386***	0.2652***	0.1292***	0.2803***	0.2592***	0.2241***	0.9644***	0.6268***
	(0.0449)	(0.0290)	(0.0232)	(0.0869)	(0.0395)	(0.0382)	(0.0392)	(0.0401)	(0.0260)	(0.0671)	(0.0816)	(0.0533)
Constant	−23.9342***	−10.2807***	−10.1386***	−81.0662***	−41.1798***	−46.5203***	12.0006***	5.3711*	10.2045***	3.2702	−1.8693	−1.6098
	(3.5162)	(2.3826)	(1.8548)	(10.0236)	(4.8246)	(4.6118)	(2.7259)	(2.9156)	(1.8529)	(3.2534)	(4.1868)	(2.5861)
Observations	1,413	1,442	1,442	420	436	436	502	508	508	491	498	498
R-squared	0.5913	0.5641	0.6666	0.5169	0.6794	0.6955	0.8859	0.6145	0.7793	0.8063	0.5536	0.7396
Number of panel_id	202	203	203	67	67	67	69	69	69	66	67	67

Source Authors' own calculations

model. The most vital variable is the exports, as manufacturing sectors (specifically the labour-intensive sectors) accelerate its exports; it generates employment significantly at the industry level. It is starting to notice that when exports increase in the small, medium and large firms, they push the overall employment significantly in the manufacturing sector. But the role of exports is drenched with the total factor productivity of the firm. It is clearly visible that the role of productivity and exports is acting in the opposite directions in employment generation. But both are playing a significant role in the employment status. Another important aspect to notice is the role of world GDP growth as the proxy of the business cycle which impacts different kinds of employment and its coefficient value decreases as we move from small to large firms. One possible reason is large firms are serving both domestic and international markets, and if business cycle is not in favour, they always have a chance of serving the domestic market at large scale. But small businesses, especially those who are dealing in exports, have significant impact on employment due to the firm base.

Substitution between contractual and supervisory workers mainly happens in the large size firms as the exports increase, and there is a decline in the unskilled labour force and inclination in the skilled labour force. While for other sized firms, exports help to increase the employment but not significantly. Large firms are backed with a lot of capital invested but there exists a disequilibrium situation because of the unmatched skilled labour supply with the capital. With the increase in productivity, contractual employment decreases, especially in small-sized firms. It is noticed that medium firms are more aligned to hire the contractual workers. Contractual employment is pushed for more working hours leading to more output per worker. But large firms do not rely on the contractual employment as their export base increases. This is because they can afford technology and are in a better position to provide the benefits and hire permanent staff. So the increase in exports in large firms would increase the supervisory and managerial staff significantly. Thus, the final increase in employment is a function of factor intensity, export, business cycle and productivity growth and the size of firm as well.

We can conclude that Indian large firms are mostly dependent on the capital intensity. They have the potential to hire more workers but with respect to capital, labour is relatively less and is decreasing in large size firm due to the advancement in the technology. Large firms are majorly linked with the export growth that increases the employment. With the increase in the world GDP growth, large firms are in better position to hire supervisory workers and fire the contractual workers. Role of productivity is setting back with the presence of large capital unmatched with skilled labour. Large firms have the potential to the increase the employment with exports, but it can be increased with the right set of skills in the labour force that makes difficult for large firms to substitute capital for labour. Moving towards medium-sized firms, where capital is not too much, they equivalently rely majorly on employees. They prefer hiring the supervisory workers to enhance the exports. Here, the role of the exports starts decreasing, and the role of productivity and business cycle increases as compared to large firms. With the last category of small firms, the role of productivity comes to the main stage, here capital is less and small firms largely rely on the workers. Given the appropriate skill set and capital, small and medium firms have the greater potential to increase the exports and employment in the Indian economy, especially in favourable business cycle environment. Indian economy suffers right now from the lack of adequate skills that act as a hindrance in creating employment in the large-scale firms. This makes the large firms to substitute labour for capital and somewhere rigid labour market regulations are also to blame at. While small and medium firms have the potential to hire but these suffer from the adequate capital problem to enhance the export base of the country using indigenous employees.

6 Conclusion

The paper using ASI factory-level data is to explain the stylised facts of employment trend in Indian manufacturing industry with a special focus on exporting industries. Though employment growth in exporting industries has been higher than the manufacturing sector as a whole during the period 2008/09–2015/16, it has been significantly different with respect to the size of the firms. This paper unearthed the complex relationship between export and employment. It has been noticed that final impact on employment generation due to rise in exports is dependent on the progress in other parameters as well like wherever labour-intensive firms are present, the demand of the supervisor and managerial workers is more. For sure, there is a demand for skilled workers in the Indian tradable sector but due to its unavailability, large firms try to substitute labour with capital. However, the technology infusion productivity has also increased in some sectors. Hence, the relationship between export growth and employment generation is conditional. As export growth is a function of the business cycle, it is important to note that global volatility also affects employment but its effect depends on variables such as productivity, factor intensity and size of the firm. Indian firms are trapped in the vicious cycle of capital, skills, firm size, productivity and factor intensity. And the government could help to get out of this cycle by training people and bringing upgraded technology wherever required.

Acknowledgments This chapter has been adapted from the authors' working paper, "'India's Trade Sensitive Employment Analysis at the Sectoral Level"', July 2018, IIFT Working Paper No: EC-18-34, http://cc.iift.ac.in/research/Docs/WP/34.pdf

Appendix

List of variables used in paper, necessary variables are deflated with WPI:

- **Capital (K)**: It is the capital stock. This we have calculated using the perpetual inventory accumulation following the idea proposed by Srivastava (1996) and Nag (2005). Model identifies the initial investment, constant growth rate of capital stock from the data of gross fixed capital and accumulated depreciation. To get capital, the net values closing of all the fixed assets of firms are taken, which includes land, building, transport equipment, plant and machinery, computer equipment including software, pollution control equipment, others and capital work in progress. It is provided in Block-C of ASI data set.

- **Labour (L)**: ASI provides the data in its Block-E regarding employment and labour cost. For this, it classifies labour as following:

  1. **Female**: Female workers employed directly
  2. **Male**: Male workers employed directly
  3. **All directly employed**: 1 + 2
  4. **Contractual workers**: Workers employed through contractors
  5. **Supervisor workers**: Supervisory and managerial staff
  6. **All workers**: 3 + 4 + 5 + unpaid family members/ proprietor/ coop. members + other employees.

- **Wages (w)**: Wages/salaries (in Rs.) are given in Block-E of ASI data set for all types of workers discussed above.
- **Material (M)**: Stock of raw materials is used as input. Raw materials and components and packing materials are the variable used to calculate the stock of raw material, by taking its closing value difference from opening value. It is given in Block D of ASI which tells about the opening and closing balance of working capital and loans.
- **Output (Y)**: It is the output. Ex-factory value of output is given in the ASI data for each firm which is considered as output variable at current prices.
- **Accumulated depreciation (AD)**: As ASI reports the book value of the fixed assets, so, having difference between net and gross closing capital, we get the accumulated depreciation.
- **Depreciation (Dep)**: It is defined for time period t as follows: $\text{Dep}_t = \text{AD}_{t+1} - \text{AD}_t$.
- **Gross fixed assets (GFA)**: It is defined with the gross closing value of all fixed assets.
- **Depreciation rate** (δ_t): It tells the rate at which fixed assets are depreciated.
- **Investment (I)**: Investment in any time (t) is defined as the difference between gross capital closing and opening.
- **Total factor productivity (TFP)**: It is the share of output not expounded by the extent of inputs used in production.

References

Aho, C. M., & Orr, J. A. (1981). Trade-sensitive employment: Who are the affected workers? *Monthly Labor Review, 104*, 29–35.

Cornwell, C., Schmidt, P., & Sickles, R. C. (1990). Production frontiers with cross-sectional and time-series variation in efficiency levels. *Journal of Econometrics*. https://doi.org/10.1016/0304-4076(90)90054-W.

Das, D., Wadhwa, D., & Kalita, G. (2009). *The employment potential of labor intensive industries in India's organized manufacturing* (No. 236).

Grossman, G. M., & Helpman, E. (1991). Trade, knowledge spillovers, and growth. *European Economic Review*. https://doi.org/10.1016/0014-2921(91)90153-A.

Hasan, R., Mitra, D., Ranjan, P., & Ahsan, R. N. (2012). Trade liberalization and unemployment: Theory and evidence from India. *Journal of Development Economics*. https://doi.org/10.1016/j.jdeveco.2011.04.002.

Kapoor, R. (2016). *Technology, jobs and inequality evidence from India's manufacturing sector* (No. 313).

Kucera, D., Roncolato, L., & von Uexkull, E. (2012). Trade contraction and employment in India and South Africa during the global crisis. *World Development*. https://doi.org/10.1016/j.worlddev.2011.11.003.

Mehrotra, S., Parida, J., & Singh, S. G. A. (2014). Explaining employment trends in the Indian economy : 1993–94 to 2011–12. *Economic & Political Weekly, XLIX*, 49–57.

Milner, C., & Wright, P. (1998). Modelling labour market adjustment to trade liberalisation in an industrialising economy. *Economic Journal*. https://doi.org/10.1111/1468-0297.00301.

Nag, B. (2005). Impact of capacity utilisation and slow adjustments of Quasi-fixed factors on productivity and efficiency measurement: An experiment with Indian pharmaceutical industry. *Journal of Pharmaceutical, Finance, Economics and Policy, 14*, 69–73.

Orbeta, A.C. (2002). Globalization and employment: The impact of trade on employment level and structure in the Philippines. In PIDS Discussion Paper Series, No. 2002–04. Philippine Institute for Development Studies (PIDS), Makati City.

Rattsø, J., & Torvik, R. (1998). Zimbabwean trade liberalisation: Ex post evaluation. *Cambridge Journal of Economics*. https://doi.org/10.1093/oxfordjournals.cje.a013719.

Revenga, A. (1999). *Employment and wage effects of trade liberalization: The case of Mexican manufacturing* 15. https://doi.org/10.1596/1813-9450-1524

Srivastav, V. (1996). *Liberalization productivity and competition: A panel study of Indian manufacturing*. Oxford University Press.

Vashisht, P. (2015). *Creating manufacturing jobs in India : Has openness to trade really helped?* (No. 303).

Veeramani, C., Dhir, G. (2017). *Reaping gains from global production sharing domestic value addition and job creation by Indian exports domestic value addition and job creation by Indian exports reaping gains from global production sharing, in: IARIW-ICIER conference.*

Vivarelli, M. (2002). *Globalisation, skills and within-country inequality in developing countries, in: Draft for ILO Project on understanding globalisation, employment and poverty reduction.* Geneva: ILO.

Wagner, J. (2002). The causal effects of exports on firm size and labor productivity: First evidence from a matching approach. *Economics Letters, 77*, 287–292. https://doi.org/10.1016/S0165-1765(02)00131-3.

Chapter 14 Trade Liberalization and Poverty Alleviation in Nigeria: The Complementary Role of Institutions

Muftau Olaiya Olarinde and A. A. Bello

1 Introduction

There has been a renew interest in global economic integration, in particular trade liberalization as a development strategy by most policy makers. This was based on the intuition that both international and national equality will be achieved through trade increasing relative wages in labor-abundant economies and lowering them in labor-scarce countries. Above all, it raises real income of trading countries and ensuring the efficient allocation of nations and world's resource endowment (Todaro & Smith, 2011). The traditional trade theory is of the view that long-term effect of trade policy (in particular tariff) aimed at improving the welfare of the poor either in a capital-endowed economy, exporting capital-intensive goods or labor endowed country, exporting labor-intensive goods will result into higher rate of return to capital or labor as the case may be. The higher rate of return to factors will be in the short-run impact the relative price of imported goods (specifically in the import competing sector) positively and encouraging transfer of capital and labor from the export sector to the import sector in the long run. The reallocation of factors between sectors specifically in a capital-rich economy will ensure higher capital–labor ratio in both sectors, resulting in long-term effects of higher marginal product of labor and declining marginal product of capital in both sectors. The increase in marginal product of labor will translate into increase in real wage rate for workers that form the bulk of the poor and a declining return on capital in real term (Sodersten & Geoffery, 1994).

M. O. Olarinde (✉) · A. A. Bello
Department of Economics, Faculty of Social Sciences, Usmanu Danfodiyo University, Sokoto, Nigeria
e-mail: olarinde.muftau@udusok.edu.ng

A. A. Bello
e-mail: abdghanbel@yahoo.co.uk

P. Lakhanpal et al. (eds.), *Trade, Investment and Economic Growth*,
https://doi.org/10.1007/978-981-33-6973-3_14

However, the present growth experience of many developing countries creates doubt in the above prediction of neoclassical trade theories and provides evidence in support of the opposing view. They argued that through redistribution, trade liberalization policy could actually result to growth in income but fail to ensure increase in wages of unskilled labor even in a labor-abundant country, thereby widening the gap of inequality between the rich and the poor, as well as increasing rate of poverty in developing economies (Topalova, 2007). The above assertion vividly portrayed the present poor state of development in African continent most especially Nigeria with a considerable level of economy openness.

Nigeria is an oil-rich economy and a labor abundant with oil proceeds accounting for the largest percentage of its total GDP. Although at independence and early 1970s, Nigeria's major exports were non-oil agricultural produce. Between 1970 and 1985, crude oil exports surpassed this feat and the sector accounted for about 93% of the total exports, and by 1998, it is increased to 96.05, by 2012 it experienced an insignificant decline in its figures by 1.05%. Despite all efforts toward diversifying the economy away from oil, the total of value of crude oil export in the country still remains high with a figure of 79.9% as at second quarter of 2016. Over this period, the share of non-oil exports declined to 4.0% in the same year. Within the non-oil exports, cocoa accounted for about 61.1% in the 1970s, and between 1986 and 1998, its share declined to 30.0%, (Mordi et al., 2010; NBS, 2017; Index Mundi, 2017). Overall, the non-oil export performance was discouraging. More disappointing was the total exists of some products such as groundnuts, cotton, hides and skin and palm oil among others. While the exports basket has been on the increase due to oil and gas exports, the import basket has been following the same trend. Most importantly, between 1980 and 1984 before the introduction of SAP, the importations of consumer goods top the list of imports. The import bill which averaged US$ 5899 million in 1986 increased to US$ 18,172.86 million by 2007. As at the end of the second quarter of 2016, the total import bill rose by 38.1% from the preceding year value.

In order to curtail this trend, a number of trade policy measures have been introduced in Nigeria targeted at restricting import volume to the available foreign exchange earning along with supply-side measures to boost exports, a strategy that has been dynamic. The dynamic nature of the external trade policy takes the form of a tightened exchange control from 1976 to 1979, between 1980 and 1986 the policy thrust was in favor of trade liberalization, and by early 1990 the policy was abandoned. Again, in July 1996 a liberalized trade regime became the policy thrust of the government. In the recent time, the trade policy adopted was contained in a circular released in June 23, 2016, by the Central Bank of Nigeria excluding importers of some foods and agricultural items from accessing forex at the official rate of exchange (Export.gov, 2016; Mordi et al., 2010).

On the whole, it can be said that Nigeria keys into the wave of trade liberalization as a condition for financial aid from international financial institutions. This was required to overcome its poor state of the macroeconomic environment necessitated by the global economic crisis in the 1980s (Mordi et al., 2010). Also, the adoption of common external tariff (CET) under the Economic Community of West African States (ECOWAS) in 2005 which came into effect in 2015 marked another era of a new

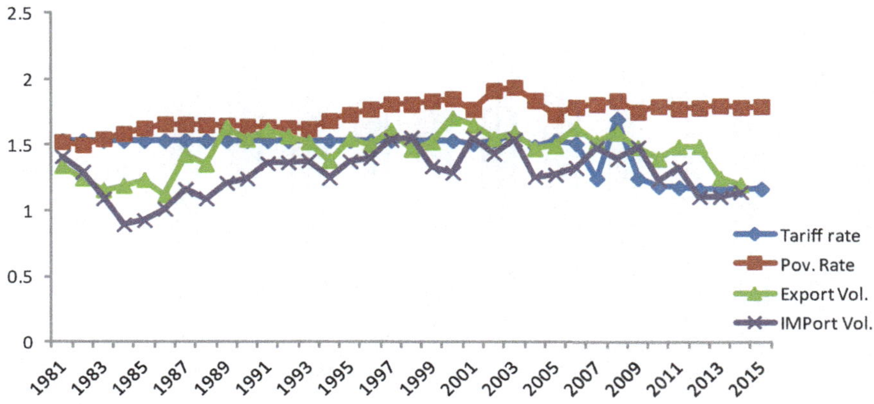

Fig. 1 Trend of annual consumer tariff rate, trade volume and poverty rate in Nigeria (1981–2015). *Source* Authors Computation using Data from World Bank, (2014), World Bank, WITS 2016 NBS, Various Issues. **Note* Data have been transformed into log values

trade policy regime in the country. The outcome of the above is an increasing degree of openness of the economy, with very poor macroeconomic outcomes, making an oil-rich country one of the poorest economies of the world. For instance, the trend of Nigeria imports tariff rates, which stood at 150% in 1999 reduced to 50% and 35% by 2008 and 2013, respectively, while weighted average tariff rate on consumer goods also experienced the same trend, declining from 38.28 to 17.82% and 14.87% over the same periods (World Bank, WITS 2016). Disappointedly, the worsened standard of living of most households only experienced a marginal improvement with percentage of the population below the poverty line declining from 64.2% in 2004 to just 62.0% in 2010 (see Fig. 1) while its level of inequality continues to get worsened as shown by Gini coefficient figures of 40.6 in 2003, increasing to 42.97 in 2009 (UNDP, 2015).

In the same vein, commencing from 1991, import price has been on the increase, in most cases higher than export prices, a scenario that has resulted in falling standard of living due to increasing level of consumer prices (see Fig. 2). Statistics available pointed to the fact that the marginal improvement achieved in the rate of poverty will be unsustainable and that a disappointing situation is evident in the near future to come. For example, between the years 2002 and 2011, the country recorded an average unemployment rate of 51.2% of the total population, higher than the rate in other countries in the region (UNDP, 2012). A careful look at the country-specific level of unemployment among the low- and middle-income countries portrays a clearer picture of worsening state of employment with Nigeria, having a rate of unemployment that is higher than that of Libya at 23.95, Malaysia 3.7%, Brazil 6.4% and Egypt at 11.85 in 2011 (UNECA, 2012; WDI, 2013).

The above scenarios create uncertainty on the postulates of trade theories, leaving the question of how trade liberalization impacts poverty at the mercy of empirical investigation. Empirical literature examining the effect of trade liberalization on

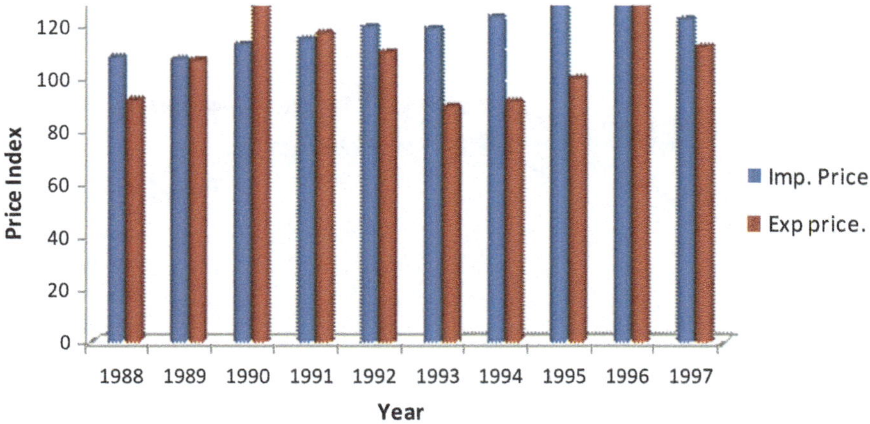

Fig. 2 Figure showing Trend of Import and Export prices in Nigeria (1988–1997). *Source* Author's Computation using Data from World Bank (2016)

poverty is highly debated, and the empirical evidences are conflicting (see Geoferrey & Kamau, 2001; Pineopi & Nina, 2004; Topalova, 2007; Goff & Singh, 2012; Imran & Imran, 2013) and specifically on Nigeria are Olofin, Adenikinju and Iwayemi (2001), Nwafor et al. (2005), Adeoye (2008), Ayinde, (2013), Uexkull and Shui (2014) and Eric (2015). One noticeable gap in previous studies with the exception of Goff and Singh (2012) is that the scholars assumed the link between trade and poverty to be direct. In actual sense, the impacts of trade policy on poverty may act through other complimentary factors like institution and level of education indicating an indirect relationship (Winters, 2004 as cited by Goff & Singh, 2012). Examining this relationship, the possibility of nonlinearity was not considered, a situation that might impair the validity of inferences, and this provides an intuition for the present study.

Also, previous empirical papers (Nwafor et al., 2005; Adeoye, 2008; Ayinde, 2013; Eric, 2015) assumed the link between trade deregulation and poverty to be static, whereas policy and economic activities change overtime and as such their shock is dynamic with varying intensity, a situation in which a technique based on static analysis could not be handled. This gap is covered in this study by estimating a time-varying parameter (TVP) based on state-space model using Kalman filter approach. Therefore, the present study examined the impacts of trade liberalization on poverty taking into consideration the likelihood of structural breaks in the behavior of the series. Specifically, the paper intends to investigate the responses of poverty to shocks in trade liberalization as well the impact of its complementary factors on poverty in Nigeria. To achieve these objectives, the paper has been divided into various sections. Following this section is the review of relevant literature, Sect. 3 dwells on methodology while Sect. 4 contains data analysis, and Sect. 5 concludes and proffers recommendations.

2 Literature Review

2.1 Review of Theoretical and Empirical Literature

Defining liberalization as it relates to trade is as difficult as measuring the extent of liberalization itself. This is due to the fact that even if all restrictive policies are known, the knowledge of the depth of implementation may not be known. In view of this, trade liberalization could be taken to be reduced or partial removal of the institutional barriers to trade, which alter prices of both foreign and domestic goods, ensuring an unvarying policy treatment between different economic activities and allowed for competitive market (Winters, 2000a).

As difficult as it is in defining liberalization so also the concept of poverty. Poverty could be likened to a situation in which an individual was deprived of the basic necessities of life required for a minimally acceptable standard of living. These include needs for food and other basic necessities of life like health, education and essential public goods (Kankwenda et al., 2000). For the purpose of this study, poverty will be viewed from the perspective of income, therefore an individual is considered to be poor if his or her consumption falls short of a predetermined poverty line and as such, he or she does not have sufficient income to achieve a certain level of well-being.

Theories explaining the trade–poverty link can be grouped into two main strands; mainstream theory of trade and new trade theory, each with different explanations about the trade internal distributional effects and how it impacts the poor. For instance, Stopler-Samuelson (1941), Samuelson (1948, 1949) theorem on long-term effect of tariff based on assumption of a capital-endowed economy, an offshoot of Heckscher-Ohlin neoclassical orthodox trade model, states that in a two inputs (capital and labor), two countries and two commodities model, a country will have relative opportunity in relatively intensive goods produced through relatively abundant factor (*capital-intensive goods*). The comparative advantage enjoyed in the form of higher rate of return to capital due to increase in the relative price of imported goods (specifically in the import competing sector) resulting into optimum reallocation of factors between sectors and thus a higher marginal product of labor and declining marginal product of capital. The increase in the marginal product of labor will translate into increasing real income of the factor with which the country is well endowed and a decrease in that of the scarce input, thereby resulting increasing income and declining trend of poverty (Samantha & Nicollete, 2006).

The new trade theory as developed by Winters (2000a, b) and further expanded by McCulloch et al. (2001) extends orthodox neoclassical trade theory and posits that understanding the trade–poverty link goes beyond providing restrictive assumption but required detailed knowledge of three different transmission channels through which trade can be linked to poverty. These channels are price mechanism channel, enterprise channel and government policy channel (McCulloch et al., 2001).

Explaining the price transmission channel, Winters (2000b) used as a case study, a household operating on both sides of the market in an economy, (consumer and producer) in which trade liberalization is expected to affect the prices of export goods as well as import substitutes. The overall impacts depend on either the underprivileged is a final consumer or producer of commodities whose price has been affected. A rise in the price of good of which the household is a final producer and a decline in the price of which is a final consumer will definitely result in increase welfare and vice versa (PRUS, 2001).

Providing for the role of institutions, Winters (2000b) opined that the price pass through might not be direct due to the way channel of distribution is set up in the absence of effective institutions. In an economy, tradable goods have to pass through different borders, adding to the production cost at each stage, thus reducing the price reduction benefit expected to be gained by the poor. In other cases, a net producer of exported goods might not experience any increase in price due to liberalization if the middlemen retain the increase in price as a profit. Also, in a situation where economic liberalization eliminates certain market institutions (Marketing Board), creating a missing market and leaving small farmers at the mercy of private agents, the poor farmers can completely be isolated both in the existing market and new market opportunities. Therefore, efficient institutions are required to remove administrative bottlenecks that can add to cost, safeguard poor producers from exploitation of private gents and market failure (McCulloch et al., 2001). Mukhopadhyay (2002) submits that unguided liberalization without adequate government policies and strong institutions to safeguard the system against market failure can result into doom for the poor in the periphery. This was the case in South Africa, where liberalization was associated with declining rate of employment, increasing prices of commodities that are basically for the underprivileged.

Tracing the impact of trade on poverty through enterprise channel as it affects wages and employment, the theory posits that the elasticity of labor supply determines the extent at which fluctuations in prices of goods jointly produced by a firm and others will result into changes in wages and employment (Winters, 2000b). If the supply of labor in a liberalized economy is perfectly inelastic, a change in price will only be reflected in increase wages but not in employment level because works compete with leisure (Branson, 1989). Conversely, in a state of perfectly elastic supply of labor, the impact will be purely employment-driven based since wages are assumed to be sticky downward as argued by the Keynesians. Increased prices encourage higher output, real wage remains unchanged, and this translates into an increase rate of employment, thereby reducing poverty rate, but with a neutral wage effect (Bannister and Thugge, 2001).

In the third channel, trade liberalization may impact government expenditure through tax revenue. The increasing government spending on social safety net and transfer through increased tax revenue will influence positively household income. A liberalized trade with a declining impact on government spending due to dwindling revenue could end up making the poor worse off. On the other hand, in order to compensate for the loss in revenue, an attempt by the government to increase charges and other taxes like value-added tax might be considered; if these taxes affect goods consumed by the poor, the outcome will be poverty inducing (Winters, 2000b). Providing a counter argument on the above submission, Bannister and Thugge (2001) submit that lower tariff rates due to trade liberalization may increase trade volume, reduce incentives for smuggling, thereby increases total traded goods and consequently also increases revenue. This preposition may be far from reality in most developing countries most especially in Nigeria characterized by economic rigidity where reduction in tariff due to trade Liberalization might have a declining impact on revenue. Therefore, the nature of the influence in various countries depends on the types of the markets (perfect or imperfect), the strategic behavior of the firm, the nature of the institution of a country and the level of diversification among others.

Providing an empirical evidence in support of various channels through which trade could impact poverty as postulated by the new trade theory, Yoon and Nguyen (2006) using simple descriptive statistics as method of data analysis conclude that the effects of trade liberalization on poor households in Vietnam could be transmitted through economic growth, enterprises, market and government. The study further revealed that the import substitution policy has failed in improving the welfare of the poor. This is because the increased level of industrialization achieved is insufficient to generate increased labor demand and the most important economic resources owned by the poor.

Hala (2012) examines the link between trade openness and poverty reduction in Egypt, using simple descriptive statistics to analyze data covering a period of 1999–2012. The paper revealed that the removal of trade restriction alone could not ensure an optimum declining impact of openness on poverty. Therefore, trade liberalization needs to be combined with relevant policies related to infrastructure and institutional development, safety nets, adequate financial support and labor mobility in order to reduce the number of the poor.

Using an historical data covering a period of 1974–2001, Guillermo and Marcelo (2006) investigate whether the impacts of trade on skill premium depend on other complementary policies in Argentina. It was confirmed that education, governance (proxy for institutions), labor market and firm entry flexibility have a positive significant influence on poor income both as a variable and when interacted with the openness. The paper concludes that the impact of liberalized trade is dynamic over the different periods and policy complementarities in the form of education, access to credit, strong institutions among others can ensure that the underprivileged gained from poverty reducing trade reforms. Dahai and Shantong (2014) investigated the impact of globalization (through its influence on the exchange rate) on welfare of Chinese households' consumption. The authors adopted feasible generalized least squares method to evaluate the effects of the renminbi appreciation on domestic prices and consumption. The results confirm that appreciation of renminbi is negatively related to prices of consumer goods in China. However, the poor households do not benefit much from the currency appreciation compared to that of the wealthy families.

In an Africa-related study, Dorosh and Sahn (1999) looked at the linkage between trade and exchange rate liberalization on poverty and income among some selected African countries using social accounting matrices (SAMS) for the period 1989–1993. Findings revealed that openness and liberalization of exchange rate benefit the low-income families, both in urban and rural areas. Producing the same result is a study by Decalawe et al. (1999) on the impact of export crop prices and import tariff on the level of poverty among African, the result of computable general equilibrium shows that reductions in import tariffs positively influence alleviation of poverty.

Building on the methodological approaches of earlier studies, Olayinka (2014) carried out a research on the nexus between domestic prices and wages and their combine effects on household welfare in Nigeria. Feasible generalized least square (FGLS) based on cross-sectional time series was used to estimate different models including interacting term (distance and tariff). The result revealed that tariff reduction benefits the consumers of agricultural products through the ECOWAS CET. This benefit tends to decline as they interact distance with tariff, and that households that are closer to the ports greatly benefit more. In relation to the wage-earning channel, the result further revealed that the country wage rate is not associated with falling domestic prices.

Examining the prospects of the ECOWAS CET in relation to changes in tariff and its impact on total export and revenue for Nigeria using a trade model based on partial equilibrium with imperfect substitution between imports under three scenarios. Uexkull and Shui (2014) simulation results revealed, that the whole setup of CET based on removal of import restriction will result in significant improvement in Nigerian consumer's welfare with a reduction in consumption prices with about 2.4%. Contrary to the above, imposition of ban and tariffs on certain imports and applying CET on non-prohibited goods will result into increasing prices and further worsened the welfare of the poor. On the job creation impact of CET, it was revealed that the employment creation rate of regional exporters is faster than that of global and domestic exporters. Providing support for the role of institutions, Eric (2015) using FMOLS concludes that there exists a significant negative relationship between trade liberalization and level of development in Nigeria, while both export and import impact growth positively. The paper recommends for strong institutions capable of eradicating corrupt practices.

Following a different approach, Akinlo et al. (2013) adopted GMM technique to analyze time series data over a period of 1980–2009 with focus on the effect of trade openness on poor household in Nigeria. The findings revealed that trade liberalization does not significantly reduce poverty, with the exception of trade openness that marginally exerts a downward trend on poverty rate. These findings were later refuted by Ogungbowa and Eburajolo (2014) with empirical evidence obtained from their error correction model indicating that globalization will result into a significant declining trend in the poverty rate in Nigeria.

2.2 Theoretical Framework

The basic theoretical model for this study follows Mcculloch et al. (2001) and Arne et al. (2007) with little modification. The framework identifies three basic channels (enterprise, distribution and government channels) through which trade impacts welfare of the poor and incorporates institutional and educational factors as endogenous factors which serve as complements to trade liberalization. Trade policy in the form of tariffs or taxes will have a short-run impact, firstly on boarder prices and then on retail prices through distribution channels. The nature of the impact depends on the objective behind the imposition of tariffs. A reduction in tariffs on import is expected to have declining impact on boarder prices with its multiplier effects on retail prices (Fig. 3).

Tracing the effect of tariff and tax policies, the figure shows a lower tariff rate will affect the boarder price of factors (in particular goods produced by the poor) resulting in lower cost of production and firm's (producer's) profitability. Tax policy informs of tax holidays will also exert the same impact on the production cost through the government channel. The pass-through effects of both channels (distributional and government channels) will result into increasing levels of investment, employment opportunities and income.

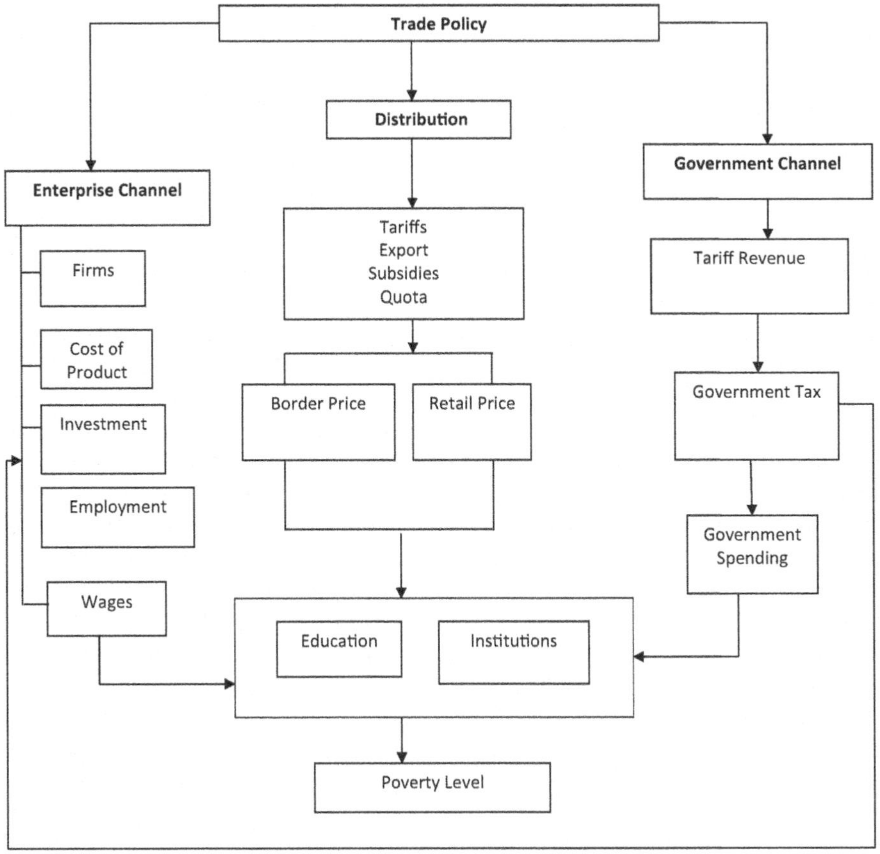

Fig. 3 Trade policy and poverty interaction. *Source* Author's Concept

The long-run objectives behind trade liberalization using tariffs and taxes as instruments are to improve the welfare of the poor as a consumer from the consumption side and as producers from the factors market. Therefore, trade liberalization changes the prices (boarder and retail prices) that the poor face both as consumers and producers. It also ensures improved incomes for the poor since they are mostly a supplier of human efforts. The figure shows that the long-run benefits of trade liberalization might not be automatic, but depends on the complementary roles played by institutions and quality of education of the set of people that the policy is meant to benefit. In an environment of weak institutions, the price reduction benefits that are expected to be gained through distributional channel may be missing if the poor are left at the mercy of the profit maximizing agents. Also, the employment and increasing wage benefits as a result of falling production cost might fail to benefit the poorly educated workers. This is particularly so in the world of technology innovation that requires professional skills. In conclusion, the nature of the long-run impact of trade policy on the poor depends on both the educational and institutional qualities that are available.

3 Methodology

3.1 Data Sources and Description of Variables

Annual time series data for the period 1981–2015 were used in the study. A broad investigation of the literature shows different proxies that have been used as a measure of trade liberalization. This has been grouped into outcome-based captured by trade data and incidence-based measures using tariff data (Spilimbergo et al., 1999; Calderón et al., 2005 as cited by Golf & Singh, 2012). For the present study, trade liberalization will be measured both as outcome-based and incidence-based (Marta et al., 2009). As incidence-based, weighted average tariff on consumer goods source from World Bank (World Bank, WITS 2016) was used, and this is predicated on the fact that significant period of study falls within the periods of structural adjustment program (SAP) during which policy of deregulation was adopted and the introduction of ECOWAS CET that compel all members' countries to remove almost all tariffs on intra ECOWAS trade. Although ECOWAS market for Nigeria remains insignificant when compared to the global trading partners, the fact that regional exporters just like the domestic firms create more job opportunities and thus increase sources of income compared to the global exporter (Uexkull & Shui, 2014) makes this a significant factor. Also, developing countries are major producers of primary products of which Nigeria is not an exception. The producers of these commodities are significantly farmers; therefore, a change in the rate of tariff on any of the products will impact significantly the earnings of both producers and consumers of such commodities. Globalization has been found to typically increase the volume of trade and ensure availability of varieties of goods which presents consumers the freedom to make choices among competing goods at a cheaper price. Consequently, trade liberalization is also measured as the value of exports plus imports as a percentage of GDP (Akinlo et al., 2013). Poverty headcount index has been defined as number of household members that fall below the poverty line (Kankwenda et al., 2000), and in the present study it is measured as percentage of the total population below poverty line sourced from World Bank mega data line 320 (2014).

Level of education is proxy by secondary school enrollment measured in percentages. It is expected that the level of education of workers in a country determines the rate at which such worker acquired new skills needed to meet up with modern day labor demand due to globalization. Monetary policy proxy by the rate of inflation is considered more appropriate compared to interest rate, due to its relative influence on consumer goods prices, mostly patronized by low-income groups. Also, a larger percentage of this group of people resides in the rural areas with little access to financial facilities, thus, they care less about the rate of interest. The financial development which determines the capacity of a country to absorb financial inflow due to openness is captured by broad money as ratio of the total GDP source from World Bank (2014). In order to measure the effect of level of economic development on poverty, real growth in income proxy by real GDP is considered to be appropriate.

Quality of service delivery proxy by electricity consumption (in kilowatts) per capita was used as a measure of institutional quality (Ndebbio, 2006; Udah, 2010), source from World Bank (2014). The use of this indicator is considered more appropriate and free from criticisms of subjectivity mostly associated with the use of indexes. Also, the indicator is considered more superior to other institutional indicators based on three major reasons. First, the effectiveness of policy implementation determined by the quality of social institutions and the level of public acceptance of this policy can be evaluated based on the indicators. Also, the availability of energy has a great bearing on the sources of income as well as the overall welfare of the poor. In light of this, the ability to provide essential public services achievable through strong institution is germane in determining the poverty level in a country. For annual weighted average tariff on consumer goods and other variables, four years moving average figure were used for years in which data were unavailable.

3.2 Model Specification and Estimation Procedure

In other to capture the responses of poverty to shocks from trade policy on one hand, and how liberalization impacts poverty on the other, the following baseline model in its dynamic nature was specified and estimated with two distinct techniques: state-space model and fully modified OLS.

$$\text{pov} = \beta_0 + \beta_i \text{X}i + \sum_{i=-p}^{p} \delta_i \Delta \text{X}_{t-i} + \varepsilon_i \tag{1}$$

where β_0 and δ_i,δ_p are parameters to be estimated, and ε_i is the error term assumed to be normally and identically distributed. X is a vector of regressors, and Δ is the lag operator. Expressing Eq. (1) in terms of the regressors in an estimable form, we have

$$\text{pov} = \beta_0 + \beta_1\text{tlib} + \beta_2\text{opens} + \beta_3\text{rgdp} + \beta_4\text{ins} + \beta_5\text{edu} + \beta_6\text{fdep} + \varepsilon_t \quad (2)$$

Introducing the interacting term in Eq. (2) gives Eq. (3)

$$\begin{aligned}\text{pov} = \beta_0 + \beta_1 t\text{lib} + \beta_2\text{opens} + \beta_3 rgdp + \beta_4 f\text{dep} \\ + \beta_5\text{edu} + \beta_6\text{ins} + \beta_7 t\text{lib} * \chi_{5-6} + \varepsilon_t \end{aligned} \quad (3)$$

where POV represents poverty, and TLIB and OPENS denote trade liberalization (proxy by average tariff rate and openness index, respectively). inf, rgdp, edu, fdep, ins and ε_t represent inflation, real GDP, level of education, financial development, institutions and error term that is expected to be white noise, respectively, while $\chi_{5\text{-}6}$ are the set of variables interacted with trade liberalization. This is grounded on the intuition that the poverty reducing impacts of trade might not be direct but operate or be impaired through the quality of institutions and level of education in the country. $\beta_1 \dots \beta_7$ are the coefficients to be estimated. In order to guide against problems of serial autocorrelation and heteroskedaciticy in the model, all the variables were transformed into their natural log with the exception of openness and inflation that were expressed in rates (Jalilian et al., 2007).

The estimation of Eq. (2) commenced with the test of stationarity of the series is used in the model. Two traditional and one modern unit root tests were employed; the traditional tests used in the paper are and Phillips-Perron (PP) and Augmented Dickey-Fuller (ADF). The two traditional tests were used to test for consistency and where conflicts exist, to decide on the most appropriate option (see Hamilton, 1994). Confirming the stationarity of the series through unit roots test with structural break becomes imperative in a model set out to explain the dynamics between trade policy and household welfare that may likely be affected through structural changes. This is important, because the correct assessment of any policy that can result in significant structural changes depends on the knowledge of the break dates (Piehl et al., 1999). In view of the above, Perron (1997) framework which deals with unit roots with structural breaks was estimated to further investigate the stationarity of the variables employed.

The test of unit root was immediately followed by test of co-integration. Following the Johansen et al. (2000) test procedure, we accounted for the possible breaks in the model before the conclusion was drawn. The technique involves an extension of the standard vector error correction model (VECM) which takes into account the probable exogenous breaks (in the form of dummy) in the levels and trends of the deterministic components of a vector-valued stochastic process.

Using the response surface method, it generates the probability value with likely break dates based on the asymptotic distribution of the likelihood ratio (LR) or trace statistic for co-integration. The confirmation of the existence of co-integration was followed by estimation of Eq. (3). Conventionally, if series is co-integrated, static OLS is consistent, but one shortcoming associated with the technique is that it is prone to produce non-Gaussian asymptotic distribution estimates, display asymptotic bias and are functions of non-scalar nuisance parameters. To make up for the shortcomings, we adopted fully modified OLS (FMOLS) developed by Phillips and Hansen (1990). The techniques do away with problems caused by correlation between the co-integrating equation and stochastic regressors in the long run through the employment of semiparametric correction.

In an attempt to investigate the responses of poverty due to shocks in trade liberalization and other explanatory factors, the state-space model (SSM) solved by Kalman filter (1960) was estimated. The state-space model originally developed by engineers to control linear systems enclosed most of classical linear and Box–Jenkins models. The model has been used extensively in the representation of autoregressive integrated moving average model (ARIMA), modeling of unobservable components as well as estimating time-varying parameter (TVP). Authors like Nelson and Kim (1988) and Pavel and Annia (2008), Moshen and Rafiel (2014) have used the latter approach in modeling time series data; the same approach is adopted for the present study.

Estimating a state-space model (SSM), two equations need to be specified, i.e., state and observed equations. The measurement (observed) equation defines the linkage between observed variables and unobservable state variables. For instance, taking X^t as a function of the random variables $\beta_t = \beta_{\text{it}}, \beta_{2t}, \ldots \beta_{nt}$. where $\beta_t =$ vector of state variables, which occur at (t), but (t) is unobservable (latent). Then we have the following measurement or observation equation,

$$\text{Observation equation:} X_t = y_t \beta_t + \varepsilon_t \tag{4}$$

where ε_t is i.i.d, white noise sequence with zero mean and variance $\varepsilon_t \sigma_\varepsilon^2$.

The state equation will be specified as

$$\beta_{t+1} = F\beta_t + \eta_{t+1} \tag{5}$$

where $\eta_t \sim$ i.i.d. N (0,Q), $E(\varepsilon_t, \eta_t.) = 0$(mutually independent) and F is a vector of constant with order $K\ X\ K$. Equation (4) describes how the observation depends on the state vector while Eq. (5) shows the external shocks that entered into the system. This can be changed in policy shift at time t (Moshen and Rafiei, 2014).

In Eq. (4), X_t is a vector of 1×1 and represents the explained variable in our case poverty, which is measured at the time t. β_t is a vector of $K \times 1$ unobservable state variable. y_t is a vector $1 \times\ k$of observed exogenous variables (TLIB, EDU, GDPPC) that connect the observable vector X_t with the unobservable vector β_t; the ε_t of order 1×1 and the vector η_t of order $k \times 1$ stand for residuals in the observed and unobserved equations, respectively, that are independent and normally distributed with zero mean.

It is assumed that the state vector element $\beta_{1t} = \beta_{1(t-1)} + \beta_{2(t-2)} + \eta_t$ is a moving average (MA) of its pass values making the new state vector a linear combination of the previous state vector and of process of error. Using Eq. (2), expressing a long-run association between poverty, trade liberalization, education and real GDP per capita in its dynamic form, we re-specified the model by attaching "t" as an index to each of the coefficients. This results in Eq. (6) as specified below:

$$\text{pov}_t = \beta_{0t} + \beta_{1t}\text{tlib} + \beta_{2t}\text{edu} + \beta_{3t}\text{rgdp} + \beta_{4t}\inf + \varepsilon_t \tag{6}$$

Therefore, $\beta_{1t} \ldots \beta_{4t}$ are state variables that are unobservable. Estimating the state-space model required that the series are I (1) and co-integrated. Also, the presence of deterministic variable is important for establishing a long-run relationship, and this was captured by independent term which also varies with time (Pavel & Annia, 2008). Equation (6) is then expressed in a state-space representation as follows:

Observed equation:

$$\text{pov}_t = \left[\, 1 \ \log\ \text{tlib} \ \log\ \text{edu} \ \text{rgdp} \ \inf \,\right] \begin{bmatrix} \beta_{0t} \\ \beta_{1t} \\ \beta_{2t} \\ \beta_{3t} \\ \beta_{4t} \end{bmatrix} + \varepsilon_t$$

State equation

$$\begin{bmatrix} \beta_{0t} \\ \beta_{1t} \\ \beta_{2t} \\ \beta_{3t} \\ \beta_{4t} \end{bmatrix} = \begin{bmatrix} \alpha \\ 0 \\ 0 \\ 0 \\ 0 \end{bmatrix} + \begin{bmatrix} 1\,0\,0\,0\,0 \\ 0\,1\,0\,0\,0 \\ 0\,0\,1\,0\,0 \\ 0\,0\,0\,1\,0 \\ 0\,0\,0\,0\,1 \end{bmatrix} + \begin{bmatrix} 0 \\ \delta_t \\ \eta_t \\ \omega_t \\ \phi_t \end{bmatrix}$$

We should note that the coefficients of $\beta_{1t} \ldots \beta_{4t}$ exhibit random walk behavior and with a permanent disturbances term. If β_t tends to zero, then the coefficient will be said to be constant and not dynamic in nature.

4 Result and Discussion

4.1 Pre-estimation Results

The results of both the conventional unit root tests and that of unit root test with structural break are presented in Table 1 panel A and B, respectively. The results indicate

Table 1 Unit root tests

Panel A: Traditional unit root test results (with intercept and trend)

At level			At first difference	
Variable	ADF	PP	ADF	PP
LOGTLIB	−0.8703 (0.9474)	−3.8038** (0.0286)	−7.6875*** (0.0000)	−12.8434*** (0.000)
OPENS	−2.3862 (0.3797)	−2.3294 (0.4078)	5.3418*** (0.0012)	−10. 4310*** (0.0000)
LOGPOV	−2.1041 (0.5252)	−2.0262 (0.5666)	−6.1001*** (0.0001)	−12.5491*** (0.0000)
LOGINS	−3.2552 (0.0941)	−3.4051 (0.0674)	−8.6673*** (0.000)	−8.9042* (0.0000)
LGDPPC	−2.6529 (0.2611)	−2.6471 (0.2634)	−5.3781*** (0.0001)	−5.4032*** (0.000)
INF	−3.45187 (0.0661)	-2.7634 (0.2197)	-5.7469*** (0.0002)	-10.5522*** (0.0000)
EDU	-1.8007 (0.6825)	−2.0509 (0.5535)	−4.7997*** (0.0026)	−4.7372*** (0.0031
M2/GDP	−2.5001 (0.3261)	−2.5405 (0.3080)	−5.3801*** (0.0006)	−5.8779*** (0.0002)

Panel B Unit root tests with structural break

	Innovative Outlier Model			Additive Outlier Model		
Variable	*t*-statistics	Break date	Lag	*t*-statistics	Break date	Lag
LOGTLIB	−17.4636	2006	7	−4.8628 (0.051)	1996	0
OPENS	−4.0656 (0.3319)	2009	0	−3.5453 (0.6648)	2007	0
LOGPOV	−3.7906 (0.5062)	2003	0	−3.9269 (0.4186)	2003	0
LOGINS	4.6472 (0.0831)	1996	0	−3.9362 (1786)	2004	0
LGDPPC	−3.4433 (0.4384)	1999	0	−2.9905 (0.9142)	1992	0
EDU	−3.3649 (0.7697)	2004	8	−3.1462 (0.8643)	2010	4
M2/GDP	0.8082 (>0.99)	2009	0	−4.9667** (0.0365)	1999	8
ΔLOGTLIB	18.5410*** (<0.01)	2007	8	−4.9519*** (<0.01)	1996	8
ΔOPENS	−6.6817*** (<0.01)	2003	8	−8.4347*** (<0.01)	2001	0
ΔLOGPOV	−6.4872*** (<0.01)	2004	0	−7.5839*** (<0.01)	2005	0

(continued)

Table 1 (continued)

Panel B Unit root tests with structural break

	Innovative Outlier Model			Additive Outlier Model		
Variable	*t*-statistics	Break date	Lag	*t*-statistics	Break date	Lag
ΔLOGINS	−10.1961*** ((<0.01)	2002	1	−9.3385*** (<0.01)	1999	0
ΔLGDPPC	−7.0508*** ((<0.01)	2003	0	−7.0847*** (<0.01)	2005	0
ΔEDU	−5.3134** (0.0118)	2000	0	−5.5695*** (<0.01)	2000	0
ΔM2/GDP	−3.3716 (0.4592)	2001	0	−5.775*** (<0.01)	1998	0

Note *** and ** indicate significant at the 1% and 5% levels, respectively. The asymptotic critical values of Vogelsang (1993) unit root test for model C (in Panel B) at 1%, and 5% are −5.719131 and −5.175710, respectively
Source Authors' computations

that all the variables were difference stationary. More importantly, the estimation of stationarity tests with unknown break dates revealed that there were significant structural breaks in the trend of the series in 1995, 1998 and in 2001 through 2008. During these periods specifically between 1995 and 2001, there were tariff reforms aimed at ensuring optimum allocation of resources in which the country has comparative advantage, while in 2002 export promotion strategies were adopted for an enlarge market through product diversification (Mordi et al., 2010). Above all, the conclusion that could be drawn from both approaches is that on the average, all the series were not level stationary but difference stationary.

The stationarity of the series at I (1) provides the theoretical bases for the test of co-integration using Johasen et al. (2000) approach. In this respect, an ordinary VAR model was first estimated in order to ascertain the optimum lag length and reliability of the model based on stability, serial autocorrelation and heteroskedacity tests, the result of which provides evidence in support of the robustness and stability of the model (see Table 1D, Panel A-D of the appendix). The result of the optimum lag selection indicates an optimum lag of one as shown in Table (1C), consequently the test for co-integration was carried out. Doing this, correct intervention dummies were introduced to account for the break dates identified in the results presented in Table 1 panel B. The co-integration test results presented in Table 1E of the appendix adopting Jahansen et al. (2000) suggest the acceptance of alternative hypothesis, indicating the existence of a long-run association between the series in the model. The results show that there are at least three co-integrating vectors at 1% level of significance.

4.2 Analysis of the Inferential Statistics Results

Having confirmed the existence of co-integration among the series in the model, we estimated a FMOLS model and the estimated co-integrating coefficients are as shown in Table 2.

Table 2, model (1), represents the result of our base line Eq. (2). From the result, trade liberalization measured as incidence based has positive, but insignificant impact (LOGTLIB) while as outcome-based measures (OPENS) its exhibits positive significant impact on poverty at 1% level of significance in consistent with the work of Goff and Singh, (2012), Beck et al. (2007) but refuting the work of Yoon and Nguyen (2009) and that of Olayinka (2014). This implies that greater trade openness measured either in terms of tariff reduction or increased volume of goods and services is not a declining function of level of poverty. Quality of institution measured as quality of service delivery indicates an insignificant negative impact on the level of poverty.

Table 2 Fully modified OLS regression results

Dep. variable: POV	Model 1		Model 2		Model 3	
Variable	Coefficient	*t*-Statistic	Coefficient	*t*-Statistic	Coefficient	*t*-Statistic
Constant	1.621777*	1.688509	–	–	–	–
OPENS	0.49811***	4.538754	0.54274***	4.95828	0.514677***	5.15824
LOGTLIB	0.151278	0.783291	1.48626***	2.88461	1.627303***	3.49186
EDU	0.01635***	2.521316	0.07040***	2.88461	0.01856***	3.13194
LOGINS	−0.07776	−0.26927	0.06372	0.20264	0.83938*	1.81198
LGDPPC	−0.241879	−0.77005	−0.48025	−1.60328	−0.365636	−1.30955
M2_GDP	0.000149	0.043059	–	–	–	–
INF	–	–	−0.00099	−0.98311	−0.000374	−0.40872
LOGTLIB_ED			−0.036482**	−2.39869	–	–
LOGTLIB_INS			–	–	−0.71728**	−2.81313
Diagnostics						
R^2		0.613133		0.5542		0.61873
Adjusted R^2		0.527163		0.4551		0.5339
S.E. of regression		0.071580		0.07683		0.0711
Long-run variance		0.007660		0.00714		0.00588
Hansen LC Statistics		3.7977 (0.001)		0.914992 (0.0545)		0.930662 (0.0508)
Jarque Bera		1.23717 (0.5387)		0.5853 (0.7463)		0.8284 (0.6608)

Note ***, ** and * denote significant at the 1%, 5% and 10% levels, respectively
Source Authors' computations

The insignificant of the impact may be alluded to the fact that institution on its own cannot engineer the process of a declining rate of poverty, but can only act as complimentary factors for poverty reduction policy. Real income per capita (LGDPPC) is negative, but insignificant, indicating that the more developed an economy is, the lower the level of poverty in such economy (Goff & Singh, 2012). The insignificant impact of the variable under consideration reflects the reality of the Nigeria growth experience where growth in income has been confirmed to be non-inclusive and thus not pro-poor.

Level of education also has a significant poverty-inducing effect against our a priori and in line with the earlier empirical result of Guillermo and Marcelo (2006). It is expected that higher level of education should be able to equip an individual with necessary skills which increases worker mobility and easy adaptation to modern day labor requirement, thereby increases job security. But disappointedly, the quality of education in Nigeria has experienced a declining trend in the last decade, making graduate unemployable in the labor sector. Increasing level of education devoid of entrepreneurship skills in an environment that is not investment friendly would not have a declining impact on poverty. This assertion is supported by the data released by the National Bureau of Statistics which show that poverty is more among the family head with higher levels of education (NBS, 2012). Financial development has a positive insignificant impact on poverty, indicating that the level of financial development in the country has not evolved to such a level that can be pro-poor. Worthy of note is the facts that a lot of services provided by the financial intermediaries have not been pro-poor. A pro-poor financial service should be able to make available for the poor loan at a cheaper rate. This is predicated on the belief that easier access to cheaper credit may allow the poor to benefit more from trade liberalization.

Model (2) and (3) presented results with the interaction terms, the results of which provide evidence in support of trade policy complementarity: Looking at trade openness, the results mimicked its earlier behavior exhibited in Model (1) indicating that both measures of trade liberalization are not significantly poverty reducing in line with Goff and Singh (2012), Beck et al. (2007) and Kpodar and Singh (2011). They suggest that openness cannot be linked to either lower or higher levels of poverty. Following the same trend is the coefficient of level of education which also indicates that increasing rates of poverty are associated with a higher level of education. Further into the result, quality of institutions and levels of economic development is insignificantly associated with lower levels of poverty. The coefficient of inflation tends to suggest that price level is poverty reducing corroborating the earlier findings by Carmen and Ganoza (2014).

Interacting trade liberalization with level of education resulted in change in sign and significant levels of the effect of liberalization complimented with level of education. The result revealed that a unit change in LOGTLIB_ED would result into 4% fall in poverty rates, providing empirical support for earlier researches. The conclusion that could be drawn is that effort toward poverty alleviation using trade policy will remain elusive except in an economy where the right mix of education is present. It should be noted that for an economy to optimize the benefits that will present itself through trade policy, qualitative education becomes imperatives. This is in line with the result of Guillermo and Marcelo (2006), in which openness interacted with education positively impact and level of real income of the poor.

In Model (3), there is no significant difference in the relationship between the two proxies of trade liberalization, inflation, financial development and poverty from their earlier behaviors. The behavior of institutional variable proxy by quality of service delivery continues to modulate between positive and negative impacts. In the present study, institution tends to be a positive function of poverty at 10% level of significance. Surprisingly not, the nature of the institution in the country has been extractive rather than inclusive overtime, which encourages rent seeking behavior among public office holders and thus poverty inducing. Interacting institutional variables with trade liberalization provides an interesting result. The result revealed that trade liberalization in an environment characterized by an efficient institution will result into about 7.0% fall in the rate of poverty. It is believed that for gains from trade to translate into a reduction in poverty rate, such gains must be evenly distributed among the citizens, the achievement of which will be elusive in the absence of qualitative institutions. Therefore, strong institutions are critical for the effectiveness of poverty reducing trade impact. The changed in sign when interacted with trade liberalization indicates that the impact of trade on poverty might be indirect operating through qualitative and efficient institutions. Therefore, institutions remain a complementary variable for the gain from trade to be pro-poor, providing an empirical support for the argument advanced by McCulloch et al. (2001). They argued, in a situation where trade liberalization allows for the operation of the price mechanism and leaving small farmers at the mercy of private agents, the poor farmers can completely be isolated or exploited both in the existing market and new market opportunities. This could only be avoided only in an economy where there is strong institution which ensures protection of property rights; otherwise the positive impact of trade reform on poor farmers will be negligible or become worse off.

The goodness of fits of all the models estimated is adequate. On the average, the explanatory variables employed in the models account for about 55, 55 and 61% change in poverty level for model one to three, respectively. The Hansen stability tests also indicate that the alternative hypothesis of existence of co-integration among the series could not be rejected while the standard error of the regressions is also adequate. The insignificant Jarque–Bera statistics also indicate normality of the model (Table 3).

The time-varying parameter estimate when interpreted based on the nature of the relationship between the series mimics the earlier result obtained in model (1) using fully modified OLS. The results revealed that trade liberalization and level of education are positive function of poverty, although the coefficient of education turns to be insignificant using this approach. Level of economic development and inflation rate maintained their behaviors in relation to the level of poverty with a significant poverty reducing impact of real GDP. It is expected that an increase in per capita income of an individual will definitely translate into higher purchasing power and ability to provide for the basic necessities of life, like health services, feeding, clothing, decent shelter and qualitative education among others. All of which ensures improved standard of living and reducing levels of poverty.

Table 3 Result of time-varying parameters

Space-state model result				
Coeeficient	Final State	Root MSE	*z*-Statistic	Prob
LOGTLIB	11.27***	866.0254	13.62000	0.0000
EDU	40.34	866.0254	0.466853	0.6406
LGGDPPC	−25.28***	866.0254	−2.988651	0.0028
INFL	−55.57***	866.0254	−11.06732	0.0000
Log likelihood	−1099	Akaike info criterion		615.72
Parameters	0	Schwarz criterion		624.81
Diffuse priors	4	Hannan–Quinn criteria		613.70

***represent significant at 1%

Source Authors Computation using Eviews 9.

The paper goes further to estimate one period ahead forecast of the response of poverty to socks in policy as shown in Fig. 4. The poverty models with time-varying coefficients show how poverty is responding to shocks from other variables, thus a suitable approach for representation of structural changes. The figure revealed that throughout the forecast periods, trade policy tends to produce a negative result in an effort toward alleviating poverty, thus coefficient of the poverty remains negative. The figure explains the years where poverty experienced a sharp upward movement and a mild reduction in poverty rates. Between 1985 and 2000, the parameter varies slightly and so the rate at which level of poverty fluctuates could be said to be

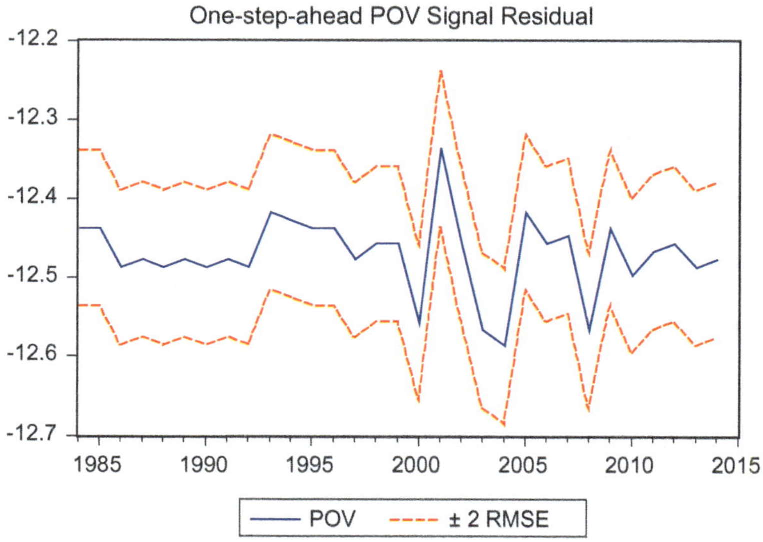

Fig. 4 One period ahead forecast error of the Kalman filter estimate 1981–20. *Source* Authors' Computation using Eviews 9.0

relatively stable. It should be noted that during these periods, specifically between 1995 and 2001, there were different tariff reforms which aimed at protecting certain sector of the economy over which the country enjoys relative advantage and ensures optimum distribution of resources. During the period, the weighted average tariff for the country experienced a declining trend. The rate fell from 34.3% in 1988 to 20.4% in 1998. The bulk of these tariffs were for manufacturing sector capable of generating employment opportunities and income. During this period, it could be said that the policy had been able to keep a check at least on the rate of poverty in the country.

A further analysis of the figure shows that in the year 2000, the poverty rate was highly volatile with a very sharp rise and fall between 2000 and 2006 and the trend continued until around 2009 when it becomes relatively stable. It should be noted that during the period, 2002–2007, export promotion policies were adopted to provide support for exporters and encourage diversification. In 2006, destination inspection of goods was introduced that was relatively imported restrictive in nature. The period also marked the era of a substantial reduction in tariffs on chemicals ranging from 15 and 80% based on the strategic importance attached to chemical products (Mordi et al., 2010). Overall, various tariff policies adopted during the period aimed at improving Nigeria balance of trade through discouragement of non-essential imports and generate revenue. These inconsistencies in policies provide an explanation behind sharp movements in response of poverty to shocks from policies. On the whole, going by Fig. 4, trade liberalization has failed in reducing the rate of poverty, but rather modulating between the negative values over the forecast period.

5 Summary and Conclusion

Adopting fully modified ordinary least squares (FMOLS) as a method of data analysis along with state-space model solved with Kalman filter, the paper explores the impacts of trade liberalization on the level of poverty with an emphasis on Nigeria, for the period 1981–2015. Also, there exists among the variables, a long-run equilibrium association.

The result of the empirical analyses of this study suggests that trade reform in terms of liberalization has a long-run beneficial impact on the poor. Level of education, quality of institution and financial development are also poverty inducing with the exception of inflation that tends to drag down poverty rate, though insignificant in its impacts. The result further revealed that the direct influence of trade liberalization on poverty will remain insignificant except when complimented with strong institutions and qualitative education, thus indicating an indirect impact. The adoption of a liberal trade policy through tariff reduction should be based on a holistic approach to combat poverty. Gains from trade in terms of availability of goods at lower prices, employment opportunity, increase return on labor most especially in the labor-intensive sector, improved terms of trade and efficient and equalization of resource distribution capable of expanding opportunities for the poor will not be optimized unless complimented with other relevant factors like qualitative institution and education. It is thus concluded that in Nigeria, trade liberalization has been poverty inducing rather than reducing the number of the poor and the impact of the former on the latter is statistically significant. The result of the time-varying parameter estimate also mimics the results obtained from FMOLS, with poverty responding to shocks from trade policy negatively.

Therefore, to optimized the benefits of trade liberalization in alleviating poverty, it is recommended that efforts toward improving the quality of education in the country become imperatives and this should be pursued along with building a qualitative institution.Specifically, overhauling of the educational curricula capable of instilling in an individual skill in identifying opportunities and venture into risk where others do not as well as improvement in service delivery by the government are required. In this context, the integration and consistency of trade policy with all complimentary variables are germane to guarantee a significant reduction in the number of the poor. On a final note, trade policies that are selective in nature which could ensure availability of cheaper commodities specifically those consumed by the poor and inputs for the real sector of the economy in order to expand productivity and employment opportunities should be encouraged.

References

Adeoye, T. A. (2008). *International trade and poverty reduction in Nigeria.* An M.Sc. Dissertation submitted to the Department of Economics and Development Studies, College of Business and Social Sciences, Covenant University, Ota, Ogun State, Nigeria (Unpublished).

Akinlo, E. A., Adeleke, G., & Aremo, A. (2013). The effect of trade liberalization on some selected poverty indicators in Nigeria (1980–2009): Generalised method of moments (GMM) approach. *American Journal of Economics, 3*(5), 199–209.

Branson, H. W. (1989). *Macroeconomic theory and policy.* New York: Harper and Row Publishers.

Carmen, C. M. J., & Ganoza, A. M. V. (2014) Estimation of the pass-through and welfare effects of the tariff reduction for yellow corn in Peru between 2000 and 2011. In *Proceeding of the United Nation Conference on Trade and Development (UNCTAD) with the theme Trade Policies, Household Welfare and Poverty Alleviation Case Studies from the Virtual.* New York, Geneva: Institute Academic Network. UNCTAD/GDS/2014/3

Dahai, F., & Shantong, L. (2014). The consumption effect of the renminbi appreciation in rural China. Trade policies, household welfare and poverty alleviation: Case studies from the virtual institute academic network. In *United Nations Conference on Trade and Development (UNCTAD)* UNCTAD/GDS/2014/3.

Decalawe, G., Partry, M., Savard, K., & Thorbecke, G. (1999). Environmental impacts of a North American free trade agreement. In P. M. Garber (Ed.), *The Mexico-US free trade agreement.* Cambridge: MA MIT Press.

Dorosh, M., & Sahn, P. (1999) Trade openness and income inequality in developing countries. *CSGR Working Paper Series 232/07.*

Eric, O. O. (2015). Trade liberalization and economic growth in Nigeria: Do concern matters? *3*(6), 306–311.

Export.gov. (2016). Nigeria—Agriculture. Published on 20th of June, 2016, https://www.export.gov/apex/article2?id=Nigeria-Agriculture

Geoferry, J. B., & Kamau, T. (2001). International trade and poverty alleviation. IMF Working Paper No. WP/01/54, May 2001

Goff, M. L., & Singh, R. J. (2012). Does trade reduce poverty? A view from Africa. Presented at Centre *for the Study of African Economies Conference.* Oxford.

Guillermo, P., & Marcelo, O. (2006) Trade liberalization, inequality and poverty reduction in Latin America. Paper presented at ABCDE. San Petersburg.

Hala, M. S. (2012). Trade policy and poverty eradication (with special reference to the Egyptian Case), Paper presented to the *joint research workshop-paris 1 University and Cairo University*

Hamilton, J. D. (1994). *Time Series Analysis.* Princeton: Princeton University Press.

Imran, S. C., & Imran, F. (2013). Trade liberalization reduce poverty and inequality? Empirical evidence from Pakistan. *Pakistan Journal of Commerce and Social Sciences, 7*(3), 569–587.

Johansen, S., Mosconi, R., & Nielsen, B. (2000). Cointegration analysis in the presence of structural breaks in the deterministic trend. *Econometrics Journal, 3,* 216–249.

Kalman, R. E. (1960). A new approach to linear filtering and prediction problems. *Journal of Basic Engineering, 82*(1). New York: American Society of Mechanical Engineering.

Kankwenda, M., Gregoire, L., Legros, H., & Ouedraogo, H. (2000). *Poverty eradication: Where stands Africa?* London: Economica Ltd. United Nation Development Programme.

Marta, C., Marta, M., & Aude, S. (2009). trade liberalization, inequality and poverty in Brazillian states. Paris: Document de travail, Institute de recherche pour le development, dauphine University. DT/2010–02.

Mcculloch, N., Winters, L. A., & Cirera, X. (2001). *Trade liberalization and poverty: A Handbook.* London: CEPR and DFID.

Mordi, N. O. C., Abwaku, E, & Banji. S. A. (2010). *The changing structure of the Nigerian economy* (pp, 257–262). The Research Department, Central Bank of Nigeria.

Moshen, M., & Rafiei, F. (2014). Energy consumption and economic growth: Kalman filter approach. *International Journal of Academic Research in Economics and Management Sciences, 3*(3), 204–210.

Mukhopadhyay, S. (2002). Consumer demand in South Africa. Paper presented at the trade and industrial policy strategies (TIPS). Annual Forum, Glenburn Lodge, Muldersdrift.

National Bureau of Statistics. (2012). *Annual abstracts of statistics.* Abuja: National Bureau of Statistics.

National Bureau of Statistics (NBS). (2017). *Foreign trade statistics.* Abuja: NBS.

Ndebbio, J. E. U. (2006). *The structural economic dimensions of underdevelopment associated vicissitudes and imperatives: Agenda for positive change.* Nigeria: Saesprint Publishers.

Nwafor, M., Kanayo, O., & Adenikinju, A. (2005). The impact of trade liberalization on poverty in Nigeria: micro simulation in a CGE model. Interim report to the poverty and economic policy (PEP) research network. Paper presented during the 4th PEP Research network general meeting. Colombo.

Okungbowa, F. O. E., & Eburajolo, O. C. (2014). Globalization and poverty rate in Nigeria: An empirical analysis. *International Journal of Humanities and Social Science, 4*(11), 126–135.

Olayinka, I. K. (2014). The welfare impact in Nigeria of the ECOWAS common external tariff: A distributional effects analysis. *Proceeding of the united nation conference on trade and development (UNCTAD)* with the theme trade policies, household welfare and poverty alleviation case studies from the virtual institute academic network. New York, Geneva UNCTAD/GDS/2014/3.

Olofin, S., Adenikinju, A., & Iwayemi, A. (2001). A computable general equilibrium analysis of Nigeria's trade competitiveness. *CEAR Research Paper No 2001/01.*

Pavel, V. A., & Annia, F. F. (2008). Trade-Growth Relationship in Cuba: Estimation Using the Kalman Filter. *CEPAL Review, 94,* 97–116.

Perron, P. (1997). Further evidence on breaking trend functions in macroeconomic variables. *Journal of Econometrics, 80,* 355–385.

Phillips Peter, C. B., & Hansen, B. E. (1990). Statistical inference in instrumental variables regression with I (1) processes. *Review of Economics Studies, 57,* 99–125.

Piehl, A. M., Cooper, S. J., Braga, A. A., & Kennedy, D. M. (1999). Testing for structural breaks in the evaluation of programs. NBER working paper 7226.

Pineopi, K. G., & Nina, P. (2004). Trade, inequality, and poverty: What do we know? Evidence from recent trade liberalization episodes in developing countries. Paper presented at the 2004 Brookings trade forum on "globalization, poverty & inequality: Research Unit at Sussex University of Sussex Brighton.

PRUS (Poverty Research Unit At Sussex). (2001). *Trade and poverty*. Available at: www.sussex.ac.uk/Units/PRU/notes5.pdf. [15th June 2016].

Samantha, D., & Nicolette, C. (2006). Theoretical approaches to the analysis of trade and poverty and a review of related literature on South Africa. *Trade and poverty project, Southern Africa labor and development research unit.*

Samuelson, P. A. (1948). International Trade and the equalisation of factor prices. *the Economic Journal, 58*(230), 163–184.

Sodersten, B. O., & Geoffery, R. (1994). *International economic* (3rd ed.). London: Palgrave Macmillan.

Spilimbergo, A., Juan Londonõ, L., & Miguel Londonõ, S. (1999). *Journal of Development Economics, 59,* 77–101.

Stolper, W., & Samuelson, P. A. (1941). Protection and REAL WAGES. *Review of Economic Studies, 9,* 58–73.

Todaro, M. P., & Smith, S. C. (2011). *Economic development* (11th ed.). England: Addison-Wesley, Harlow.

Topalova, P. (2007). Trade liberalization, poverty and inequality: Evidence from Indian districts. In A. Harrison (Ed.), *Globalization and poverty*. Chicago and Cambridge MA: University of Chicago Press and NBER. Paper No. 6–1 https://www.nber.org/books-and-chapters/globalization-and-poverty or https://www.nber.org/chapters/c0110.

Uexkull, E. V., & Shui, L. (2014). Implementing the ECOWAS common external tariff challenges and opportunities for Nigeria. African trade practice. World bank working paper series, No. 5.

Udah, E. B. (2010). Industrial development, electricity crisis and economic performance in Nigeria. *European Journal of Economics, Finance and Administrative Sciences, 18,* 105–121.

UNECA. (2012). Economic transformation for Africa's development", *United Nations, Economic Commission for Africa,* Macroeconomic policy Division, C-10 Meeting April. Washington D, C.

United Nation Development Project (UNDP). (2012). List of countries by human development index, *United Nation Development Project* Download from the Web https://en.wikipedia.org/wiki/List_of_countries_by_Human_Development_Index [20/5/2016].

United Nation Development Project (UNDP). (2015). Human development report. hdr.undp.org/sites/.../hdr.../NG... downloaded from the web on 27th April, 2016.

Winters, L. A. (2000a). Trade liberalization and poverty. *PRUS Working Paper No. 7,* Poverty Research Unit at Sussex, University of Sussex Falmer, Brighton. BN198, 2000.

Winters, L. A. (2000b) Trade, trade policy, and poverty: what are the links? *Centre for economic policy research paper* No. 2382.

World Bank WTIS. (2016). World Bank World Integrated Trade Solution (WITS) database, available at: https://wits.worldbank.org/wits.downloaded on 22/06/2016.

Yoon, H., Nguyen, K. D. (2009). *Trade liberalization and poverty the World Economy* (pp. 934–964). https://doi.org/10.1111/j.1467-9701.2009.01183.

Chapter 15
Trade Liberalization, Growth and Poverty: Empirical Analysis for India

M. Pant and N. Dhamija

1 Introduction

The effects of globalization on poverty have been important areas of concern for policy-makers and researchers alike, especially for developing countries. The developed and developing countries are increasingly trading with each other, and many developing countries are also experiencing high-income growth rates. Over the last few decades, there is evidence of robust decline in absolute income poverty, but the inequality is rising (Alvaredo & Gasparini, 2015). A pertinent question is whether this globalization process, especially openness of trade, reduces poverty?

India initiated the process of liberalization as a response to the severe balance of payments and fiscal crisis of 1991. The trade liberalization reforms reduced tariffs and non-tariff barriers and the gradual reduction of control over exchange rate. This led to significant increase in India's trade/GDP ratio and also in its share of merchandise trade, in the last two decades. The growth rate of real GDP per capita also increased sharply in the post liberalization period. There is no denying the fact that poverty has declined steadily in India since 1990s. The decline was observed in both rural and urban sectors of the economy. The trend in inequality, however, is not so encouraging, and inequality has been rising, more so in the urban sector. It is hence important to enquire and analyse the role played by the process of trade liberalization and accompanying increase in trade volumes, in the observed reduction of poverty. The present study thus focusses on analysing the impact of trade liberalization and accompanying increase in trade volumes on poverty in India.

M. Pant
Indian Institute of Foreign Trade (IIFT), Delhi, India
e-mail: mpant101@gmail.com

N. Dhamija (✉)
Hindu College, University of Delhi, Delhi, India
e-mail: dhamijanidhi@yahoo.com

P. Lakhanpal et al. (eds.), *Trade, Investment and Economic Growth*,
https://doi.org/10.1007/978-981-33-6973-3_15

According to Winters (2000) and Winters et al. (2004), the relationship between trade liberalization and poverty is not direct and operates via different channels, classified as static (further categorized into households, distribution, factor markets and government) and dynamic (via growth and inequality) impacts of trade openness on poverty. The dynamic channel of growth is considered to be more important channel in the literature, the channel operating through two causal relations—trade promotes growth and growth leads to decline in poverty.

According to Bourguignon (2003), growth and income distributions have to be studied simultaneously for analysing poverty reduction, depicted by the poverty–growth–inequality (PGI) triangle. The reverse causality is present not only between growth–inequality relationship but also between trade openness and growth (Rodriguez & Rodrik, 1999). This paper attempts to analyse the relation between trade liberalization and poverty by estimating a simultaneous equation model using panel data for 21 major states of India for years 1993–94, 2004–05, 2009–10 and 2011–12.

The study is structured as follows: Sect. 2 presents the brief review of empirical studies; Sect. 3 presents the analytical framework and the econometric model to be estimated; Sect. 4 provides definitions of the variables and sources of the data; Sect. 5 presents and discusses the results; and Sect. 6 concludes.

2 Review of Empirical Literature

There is a high level of interest in studying the effect of trade and trade liberalization on poverty and inequality, over the last several years (Winters et al., 2004, Goldberg & Pavnick, 2007). There are various studies on the subject, and they vary across many dimensions.

A number of cross-country studies based on macro analysis have attempted to understand the effect of trade reforms on economic growth (Dollar, 2001; Sachs & Warner, 1995; Edwards, 1998; Wacziarg & Welch, 2003; Harrison, 2006). These studies found that trade openness leads to rapid growth. More recently, Villaverde & Maza (2011) also showed that economic globalization has led to a higher growth and also to the convergence of income globally. On the other hand, certain studies have refuted this hypothesis (Rajan, 2002; Ravallion, 2004; Rodriguez & Rodrik, 1999 and Harrison & Hanson, 1999), suggesting that there is no clear and direct relationship between trade liberalization and growth. McKay et al. (2000) argued that country's domestic conditions, the way of implementing trade reforms and other complementary policies followed, play an important role.

The empirical studies analysing this relationship for India also found contradictory results (Marelli & Signorelli, 2011; Chatterji et al., 2013; Mallick, 2008; Sarkar, 2005, 2008; Dash & Sharma, 2008). Singh (2010) provides a comprehensive review of the extensive literature.

There is, however, consensus that growth leads to decline in poverty levels as given by Dollar & Kraay (2002), Ravallion (2004), Ravallion & Chen (1997), etc.

Ravallion (2001) found that an increase in the per capita income by 1% can lead to average decline of proportion of poor people by about 2.5%.

In India, this hypothesis seemed to be relevant during the 1980s as the experience suggests that economic growth typically reduced poverty levels (Datt & Ravallion, 2002). However, there is debate about what happened to poverty post 1991. According to Bhalla (2000), there has been greater fall in poverty in the 1990s as compared to the pre-reform period, whereas Sen (2001) argued that there has been no decline in poverty in post 1990 period (poverty would have also increased). Datt & Ravallion (2002) showed that the poverty reduction in 1990s was at the same rate as was observed in 1980s. A more recent study by Datt & Ravallion (2011) calculated the growth elasticity of poverty and found the elasticity to be similar for both pre- and post-reforms period for the Indian economy.

The researchers such as Dreze & Sen (2013), however, argue that growth is necessary but not sufficient for poverty reduction. In the presence of widening income inequalities accompanying growth, this relationship can reverse. Most of the empirical work supports the argument that inequality falls when the economy grows (Ravallion & Datt, 2002; Ravallion, 2001).

Topalova (2008) and Cain et al. (2010a) analysed the change in poverty in India, by decomposing it into growth effect and distribution effect for 1983–2004 period. Their studies showed that redistribution helped to enhance the poverty reduction in 1983–93, particularly in the rural areas. In the later post-reform period, the distribution effect significantly reduced the extent of poverty reduction in rural as well as urban areas. Radhakrishna et al. (2013) examined the factors contributing to decline in poverty between 1993–94 and 2009–10 and found that the poverty would have fallen more (by about 2 percentage points) in 2009–10 if the inequalities of the states were maintained at the levels of the year 1993–94.

One of the important concerns is that the pattern of growth emerging from open trade policies is biased towards the rich and worsens the economy's income distribution (McCulloch et al., 2001). The studies provide substantial evidence that liberalization can cause increase in inequality (between and within countries) in both income and assets (Kanji & Menon-Sen, 2001). Other studies like Edwards (1998) and Dollar & Kraay (2004), however argue against.

For the Indian economy, Mitra (2016) claimed that the tariff reductions were found to be increasing inequality in a statistically significant way for the period of 1981–2013. However, similar analysis for the sub-national level was followed in Krishna & Sethupathy (2011) and Topalova (2005). Their results showed that inequality remained unaffected with trade liberalization.

Topalova (2005), Cain et al. (2010a) and Hasan et al. (2007) analysed the relationship between trade liberalization and poverty levels of India in a single equation (reduced form framework) by assuming explanatory variables as exogenous. However, this framework suffers from the limitation of relating trade policy directly to poverty reduction without specifying the underlying model for such a relationship. Topalova (2005) showed that in rural districts (where industries exposed to liberalization were found in higher concentration), the incidence of poverty and also gap in poverty increased due to liberalization of trade. However, no statistically significant relation was found for urban areas. Hasan et al. (2007) and Cain et al. (2010a) indicated that incidence of poverty on average was increasing with respect to protection over time and across states.

From the review above, it can be concluded that the direct impact of trade openness on poverty has been ambiguous. It is also difficult to reach a definitive conclusion about the impact of trade liberalization on income growth, in contrast to well-established positive effect of growth on poverty. However, the effect of growth on inequality has been quite substantial but trade openness has not been found to be significantly affecting inequality.

3 Analytical Framework and Model

The model of this study builds on poverty–growth–inequality triangle (also known as development triangle) of Bourguignon (2003) given below. According to it, decline in poverty at any point of time is determined by the growth rate of average income of the population and the change in income distribution. Thus, growth and income distributions have to be studied simultaneously for analysing poverty reduction (Fig. 1).

The interactions among these three variables lead to the following relations: First, consider the growth and poverty relationship. There is no dispute about the role of growth in poverty reduction. A higher growth (given the constant level of inequality) would lead to fall in poverty. But how much of growth actually trickles down to the poor is measured by the growth elasticity of poverty. However, inequality changes accompanying growth will determine the extent to which economic growth translates into fall in poverty.

Second is the impact of inequality on poverty. There is again no ambiguity in this relationship as less inequality (at a given rate of growth) would lead to reduction in poverty. In fact, these last two effects reinforce each other for poverty reduction.

Third is the effect of growth on inequality. There are many ways in which growth impacts inequality, most famously given by Kuznets 'inverted U curve', Todaro's 'trickle-down' theory and Lewis model. This hypothesis was found to be true across countries in studies focussing on the decade of 1960s and 1970s. In the subsequent evolution of inequality across countries, this empirical relationship was not

Fig. 1 Poverty–growth–inequality triangle. *Source* Reproduced from Bourguignon (2003) for easy reference

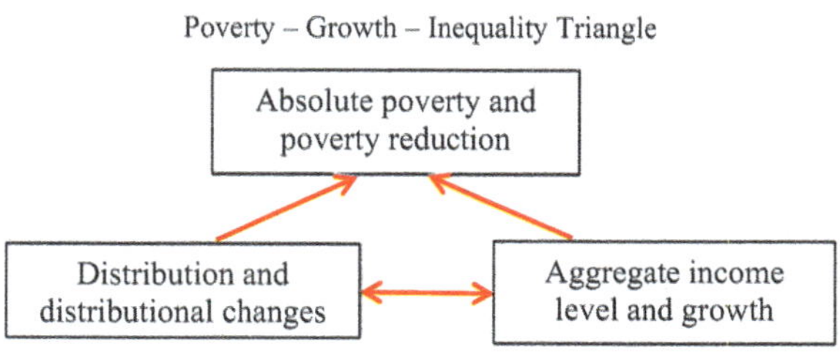

found (Deininger & Squire, 1996). However, it does not imply that there is no significant effect of growth on inequality but perhaps indicates the importance of domestic factors in determining this relationship and limitation in generalizing it across countries (Bouguignon, 2003).

Fourth is the effect of inequality on growth, which is ambiguous in literature. Kaldor (1956) argued that inequality is beneficial for higher growth. Higher rate of inequality favours higher savings rate (as richer population save more than the poorer population) and hence the rate of investment and growth. There are also various counteracting channels such as inequality induces crime and political stability; the impact on voting patterns and fiscal policy followed as a response; effect on the composition of investment; fall in human capital (as poor would have lower investment in human capital); reduction in the domestic market size and the impact on the quality of institutions (Janvry & Sadoulet, 2016).

According to Bourguignon (2003), due to the presence of reverse causality in growth–inequality relation, empirical verification from 'growth' equation by taking inequality as an independent variable would produce ambiguous results (because of endogeneity bias). One way out of this ambiguity is to try estimate the 'structural' model of the growth-inequality relationship formalizing various factors discussed above on the distributional consequences of growth.

The main objective of the paper is to study the impact of trade openness on poverty in India. For this, it superimposes trade openness on the PGI triangle (and relations depicted there), as the impact of trade openness on growth, and therefore, poverty cannot be meaningfully studied independent of these relations.

The theory of trade is ambiguous about effect of trade openness on growth. Theoretically, the models supporting the argument are given by Harrod and Domar (trade is characterized as 'engine of growth'), Romer (endogenous growth theory) and Todaro (trickle-down theory of growth). The counteracting arguments indicating no direct link between them have been argued by Solow and neoclassical growth models. On the other hand, division of total output of the economy is between domestic output and exports. Hence, exports are determined by size of the country and its economic growth. Imports can also increase the productivity due to reduction in shortages and provisioning of better inputs and newer technology. Also, imports are part of consumption in the economy and comprise largely 'income elastic' goods. Hence, per capita income increase would lead to increase in the share of imports and even in the share of exports, to pay for the rising imports (Esfahani, 1991). Thus, both exports and imports not only affect growth but get affected by it as well.

The reverse causality is thus present between trade openness and growth, similar to growth–inequality relationship. To account for these interrelations, the present study adopts a simultaneous equations model of four structural equations, for the four endogenous variables.[1]

$$\begin{aligned}\mathrm{PI}_{\mathrm{it}} &= \alpha_0 + \alpha_1\,\mathrm{PCNSDP}_{\mathrm{it}} + \alpha_2\mathrm{PCGovtExp}_{\mathrm{it}} + \alpha_3\mathrm{Agr}_{\mathrm{it}} \\ &\quad + \alpha_4\mathrm{Pop}_{\mathrm{it}} + \alpha_5\mathrm{INE}_{\mathrm{it}} + \alpha_6\mathrm{Infl}_{\mathrm{it}} + \varepsilon_{1it} \qquad (1)\end{aligned}$$

[1]Natural logs of all variables are taken.

$$\begin{aligned}\text{PCNSDP}_{\text{it}} = \beta_0 + \beta_1\,\text{Trade}_{\text{it}} + \beta_2\,\text{Wkg}_{\text{it}} + \beta_3\,\text{GradPop}_{\text{it}} \\ + \beta_4\,\text{PCGovtExp}_{\text{it}} + \beta_5\,\text{INE}_{\text{it}} + \beta_6\,\text{Infl}_{\text{it}} + \varepsilon_{2it}\end{aligned} \quad (2)$$

$$\begin{aligned}\text{Trade}_{\text{it}} = \theta_0 + \theta_1\text{PCNSDP}_{\text{it}} + \theta_2\text{PCCapExp}_{\text{it}} + \theta_3\text{Credit}_{\text{it}} \\ + \theta_4\text{Pop}_{\text{it}} + \theta_5\text{Infl}_{it+} + \varepsilon_{3it}\end{aligned} \quad (3)$$

$$\begin{aligned}\text{INE}_{\text{it}} = \eta_0 + \eta_1\text{PCNSDP}_{\text{it}} + \eta_2\text{Trade}_{\text{it}} + \eta_3\text{PCCapExp}_{\text{it}} \\ + \eta_4\text{GradPop}_{\text{it}} + \eta_5\text{Pop}_{\text{it}} + \eta_6\text{Infl}_{\text{it}} + \varepsilon_{4\text{it}}\end{aligned} \quad (4)$$

The four endogenous variables are as follows:

PI = poverty indicator (taken as poverty incidence)
PCNSDP = per capita net state domestic product
Trade = trade openness measure (trade as a percentage of GDP)
INE = consumption inequality measure (Gini coefficient).
The exogenous variables in the model are as follows:
PCGovtExp = per capita government expenditure (taken as a measure of fiscal policy)
Agr = share of agricultural sector in GDP (taken as a measure of growth of rural sector in the economy)
Pop = rate of growth of population
Infl = rate of inflation (CPI-IW) (taken as a measure of other macroeconomic factors)
Wkg = proportion of working population (in the age group 15–59) (taken as a measure of labour force)
GradPop = proportion of graduates and above in the population (more than 6 years of age) (taken as a measure of human capital)
PCCapExp = per capita capital expenditure of the government (taken as a measure of investment)
Credit = private credit/GDP (taken as an indicator of financial deepening).

The model is specified based on the relevant theoretical and empirical research literature. The dependent variable of each equation comprises the endogenous variables of the model, and rest are exogenous variables as there are no other declared endogenous variables.

In the model, poverty (Eq. 1) is determined by two endogenous variables—per capita NSDP and inequality. In addition, government per capita expenditure (especially on social and welfare schemes) is included because it plays a crucial role for poverty reduction in India. Share of output of agriculture in GDP is expected to have an impact on poverty reduction (Datt & Ravallion, 2011) and is included in the equation. Population growth is also typically assumed to affect the level of poverty adversely (Donald & Majeed, 2010). Inflation rate is a relevant variable (taken as control variable) affecting the macroeconomic relations and is important to take into account. It would affect the poverty levels as higher inflation is expected to adversely affect the poor, making it harder for them to meet the necessities of life and trapping them in the vicious circle of poverty.

Using neoclassical growth theory, PCNSDP (Eq. 2) in present model, is specified as a function of the labour force (taken as the proportion of working population), human capital (taken as proportion of graduates and above in the population), per capita government expenditure and inflation (apart from two endogenous variables—trade openness and inequality). The investment level of the economy is an important determinant but could not be included as comprehensive state wise data for investment or capital formation is not available for India.[2] To allow for the effects of trade openness on growth through other factors, Wacziarg (2001) recommends to add measure of government consumption and macroeconomic policy to the growth equation. The government consumption expenditure (which also denotes a measure of fiscal policy) and rate of inflation (to capture the overall macro environment and the monetary policy of the economy) hence are added in the equation above.

Many important determinants of a country's trade such as tariffs, exchange rate, relative price of domestic country vis-à-vis rest of the world, growth of principal trading partners, WTO and bilateral agreements of trade cannot be included in Eq. (3) which explains trade openness at the state level. Hence, important variables explaining state trade openness are taken as (apart from PCNSDP) investment (taken as per capita capital expenditure), financial deepening (taken as credit to GDP ratio), population growth rate and inflation. Investment is an important factor as infrastructural bottlenecks delay transportation of goods and also affect the quality of goods exported (Kumar, 2001). Another relevant variable is financial development as a more developed financial sector is expected to positively affect the trade balance (Hasan, 2010). Inflation captures the overall macroeconomic scenario and hence acts as the control factor, controlling for other macroeconomic variables affecting trade.

In Eq. (4), inequality is specified as a function of per capita capital expenditure, proportion of graduates and above in the population of more than 6 years of age, rate of growth of population and inflation. The equation has PCNSDP and trade openness as two other endogenous variables. Capital expenditure of the government directly influences the development and infrastructural expenditure affecting the level of inequality (Pal & Ghosh, 2007 and Topalova, 2008). The level of education of population is an important determinant of income inequality and is incorporated into the equation as the proportion of graduates and above in the population. The difference in the level of education is expected to increase the skill and productivity gaps in the working population thereby leading to more unequal distribution of income. Inflation leads to higher inequality in the existing income distribution by transferring wealth from poorer to richer sections of the population (Donald & Majeed, 2010).

[2]One way is to proxy it by taking capital expenditure of the government which will at least substitute for public investment, as there is no measure available for private investment. But it has been dropped from this equation due to high correlation with per capita government expenditure leading to the problem of multicollinearity.

4 Variables Definition and Data Sources

The definitions of variables and their data sources are detailed below.[3]

Poverty indicator: The main measure of poverty is the head count ratio or poverty rate calculated for the states of India. It is calculated by taking the proportion of population with monthly per capita expenditure below a given poverty line. The data for household consumption expenditure are collected by the National Sample Survey Office (NSSO) of India, and for period covered under the study, data are available for five thick rounds of NSSO surveys for the years 1993–94, 1999–00, 2004–05, 2009–10 and 2011–12. The present study uses poverty lines given by the Tendulkar Committee Report. Due to non-comparability of poverty estimates for the year 1999-00, this study excludes it from the empirical analysis and hence includes data for only four remaining NSSO surveys. [4]

Per capita NSDP: Real per capita NSDP is taken as the measure of income. The data source for NSDP per capita (constant prices) is Central Statistical Office (CSO). The data are available at different base year prices and converted to constant 2004–05 prices.

Trade openness: The state's total trade (i.e. exports and imports) as a percentage of NSDP is taken as a measure of trade openness for the states in India. The data for exports and imports of states are not available, and hence these variables are estimated.[5] The export orientation of each state is calculated as the share of estimated state's exports in India's total exports (based on procedures outlined in UNCTAD report (2013) and Barua & Chakraborty (2010)).

$$X_i = \left[\sum_{l=1}^{L} \frac{Y_{il}}{Y_l} * X_l \right]$$

where X_i = state i's exports; Y_{il} = state's i's output in industry l; L = total number of industries; Y_l = India's total output in industry l; X_l= India's exports of industry l. The data for state's output in different industries and total output are taken from Central Statistical Organization (CSO), and data for exports of India are taken from United Nations Commodity Trade Statistics database (UNCOMTRADE). The industries for which data have been utilized with the corresponding two digit industry codes of

[3]Three new states were formed in the year 2000, namely Chhattisgarh, Jharkhand and Uttaranchal. The new boundaries of the states are taken to maintain consistency across years, and data for the newly formed states are constructed accordingly (data adjustment done for Madhya Pradesh, Bihar and Uttar Pradesh, respectively) for period prior to the year 2000.

[4]There is a general consensus in literature that the estimates based on the 55th NSSO round are biased downwards due to a change in methodology of collecting data on household consumption expenditure (Datt & Ravallion, 2002). However, there is no agreement yet on the extent to which poverty has been underestimated.

[5]The methodology to calculate exports and imports of the states is adopted from author's another study, Dhamija (2019), and is reproduced here for ease of understanding.

ISIC (given in brackets) are (i) agriculture (01); (ii) forestry and logging (02); (iii) fishing (05); (iv) mining and quarrying (10 + 11 + 12 + 13 + 14); (v) manufacturing (15–36) and (vi) electricity, gas and water supply (40).

The total imports of the country are divided across states in accordance with the weight given by share of GSDP in total GDP of the economy for that period, to arrive at the imports of each state. [6]

$$M_i = \sum_l [M_l^* Y_i / Y] \quad i = 1 \text{ to } 21 \text{ and } l = 1 \text{ to } 6$$

where M_i= imports of state i; M_l = imports of industry l (six industries given above); Y_i = GSDP at constant prices of state i; Y = GDP at constant prices of India.

Consumption inequality: The inequality is measured by computing the Gini index of monthly per capita expenditure of each state. This is calculated using data of household consumption expenditure, collected by NSSO (as is used for the measurement of poverty indicator).

Per capita government expenditure: is calculated by adding government expenditure on both revenue and capital account. The data taken from various reports of State Finances, RBI, are available at current prices, converted to constant 2004–05 prices by using GDP deflators. Per capita government expenditure is obtained by dividing it by population.

Share of agriculture sector in total GDP: is calculated by taking GDP accruing from the agriculture sector of the state and dividing it by total GDP of the state. The data for both variables are taken from CSO.

Population growth rate: The data for population of each state are taken from Economic and Political Weekly Research Foundation (EPWRF) to calculate the annual growth rate for the years in consideration.

Inflation rate: The inflation rate is calculated using the state-specific consumer price index of industrial workers (CPI-IW) for urban areas. The data are taken from EPWRF. CPI-IW is available at different base years, which is then converted to common base year of 1982.

Proportion of working population: is calculated as the share of population aged between 15 and 59 in total population of the states and is calculated from data of specified rounds NSS employment and unemployment survey.[7]

[6]Barua and Chakraborty (2010) used the population share of state as weights, in place of GSDP share as weights, used here. They based it on the assumption of homothetic preference for imports across all states. However, according to the macroeconomic theory, imports are a positive function of income. The studies have also largely linked magnitude of imports to the size of the economy (Kumar, 2001).

[7]Sampling weights are used to derive population level for these variables.

Proportion of graduates and above in the population: (more than 6 years of age) of the states is also calculated from data of the NSS employment and unemployment survey rounds.[8]

Per capita capital expenditure: The investment level of the economy is an important factor for economic growth. Capital expenditure of each state is taken as a measure of investment as comprehensive state wise data for investment or capital formation are not available.[9] The data at current prices are taken from EPWRF and GDP deflators are used to convert in constant 2004–05 prices. Per capita is obtained by dividing it by population

Credit: Financial deepening of the state is determined by private credit given by the banks and financial institutions. Hence, private credit as a proportion of GDP is taken, and data for the same are collected from the banking statistics, RBI.

5 Analysis and Discussion of Results

5.1 Panel OLS Regression Results of the Structural Equations

The model given in Eqs. (1)–(4) is estimated using panel data for 21 states of India for the years 1993–94, 2004–05, 2009–10 and 2011–12. The simultaneous model is first estimated using the panel data OLS methodology on each equation by assuming all RHS variables to be exogenous. The results of different equations are shown in Table 1.[10]

It is important to note that in short panels where T is fixed and $N \rightarrow \infty$, the FE estimation suffers from incidental parameter problem (Neyman & Scott, 1948 and Lancaster, 2000). The estimates of individual effects ($\alpha + \mu_i$) are not consistent because as $N \rightarrow \infty$, the number of fixed effects (μ_i) increases, and as only T observations are used to estimate each parameter, it gives inconsistent estimates. In some circumstances such as nonlinear regression, binary variables regression, etc., this would also lead to inconsistent estimates of the slope parameters. However, for linear regression models, the FE estimators of slope parameters (β), which are main parameters of interest, are consistent (Baltagi, 2008).

[8]Same as above.

[9]The same approach of taking capital outlay as a proxy for investment at the state level has been followed by Bathla et al. (2015) and Nayyar (2008).

[10]The results of fixed effects and random effects specifications of each equation are not given in the paper but are available on request. The choice between the two specifications is based on Hausman test and Mundlak formulation (Greene, 2012). The Mundlak formulation is given preference over Hausman test wherever contradictory results emerge. This is because the test statistic of Mundlak formulation is based on robust covariance matrix estimator, while Hausman test statistic is based on non-robust covariance matrix estimator.

Table 1 Panel data OLS estimates

Explanatory variables	L. PI	L. PCNSDP	L. Trade	L. Gini
L. PCNSDP	−1.3893		0.8577	0.0602
	(−7.64)***		(6.40)***	(0.60)
L. Trade		0.6610		−0.0683
		(3.87)***		(−0.55)
L. Gini	0.7377	0.1264		
	(1.77)*	(0.66)		
L. PC government	0.0152	0.0010		
expenditure	(1.69)	(0.07)		
L. PC capital expenditure			0.0261	0.0149
			(1.93)*	(2.05)*
L. Share of credit			0.1050	
			(0.62)	
L. Share of agriculture	−0.2133			
	(−1.14)			
L. Population growth rate	−0.0695		0.0381	−0.0040
	(−0.81)		(0.79)	(−0.15)
L. Working population		0.4723		
proportion		(1.52)		
L. Proportion of graduates		0.2372		0.1290
		(1.78)*		(1.78)*
L. Inflation	0.0538	0.0658	−0.0220	−0.0273
	(1.17)	(2.20)**	(−0.69)	(−2.09)**
Constant	15.3349	5.0527	−5.813	2.8027
	(5.50)***	(3.81)***	(−6.75)***	(3.63)***
Year dummies	No	No	No	No
F—test statistic	F(6,20) = 97.94 Prob > F = 0.00	F(6,57) = 99.38 Prob > F = 0.00	F(5,20) = 104.32 Prob > F = 0.00	F(6,57) = 6.86 Prob > F = 0.00
R square	0.80	0.91	0.90	0.42
Selected model	**FE**	**FE**	**FE**	**FE**
F-statistic for state dummies	F(20, 57) = 5.30 Prob > F = 0.00	F(20, 57) = 8.43 Prob > F = 0.00	F(20, 58) = 18.99 Prob > F = 0.00	F(20, 57) = 4.31 Prob > F = 0.00

(continued)

Table 1 (continued)

Explanatory variables	L. PI	L. PCNSDP	L. Trade	L. Gini
Observations	84	84	84	84

Notes '***', '**' and '*' imply level of significance of 1, 5 and 10%, respectively
The numbers in parentheses are '*t*' statistic corresponding to robust standard errors
The *R* square is within *R* square
Source Author's own calculations

5.2 Panel 2SLS Results of the Structural Equations

The Eqs. (1) to (4) above have endogenous variables on the RHS that are correlated with the error terms, therefore the estimates using FE and RE methods would be inconsistent. This is termed as 'simultaneity-bias'. The leading method to obtain consistent estimates of the parameters of simultaneous equations models is the instrumental variable (IV) method such as two-stage least squares (2SLS). The 2SLS method addresses problem of endogeneity of RHS variables with the help of an instrument obtained by linear combination of all other exogenous variables in the model.

There are two widely used instrumental variable (2SLS) methods for panel data: fixed effects 2SLS (FE2SLS) and random effects 2SLS (RE2SLS). These estimators are presented in Baltagi (2008). Hausman (1978) suggested a test for the comparison between FE and RE estimators in panel regression, to help choose between them. This test can be generalized to choose between FE2SLS and RE2SLS estimators (Baltagi, 2008). This 2SLS estimator is consistent but not fully efficient as it ignores cross-equation relationships between error terms and any omitted endogenous variables. The 2SLS estimates of the four structural equations are presented in Table 2.[11]

The above results support the main hypothesis of the study that trade openness leads to poverty reduction via its influence on growth and inequality. Inequality (at least empirically) is shown not playing a significant role in affecting per capita income, trade openness or poverty incidence, as the coefficients are not found to be significant. The total effect (both direct and indirect) of any variable on poverty can be obtained by two components: (a) coefficient of the variable of interest (which estimates elasticity) in the poverty equation and (b) coefficients (elasticities) of other variables which are affected by the variable of interest in the poverty equation (Bathla et al., 2015). The total effect of trade openness on poverty is calculated from 2SLS results, using the Formula: [12]

[11]The results of FE and RE specifications along with Hausman test to choose final model for each equation are given in Appendix 1.

[12]Note that this calculation of the impact of trade openness on poverty can only be taken as impact effects including both indirect channels into account (as there is no direct channel of effect in the model) but omitting the feedback effect from PCNSDP (as this omits the feedback effect from PCNSDP to trade and from PCNSDP to inequality).

Table 2 Panel data 2SLS estimates

Explanatory variables	L. PI	L. PCNSDP	L. Trade	L. Gini
L.PCNSDP	−1.2233		0.9755	−0.0855
	(−4.51)***		(9.16)***	(−0.80)
L. Trade		1.3937		−0.1426
		(4.50)***		(−1.06)
L. Gini	−0.5577	−0.3913		
	(−0.67)	(−0.43)		
L. PC government	0.0271	−0.0063		
expenditure	(1.24)	(−0.30)		
L. PC capital expenditure			0.0143	0.0178
			(0.92)	(1.70)*
L. Share of credit			−0.0045	
			(−0.04)	
L. Share of agriculture	−0.2817			
	(−1.92)*			
L. Population growth rate	−0.0615		0.0343	−0.0260
	(−0.81)		(0.79)	(−0.97)
L. Working population		0.6570		
proportion		(0.99)		
L. Proportion of graduates		−0.2228		0.2744
		(−0.93)		(1.96)**
L. Inflation	0.0042	−0.0232	−0.0261	−0.0008
	(0.05)	(−0.33)	(−0.71)	(−0.02)
Constant	18.2530	4.4621	−6.5667	4.2661
	(7.46)***	(1.46)	(−9.25)***	(3.83)***
Year dummies	No	No	No	No
F-test statistic	Wald chi2 (6) = 179.5 Prob > chi2 = 0.00	Wald chi2 (6) = 334431 Prob > chi2 = 0.00	Wald chi2 (6) = 61414 Prob > chi2 = 0.00	Wald chi2 (6) = 46.05 Prob > chi2 = 0.00
R Square	0.69	0.84	0.34	0.31
Selected model	**RE**	**FE**	**FE**	**RE**

(continued)

Table 2 (continued)

Explanatory variables	L. PI	L. PCNSDP	L. Trade	L. Gini
Observations	84	84	84	84

Notes '***', '**' and '*' imply level of significance of 1%, 5% and 10%, respectively
The numbers in parentheses are '*t*' (*Z*) statistic for FE (RE) estimates with non-robust standard errors
Within (Overall) *R* square is given for FE (RE) models
Source Author's own calculations

$$\frac{d\text{Poverty}}{d\text{Trade}} = \frac{\partial\text{Poverty}}{\partial\text{PCNSDP}}\left(\frac{\partial P\text{CNSDP}}{\partial\text{Trade}}\right) + \frac{\partial\text{Poverty}}{\partial\text{PCNSDP}}\left(\frac{\partial\text{PCNSDP}}{\partial\text{Gini}} * \frac{\partial\text{Gini}}{\partial\text{Trade}}\right) + \frac{\partial\text{Poverty}}{\partial\text{Gini}}\left(\frac{\partial\text{Gini}}{\partial\text{Trade}}\right)$$

The total effect of trade openness on poverty incorporating only indirect effect (as there is no direct effect) is thus, equal to -1.64 from 2SLS results. If only significant effects are taken into account in the calculation, then only first term will be nonzero and hence trade elasticity of poverty would be equal to -1.7. Thus, with such a high elasticity, trade openness is expected to play a significant role in poverty reduction through its impact on per capita income of the states.

5.3 Discussion of Regression Results

The simultaneous equations model depicts the important interdependencies among the four endogenous variables. These are indicated in Table 3 depicting the relations found to be significant/insignificant in both OLS and 2SLS estimates. The nature of significance of coefficients depicting interrelationships between endogenous variables is the same in both OLS and 2SLS results, except in one case. These

Table 3 Significance of relationships between the endogenous variables of the model

	Equation for							
RHS Endogenous variables	PI		PCNSDP		Trade		Gini	
	OLS	2SLS	OLS	2SLS	OLS	2SLS	OLS	2SLS
PCNSDP	√	√			√	√	n.s	n.s
Trade			√	√			n.s	n.s
Gini	√	n.s	n.s	n.s				

Notes
√ Depicts significant relations
n.s implies non-significant relations
Source Author's own calculations

relationships are robust to the inclusion of state fixed effects in the empirical analysis, implying that both within states and across states, these associations exist.

The first important relationship is responsiveness of poverty to increase in per capita income. This is a well-established hypothesis. Much evidence points in the direction of how growth is essential for poverty reduction (Dollar & Kray, 2002, 2013. For the Indian economy, Ravallion & Datt (1996), Datt & Ravallion (2011), Radhakrishna et al. (2013) and Datt et al. (2016) estimated the elasticity of poverty with respect to net domestic product per capita, stating that economic growth had typically been poverty reducing in India. In our results, this elasticity is −1.22 for the period of 1993–94 to 2011–12.

The results above show that Gini coefficient is neither affecting PCNSDP, nor getting affected by it. Many studies employing cross-section data (listed in Benabou, 2000) confirm the Kuznets hypothesis of negative impact of growth on inequality. However, Radhakrishna et al. (2013) estimated impact of GDP on inequality of the states of India for the period of 1993-94–2009-10, found the coefficient to be significant and elasticity value of 0.27. According to the World Development Report (2006), growth has on average no impact on inequality. This apparent difference in the results of various studies can be due to some methodological problems such as OLS results being inconsistent in the presence of endogeneity, measurement error bias and omitted variable bias. Banerjee & Duflo (2003) attempted to explain this contrasting evidence for both sets of studies (using either cross section or panel data) stated that there exist a nonlinear relation between growth and inequality.

Our results show the absence of significant causal relationships between PCNSDP and inequality, and hence inequality is not expected to adversely affect poverty. According to Bourguinon (2003), inequality would not adversely affect the reduction in poverty only if the country grows at a rate high enough to offset the impact of inequality. However, many observers have noted increase in inequality in the Indian economy and considered it to be one of the important factors dampening the impact of growth on poverty especially for the post-reform period. Topalova (2005) and Radhakrishna et al. (2013) claimed that poverty reduction would have been much higher at all India level (and also for urban and rural areas) if inequality had not been growing at such a high rate.

Another important relationship for the present analysis is between trade openness and per capita income, which is a two-way relation. Both relations are found to be positive and significant. So, it is not only that trade openness promotes growth, but also higher per capita income pushes up trade. As already discussed, the literature gives mixed evidence on this relation. Chandra (2002, 2003) and Dhawan & Biswal (1999) largely employed time series data and supported the two-way causality of these variables (more so between income and export growth). Chatterji et al. (2013), Marelli & Signorelli (2011) and Paul & Das (2012), studying the period of post 1980s, found supporting evidence of the positive relation between trade openness and growth.

One can draw an important inference from the results that the estimated values of both sides of causal relations between trade openness and per capita NSDP are higher for panel data 2SLS results than panel data OLS results. Thus, even after accounting for trade endogeneity states with higher trade openness experience higher per capita incomes.[13]

In our results, trade openness does not impact inequality in any significant way. In a cross-sectional study for the period of 1981–2013, Mitra (2016) found that trade as a percentage of GDP had insignificant impact on inequality but tariff reductions led to increase in inequality. These results remained consistent even when country effects and time effects were included in the regression. But in a study by Krishna & Sethupathy (2011), which focussed on the states of India and incorporated Theil measure of inequality (and not Gini coefficient), the impact of tariffs on inequality was not found to be significant. This was also supported by Topalova (2005) for inequality at the district level for India.

6 Conclusion

This paper attempted to empirically analyse the impact of trade openness on poverty. It builds on PGI triangle proposed by Bourguignon (2003) to determine the impact of trade openness on poverty through its effects on growth and inequality and examine the interrelations among these four relevant variables. The structural equation model (SEM) consisting of a system of four Eqs. (1)–(4) of Sect. 3 is estimated from panel data for 21 major states in India. Both OLS and 2SLS estimates of the four equations are presented.

The key relations (among endogenous variables) emerging from the empirical analysis are as follows:

(1) There is a negative relation between PCNSDP and poverty incidence and hence the higher the PCNSDP of a state, the lower is its poverty incidence.
(2) There is a positive relation between trade openness and PCNSDP. So the states which are trading more experience higher PCNSDP. Also, PCNSDP positively influences trade openness.

From these two statements, one can conclude that trade openness leads to poverty reduction through its positive effect on growth.

(3) The two-way relation between PCNSDP and inequality is not found to be significant.
(4) The relation between trade openness and inequality is also not found to be significant.

[13]Frankel and Romer (1999), in their cross-section study of 150 countries for the year 1985, found the similar pattern in OLS and IV estimates of the coefficient of trade openness on per capita income. Irwin and Tervio (2002) also checked for the consistency of results of Frankel and Romer (1999) and found that instrumenting trade openness led to higher positive effect of trade openness on per capita income. However, they stated that this implied that either trade openness was not measured correctly and/or it was not a good proxy for other factors that increased income due to interactions between nations.

Thus, trade openness of the states would not affect inequality and through this channel would have no effect on PCNSDP and hence poverty. This channel with the possibility of negative impact on poverty is not found to be significant in the results. Hence, one can say with some confidence that trade openness through its impact on PCNSDP (and no impact on inequality from either trade openness or PCNSDP) would be beneficial for reduction in poverty incidence.

However, one needs to be careful in interpreting this result of no impact of inequality on income and poverty incidence. Though poverty ratio has fallen in India, the number of poor has gone up over the years. According to Nayyar (2013), this trend has been observed in both Africa and Asia (despite rapid economic growth). The literature also points to a nonlinear relation between PCNSDP and inequality, which has not been tested in this study. According to it, inequality negatively influences per capita income after a certain level of growth, and in that case, higher inequality would adversely affect not only growth but also poverty incidence. Thus, it would be imperative for the economy to control the rising inequality. If it remains unchecked, it can become detrimental for the growth prospects of the economy and eventually can arrest the observed fall in poverty.

The majority view of the literature as well as the present empirical analysis point towards the importance of trade liberalization for growth and poverty reduction. It is desirable not to place too much emphasis on globalization and exports as an easy path to rapid economic growth and development. Rodrik et al. (2004) have shown the importance of domestic strategy, which includes building institutions and focussing on human and physical investment, to fully exploit the beneficial effects of trade openness, thus concluding that openness is a means to an end and not an end in itself.

Appendix 1

See (Tables 4, 5, 6 and 7)

Table 4 Panel data 2SLS estimates—poverty equation

Variables	Fixed effects (1)	Random effects (2)	Final_Random effects (3)
L.PCNSDP	−1.3712	−1.2233	−1.2233
	(−2.84)***	(−4.51)***	(−4.51)***
L. Gini	−0.4849	−0.5577	−0.5577
	(−0.40)	(−0.67)	(−0.67)
L. PC government expenditure	0.0327	0.0271	0.0271
	(1.16)	(1.24)	(1.24)
L. Share of agriculture	−0.3271	−0.2817	−0.2817
	(−1.08)	(−1.92)*	(−1.92)*
L. Population growth rate	−0.0941	−0.0615	−0.0615
	(−1.21)	(−0.81)	(−0.81)
L. Inflation	0.0222	0.0042	0.0042
	(0.19)	(0.05)	(0.05)
Constant	19.5708	18.2530	18.2530
	(5.05)***	(7.46)***	(7.46)***
Within *R* square	0.75	0.74	0.74
Between *R* square	0.69	0.69	0.69
Overall *R* square	0.69	0.69	0.69
F-test statistic	Wald chi2 (6) = 17093 Prob > chi2 = 0.00	Wald chi2 (6) = 179.59 Prob > chi2 = 0.00	Wald chi2 (6) = 179.5 Prob > chi2 = 0.0000
Hausman *p* value $	0.63		
Selected model	Random effects		
Observations	84	84	84

Notes '***', '**' and '*' imply level of significance of 1, 5 and 10%, respectively
The numbers in parentheses are '*t*' (*s*) statistic for FE (RE) estimates with non-robust standard errors
Source Author's own calculations

Table 5 Panel data 2SLS estimates—income equation

Variables	Fixed effects (1)	Random effects (2)	Final_Fixed effects (3)
L. Trade	1.3937	0.1007	1.3937
	(4.50)***	(0.26)	(4.50)***
L. Gini	−0.3913	−1.3267	−0.3913
	(−0.43)	(−1.82)*	(−0.43)
L. PC government expenditure	−0.0063	0.0516	−0.0063
	(−0.30)	(2.63)***	(−0.30)
L. Working population proportion	0.6570	2.3313	0.6570
	(0.99)	(3.13)***	(0.99)
L. Proportion of graduates	−0.2228	0.9572	−0.2228
	(−0.93)	(4.08)***	(−0.93)
L. Inflation	−0.0232	0.0096	−0.0232
	(−0.33)	(0.11)	(−0.33)
Constant	4.4621	2.8532	4.4621
	(1.46)	(0.69)	(1.46)
Within *R* square	0.84	0.80	0.84
Between *R* square	0.00	0.86	0.00
Overall *R* square	0.17	0.83	0.17
F-test statistic	Wald chi2 (6) = 334431 Prob > chi2 = 0.00	Wald chi2 (6) = 345.94 Prob > chi2 = 0.00	Wald chi2 (6) = 334431 Prob > chi2 = 0.00
Hausman *p* value $	0.00		
Selected model	Fixed effects		
Observations	84	84	84

Notes Same as Table 1

Table 6 Panel data 2SLS estimates—trade openness equation

Variables	Fixed effects (1)	Random effects (2)	Final_Fixed effects (3)
L.PCNSDP	0.9755	0.8049	0.9755
	(9.16)***	(6.62)***	(9.16)***
L. PC capital expenditure	0.0143	0.0174	0.0143
	(0.92)	(0.83)	(0.92)
L. Share of credit	−0.0045	−0.1369	−0.0045
	(−0.04)	(−1.20)	(−0.04)
L. Population growth rate	0.0343	−0.0173	0.0343
	(0.79)	(−0.29)	(0.79)
L. Inflation	−0.0261	0.0472	−0.0261
	(−0.71)	(0.89)	(−0.71)
Constant	−6.5667	−4.5279	−6.5667
	(−9.25)***	(−5.21)***	(−9.25)***
Within R square	0.90	0.88	0.90
Between R square	0.10	0.14	0.10
Overall R square	0.34	0.38	0.34
F-test statistic	Wald chi2 (6) = 61414 Prob > chi2 = 0.00	Wald chi2 (6) = 181.08 Prob > chi2 = 0.00	Wald chi2 (6) = 61414 Prob > chi2 = 0.0000
Hausman p value $	0.00		
Selected model	Fixed effects		
Observations	84	84	84

Notes Same as Table 1

Table 7 Panel data 2SLS estimates—inequality equation

Variables	Fixed effects (1)	Random effects (2)	Final_Random effects (3)
L.PCNSDP	−0.0860	−0.0855	−0.0855
	(−0.46)	(−0.80)	(−0.80)
L. Trade	0.2522	−0.1426	−0.1426
	(0.80)	(−1.06)	(−1.06)
L. PC capital expenditure	0.0096	0.0178	0.0178
	(0.94)	(1.70)*	(1.70)*
L. Population growth rate	−0.0195	−0.0260	−0.0260
	(−0.59)	(−0.97)	(−0.97)
L. Proportion of graduates	−0.0045	0.2744	0.2744
	(−0.03)	(1.96)**	(1.96)**
L. Inflation	−0.0398	−0.0008	−0.0008
	(−1.35)	(−0.02)	(−0.02)
Constant	3.4608	4.2661	4.2661
	(2.92)***	(3.83)***	(3.83)***
Within *R* square	0.31	0.34	0.34
Between *R* square	0.08	0.30	0.30
Overall *R* square	0.02	0.31	0.31
F-test statistic	Wald chi2 (6) = 125869 Prob > chi2 = 0.00	Wald chi2 (6) = 46.05 Prob > chi2 = 0.00	Wald chi2 (6) = 46.05 Prob > chi2 = 0.00
Hausman *p* value $	0.64		
Selected model	Random effects		
Observations	84	84	84

Notes Same as Table 1

References

Alvaredo, F., & Gasparini, L. (2015). Recent trends in inequality and poverty in developing Countries. In A. Atkinson, & F. Bourguignon (Eds.), *Handbook of income distribution,* Vol. 2.

Baltagi, B. H. (2008). *Econometric analysis of panel data* (4th ed.). New York: Wiley.

Banerjee, A. V., & Duflo, E. (2003). Inequality and growth: What can the data say? *Journal of Economic Growth, 8,* 267–299.

Barua, A., & Chakraborty, P. (2010). Does openness affect regional inequality? A case study for India. *Review of Development Economics, 14*(3), 447–465.

Bathla, S., Yu, B., Thorat, S., & Joshi, P. (2015). *Accelerating agricultural growth and poverty alleviation through public expenditure: The experience of India*", Paper presented in 29th International Conference of Agricultural Economists, Milan, Italy.

Benabou, R. (2000). Unequal societies: Income distribution and the social contract. *American Economic Review, 90*(1), 96–129.

Bhalla, S. (2000). Growth and poverty in India: Myth and reality. Available at http://www.oxusresearch.com/economic.asp.

Bourguignon, F. (2003). The poverty-growth-inequality triangle. *Paper presented at the Conference on Poverty, Inequality and Growth, on November 13, 2003*, Paris, sponsored by the Agence Française de Dévelopment and the EU Development Network.

Cain, S. J., Hasan, R., & Mitra, D. (2010a). Trade liberalization and poverty reduction: New evidence from Indian States. *Working Paper No. 2010–3, Columbia Program on Indian Economic Policies.*

Chandra, N. (2002). Export growth and economic growth: An investigation of causality in India. *Indian Economic Journal, 49*(3), 64–73.

Chandra, N. (2003). Reinvestigating export-led growth in india using a multivariate cointegration framework. *Journal of Developing Areas, 37*(1), 73–86.

Chatterji, M., Mohan, S., Dastidar, S. G. (2013). Relationship between trade openness and economic growth of India: A time series analysis. *Working Paper No. 274, Dundee Discussion Papers in Economics*, University of Dundee.

Dash, R. K. & Sharma, C. (2008). Government expenditure and economic growth in India. *The IUP Journal of Public Finance, 6*, 60–69.

Datt, G., & Ravallion, M. (2002). Is India's economic growth leaving the poor behind? *Journal of Economic Perspectives, 16*(3), 89–108.

Datt, G., & Ravallion, M. (2011). Has India's economic growth become more pro-poor in the wake of economic reforms? *World Bank Economic Review, 25*(2), 157–189.

Datt, G., Ravallion, M., & Murgai, R. (2016). Growth, urbanization and poverty reduction in India. *Working Paper No. 21983, NBER Working Paper Series*, National Bureau of Economics Research.

Deininger, K., & Squire, L. (1996). A new data set measuring income inequality. *World Bank Economic Review, 10*(3), 565–591.

Dhamija, N. (2019). Trade liberalization and unemployment in India: A state level analysis. *MPRA Paper 95001*, Germany: University Library of Munich.

Dhawan, U., & Biswal, B. (1999). Re-examining export-led growth hypothesis: A multivariate cointegration analysis for India. *Applied Economics, 31*(4), 525–530.

Dollar, D. (2001). *Globalization, inequality and poverty since 1980.* Washington, DC: Background paper, World Bank.

Dollar, D., & Kraay, A. (2002). Growth is good for the poor. *Journal of Economic Growth, 7*(3), 195–225.

Dollar, D., & Kraay, A. (2004). Trade, growth, and poverty. *The Economic Journal, 114*(493), 22–49.

Dollar, D., Kleineberg, T., & Kraay, A. (2013). Growth still is good for the poor. *Policy Research Working Paper, No. 6568*, World Bank.

Donald, M. R. & Majeed, M. T. (2010). Distributional and poverty consequences of globalization: A dynamic comparative analysis for developing Countries, *SIRE Discussion Paper No. 2010–62*, Scottish Institute for Research in Economics.

Dreze, J., & Sen, A. (2013). In: An uncertain glory: India and its contradictions. Princeton University Press.

Edwards, S. (1998). Openness, productivity and growth: What do we really know? *The Economic Journal, 108*, 383–398.

Esfahani, H. S. (1991). Exports, imports and economic growth in semi-industrialized Countries. *Journal of Development Economics, 35*, 93–116.

Goldberg, P., & Pavcnik, N. (2007). Distributional effects of globalization in developing countries. *Journal of Economic Literature, 45*(1), 39–82.

Greene, W. H. (2012). In *Econometric analysis*. 7th edn. Pearson.

Harrison & Hanson. (1999). Who gains from trade reform? Some remaining puzzles. *Working Paper No. 6915, NBER Working Paper Series*, National Bureau of Economics Research.

Harrison, A. (2006). Globalization and poverty. *Working Paper No. 12347, NBER Working Paper Series*, National Bureau of Economics Research.

Hasan, R., Mitra, D., & Ural, B. P. (2007). Trade liberalization, labour-market institutions and poverty reduction. IN *India policy forum 2006–07*, (Vol. 3), India: National Council of Applied Economic Research.

Hausman, J. A. (1978). Specification tests in econometrics. *Econometrica, 46*, 1251–1271.

Janvry, A. D. & Sadoulet, E. (2016). *Development economics—theory and practice*. Routledge.

Kaldor, N. (1956). Alternative theories of distribution. *The Review of Economic Studies, 23*(2), 83–100.

Kanji, N. & Menon-Sen, K. (2001). What does the feminisation of labour mean for sustainable livelihoods. *Unpublished paper, International Institute for Environment and Development.*

Krishna, P. & Sethupahy, G. (2011). Trade and inequality in India. *Working Paper No. 17257, NBER Working Paper Series*, National Bureau of Economics Research.

Kumar, N. (2001). India's trade in 2020: *A mapping of relevant factors*. Paper prepared for the Committee on Vision 2020 for India, Planning Commission, Government of India.

Lancaster, T. (2000). The incidental parameter problem since 1948. *Journal of Econometrics, 95*, 391–413.

Mallick, H. (2008). Government spending, trade openness and economic growth in India: A time series analysis. *eSocialSciences Working Paper No. 1809.*

Marelli, E., & Signorelli, M. (2011). China and India: Openness, trade and effects on economic growth. *The European Journal of Comparative Economics, 8*(1), 129–154.

McCulloch, N., Winters, L. A., & Cirera, X. (2001). *Trade liberalisation and poverty: A handbook*. UK: Centre for Economic Policy Research.

McKay, A., Winters, L. A. & Kedir, A. M. (2000). A review of empirical evidence on trade, trade policy and poverty. *DFID White Paper on Eliminating Poverty: Making Globalisation Work for the Poor*, UK.

Mitra, D. (2016). Trade poverty and inequality. In J. Bhagwati, P. Krishna & A. Panagariya (Eds.), *The World trade system-trends and challenges*. MIT Press.

Nayyar, D. (2013). IN *Catch up: Developing countries in the World economy*. Oxford University Press.

Nayyar, G. (2008). Economic growth and regional inequality in India. *Economic and Political Weekly, 43*(6), 58–67.

Neyman, J., & Scott, E. L. (1948). Consistent estimation from partially consistent observations. *Econometrica, 16*(1), 1–32.

Pal, P., & Ghosh, J. (2007). Inequality in India: A survey of recent trends. *DESA Working Paper No. 45*, Department of Economic and Social Affairs, United Nations.

Paul, B., & Das, A. (2012). Export-led growth in india and the role of liberalization. *Margin: The Journal of Applied Economic Research, 6*(1), 1–26.

Radhakrishna, R., Ravi, C., & Reddy, B. (2013). Assessment of well-being in multidimensional perspective in post reform period. *Indian Economic Review, 48*(1), 131–166.

Rajan, R. (2002). *Trade liberalization and poverty in Asia: Issues and policy options*. Paper presented at the Fourth Asia Development Forum, co-sponsored by the Asian Development Bank, KDI, KIEP and the World Bank, Seoul on November 3–5.

Ravallion, M., & Chen, S. (1997). What can new survey data tell us about recent changes in distribution and poverty? *World Bank Economic Review, 11*(2), 357–382.

Ravallion, M., & Datt, G. (1996). How important to India's poor is the sectoral composition of economic growth? *World Bank Economic Review, 10*(1), 1–25.

Ravallion, M. (2001). Growth, inequality and poverty: Looking beyond averages. *World Development, 29*, 1803–1815.

Ravallion, M. (2004). Competing concepts of inequality in the globalization debate. In Susan M. Collins & Carol Graham (Eds.), *Brookings trade forum: 2004–Globalization, poverty and inequality*. Washington, D.C: Brookings Institution Press.

Ravallion, M., & Datt, G. (2002). Why has economic growth been more pro-poor in some states of India than others? *Journal of Development Economics, 68*, 381–400.

Rodriguez, F., & Rodrik, D. (1999). Trade policy and economic growth: A sceptic's guide to the cross-national evidence. *Working Paper No. 7081, NBER Working Paper Series*, National Bureau of Economics Research.

Rodrik, D., Subramanian, A., & Trebbi, F. (2004). Institutions rule: The primacy of institutions over geography and integration in economic development. *Journal of Economic Growth, 9*, 131–165.

Sachs, J. D. & Warners, A. (1995). Economic reform and the process of global integration. *Brookings Papers on Economic Activity I*, Washington D.C: Brookings Institution.

Sarkar, P. (2005). Is there any impact of trade liberalisation on growth? Experiences of India and Korea. MPRA Paper No. 5177, Munich Personal RePEc Archive.

Sarkar, S. (2008). Trade openness and growth: Is there any link? *Journal of Economic Issues, 42*(3), 763–785.

Sen, A. (2001). Estimates of consumer expenditure and its distribution: Statistical priorities after the NSS 55th round. *Economic and Political Weekly, 35*(51), 4499–4518.

Singh, T. (2010). Does international trade cause economic growth? A survey. *The World Economy, 33*(11), 1517–1564.

Topalova, P. (2005). Trade liberalization, poverty and inequality: Evidence from Indian districts. *Working Paper 11614, NBER Working Paper Series*, National Bureau of Economic Research.

Topalova, P. (2008). *India: Is the rising tide lifting all boats?. IMF Working Paper No. WP/08/54*, International Monetary Fund.

UNCTAD. (2013). *How are the poor affected by international trade in India: An empirical approach*, United Nations.

Villaverde, J., & Maza, A. (2011). Globalisation, growth and convergence. *The World Economy, 34*(6), 952–971.

Wacziarg, R., & Welch, K. H. (2003). Trade liberalization and growth: New evidence. *Working Paper No. 10152, NBER Working Paper Series*, National Bureau of Economics Research.

Wacziarg, R. (2001). Measuring the dynamic gains from trade. *World Bank Economic Review, 15*(3), 393–429.

Winters, L. A. (2000). Trade, trade policy, and poverty: What are the links? *World Economy, 25*(9), 1339–1367.

Winters, L. A., McCulloch, N., & McKay, A. (2004). Trade liberalization and poverty: The evidence so far. *Journal of Economic Literature, 42*, 72–115.

World Development Report. (2006). *Equity and Development*, World Bank.

Chapter 16
An Analysis of Labour-Intensive Exports to USA: Unlocking India's Potential

Vijaya Katti

1 Background

The USA happens to be the leading import market of the world. Its share in the global import has remained fairly constant, at 13.2 and 13.6% during 2008 and 2017, respectively. It has been noticed that China's penetration in the US market is growing over the years, with the country's share in US imports rising from 16.5% in 2008 to 21.8% in 2017. In that comparison, India's penetration in the US market has been fairly slow, rising from 1.2% in 2008 to 2.1% in 2017. Even during 2016–17, US import from China increased at a rate of 8%, as compared to the corresponding figure of 7% from India.

The high growth volume of US import from China has caused the bilateral trade deficit to move in China's favour. It has been noticed that trade deficit has reached a figure of $375 billion in 2017, with US exports to and imports from China standing at $130 billion and $505 billion, respectively. The lop-sided trade pattern recently triggered the USA to increase tariff protection on several imported goods. As a result of these measures, import in value terms from China has declined from $46.19 billion in December 2017 to $39.75 billion in March 2018 (US Census Bureau 2018).

Over the years, Indian export pattern to USA is becoming more value-added in nature, which is reflected in the rising share of the country in US imports. Given the growing importance of the US market for Indian exports, it deserves the analysis whether India would be able to occupy the space vacated by China. The profile of various competitors of India for the products in labour-intensive sectors needs to be analysed. Finally, possibilities of employment generation through boosting exports of these products to the USA need to be explored.

Against this background, this paper has examined the possibility of India gaining an important position and trying to occupy the space which is being vacated by China

V. Katti (✉)
Indian Institute of Foreign Trade, New Delhi, India
e-mail: vijayakatti@iift.edu

P. Lakhanpal et al. (eds.), *Trade, Investment and Economic Growth*,
https://doi.org/10.1007/978-981-33-6973-3_16

in USA because of US-China trade war. Small and **medium industries including** handicrafts, leather, gems and jewellery, textiles, handlooms, etc., have been playing a very important role in Indian economy. Almost 45% of India's merchandise exports are being carried out by these industries belonging to mostly the unorganized sector. They are labour-intensive. Employment generation is possible with these items, and they can help in India's better economic development.

2 Objectives of This Paper are as Follows

- To study the pattern of imports of USA from different countries which are India's competitors in US market.
- To explore the possibility of India occupying the vacated space by China.
- To analyse India's export performance in key labour-intensive sectors and recommend policies to enhance exports and employment of select products.
- To identify the impediments for India in increasing its export share substantially and provide necessary policy remedies to boost Indian exports significantly which in turn will generate more employment opportunities.

To identify Indian potential of labour-intensive good exports to USA, four HS codes have been selected:

- **HS Code 42**—Articles of leather; saddlery and harness; travel goods, handbags and similar containers; and articles of animal gut (other than silkworm gut).
- **HS Code 61**—Articles of apparel and clothing accessories, knitted or crocheted.
- **HS Code 64**—Footwear, gaiters and the like; parts of such articles.
- **HS Code 71**—Natural or cultured pearls, precious or semi-precious stones, precious metals, metals clad with precious metal and articles thereof; imitation jewellery; coin.

(source for HS codes and commodities names—DGFT https://www.dgft.gov.in/CP/***).***

3 Methodology

The following indices have been selected to compare Indian position in the context of US imports from world:

1. **Export Intensity Index (EII)**: This is a very important index which indicates whether a region's exports are more as a percentage to a specified destination compared to the average of the world.
2. **Export Specialization Index (ESI)**: The index measures whether a country is exporting one product more intensively to the other, in terms of proportional importance in the export basket.

3. **Revealed Trade Barrier (RTB) Index**: This particular index examines whether a country exports more of a product as a percentage to a particular destination compared to the world on an average.
4. **Revealed Comparative Index (RCI)**: The RCI is defined as the ratio of two shares. The numerator is the share of a country's total exports of the commodity of interest in its total exports. The denominator is share of world exports of the same commodity in total world exports.
5. **Export Similarity Index (E SIM)**: This particular index is nothing but the summation of export categories of the smaller of the sectoral export shares and that in comparison as a percentage of every country under the study.
6. **Trade Complementary Index (TCI)**: This particular index indicates the sum of total absolute value of the difference which is there in import category shares and that of export shares of different countries under the study and the whole divided by two. Normally, this index has been converted to a percentage form.

Note EII, ESI, RTB, RCI, E SIM and TCI of four select product categories have been calculated, and results and analysis for each product are given in the paper to highlight the possibility of India getting space in US market and capturing the same.

******Formulas for these indices have been given in Annexure*** 1. ***Graphical presentation of comparative position of India vis-à-vis other countries which are exporting these products to USA in last five years is given in Annexure*** 2.

4 Use of Indices Across Different Countries and HS Codes

It is worth mentioning that different sets of countries are chosen for comparison for same HS code with this research methodology. This is because certain indices like RCA are independent, others like TCI are calculated with trade partner country, and rest indices like export similarity index are generally calculated with an L2 competitor country. Hence, the purpose of each of the indices being different calls for different sets of countries. The insights drawn from these comparisons are then used for a collective analysis.

5 India-US Relations—Current Scenario

The USA occupies a very important position as India's trading partner. It comes into the second number, and last year India has become its 10th largest trading partner. In an attempt to move forward in the positive relationship, India and USA have signed the Logistics Exchanged Memorandum of Agreement and USA has been declared as a major defence partner by India. In 2015, both countries have renewed their 10-year Defense Framework Agreement that was signed on 2005. The collaborations between Indian and American businesses have enhanced particularly in information and communications technology (ICT), engineering and medical sectors.

Cordial Indo-US trade relations are certainly going to be very important for long-lasting and positive influence on the future world system, and this is the firm belief of premiers of both the nations that this will not only bring in stability but also boost the drive for democracy, propel prosperity resulting in peace across the world. India-US trade relations' major characteristics are as follows:

- US Commerce Secretary and USTR visits in this particular year have given a boost to India-US trade relations, and issues of mutual interest including various issues on the Doha Round of Multilateral Trade Negotiations have been highlighted within the same.
- More transparent US licensing arrangement for Indian imports of sensitive items and technology have been enabled by the next steps in strategic partnership. This has given rise to the higher level of high-tech trade between the two countries.
- India-US relations have been characterized by the outsourcing of knowledge work to India by various US-based companies. This has resulted in higher level of production and services between India and USA and influenced the general price level in the interest of consumers in both countries.
- Sectors including telecom, IT, infrastructure, energy and knowledge industries like pharmaceuticals and biotechnology have received priority for economic cooperation between India and the USA. General Electric, Whirlpool, Ford (India), 3 M, Tecumseh Products (India) Limited, Pepsi, Proctor and Gamble (India), Microsoft, Intel and IBM Corporation have been some important multinational corporations of USA which are doing a profitable business in India.

Total two-way goods trade between India and the USA has been $74.3 billion during 2017, and India is now occupying the position as 9th largest goods trading partner of USA. The deficit in trade in services of the USA with India was of the order of $4.4 billion in 2017. USA is 15th largest goods export market in 2017. US goods export to India was worth $25.7 billion, and the level was 18.7% higher compared to 2016 and 71.6% from 2007. In 2017, US exports to India accounted for 1.7% of overall US exports.

6 Exports

The 15th largest goods export market in 2017, India has accounted for 1.7% of overall US exports in 2017. Top export categories at 2-digit level of HS in 2017 included a variety of products, e.g. precious metal and stone (diamonds) ($7.0 billion), mineral fuels ($2.8 billion), aircraft ($2.2 billion), machinery ($2.1 billion), and optical and medical instruments ($1.4 billion). US total exports of agricultural products to India totalled $1.6 billion in 2017. Leading domestic export categories include: tree nuts ($738 million), cotton ($435 million), fresh fruit ($104 million), pulses ($53 million) and dairy products ($43 million). US exports of services to India were an estimated

$23.7 billion in 2017, 15.2% ($3.1 billion) more than 2016 and 174% greater than 2007 levels. Leading services exports from the USA to India were in the travel, intellectual property (computer software, audio and visual-related products) and transport sectors.

7 Imports

India was the USA's 11th largest supplier of goods imports in 2017. US goods imports from India totalled $48.6 billion in 2017, up 5.6% ($2.6 billion) from 2016 and up 101.9% from 2007. US imports from India accounted for 2.1% of overall US imports in 2017. The top import categories (2-digit HS) in 2017 were: precious metal and stone (diamonds) ($10 billion), pharmaceuticals ($6.1 billion), mineral fuels ($2.7 billion), machinery ($2.5 billion) and miscellaneous textile articles ($2.5 billion). US total imports of agricultural products from India totalled $2.6 billion in 2017. Leading categories include: spices ($272 million), tree nuts ($236 million), essential oils ($182 million), rice ($178 million), and processed fruit and vegetables ($125 million). US imports of services from India were an estimated $28.1 billion in 2017, 9.0% ($2.3 billion) more than 2016 and 183% greater than 2007 levels. Telecommunications, computer and information services, research and development, and travel sector have been identified as leading services imports from India to the USA.

8 Trade Balance

Trade in Goods: Total trade growth between the two countries in two years time period, i.e. 2016 to 2017, has been of the order of 9.7%. Absolute figures have been $25.7 billion US exports to India and $48.6 billion imports from India. An impressive growth of exports at the rate of 18.8% was experienced, and imports of goods from India rose by 5.4% from the 2016 level. Obviously, the trade deficit with India came down from 2016 to 2017 with the figures of $22.9 billion (2017) over the previous year's $24.5 billion.

Trade in Services: The USA's services trade deficit with India was ($5.6 billion in 2017), up 7.4% from the 2016 level of ($5.1 billion). Bilateral trade in services at ($51.8 billion) grew 11.5% over the previous year, with ($23.2 billion worth US exports to India and $28.7 billion) imports from India. 2017 US exports of services to India growth at 12% were balanced with (11.1% growth in U.S. imports from India), exhibiting a stable and consistent engagement on service trade from both sides.

Analysis has been undertaken with the help of various indices for 4 product groups. Each index is calculated product by product, and results in terms of strong competitor, etc., have been furnished for each product country-wise.

9 Export Intensity Index (EII)

***HS 42*: Articles of leather; saddlery and harness; travel goods, handbags and similar containers; and articles of animal gut (other than silkworm gut)**

- Mexico has the highest flow of trade with USA among all countries, but the value has decreased over the years due to more stringent laws of trade imposed by USA.
- Next come Philippines, Indonesia and Vietnam which have good trade flow with USA. These countries can improve their share in US market with better laws as China's exports to USA are declining.
- Trade war and retaliatory tariffs have been threatening US hide, skin export survival: US hides, skins and leather products would also face tariffs of either 5% or 25% from China. China and other trading partners did not undertake retaliatory tariffs (U.S. Hide, Skin and Leather Association).
- China is likely to face problems due to duty hike 5–25%.
- India has to compete with Mexico and others.

***HS 61*: Articles of apparel and clothing accessories, knitted or crocheted**

- China's export intensity index is increasing despite slowing down of textile exports to USA. On the other hand, Vietnam is making room in export intensity index in last 5 years as it fell continuously.
- India's export intensity index has been more or less stagnant, but countries like Cambodia are losing out continuously in last 5 years. Hence, India has a chance to attain optimum share.
- Export intensity when it comes to textile exports to US, EII of Honduras decreased significantly in last 5 years and hence has relatively become the player with lowest intensity in textile exports out of all the major players.
- Export intensity index of Vietnam, Cambodia and Honduras is decreasing, so India can occupy that space in textiles.

***HS 64*: Footwear, gaiters and the like; parts of such articles**

- Mexico has the highest flow of trade with USA among all countries and remains stable.
- Next come Dominican Republic, Vietnam, Indonesia, China and India which have good trade flow with USA, could be increased with better laws and can use the fact that China's share is slowing in imports of USA.
- Export flow between USA and Italy is the least followed by Spain.
- Mexico, Dominican Republic, Vietnam, Indonesia and China are strong competitors of India.
- Italy and Spain are not strong, and India can take space.

HS 71*: *Natural or cultured pearls, precious or semi-precious stones, precious metals, metals clad with precious metal and articles thereof; imitation jewellery; coin

- EII values greater than 1 indicate export flow between countries/regions is larger than expected given their importance in world trade.
- Mexico has the highest flow of trade with USA among all countries, but the value has decreased over the years due to more stringent laws of trade imposed by USA.
- Next come Israel, Canada, Peru and India which have good trade flow with USA, could be increased with better laws and can use the fact that China is slowing its exports to USA.
- Export flow between USA and Belgium is the least followed by South Africa.
- Mexico is the strong competitor, but value has decreased due to strong laws imposed by USA.
- In case of Israel, Canada and Peru, EII is declining.
- Similarly, China is slowing so India stands a better chance to increase its exports to USA.

10 Export Specialization Index (ESI)

HS 42*: *Articles of leather; saddlery and harness; travel goods, handbags and similar containers; articles of animal gut (other than silkworm gut)

- The export specialization (ES) index is nothing but a slightly modified RCA index. The denominator is usually measured by specific markets or partners in this. This specialization aims at giving the information about the products on revealed specialization in the export sector of a particular country. The index measures whether a country is exporting one product more intensively to the other, in terms of proportional importance in the export basket.
- As far as trade shares are concerned, high or low specialization indices and changes over the time normally reflect various factors which are other than trade policy-related matters.
- Export specialization index of China for HS-42 has been decreasing over the years, and this is a good opportunity for other players to step in.
- ESI for India has been steadily increasing for the past three years, indicating India could be a good alternative to China for US imports of hides and skins.
- Export specialization is improving for India, and India can take space of China as ESI for China decreasing.

HS 61*: *Articles of apparel and clothing accessories, knitted or crocheted

- India has a greater modified revealed comparative advantage, i.e. export specialization index in exporting textiles to USA w.r.t China, and yet it is not able to catch up with the space being vacated by China.

- India's ESI has been fluctuating and is back to original levels in last 5 years, whereas that of China has been continuously decreasing.
- The export specialization index of Vietnam, India and Cambodia has been increasing over the last 5 years as well.
- Hence, an interesting trend can be seen here in terms of a lot of players moving in simultaneously to fill in the export space being vacated by China in textiles.
- India is improving and occupied the space of China where Vietnam is decreasing.

HS 64: ***Footwear, gaiters and the like; parts of such articles***

- India can boost the exports of the product to USA, Dominican Republic for which ESI value trend increased over the years.
- Vietnam and Mexico take a value between 0 and 1. Values greater than 1 indicate export specialization in these countries for this product.
- India increasing—Mexico and Vietnam between 0 and 1 so India can perform and dominate.

HS 71: ***Natural or cultured pearls, precious or semi-precious stones, precious metals, metals clad with precious metal and articles thereof; imitation jewellery; coin***

- The index measures whether a country is exporting one product more intensively to the other, in terms of proportional importance in the export basket.
- There can be a boost to the exports of the product to USA from South Africa, Mexico for which ESI value trend has increased over the years.
- India, Israel and Belgium take a value between 0 and 1. Values greater than 1 indicate export specialization in these countries for this product.
- ESI of India, Israel and Belgium is increasing.

11 Revealed Trade Barrier (RTB) Index

HS 42: ***Articles of leather; saddlery and harness; travel goods, handbags and similar containers; articles of animal gut (other than silkworm gut)***

- Mexico has a value lesser than 1 which indicates that Mexico is exporting this commodity relatively more as compared to the rest of the world than it is to USA, possibly due to low barriers.
- Vietnam and Philippines have seen increasing trade barriers over the last five years.

HS 61: ***Articles of apparel and clothing accessories, knitted or crocheted***

- India enjoys an advantage in having lower trade barriers to export textiles to USA compared to other countries. China has trade barriers at same level, and Mexico has even lower than that. Over the period of last 5 years, trade barriers against

textile exports from India to USA have increased, whereas they have decreased in case of Vietnam and Indonesia.
- Vietnam and Indonesia have managed quite well to decrease trade barriers faced. India should also try to negotiate a better agreement to counter trade barriers faced in USA while exporting textile products.
- Exceptionally low trade barriers faced by Mexico are a huge threat to Indian exports due to geographical vicinity of Mexico to USA.
- Mexico is a member of NAFTA, i.e. one more reason why Mexico enjoys low trade barriers from USA.

HS 64*: *Footwear, gaiters and the like; parts of such articles

- As the destination is USA, it can be seen that USA imports more of this product from India, China, Italy and Dominican Republic. Hence, these can be alternative options for USA to import if China restricts its trade to USA.
- Mexico and Vietnam with values lesser than 1 show that India is exporting this commodity exported relatively more to the rest of the world than it is to these countries. This can be attributed to trade barriers.
- India–China, Dominican Republic and Italy; India can take space of China.

HS 71*: *Natural or cultured pearls, precious or semi-precious stones, precious metals, metals clad with precious metal and articles thereof; imitation jewellery; coin

- As the destination is USA, it can be seen that USA imports more of this product from Israel, South Africa, Peru, India, Belgium. Hence, these can be alternative options for USA to import if China restricts its trade to USA.
- Mexico, China and Canada with values lesser than 1 show that India's export of this commodity is greater to the world than it is to these countries. This can again be attributed to trade barriers therein.
- Exports of Israel, Peru, South Africa and Belgium are very high to compete, so India can compete with China.

12 Export Similarity Index (E SIM)

HS 42*: *Articles of leather; saddlery and harness; travel goods, handbags and similar containers; articles of animal gut (other than silkworm gut)

- India faces high structural competition from Hong Kong and Vietnam, apart from China. While leather exports from China declined by about 11% in 2016-17, exports from Vietnam increased by nearly 46%.
- India's leather production of 2.5 million sqft accounts for 13% of global leather production. It manufactures products worth $18 billion out of which 90% consumed locally and India is world's second largest producer of footwear and

leather garments after China, and fifth largest exporter of leather goods and accessories.

- India's competitors are Hong Kong, Vietnam and China

HS 61*: *Articles of apparel and clothing accessories, knitted or crocheted

- Although China is slowing down in absolute terms, the competitive profile of China for textile and clothing exports to USA is becoming relatively stronger.
- Bangladesh has a strongest and stable competitive profile against India in exporting textile products to USA. The competitiveness of Turkey is decreasing over last 5 years and that of Italy is increasing.

HS 64*: *Footwear, gaiters and the like; parts of such articles

- India faces high structural competition from Hong Kong, Turkey, Italy and Spain in service trade (higher when compared to China).
- Competition to India has been consistent over years in case of Turkey and Italy, while it has been decreasing in case of Cambodia and Vietnam.
- China and Vietnam show a low competition to India in this trade.
- Intra-industry trade is possible with Vietnam and Cambodia and to some extent with China with reduced hurdles.
- This representation however does not consider the level of exports, so can be misleading when the size of the economies is considered and it would be very different. It is subject to aggregation bias.

HS 71*: *Natural or cultured pearls, precious or semi-precious stones, precious metals, metals clad with precious metal and articles thereof; imitation jewellery; coin

- India faces high structural competition from Hong Kong, Turkey, Italy and Cambodia in service trade (higher when compared to China).
- Competition to India has been consistent over years in case of Hong Kong and Cambodia, while it has been decreasing in case of Italy and Turkey.
- Spain, Germany and Switzerland show a low competition to India in this trade.
- Intra-industry trade is possible with Spain, Germany and Switzerland and to some extent with Turkey with reduced hurdles.
- The representation does not consider the level of exports. That is why, this can give the misleading picture when the size of the economies considered is very different. It is subject to the aggregation bias because of that fact.

13 Trade Complementary Index (TCI)

HS 42*: *Articles of leather; saddlery and harness; travel goods, handbags and similar containers; articles of animal gut (other than silkworm gut)

- The extent to which the export profile of a report compliments the importer profile of a partner is evaluated with the help of the trade complementarity index. In this context, whenever the profiles are strongly complementary, this may be indicative of the fact that the sources of growth might be exploitable.
- Range: 0 to 100—Within this index, score of 100 indicates that these are ideal trading partners and a score of 0 indicates that the two countries are absolute competitors of each other.
- Normally, those countries which are geographically far away from each other or which are incurring high cost of transportation and transaction cost may not prove to be ideal trading partners despite a high complementarity index.
- This index may reveal the aggregation bias.
- India has shown a lot of improvement on this front in recent years, while China's TCI has been more or less constant. Indonesia too has seen its TCI steadily rises over the years.

HS 61*: *Articles of apparel and clothing accessories, knitted or crocheted

- Stagnant export profile of China w.r.t USA in terms of trade complementary index indicates structural potential for other players to increase the share.
- India's position is worse than China as India's profile is stagnant since last 5 years as against China's which is stagnant since last 3 years.
- Vietnam, Cambodia and Bangladesh are catching up in making the export profile more attractive to w.r.t USA in last 5 years.
- This indicates India's export profile also has a structural stagnancy.
- Incentives to not only export but skill development and technology transfer are required to make better textile products.

HS 64*: *Footwear, gaiters and the like; parts of such articles

- Overall demand orientation of Cambodia and Indonesia is highly correlated to supply orientation of USA. Next best orientation is that of China, El Salvador, Mexico and India.
- These countries should look for opportunity to push huge volumes and gain more share in country import basket.
- USA should try to build a revealed comparative advantage with Indonesia, Cambodia, El Salvador, India and Mexico compared to China in terms of cost leadership or negotiating better tariff rates and trade agreements.
- China, El Salvador, Mexico and India—increasing TCI. Hence, India stands a chance to gain.

HS 71*: *Natural or cultured pearls, precious or semi-precious stones, precious metals, metals clad with precious metal and articles thereof; imitation jewellery; coin

- Overall demand orientation of India is highly correlated to supply orientation of USA. Next best orientation is that of Canada and Belgium.

- Next come Israel, Mexico and South Africa which are better correlated with USA when compared to China.
- These countries should look for opportunities to push huge volumes and gain more share in country import basket.
- USA should try to build a revealed comparative advantage with Canada, Belgium, Israel, Mexico, South Africa and India as compared to China in terms of cost leadership or negotiating better tariff rates and trade agreements.

14 Revealed Comparative Index (RCI)

HS 42*: *Articles of leather; saddlery and harness; travel goods, handbags and similar containers; articles of animal gut (other than silkworm gut)

- Over 2013-2015, RCA for India has had a minimal increase, while for China it has gone down steadily.
- Italy and Vietnam have also seen drops, while Philippines has managed to increase its RCI.
- CHINA WAGE INCREASES—China experienced limited expansion in world markets because of the wage increases specially for labour-intensive products in recent years. Other Asian partners including Bangladesh and Vietnam, however, gained relatively in a better manner compared with India.
- When in the context of apparel and leather products, Bangladesh and Vietnam have obviously been more competitive, compared to India.
- China gone down; India minimal increase; Italy and Vietnam—drop leather apparel; India to compete with Bangladesh and Vietnam.
- China wage increase—India can take space.

HS 61*: *Articles of apparel and clothing accessories, knitted or crocheted

- India has a greater revealed comparative advantage in exporting textiles to USA w.r.t China, and yet it is not able to catch up with the space being vacated by China.
- India's RCI has been constant, whereas that of China has been decreasing over the last 5 years.
- The interesting trend is that RCI of many top 10 countries has been decreasing over last five years except Egypt.
- Hence, India can also collaborate with Egypt in building a better RCI for exporting textiles to USA. The labour-intensive industry needs a combined effort in terms of skilling for gaining advantage.

15 Policy Boost Required for Competing This Following Countries

India needs to compete with the following countries:

- **HS 42** (***Articles of leather; saddlery and harness; travel goods, handbags and similar containers; articles of animal gut (other than silkworm gut)***: China, Vietnam, Italy, France, Philippines, Indonesia, Mexico, Turkey, Cambodia, Spain, Hong Kong, Bangladesh, El Salvador, Honduras, Nicaragua, Sri Lanka.
- **HS 61** (***Articles of apparel and clothing accessories, knitted or crocheted***): China, Vietnam, Salvador, Honduras, Nicaragua, Bangladesh, Mexico, Turkey, Cambodia, Spain, Hong Kong, Sri Lanka, Jordan, Pakistan, Egypt.
- **HS 64** (***Footwear, gaiters and the like; parts of such articles***): China, Vietnam, Indonesia, Italy, Mexico, Cambodia, Dominican Republic, Spain, Brazil, Hong Kong, Germany, Honduras, Nicaragua, Sri Lanka.
- **HS 71** (***Natural or cultured pearls, precious or semi-precious stones, precious metals, metals clad with precious metal and articles thereof; imitation jewellery; coin)***: China, Belgium, Canada, Israel, Mexico, SA, Peru, Turkey, Cambodia, Hong Kong, Spain, Germany, Switzerland, USA.
- China, Vietnam, Cambodia, Mexico, Hong Kong and Spain are the common countries which are appearing as exporters to USA for all the four HS codes.
- India better than China—China decreasing other countries declining except Egypt.

16 India Vis-à-Vis Competitors

The USA happens to be the leading import market of the world. Its share in the global import has remained fairly constant, at 13.2 and 13.6% during 2008 and 2017, respectively. It has been noticed that China's penetration in the US market is growing over the years, with the country's share in US imports rising from 16.5% in 2008 to 21.8% in 2017. India's penetration in the US market has been fairly slow, rising from 1.2% in 2008 to 2.1% in 2017. Even during 2016–17, US import from China increased at a rate of 8%, as compared to the corresponding figure of 7% from India.

The high growth volume of US import from China has caused the bilateral trade deficit to move in China's favour. It has been noticed that trade deficit has reached a figure of $375 billion in 2017, with US exports to and imports from China standing at $130 billion and $505 billion, respectively. The lop-sided trade pattern recently caused the USA to increase tariff protection on several imported goods. As a result of these measures, import in value terms from China has declined from $46.19 billion in December 2017 to $39.75 billion in March 2018 (US Census Bureau 2018).

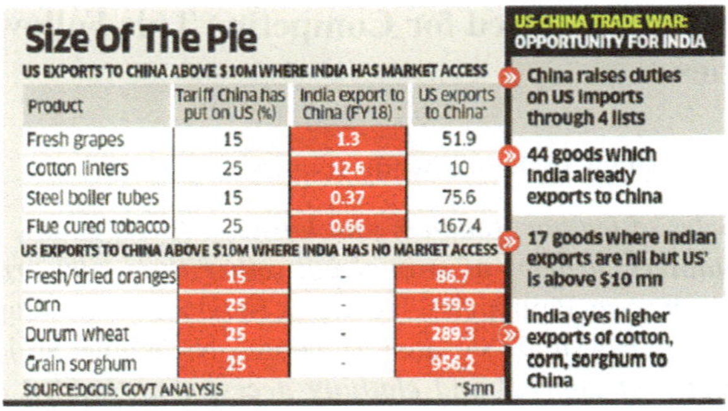

Size Of The Pie

US EXPORTS TO CHINA ABOVE $10M WHERE INDIA HAS MARKET ACCESS

Product	Tariff China has put on US (%)	India export to China (FY18)*	US exports to China*
Fresh grapes	15	1.3	51.9
Cotton linters	25	12.6	10
Steel boiler tubes	15	0.37	75.6
Flue cured tobacco	25	0.66	167.4
US EXPORTS TO CHINA ABOVE $10M WHERE INDIA HAS NO MARKET ACCESS			
Fresh/dried oranges	15	-	86.7
Corn	25	-	159.9
Durum wheat	25	-	289.3
Grain sorghum	25	-	956.2

SOURCE: DGCIS, GOVT ANALYSIS *$mn

US-CHINA TRADE WAR: OPPORTUNITY FOR INDIA

- China raises duties on US imports through 4 lists
- 44 goods which India already exports to China
- 17 goods where Indian exports are nil but US' is above $10 mn
- India eyes higher exports of cotton, corn, sorghum to China

Economic growth gets a boost by export and augments employment of India's growing workforce. Low and manufacturing space being vacated by China is being captured by Vietnam, South Korea and Indonesia as they are becoming more competitive. India needs to take into consideration this aspect and take certain immediate steps to make sure that India's position does not deteriorate further.

17 Exports Declining in Labour-Intensive Sectors

India's exports are not picking up, that too at a time when the global environment is becoming more conducive for trade. The reason is not weak currency, but the lack of competitiveness. Exports from the labour-intensive sectors are not only important for the generation of foreign revenue, but the sectors need a boost for creating more jobs. Vietnam, South Korea and Indonesia have taken lot of advantage of the situation which is changed because of the stronger trading environment. However, India has not been able to put that advantage. India has not experienced any major improvements in terms of national competitiveness in the context of manufacturing sector. Manufacturing–export–GDP ratio and manufacturing trade balance have deteriorated.

There are combinations of factors that are leading to the slowdown in this sector, including lack of diversification, dynamism and low level of competitiveness; the slow growth of the labour-intensive sectors is also caused by domestic developments such as the ham-handed implementation of the GST. "The implementation of GST and the associated glitches have hit the small and medium-scale enterprises the hardest, derailing growth in sectors such as textiles, gems and jewellery, and leather, where such enterprises dominate the supply chain".

Textiles, jewellery and other labour-intensive export sectors face slowdown

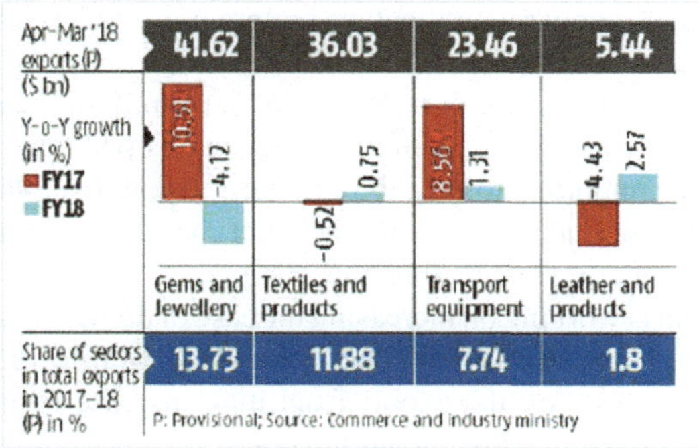

Textile Industry.

India has been earning foreign exchange through the textile export sector of the order of third largest foreign exchange earner in the country. India's top foreign exchange earner has been petroleum products at the top followed by gems and jewellery as foreign exchange earners. There has been slight increase of 0.75% in 2017-18 after a contraction of past two years. Apparel manufacturing, the largest segment within textiles, registered a decline for the 11th straight month till March 2018. The sector currently employs 12.9 million workers, and the ongoing slide has hit several clusters. Bangladesh and Vietnam have exhibited growth in apparel exports, whereas India has been struggling hard due to the stagnation in exports.

18 Impediments in the India-US Trade Relations

- High tariff rates on imports.
- High surcharges and taxes on a variety of imports.
- Non-tariff barriers on US exports to India.
- Labour-intensive products are increasing in terms of imports which may experience severe impact on employment.
- Rigours of GST could not be managed by small and medium-sized exporters. They found it difficult to cope up. The problem was triggered because of demonetization.
- Vietnam got a further push in the global apparel trade because of (a) the modified Trans-Pacific Partnership and (b) the EU-Vietnam Free Trade Agreement.

19 Suggestion to Increase Its Competitiveness

- First, it will need to improve logistics to increase efficiency, in terms of both the time and costs involved.
- Second, the government will need to move forward with reforms in the factor market.

- Indian firms in the apparel and leather sectors are smaller than those in China, Vietnam and Bangladesh.
- Third, while there is a threat of rising protectionism, India needs to be prepared to protect its interests without compromising on its open trade policy.
- Fourth, it will be important to keep the currency competitive. This is not to suggest that India needs an undervalued currency, but the Reserve Bank of India (RBI) should not allow the rupee to appreciate sharply.
- The government is working on increasing the ease of doing business, which should also help India's exports. Policymakers would do well to increase the pace of reforms as challenges on the export front may increase owing to the growing threat of protectionism and rising automation.
- The current stringent laws of the US economy likely contributed to the decreased growth of US imports of gems and jewellery. From ESI calculations above, Mexico, Canada and South Africa are most prospective countries for USA to import gems and jewellery but again US recent restriction on Mexico comes into play. This is proved even from TCI calculations where they have index values greater than that of China.
- The Jewellers Vigilance Committee in USA is a private association which states that personal imports of these items are usually cleared informally and do not require a custom bond. There are sanctions against diamonds imported from Sierra Leone, Angola, Liberia and other countries.

*******Sector-specific problems which are putting constraints on Indian competitiveness with respect to all these 4 sectors need to be addressed at micro-level. For more detail, please see the reference no. 8,9,10 below.***

Acknowledgements **** Note—Thanks to the following students of IIFT MBA (IB) (2017-19) for their contribution in the paper*:**

- Darshansabalpara
- Annie John C S
- KavyasriJadala
- Priya Kaur Dhamrait
- Sachin Prabhakar
- Shilpa A R
- Lokesh M K.

Annexure 1

1. **Trade Complementarity Index**

$$\left[1-\left(\sum\left|\frac{\sum_w m_{iwd}}{\sum_w M_{wd}}-\frac{\sum_w x_{isw}}{\sum_w M_{sw}}\right|\right)\div 2\right]\times 100$$

m—import; *x*—export; *d*—domestic country; *w*—world

Definition The sum of the absolute value of the difference between the import category shares and the export shares of the countries under study is divided by two. The index is converted to percentage form.

2. **Export Similarity Index**

$$\sum_i \min\left(\frac{\sum_w x_{isw}}{\sum_w X_{sw}}, \frac{\sum_w x_{idw}}{\sum_w X_{dw}}\right) \times 100$$

The index is the sum over export categories of the smaller of the sectoral export shares (as a percentage) of each country under study.

3. **Revealed Comparative Advantage Index**

$$\frac{\sum_s x_{isd} / \sum_d X_{sd}}{\sum_{wd} x_{iwd} / \sum_{wd} X_{wd}}$$

The RCA index is defined as the ratio of two shares. The numerator is the share of a country's total exports of the commodity of interest in its total exports. The denominator is share of world exports of the same commodity in total world exports.

4. **Export Intensity Index**

$$XII_{ij} = \frac{x_{ij}/X_{iw}}{x_{wj}/X_{ww}}$$

x_{ij} is the dollar value of exports of country/region *i* to country/region *j*,
X_{iw} is the dollar value of the exports of country/region *i* to the world,
x_{wj} is the dollar value of world exports to country/region *j*, and
X_{ww} is the dollar value of world exports.

Definition EII tells one whether or not a region exports more (as a percentage) to a given destination than the world does on average.

5. **Revealed Trade Barrier Index**

$$RTB_{ik}^{j} = \frac{M_{ik}^{j}}{\sum_k M_{ik}^{j}} / \frac{\sum_i M_{ik}^{i}}{\sum_i \sum_k M_{ik}^{j}}$$

M^{j}_{ik} is the dollar value of country *j*'s import from country *i* of product *k*,
ΣM^{j}_{ik} is the dollar value of the imports of country *j* of all products from country *i*,
ΣM^{j}_{ik} is the dollar value of country *j*'s import of product *k* from the world, and
$\Sigma\ \Sigma M^{j}_{ik}$ is the dollar value of the imports of country *j* of all products from the world.

Definition RTB tells one whether or not a country exports more of a product (as a percentage) to a given destination than the world does on average.

6. **Export Specialization Index**

$$ES = \left(X_{ij}/X_{it}\right)/\left(X_{kj}/X_{kt}\right)$$

X_{ij} is the export of product *i* from country *j* (to country *t*).
X_{it} is the export of product *i* from country *t* (to country *j*).
X_{kj} is the total export of country *j* to country *t*.
X_{kt} is the total export of country *t* to country *j*.

Definition The index measures whether a country is exporting one product more intensively to the other, in terms of proportional importance in the export basket.

Annexure 2

Export Intensity Index (EII) for all the four HS Codes

HS Code 42

EXPORT INTENSITY INDEX:

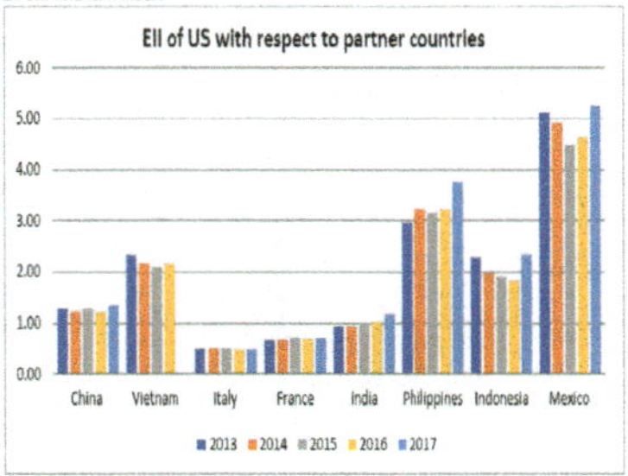

EII
HS Code 61

EII
HS Code 64

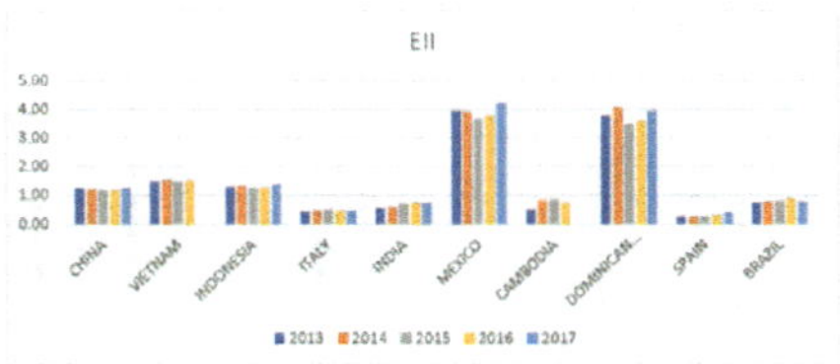

EII
HS Code 71

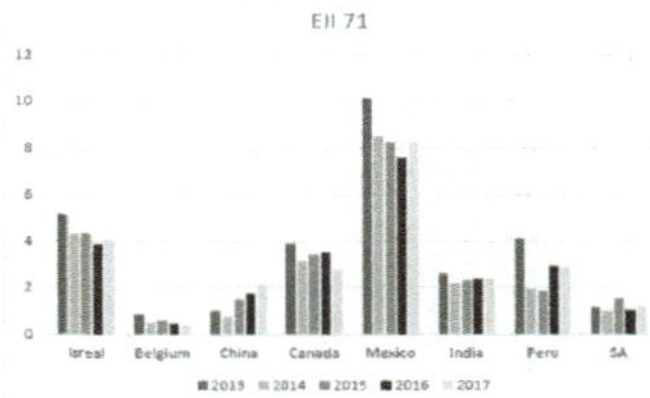

Export Specialization Index (ESI) for all the four HS Codes

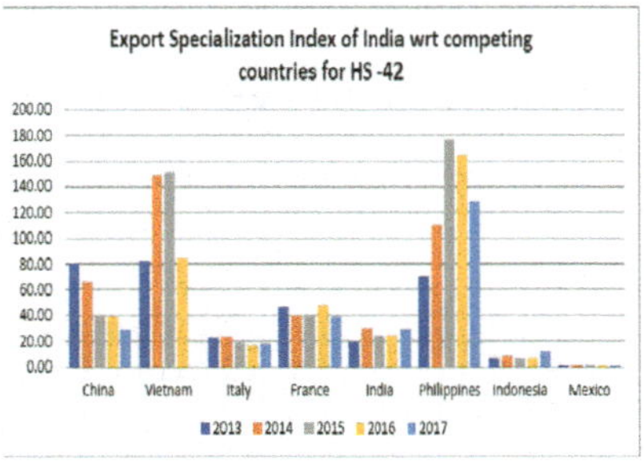

ESI
HS Code 61

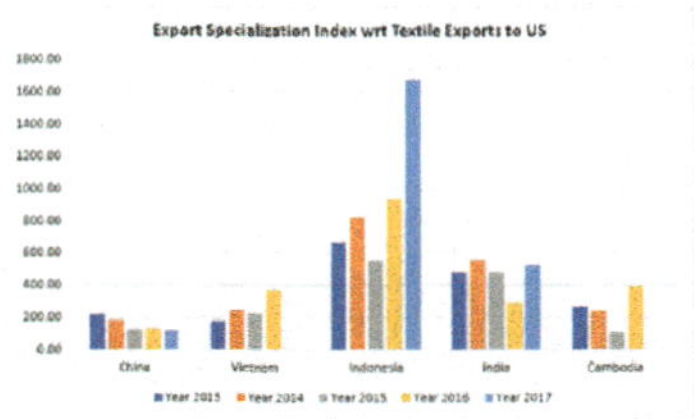

ESI
HS Code 64

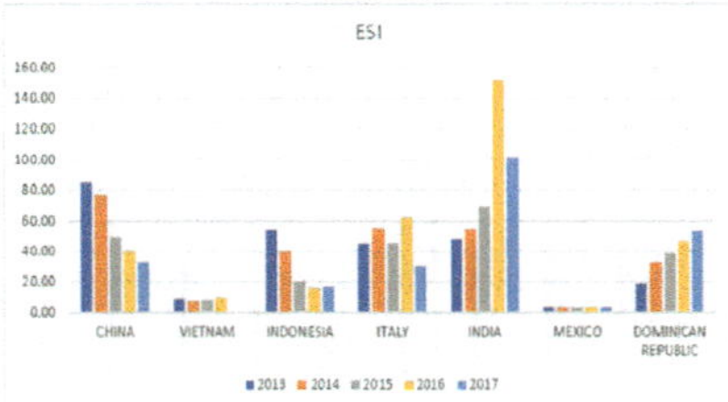

ESI
HS Code 71

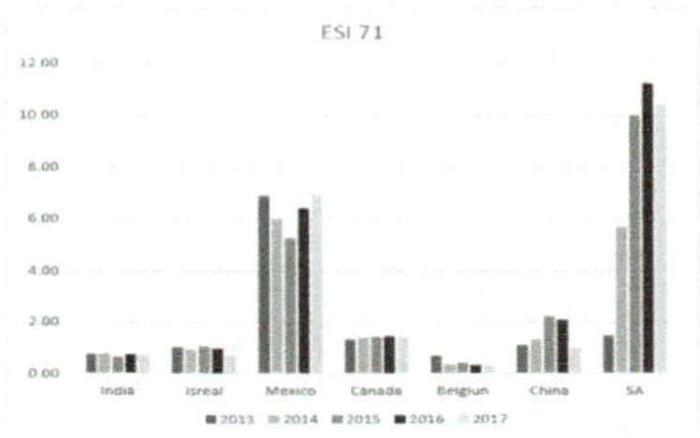

Revealed Trade Barrier Index (RTB) for all the four HS Codes

HS 42

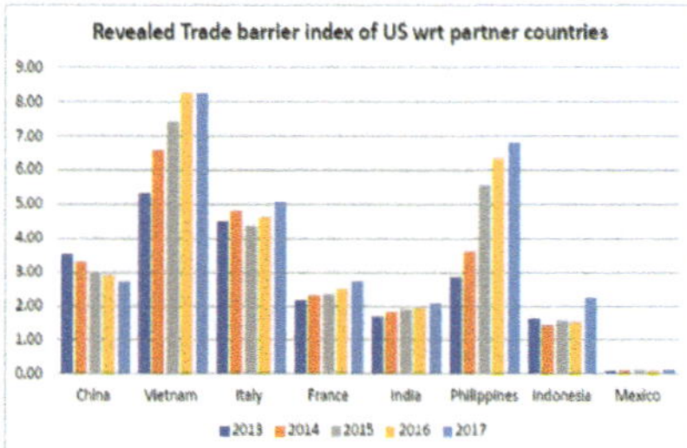

RTB HS Code 61

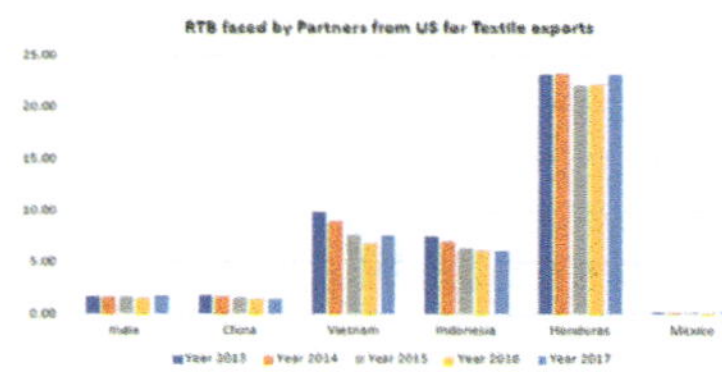

RTB HS Code 64

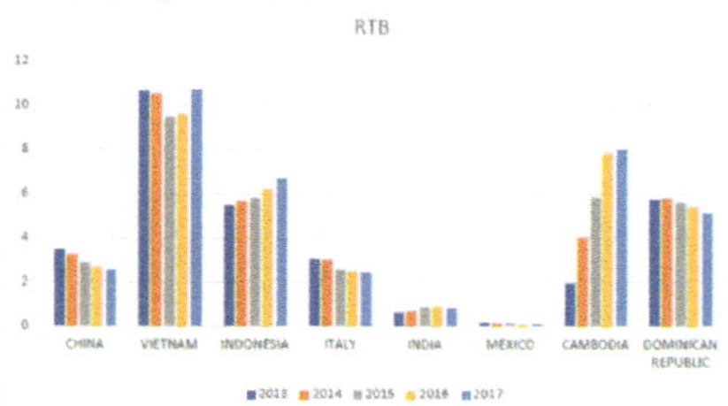

RTB HS Code 71

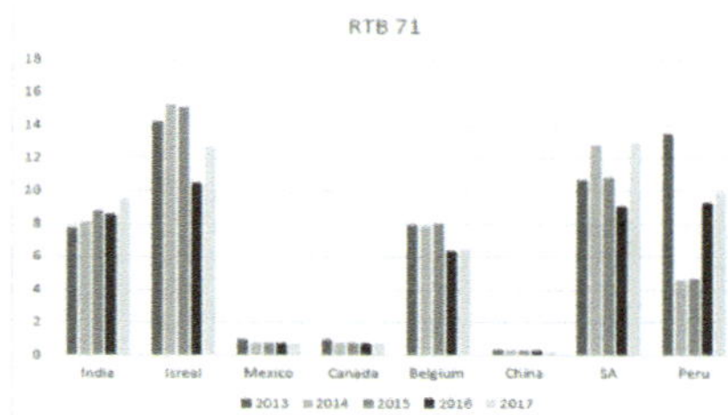

Export Similarity Index (E SIM) for all the four HS codes

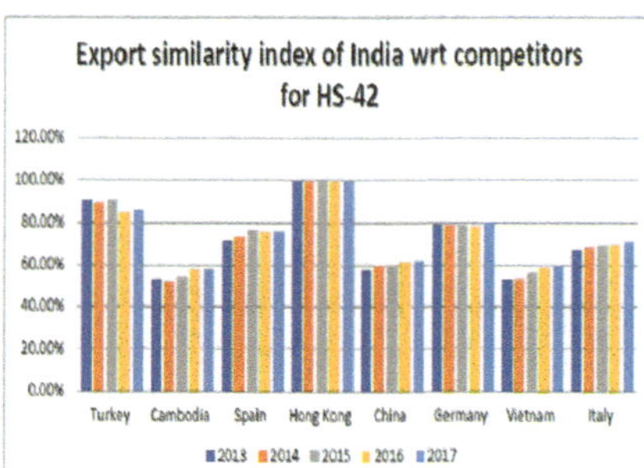

E SIM HS Code 61

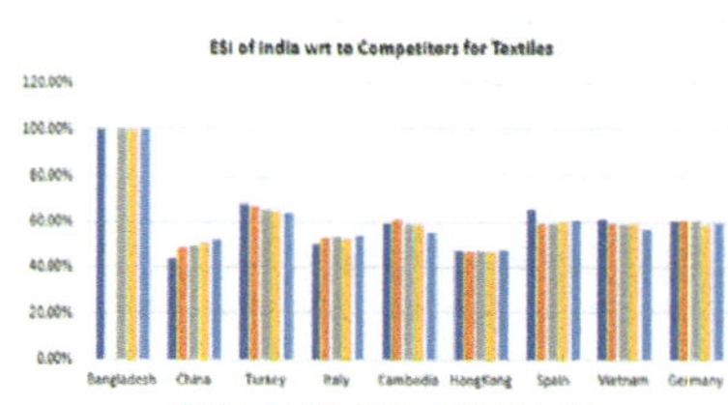

E SIM HS Code 64

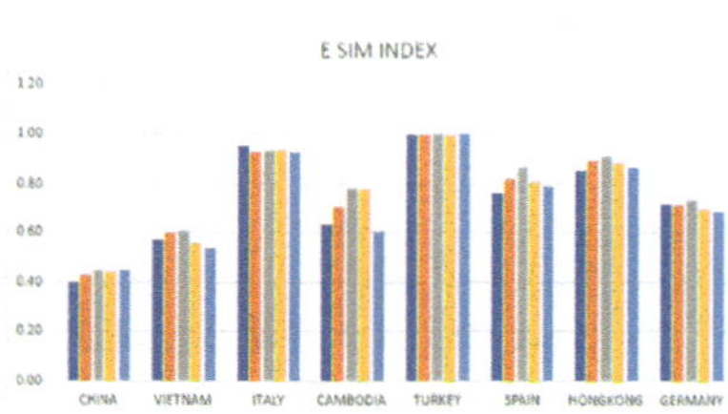

E SIM HS Code 71

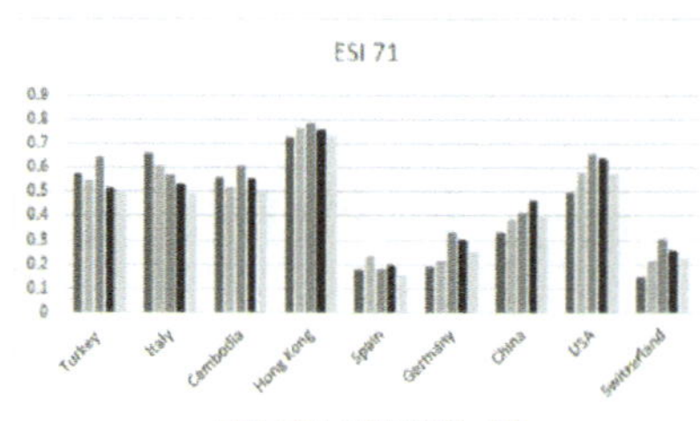

Trade Complementary Index (TCI) for all the four HS Codes

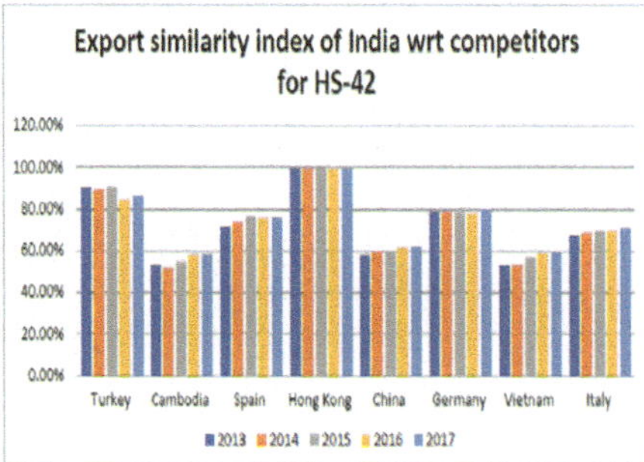

E SIM HS Code 61

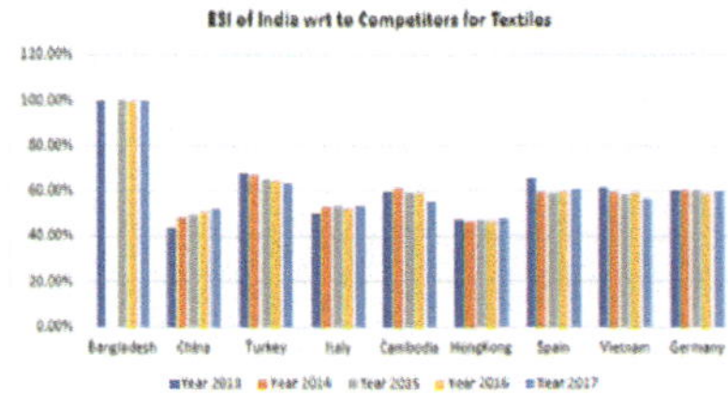

E SIM HS Code 64

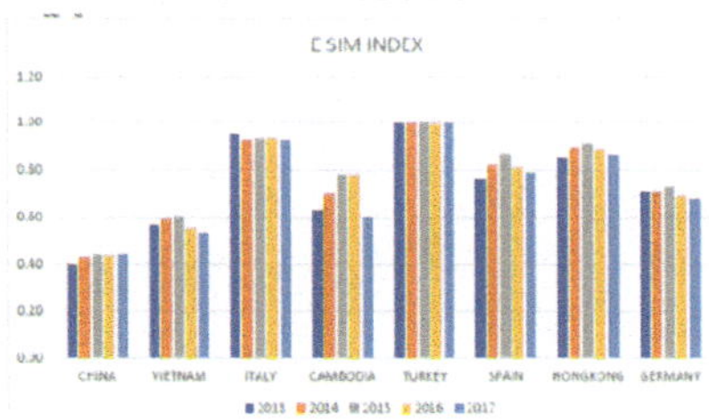

E SIM HS Code 71

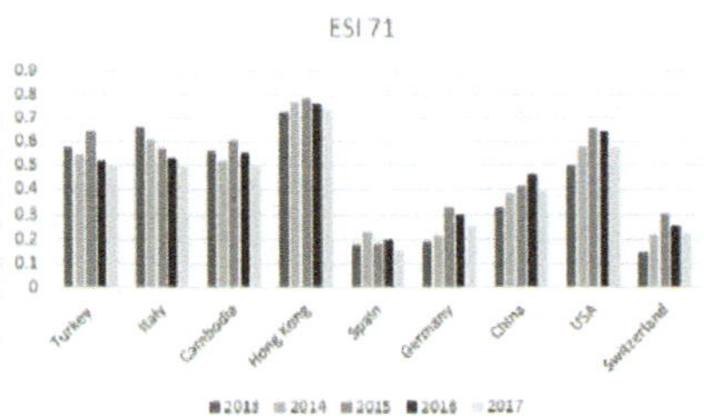

Revealed Comparative Advantage (RCA) for Two HS Codes

HS Code 42

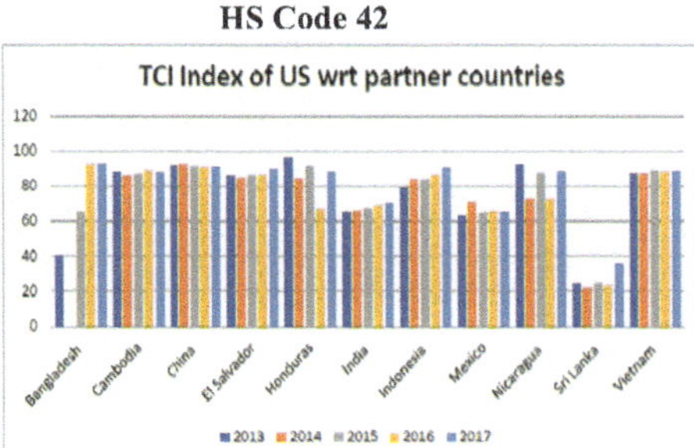

HS Code 61

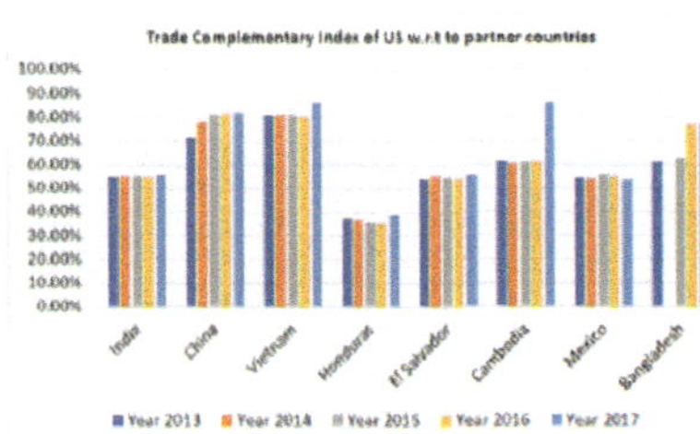

References

WITS, World Bank Database (https://wits.worldbank.org/).

WDI, World Bank Database (http://data.worldbank.org/data-catalog/world development-indicators).

WTO Database (http://stat.wto.org/Home/WSDBHome.aspx?Language=E).

UNCTAD Database (http://unctadstat.unctad.org/EN/).
US Census Bureau. (2018). https://www.census.gov/foreign-trade/balance/c5700.html#2018.
https://www.sustainablegemstones.org/blog/2018/1/23/a-study-on-problems-faced-by-exporters-of-gems-and-jewellery-industry.
https://economictimes.indiatimes.com/industry/miscellaneous/leather-and-leather-footwear-export-facing-massive-challenges/articleshow/60955318.cms.
https://crimsonpublishers.com/tteft/pdf/TTEFT.000538.pdf.

Chapter 17
UNECE Agreements on Harmonization of Vehicle Standards and India: Empirical Results and Policy Implications

D. Chakraborty and B. Nag

1 Introduction

In India, the industrialization drive, particularly since the nineties, has been closely watched by the policymakers with one crucial long-term concern, i.e., whether the growing technology intensity in a sector may displace more workers vis-à-vis the newer employment opportunities generated. Automotive sector is a prime example of this complex interface between long-term global competitiveness concerns and domestic equity considerations. On the one hand, while the presence of the labor-intensive upstream segments generates significant employment among the small and medium enterprises (SMEs) in auto-clusters (Barnes, 2018), the downstream segment, i.e., assembling in the capital-intensive brands (e.g., the 2-wheeler/ 4-wheeler producing corporates), is increasingly adopting automation in line with global trends (Miglani, 2019).

Given the modest competitiveness scenario, since early nineties the need to ensure FDI inflow and technology transfer in the sector was noted. It is important to understand how India perceived the automobile sector's growth path in the long run. Recognizing the high employment generation capability of the automobile sector, Government of India has always accorded it with growth opportunities, yet protecting the same from possible global challenges. For instance, the FDI inflow-related policies in the sector were gradually reformed since nineties. However, the restrictive framework, particularly the non-automatic import licenses on imports of automobiles as completely built units (CBUs) and certain parts and components, and the system of granting import licenses only to local joint venture manufacturers who had

D. Chakraborty (✉)
Indian Institute of Foreign Trade, Kolkata, India
e-mail: debashis@iift.edu

B. Nag
Indian Institute of Foreign Trade, New Delhi, India
e-mail: biswajit@iift.edu

P. Lakhanpal et al. (eds.), *Trade, Investment and Economic Growth*,
https://doi.org/10.1007/978-981-33-6973-3_17

signed a Memorandum of Understanding (MoU) with the government, promising to conform to the local content and export balancing requirements, were successfully challenged by the EU at the WTO dispute settlement body (DSB) (WTO, 2002).

The National Auto Policy (2002), which was released after India's defeat at the WTO DSB, understandably stressed on building of competitiveness through internal structural changes for obvious reasons, '.. modernization of the industry and facilitate indigenous design, research and development' (GoI, 2018). Though the tariff barriers continued, the objective of the government gradually moved toward attracting more FDI and facilitates relocation of global auto majors in the country, as evident from the Automotive Mission Plan (AMP) 2006–16 documents. For fulfilling this objective, while recognizing the global trends, the government slowly reformed the auto-sector by lowering tariff and tried to create a facilitating policy environment for the local players across all tiers (Nag et al., 2007). However, the competitiveness still remained a concern area (Badri Narayanan & Vashisht, 2008). To encourage FDI and technology transfer further, India removed the much-contested no objection certificate (NOC) requirement from the domestic partner, which was mandatory to obtain before a foreign auto-major can initiate a new wholly owned subsidiary in the country (Tendulkar & Bhavani, 2012). The removal of the NOC requirement in 2011, which was introduced in 1998, crucially marks the change in policy emphasis. In addition, from 2010–11 onward India joined a number of regional trade agreements (RTAs) spread across East and Southeast Asia (Chaisse et al., 2011), which increased the appeal of the country as a final assembly location for foreign investors. The cumulative effects of the domestic economic growth, tariff reforms undertaken both unliterally and through the RTAs and the gradual improvements in ease of doing business helped India to draw significant FDI inflows from global OEMs, while local OEMs also expanded their operation. These developments, which also created incremental employment of 25 million, enabled India to consolidate its position as a global hub for passenger vehicle production (SIAM, 2016).

The policy focus on the automotive sector continued even in the subsequent period, when it was included as a focus industry under the 'Make in India' (MII) initiative in 2014. The MII envisioned to foster growth in the sector by developing the country as a global manufacturing hub in general and automobile hub in particular, though enhanced foreign investment and technology transfer. The policy facilities extended to the Indian auto firms under the MII initiative included a diverse set of policies, including: automatic approval of FDI inflows (GoI, 2015), removal of minimum investment criteria (IBEF, 2018), fiscal supports (GoI, 2016), financial supports including the supports through Merchandise Export Incentive Scheme (MEIS) (MII, undated), etc. In particular, for facilitating innovation and quality improvement, funds worth INR 3727 crore under the National Automotive Testing and R&D Infrastructure Project (NATRiP) have been arranged (GoI, 2016).

It is anticipated that the cumulative effects of the aforesaid policies would enhance the competitiveness of the Indian automobile sector. Emboldened by these policy reforms, the AMP 2016–26 envisioned that by 2026 the global standing of Indian automotive sector may improve to, 'among the top three of the world in engineering, manufacture and export of vehicles and auto components ... growing in value to over

12% of India's GDP, and generating an additional 65 million jobs' (SIAM, 2016). Along similar lines, the National Auto Policy (2018) estimated that India might emerge among the top three auto-exporting nations while increasing, '… exports to 35–40% of the overall output and become one of the major automotive export hubs in the world… a global hub for research and development' (GoI, 2018). The potential opportunities for the sector are currently being reviewed closely (Krishnan and Dayasindhu, 2020), particularly in light of the government's recent launch of 'Atmanirbhar Bharat Abhiyan' in May 2020 (GoI, 2020).

Despite the intense pace of policy interventions in India over the last two decades, as evident from the analysis so far, it is observed that the country is still among the mid-level players in the global automobile value chain. There is a need to evaluate India's trade opportunities in automobile sector not only through the simple prism of tariff and FDI policy reforms, but also from the perspective of global standard harmonization. Keeping note of the existing set of United Nations Economic Commission for Europe (UNECE) standards, the current article is arranged along the following lines. Firstly, the article provides a brief overview of the UNECE forum discussions on harmonization of vehicle regulations under the WP.29 Forum. Secondly, Indian participation in the UNECE forums so far are briefly noted. Thirdly, Indian involvement in global trade on this front is briefly narrated. Fourthly, the possible non-tariff barriers (NTBs) on imports of auto-components in select partner countries with different UNECE membership backgrounds are analyzed. Fifthly, the possible impacts of tariff reforms on select auto-products in trade with the European Union (EU) are presented. Finally, based on the observations, certain policy conclusions are drawn.

2 UNECE Forums and India

The intra-industry trade (IIT), i.e., simultaneous export and import of industrial products within narrower classifications, was observed in the developed countries from fifties, given the rising cross-border trade in parts and components. The rising trade in industrial products in turn created demand for product quality harmonization across countries. In Europe, the demand for such harmonization led to creation of a forum within UNECE for securing mutual recognition of the approval of equipment and parts of motor vehicles in 1958, under the aegis of the WP.29. The UNECE discussion forum intends to: (i) improve vehicle safety (both passive and active road transport safety), (ii) protect the environment by controlling relevant pollution standards (e.g., air quality and noise-related), (iii) promote energy efficiency (through engine efficiency and other abatement standards) and (iv) increase anti-theft performance (UNECE, undated a). The UNECE 1958 Agreement, which is primarily managed by the European countries, covers 120 technical regulations on road and passenger safety (UNECE, undated b). A second agreement was introduced in 1997 on periodic technical inspections, which is managed by Russia and mainly has the Commonwealth of Independent States (CIS) countries as members. The last and final agreement came to force in 1998 with explicit US patronage and focused on mutual recognition of standards and harmonization of global technical regulations. There are 20 Global Technical Regulations (GTRs) under the UNECE 1998 Agreement (UNECE, undated c).

A major advantage of joining a UNECE agreement is that trade flows with another member country become smoother, without multiple checks and hindrances at the border. On the face of it, there should be high demand for the UNECE forum memberships. However, the 1958, 1997 and 1998 agreements have only 53, 15 and 38 members, respectively. The continent-wise details of the members in these three agreements are reported in Annex 1. It is clearly visible from the table that while in Africa and Asia the spread of UNECE membership is quite narrow, Latin America has altogether shied away from the forum so far. On the other hand, the membership has been deeper in North America and European countries. The cautious approach adopted by the developing countries and less developed countries (LDCs) so far can be explained by their threat perceptions. It is true that the UNECE agreements are laden with certain flexibilities in terms of right to implement specific technical regulations, in line with the national priorities (EC, 2015). However, the framework regarding decision-making across UNECE forums is not similarly democratic. For instance, UNECE 1958 can introduce a new regulation or amend an existing one, if such a motion is passed by a two-third voting majority among the member countries. Given the predominance of the European counties in the forum, they can technically influence the decision-making process. Conversely, the 1998 Agreement operates only by consensus and any change of rules cannot be dictated by any particular member or group of countries (Ramos, 2011). Given the concerns related to future decision-making, joining UNECE (1958) therefore can pose a challenge for India (Chakraborty et al., 2020).

The passenger safety concerns are currently dealt in India through the *Motor Vehicle Act* (1988), and its periodic amendments as well as the Central Motor Vehicle Rules (CMVR) are under the aegis of the Ministry of Road Transport and Highways (MoRTH). Moreover, a National Standing Committee (NSC) under the Chairmanship of Joint Secretary (MoRTH), helped by multiple stakeholders (including different ministries and test agencies), plays a crucial role in the decision-making process (UNECE, 2012).

With the domestic standard-setting structure in place, India until late nineties did not feel the pressing need of joining any of the UNECE forums. However, in the new millennium as the country aspired to emerge as both an exporter of auto-components and global auto-assembly hub (Exim Bank, 2017), the need to align with an international standard became apparent. The country initially joined WP.29 as an observer in 2003, before becoming a full-fledged member of UNECE 1998 Agreement in April 2006, and agreeing to bring conformity between domestic standards with UN GTRs (Marathe, 2008). Amendments in the CMVR are followed after joining UNECE 1998 forum (GoI, 2017), and it has been observed that 'currently India has more than 70% safety regulations which are either partially or fully aligned with GTRs and UN Regulations while keeping in view the Indian specific driving and environmental conditions' (GoI, 2018). Moreover, the recent move toward Bharat Stage (BS) VI emission norms improved the domestic compliance scenario further (ICCT, 2016).

Over the last fourteen years, India has been approached by the EU members for joining the 1958 Agreement at times (Sen, 2009), highlighting the improved safety for both car occupants and pedestrians that can be secured therein (OECD-UNECE, 2016). The EU has also tried to engage with India through various activities under the UNECE 1958 Agreement (Philippe, 2012). It is expected that the negotiating pressure would surface in the future again, as the two sides are set to resume the RTA negotiations (The Hindu, 2020). However, India is unlikely to humor EU soon owing to a number of reasons, namely: the discomfort with the reciprocity requirement embedded within the UNECE 1958 framework (GoI, 2018), potential adjustment problems to be faced by Tier III and Tier IV component manufacturers under the UNECE 1958 regime (Barnes, 2018) and incomplete legal reforms for preparing the domestic setup for the procedural requirements (Marathe, 2008).

3 Evidence from India's Trade Flows

Table 1 shows how India's trade share has evolved in global automotive product and transport equipment (HS 87) trade the last two decades. For understanding the temporal dimension, the time range is divided into four periods, namely: 2001–05, 2006–10, 2011–15 and 2016–19. It can be observed that before joining the UNECE 1998 forum in 2006, India's share in global trade had been modest. In the subsequent period, the country's share in global export and imports increased considerably over 2006–10 to 2011–15. However, the change in export share has been slower over the next period range (over 2011–15 to 2016–19), while import share remained almost constant. During 2019, India's rank in global export and import canvas in the automobile category has been 22 and 46, respectively.

Table 2 shows the top twenty export and import partners of India in terms of their importance in the trade basket, also viewed in light of their UNECE forum affiliation. It is revealed that India's export partners primarily consist of countries with common membership in both UNECE 1958 and 1998 Agreements, i.e., are contracting parties to both agreements (Common CP) and countries without membership in any UNECE agreement. USA (UNECE 1998 member) and Thailand (UNECE 1958 member) are also among the major export destinations of India. While India's trade relation with USA is deep-routed, Thailand is part of the Indo-ASEAN FTA that India has entered into in 2010. Along similar lines, predominance of these two groups is observed among the import sources as well. While two countries belonging to the UNECE 1958 Agreement (Belgium and Thailand) are among the import sources, import from only Thailand has increased over the period, owing to the deepened RTA relationship. It can be noted that countries characterized by only UNECE 1958 membership are generally not among India's major trade partners in this product category.

It has been noted that in addition to the finished automobile products (HS 87), auto-components (represented by tariff lines at HS 6-digit level and covered by

Table 1 Presence in world automotive products and transport equipment (HS 87) trade—India and top players

Global exports (average % share)						Global imports (average % share)					
Rank in 2019	Countries	2001–05	2006–10	2011–15	2016–19	Rank in 2019	Countries	2001–05	2006–10	2011–15	2016–19
1	Germany	18.59	18.83	18.45	17.30	1	USA	25.11	17.76	18.91	20.26
2	Japan	14.49	13.41	11.08	10.14	2	Germany	7.60	7.84	7.45	8.47
3	USA	9.61	9.00	9.78	8.90	3	China	1.27	2.72	5.57	5.21
4	Mexico	4.06	3.93	5.80	7.29	4	UK	7.85	6.15	5.29	5.05
5	China	1.23	2.98	4.35	4.74	5	Canada	6.37	5.32	5.20	4.94
6	Korea, Republic of	3.35	4.30	5.30	4.27	6	France	5.59	5.62	4.42	4.61
7	Canada	8.14	4.88	4.42	4.27	7	Belgium	3.97	3.93	3.37	3.64
8	Belgium	4.88	4.00	3.34	3.45	8	Mexico	2.58	2.26	2.53	2.91
9	Spain	4.85	4.40	3.65	3.77	9	Italy	4.91	4.52	2.76	3.24
10	France	7.00	5.12	3.61	3.52	10	Spain	4.70	4.00	2.64	3.00
11	UK	4.19	3.64	3.75	3.61	11	Netherlands	2.01	1.92	1.91	2.22
12	Italy	3.47	3.36	2.81	2.91	12	Australia	1.65	1.98	2.10	1.90
13	Czech Republic	1.18	1.92	2.23	2.63	13	Poland	0.89	1.41	1.22	1.55
14	Netherlands	1.49	1.41	1.48	1.92	14	Japan	1.62	1.32	1.52	1.55
15	Poland	0.87	1.87	1.66	1.88	15	Russian Federation	0.68	2.46	2.56	1.42
22	India	0.23	0.55	0.97	1.14	46	India	0.07	0.25	0.37	0.37

Source Computed from Trade Map Data, ITC (undated)

Table 2 India's trade in automotive products and transport equipment (HS 87)—top partners

Export							Import						
Sl. no.	Country	Average share (%)				UNECE membership	Sl. no.	Country	Average share (%)				UNECE membership
		2001–05	2006–10	2011–15	2016–19				2001–05	2006–10	2011–15	2016—19	
1	USA	12.95	10.14	8.73	12.53	1998	1	China	2.56	15.01	21.75	24.26	1998
2	Mexico	3.76	1.86	5.15	10.94	None	2	South Korea	23.17	23.05	14.58	13.88	Common CP
3	South Africa	3.07	5.20	6.81	4.95	Common CP	3	Germany	10.78	12.95	16.99	15.16	Common CP
4	Bangladesh	4.53	2.92	3.44	5.44	None	4	Japan	19.27	16.43	11.37	10.00	Common CP
5	Nepal	3.38	1.82	1.88	4.18	None	5	Thailand	3.65	3.39	6.67	8.31	1958
6	Saudi Arabia	0.83	0.91	1.12	2.29	None	6	USA	5.13	2.79	4.24	5.48	1998
7	Nigeria	2.93	1.95	3.30	2.20	Common CP	7	Singapore	0.86	0.74	0.22	1.93	None
8	United Arab Emirates	3.01	2.79	2.54	2.25	None	8	Sweden	1.55	2.68	1.75	2.21	Common CP
9	Germany	3.73	4.43	2.44	2.65	Common CP	9	Mexico	0.15	0.58	0.83	1.59	None
10	Indonesia	1.13	1.79	1.70	2.51	None	10	UK	4.55	1.90	2.56	2.41	Common CP
11	Sri Lanka	8.00	6.24	5.55	3.10	None	11	Italy	4.86	2.74	2.65	2.15	Common CP

(continued)

Table 2 (continued)

Export							Import						
Sl. no.	Country	Average share (%)				UNECE membership	Sl. no.	Country	Average share (%)				UNECE membership
		2001–05	2006–10	2011–15	2016–19				2001–05	2006–10	2011–15	2016—19	
12	Italy	5.54	6.49	3.04	2.69	Common CP	12	Indonesia	1.04	0.58	1.14	1.82	None
13	Colombia	1.62	2.54	3.05	1.80	None	13	Belgium	1.02	0.38	0.51	0.79	1958
14	UK	6.01	4.90	4.95	2.89	Common CP	14	France	1.11	1.12	1.57	1.03	Common CP
15	Brazil	0.53	0.69	1.45	1.52	None	15	Viet Nam	0.00	0.16	0.67	0.82	None
16	Turkey	1.40	1.93	3.51	2.83	Common CP	16	Spain	0.78	0.79	2.08	1.14	Common CP
17	Philippines	0.75	0.95	1.49	1.57	None	17	Brazil	3.77	0.73	0.54	0.52	None
18	Thailand	0.79	1.48	1.97	1.51	1958	18	Turkey	0.66	0.49	0.60	0.46	Common CP
19	Viet Nam	0.12	0.12	0.70	1.15	None	19	Netherlands	0.76	0.37	0.43	0.48	Common CP
20	Japan	0.52	0.41	0.90	1.27	Common CP	20	United Arab Emirates	0.36	0.06	0.11	0.18	None

Source Computed from Trade Map Data, ITC (undated)

both the 1958 and 1998 standards) are spread across nine product groups, namely: plastic products (HS 39), rubber products (HS 40), glass and glassware (HS 70), articles of iron and steel (HS 73), miscellaneous articles of base metal (HS 83), machinery and equipment (HS 84), electrical equipment (HS 85), vehicle and parts and accessories thereof (HS 87) and sign, cushion, etc. (HS 94) (IIFT, 2017). This HS classification is explained by the dominance of material content over functionality. Table 3 summarizes India's trade direction in these product categories with respect to the UNECE membership. The analysis is done separately for the auto-components spread across categories as a collective group and automotive products. Two time periods, namely 2009-13 and 2014-18, have been considered here, both of which depict the dynamics in the aftermath of India's UNECE 1998 Agreement accession. A couple of interesting observations emerge from the analysis. First, during 2014-18 while India's relative exports of auto-components to the UNECE 1998 member countries have increased, the same to other three groups have come down moderately. Second, in case of automotive products, the export focus has considerably gravitated toward UNECE 1998 members as well as non-member countries. The observation can be explained by the growing importance of many developing countries and LDCs in India's value-added exports, who are not conforming to any UNECE standards. Third, India's imports of auto-components have increased from both UNECE 1998 members and non-member countries, perhaps underlining the importance of both quality harmonization and cost-competitiveness considerations. Finally, in case of automobile products, only the relative importance of the countries with affiliation to both the UNECE provisions (i.e., Common CPs) has come down. The result

Table 3 India's trade direction in automobile-related products by UNECE membership

Country groups by UNECE membership	Trade in auto-components (across chapters)				Trade in automotive products and transport equipment (HS 87)			
	Average share (%)				Average share (%)			
	Export		Import		Export		Import	
	2009–13	2014–18	2009–13	2014–18	2009–13	2014–18	2009–13	2014–18
UNECE 1958	9.16	8.62	12.01	10.76	8.71	5.81	10.00	11.54
UNECE 1998	22.78	25.20	24.26	32.60	8.95	11.88	22.92	28.87
Membership in both UNECE 1958 and 1998	35.92	34.96	57.14	49.55	37.14	28.64	61.80	52.79
Countries with no UNECE affiliation	32.24	31.25	6.67	7.14	45.19	53.67	5.29	6.79

Source Chakraborty et al., (2020)

underlines the evolving importance of the UNECE 1998 membership for both India's exports and imports.

The increasing two-way trade of India in automotive products and the associated trade integration can be understood from the bilateral 'intra-industry trade' (IIT) index that measures the level of trade overlap in product categories. The IIT index can be computed by following *Grubel and Lloyd* measure, by considering the simultaneous export and import data for any given country pairs (Grubel & Lloyd, 1975). The Grubel–Lloyd uncorrected (GLU) and Grubel–Lloyd corrected (GLC) indices of IIT, at a HS 2-digit level of classification, can be calculated by using the following formula:

$$\mathrm{GLU} = \frac{\sum_i (X_{ij} + M_{ij}) - \sum_i |X_{ij} - M_{ij}|}{\sum_i (X_{ij} + M_{ij})} \times 100$$

$$\mathrm{GLC} = \frac{\sum_i (X_{ij} + M_{ij}) - \sum_i |X_{ij} - M_{ij}|}{\sum_i (X_{ij} + M_{ij}) - |\sum_i X_{ij} - \sum_i M_{ij}|} \times 100$$

Here, X_{ij} and M_{ij} denote the value of export and imports of the ith country (here, India) with the jth partner (say, USA) at HS 4-digit level, respectively. The IIT index calculated in this manner could vary between 0 and 100. When exports exactly match corresponding imports at each HS 4-digit classification (e.g., HS 87), it signifies growing production integration between the two countries and the IIT value reaches 100. On the other hand, when either of export or import is zero, this implies specialization patterns in both countries are rather in complementary sectors and the IIT index takes the value of zero. The GLC index corrects for aggregate trade imbalances, if any. Interestingly, despite the trade being of IIT-type, the GLC index can take the value of 100 if the exports or imports are greater than the other series for all the HS 4-digit headings within the HS 2-digit chapters. It is expected that when two countries enter into FTAs (i.e., resulting into tariff reforms) or any form of trade facilitation agreement (i.e., resulting from a quality harmonization, like the ones specified under the UNECE forum discussions), IIT-type trade deepens as firms from both countries may engage into trade in parts and components and intermediate products across the border, due to lower cost of doing business.

It has been noted that India's bilateral IIT in automobile sector has increased over the period (Aggarwal & Chakraborty, 2019; Srivastava & Sen, 2015). The current analysis computes the IIT index involving four countries, namely: Germany and Japan (UNECE, 1958 and 1998 common membership), Thailand (UNECE, 1958 member) and USA (UNECE, 1998 member), so as to compare the country's relative performance with each group. Moreover, while Japan and Thailand are in RTA relationship with India, both Germany (as EU member) and USA have expressed willingness to enter into preferential trade relations with India in coming future. The IIT results are noted in Table 4. While rise in the IIT index over the period had been noticed, indicating deeper production integration with these countries, the decline in the index value during some years signifies growing divergence between the export and import series. India's trade performance largely remained modest against the

Table 4 India intra-industry trade index with select trade partners in automotive products and transport equipment (HS 87)

Trade partner	2001	2005	2010	2015	2019
Grubel–Lloyd uncorrected index					
Germany	78.60	74.25	56.66	47.08	62.80
Japan	12.60	13.67	11.19	40.01	50.32
Thailand	56.10	75.74	91.70	62.45	66.19
USA	17.11	16.56	21.95	26.91	20.13
Grubel–Lloyd corrected index					
Germany	83.25	76.74	97.90	97.32	83.09
Japan	100.00	95.89	100.00	94.70	73.71
Thailand	92.16	89.34	94.70	92.00	88.83
USA	73.61	78.55	57.56	93.25	92.79
Sectoral trade balance (Indian perspective)					
Germany	Positive	Negative	Negative	Negative	Negative
Japan	Negative	Negative	Negative	Negative	Negative
Thailand	Positive	Negative	Negative	Negative	Negative
USA	Positive	Positive	Positive	Positive	Positive

Source Computed from Trade Map Data, ITC (undated)

partners (reflected in trade deficits), barring the exception of the USA, where India enjoyed a positive trade balance. Interestingly for two years (2001 and 2010), the GLC value with Japan had been 100, signifying that Japan enjoyed a strong advantage in trade with India across all the HS 4-digit product lines within HS 87. While the IIT indices underline growing trade integration of India with the partners, the predominance of trade deficit is an area of policy concern.

4 Non-tariff Barriers on Indian Auto-Component Exports

The UNECE 1958 standards cover several major functional areas of the automobile, including: engine and emission system; crash-related (front and rear underrun protection, etc.); strength of the superstructure; safety belt-related (child safety, seating position, etc.) and airbags; alarm/ warning system; heating and climate control system; braking mechanism/ speed limiting devices; and so on (IIFT, 2017; Chakraborty et al., 2019). It may be noted that Germany (as part of the EU) and USA generally have lower tariffs on auto-components, while Japan and Thailand enjoy a preferential trade relationship with India. There is a need to assess whether the accession to UNECE 1998 Agreement might help India to bypass the possible NTBs (both explicit policies, e.g., specified domestic standards and non-transparent administrative measures) in these markets. The tariff equivalent of the NTBs on auto-components at HS 6-digit level in the four countries considered earlier is determined through the price ratio method proposed by Bradford (2003), which is a two-step process. First, the ratio of an importing country's producer price to the world price is calculated:

$$ppr_{ij} = \frac{p_{ij}^{p}}{p_{i}^{w}}$$

where ppr_{ij}, p_{ij}^{p} and p_{i}^{w} represent the preliminary protection index of good i in country j (the importer), producer price of good i in country j and the corresponding world price, respectively. In line with existing literature, the average export price in an importer (say, Germany) has been used in place of the domestic price (Ardakani et al., 2009). Similarly, the lowest import price faced by Germany has been considered as the proxy for world price (Bradford, 2003). The idea is that if a UNECE 1958 member country (e.g., Thailand) operates in a higher-quality plane, it would inflate the sectoral domestic price, given the higher compliance requirements. Compared with respect to world, the PPR ratio reflects the policy-induced NTBs. However, in the presence of high tariff barriers, the ppr_{ij} may fail to capture the actual protection scenario. Hence, in the second step, the final NTB equivalent can be calculated by the following Formula:

$$pr_{ij} = \max\left(ppr_{ij}, 1 + tar_{ij}\right)$$

where tar_{ij} and pr_{ij} are the applied tariff on the particular HS 6-digit level product and final NTB equivalent of good i in country j, respectively.

The NTB equivalent analysis involving all the auto-components across HS sections for the four countries over 2009–13 and 2014–18 period is reported in Table 5, as obtained from Chakraborty et al., (2020). The third column shows India's RTA relationship with a partner, underlining possible emergence of mutual recognition agreements (MRAs). The purpose of considering two separate periods is to understand any systemic difference in the NTB behavior of partners shortly after India's accession to UNECE 1998 and after launching of the MII initiative at home. The last column shows the number of auto-components imported by a particular country during the two periods. The constructed NTB equivalents are arranged in six distinct ranges: 0–5, 5–10, 10–20, 20–50, 50–100 and greater than 100%, respectively, for understanding the distribution of stringency pattern in a partner country. It is clearly observed from the table that cutting across UNECE membership profile, the NTB equivalent has not come down significantly. On the contrary, the standard-related trade barriers in the top range (greater than 100%) have increased for both USA (UNECE, 1998 member) and Thailand (UNECE, 1958 member). The results underline that incidence of high NTBs can hinder India's export opportunities in several partner countries, irrespective of their membership in UNECE forums.

Table 5 NTB equivalent estimates for auto-components for select trade partners

	2009-13									
Country	UNECE membership	RTA partnership with India	Analysis	NTB equivalent range (%)						Total number of products
				0–5	5–10	10–20	20–50	50–100	>100	
USA	UNECE 1998	None	Number of auto-components	17	9	11	18	9	19	83
			Composition (%)	(20.48)	(10.84)	(13.25)	(21.69)	(10.84)	(22.89)	(100)
Germany	Common CP	BTIA (negotiations since 2007)	Number of auto-components	0	0	0	2	15	67	84
			Composition (%)	(0.00)	(0.00)	(0.00)	(2.38)	(17.86)	(79.76)	(100)
Japan	Common CP	India-Japan CEPA (since 2011)	Number of auto-components	5	2	3	6	18	50	84
			Composition (%)	(5.95)	(2.38)	(3.57)	(7.14)	(21.43)	(59.52)	(100)
Thailand	UNECE 1958	India-ASEAN FTA (since 2010)	Number of auto-components	0	6	8	23	23	24	84
			Composition (%)	(0.00)	(7.14)	(9.52)	(27.38)	(27.38)	(28.57)	(100)
	2014-18									
Country	UNECE membership	RTA partnership	Analysis	NTB equivalent range (%)						Total products
				0–5	5–10	10–20	20–50	50–100	>100	
USA	UNECE 1998	None	Number of auto-components	14	4	6	11	11	40	86
			Composition (%)	(16.28)	(4.65)	(6.98)	(12.79)	(12.79)	(46.51)	(100)
Germany	Common CP	BTIA (negotiations since 2007)	Number of auto-components	0	0	0	6	16	65	87
			Composition (%)	(0.00)	(0.00)	(0.00)	(6.90)	(18.39)	(74.71)	(100)

(continued)

Table 5 (continued)

	2009-13									
Country	UNECE membership	RTA partnership with India	Analysis	NTB equivalent range (%)						Total number of products
				0–5	5–10	10–20	20–50	50–100	>100	
Japan	Common CP	India-Japan CEPA (since 2011)	Number of auto-components	6	2	4	7	19	49	87
			Composition (%)	(6.90)	(2.30)	(4.60)	(8.05)	(21.84)	(56.32)	(100)
Thailand	UNECE 1958	India-ASEAN FTA (since 2010)	Number of auto-components	1	8	3	12	18	45	87
			Composition (%)	(1.15)	(9.20)	(3.45)	(13.79)	(20.69)	(51.72)	(100)

Source Chakraborty et al., (2020)

5 Tariff Reforms: Smart Simulation Results

As noted earlier, India has recently initiated talks with the EU on entering into an RTA. There is a need to understand how the reduction of tariffs on various auto-components and final products may influence the corresponding trade flows. In line with existing literature, a simulation exercise for that purpose has been undertaken with the help of the WITS-SMART database, a partial equilibrium modeling tool (Nag & Chaturvedi, 2019). In the partial equilibrium framework under WITS-SMART, only the effects of tariff reforms (i.e., reduction of the duty to 0%) in the import-recipient country (i.e., EU/ India), where the tariff policy has been liberalized, are considered. The effects of the hypothesized policy change (which involves tariff reduction in the current example) in other markets (e.g., Malaysia) are not considered.

Under the WITS-SMART framework, the supply side is centered on the assumption that export supply of a HS 6-digit product is a function of its price in the export market. It is further assumed that export supply curves are flat; i.e., world prices are exogenous in the constructed framework. Therefore, given inherent comparative advantage, the reduction of tariff in the reporter (i.e., importer) market would facilitate exports from the partner (i.e., exporter) country. On the demand side, the WITS-SMART model is based on Armington assumption on consumer behavior, which in particular highlights the imperfect substitutability of the ith product (at HS 6-digit level) coming from different partner countries. The crux of the assumption is the postulated difference in varieties originating from different import sources, leading to a positive substitution elasticity. The Armington assumption implies that any bilateral tariff liberalization through preferential rules of origin (ROO) would not lead to complete shift in import pattern from a group of importers to the RTA partner, which is receiving the preferential tariff treatment in the aftermath of the policy change.

In the current context, a number of prominently traded auto-products are selected and the possible effects of significant tariff reforms (lowered down to to 0%) on their trade are considered. First, the effect is considered in the EU market (i.e., analyzing effects on Indian exports to EU), followed by the same exercise for India (i.e., on EU exports to India). While the WITS-SMART simulations run with zero tariff specifications reports a set of tables including the trade effects for all the exporting countries (trade creation and trade diversion), revenue effect, welfare effect, etc., the current analysis only focuses on the export change for India (as exporter) in the EU market (as importer) and vice versa.

The summarized WITS-SMART simulation results on Indian exports in the EU market are reported in Table 6. Based on growth rate of exports in the pre- and post-tariff liberalization period, the results are segregated under three groups and reported accordingly. Two products fall under the high growth category, which is defined as export changes above 10%. Nine products come under the medium export growth category, which is falling within the 5–10% range. Finally, for eleven products, the expected growth rate has been defined as low; i.e., the products falling under this

Table 6 Effect of reduction in tariff for select Indian automobile exports in European union market

Sl. no.	HS code	Exports before	Exports after	Export growth	EU average percentage share in Indian exports	
		USD million		(% change)	2010–14	2015–19
High export growth						
1	840820	89.72	100.35	11.84	56.82	27.39
2	870840	44.70	49.28	10.24	10.77	20.11
Medium export growth						
3	870850	124.82	136.05	9.00	40.46	26.61
4	840790	0.67	0.73	8.13	39.08	10.90
5	870894	14.62	15.80	8.03	29.37	12.68
6	840733	5.54	5.89	6.32	35.58	0.12
7	870810	7.34	7.79	6.16	23.07	16.46
8	870895	0.96	1.01	5.65	23.96	0.46
9	840734	0.74	0.77	5.19	2.70	0.70
10	870830	142.44	149.78	5.15	46.79	31.10
11	870880	40.22	42.27	5.09	23.56	18.72
Low export growth						
12	853939	0.21	0.22	2.98	28.50	16.48
13	853921	18.34	18.88	2.95	64.64	66.54
14	853929	1.63	1.68	2.93	9.25	4.96
15	853990	1.62	1.67	2.82	17.15	22.71
16	850520	0.86	0.89	2.68	56.00	55.07
17	853931	6.90	7.09	2.65	49.78	17.40
18	853910	0.20	0.20	2.53	3.37	5.62
19	853922	5.07	5.19	2.42	56.07	0.00
20	851120	0.33	0.33	2.00	41.60	15.54
21	840731	0.02	0.02	1.94	17.26	20.69
22	840732	0.05	0.05	1.81	9.75	0.05

Source Own Estimation

list have witnessed export growth below 5%. It appears that for several machinery-related and electrical products, India is not expected to witness a high export growth in the EU market, even when the tariff barriers are totally liberalized. The underlying reason can be explained by two arguments. First, the import tariff in most of the product categories in EU is already zero or near zero. Hence, benefits arising from pure tariff reforms are not going to be much for Indian exports. Second, India might witness a stiff challenge from competitors in the EU market, particularly from the UNECE 1958 members (e.g., CIS countries, Malaysia, South Africa), who have already undertaken the necessary investments to align their production and safety standards with the EU requirements. Just to understand the real opportunities for Indian auto-component exports, in the last two columns, the share of the EU players in Indian exports is compared. It is observed that among the twenty-two products considered in the analysis, the share of the EU in Indian exports has increased only for five products.

The WITS-SMART simulation results on impact of the tariff reforms on Indian imports are summarized next in Table 7. It is observed that for eleven products the expected export growth of the EU countries would be in high growth category (i.e., export growth in excess of 10%), and five products fall under the medium and low

Table 7 Effect of reduction in tariff for select European Union automobile exports in Indian market

Sl. no.	HS code	Exports before	Exports after	Export growth	EU average percentage share in Indian imports		Average tariff barrier (%)	
		USD million		(% change)	2010–14	2015–19	2010–14	2015–19
High export growth								
1	870324	49.46	2554.67	5064.99	90.8	86.0	92.0	86.0
2	870333	43.78	900.87	1957.85	71.8	66.8	92.0	86.0
3	870332	70.99	775.25	992.10	65.0	94.1	92.0	86.0
4	840820	272.37	758.29	178.40	29.8	22.4	7.5	10.5
5	870840	175.46	299.77	70.85	34.3	19.6	10.0	12.0
6	870830	55.13	90.85	64.79	37.9	33.5	10.0	12.0
7	870829	184.41	249.55	35.32	50.3	38.8	10.0	12.0
8	870893	31.58	40.44	28.03	40.3	43.6	10.0	12.0
9	870894	33.82	42.96	27.00	19.8	23.8	10.0	12.0
10	392690	123.98	144.96	16.92	20.3	20.3	10.0	10.3
11	848180	312.11	343.39	10.02	44.2	35.8	7.5	7.5
Medium export growth								
12	870850	74.90	80.68	7.72	35.9	41.8	10.0	12.0
13	851220	55.30	59.32	7.27	47.8	36.7	9.2	10.3
14	848340	119.51	127.58	6.75	45.7	37.0	7.5	7.5
15	840999	241.80	257.56	6.52	45.5	40.7	7.5	10.5
16	870790	28.57	30.17	5.61	27.9	82.4	10.0	11.0
Low export growth								
17	840734	33.29	34.74	4.33	23.7	23.1	7.5	10.5
18	840890	140.49	145.78	3.76	47.8	46.3	7.5	10.5
19	848360	56.33	56.68	0.61	54.7	54.3	7.5	7.5
20	870899	553.21	555.22	0.36	29.8	30.6	10.0	12.0
21	842119	30.09	30.09	0.00	56.2	58.9	6.7	7.5

Source Own Estimation

growth categories each. The observation can be explained by the following drivers. First, given the longer operational duration and deeper spread of standards, the EU products might be on a higher-quality plane vis-à-vis the Indian varieties and other import sources. Given the fact that the EU is exporting high-value final products as well as crucial auto-components, for which there might be limited competition in the Indian market, the relatively higher growth rates become apparent. Second, as observed from the table, the average tariff rates in India are quite high for several product categories. In fact, in some cases the average tariffs have increased during 2015–19 vis-à-vis the corresponding 2010–14 period. It is observed that among the twenty-one products considered in the analysis, the share of the EU in Indian imports has increased only for eight products, which can be part explained by tariff barriers. Hence, tariff reforms would significantly reduce the landed price of EU imports in the Indian market.

So, the conclusion is that reduction of tariff barriers in the EU market is not going to provide significant market access to Indian exports, as reflected through simulation exercise. The result can be explained by the stiff competition in the EU market from countries already complying with the UNECE 1958 standards. On the other hand, the EU exporters are expected to gain significantly in the Indian market given the higher tariff barriers as well as product quality harmonization. The decision to go for RTAs with the EU, therefore, needs to be viewed in this light.

6 In Lieu of Conclusion

Nag (2011) depicted India's emerging participation in global value chain in early 2000 with an indication of technological upgrading, especially through 'learning by doing' and 'learning by exporting.' Several Indian tier 1 suppliers have also improved their global position since the study was conducted. India's export of components to Europe and America has experienced a rising trend who mostly follow UNECE standards. However, increasing NTBs, especially regulatory barriers and standard-related restrictions is still a major obstacle. India's prospect of increasing exports depends on its agility to respond to the evolving standards in major auto-importing countries. This brings up a strategic question of focusing on *Atmanirbhar Bharat* (Self-reliant India) with appropriate technology versus accepting UNECE 1958 with an expectation of more FDI inflow to India from Europe in the sector. The decision is delicate as India's exports to many non-members of UNECE forums on automobile safety standard harmonization have also increased. We also need to remember that UNECE 1998 provides more flexibility in developing common standards unlike 1958 Agreement. At the same time, it is also noteworthy that several new members of UNECE 1958 are slow in adopting the recommended standards. One option for India could be to enter into a tough negotiation with UNECE 1958 members for adopting UNECE 1998 kind of structure or provide sufficient flexibility to India.

Given the level of potential NTBs in the partner countries cutting across UNECE profile, deliberate inaction from India may not be a prudent option for the country, particularly when India is toying with the idea of entering into an RTA with the EU. It is apparent from the observed WITS-SMART simulation results that as far as the auto-sector is concerned, the proposed bloc might help EU more vis-à-vis India. It might also be noted that the difference in perspectives over tariff reforms under automobile sector earlier hindered the EU-India Bilateral Trade and Investment Agreement (BTIA) negotiations (Chaisse & Chakraborty, 2014). Discussions are also on the feasibility of an Indo-US FTA, which is a UNECE 1998 partner. However, as evident from the analysis, the presence of some form of NTBs in the US market cannot be ruled out as well. Finally, one of the expectations behind India's decision to join the Indo-ASEAN FTA was to deepen participation in the East and Southeast Asian production networks. However, this aspiration of India has only been modestly fulfilled so far (Nag, 2016). While this may partly result from the modest price competitiveness of the country in semi-processed and intermediate product categories vis-à-vis ASEAN players, the role of divergence in product standards cannot be ruled out. In particular, the ASEAN members have decided in 2015 that the bloc's sectoral MRA would be based on UNECE 1958 standards, though only Malaysia and Thailand are currently members in that forum. As the other eight ASEAN members are not CPs in any UNECE forum, the bloc has decided to deviate from strict conformity with UNECE 1958 standards in short run by introducing certain flexibilities (Thai Auto, undated). The speed of implementing the UNECE 1958 technical standards is quite fast in several ASEAN countries (Scoles, 2016), which can be a long-run concern for India. It may be noted that India's auto-sector-specific trade balances with several East and Southeast Asian partners are negative irrespective of UNECE spectrum, e.g., Thailand (membership in UNECE 1958), Japan and South Korea (membership in both UNECE 1958 and 1998) and China (membership in UNECE 1998). More export focus toward African and Latin American countries, presently not part of any agreement, may also be considered while developing India's comprehensive strategy. In particular, India's sectoral trade relations with Mexico in this regard are encouraging.

Annex 1

Membership in various UNECE agreements on vehicle safety

Sl. no.	UNECE agreement	Number of members	Member countries by continent				
			Asia and Pacific	CIS	Europe	North America	Africa

(continued)

(continued)

Sl. no.	UNECE agreement	Number of members	Member countries by continent				
			Asia and Pacific	CIS	Europe	North America	Africa
1	UNECE (1958)	53	Australia, Japan, Malaysia, New Zealand, Republic of Korea, Thailand	Armenia, Azerbaijan, Belarus, Georgia, Kazakhstan, Republic of Moldova, Russian Federation, Ukraine	Albania, Austria, Belgium, Bosnia and Herzegovina, Bulgaria, Croatia, Czechia, Denmark, Estonia, European Union, Finland, France, Germany, Greece, Hungary, Italy, Latvia, Lithuania, Luxembourg, Montenegro, Netherlands, North Macedonia, Norway, Poland, Portugal, Romania, San Marino, Serbia, Slovakia, Slovenia, Spain, Sweden, Switzerland, Turkey, UK of Great Britain and Northern Ireland	–	Egypt, Nigeria, South Africa, Tunisia

(continued)

(continued)

Sl. no.	UNECE agreement	Number of members	Member countries by continent				
			Asia and Pacific	CIS	Europe	North America	Africa
2	UNECE (1997)	15	–	Belarus, Georgia, Kazakhstan, Republic of Moldova, Russian Federation, Ukraine	Albania, Bulgaria, Estonia, Finland, Hungary, Netherlands, Romania, San Marino	–	Nigeria
3	UNECE (1998)	38	Australia, China, India, Japan, Malaysia, New Zealand, Republic of Korea	Azerbaijan, Belarus, Kazakhstan, Republic of Moldova, Tajikistan, Russian Federation, Uzbekistan	Cyprus, European Union, Finland, France, Germany, Hungary, Italy, Lithuania, Luxembourg, Netherlands, Norway, Romania, San Marino, Slovakia, Slovenia, Spain, Sweden, Turkey, UK of Great Britain and Northern Ireland	Canada and USA	Nigeria, South Africa, Tunisia

(continued)

(continued)

Sl. no.	UNECE agreement	Number of members	Member countries by continent				
			Asia and Pacific	CIS	Europe	North America	Africa
4	Common Membership in UNECE (1958) and (1998) Agreements	31	Australia, Japan, Malaysia, New Zealand, Republic of Korea	Azerbaijan, Belarus, Kazakhstan, Republic of Moldova, Russian Federation	European Union, Finland, France, Germany, Hungary, Italy, Lithuania, Luxembourg, Netherlands, Norway, Romania, San Marino, Slovakia, Slovenia, Spain, Sweden, Turkey, UK of Great Britain and Northern Ireland	–	Nigeria, South Africa, Tunisia.

Source Obtained from http://www.unece.org/transport/international-agreements/contracting-parties.html (accessed September 23, 2020)

References

Aggarwal, S. and D. Chakraborty (2019), 'Which Factors Influence India's Intra-Industry Trade? Empirical Findings for Select Sectors', Global Business Review, available at: https://journals.sagepub.com/doi/10.1177/0972150919868343 (accessed March 11, 2021).

Ardakani, Z., Yazdani, S., & Gilanpour, O. (2009). Studying the effects of non-tariff barriers on the export of the main agricultural products of Iran. *American Journal of Applied Sciences, 6*(7), 1321–1326.

Thai Auto.(undated). see ASEAN MRA and Implementation Status. http://www.thaiauto.or.th/2012/Automotive-Summit/doc/ppt/2015/25-6-15/203_PM/10.ASEAN%20MRA%20and%20status%20of%20Implementation%20Rev%201.pdf.

Badri Narayanan, G., & Vashisht, P. (2008). *Determinants of competitiveness of the indian auto industry*. Working Paper No. 201, New Delhi: Indian Council for Research on International Economic Relations.

Barnes, T. (2018). *Making cars in the new India: Industry*. New Delhi: Precarity and Informality Cambridge University Press.

Bradford, S. (2003). Paying the price: Final goods protection in OECD countries. *The Review of Economics and Statistics, 85*(1), 24–37.

Chaisse, J., & Chakraborty, D. (2014). The evolving and multilayered EU-India investment relations: Policy conjectures and regulatory issues. *European Law Journal, 20*(3), 385–422.

Chaisse, J., Chakraborty, D., & Nag, B. (2011). The three-pronged strategy of india's preferential trade policy—A contribution to the study of modern economic treaties. *Connecticut Journal of International Law, 26*(2), 415–455.

Chakraborty, D., Chaisse, J., & Hussain, Z. (2019). Non-Tariff barriers on auto-components exports: application of select indices. In B. Nag & D. Chakraborty (Eds.), *India's trade analytics: Patterns and opportunities* (pp. 299–315). New Delhi: Sage.

Chakraborty, D., Chaisse, J., & Pahari, S. (2020). Global auto industry and product standards: A critical review of India's economic and regulatory experience. *Journal of International Trade Law and Policy, 19*(1), 8–35.

European Commission. (2015). *Study on the impact of the revision of the UNECE 1958 Agreement on the global competitiveness of the EU automotive industry,* EC, Luxembourg.

Export Import Bank of India. (2017). *The Indian automotive industry: An international trade perspective*, Working Paper No. 59, Mumbai: EXIM Bank.

Government of India. (2020). PM gives a clarion call for Atmanirbhar Bharat. https://pib.gov.in/PressReleseDetail.aspx?PRID=1623391.

Government of India. (2018). *National auto policy' (Draft).* New Delhi: Ministry of Heavy Industries and Public Enterprises.

Government of India. (2017). Lok Sabha Unstarred Question No.4313 (to be answered on 28.03.2017), Department of Heavy Industry, New Delhi: Ministry of Heavy Industries and Public Enterprises.

Government of India. (2016). *Make in India: Automotive sector-achievements report.* New Delhi: Department of Industrial Policy and Promotion and Department of Heavy Industries.

Government of India. (2015). *Foreign trade policy 2015-20'.* New Delhi: Department of Commerce, Ministry of Commerce and Industry.

Grubel, H. G., & Lloyd, P. J. (1975). *Intra-industry trade: The theory and measurement of international trade in differentiated products.* London: The Macmillan Press Limited.

India Brand Equity Foundation.(2018). *Automobiles sector* IBEF, New Delhi. https://www.ibef.org/download/Automobiles-January-2018.pdf.

Indian Institute of Foreign Trade. (2017). *Trade impact of WP 29 on India.* New Delhi: Report Submitted to Society for Indian Automobile Manufactures (SIAM).

International Council on Clean Transportation. (2016). *India bharat stage VI emission standards.* ICCT, Washington DC: Policy Update.

International Trade Centre (undated). *Trade Map database.* Available at http://www.trademap.org/Index.aspx. (Accessed September 8, 2016).

Innovation, Economic Development, and Intellectual Property in India and China. (pp. 439–463) Cite as.

Krishnan, R. T. & Dayasindhu, N. (2020). Indian motorcycle industry: A role model for Atmanirbhar Bharat?.https://www.iimb.ac.in/sites/default/files/2020–08/Indian-motorcycle.pdf.

Make in India (undated). *Automobile: Financial support.* http://www.makeinindia.com/sector/automobiles.

Marathe, S. (2008, June 26). WP 29 1958 agreement: A view from India. Presentation at the Special Session to commemorate the 50th Anniversary of the 1958 agreement, Geneva.

Miglani, S. (2019). The growth of the indian automobile industry: Analysis of the roles of government policy and other enabling factors. In K. Liu & U. S. Racherla (Eds.), *Innovation, economic development, and intellectual property in India and China: Comparing six economic sectors.* Singapore: Springer.

Nag, B. (2016). Emerging production network between India and ASEAN: An analysis of value-added trade in select industries. In D. Chakraborty & J. Mukherjee (Eds.), *Trade, investment and economic development in Asia: Empirical and policy issues* (pp. 41–67). Abingdon: Routledge.

Nag, B. (2011).Trade liberalization and international production networks: Experience of the Indian automotive sector. In *Asia-pacific research and training network on trade (ARTNeT) study on 'fighting irrelevance: The role of regional trade agreements in international production networks in Asia.* Bangkok: United National Economic and Social Commission on Asia and the Pacific

Nag, B., Banerjee, S., & Chatterjee, R. (2007*). Changing features of the automobile industry in Asia: Comparison of production, trade and market structure in selected countries,* ARTNeT Working Paper No 3707, UNESCAP, Bangkok.

Nag, B., & Chaturvedi, P. (2019). Implication of tariff reduction through partial simulation using SMART: An analysis of india's import of passenger vehicles from Japan and Germany. In B. Nag & D. Chakraborty (Eds.), *India's trade analytics: Patterns and opportunities* (pp. 319–332). New Delhi: Sage.

Organisation for Economic Co-operation and Development and United Nations Economic Commission for Europe. (2016). *International regulatory co-operation and international organisations: The case of the United nations economic commission for Europe (UNECE).* Paris: OECD and UNECE.

Philippe, J. (2012). *Review of the 1958 Agreement and IWVTA: EU objectives and perspectives,* Presentation at the EU-Japan Policy Seminar. https://www.eu-japan.eu/sites/eu-japan.eu/files/presentation_23052012_jean.pdf

Ramos, J. (2011, November 9). In *The UNECE World forum for harmonization of vehicle regulations (WP.29).* Geneva: Presentation at the World Trade Organization (WTO), TBT Committee.

Scoles, S. D. (ed) (2016). Harmonization of standards and mutual agreements on conformity assessment in Indonesia, Malaysia, Thailand and Vietnam. Research Project Report No. 15, Jakarta: Economic Research Institute for ASEAN and East Asia

Sen, S. (2009). *Non-Tariff Barriers in Automotive Industry.* Society of Indian Automobile Manufacturers. https://bis.gov.in/other/SIAM-NTB.pdf.

Society for Indian Automobile Manufactures. (2016). *Automotive mission plan: 2016-26—A curtain raiser.* New Delhi: SIAM.

Srivastava, S., & Sen, R. (2015). Production fragmentation in trade of manufactured goods in India: Prospects and challenges. *Asia-Pacific Development Journal, 22*(1), 33–66.

Tendulkar, S. D., & Bhavani, T. A. (2012). *Understanding reforms: Post-1991 India.* New Delhi: Oxford University Press.

The Hindu. (2020, July 14). EU-India summit to launch talks on resuming FTA negotiations, Chennai.

United Nations Economic Commission for Europe. (2012). In *world forum for harmonization of vehicle regulations (WP.29): How it works, how to join it,* (3rd ed.), UN, New York and Geneva.

United Nations Economic Commission for Europe (undated a). *WP.29-Introduction.* https://www.unece.org/trans/main/wp29/introduction.html.

United Nations Economic Commission for Europe.(undated b). UN Vehicle Regulations-1958 Agreement. https://www.unece.org/?id=39146.

United Nations Economic Commission for Europe (undated c). (1998). Agreement on Global Technical Regulations (GTRs). https://www.unece.org/trans/main/wp29/wp29wgs/wp29gen/wp29glob_registry.html.

World Trade Organization. (2002). DS146: India—Measures affecting the automotive sector (Complaint by EU). https://www.wto.org/english/tratop_e/dispu_e/cases_e/ds146_e.htm.

Part IV
Analysis of Sector Level Growth and Development in India

Chapter 18
Is 'Make in India' A Success? A Review from the Electronics Sector in India

S. Roy Chowdhury and S. Rastogi

1 Introduction

India's electronics and IT hardware manufacturing sector comprises close to 3,500 electronics manufacturing and 250,000 small units engaged in electronics manufacturing either directly or indirectly (DeitY, 2010). India produces only a minuscule amount of electronics compared to global production. The global production was valued at USD 2149 billion in 2012, out of which India produced goods valued at only approximately USD 28 billion or 1.3% of the global production. China produced 28%, and USA produced 29% of the global production in the year 2012 (EXIM, 2015). Owing to the rising middle class in the country, combined with changing lifestyle pattern and better access to credit facilities, demand for electronics goods has been rising at a rapid pace in India over the recent years (IBEF, 2015). The electronics demand is estimated to reach USD 400 billion by the year 2020 from mere USD 45 million in 2009 data (DeitY, 2010).

The estimated production of the electronics sector will reach approximately USD 104 billion in 2020, leaving a gap of USD 296 billion. The sector is estimated to be able to attract USD 100 billion of foreign direct investment (DeitY, 2010). Through Make in India, a fresh policy approach is sought to fill this wide gap between demand and supply. This sector provides a huge scope for employment as well. Employment in this sector was less than a million in the year 2009. The objective of the policies is not only to increase production but also to create 28 million jobs in the sector by 2020 and enhancing human capital by producing 2500 researchers annually (IBEF, 2015).

S. Roy Chowdhury (✉) · S. Rastogi
IIM Indore, Rau Pithampur Road, Indore 453556, India
e-mail: f17sanchitar@iimidr.ac.in

S. Rastogi
e-mail: srastogi@iimidr.ac.in

P. Lakhanpal et al. (eds.), *Trade, Investment and Economic Growth*,
https://doi.org/10.1007/978-981-33-6973-3_18

The primary policies of the government aimed at promoting the electronics industry are Electronic Manufacturing Cluster Scheme, schemes focused on trade such as Reduced Export Obligation and promoting Export Oriented Units, and Manufacturing Special Incentive Package Scheme. The Make in India campaign has provided the electronics manufacturing sector a well-needed push to harness foreign direct investment as well as domestic investment. The overarching objective of our study is to observe whether the policy push under the Make in India campaign has been successful in increasing electronics exports and reducing import to date.

In Sect. 2 of the paper, the objective of Make in India and associated specific policy steps for electronics sector are presented. Section 3 details the data and methodology used. Section 4 presents the results and analyses. Section 5 concludes with overall comments.

2 Make in India and Related Policies

The primary goal of the Make in India campaign is to make India the manufacturing hub of the world. Various policies under the campaign aimed at promoting manufacturing units. On the one hand, with the rise in manufacturing of intermediate and final goods, the export of the country can be expected to rise; on the other hand, the manufactured goods can help substitute imports. The campaign was expected to accomplish all the objectives within a short duration by the then government. The economy anticipated a drastic change with a rapid rise in the growth rate. Therefore, it is one of the most dominant campaigns which needs to be studied to assess the success rate. However, to the best of our knowledge, no study has been conducted to understand the effect of the campaign on the trade balance of the country for any of the sectors so far. We have attempted to study the impact of the umbrella policy of Make in India.

The electronics sector has been considered as one of the priority sectors under the Make in India initiative (DeitY, 2012). The Indian electronics sector is broadly divided into six segments, based on end use and valuation, which is depicted in Fig. 1. Due to the increasing upward pressure of labor wages in China, other Asian countries, like Vietnam, Cambodia, and India, are gaining popularity as possible manufacturing hubs. These countries have favorable product demand, labor cost, and government

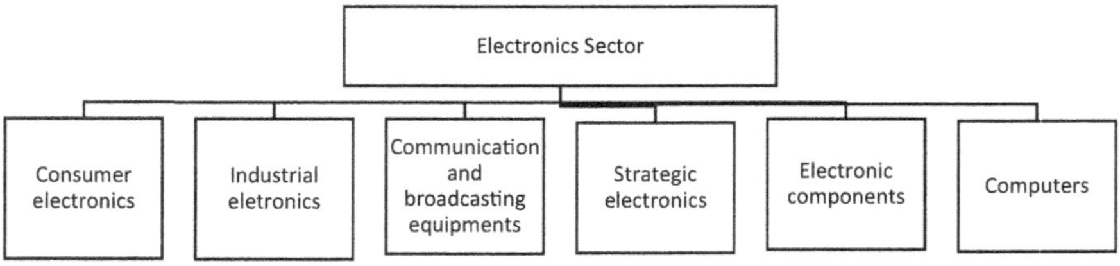

Fig. 1 Six segments of the Indian electronics sector. *Source* DeitY, (2012)

policies. From the year 2012, the Government of India has been trying to use the abundant young talent and low wages to make India globally competitive in the electronics sector. The government's objective is to close the demand–supply gap and reach USD 400 billion worth of production by 2020 (IBEF, 2017).

2.1 Policy Measures Adopted by the Government

The Government of India has come up with a variety of policies to enable and encourage the expansion of Electronics System Design and Manufacturing (ESDM) sector in India. The policy purpose is to enhance production capacity as well as production diversity in the sector to meet the domestic demand indigenously and to gain a share of the global electronics trade. The policy steps, as stated in NSDC (2011) report, include:

1. Special purpose vehicles for ESDM
2. M-SIPS or Manufacturing Special Incentive Package Scheme
3. Electronics Hardware Technology Park (EHTP) Scheme
4. The National Policy on Electronics
5. 100% FDI permitted through automatic route in most sectors including ESDM according to the consolidated FDI policy 2015
6. Implementation of ITA-I (Information Technology Act) under WTO
7. Reduced export obligation (EO) for domestic procurement under Export Promoting Capital Goods (EPCG) Scheme
8. Export-Oriented Unit (EOU) Scheme.

There are various skill development initiatives undertaken under the ESDM Scheme toward the goal of the creation of 28 million jobs, including:

1. Under the National Policy on Electronics, the objectives for human resource development include significant enhancement in the availability of skilled manpower in ESDM.
2. A scheme to support 3000 additional Ph.D., which includes 1500 in ESDM sector, was approved in 2014 at an estimated cost of USD 57 billion.
3. A scheme of financial assistance from the center to set up seven electronics and information and communications (ICT) academies in institutions.
4. A scheme of financial aid to select states/UTs (selected by an Empowered Committee based on proposals received).
5. The National Institute for Electronics and Information Technology (NIELIT) launched a project 'Capacity building in the areas of Electronic Design and Production Technology.'
6. A project entitled 'Special Manpower Development Program for Chips to Systems' has been approved by the Department of Electronics and Information Technology (DeitY).

7. DeitY approved a project for skill development in electronics hardware.[1]

3 Data Collection and Methodology

To understand the impact of Make in India and associated policy measures, we consider the changes in exports and imports as the proxy for the responsiveness of the umbrella campaign of Make in India. We choose the electronics products based on their six-digit HS codes. The HS code 85 is termed as 'electrical and electronics goods.' We consider the list of all the items with HS code starting with 854, and 49 items were found in this list. The generalized product categories listed as 'others' are removed, and finally, 46 items are chosen for further study. These 46 products made up around 1% of the total imports in 2009 and 2% in 2017, and approximately 0.6% of total Indian exports. The products along with their HS codes are listed in Appendix 1. We chose the time frame from the financial year 2009–2017 to distinguish between pre- and post-policy impact. Data for imports and exports in terms of billions USD for relevant items are collected from the Ministry of Commerce, Government of India, Web site.

For all the products, line graphs for the change in exports and imports over the years are plotted from the year 2009–2017 (refer to Appendix 2, Figs. 2 to 47). The results obtained are inconclusive due to high volatility. Therefore, we apply difference-in-difference (DID) method to examine the effects of the policies in the sector under consideration.

The Make in India campaign primarily came into effect in the year 2014. Hence, we consider years 2009–2014 as the control period and years 2015–17 as the treatment period. The CAGR from the pre-campaign period is expected to continue without policy, and the difference in CAGR with post-campaign is calculated to determine the effect of the policies. We use Eqs. (1)–(6) to calculate the required values (Table 1).

$$\text{Imports CAGR}_{\text{expected}} = \frac{\frac{(\text{Imports}_{2009-10} - \text{Imports}_{2014-15})}{\text{Imports}_{2009-10}} \times 100}{5} \quad (1)$$

$$\text{Imports CAGR}_{\text{actual}} = \frac{\frac{(\text{Imports}_{2014-15} - \text{Imports}_{2017-18})}{\text{Imports}_{2014-15}} \times 100}{3} \quad (2)$$

$$\text{Difference} = \text{Imports CAGR}_{\text{actual}} - \text{Imports CAGR}_{\text{expected}} \quad (3)$$

[1]Details of the policies are available at: IESA (2017).
https://meity.gov.in/writereaddata/files/Executive%20Summary%20of%20the%20IESA%20EY%20Report.pdf.
https://meity.gov.in/writereaddata/files/Electronics_IT_Hardware_NSDC_Report_1732011%20%281%29.pdf.

Table 1 DID results on imports

HS code (1)	2009–2010 (2)	2014–2015 (3)	Expected CAGR (4)	Actual CAGR (5)	Difference (6)	Expected 2017–18 values (7)	Actual 2017–2018 values (8)
854011	165.34	81.40	−10.15	−32.62	−22.46	59.04	1.75
854020	10.54	17.64	13.47	−26.68	−40.15	25.77	3.52
854040	2.55	0.87	−13.18	7.28	20.46	0.57	1.06
854060	1.43	0.36	−14.97	27.78	42.74	0.22	0.66
854071	1.23	2.94	27.80	0.79	−27.01	6.14	3.01
854079	2.39	7.45	42.34	−30.65	−72.99	21.49	0.60
854081	0.93	0.32	−13.12	−19.79	−6.67	0.21	0.13
854089	2.62	2.32	−2.29	3.88	6.17	2.16	2.59
854091	18.65	0.23	−19.75	−20.29	−0.54	0.12	0.09
854099	11.25	5.85	−9.60	−13.39	−3.79	4.32	3.50
854110	127.31	154.19	4.22	5.78	1.55	174.56	180.91
854121	4.17	4.08	-0.43	61.93	62.36	4.03	11.66
854129	113.83	221.81	18.97	2.30	−16.67	373.52	237.12
854130	26.29	56.41	22.91	−2.87	−25.79	104.75	51.55
854140	329.65	1041.31	43.18	100.61	57.44	3056.31	4184.40
854150	16.66	15.06	−1.92	−4.67	−2.75	14.21	12.95
854160	23.16	35.64	10.78	−0.60	−11.38	48.45	35.00
854190	26.86	11.56	−11.39	64.59	75.98	8.04	33.96
854231	525.62	728.87	7.73	17.02	9.29	911.39	1101.04
854232	92.88	128.98	7.77	−4.97	−12.75	161.46	109.73
854233	19.53	11.21	−8.52	65.77	74.29	8.58	33.33
854290	82.45	30.07	−12.71	−17.54	−4.83	20.00	14.25
854310	4.32	2.41	−8.84	69.16	78.00	1.83	7.41
854320	10.50	24.06	25.83	−5.54	−31.37	47.93	20.06
854330	14.51	20.25	7.91	30.58	22.67	25.45	38.83
854370	246.12	499.92	20.62	−3.28	−23.90	877.41	450.74
854390	109.60	123.57	2.55	0.77	−1.78	133.26	126.44
854411	75.00	84.54	2.54	−4.71	−7.25	91.16	72.60
854419	120.24	95.24	−4.16	5.87	10.02	83.85	112.00
854420	153.57	115.40	−4.97	−5.52	−0.55	99.03	96.28
854430	34.14	85.09	29.85	9.23	−20.62	186.29	108.65
854442	37.60	93.12	29.53	38.04	8.51	202.38	199.40
854449	183.96	245.78	6.72	7.42	0.70	298.74	300.50
854460	53.33	186.47	49.93	−20.67	−70.60	628.46	70.85

(continued)

Table 1 (continued)

HS code (1)	2009–2010 (2)	2014–2015 (3)	Expected CAGR (4)	Actual CAGR (5)	Difference (6)	Expected 2017–18 values (7)	Actual 2017–2018 values (8)
854470	31.69	42.21	6.64	7.79	1.15	51.19	52.07
854511	61.10	42.83	−5.98	−10.26	−4.28	35.60	29.65
854519	72.38	84.06	3.23	−18.45	−21.68	92.46	37.53
854520	6.79	15.94	26.95	5.71	−21.24	32.61	18.67
854590	10.77	11.45	1.26	53.92	52.65	11.89	29.97
854610	2.70	7.26	33.78	−29.71	−63.48	17.38	0.79
854620	17.93	10.95	−7.79	5.66	13.45	8.59	12.81
854690	46.93	60.43	5.75	15.99	10.23	71.47	89.41
854710	2.27	5.24	26.17	−5.79	−31.96	10.52	4.33
854720	40.49	86.83	22.89	14.65	−8.24	161.14	124.99
854790	30.87	38.04	4.65	−2.68	−7.33	43.59	34.98
854810	0.76	38.40	990.53	62.00	−928.53	49801.18	109.82

Source Ministry of Commerce and Industry, Government of India (MCI, 2018) (columns 1–3), authors' calculation (column 4–8)

$$\text{Exports CAGR}_{\text{expected}} = \frac{\frac{(\text{Exports}_{2009-10} - \text{Exports}_{2014-15})}{\text{Exports}_{2009-10}} \times 100}{5} \quad (4)$$

$$\text{Exports CAGR}_{\text{actual}} = \frac{\frac{(\text{Exports}_{2014-15} - \text{Exports}_{2017-18})}{\text{Exports}_{2014-15}} \times 100}{3} \quad (5)$$

$$\text{Difference} = \text{Exports CAGR}_{\text{actual}} - \text{Exports CAGR}_{\text{expected}} \quad (6)$$

Applying DID method, we calculate the CAGR for every product from 2009–10 to 2014–15 (columns 4 in Tables 2 and 3) using Eqs. (1) and (4). We consider this value as the expected cumulative annual growth rate of import and export, respectively, for the next years, if there had not been any policy change. Based on the value of CAGR obtained, we calculate the expected 2017–18 import and export values (columns 7). However, 'Make in India' campaign was launched in 2014. Hence, we determine the changed actual CAGR for the years 2014–15–2017–18 using Eqs. (2) and (5). The difference in the actual and the expected CAGR is used as an indicator for the effectiveness of the campaign. The difference is represented in columns (6), which is obtained using Eqs. (4) and (6). The results for import analysis are shown in Table 1, and that for exports are shown in Table 2.

Table 2 DID results on exports

HS code (1)	2009–2010 (2)	2014–2015 (3)	Expected CAGR (4)	Actual CAGR (5)	Difference (6)	Expected 2017–18 values (7)	Actual 2017–2018 values (8)
854011	2.30	2.78	4.17	−5.64	−9.81	3.14	2.31
854020	1.25	0.87	−6.08	−27.59	−21.51	0.72	0.15
854040	0.20	0.01	−19.00	33.33	52.33	0.01	0.02
854060	0.05	0.00	−20.00	NA	NA	0.00	0.00
854071	0.22	0.00	−20.00	NA	NA	0.00	0.03
854079	0.29	0.68	26.90	−24.02	−50.92	1.39	0.19
854081	0.00	0.02	NA	50.00	NA	NA	0.05
854089	1.81	1.53	−3.09	−28.32	−25.23	1.39	0.23
854091	0.67	0.80	3.88	−25.00	−28.88	0.90	0.20
854099	0.73	1.98	34.25	−22.90	−57.14	4.79	0.62
854110	2.23	2.16	−0.63	14.66	15.29	2.12	3.11
854121	1.26	0.69	−9.05	2.42	11.46	0.52	0.74
854129	4.41	3.71	−3.17	0.36	3.53	3.37	3.75
854130	2.77	0.96	−13.07	10.76	23.83	0.63	1.27
854140	359.86	179.12	−10.05	−5.67	4.37	130.38	148.65
854150	16.65	16.28	−0.44	−6.41	−5.96	16.06	13.15
854160	6.52	30.80	74.48	−21.88	−96.36	163.60	10.58
854190	4.55	4.50	−0.22	0.15	0.37	4.47	4.52
854231	23.07	22.84	−0.20	2.52	2.72	22.70	24.57
854232	14.53	10.99	−4.87	−18.65	−13.78	9.46	4.84
854233	0.94	0.90	−0.85	0.00	0.85	0.88	0.90
854290	20.22	10.33	−9.78	−25.72	−15.94	7.59	2.36
854310	0.97	0.43	−11.13	−21.71	−10.57	0.30	0.15
854320	9.52	5.46	−8.53	11.84	20.37	4.18	7.40
854330	4.16	1.93	−10.72	−9.67	1.05	1.37	1.37
854370	31.40	29.75	−1.05	28.83	29.88	28.82	55.48
854390	41.06	99.31	28.37	−16.96	−45.33	210.09	48.79
854411	50.42	60.88	4.15	2.26	−1.89	68.78	65.01
854419	34.67	73.43	22.36	−3.86	−26.22	134.52	64.92
854420	15.28	30.09	19.38	−21.34	−40.72	51.20	10.83
854430	34.74	162.88	73.77	8.41	−65.36	854.67	203.98
854442	16.71	41.41	29.56	13.44	−16.12	90.06	58.11
854449	55.12	45.31	−3.56	111.75	115.31	40.64	197.21
854460	89.62	248.60	35.48	−1.06	−36.54	618.18	240.71

(continued)

Table 2 (continued)

HS code (1)	2009–2010 (2)	2014–2015 (3)	Expected CAGR (4)	Actual CAGR (5)	Difference (6)	Expected 2017–18 values (7)	Actual 2017–2018 values (8)
854470	40.13	29.96	−5.07	−4.65	0.42	25.63	25.78
854511	160.43	237.88	9.66	27.17	17.51	313.65	431.77
854519	4.05	3.33	−3.56	−10.61	−7.06	2.99	2.27
854520	3.32	5.32	12.05	−4.51	−16.56	7.48	4.60
854590	2.36	5.66	27.97	−0.53	−28.50	11.86	5.57
854610	0.79	0.32	−11.90	82.29	94.19	0.22	1.11
854620	44.34	36.36	−3.60	9.76	13.36	32.57	47.01
854690	16.30	30.98	18.01	12.64	−5.37	50.92	42.73
854710	3.19	1.61	−9.91	−17.18	−7.28	1.18	0.78
854720	2.37	7.31	41.69	27.77	−13.92	20.79	13.40
854790	81.36	59.77	−5.31	−14.73	−9.43	50.75	33.35
854810	1.15	0.13	−17.74	30.77	48.51	0.07	0.25

Source Ministry of Commerce and Industry, Government of India (MCI, 2018) (columns 1–3), authors' calculation (column 4–8)

4 Results and Analysis

Table 1 represents the results of difference-in-difference on imports. In Table 1, a negative actual CAGR represents that the rate of growth of import for a particular commodity has been negative, or there has been a fall in imports from 2014–15 to 2017–18. Similarly, a positive CAGR represents a rise in imports over the years. When we calculate the difference between the actual and expected CAGR, it shows the import performance of the commodity above its expected value. Hence, a negative difference is desirable, as it shows a positive effect in terms of trade.

From the above results, we see that column 6 has 28 negative values and 18 positive values. It implies that the imports for 28 commodities have fallen over expected figures from 2014 to 2017 whereas 18 commodities have witnessed an increase in imports.

Table 2 represents the difference-in-difference results in exports. The exports are expected to move in the opposite direction of the imports. In Table 2, a positive actual CAGR represents that the rate of growth of export for a particular commodity has been positive, or there has been a comparative rise in exports over the expected trend from 2014–15 to 2017–18. Similarly, a negative CAGR represents a fall in exports over the years. When we calculate the difference between the actual and expected CAGR, it shows the export performance of the commodity above its expected value. Hence, a positive difference is desirable for exports, as falling exports would hurt the terms of trade.

Table 3 Overall impact of Make in India policies on the trade of electronics commodities

HS code (1)	Commodity (2)	Import CAGR difference (actual-expected) (3)	Export CAGR difference (actual-expected) (4)	Final impact of campaign (5)
854011	Cathode ray TV picture tubes, including video monitor cathode ray tube color	−22.46	−9.81	Inconclusive
854020	TV camera tube image convertors and intensifiers; other photocathode tubes	−40.15	−21.51	Inconclusive
854040	Data/graphic display tubes, color, with a phosphor dot screen pitch < 0.4 mm	20.46	52.33	Inconclusive
854060	Other cathode ray tubes	42.74	NA	Inconclusive
854071	Magnetrons	−27.01	NA	Inconclusive
854079	Other microwave tubes (e.g., traveling wave tube carcinotrons), excel grid-controlled tubes	−72.99	−50.92	Inconclusive
854081	Receiver/amplifier valves and tubes	−6.67	NA	Inconclusive
854089	Other valves and tubes	6.17	−25.23	Negative impact
854091	Parts of cathode ray tubes	−0.54	−28.88	Inconclusive
854099	Other parts of the tubs and valves of hdg 8540	−3.79	−57.14	Inconclusive
854110	Diodes, other than photosensitive or light-emitting diodes	1.55	15.29	Inconclusive
854121	Transistors, other than photosensitive transistors with a dissipation rate of less than 1 W	62.36	11.46	Inconclusive
854129	Other transistor, other than photosensitive transistors	−16.67	3.53	Positive impact
854130	Thyristors, diacs, and triacs, other than photosensitive devices	−25.79	23.83	Positive impact

(continued)

Table 3 (continued)

HS code (1)	Commodity (2)	Import CAGR difference (actual-expected) (3)	Export CAGR difference (actual-expected) (4)	Final impact of campaign (5)
854140	Photosensitive semiconductor devices including photovoltaic cells w/n assembled in modules/made up into panels; light-emitting diodes	57.44	4.37	Inconclusive
854150	Other semiconductor devices	−2.75	−5.96	Inconclusive
854160	Mounted piezoelectric crystals	−11.38	−96.36	Inconclusive
854190	Parts of items of hdng 8541	75.98	0.37	Inconclusive
854231	Processors and controllers, whether or not combined with memories, converters, logic circuits, amplifiers, clock	9.29	2.72	Inconclusive
854232	Memories	−12.75	−13.78	Inconclusive
854233	Amplifiers	74.29	0.85	Inconclusive
854290	Parts of electronic integrated circuits and micro-assemblies	−4.83	−15.94	Inconclusive
854310	Particle accelerators:	78.00	−10.57	Negative impact
854320	Signal generators	−31.37	20.37	Positive impact
854330	Machines and apparatus for electroplating, electrolysis/electrophoresis	22.67	1.05	Inconclusive
854370	Other machines and apparatus:	−23.90	29.88	Positive impact
854390	Parts of articles of heading 8543	−1.78	−45.33	Inconclusive
854411	Winding wire of copper	−7.25	−1.89	Inconclusive
854419	Winding wires of other metals/substances, excel copper	10.02	−26.22	Negative impact
854420	Coaxial cable and other coaxial electrical conductors	−0.55	−40.72	Inconclusive

(continued)

Table 3 (continued)

HS code (1)	Commodity (2)	Import CAGR difference (actual-expected) (3)	Export CAGR difference (actual-expected) (4)	Final impact of campaign (5)
854430	Ignition wiring sets and other wiring sets of a kind used in vehicle aircraft/ships	−20.62	−65.36	Inconclusive
854442	Other electric conductors < 1000 v fitted with connectors:	8.51	−16.12	Negative impact
854449	Other electric conductors < 1000 v not fitted with connectors:	0.70	115.31	Inconclusive
854460	Other electric conductors, for a voltage exceeding 1000 v	−70.60	−36.54	Inconclusive
854470	Optical fiber cables	1.15	0.42	Inconclusive
854511	Electrodes of a kind used for furnaces	−4.28	17.51	Positive impact
854519	Other electrodes	−21.68	−7.06	Inconclusive
854520	Brushes	−21.24	−16.56	Inconclusive
854590	Other articles used for electrical purposes	52.65	−28.50	Inconclusive
854610	Electrical insulators of glass	−63.48	94.19	Positive impact
854620	Electrical insulators of ceramics	13.45	13.36	Inconclusive
854690	Electrical insulators of other materials	10.23	−5.37	Negative impact
854710	Insulating fittings of ceramics	−31.96	−7.28	Inconclusive
854720	Insulating fittings of plastics	−8.24	−13.92	Inconclusive
854790	Other insulating fittings	−7.33	−9.43	Inconclusive
854810	Waste and scrap of primary cells, batteries, and electric accumulators, spent primary cell batteries and spent electric accumulators	−928.53	48.51	Positive impact

Source Ministry of Commerce and Industry, Government of India (MCI, 2018) (columns 1–2), authors' calculation (column 3–5)

We find that exports have increased over the expected trend for 20 products and have fallen from the expected trend for the remaining 26 products for the period from 2014 to 2017.

To understand the overall impact of the Make in India campaign and associated policies, we compare the import CAGR difference and the export CAGR difference in Table 3. A negative (positive) value in column 3 of Table 3 indicates the CAGR of import of the particular commodity has fallen (risen) from pre-campaign and post-campaign period and has benefitted (harmed) the trade balance of India. Similarly, for the export, a positive (negative) value in column 4 of Table 3 indicates the CAGR of export of the particular commodity has risen (fallen) from pre-campaign and post-campaign period and has benefitted (harmed) the trade balance of India.

For the products that witnessed a rise in export and a fall in import, the campaign is labeled to be successful (positive impact). For products that witnessed a fall in export and a rise in import, the campaign is labeled to be unsuccessful (negative impact). The products that show diverging trends for both (export and import simultaneously rising or falling), the campaign is labeled as inconclusive. From the above table, we see that the campaign has been clearly successful for only seven products and unsuccessful for five products. For the rest of the 34 items, the results are inconclusive. The rising imports and falling exports for these five items might be due to the nature of these items. These can be components which are used to produce some other final products. The production of such final products might have seen an increasing trend. The reason behind the trend might be because additional manufacturing has been successful to cater to domestic demand for most products, but excess supply has not been reached, which can promote export. Hence, imports have fallen, with no or negative change in exports.

5 Conclusion

We attempt to study the overall effect of the ‘Make in India’ umbrella campaign on the electronics sector of India. Since Make in India as a policy has been focused on export promotion and import substitution, we analyze the export and import figures for 46 commodities from the sector as a proxy for growth in manufacturing, and as with the rise in local manufacturing, exports (imports) are expected to rise (fall). We employ difference-in-difference method to measure the deviation of exports and imports from their expected trend values. This is the first study which attempted to assess the performance of the ‘Make in India’ campaign.

We find that Make in India has been successful for a few products and unsuccessful for a few of them. However, no significant result could be drawn for 34 out of 46 items in the electronics sector of India. The inconclusive trend might be a result of the short lag available post the policy initiative. Further, it is also possible that one sector benefitting from the policy initiative may create a stronger input demand in another sector, leading to an increase or decrease in both the numbers for exports and imports. The increased production may have been successful in substituting imports for the domestic market but unsuccessful in producing enough surplus to improve export and cater to international demand.

The study has a few limitations, which can be addressed in the future research. We have considered only the electronics sector for the analysis. Further, we analyzed the export and import figures in isolation from the other macroeconomic variables, which may have led to inconclusive or biased results. A similar analysis can be carried out on other sectors to observe the differences in the impact of the initiative. The data time frame is limited as Make in India was launched only four years back. With more data points in the future, a more conclusive study can be conducted.

Appendix 1

The list of all the product names with HS codes under study

HS code	Product name
854011	Cathode ray TV picture tubes, including video monitor cathode ray tube color
854020	TV camera tube image convertors and intensifiers; other photocathode tubes
854040	Data/graphic display tubes, color, with a phosphor dot screen pitch <0.4 mm
854060	Other cathode ray tubes
854071	Magnetrons
854079	Other microwave tubes (e.g., traveling wave tube carcinotrons), excel grid-controlled tubes
854081	Receiver/amplifier valves and tubes
854089	Other valves and tubes
854091	Parts of cathode ray tubes
854099	Other parts of the tubs and valves of hdg 8540
854110	Diodes, other than photosensitive or light-emitting diodes
854121	Transistors, other than photosensitive transistors with a dissipation rate of less than 1 W
854129	Other transistor, other than photosensitive transistors
854130	Thyristors, diacs, and triacs, other than photosensitive devices
854140	Photosensitive semiconductor devices including photovoltaic cells w/n assembled in modules/ made up into panels; light-emitting diodes
854150	Other semiconductors devices
854160	Mounted piezoelectric crystals
854190	Parts of items of hdng 8541
854231	Processors and controllers, whether or not combined with memories, converters, logic circuits, amplifiers, clock
854232	Memories
854233	Amplifiers

(continued)

(continued)

HS code	Product name
854290	Parts of electronic integrated circuits and micro-assemblies
854310	Particle accelerators:
854320	Signal generators
854330	Machines and apparatus for electroplating, electrolysis/electrophoresis
854370	Other machines and apparatus:
854390	Parts of articles of heading 8543
854411	Winding wire of copper
854419	Winding wires of other metals/substances, excel copper
854420	Coaxial cable and other coaxial electrical conductors
854430	Ignition wiring sets and other wiring sets of a kind used in vehicle aircraft/ships
854442	Other electric conductors <1000 v fitted with connectors:
854449	Other electric conductors <1000 v not fitted with connectors:
854460	Other electric conductors, for a voltage exceeding 1000 v
854470	Optical fiber cables
854511	Electrodes of a kind used for furnaces
854519	Other electrodes
854520	Brushes
854590	Other articles used for electrical purposes
854610	Electrical insulators of glass
854620	Electrical insulators of ceramics
854690	Electrical insulators of other materials
854710	Insulating fittings of ceramics
854720	Insulating fittings of plastics
854790	Other insulating fittings
854810	Waste and scrap of primary cells, batteries, and electric accumulators, spent primary cell batteries and spent electric accumulators

Source Ministry of Commerce and Industry, Government of India (MCI, 2018)

Appendix 2

See Figs. 2, 3, 4, 5, 6, 7, 8, 9, 10, 11, 12, 13, 14, 15, 16, 17, 18, 19, 20, 21, 22, 23, 24, 25, 26, 27, 28, 29, 30, 31, 32, 33, 34, 35, 36, 37, 38, 39, 40, 41, 42, 43, 44, 45, 46 and 47.

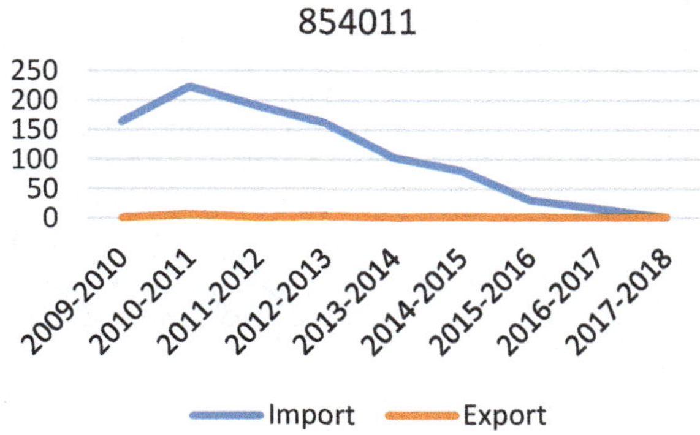

Fig. 2 Import–export for HS code 854011

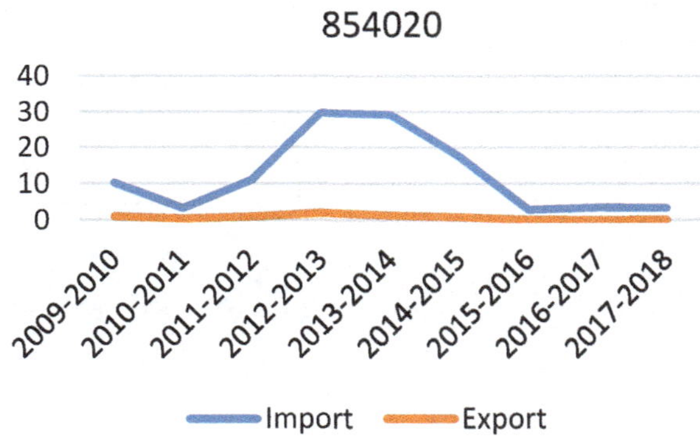

Fig. 3 Import–export for HS code 854020

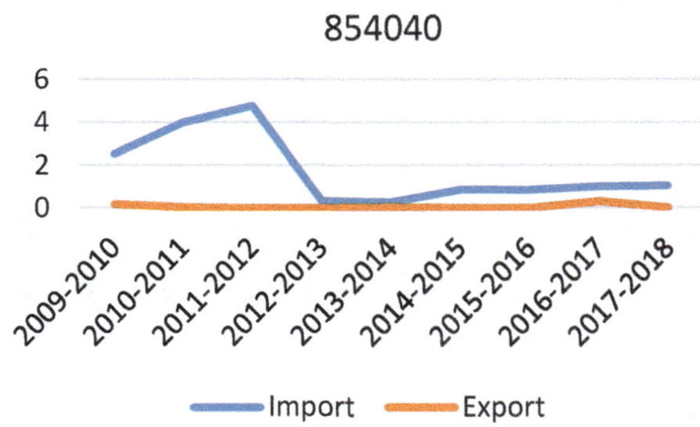

Fig. 4 Import–export for HS code 854040

Fig. 5 Import–export for HS code 854060

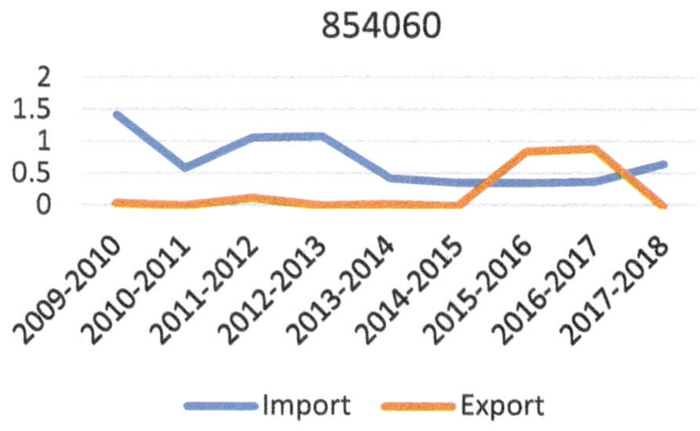

Fig. 6 Import–export for HS code 854071

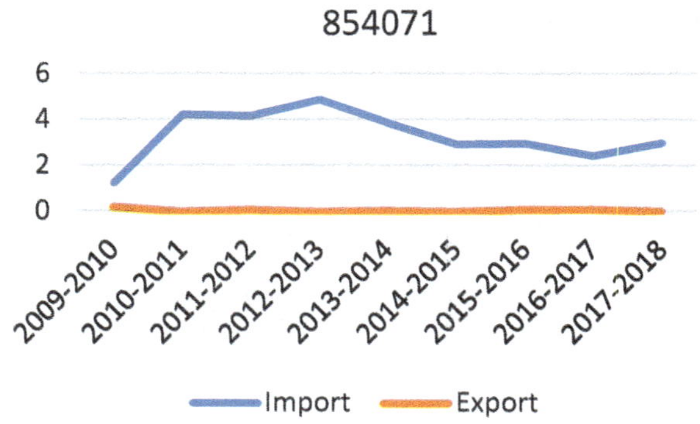

Fig. 7 Import–export for HS code 854079

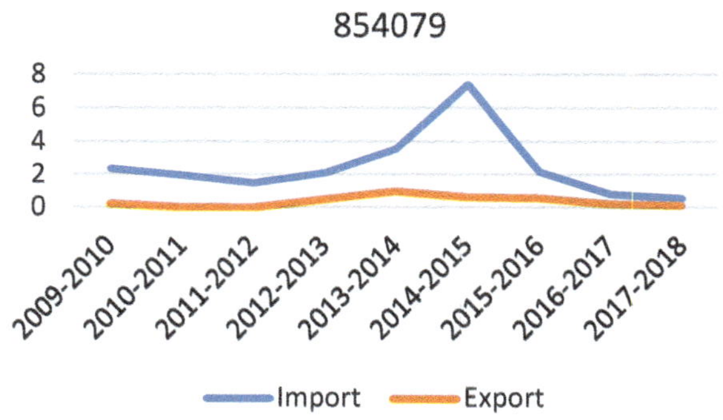

Fig. 8 Import–export for HS code 854081

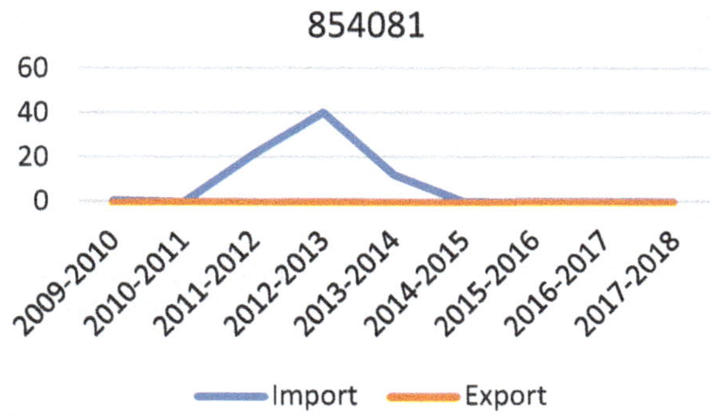

Fig. 9 Import–export for HS code 854089

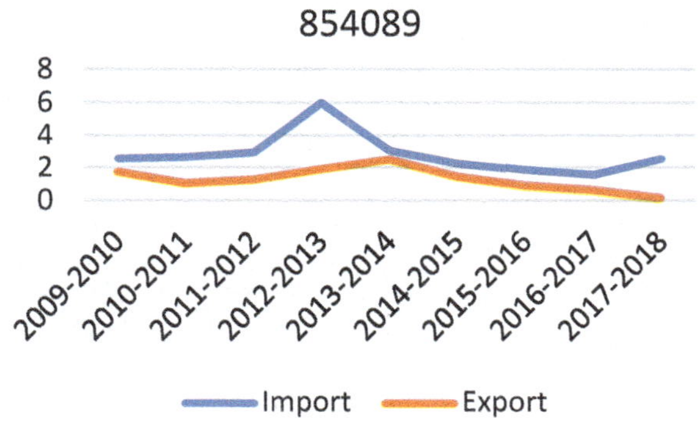

Fig. 10 Import–export for HS code 854091

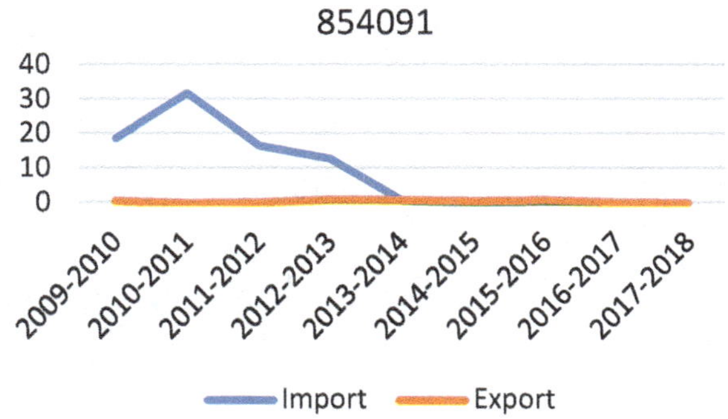

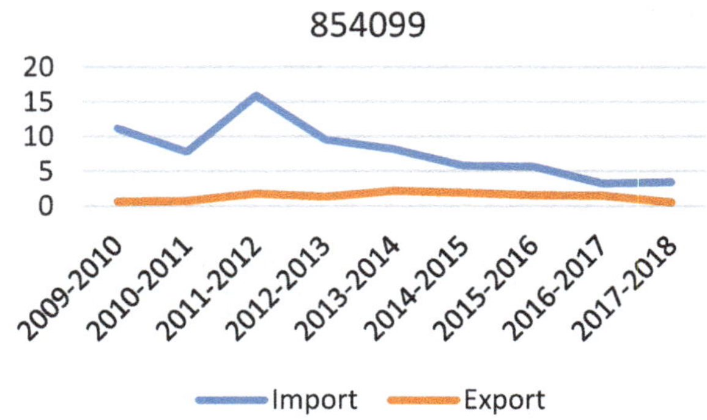

Fig. 11 Import–export for HS code 854099

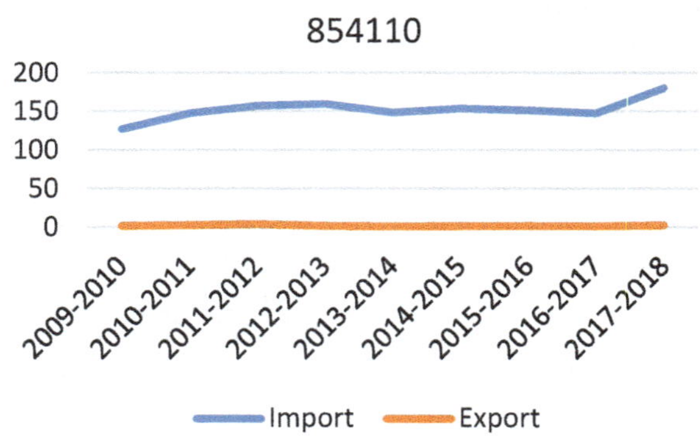

Fig. 12 Import–export for HS code 854110

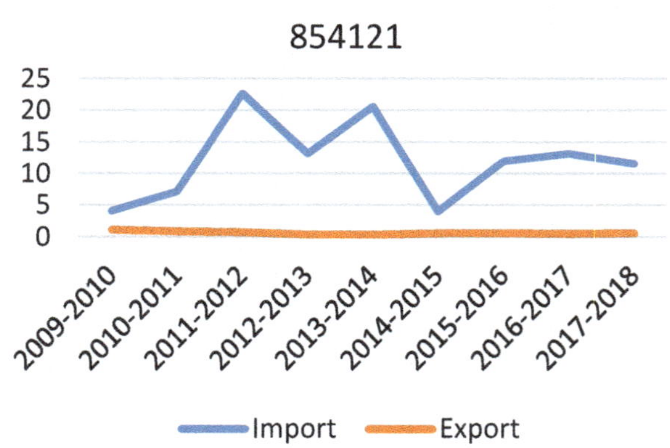

Fig. 13 Import–export for HS code 854121

Fig. 14 Import–export for HS code 854129

Fig. 15 Import–export for HS code 854130

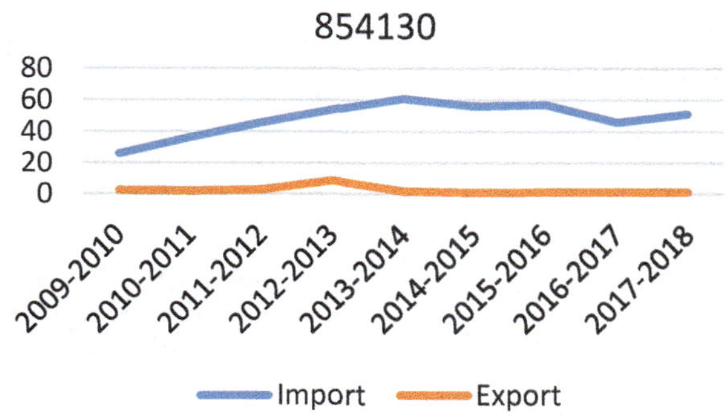

Fig. 16 Import–export for HS code 854140

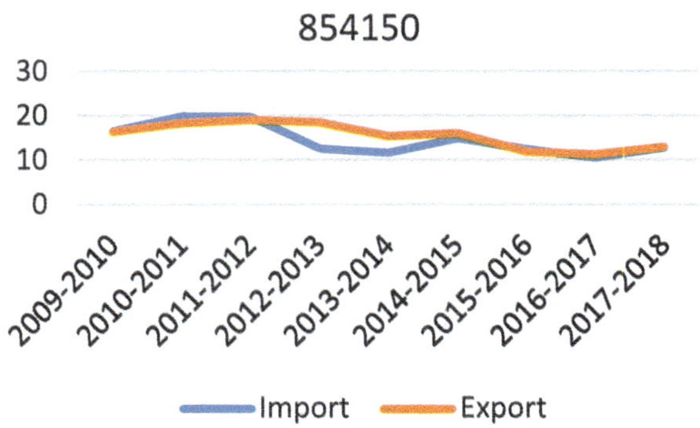

Fig. 17 Import–export for HS code 854150

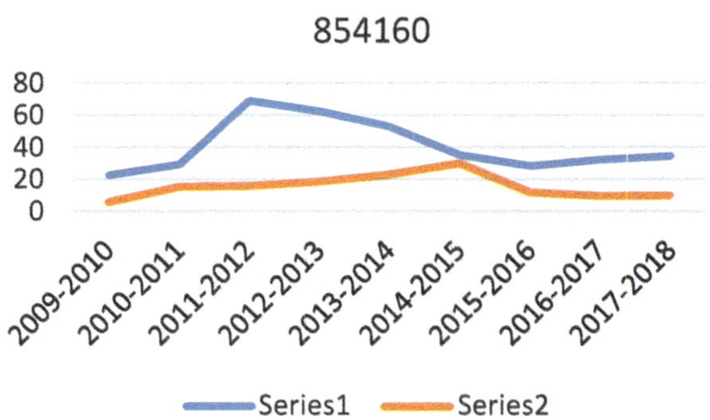

Fig. 18 Import–export for HS code 854160

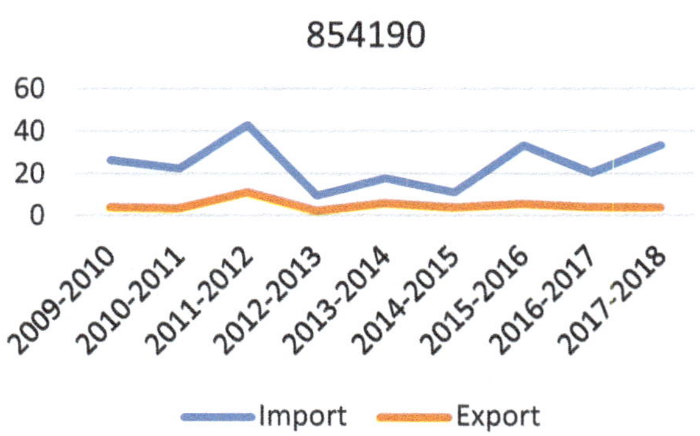

Fig. 19 Import–export for HS code 854190

Fig. 20 Import–export for HS code 854231

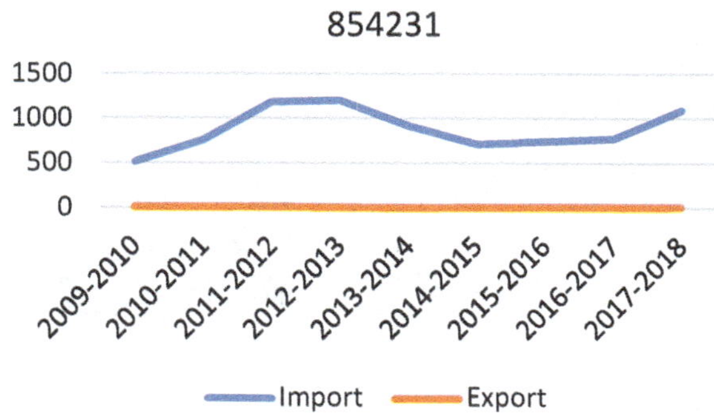

Fig. 21 Import–export for HS code 854232

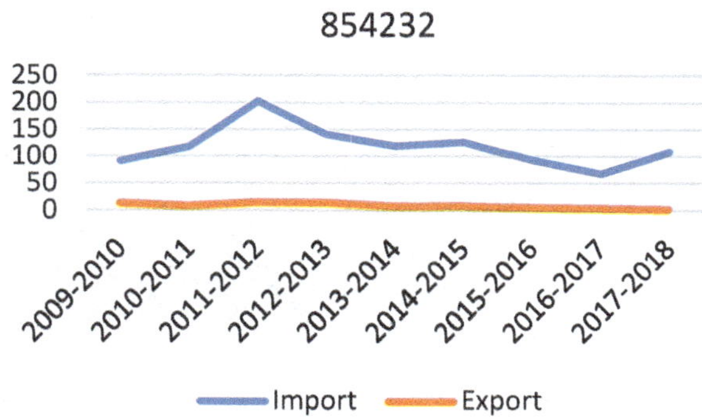

Fig. 22 Import–export for HS code 854233

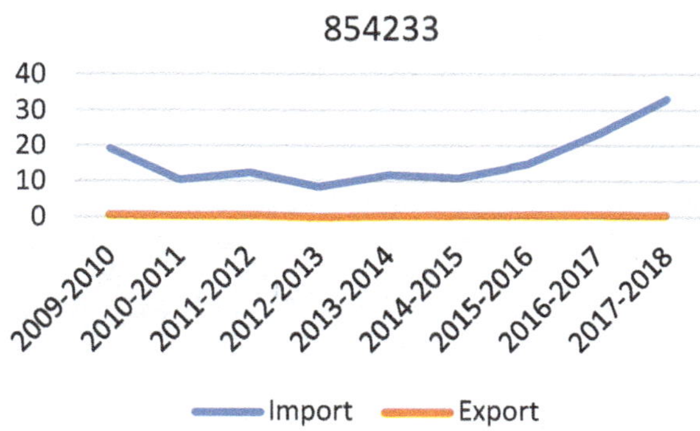

Fig. 23 Import–export for HS code 854290

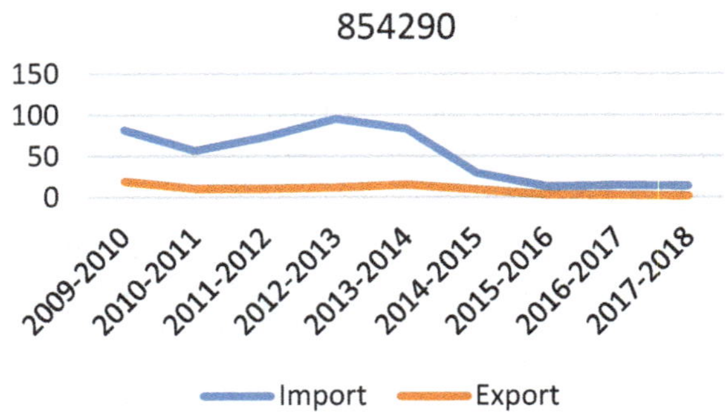

Fig. 24 Import–export for HS code 854310

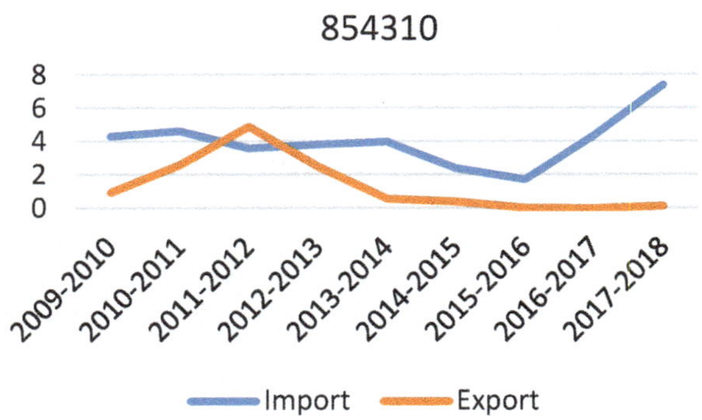

Fig. 25 Import–export for HS code 854320

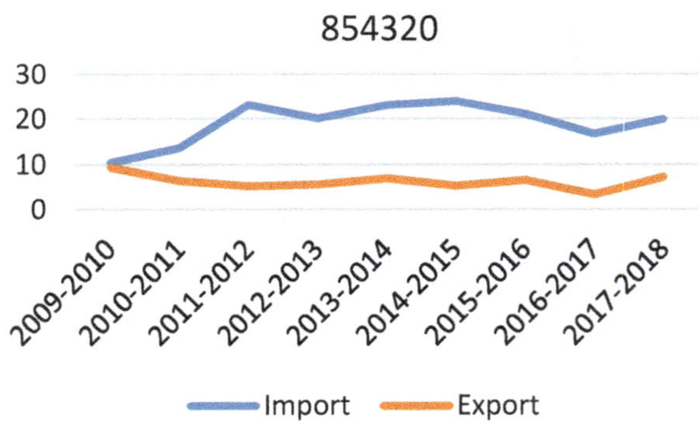

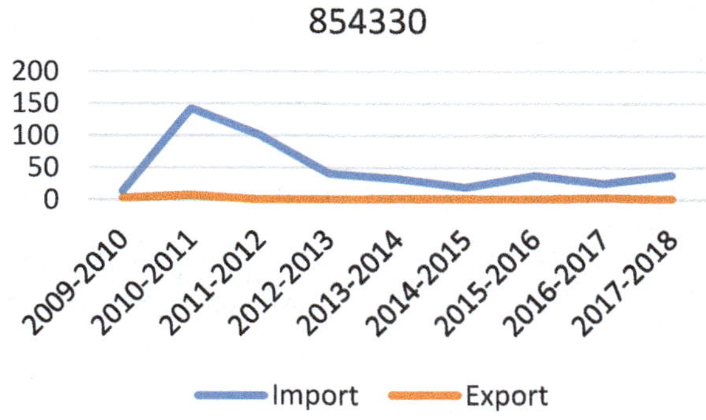

Fig. 26 Import–export for HS code 854330

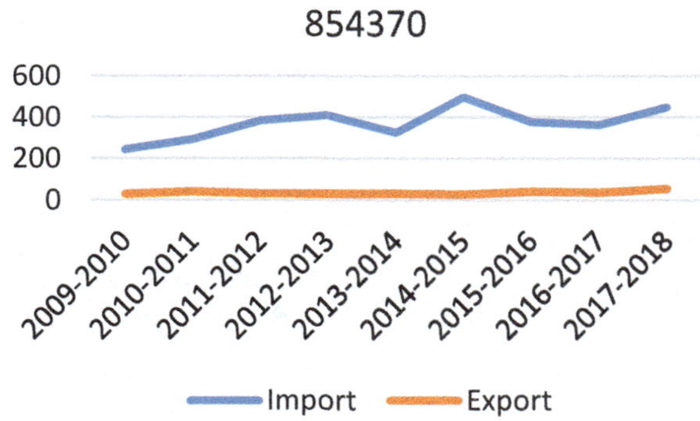

Fig. 27 Import–export for HS code 854370

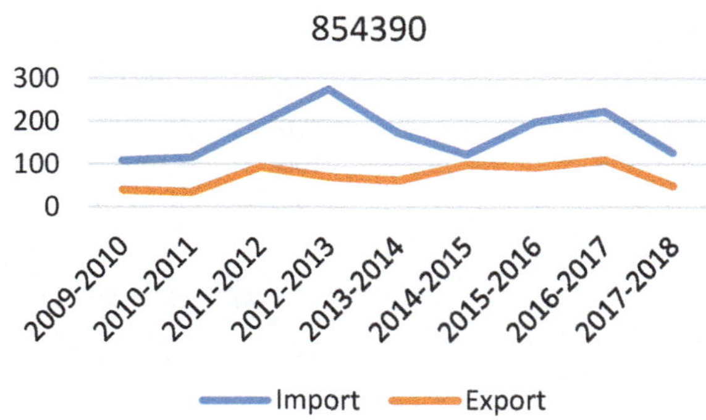

Fig. 28 Import–export for HS code 854390

Fig. 29 Import–export for HS code 854411

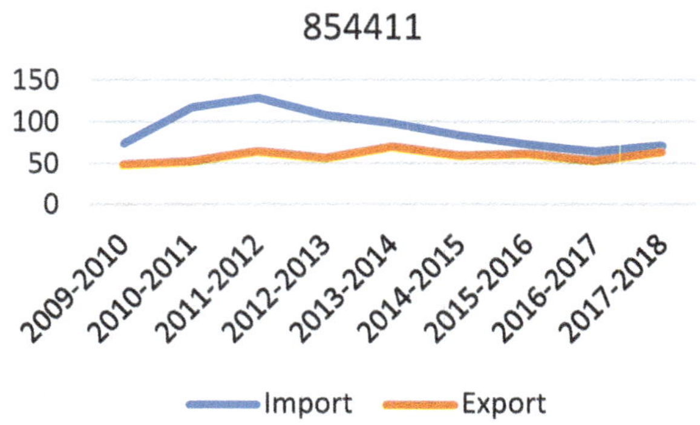

Fig. 30 Import–export for HS code 854419

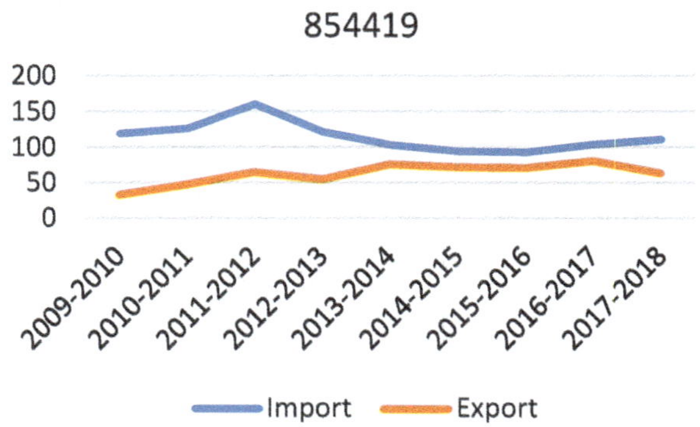

Fig. 31 Import–export for HS code 854420

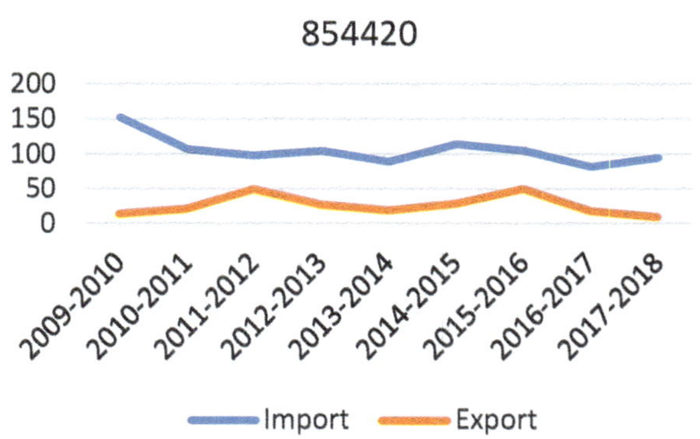

Fig. 32 Import–export for HS code 854430

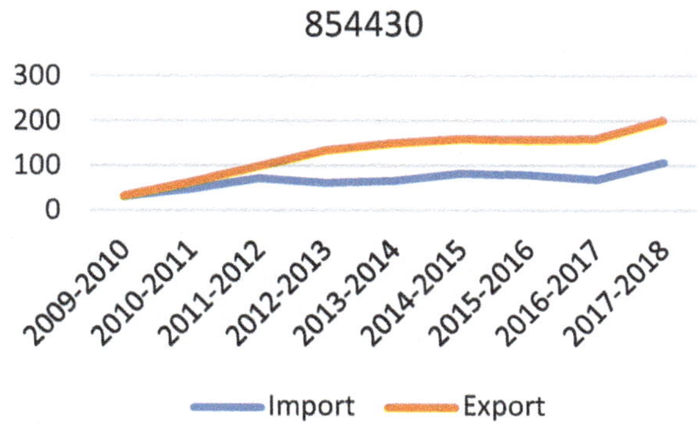

Fig. 33 Import–export for HS code 854442

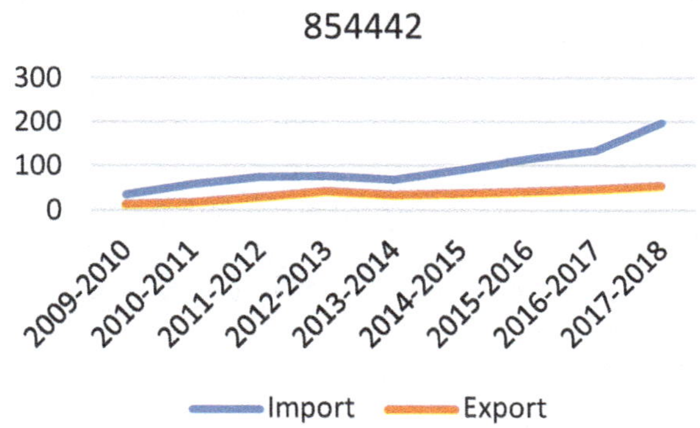

Fig. 34 Import–export for HS code 854449

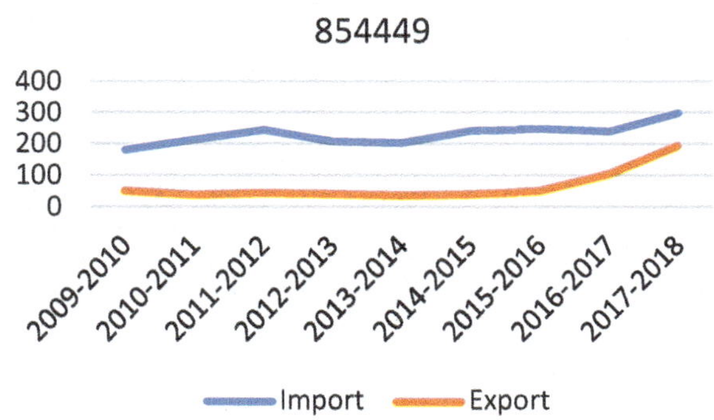

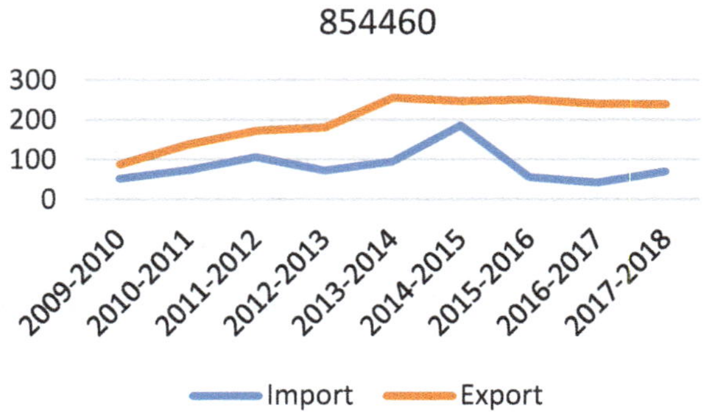

Fig. 35 Import–export for HS code 854460

Fig. 36 Import–export for HS code 854470

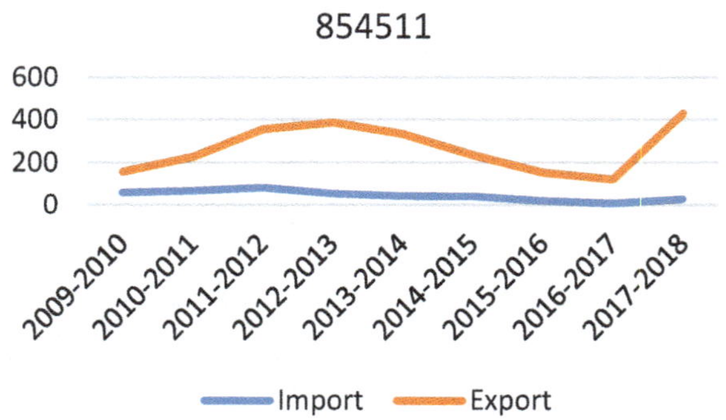

Fig. 37 Import–export for HS code 854511

Fig. 38 Import–export for HS code 854519

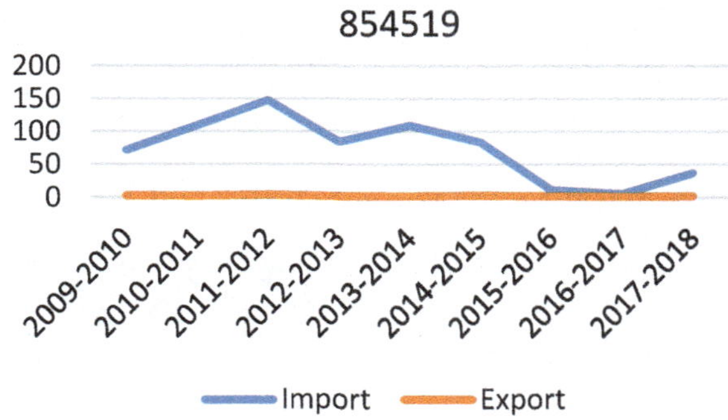

Fig. 39 Import–export for HS code 854520

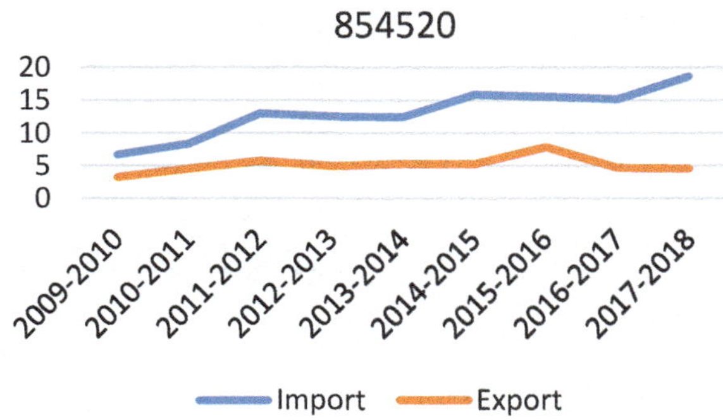

Fig. 40 Import–export for HS code 854590

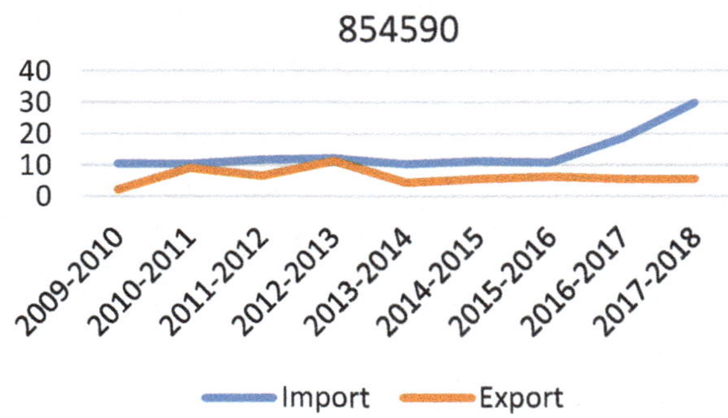

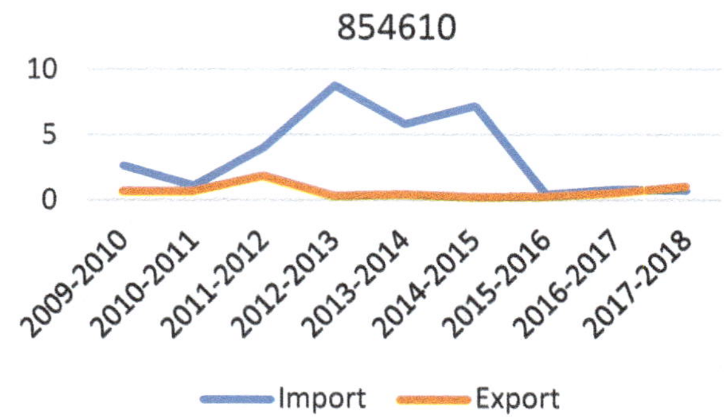

Fig. 41 Import–export for HS code 854610

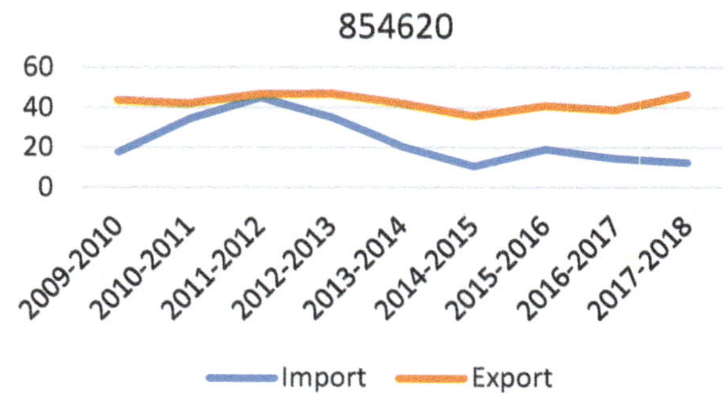

Fig. 42 Import–export for HS code 854620

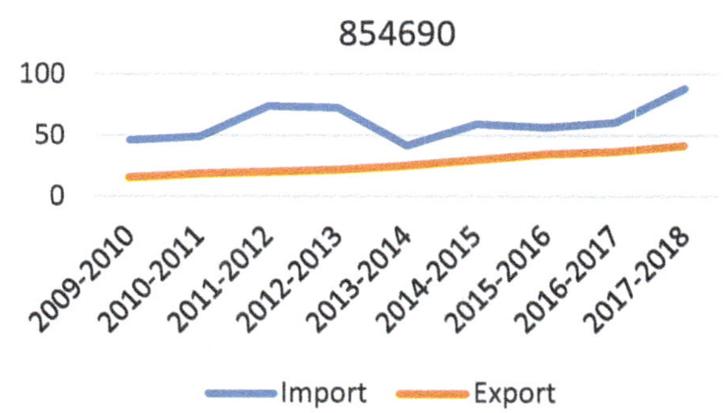

Fig. 43 Import–export for HS code 854690

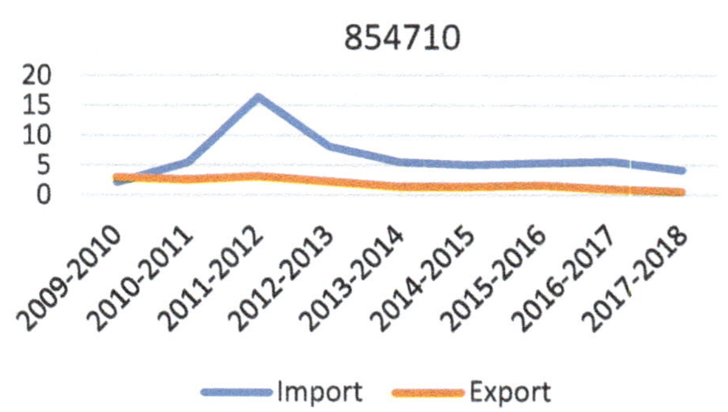

Fig. 44 Import–export for HS code 854710

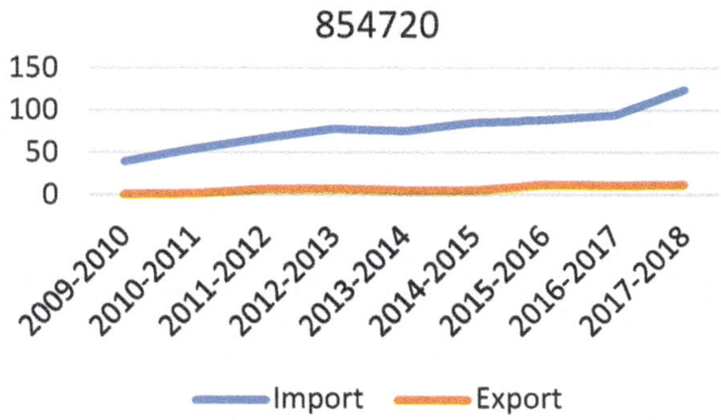

Fig. 45 Import–export for HS code 854720

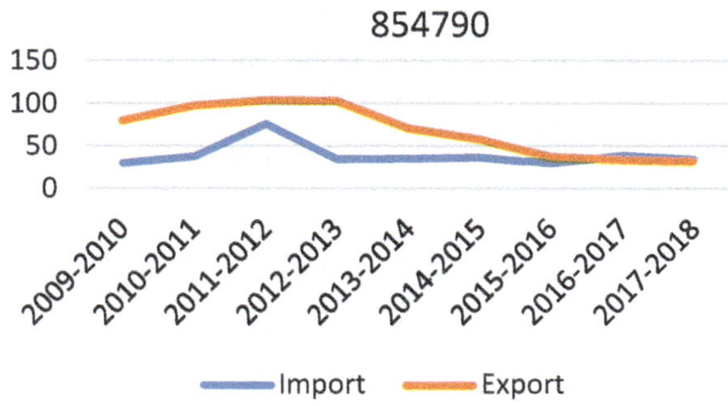

Fig. 46 Import–export for HS code 854790. *Source* MCI, (2018)

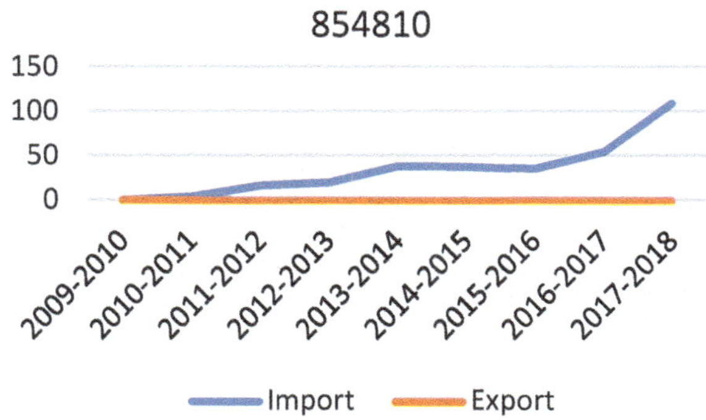

Fig. 47 Import–export for HS code 854810

References

DeitY. (2010). The Ministry of Electronics and Information Technology, Government of India -Report of Task Force to suggest measures to stimulate the growth of IT, ITES and Electronics Hardware manufacturing industry in India. Retrieved from https://meity.gov.in/writereaddata/files/Suggest%20Measures%20to%20stimulate%20growth%20of%20IT,%20ITES%20and%20Electronics%20Hardware%20Manufacturing%20Industry%20in%20India%20(2009)%20(4961%20KB)(1).pdf. Accessed on July 5, 2018.

DeitY. (2012). The Ministry of Electronics and Information Technology, Government of India, 2012. Promotion of Electronics/ IT Hardware Manufacturing (Annual Plan 2012–13). Retrieved from https://meity.gov.in/writereaddata/files/Annual%20Plan%202012-13%20_Promotion%20of%20Electronics%20IT%20Hardware%20Manufacturing%20(2012)%20(23%20KB)(1).pdf. Accessed on July 27, 2018.
EXIM. (2015). Export–Import Bank of India–Indian Electronic Goods Industry: Neutralizing Trade Deficit with China. Retrieved from https://www.eximbankindia.in/Assets/Dynamic/PDF/Publication-Resources/ResearchPapers/Hindi/7file.pdf. Accessed on July 15, 2018.
IBEF. (2015). India Brand Equity Foundation–Electronics. Retrieved from https://www.ibef.org/download/Electronics-March-2015.pdf. Accessed on July 30, 2018.
IBEF. (2017). India Brand Equity Foundation–Electronics. Retrieved from https://www.ibef.org/download/Electronics-June-2017.pdf. Accessed on August 28, 2018.
IESA. (2017). Indian Electronics and Semiconductor Association - Indian Electronics Industry Update. Retrieved from https://meity.gov.in/writereaddata/files/Executive%20Summary%20of%20the%20IESA%20EY%20Report.pdf. Accessed on August 5, 2018.
MCI. (2018). Ministry of Commerce & Industry, Government of India–Export Import data Bank. Retrieved from https://commerce-app.gov.in/eidb/. Accessed on August 1, 2018.
National Skill Development Cooperation. (2011). Human Resource and Skill Requirements in the Electronics and IT Hardware Industry. Retrieved from https://meity.gov.in/writereaddata/files/Electronics_IT_Hardware_NSDC_Report_1732011%20%281%29.pdf. Accessed on August 21, 2018.

Chapter 19
Financial Inclusion and Telecommunication in India : A Study on Spillover Effect

Taufeeque Ahmad Siddiqui and Kashif Iqbal Siddiqui

1 Introduction

Literature has established an apparent positive relationship between efficient financial services and economic growth. The Indian economy is one of the fastest-growing in the world. The key to the inclusive growth of the country depends upon the status of the rural population. According to the census 2011, nearly 70% of the Indian population live in rural areas. Financial inclusion is an effort to bring these rural populations into the mainstream line. Financial inclusion has been a significant policy concern for governments across the world.

Chakrabarty (2011) defines financial inclusion as 'the process of ensuring access to appropriate financial products and services needed by vulnerable groups such as weaker sections and low-income groups at an affordable cost fairly and transparently by mainstream institutional players'. Rural poor struggle with inadequate access to finance (Siddiqui and Siddiqui, 2020). There are various initiatives taken by the Government of India and the Reserve Bank of India, such as no-frills accounts, branch expansion, relaxed KYC norms, correspondent banking, and electronic payment to achieve the objectives of financial inclusion in India. The government is also making efforts to promote financial inclusion through the Direct Benefit Transfer scheme, Pradhan Mantri Jan Dhan Yojna, and various other social upliftment schemes. As of June 24, 2020, 39.57 crore beneficiaries have opened their accounts under PMJDY, making this scheme as one of the most extensive financial inclusion programs in the world (PMJDY, 2020).

Improving technology has accelerated the use of cellular phones to access financial services. In terms of the number of subscribers, the Indian telecom industry is

---

T. A. Siddiqui · K. I. Siddiqui (✉)
Centre for Management Studies, Jamia Millia Islamia, New Delhi, India
e-mail: kshfsiddiqui@gmail.com

T. A. Siddiqui
e-mail: taufeeque@gmail.com

P. Lakhanpal et al. (eds.), *Trade, Investment and Economic Growth*,
https://doi.org/10.1007/978-981-33-6973-3_19

the second largest in the world (GSMA, 2017). The sector has witnessed exponential growth over the last few years. The overall teledensity of India is 88.56%, whereas rural teledensity is 56.67% (TRAI, 2020). Rural regions are well covered by telecommunications networks and are now seeing growing penetration of smartphones and computers. Increased teledensity has reduced the digital divide between rural and urban India. The extraordinary growth of cellular telephony in India provides an opportunity that can be harnessed to expand access to financial services to unbanked sections of the population. The growth of the telecommunications infrastructure, particularly the penetration of cell phones, has provided an opportunity to provide financial inclusion (Mishra and Bisht, 2013). Hence, telecom can play an active role in providing significant support for the growth and transformation of the banking industry in rural areas. The latest technology, along with telecom infrastructure, may play a significant role in the financial inclusion revolution.

2 Brief Literature Review

Bagli and Dutta (2012), in their study, attempted to find out how fairly Indian states have delivered as far as financial inclusion is concerned. A rotated principal component analysis methodology was applied to compute a comprehensive measure of financial inclusion for every state. According to the study, the computed values of the composite index of financial inclusion inferred that so far, the financial inclusion of the states in India is not encouraging. The study also confirms the strong positive relationship between human development and financial inclusion in India.

Andrianaivo and Kpodar (2012), in their paper, tried to find out whether the mobile phone development boosts economic growth through better financial inclusion. The results of the estimation through GMM estimators revealed that mobile telephone development contributes to economic growth in Africa. They further added that mobile phone penetration has the potential to improve financial inclusion by providing cost-effective financial services to the poor and the unbanked.

Chakravarty and Pal (2013) developed an index to measure financial inclusion. They use panel data econometrics techniques to examine the effects of major banking policies on financial inclusion across states in India from 1972 to 2009. It was reported that during 1977–1990, the social banking policy played a crucial role in fostering financial inclusion across Indian states. Financial inclusion levels are significantly influenced by a region's economic development and its structure. They recommended geographic penetration of banking services and the availability of credit as two policy objectives to foster financial inclusion across Indian states.

CRISIL (2015) measured the degree of financial inclusion in India in the form of an index. CRISIL evaluated financial inclusion at the national/regional/state as well as district levels. Nine districts hit the Inclusix score of 100. Six are from Kerala, namely, Pathanamthitta, Alappuzha, Ernakulam, Kottayam, Thiruvananthapuram, and Thrissur. Karaikal and Mahe are from Pondicherry and Coimbatore from Tamil Nadu.

Wang and Guan (2017) examine the status of financial inclusion using the World Bank Global Findex database across the countries. The results based on access and usage as a dimension of financial inclusion indicate a high level of financial inclusion in European and North American countries. They further studied the factors associated with financial inclusion using spatial regression. Income, education, and communication instruments are the main demand-side factors of financial inclusion. Additionally, financial depth and banking health are the supply side factors explaining the level of financial inclusion.

Chikalipah (2017) investigated the determinants of financial inclusion in Sub-Saharan Africa using the World Bank Global Findex database, 2014. Financial inclusion was considered as a dependent variable represented by the ratio of the population with a bank account in the country. Literacy, GDP growth, population density, infrastructure, and GNI per capita are the independent variables used in the study. Literacy, GDP growth, and GNI per capita have a significant and positive impact on financial inclusion. The study concludes that enhancing literacy will strengthen financial inclusion in SSA countries.

Siddiqui and Siddiqui (2017), in their paper, analyzed the effect of telecom services on financial inclusion in Haryana by moderating the impact of education. A sample of 200 was analyzed using SmartPLS. Outcomes of the study reveal a significant impact of telecom services on financial inclusion. They have suggested that the synergy and collaboration between telecom and the financial institution can be instrumental in reaching the unbanked. In a similar study, Siddiqui and Siddiqui (2018) scrutinize the role of telecom and socioeconomic constructs to achieve financial inclusion.

Chatterjee and Das (2019), in their article, examine the role of information and communication technology in the dissemination of financial inclusion in India. The results indicate that technology plays a vital role in the diffusion of financial inclusion in India. They also added that older people in rural and urban areas are still not familiar with the Internet and mobile phones, which exclude them from the telecom revolution.

In a similar study, Fanta and Makina (2019) examine the relationships between financial inclusion and technology. They have considered the Internet, mobile, telephone, and ATMs as components of technology, whereas the account ownership, electronic fund transfer, and deposits as a percentage of GDP as components of financial inclusion. The results indicate a positive association between financial inclusion and technology. Technology fosters the access and usage of financial services.

Various aspects related to financial inclusion and telecommunication have been covered individually in past studies. Some of the studies which are focused on telecom are Kaur and Malhotra (2014), Ketkar et al. (2014) and Andrianaivo and Kpodar (2012). Conversely, some vital studies based on financial inclusion are Chikalipah (2017), Stephen and Tom (2015), and Aduda and Kalunda (2012). Moreover, the studies cover both the realms with some other related aspects, such as economic development. Such studies are Scott et al. (2005), Nino-zarazua and Copestake (2008), Adeola and Evans (2017), and Stephen and Tom (2015). To the best of the authors' knowledge, minimal research is available, which links telecom and financial inclusion directly. The present study is based on the causal relationship between telecom and financial inclusion, comparing two entirely different states.

3 Objectives

- To evaluate the impact of awareness about banking services, the ability to use banking services and usage of banking services on the awareness about telecom services, the ability to use telecom services, and usage of telecom services in Bihar and Kerala.
- To assess the impact of awareness about telecom services, the ability to use telecom services and usage of telecom services on the awareness about banking services, the ability to use banking services, and usage of banking services in Bihar and Kerala.

4 Hypothesis

- H01: There is no significant impact of the awareness about banking services, the ability to use banking services, and the usage of banking services on the awareness about telecom services, the ability to use telecom services, and the usage of telecom services in Kerala.
- H02: There is no significant impact of the awareness about telecom services, the ability to use telecom services, and the usage of telecom services on awareness about banking services, the ability to use banking services, and the usage of banking services in Kerala.
- H03: There is no significant impact of the awareness about banking services, the ability to use banking services, and the usage of banking services on awareness about telecom services, the ability to use telecom services, and the usage of telecom services in Bihar.
- H04: There is no significant impact of the awareness about telecom services, the ability to use telecom services, and the usage of telecom services on awareness about banking services, the ability to use banking services, and the usage of banking services in Bihar.

5 Research Methodology

In the current study, primary data were collected through a schedule from four randomly selected villages from Kerala and Bihar. Karanthur and Kanthapuram are the two villages representing the Calicut district of Kerala, whereas Chaparia and

Jagatpur are two villages from Madhubani district of Bihar. Two hundred samples each from the two states were collected, making the sample size of 400. A household is the sampling unit used for the study. Kerala is ranked top and Bihar as the bottom on CRISIL Inclusix score published by CRISIL (CRISIL, 2015). Thus, the comparison would be fruitful.

Smart PLS is used to test the hypothesis. This software package is one of the leading tools for partial least square structural equation modeling (Ringle et al., 2015; Sarstedt et al., 2014).

Hair et al. (2011) recommend the minimum sample size required for the multivariate analysis technique of partial least square structural equation modeling. The minimum sample size should be equal to ten times the highest number of indicators used to measure one construct. In the present study, 8 is the maximum indicator loaded on a latent construct, and therefore, minimum required sample to run the SEM will be 80.

Formative and reflective indicators are the two measurements model in SEM (Edwards and Bagozzi, 2000). A formative indicator is a function of the indicators of a latent variable, whereas a reflective indicator is a function of the latent variable. In the case of a reflective indicator, change in a latent construct can determine the changes in the value of its indicators (Hair et al., 2012). Hence, all the research indicators are reflective of the current study.

In the present study, four hypothesized models have been developed. There are six constructs used for the study. The ability to use banking services, the awareness about banking services, and the usage of banking services are constructs representing financial inclusion. In the same way, the constructs for telecommunication are the ability to use telecom services, the awareness about telecom services, and the usage of telecom services. The constructs consist of 38 indicators. The list is depicted in Appendix 1.

In two models (model 1 and model 3), telecommunication is an endogenous variable, and financial inclusion is the exogenous variable for Kerala and Bihar, respectively. Likewise, another two models (model 2 and model 4) have financial inclusion as the dependent construct and telecommunication as an independent construct for Kerala and Bihar, respectively.

6 Analysis

The inner and outer models are the two sub-models in structural equation modeling. The inner model stipulates the relationship between an independent and dependent construct that is known as a structural model. The measurement model specifies the relationship between latent constructs and their indicators, which is an outer model. Both outer and inner models are analyzed to confirm the relationship.

Model 1: Financial inclusion as independent and telecom as dependent construct (Kerala)

and

Model 2: Telecom as independent and financial inclusion as dependent construct (Kerala).

Indicator Reliability

Hulland (1999) recommended that indicator loading should be higher than 0.70. An indicator loading of 0.40 is also acceptable for exploratory research. The item with loading ranging from 0.40 to 0.70 should be reviewed and may be retained if they improve the value of composite reliability.

Table 1 summarizes factor loading of the indicators of model 1 as well as model 2. 'DB', 'DO', 'FUCC', 'WMS', UMFW', 'NFAC', and 'NFRC' with a factor loading of 0.322, 0.260, 0.217, 0.659, 0.371, 0.330, and 0.418, respectively, are eliminated due to lower indicator loadings. The deletion of the indicators mentioned above from the reflective scale leads to significant changes in the composite reliability and convergent validity of the latent constructs. Out of the 38 indicators, nine are dropped from the original model to improve reliability and validity.

Internal Consistency Reliability

Composite reliability is the measure of internal consistency reliability. Composite reliability should be higher than 0.70, and 0.60 is considered acceptable for exploratory research (Bagozzi and Yi, 1988). Table 1 depicts the composite reliability of all the constructs of model 1 and model 2. The constructs AUTS, AWTS, UTS, AUBS, AWBS, and UBS with a value of 0.827, 0.896, 0.820, 0.938, 0.896, and 0.827, respectively, are above the stated limit.

Convergent Validity

For assessing convergent validity, the value of the average variance extracted (AVE) for each latent construct should be examined. According to Bagozzi and Yi (1988), the average variance extracted should be higher than 0.50, which means that the latent variables capture at least 50% of measurement variance. Table 1 also represents the value of the average variance extracted for model 1 and model 2. All the constructs have a value higher than 0.50. The ability to use banking services (AUBS), ability to use telecom services (AUTS), awareness about banking services (AWBS), awareness about telecom services (AWTS), usage of banking services (UBS), and usage of telecom services (UTS) with AVE value of 0.792, 0.707, 0.524, 0.552, 0.547, and 0.552, respectively, are above the threshold limit.

Discriminant Validity

Discriminant validity is the degree to which the measure of a single construct is distinct from the other constructs of a model (Campbell and Fiske, 1959). 'Square

Table 1 Accuracy analysis statistics of model 1 and model 2

Constructs	Indicators loadings			Composite reliability		AVE	
	Indicators	Original	Modified	Original	Modified	Original	Modified
UBS	DB	0.322		0.771	0.827	0.329	0.547
	DO	0.26					
	DS	0.601	0.702				
	FUAC	0.793	0.811				
	FUCC	0.217					
	WMATM	0.798	0.791				
	WMC	0.593	0.641				
	WMS	0.659	0.659				
AWBS	KAC	0.823	0.823	0.895	0.896	0.524	0.524
	KACC	0.849	0.85				
	KAMF	0.475	0.48				
	KARD	0.687	0.691				
	KASA	0.823	0.824				
	KATM	0.74	0.737				
	KATMS	0.728	0.726				
	KIB	0.585	0.581				
AUBS	NFATM	0.913	0.916	0.952	0.938	0.8	0.792
	NFC	0.928	0.944				
	NFCC	0.739	0.766				
	NFDM	0.93					
	NFWC	0.947	0.921				
AUTS	NFAC	0.33		0.701	0.828	0.4	0.707
	NFAI	0.828	0.848				
	NFRC	0.418					
	NFSP	0.795	0.833				
UTS	UMFE	0.864	0.871	0.787	0.82	0.445	0.542
	UMFG	0.613	0.623				
	UMFI	0.821	0.853				
	UMFW	0.371					
	UMSA	0.539	0.539				
AWTS	MK2G	0.818		0.911	0.896	0.564	0.552
	MKID	0.736	0.756				
	MKMB	0.795	0.784				
	MKMNP	0.62	0.651				
	MKMP	0.668	0.665				

(continued)

Table 1 (continued)

Constructs	Indicators loadings			Composite reliability		AVE	
	Indicators	Original	Modified	Original	Modified	Original	Modified
	MKMS	0.774	0.79				
	MKRO	0.805	0.769				
	MKSS	0.768	0.771				

Source Compiled by Authors

Table 2 Discriminant validity for model 1

	AUBS	AUTS	AWBS	AWTS	UBS	UTS
AUBS	**0.890**					
AUTS	0.693	**0.841**				
AWBS	0.788	0.742	**0.724**			
AWTS	0.729	0.694	0.714	**0.743**		
UBS	0.592	0.582	0.740	0.490	**0.737**	
UTS	0.346	0.427	0.430	0.554	0.500	**0.736**

Source Compiled by Authors

root of each construct's AVE should be higher than the correlation with any other construct' (Fornell and Larcker, 1981). Table 2 captures the discriminant validity of model 1. The values of the square root of the AVE of each construct are marked as bold. For UBS-AWBS, the value is problematic, but it can be ignored (Rahim and Magner, 1995). Hence, the overall discriminant validity of the model is acceptable.

Similarly, Table 3 encapsulates the discriminant validity values for model 2. All the values of correlation among the constructs are less than the value of the square root of AVE. The results confirm the discriminant validity of the constructs.

Table 3 Discriminant validity for model 2

	AUBS	AUTS	AWBS	AWTS	UBS	UTS
AUBS	**0.890**					
AUTS	0.693	**0.841**				
AWBS	0.789	0.743	**0.724**			
AWTS	0.731	0.696	0.718	**0.743**		
UBS	0.554	0.568	0.699	0.413	**0.737**	
UTS	0.369	0.450	0.437	0.591	0.469	**0.736**

Source Compiled by Authors

Multicollinearity

The Variance Inflation Factor (VIF) measures multicollinearity severity in the regression analysis. Hair et al. (2011) recommended the VIF values should be less than or equal to 5. All the values are within a specified limit of 5 for VIF (inner) as well as VIF (outer). Two indicators 'MK2G' and 'NFDM' with a factor loading of 0.818 and 0.929, respectively, are removed from the modified model due to high VIF value. Hence, from the results, it can be concluded that there is a low level of collinearity among the predictor variables.

Path Analysis

The path of the current model is examined through bootstrapping in smartPLS that represents the hypothesized relationships between the constructs. Out of nine paths, four paths are statistically significant at a significance level of 5 percent, with a T statistics value greater than 1.96. Table 4 shows the significance of path coefficients.

There is a significant impact of the ability to use banking services on the awareness about telecom services, the awareness about banking services on the ability to use telecom services, the awareness about banking services on the awareness about telecom services, and the ability to use banking services on the usage of telecom services.

Similarly, Table 5 shows the path coefficient. Out of nine paths, six are significant

Table 4 Path coefficient for model 1

	Original sample (O)	Sample mean (M)	Standard deviation (STDEV)	T statistics (|O/STDEV|)	*P* values
AUBS → AUTS	0.284	0.275	0.163	1.744	0.082
AUBS → AWTS	0.442	0.441	0.131	3.385	0.001
AUBS → UTS	0.010	−0.012	0.106	0.090	0.928
AWBS → AUTS	0.469	0.475	0.139	3.371	0.001
AWBS → AWTS	0.434	0.442	0.161	2.692	0.007
AWBS → UTS	0.127	0.140	0.159	0.796	0.427
UBS → AUTS	0.067	0.058	0.124	0.540	0.589
UBS → AWTS	−0.092	−0.107	0.121	0.763	0.446
UBS → UTS	0.401	0.418	0.122	3.288	0.001

Source Compiled by Authors

Table 5 Path coefficient for model 2

	Original sample (O)	Sample mean (M)	Standard deviation (STDEV)	T statistics (|O/STDEV|)	*P* values
AUTS → AUBS	0.366	0.347	0.123	2.968	0.003
AUTS → AWBS	0.472	0.477	0.128	3.681	0.000
AUTS → UBS	0.521	0.521	0.153	3.403	0.001
AWTS → AUBS	0.547	0.537	0.133	4.104	0.000
AWTS → AWBS	0.394	0.376	0.155	2.547	0.011
AWTS → UBS	−0.136	−0.150	0.181	0.749	0.454
UTS → AUBS	−0.119	−0.099	0.092	1.296	0.195
UTS → AWBS	−0.008	0.014	0.091	0.085	0.932
UTS → UBS	0.315	0.334	0.123	2.566	0.011

Source Compiled by Authors

in model 2 at a 5% significance level. The ability to use telecom services affects the ability to use banking services, awareness about banking services, and the usage of banking services. Similarly, awareness about telecom services significantly affects the ability to use banking services and awareness about banking services. Likewise, the usage of telecom services affects the usage of banking services. Figures 1 and 2 show the path diagram for model 1 and model 2, respectively.

Coefficient of Determination

The coefficient of determination (R^2) explains the proportion of the variance of one variable that another variable might predict. The value of R^2 ranges from zero to one. The value of 0.25, 0.50, and 0.75 denoted as weak, moderate, and strong, respectively (Hair et al., 2011). Table 6 depicts the value of R^2 for model 1 and model. R^2 values for the construct AUTS, AWTS, and UTS of model 1 are 0.369, 0.273, and 0.138, respectively. AUTS and AWTS have a moderate coefficient of determination, whereas UTS has a weak coefficient of determination. Similarly, R^2 values for the dependent constructs of model 2 are AUBS (0.609), AWBS (0.630), and UBS (0.388). All three constructs have a moderate coefficient of determination.

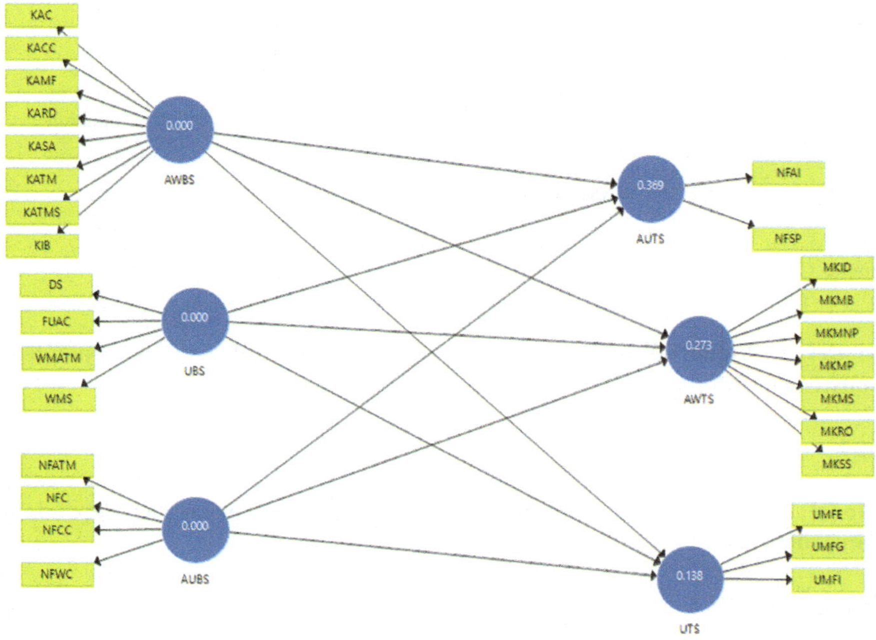

Fig. 1 Path diagram for model 1. *Source* Authors

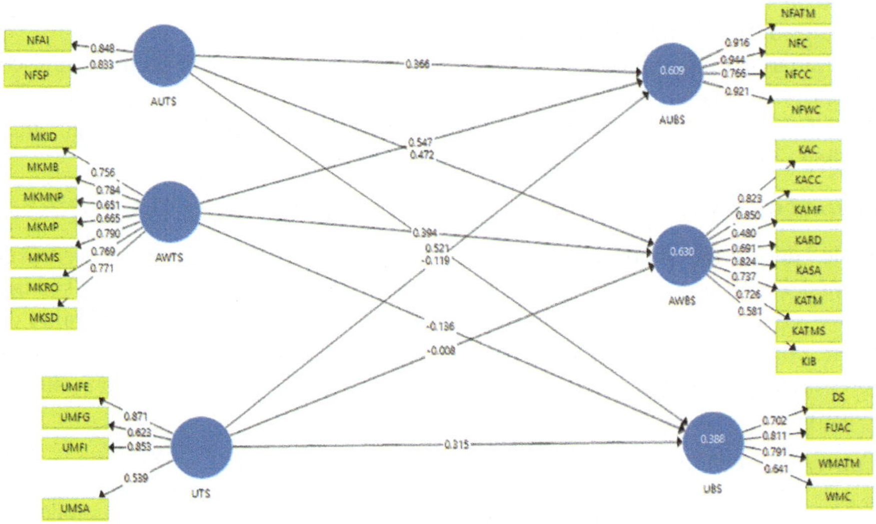

Fig. 2 Path diagram for model 2. *Source* Authors

Table 6 R^2

Model 1			Model 2		
Dependent constructs	R^2	Coefficient of determination	Dependent constructs	R^2	Coefficient of determination
AUTS	0.369	Moderate	AUBS	0.609	Moderate
AWTS	0.273	Moderate	AWBS	0.630	Moderate
UTS	0.138	Weak	UBS	0.388	Moderate

Source Compiled by Authors

Model 3: Financial inclusion as independent and telecom as dependent constructs (Bihar)

and

Model 4: Telecom as independent and financial inclusion as dependent constructs (Bihar).

Indicator Reliability

Table 7 encapsulates the values of the indicator loadings of model 3. All the values of loadings are within the specified limit. FUCC is dropped due to the unit matrix problem. Two indicators, i.e., DS and NFAC, are dropped due to lower indicator loadings of 0.378 and 0.302, respectively.

Similarly, Table 8 indicates the values of the outer loadings of both the revised and original model for model 4. The indicators, i.e., DS (0.337), UMSA (0.347), and NFAC (0.305), are dropped due to lower outer loadings. NFDM having an outer loading of 0.955 is dropped due to high VIF value from the model.

Internal Consistency Reliability

Table 7 depicts the composite reliability for the dependent and independent constructs of model 3. The composite reliability for constructs in the modified model is the above-recommended limit. Likewise, Table 8 represents the composite reliability of all the constructs of the model 4. They satisfy the required threshold value. Therefore, high internal consistency reliability levels were demonstrated among all six constructs.

Convergent Validity.

Tables 7 and 8 represent the value of the average variance extracted for models 3 and 4, respectively. All the constructs have a value higher than 0.50. Thus, all the constructs meet the required limit.

Discriminant Validity

Tables 9 and 10 show the discriminant validity statistics for model 3 and model 4, respectively. The square root of AVE of each construct is represented in bold, and

Table 7 Accuracy analysis statistics for model 3

Constructs	Indicators loadings			Composite reliability		AVE	
	Indicators	Original	Modified	Original	Modified	Original	Modified
UBS	DB	0.803	0.801	0.844	0.857	0.458	0.514
	DO	0.539	0.566				
	DS	0.378					
	FUAC	0.634	0.658				
	FUCC						
	WMATM	0.922	0.915				
	WMC	0.428	0.432				
	WMS	0.821	0.816				
AWBS	KAC	0.856	0.853	0.938	0.927	0.631	0.62
	KACC	0.649	0.654				
	KAMF	0.589	0.598				
	KARD	0.868	0.867				
	KASA	0.863	0.859				
	KATM	0.83	0.826				
	KATMS	0.888	0.889				
	KIB	0.659	0.667				
AUBS	NFATM	0.95	0.941	0.909	0.888	0.683	0.637
	NFC	0.729	0.782				
	NFCC	0.395	0.445				
	NFDM	0.953					
	NFWC	0.958	0.923				
AUTS	NFAC	0.302		0.869	0.897	0.547	0.674
	NFAI	0.907	0.924				
	NFRC	0.59	0.562				
	NFSP	0.833	0.839				
UTS	UMFE	0.887	0.884	0.89	0.89	0.637	0.637
	UMFG	0.907	0.904				
	UMFI	0.933	0.933				
	UMFW	0.765	0.771				
	UMSA	0.343					
AWTS	MK2G	0.913	0.912	0.928	0.928	0.593	0.593
	MKID	0.887	0.886				
	MKMB	0.9	0.899				
	MKMNP	0.65	0.656				
	MKMP	0.551	0.557				

(continued)

Table 7 (continued)

Constructs	Indicators loadings			Composite reliability		AVE	
	Indicators	Original	Modified	Original	Modified	Original	Modified
	MKMS	0.636	0.639				
	MKRO	0.829	0.826				
	MKSS	0.717	0.766				

Source Compiled by Authors

correlation among the constructs is represented as non-diagonal elements. There is some problem in the discriminant validity for AUTS-AUBS, AWBS-AUBS, AWTS-AUBS, AWTS-AUTS, AWTS-AWBS as the values of correlations among the constructs are more than the square root of AVE of the respective construct. It can be accepted (Rahim and Magner, 1995). Rest all the other relationships satisfy the discriminant validity criteria.

Multicollinearity

The indicator 'NFDM' with VIF outer value of 89.662 is dropped from the modified model 3 due to high collinearity. The VIF values in the remaining cases are below 5. Similarly, two indicators, MK2G (12.239) and NFDM (5.96), are dropped due to high VIF values in model 4. All the values of the VIF (outer) and VIF (inner) are within the above-mentioned limit in the modified model. Hence, it can be concluded that there is a low level of collinearity among the predictor variables.

Path Analysis

Table 11 encapsulates the values of path analysis. Model 3 has all the significant paths except 2.

The two insignificant paths are the awareness about banking services with the usage of telecom services and the usage of banking services with the ability to use telecom services. Table 12 shows the path relationship statistics for model 4 also. Out of nine paths, seven paths are significant at a 5% significance level. AUTS positively impacts AUBS. AWTS has a significant impact on AUBS, AWBS, and UBS.

Similarly, UTS positively impacts AUBS, AWBS, and UBS. Also, the relationship of the ability to use telecom services (AUTS) with the awareness about banking services (AWBS) and the usage of banking services is not significant. Figures 3 and 4 indicate the path relationship of model 3 and model 4, respectively.

Coefficient of Determination

Table 13 shows the value of R^2 for Model 3 and Model 4. AUTS and UTS have a moderate coefficient of determination, whereas AWTS with an R^2 value of 0.822 indicates a strong coefficient of determination in Model 3. Similarly, AUBS (0.807) and AWBS (0.798) have a strong coefficient of determination, while the coefficient of determination for UBS (0.693) is moderate in Model 4.

Table 8 Accuracy analysis statistics for model 4

Constructs	Indicators loadings			Composite reliability		AVE	
	Indicators	Original	Modified	Original	Modified	Original	Modified
UBS	DB	0.803	0.801	0.844	0.857	0.458	0.514
	DO	0.539	0.566				
	DS	0.337					
	FUAC	0.64	0.658				
	FUCC						
	WMATM	0.92	0.915				
	WMC	0.422	0.432				
	WMS	0.835	0.816				
AWBS	KAC	0.853	0.853	0.938	0.938	0.632	0.632
	KACC	0.654	0.654				
	KAMF	0.598	0.598				
	KARD	0.867	0.867				
	KASA	0.859	0.859				
	KATM	0.826	0.826				
	KATMS	0.889	0.889				
	KIB	0.666	0.667				
AUBS	NFATM	0.951	0.941	0.909	0.868	0.683	0.636
	NFC	0.726	0.782				
	NFCC	0.387	0.445				
	NFDM	0.955					
	NFWC	0.959	0.923				
AUTS	NFAC	0.305		0.869	0.897	0.547	0.64
	NFAI	0.906	0.924				
	NFRC	0.589	0.562				
	NFSP	0.834	0.839				
UTS	UMFE	0.883	0.884	0.89	0.89	0.636	0.636
	UMFG	0.903	0.904				
	UMFI	0.932	0.933				
	UMFW	0.772	0.771				
	UMSA	0.347					
AWTS	MK2G	0.913	0.912	0.928	0.928	0.593	0.593
	MKID	0.886	0.886				
	MKMB	0.899	0.899				
	MKMNP	0.653	0.656				
	MKMP	0.555	0.557				

(continued)

Table 8 (continued)

Constructs	Indicators loadings			Composite reliability		AVE	
	Indicators	Original	Modified	Original	Modified	Original	Modified
	MKMS	0.637	0.639				
	MKRO	0.827	0.826				
	MKSS	0.758	0.766				

Source Compiled by Authors

Table 9 Discriminant validity for model 3

	AUBS	AUTS	AWBS	AWTS	UBS	UTS
AUBS	**0.798**					
AUTS	0.808	**0.821**				
AWBS	0.890	0.790	**0.787**			
AWTS	0.869	0.846	0.879	**0.770**		
UBS	0.774	0.719	0.736	0.766	**0.737**	
UTS	0.717	0.622	0.658	0.661	0.741	**0.798**

Source Compiled by Authors

Table 10 Discriminant Validity for model 4

	AUBS	AUTS	AWBS	AWTS	UBS	UTS
AUBS	**0.798**					
AUTS	0.811	**0.800**				
AWBS	0.889	0.782	**0.795**			
AWTS	0.870	0.847	0.883	**0.770**		
UBS	0.774	0.712	0.753	0.767	**0.717**	
UTS	0.718	0.602	0.683	0.665	0.744	**0.798**

Source Compiled by Authors

7 Conclusion and Implication

Financially excluded individuals seem unable to engage in the country's social and economic activities, leading to inequalities (Aduda and kalunda, 2012). This study aims to explore the link between financial inclusion and telecommunication. The study has proposed a causal model to show the relationship between the awareness, ability, and usage of banking services with awareness, ability, and usage of telecom services using PLS structural equation modeling. For the study, the primary survey was conducted in Bihar and Kerala states of India.

There is a noticeable impact of telecommunication on financial inclusion in the case of both the states (Kerala and Bihar). The usage of telecom services positively

Table 11 Path coefficient for model 3

	Original sample (O)	Sample mean (M)	Standard deviation (STDEV)	T statistics (|O/STDEV|)	*P* values
AUBS → AUTS	0.394	0.392	0.167	2.360	0.019
AUBS → AWTS	0.314	0.317	0.122	2.562	0.011
AUBS → UTS	0.361	0.349	0.173	2.090	0.037
AWBS → AUTS	0.292	0.293	0.141	2.069	0.039
AWBS → AWTS	0.469	0.470	0.109	4.298	0.000
AWBS → UTS	−0.005	−0.007	0.168	0.028	0.978
UBS → AUTS	0.199	0.200	0.120	1.659	0.098
UBS → AWTS	0.179	0.175	0.078	2.282	0.023
UBS → UTS	0.464	0.483	0.100	4.663	0.000

Source Compiled by Authors

Table 12 Path coefficient for model 4

	Original sample (O)	Sample mean (M)	Standard deviation (STDEV)	T statistics (|O/STDEV|)	*P* values
AUTS → AUBS	0.231	0.233	0.107	2.170	0.030
AUTS → AWBS	0.101	0.097	0.091	1.190	0.268
AUTS → UBS	0.166	0.154	0.141	1.178	0.239
AWTS → AUBS	0.519	0.517	0.119	4.348	0.000
AWTS → AWBS	0.688	0.691	0.103	6.666	0.000
AWTS → UBS	0.354	0.357	0.133	2.667	0.008
UTS → AUBS	0.234	0.233	0.069	3.380	0.001
UTS → AWBS	0.164	0.166	0.072	2.266	0.024
UTS → UBS	0.408	0.420	0.073	5.580	0.000

Source Compiled by Authors

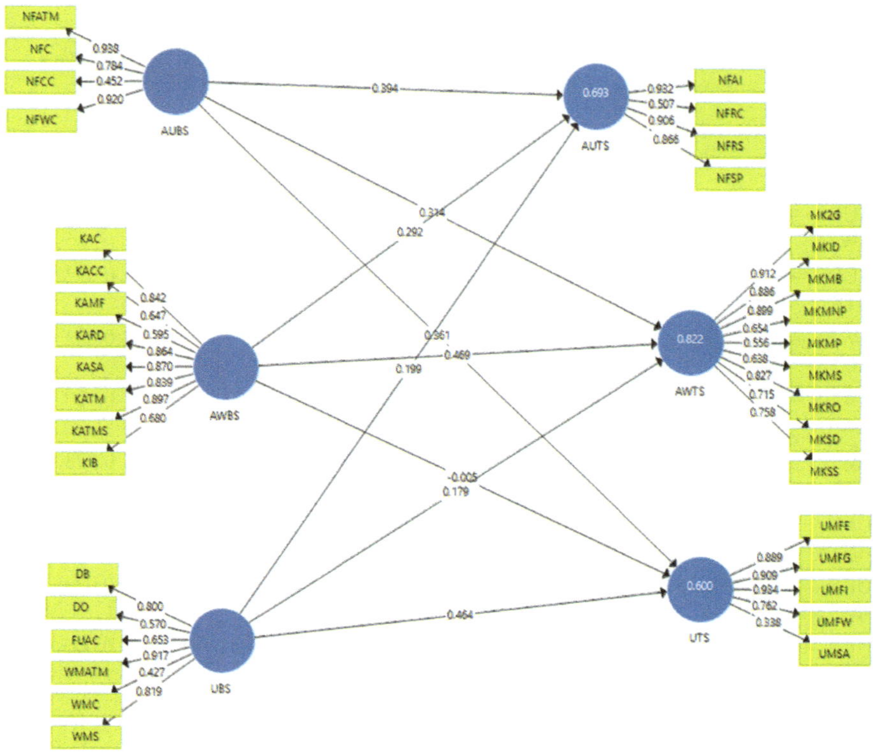

Fig. 3 Path diagram for model 3. *Source* Authors

impacts the usage of banking services. The ability to use telecom services positively impacts the awareness about banking services, the ability to use banking services, and the usage of banking services. Similarly, the awareness about telecom services positively impacts the awareness about banking services and the ability to use banking services. Out of nine, six paths are significant for both the states. Thus, the relation is more or less the same irrespective of the stage of development in both the states.

Similarly, the impact of financial inclusion on telecom is visible in both states. The ability to use banking services and awareness about banking services positively impacts the awareness of telecom services. In the same way, awareness about banking services impacts the ability to use telecom services, whereas the ability to use banking services impacts the usage of telecom services. Hence, four paths are significant in both states. Therefore, the results are approximately similar irrespective of the level of development in the states.

The results point toward the need for rigorous and cooperative steps by both the industries as there is a causal relation between telecom and financial inclusion in both the states. It indicates that despite the difference in the development of the state, the impact is apparent. Although the impact of telecom on financial inclusion is comparatively more, the reverse is also significant.

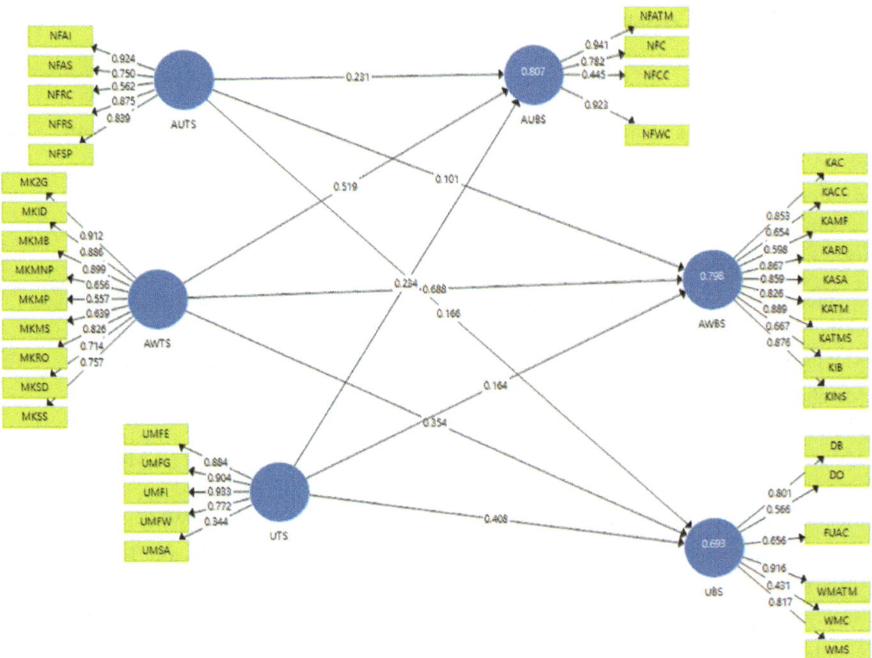

Fig. 4 Path diagram for model 4. *Source* Authors

Table 13 R^2 for model 3 and model 4

Model 3			Model 4		
Dependent constructs	R^2	Coefficient of determination	Dependent constructs	R^2	Coefficient of determination
AUTS	0.693	Moderate	AUBS	0.807	Strong
AWTS	0.822	Strong	AWBS	0.798	Strong
UTS	0.600	Moderate	UBS	0.693	Moderate

Source Compiled by Authors

If the banks/financial institutes and telecom companies strategically support each other, it will certainly pay them back. The banks can help telecom players in several ways, for instance, financing smartphones on affordable and customized installments, playing an influential role in telecom infrastructure, mainly in rural areas. The banks joining telecom companies can initiate financial awareness and literacy programs in villages.

Appendix 1 (Constructs with Their Respective Indicators)

Telecom constructs and their indicators	Financial inclusion constructs and their indicators
Awareness about telecom services (AWTS)	*Usage of banking services (UBS)*
Member having knowledge of 2G/3G (MK2G)	Deposited by business or employment (DB)
Member having knowledge of ISD (MKID)	Deposited by self (DS)
Member having knowledge of MB/GB (MKMB)	Frequency of using ATM card (FUAC)
Member having knowledge of SMS (MKMS)	Deposited by others (DO)
Member having knowledge of MNP (MKMNP)	Withdraw money by ATM (WMATM)
Member having knowledge of mobile banking (MKMP)	Withdraw money by check (WMC)
Member having knowledge of STD (MKSS)	Withdraw money by self (WMS)
Member having knowledge of roaming (MKNP)	Frequency of using credit card (FUCC)
Ability to use telecom services (AUTS)	*Ability to use banking services (AUBS)*
Number of family member able to call (NFAC)	Number of family can use check (NFC)
Number of family member able to receive call (NFRC)	Number of family member can use ATM (NFATM)
Number of family member able to send SMS (FASP)	Number of family member can use credit card (NFCC)
Number of family member able to use internet (NFAI)	Number of family member can withdraw cash (NFWC)
Usage of telecom services (UTS)	Number of family can deposit money (NFDM)
Work-related use of mobile phone (UMFW)	*Awareness about banking services (AWBS)*
Use of mobile phone for entertainment (UMFE)	Knowledge about check (KAC)
Use of mobile phone for internet (UMFI)	Knowledge about credit card (KACC)
Use of mobile phone for social activities (UMSA)	Knowledge about mutual fund (KAMF)
Use of mobile phone for games (UMFG)	Knowledge about RD&FD (KARD)
	Knowledge about saving account (KASA)
	Knowledge about ATM/debit card (KATM)
	Knowledge about ATM services (KATMS)
	Knowledge about internet banking (KIB)

References

Adeola, O., & Evans, O. (2017). Financial inclusion, financial development, and economic diversification in Nigeria. *The Journal of Developing Areas, 51*(3), 1–15. http://dx.doi.org/10.1353/jda.2017.0057.

Aduda, J., & Kalunda, E. (2012). Financial inclusion and financial sector stability with reference to Kenya: A review of literature. *Journal of Applied Finance and Banking, 2*(6), 95–120.

Andrianaivo, M., & Kpodar, K. (2012). Mobile phones, financial inclusion, and growth. *Review of Economics and Institutions, 3*(2), 1-30. https://www.rei.unipg.it/rei/article/view/75.

Babajide, A. A., Adegboye, F. B., & Omankhanlen, A. E. (2015). Financial inclusion and economic growth in Nigeria. *International Journal of Economics and Financial Issues, 5*(3), 629–637. http://eprints.covenantuniversity.edu.ng/id/eprint/5426.

Bagli, S., & Dutta, P. (2012). A study of financial inclusion in India. *Radix International Journal of Economics & Business Management, 1*(8), 1–18.

Bagozzi, R. P., & Yi, Y. (1988). On the evaluation of structural equation models. *Journal of the Academy of Marketing Science, 16*(1), 74–94. https://doi.org/10.1007/BF02723327.

Campbell, D. T., & Fiske, D. W. (1959). Convergent and discriminant validation by the multitrait-multimethod matrix. *Psychological Bulletin, 56*(2), 81–105. https://doi.org/10.1037/h0046016.

Chakrabarty, K. C. (2011). Financial inclusion. In *Seminar on financial inclusion: Partnership between banks, MFIs and communities, New Delhi* (Vol. 14).

Chakravarty, S. R., & Pal, R. (2013). Financial inclusion in India: An axiomatic approach. *Journal of Policy Modeling, 35*(5), 813–837. https://doi.org/10.1016/j.jpolmod.2012.12.007.

Chatterjee, A., & Das, S. (2019). Information communication technology diffusion and financial inclusion: An inter-state analysis for India. *Innovation and Development*, 1–23. https://doi.org/10.1080/2157930X.2019.1678803.

Chikalipah, S. (2017). What determines financial inclusion in Sub-Saharan Africa? *African Journal of Economic and Management Studies, 8*(1), 8–18. https://doi.org/10.1108/AJEMS-01-2016-0007.

CRISIL. (2015). CRISIL Inclusix: An index to measure India's progress on financial inclusion. Available at: https://www.crisil.com/content/dam/crisil/crisil-foundation/generic-pdf/CRISIL-Inclusix-Volume-III.pdf.

Edwards, J. R., & Bagozzi, R. P. (2000). On the nature and direction of relationships between constructs and measures. *Psychological Methods, 5*(2), 155–174. https://doi.org/10.1037/1082-989X.5.2.155.

Fanta, A. B., & Makina, D. (2019). The relationship between technology and financial inclusion: Cross-sectional evidence. In D. Makina (Ed.), *Extending financial inclusion in Africa* (pp. 211–230). Academic Press. https://doi.org/10.1016/B978-0-12-814164-9.00010-4.

Fornell, C., & Larcker, D. F. (1981). Structural equation models with unobservable variables and measurement error: Algebra and statistics. *Journal of marketing research, 18*(3), 382–388. https://doi.org/10.1177%2F002224378101800313.

Hair, J. F., Ringle, C. M., & Sarstedt, M. (2011). PLS-SEM: Indeed a silver bullet. *Journal of Marketing Theory and Practice, 19*(2), 139–152. https://doi.org/10.2753/MTP1069-6679190202.

Hair, J. F., Sarstedt, M., Pieper, T. M., & Ringle, C. M. (2012). The use of partial least squares structural equation modeling in strategic management research: A review of past practices and recommendations for future applications. *Long Range Planning, 45*(5–6), 320–340. https://doi.org/10.1016/j.lrp.2012.09.008.

Hulland, J. (1999). Use of partial least squares (PLS) in strategic management research: A review of four recent studies. *Strategic Management Journal, 20*(2) 195–204. https://doi.org/10.1002/(SICI)1097-0266(199902)20:2%3C195::AID-SMJ13%3E3.0.CO;2-7.

Kaur, K., & Malhotra, N. (2014). Telecommunication and economic growth in India: Causality analysis. *International Journal of Research in Business Management, 2*(5), 31–46.

Ketkar, S. P., Shankar, R., & Banwet, D. K. (2014). Telecom KYC and mobile banking regulation: An exploratory study. *Journal of Banking Regulation, 15*(2), 117–128. https://doi.org/10.1057/jbr.2013.1.

Mishra, V., & Bisht, S. S. (2013). Mobile banking in a developing economy: A customer-centric model for policy formulation. *Telecommunications Policy, 37*(6–7), 503–514. https://doi.org/10.1016/j.telpol.2012.10.004.

Nino-Zarazua, M. M., & Copestake, J. (2008). Financial inclusion, vulnerability, and mental models: from physical access to effective use of financial services in a low-income area of Mexico City. *Savings and Development, 32*(4), 353–379. https://www.jstor.org/stable/41406477.

PMJDY. (2020). Progress Report. Available at: https://www.pmjdy.gov.in/account.

Rahim, M. A., & Magner, N. R. (1995). Confirmatory factor analysis of the styles of handling interpersonal conflict: First-order factor model and its invariance across groups. *Journal of Applied Psychology, 80*(1), 122-132. https://doi.org/10.1037/0021-9010.80.1.122.

Ringle, C. M., Wende, S., & Becker, J. M. (2015). SmartPLS 3. *Boenningstedt: SmartPLS GmbH,* https://www.smartpls.com.

Sarstedt, M., Ringle, C. M., Smith, D., Reams, R., & Hair, J. F., Jr. (2014). Partial least squares structural equation modeling (PLS-SEM): A useful tool for family business researchers. *Journal of Family Business Strategy, 5*(1), 105–115. https://doi.org/10.1016/j.jfbs.2014.01.002.

Scott, N., Garforth, C., Jain, R., Mascarenhas, O., & McKemey, K. (2005). The economic impact of telecommunications on rural livelihoods and poverty reduction: A study of rural communities in India (Gujarat), Mozambique and Tanzania. Commonwealth Telecommunications Organization for UK Department for International Development.

Siddiqui, T. A., & Siddiqui, K. I. (2018). Scrutinizing Status of Financial Inclusion using Structural Equation Modeling. *Asian Journal of Research in Business Economics and Management, 8*(1), 90–100. https://doi.org/10.5958/2249-7307.2018.00008.7.

Siddiqui, T. A., & Siddiqui, K. I. (2020). FinTech in India: An analysis on impact of telecommunication on financial inclusion. *Strategic Change, 29*(3), 321–330. https://doi.org/10.1002/jsc.2331.

Siddiqui. T. A., & Siddiqui. K. I. (2017). Determining effect of telecom services on financial inclusion in Haryana using SEM. In M. K. Barua, U. Lenka, K. V. Pandya & P. N. Sinha (Eds.), *International Conference on Research and Business Sustainability* (pp. 436–441). New Delhi, Delhi: Excellent Publishing House.

Stephen, N., & Tom, T. R. (2015). The Role of Cooperative Banks in Financial Inclusion. *IUP Journal of Bank Management, 14*(3), 55-64.

GSMA (2017). The Mobile Economy. Available at: https://www.gsmaintelligence.com/research/?file=9e927fd6896724e7b26f33f61db5b9d5&download.

TRAI. (2020). Available at: https://main.trai.gov.in/sites/default/files/PR_No.17of2020.pdf.

Wang, X., & Guan, J. (2017). Financial inclusion: Measurement, spatial effects and influencing factors. *Applied Economics, 49*(18), 1751–1762. https://doi.org/10.1080/00036846.2016.1226488.

Chapter 20
Environmental Efficiency and Trade Theory: Evidence from Indian Metal Sector

M. Prasad and T. Mishra

1 Introduction

Metal sector is one of the important sectors to help India improve the share of the manufacturing sector in economy's output to 25% by 2022. The sector has potential to grow with low average per capita ferrous and non-ferrous metal consumption. At present, the sector contributes more than 2% of the nation's GDP and is the third largest producer of crude steel in the world (The Energy and Resources Institute, 2013). The sector has an output multiplier effect of 1.4× on GDP and increase employment by multiplier effect of 6.8× (Ministry of Steel, 2012).

Going forward, Ministry of Steel and Mines, is targeting a production of 300 million tons of steel by 2025 (Ministry of Steel, 2012). Further, in order to accomplish government's target of 100% village electrification, infrastructure development of railways, irrigation, will lead to higher demand of metal products such as poles, structural steel, wires, electrical steel. Apart from the significant potential to contribute towards economic development, the sector is also a key contributor to the nation's emission profile. As per the sectoral emission inventory, metal sector and others (cement, refineries and petrochemicals, fertilizer) contribute more than half of the industrial emissions (like CO_2, SO_2, NO_x and $PM_{2.5}$) in India over last the several decades (Sadavarte & Venkataraman, 2014). The sector is highest in terms of energy intensity, consuming 15.01% of total industrial energy in India (Central Statistics Office, 2017) and meets its most of the energy requirement from fossil fuels that add to industrial emissions. Also, the firms in the metal sector are classified under the red category by pollution control boards on account of high pollution intensity (Ministry of Environment and Forest, 2015).

M. Prasad (✉) · T. Mishra
India Institute of Technology, Bombay, India
e-mail: mousamiprasad@gmail.com

T. Mishra
e-mail: truptimishra@iitb.ac.in

P. Lakhanpal et al. (eds.), *Trade, Investment and Economic Growth*,
https://doi.org/10.1007/978-981-33-6973-3_20

Managing economic growth along with environmental concerns is, therefore, a challenge in energy-intensive sectors like metal. On one hand, there are proponents of increasing growth by economic integration in the form of foreign direct investment and trade; while on the other hand, the evidence of the impact of the economic integration of environmental issues remains an area of debate. Economic integration is defined as the free flow of (a) goods and services and (b) capital. One of the most commonly used indicators for economic integration is trade (Marginean, 2015; OECD, 2018). However, the empirical evidence of trade on firms' environmental impacts remains mixed in the case of developed countries and less investigated in the case of developing nations. In India, Mukhopadhyay and Chakraborty (2005) found that trade liberalization did not result in pollution-intensive economic growth using country-level data. A more recent study by Jayanthakumaran et al. (2012), however, did not find a clear relationship between emission intensity and trade either in the short run or in the long run.

This study, therefore, examines the impact of economic integration, indicated by trade and environmental efficiency of firms in one of the most energy and pollution-intensive sector. Environmental efficiency measures the firms' impact on the environment and indicates the environmental performance of firms.

The remainder of the paper is organized as follows. The next section presents the literature review followed by methodology in Sect. 3. Section 4 provides the results and discussion, and finally, conclusions is discussed in Sect. 6.

2 Literature Review

The literature on the role of trade suggests that there exists a mixed relationship between exports and environmental efficiency (Taskin & Zaim, 2001). A literature review of previous empirical findings suggests that some studies have found, trade led by exports, promote accelerated extraction of natural resources and increase energy consumption, to support increased production demand. Also, the firms in countries with stringent environmental regulations may shift some production to the countries with laxity in the environmental regulations. This effect is known as 'pollution haven' hypothesis, and the growth resulting from such expansion is pollution-intensive growth (Jayanthakumaran et al., 2012; Mukhopadhyay & Chakraborty, 2005). According to this view, trade is likely to have a negative impact on environmental efficiency. However, some studies suggest a positive link between exports and environmental efficiency. As per these studies, trade increases competitiveness of firms as foreign customers may put pressure them to adopt environmental management practices. This influences firms to make optimum utilization of resources like energy, which can improve their environmental efficiency (Taskin & Zaim, 2001).

In India, the empirical evidence on the role of trade is mixed. However, many studies have found that foreign customers create market pressure for firms to adopt environmental practices (Sandhu et al., 2012; Singh et al., 2015). This suggests that firms engaging in trade are likely to have better environmental practices, which will reduce their environmental impacts and improve efficiency. Also, the nation addresses the environmental concerns by (a) command and control mechanism like Air Act, Water Act that mandates firms to emit within prescribed limits; (b) disclosure programs like social responsibility disclosure report, business responsibility report and (c) market-based instruments like perform-achieve-trade that requires firms to reduce their energy intensity within a given time period. These policies may act as a deterrent for firms looking to use India as a pollution haven. With this background, we posit a positive relationship between trade and environmental efficiency.

3 Research Methodology

This is a descriptive study examining the impact of trade on environmental efficiency of firms in an energy-intensive sector: metal sector. The unit of analysis is firm.

3.1 Data Sample

Metal firms were classified based on the National Industry Classification (NIC). It includes firms from iron and steel sector, non-ferrous and metal casting. Out of this, we shortlisted the metal firms based on the following criteria:

(a) The firms should have published annual reports during the financial year 2006–07 to 2014–15.
(b) The firms should have disclosed information on fuel-wise energy consumption.

Firms that were incorporated between 2006–07 and 2014–15 were excluded to keep the firms the same over the study period. This was done to enable firm-wise efficiency comparison over the years. The process resulted in unbalanced panel data. The details of year-wise sample firms are presented in Table 1.

The period of study was 2006–07 to 2014–15, to provide a comprehensive dataset for examining the relationship. Also, the selected time period covers the major environmental policies that impacted metal sectors.

3.2 Variables and Their Measurement

Trade: Previous studies in the Indian context suggest that foreign customers create market pressure for firms and influence them to adopt environmental standard/practices. This is likely to reduce emissions and improve environmental efficiency. The trade variable is measured as a dummy variable that takes a value of 1 if the firm has exports or imports in that year and 0 otherwise.

Table 1 Study sample description

No. of firms	2006–07	2007–08	2008–09	2009–10	2010–11	2011–12	2012–13	2013–14	2014–15
Manufacture of basic iron and steel (241)[a]	76	77	77	77	77	77	73	69	27
Manufacture of basic precious and other non-ferrous metals (242)[b]	18	18	18	18	18	18	18	18	9
Casting of metals (243)	26	26	26	26	26	26	25	22	12
Total	121	121	121	121	121	121	116	109	48

[a]Includes one public sector unit: Steel Authority of India (SAIL)
[b]Includes one public sector unit: (National Aluminium Company Limited (NALCO)
Source Authors summary

Environmental Efficiency: We estimated the environmental efficiency of the firms using output distance function and stochastic frontier analysis. Translog production function was used to model the multiple outputs and multiple input production technology. The output was measured in terms of good output: sales and bad output: emissions. The input variables were identified as labour, capital, raw materials and energy consumption. The data for the firm variables were taken from CMIE Prowess. However, the data for bad output: emissions were calculated from energy consumption as there is no firm-level emission inventory in India. The emission inventory was, therefore built for the sample firms over the given period. The average emission coefficient, considering the national fuel characteristics, is presented in Table 2.

These emission coefficients were multiplied with the type of fuels to arrive at emissions. The emissions were then used in the production function as a measure of bad output to estimate environmental efficiency. Environmental efficiency is estimated under varying assumptions of undesirable output. The details of the efficiency models are used in given below:

(a) EE1—estimates environmental efficiency under the assumption of time-varying inefficiency and uses CO_2 emission as undesirable output.
(b) EE2—estimates environmental efficiency under the assumption of time-varying inefficiency and uses CO_2, SO_2, NO_x, $PM_{2.5}$ emission as undesirable output.

Apart from the main variables of interest, trade and environmental efficiency, the firm heterogeneity literature suggests that characteristics of individual firms are also an important aspect in influencing their emission/pollution profile (Holladay, 2010). To control for this, we include firm variables like size, asset age, research and development intensity, sales-asset ratio, labour productivity, voluntary compliance to the environmental management system (EMS) and year dummies. These firm characteristics have been used most commonly in the literature on environmental efficiency and energy efficiency. The description of these variables along with their measurement is discussed below and is similar to Prasad and Mishra (2017).

Size: Large firms can adopt technological changes and environmental policies to lower their impact on the environment as they have the resources. We measure size as the natural log of sales.

Table 2 Average emission coefficient

Emissions	Solid	Liquid	Gas	Electricity
Unit	Ton	Ton	Cubic metre	MWh
CO_2 (ton)	2.242	3.089	0.002	0.675
SO_2 (kg)	6.84	19.23	19.23	7.18
NO_x (kg)	2.46	7.32	7.32	4.3
$PM_{2.5}$ (kg)	2.13	0.29	0.29	4.74

Source CO_2 – Prasad and Mishra (2017)
SO_2, NO_x, $PM_{2.5}$—(Guttikunda et al., 2014; Mittal et al., 2012; Sadavarte & Venkataraman, 2014)

Asset age—Asset age influences the emission profile, with older assets, or firms with higher asset age being associated with higher emissions as compared to young (new) plants (Khanna & Kumar, 2011). We measure the age of assets as total assets of the firm (current assets plus net plant and machinery, net land and buildings plus other non-current assets) divided by its gross assets. Gross assets include total assets plus accumulated depreciation on property, plant and equipment.

Research and Development—Firms that invest in research and development (R&D) have higher technical knowledge regarding their operations and are more innovative (Khanna & Anton, 2002). A dummy variable 1 and 0 to indicate the presence of research costs incurred by a firm is used.

Labour productivity—Labour productivity is complementary to a decreasing firm's emission intensity as higher labour productivity indicates skilled labour, which is more conversant with energy efficiency and therefore may contribute towards lower emissions (Mandal & Madheswaran, 2010).

Sales-asset ratio—Sales-asset ratio indicates capital intensity or capacity utilization (Khanna & Kumar, 2011). It indicates the efficiency with which the firm can use its asset base to generate sales. Sales-asset ratio is measured as sales divided by total assets (Khanna & Kumar, 2011).

ISO 14001—ISO 14001 represents EMS. This is a binary variable and is taken as 1 if at least one plant of the firm had ISO certification in the particular year.

3.3 Method

The regression model is specified as.

$$\text{Environmental Efficiency}_{it} = \beta_0 + \beta(\text{Trade}_{it}) + q_{it}\beta + \nu_i + \eta_{it}, i = 1, \ldots, N \text{ firms, where } \beta_0 \text{ is} \quad t = 1, \ldots, T \text{ years}$$

constant,

Trade_{it} indicates exports and imports of firm *i* in year *t*,

q_{it} is vector of observed exogenous firm-specific control variables like size, asset age, research and development, labour productivity, sales-asset ratio, EMS for firm *i* in year *t*.

ν_i is firm fixed effect,

η_{it} is error term with zero mean and constant variance.

4 Results and Findings

Table 3 presents descriptive statistics. The mean environmental efficiency of the metal sector was estimated at 72–77%, suggesting a significant potential to reduce environmental impact and improve their efficiency.

Table 3 Descriptive statistics

Variables	Mean	SD	Min	Max
EMS (Dummy)	0.42	0.49	0.00	1.00
Age of assets	0.82	0.11	0.25	1.00
Sales-asset ratio	1.25	0.80	0.00	7.31
Labour productivity	59.68	153.29	0.02	3652.56
Size (log)	8.29	2.00	4.04	13.93
R&D (Dummy)	0.21	0.40	0.00	1.00
Environmental Efficiency[a]				
EE1 (CO_2, time-varying inefficiency)	0.77	0.16	0.16	0.99
EE2 (CO_2, SO_2, NO_x, $PM_{2.5}$; time-varying inefficiency)	0.75	0.16	0.18	0.98

[a]The environmental efficiency measurement considers varying assumptions to examine the sensitivity of the results to the model specification. First model (EE1) assumed CO_2 as undesirable output, and while in second model, (EE2) SO_2, NO_x and $PM_{2.5}$ were introduced as additional emissions apart from CO_2 as undesirable output. The estimation of environmental efficiency is done using output distance approach and translog stochastic frontier
Source Authors estimates

As the dependent variable ranges from 0 to 1, and the data is the panel in nature, Tobit panel regression is used. However, for comparison purposes and robustness check, fixed effect regression is also estimated. In the present study, the estimates from fixed effect regression provide baseline results. Further, it helps to examine whether the model specification influences the results. The regression results are presented in Table 4. The results find that export has a significant positive coefficient. This suggests that firms with exports have higher environmental efficiency.

The estimates of panel Tobit regression are presented in Model 3 and Model 4 using EE1 and EE2 as a dependent variable, respectively. Export has a significant positive coefficient under both Model 3 and Model 4, suggesting the positive impact of trade on environmental efficiency. This supports the initial results of the fixed effect model.

In addition to the linear relationship examined in Model 1 to Model 4, the nonlinear relationship of the control variables is considered that might influence the relationship. Past studies have found support for the nonlinear relationship between firm size and environment performance (Mandal & Madheswaran, 2010), labour productivity and environmental impact (CO_2 emission) (Marin & Mazzanti, 2009), sales-asset ratio and environmental performance (Fujii et al., 2013). The results of fixed effect regression and Tobit regression are presented in Table 5 as Model 5 to Model 8.

The estimates presented in Model 5 and Model 6 pertain to fixed effect regression, and estimates in Model 7 and Model 8 are obtained from Tobit regression. The coefficient of export is significantly positive across all the models, suggesting that trade is associated with better environmental efficiency. This supports the initial results from the linear relationship in Table 3 and the hypothesis that there is a positive relationship between trade and environmental efficiency.

Table 4 Regression results: linear relationship

	Fixed effect regression		Tobit regression	
	DV: EE1	DV: EE2	DV: EE1	DV: EE2
	Model 1	Model 2	Model 3	Model 4
Trade	0.00687**	0.00427**	0.00715**	0.00436**
	(0.00331)	(0.00185)	(0.00327)	(0.00183)
EMS (0/1)	0.0151***	0.00585**	0.0150***	0.00590**
	(0.00449)	(0.00251)	(0.00442)	(0.00248)
Labour productivity (log)	0.00418	0.00256	0.00254	0.00214
	(0.00290)	(0.00162)	(0.00285)	(0.00160)
Sales-asset Ratio	−0.0111***	−0.00570***	−0.0101***	−0.00546***
	(0.00259)	(0.00144)	(0.00254)	(0.00143)
Asset age	0.0137	0.0124	0.00846	0.0112
	(0.0154)	(0.00862)	(0.0150)	(0.00849)
R&D (0/1)	0.00105	0.000373	0.00134	0.000470
	(0.00437)	(0.00244)	(0.00431)	(0.00241)
D1	−0.00795***	−0.00588***	−0.00822***	−0.00590***
	(0.00299)	(0.00167)	(0.00295)	(0.00165)
D2	−0.0202***	−0.0141***	−0.0208***	−0.0142***
	(0.00314)	(0.00175)	(0.00308)	(0.00173)
D3	−0.0335***	−0.0226***	−0.0344***	−0.0227***
	(0.00337)	(0.00188)	(0.00329)	(0.00186)
D4	−0.0461***	−0.0305***	−0.0471***	−0.0306***
	(0.00370)	(0.00207)	(0.00357)	(0.00203)
D5	−0.0621***	−0.0401***	−0.0633***	−0.0403***
	(0.00391)	(0.00218)	(0.00375)	(0.00214)
D6	−0.0800***	−0.0507***	−0.0815***	−0.0509***
	(0.00417)	(0.00233)	(0.00399)	(0.00228)
D7	−0.102***	−0.0627***	−0.103***	−0.0629***
	(0.00437)	(0.00244)	(0.00418)	(0.00239)
D8	−0.124***	−0.0763***	−0.126***	−0.0765***
	(0.00530)	(0.00296)	(0.00509)	(0.00290)
Size (log)	−0.0285***	−0.0177***	−0.0273***	−0.0176***
	(0.00308)	(0.00172)	(0.00283)	(0.00166)
Constant	1.031***	0.912***	1.027***	0.912***
	(0.0252)	(0.0140)	(0.0270)	(0.0194)
Observations	1001	1001	1001	1001
R^2	0.812	0.844		

(continued)

Table 4 (continued)

	Fixed effect regression		Tobit regression	
	DV: EE1	DV: EE2	DV: EE1	DV: EE2
	Model 1	Model 2	Model 3	Model 4
Number of com	121	121	121	121

Model 1 and Model 3: Environmental efficiency (under assumption of time-varying inefficiency using CO_2 emission as undesirable output) = $a_1 + B_1$ ISO 14001 + B_2 Research and Development Expenditure + B_3 Labour Productivity + B_4 Asset Age + B_5 Sales-asset Ratio + B_6 Year Dummies + B_7 Size + B_8 Trade

Model 2 and Model 4: Environmental efficiency (under assumption of time-varying inefficiency using CO_2, SO_2, NO_x, $PM_{2.5}$ emission as undesirable output) = $a_1 + B_1$ ISO 14001 + B_2 Research and Development Expenditure + B_3 Labour Productivity + B_4 Asset Age + B_5 Sales-asset Ratio + B_6 Year Dummies + B_7 Size + B_8 Trade

Standard errors in parentheses

*** $p < 0.01$, ** $p < 0.05$, * $p < 0.1$

Source Authors estimates

Apart from the trade variable, the control variable like EMS was found to have a significant positive relationship. Asset age, R&D expenses, sales-asset ratio were not significant, while labour productivity was associated with environmental efficiency in a U shape relationship. The study has implications for corporate managers and policymakers.

5 Conclusion

With increasing globalization, firms are engaged in trade with other nations. While the impact of trade on economic growth has been extensively investigated, the role of trade on the environment remains a challenging area. There are some studies finding support for trade-related environmental benefits while some studies observing environmental degradation as a result of export supported growth strategy. This study is an attempt to provide empirical evidence on the role of trade using data from the pollution-intensive sector: metal sector.

The regression results suggest a positive relationship between trade and environmental efficiency of firms using data from the metal sector over 2006–07 to 2014–15. The positive role of trade suggests that the market pressure influences firms, improves their environmental efficiency plausibly by adopting cleaner production. This results in lowering the firms' emission and improves their environmental efficiency. Policymakers may find merit in promoting export within the sector as the foreign customers create market pressure that influences the firm behaviour towards environment protection.

Table 5 Regression results: nonlinear relationship

	Fixed effect regression		Tobit regression	
	DV: EE1	DV: EE2	DV: EE1	DV: EE2
	Model 5	Model 6	Model 7	Model 8
Trade	0.00581*	0.00379**	0.00611*	0.00389**
	(0.00328)	(0.00184)	(0.00324)	(0.00182)
ISO 14001(0/1)	0.0133***	0.00504**	0.0132***	0.00510**
	(0.00443)	(0.00248)	(0.00435)	(0.00245)
Labour productivity (log)	−0.0122*	−0.00566	−0.0142**	−0.00622
	(0.00698)	(0.00391)	(0.00684)	(0.00386)
Sales-asset ratio	−0.0103***	−0.00467***	−0.00993***	−0.00459***
	(0.00284)	(0.00159)	(0.00279)	(0.00157)
Asset age	0.00663	0.0161	−0.00418	0.0130
	(0.0265)	(0.0148)	(0.0258)	(0.0146)
R&D (0/1)	0.00245	0.00115	0.00270	0.00123
	(0.00430)	(0.00241)	(0.00423)	(0.00238)
D1	−0.00861***	−0.00620***	−0.00889***	−0.00622***
	(0.00293)	(0.00164)	(0.00289)	(0.00162)
D2	−0.0208***	−0.0144***	−0.0214***	−0.0144***
	(0.00309)	(0.00173)	(0.00303)	(0.00171)
D3	−0.0348***	−0.0230***	−0.0359***	−0.0232***
	(0.00337)	(0.00189)	(0.00327)	(0.00185)
D4	−0.0474***	−0.0310***	−0.0486***	−0.0311***
	(0.00368)	(0.00206)	(0.00354)	(0.00202)
D5	−0.0633***	−0.0406***	−0.0647***	−0.0408***
	(0.00390)	(0.00219)	(0.00373)	(0.00214)
D6	−0.0808***	−0.0509***	−0.0826***	−0.0512***
	(0.00418)	(0.00234)	(0.00398)	(0.00229)
D7	−0.102***	−0.0629***	−0.104***	−0.0632***
	(0.00438)	(0.00245)	(0.00417)	(0.00240)
D8	−0.126***	−0.0770***	−0.128***	−0.0774***
	(0.00533)	(0.00298)	(0.00510)	(0.00292)
Size (log)	0.0111	0.00129	0.0108	0.000974
	(0.00788)	(0.00442)	(0.00769)	(0.00435)
Labour productivity square	0.00205**	0.00105**	0.00209**	0.00107**
	(0.000832)	(0.000466)	(0.000817)	(0.000460)
Sales-asset ratio square	−0.00172*	−0.000676	−0.00191**	−0.000736
	(0.000897)	(0.000503)	(0.000883)	(0.000497)

(continued)

Table 5 (continued)

	Fixed effect regression		Tobit regression	
	DV: EE1	DV: EE2	DV: EE1	DV: EE2
	Model 5	Model 6	Model 7	Model 8
Asset age square	−0.00150	0.00752	−0.00851	0.00528
	(0.0233)	(0.0131)	(0.0230)	(0.0129)
Size square	−0.00227***	−0.00108***	−0.00218***	−0.00106***
	(0.000433)	(0.000243)	(0.000423)	(0.000239)
Constant	0.901***	0.850***	0.902***	0.852***
	(0.0390)	(0.0219)	(0.0401)	(0.0256)
Observations	1001	1001	1001	1001
R^2	0.819	0.849		
Number of com	121	121	121	121

Standard errors in parentheses
*** $p < 0.01$, ** $p < 0.05$, * $p < 0.1$
Source Authors estimates

References

Fujii, H., Iwata, K., Kaneko, S., & Managi, S. (2013). Corporate environmental and economic performance of Japanese manufacturing firms: Empirical study for sustainable development. *Business Strategy and the Environment, 22*(3), 187–201.

Guttikunda, S. K., Goel, R., & Pant, P. (2014). Nature of air pollution, emission sources, and management in the Indian cities. *Atmospheric Environment, 95,* 501–510.

Holladay, J. S. (2010). *Are exporters mother nature's best friends?* Mimeo: New York University School of Law.

Jayanthakumaran, K., Verma, R., & Liu, Y. (2012). CO_2 emissions, energy consumption, trade and income: A comparative analysis of China and India. *Energy Policy, 42,* 450–460.

Khanna, M., Anton, W. R. Q. (2002). Corporate environmental management: Regulatory and market-based incentives. *Land Economics, 78*(4), 539–558.

Khanna, M., & Kumar, S. (2011). Corporate environmental management and environmental efficiency. *Environmental and Resource Economics, 50*(2), 227–242.

Mandal, S. K., & Madheswaran, S. (2010). Environmental efficiency of the Indian cement industry: An interstate analysis. *Energy Policy, 38*(2), 1108–1118.

Marginean, S. (2015). Economic globalization: From microeconomic foundation to national determinants. *Procedia Economics and Finance, 27,* 731–735.

Marin, G., & Mazzanti, M. (2009). The dynamics of delinking in industrial emissions: The role of productivity, trade and R&D. *Journal of Innovation Economics & Management, 1*(3), 91–117.

Ministry of Steel. (2012). *National Steel Policy*, Vol. 2012.

Mittal, M. L., Sharma, C., & Singh, R. (2012). Estimates of emissions from coal fired thermal power plants in India. *International Emission Inventory Conference, 2012,* 13–16.

Mukhopadhyay, K., & Chakraborty, D. (2005). Is liberalization of trade good for the environment? Evidence from India. *Asia Pacific Development Journal, 12*(1), 109.

OECD. (2018). *Asian economic integration report 2018 toward optimal provision of regional public goods in Asia and the Pacific*. Manila.

Prasad, M., & Mishra, T. (2017). Low-carbon growth for Indian iron and steel sector: Exploring the role of voluntary environmental compliance. *Energy Policy, 100,* 41–50.

Sadavarte, P., & Venkataraman, C. (2014). Trends in multi-pollutant emissions from a technology-linked inventory for India: I. Industry and transport sectors. *Atmospheric Environment, 99*, 353–364.

Sandhu, S., Smallman, C., Ozanne, L. K., & Cullen, R. (2012). Corporate environmental responsiveness in India: Lessons from a developing country. *Journal of Cleaner Production, 35*, 203–213.

Singh, N., Jain, S., & Sharma, P. (2015). Motivations for implementing environmental management practices in Indian industries. *Ecological Economics, 109*, 1–8.

Taskin, F., & Zaim, O. (2001). The role of international trade on environmental efficiency: A DEA approach. *Economic Modelling, 18*(1), 1–17.

The Energy and Resources Institute. (2013). *TERI Energy Data Directory and Yearbook 2012/13*. New Delhi.

Chapter 21
Prospects for Air Services in Indonesia Under Modified General Agreement on Trade in Services: India–China Dimension

Anil K. Kanungo and Abhishek Jha

1 Introduction

Trade in services in recent years has emerged as a priority area for growth in world economy. Acceleration in growth due to trade in services sectors particularly in the late 1990s and 2000s has motivated, especially some developing economies such as India and a few ASEAN economies to embrace and accomplish liberalized and complementary policies to siege advantageous opportunities unfolding in the world economy. Global economy subsequently has seen modern trends of services such as outsourcing, rise of BPO, KPO[1] and numerous retail administrations. With rapid pace of globalization and busy work schedule and lifestyle, consumerism in services is gaining momentum displaying a buoyant trend which is poised to give the sector a serious boost.

This work draws from the authors' previously published work "Air Services in Indonesia: India–China Dimension" in Cambridge Journal of China Studies, Date of Publication: Volume 13, No.1, June 2018, Cambridge, UK, Pages of the Published Article: 59–73.

A. K. Kanungo (✉)
Lal Bahadur Shastri Institute of Management (LBSIM) Delhi, Plot No.-11/7, Sector-11, Dwarka, New Delhi 110075, India
e-mail: anil@lbsim.ac.in; anilkanungo@hotmail.com

A. Jha
Centre for the Study of Regional Development, Jawaharlal Nehru University, New Delhi 110067, India
e-mail: jhaeconrlae@gmail.com

[1] After low end business processing largely confined to BPO sector, global MNCs started outsourcing high value-added business services. This activity has given rise to a new trend in outsourcing, where knowledge and application of knowledge took precedence over just mechanical process, popularly came to be known as knowledge process outsourcing (KPO). KPO includes research and work on IPRs, equity and finance, analytics, market research and data management.

P. Lakhanpal et al. (eds.), *Trade, Investment and Economic Growth*,
https://doi.org/10.1007/978-981-33-6973-3_21

As proliferation of trade in goods sector is largely supported by factors like tariff reduction and non-tariff barriers, services sector is largely controlled through regulation. It is crucial to see that even if regulation is a key determinant of rise in trade in services, but such regulations need to be deregulated at certain point of time to provide boost to the sector.

While India's integration with the global services market took place primarily through US and EU market, slowdown in India's services was experienced largely due to major collapse in these markets because of global financial crisis and USA turning protectionist soon after. This propelled India to explore other markets like East and Southeast Asia to find a foothold. Southeast Asia presently looks promising having its macroeconomic fundamentals robust and stable.[2] Earlier, due to the language barrier and cultural factors, Indian organizations were traditionally doing business transactions mainly with the Western companies and not with Southeast Asian nations. Currently, the services sector in ASEAN looks promising and continues to flourish steadily. As of 2013, this sector represented about 47% of GDP on average for the ASEAN economies. Even among Cambodia, Lao PDR, Myanmar and Vietnam, the contribution of the sector is substantial. In Singapore, around 60% of GDP is contributed by the services sector. In Malaysia and the Philippines, more than half of the economy is driven by business activities in this sector. For trade in services under the ASEAN Economic Community (AEC) Blueprint 2025, negotiations are due to commence on the ASEAN Trade in Services Agreement that aims to strengthen the existing ASEAN Framework Agreement on Services (Economic Outlook for Southeast Asia, China and India 2017).[3]

This growing demand of services in Southeast Asian countries has permitted Indian firms to scout for prospects here, and as of now, Indian organizations are carrying out more business with Japan, China, and other East Asian and ASEAN nations. Scope is wide and is feasible for Indian firms to join the ASEAN production systems by utilizing information technology and enabled services to foster richer economic and business linkages.

Formation of a vibrant and efficient services sector is fast becoming a prominent feature of modern economies. For over two decades, advanced economies often contribute to about 66% of the world's GDP through services. The shift from primary sector to secondary and then followed through services has been the focal point of structural change and economic transformation for many developing economies (Nayyar, 2019). In accordance with this pattern, it is seen that many developing markets are as of now embraced serious efforts to support and develop services industries and to put in place the regulatory structures required for more integrated international services markets. India and The Association of Southeast Asian Nations (ASEAN) are largely following this pattern in an attempt to make services sector as one of the main drivers of their economic integration with the world economy and prospective trade partners. Most of the developing economies from ASEAN region and India are presently concentrating on the growth of the services sector. This

[2] World Bank data 2017.

[3] https://www.oecd.org/dev/asia-pacific/SAEO2017_PV.pdf, accessed on December 27 2017.

is evident from the fact that India's contribution of services to GDP is impressive and bordering around 63% (Kapoor, 2014), thus contributing to economic activity, employment generation and growth.

Coupled with these factors, deregulation and liberalization of the service sector and proliferation of these activities of service economy perform a critical role in securing economic growth. Currently, travel and transport services command a prominent place in the service trade of many ASEAN nations (ITC Trade Map, COMTRADE). Indonesia is at the forefront of delivering such services to an expanding consumer base. Ever since the Indonesian government deregulated the aviation industry in 2000, Indonesia's aviation division has been developing at a faster pace in terms of travelers, carriers, armadas, flights, and air terminals. Such explosion in air services is noticed when one looks at the number of carrier travelers that has expanded from 9 million in 1990 to around 90 million in 2016. The same goes for the country's carrier armadas which have multiplied more than ten-fold from 102 aeroplanes in 1990 to 1030 in 2017 (Global Business guide).[4]

Indonesia's aviation sector provides enormous investment opportunities for domestic and foreign investors. There are several potential routes which are not so far completely encouraged particularly to destinations outside Java such as in Kalimantan and Papua. Having a GDP growth rate of 5.2% in 2017 and inflation registering around 4.2%, it can be an appropriate time for India to break into Indonesian market. It is largely recognized that India's competence in services does not lie in air services so visibly as compared to sectors such as IT, computer and information services and financial, accountancy but having known that India's strength in air services is growing and Indian airline system is an active member of International Air Transport Association (IATA), it is in the realm of exploration that India can venture into providing air services to Indonesian market after its open sky policies and can operate from Indonesian base to provide air services to other Southeast Asian nation. India's signing of ASEAN agreement and its "Look East Policy"[5] may provide some stimulus to that extent.

Similarly looking at China's aviation industry, it was discovered that Chinese government is taking initiatives to create residential assembling potential, make new air terminals, give professional training to new pilots and swell domestic maintenance capacity. China's top three emerging airlines—Air China, China Southern and China Eastern—are in the present days among the world's best ten airlines in terms of

---

[4]https://www.gbgindonesia.com/en/services/article/2017/indonesia_s_aviation_industry_flying_high_11719.php, accessed on December 26 2017.

[5]The Look East policy has emerged as an important foreign policy initiative of India in the post-Cold War period. It was launched in 1991 by the Narasimha Rao government with the aim of developing political contacts, increasing economic integration and forging security cooperation with countries of Southeast Asia. The policy marked a shift in India's perspective of the world, with the strategic and economic importance of Southeast Asia to India's national interests being recognized. The second phase, which began in 2003, extends the coverage of the Look East policy from Australia to East Asia, with Association of Southeast Asian Nations (ASEAN) as its core. The new phase thus marks a shift in focus from trade to wider economic and security cooperation, political partnerships, physical connectivity through road and rail links.

passenger volume. In 2005, the CAAC had reported that it would open up China's aviation sector to both domestic and foreign investment and empower private Chinese air carriers. This intends to spur the growth of private players in the sector such as Okay aviation routes, China's first private carrier.

Geographical proximity plays a critical role in trade and commerce. China seems to have that advantage vis-à-vis Indonesia. Besides, the familiarity of culture, race and heritage will be added advantage for China to penetrate into Indonesian market.

In an augmented gravity model, Hao (2016) indicates that the distance is significantly negatively related with the air transport services. This sets against the abovesaid argument that the close geographic proximity facilitates the business. Also, the FTA have a flourishing effect on the services trade which Chinese airline undertakes in Asia–Pacific. On the whole, the air transport network in China is moving in a fast pace which signals potential competition for India in providing transport services to Indonesia.

Against this backdrop, the paper attempts to explore if Indian aviation sector can enter into the markets of Indonesia and whether they would be able to supply such services. It also tries to assess if certain value-added services in term of auxiliary air services, which may be a current requirement for Indonesia, are India in a position to deliver that? It is time that Indian services sector must develop core competence in other sectors as it has done in IT and ITES. It aims to suggest that India should take forward the potentiality of this air services in Mode 3 and Mode 2 to negotiating table as opportunity exists in these modes. India's economic growth to an extent rests on such trade and cannot be confined to IT, financial, etc. If India to experience 7% growth rate, it is imperative for the all stakeholders such as the government, policy makers, trade and industry to realize that certain sectors need serious attention and negotiation for liberalized trade to occur in sector such as air services. Then, contribution of services sector will be fully realized.

2 Analysis of Air Service Sector

Observing the business potential and trade opportunities, it is witnessed that ASEAN region has a momentous contribution of Air Transport Services[6] Industry to its GDP. It shows an upsurge and lucrative trend, marked by vigorous growth particularly in certain emerging markets of ASEAN region and more so in Singapore, Indonesia, Thailand.[7] While global air cargo still persists somewhat at abated expectations, passenger progression is showing an upward trend, and air travelers are anticipated to double by 2035.[8] Globally, the air transport industry now supports 63 million jobs and contributes US$2.7 trillion to global GDP.

---

[6] Air transport services include commercial passenger services and air cargo.

[7] World Bank Working Paper (Air Transport Annual Report).

[8] See Footnote 7.

Quality performance of the global air services sector has made investments in air transport more lucrative.

For a second year, airlines' return on capital exceeded their cost of capital on a global scale, and many mid-sized airports in emerging markets are able to attract private capital to finance the needed infrastructure expansion. Every route or every region does not experience similar or improved financial performance. For example, the Asia–Pacific carriers were able to post a benefit of US$ 900 million in 2016, African airlines lost US$ 800 million, and many African airports still witness insufficient traffic as a result not able to finance needed investments (Air Transport Annual Report, World Bank, 2016).

Considering the prospects within the ASEAN nations and competency level of Indian air services, it is desirable that with the open sky policy and approaches adopted by ASEAN countries, India is in a comfortable position to explore opportunities in that region. Now that FTA between the two is in place, India may negotiate hard to take advantage of the sector. Negotiation in services between India and ASEAN has not experienced any serious kick start yet, not even among trade and industry, but both have realized the quantum of potential exists.

Analyzing broadly the requirement of ASEAN countries' demand in services, it was found that major ASEAN countries that are currently experiencing huge demand in these sectors are Singapore, Philippines, Thailand and Indonesia. Initial analysis of data[9] and observations gave us an idea that India has competitive advantage in some of the mentioned sectors where demands of services of those sectors are quite significant in these four countries. India therefore has distinct advantage in those sectors and can cater such services at competitive prices.

One of the key players in ASEAN countries currently is Indonesia whose requirement in air services (Air transport) is enormous. Data from National Input–Output Table provided by World Input–Output database[10] give us an idea that in 2000 it was 2.28 billion US$ from domestic value addition and imports component was 0.44 billion UD$. Subsequent years onward, which means from 2001 to 2005 domestic value addition and imports contracted making the difference between the exports and imports to almost nil. From 2006 onwards, it showed a continuous increase to make domestic consumption of air services to 18.5 billion, whereas the import component prevailed at 0.53 bn US$. So, the domestic consumption of this air services and import of services witnessed a CAGR of 53 and 1.2%; whereas exponential growth of domestic consumption of air transport services was 4.01%.[11]

It is observed that the structural change[12] that happened within the domestic air services in Indonesia has given rise to a huge number of domestic aircrafts joining the competition. In a way the industry has been solidified and enormous opportunities

[9]Managed by NWO (Netherlands Organization for scientific research).

[10]See Footnote 9.

[11]Based on author's calculation by taking into account Nation WIOD database.

[12]Indonesia deregulated its transport sector, including the air transport sector after the 1998 Asian Financial Crisis. The momentum for reform in the air transport sector was provided by the enactment of the Competition Law in 1999 which led to liberalization of air services.

for local players are in place. With the reopening of the sector occurring in 2001, entry of airlines has been facilitated.

A historical perspective gives us an idea that the state-owned enterprises, Garuda Indonesia and Merpati Nusantara dominated the industry. In 1992, both captured about 90% of the market. In 1996, however, the share of these two dropped to 68% (ADB, 1997). In 1993, the government temporally closed the industry for new entry. However, the moratorium was lifted in 2001. As a result, a number of new airlines emerged. By 2004, 28 new airlines were licensed. By this time, Merpati Nusantara and Garuda Indonesia had captured about 38% of Indonesia's air travel market, while the new entrants captured 35% of the market (Damuri and Anas 2005).

This euphoria lasted for some time as some of the airlines could not sustain their services due to lack of technical capacity or because of financial constraints. Toward the end of 2016, it was noticed that about 14 airlines are still in operation and active in domestic market by providing efficient air services (Input–Output Model–value addition—This can be accessed at www.wiod.org).

Since India has entered arrangement with ASEAN and Indonesia being a vital partner in that drive, India can consider providing such air services for the Indonesian consumers. India has a competitive open sky policy where it has energized the private sector to be the key service providers. As of now around six private airlines are competing in the market showing enough resilience to keep the sector buoyant and dynamic. Household consumption of air services both in household and imports is 2.6 billion US$ in 2014 in India.[13]

Some of the important dominions where India could possibly explore its business opportunities as far as Indonesian market is concerned are related to air connectivity and air services which are elaborated below. With the liberalization policies of air services of Indonesia, and India already having a cordial and historical relationship with the country, chances of India establishing good business and trade relationship with the country are more likely.

Key areas.

1. India can become a partner in establishing digital connectivity with ASEAN economies which will cater broadband services to the countries in the region. These computerized network ventures are of vital significance and can give superior air network and air services. This may cause a transformative effect on the economy and participation between ASEAN and India.
2. India is committed to extend financial as well as technological backup for ventures that aim to secure high-speed fiber optic systems, advanced towns, digital villages, countryside broadband, national knowledge network, secured communication systems and telecom training and skill development to avoid air accidents which are currently faced Indonesian government (Damuri & Anas, 2005).
3. India adopts a General Agreement on Trade in Services (GATS) approach, which contains provisions on national treatment, market access, modes of delivery and domestic regulation.

[13] WIOD database 2016.

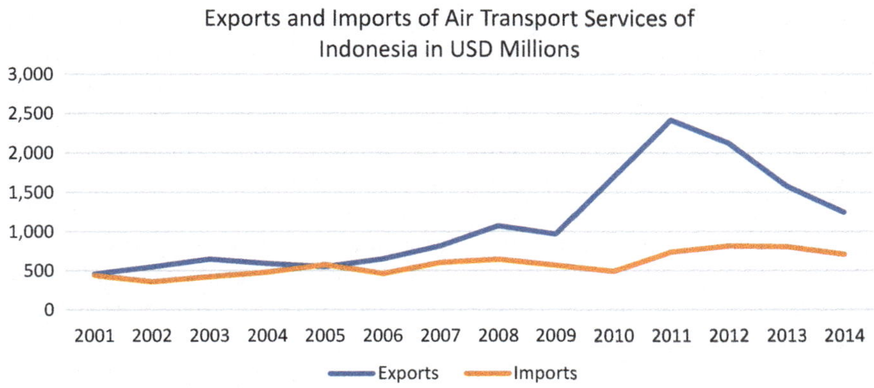

Fig. 1 Exports and imports of air transport services of Indonesia in USD Millions. *Source* National Input Output Table (NIOT), World Input Output table

3 India–Indonesia Trade Framework

Indonesia is an important services trade partner of India as India exports 10.2%[14] of services (excluding commercial air traffic as per annex GATS) to Indonesia among all ASEAN economies. In terms of value addition done in Indonesian air transport services, France and South Korea top the list, and India is unable to capitalize the opportunities thrown open by liberalization policies of Indonesia.

The air transport sector's talent to bridge Indonesia to developing nations and fast-growing cities can secure increasing economic growth of the connecting economy. As per the data provided by Oxford Economics,[15] there are 108 direct flight destinations among the ten fastest growing countries in the world, on the basis of GDP growth and 119 direct flight destinations among the 20 fastest growing countries. China is leading the league, by connecting maximum direct flights to Indonesia among the fastest growing economies followed by Vietnam and Philippines.

As per the same source, there are seven[16] direct weekly flights among the ten fastest growing cities in the world as measured by GDP growth and over 5500 direct weekly flights among the 100, growing cities but India is missing in capturing these business opportunities (Fig. 1).

Analyzing this export–import figure of air transport services of Indonesia, it is articulated that exports have truncated from 2011 to 2014 due to several policy actions of Indonesian government implemented in 2010. Few of these stringent policies include enactment of national aviation safety programme, classification of carrier services into full, medium and no frills. Apart from this, Indonesian government

[14]Calculated from ITC Trade Map, 2017.

[15]IATA, Oxford Economics IMF National Statistics, can be accessed at www.oxfordeconomics.com, accessed on December 20, 2017.

[16]Oxford Economics.

also applied surcharge if Avtur[17] price experiences consecutive surge in price.[18] Due to these convoluted policy implications, services trade of Indonesian air transport plummeted. Looking at this, now India has an opportunity to invest and expand the business of air transport services in Indonesia. The air transport subsector has also been a driver of service sector growth. Albeit smaller than the combined communication sectors, its GDP contributions have doubled in the last decade. After all, successful deregulation has again been a key driving force (Cristea et al., 2014). This argument juxtaposes the potential for Indian air transport service suppliers. An overriding step favouring deregulation will certainly generate revenues and employment in Indonesia and thus could be considered by Indonesian government as viable or doable proposal.

As per ADB Report 2016,[19] "*The rapidly expanding demand for air transport, enhanced by the upcoming ASEAN Open Skies Policy, already exceeds the capacity of many Indonesian airports, requiring extensions and new airport developments. Since airports and airline operations are typically regarded as economically and financially viable, there is little demand for external support.*"

As per the Indonesian Government policy, up to 49% of FDI in the form of foreign equity is allowed. Thus, there is a gateway for the Indian domestic business players of aviation sector to be the part of this lucrative and robust service sector mainly delivering under mode 3 (commercial presence abroad) and mode 2 (consumption abroad).[20]

4 Signing of India-ASEAN Agreement a Boost to This Opportunity

The implementation of ASEAN open sky encompasses three agreements: the ASEAN Multilateral Agreement on the Full Liberalization of Air Freight Services (MAFLAFS), the ASEAN Multilateral Agreement on Air Services (MAAS) and the ASEAN Multilateral Agreement on the Full Liberalization of Passenger Air Services (MAFLPAS). Authorization of these three agreements will permit any airlines designated by an ASEAN Member State to function both passenger and cargo scheduled services between its home economy and a point with international airport in another Member State and then to a point with international airport of a third Member State, without limitations on capacity and schedule (APEC Policy support unit) (APEC, 2017).

---

[17] Airlines aviation fuel.

[18] APEC Policy Support Unit, May 2017.

[19] https://www.opml.co.uk/sites/default/files/Growth%20in%20Indonesia_Drivers%20of%20recent%20economic%20growth.pdf

[20] The service consumer crosses the border to where the service supplier is located to purchase and consume services. Examples include holidays abroad, foreign education and overseas health care.

Here comes the role of India-ASEAN services FTA which needs to give impetus on air transport services and negotiate it in a requisite manner. The issue of enhancing air connectivity between India and Indonesia needs to be one of the pivotal themes under the India-ASEAN services policy modifications. This issue of connectivity may be taken up at the negotiating level as one of the key and front-runner agenda between the two governments. This needs to be stepped up on a fast track basis; otherwise, any other country will usurp this opportunity. There is a clear need for a comprehensive ASEAN-India Air Transport Agreement and extending it to fall into the scope of bilateral air services agreement (BASA).

Looking at increasing trade and business activities relating to air services, one of the obstacles that the Indonesian government is facing as of now is frequent air accidents. Such mishaps have the potentiality to put the industry at high risk and devoid of any expansion unless the government quickly puts in place serious measures to avoid such accidents. It was found that plethora of such mishaps are happening with Indonesian carriers. Air safety becomes a prime concern and needs to be checked if business and buoyancy of the sector are to be improved. One of the plane security assessment Web sites surveyed 407 key airlines of the world, giving each a safety tally out of seven. Of the ten airlines that scored paltry one point or less, all but one was from Indonesia. On one hand, Indonesian airport, i.e., Jakarta is considered as one of the top airports in the world which has recorded and is recording maximum number of passengers in Indonesia, and on other hand, nine out of ten airlines owned by Indonesia are ranked being least safe among the world. Detailed is mentioned below in a tabular format (Tables 1 and 2).

As safety of passengers seems to be a major concern in Indonesia, how India can provide any support services to reduce such hazards could be an area of engagement.

Table 1 The airlines awarded the lowest safety rating by the surveyed web site

1	Airlines	Country it Belongs to
1	Trigana Air Service	Indonesia
2	Batik Air	Indonesia
3	Citilink	Indonesia
4	Kalstar Aviation	Indonesia
5	Lion Air	Indonesia
6	Sriwijaya Air	Indonesia
7	Tara Air	Nepal
8	TransNusa Air Services	Indonesia
9	Wings Air	Indonesia
10	Xpress Air	Indonesia

Source www.AirlineRatings.com, accessed on December 22, 2017

Table 2 Global top 20 airports—passenger traffic 2015

Rank 2015	Country	Airport/Code	Total passengers
1	USA	Atlanta	101,491,106
2	China	Beijing	89,938,628
3	UAE	Dubai	78,010,265
4	USA	Chicago	76,949,504
5	Japan	Tokyo	75,316,718
6	UK	London	74,989,795
18	Indonesia	Jakarta	54,053,905

Source Airport traffic statistics, 2016

5 India's Strength

India can conceivably improve Indonesian air transport services by making a difference in giving way better pilot services, progressed technicalities and fair in time services. These measures may bolster the system to diminish such regular accidents. The track record and quality of services of Indian airlines such as Air India and others are way ahead in security standard compared to national carriers of Indonesia.[21] Indeed, in spite of the fact that Indonesia is an integral part of ASEAN, security proceeds to be a concern for the travelers as well as for the government. With the rate of deadly mishaps in Indonesia still being one of the highest in the world and most of its commercial aircrafts are still on the EU boycott list, the government has not acted quite positively to reduce such accidents, and apparently, there is no such significant policy in place to address this issue.

5.1 Revealed Comparative Advantage of Air Transport Services: India's Upsurge on the Ladder

India's air transport sector has so far buttressed close to 8 million jobs and contributed to $72 billion in GDP. According to IATA's recent 20-year air passenger forecast, it is estimated that India will surpass the UK to become the third largest market with 278 million passengers in 2025. Further by 2035, India is likely to be a market of 442 million passengers, with the aviation industry supporting 19.1 million jobs and contributing to $172 billion in GDP. This liberalization step in the Indian aviation market has minimized the institutional barriers which have hindered the freedom and flexibility of air transport operations among private investors. Now, competition within the aviation sector has become fiercer, the Airports Authority of India AAI and Public Private Partnership PPP in Indian airports are not only providing varied

[21] JACDEC Airline Safety Ranking 2017. In this survey, Air India stood at 40th position, whereas Indonesian airlines stood at 58th position.

services, but also attracting consumers with new infrastructure and full modern facilities (Kumar et al., 2018). It is also found that the airports managed through joint ventures are more efficient than others (Kashiramka et al., 2016). According to OECD STRI database, Indonesia has not restricted but limited the land acquisition for a foreigner to buy as far as air transport services are concerned. Thus, it can be observed India has a scope of JVs with the domestic partners or stakeholders of Indonesian airlines.

It becomes vital for us to evaluate revealed comparative advantage of air transport services exports of selected countries to compare the standing of India's comparative advantage for air transport services exports. Going by Balassa (1965), the revealed comparative advantage index (RCA) is estimated as

$$\mathrm{RCA}_{ij} = \frac{\frac{X_{ij}}{\sum i X_{ij}}}{\frac{\sum X_{ij}}{\sum i \sum j X_{ij}}}$$

where X_{ij} represents country i and exports j. $\sum_i X_{ij}$ is the sum total of exports of country i. $\sum X_{ij}$ is the world exports of jth commodity. $\sum_i \sum_j X_{ij}$ is the sum total of world exports. If the value of $\mathrm{RCA}_{ij} > 1$, it indicates that a country is competitive in export and vice versa. The index suffers from a few limitations such as unstable distribution over time, feeble ordinal ranking property and its ability to capture only exports (Yeasts 1985; Hinloopen and Van Marrewijk 2001). Further, the value of index varies from 0 to ∞ making it hard to compare the RCA of an exportable commodity having value >1. The main advantage of using RCA is that it considers the intrinsic advantage of a particular export commodity and is consistent with the changes in an economy's relative factor endowments and productivity. The disadvantage, however, is that it cannot distinguish between improvements in factor endowments and the pursuit of appropriate trade policies by a country (Batra & Khan, 2005). It also suffers from the problem of asymmetry as "pure" RCA is basically not comparable on both sides of unity as the index ranges from zero to one if a country is not specialized in a given commodity while it ranges from one to infinity if a country is specialized.

To address such limitations, several variants of Balassa index have evolved over the period of which Vollrath (1991) and Dalum et.al. (1998) indexes merit attention. Vollrath proposed three alternative measures of RCA (1) Relative trade advantage (RTA) expressed as the difference between revealed export advantage (RXA) and revealed import advantage (RMA) written as $\mathrm{RTA}_{ij} = \mathrm{RXA}_{ij} - \mathrm{RMA}_{ij}$, Where RXA $= (X_{ij}/X_t)/(X_{wj}/X_{wt})$, RMA $= (M_{ij}/M_t)/(M_{wj}/M_{wt})$ and X and M denote exports and imports. (2) Logarithmic transformation of RCA $= \ln(\mathrm{RXA}_{ij})$.

(3) Revealed competitiveness (RC) expressed as difference between logarithms of relative export advantage and relative import advantage: $\mathrm{RC} = \ln(\mathrm{RXA}_{ij}) - \ln(\mathrm{RMA}_{ij})$. A positive value of each index indicates a revealed comparative advantage, whereas a negative value indicates a revealed comparative disadvantage.

Dallum (1998) symmetrical revealed comparative advantage (SRCA) is an approximation of the log transformation of Balassa Index, ranging from -1 to $+$

1 with 0 as a neutral point. It is expressed as: $SI_{ij} = \frac{BI_{ij}-1}{BI_{ij}+1}$ where BI_{ij} is the Balassa index of country i and commodity j. Country i will have a comparative advantage for product j if the value of SRCA is greater than zero and disadvantage if it is less than zero. The distribution of Dallum index fulfills the normality assumption more often as compared to the Balassa index making it propitious to use for econometric analysis (Laursen, 1998).

As per the table, USA, UK and Germany are having high potential in revealed comparative advantage (RCA) in exports of their air transport services because their RCA is exceeding one. For India though, the value of RCA is less than 1, but in the past three years, there is an overall rise in the competitiveness of air transport services exports, hence the government may like to sign more of joint ventures at an aggressive manner, and at the same time, the government possibly can target Southeast Asia as a key traffic zones for India because large number of Indians are traveling to this region for eclectic purposes such as tourism and academics. This is expected to further surge with the kind of policies the Indian government is implementing like UDAAN scheme. In the way that Gaya, the major city in Bihar, has a center of attraction for Buddhism, hence it can provide required impetus for the Southeast Asian region's connectivity. Indian government is trying to connect and modernize regional airports, which will boost the connectivity and competitiveness and in the process of building many airports at different cities to provide better connectivity.

Looking at the Trade Map data of ITC, Indian exports of air transport services have increased from US$1.4 billion in 2009 to US $5.8 billion in 2018 registering four times increase in exports.

It can be inferred from Table 3 that top three economies such as USA, Germany and China are having more exports of air services because these three economies are having more GDPs at nominal prices compared to India which is also reflected in Table 3 as we see the exports of services in RCA of India are lower than these economies.

One of the possible reasons of India's RCA in exports of air transport services being lower is due to miniscule exports of air transport passengers. This miniscule

Table 3 Revealed comparative advantage of air transport services export

Economies	2014	2015	2016	2017	2018
China	–	–	–	0.830	1.006
France	0.874	0.826	0.824	0.765	0.849
Germany	1.082	1.086	1.134	1.158	1.436
India	0.667	0.471	0.519	0.450	0.581
United Kingdom	1.060	1.127	1.127	1.119	–
United States of America	1.524	1.476	1.428	1.360	1.695

Source Authors' calculation using ITC Trade Map Data compiled by COMTRADE

Table 4 Exports value of air transport services, in USD Billion

Economies	2014	2015	2016	2017	2018
China	–	–	–	11.390	12.962
France	14.365	12.346	12.262	12.654	11.959
Germany	19.552	17.583	18.554	21.424	22.969
India	6.311	4.299	4.808	5.013	5.761
United Kingdom	23.869	23.445	22.459	24.001	–
United States of America	68.053	65.215	62.049	65.229	67.804

Source Authors' calculation using ITC trade map data compiled by COMTRADE

value of exports of air passenger traffic in case of India is about 7.6%[22] of total air transport exports.

Table 4 mentions about the exports of air transport services in absolute terms, stating that USA tops the exports of air transports services in absolute terms, followed by UK, Germany and China. India is far behind these economies, but making concerted efforts to catch up with the other economies.

According to the Table 5, India's exports to gross world output are maximum as compared with USA and China. This clearly indicates that there is a predilection for air transport exports in the gross world output for India, although the absolute level of gross world output is lowest. This requires constructive policy intervention from the policymakers to address this issue and frame policies that would harness the sector to realize larger potential of the sector.[23]

6 Value Adding in Air Transport Services of Indonesia

Apart from standard transport air services, quality control and value addition in other auxiliary services are vital to make aviation sector resilient, timely, user friendly and secure. In the field of auxiliary services, India's performance seems to be ahead of Indonesia. This dimension is echoed in India's aviation industry when we take into account contribution of this sector to its economy. This further elaborated in two different ways, namely through taxes and investment and by using advanced

[22]As per ITC Trade Map data, India's exports for passenger air transport air services are US$ 0.444 billion, whereas air transport services exports are US$ 5.761 billion.

[23]Finance Minister Nirmala Sitharaman announced in 2019–2020 budget on July 05, 2019, that the government will re-initiate disinvestment of national carrier Air India as well as open up Foreign Direct Investment (FDI) in aviation.

There is 100% FDI allowed in aviation, but foreign airlines can only invest up to 49% in an Indian airline. Also, foreign investment in Air India is capped at 49%. The government's decision to revisit privatization of Air India follows an attempt last year that met with failure when no private player came forward to express an interest in the debt-laden carrier. https://www.thehindu.com/business/budget/union-budget-2019-20-air-india-disinvestment-set-to-take-off-again/article28298695.ece accessed on July 09, 2019.

Table 5 Exports, gross world output and % of exports to world's gross output of air transport of China, USA and India, (in USD Million)

Year	China			USA			India		
	Exports	Gross Output	% of exports to World's gross output	Exports	Gross Output	% of exports to World's gross output	Exports	Gross Output	% of exports to World's gross output
2000	3728	13,311	28.00445	22,093	123,668	17.86	753	1700	44.29
2001	4188	15,135	27.67161	18,559	107,172	17.32	650	1647	39.44
2002	4938	16,834	29.33318	17,811	100,688	17.69	714	1649	43.33
2003	6088	17,800	34.20312	16,872	109,861	15.36	943	2450	38.51
2004	8686	20,956	41.44936	20,195	120,550	16.75	1297	2723	47.62
2005	10,425	25,692	40.57823	23,423	133,590	17.53	1683	2739	61.44
2006	13,998	28,541	49.04557	25,118	145,060	17.32	2061	3374	61.06
2007	18,207	33,962	53.60898	28,611	155,997	18.34	3438	3731	92.16
2008	22,461	41,477	54.15259	36,019	165,019	21.83	3224	3224	100.00
2009	17,892	42,909	41.69694	29,909	136,328	21.94	2354	3134	75.11
2010	22,277	49,294	45.19301	35,293	153,610	22.98	3585	4374	81.96
2011	24,976	60,566	41.23705	41,345	170,379	24.27	3554	5024	70.74
2012	24,052	68,138	35.29852	45,049	178,090	25.30	2891	4851	59.59
2013	23,583	76,094	30.99213	46,625	181,418	25.70	2389	4629	51.62
2014	22,923	84,735	27.05253	48,076	188,758	25.47	2367	5016	47.18

Source Authors' Calculation based on WIOD Database (Data shown in Table 4 are till 2014 because current availability of data in WIOD database is up to 2014)

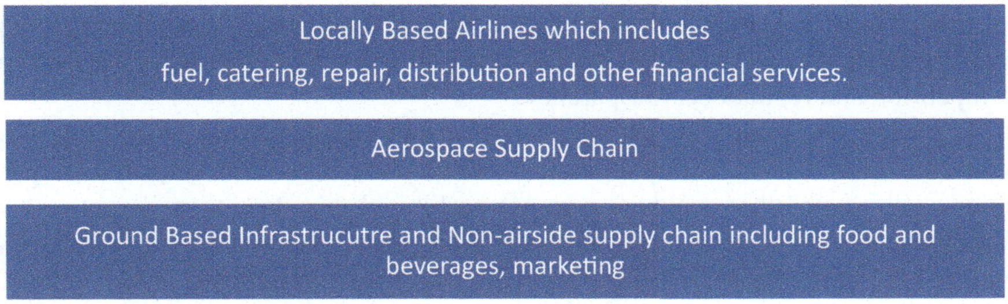

Fig. 2 Schematic diagram of value chains in Indian aviation and air transport services

technology. The Indian aviation sector rather generates more gross value addition (GVA) per employee[24] than the economy as a whole, raising the overall productivity of the economy. Such value addition, Indian government, can provide to Indonesian market through value chain.

This value addition which is foremost input of the airline business is in the realm of energy, and aircraft and its maintenance. Apart from those core inputs, the airline business also banks on other services, such as food and beverages services, trade and insurance. ICAO (2013) in its assessment of the aviation value chain suggested to include aircraft leasing services and manufacturing, air navigation services, maintenance repair and overhaul services, fuel supply, ground handling and systems for selling tickets including online systems. For Indonesia, fuel consists of 35% of the value addition followed by warehousing transport services, administrative services, retail trade of vehicles and food and accommodation services. Manufacturing food and beverages consist of 5.7% of the total value chains.[25] 4.8 billion USS[26] is the value-added exports by India to the world in terms of airlines hospitality services which could be one of the components of value addition that can be extended to the Indonesian market (Fig. 2).

Indonesian air services market has high potential as the government is determined to improve its infrastructure to promote its tourism sector (Wang et al., 2017). As demand for air services is growing in Indonesia, more and more airports are going to be built as Indonesia is a partner country of ASEAN, it will be able to connect more to the Asia Pacific region by connecting itself to the East Asian and South Asian economies where India is an emerging economy and currently well positioned because of promising growth and integration with the world economy. There seems to be synergy between India and Indonesia being further linked up through culturally and historically. India had a long historical trade relation with Indonesia. This familiarity can be exploited to increase trade realization better.

The authors also analyzed Indonesia's position in terms of services trade restrictiveness of air transport. From the OECD STRI database, it was observed that Indonesia is moderately restrictive in this sector hovering around 0.48 in a scale

[24]WIOD database 2016.

[25]According to authors' calculations from WIOD database by using NIOT.

[26]Calculated from WIOD Table.

of 0 to 1. The five parameters that need to be explained are restriction on foreign entry, restriction to movement of people, other discriminatory measures, barriers to competition and regulatory transparency.

The first component which is the restriction on foreign entry says that there is a restriction of up to 49% equity regarding foreign ownership. With respect to acquisition, it is argued that acquisition is not prohibited, but there is a limitation. A foreigner can only be granted the Right of Use or lease for a maximum of 25 years with possible extension for 20 further years. After the extension period has expired, the owner can request the renewal for the same period. An exception is in place for investment purposes, where investors can request extension and renewal of Right to Use in advance. Therefore, the investor can have the Right of Use for 90 years.

It is mandatory for an employer to appoint an Indonesian national as an associate to a foreign worker for technology and knowledge transfer purposes. The associate should also receive training to attain the same qualification as the position held by the foreign worker. This regulation exempts top executive positions or temporary/emergency foreign workers.

The second component which talks of restriction of movement of people is fairly liberal. The only requirement is to get permission from Ministry of Manpower for a foreigner to work in Indonesia. Requisite labor market test is applicable on Intra Corporate Transferees (ICT), contractual services supplier and independent services suppliers with respect to air transport services. Duration of stay for a foreigner is normally 2 years in certain circumstances, and it can be for 4 years.

The third component which is about other discriminatory restrictions is found that Indonesia does not have any restriction through the period from 2014 till 2017.

The fourth component which is barriers to competition is hardly restrictive in Indonesia. There is law on anti-monopoly and unfair competition which applies to foreign firms as well. Minimum capital requirement to establish air freight transportation company is US$ 7.5 million to be invested.

The last component which is regulatory transparency has been made liberal over last four years. Number of working days to complete all mandatory procedures to register a company has been significantly reduced from 75.5 days in 2014 to 24.9 days in 2017. For China and India, it is fairly liberal, and it takes about 27 days and 28.5 days, respectively.

The total cost to establish one company in Indonesia as a percentage income per capita has also reduced from 21.9% in 2014 to 19.4% in 2017. With respect to policies on air transport services, there is symmetry with no outliers. Table 6 provides trade restrictiveness of Indonesia and other countries. As per the Table 6, Germany seems to be most liberal in terms of air transport services and logistic cargo handling services. Indonesia is fairly less liberal in both sectors.

Table 6 Index of air transport services

Economics	Services trade restrictive index of air transport services[a]	Services trade restrictive index of logistics cargo handling services
Indonesia	0.48	0.46
China	0.48	0.41
India	0.57	0.40
USA	0.53	0.25
Germany	0.37	0.15
UK	0.39	0.16
France	0.39	0.19

[a]STRI lies between 0 and 1. 0 being least restrictive and 1 being most restrictive
Source OECD Services Trade Restrictive Index (STRI) database

7 Chinese Outlook in Indonesia's Air Transport Services

China is the world's second largest and one of the world's fastest burgeoning civil aviation markets. The industry has grown at double-digit rates for several years. From 2000 to 2014, exponential growth rate of household consumption of air transport services of China remained at 18.1[27]%. This figure is though impressive, but unable to articulate the real scenario. Comparing with world air transport services, role of Chinese's air transport services is at miniscule. Exports of China's air transport services for above-specified time period are again impressive from growth rate point of view, else is insignificant. China's air transport network is still a point-to-point network instead of a hub-and-spoke system (Qiang et al., 2014). Close to 88% of China's air transport services are utilized by the domestic passengers itself, thus indirectly making Chinese aviation sector's predilection for domestic services. Numbers reflect an enervated intra industry scenario for air services between China and Indonesia. According to WIOD, 2014 Chinese's air transport's contribution in the Indonesian's output of air transport is USD 2 million. But relatively the final consumption expenditure by households of Indonesia is USD 8 million due to Chinese input of air transport services.

Indonesian public administration and defense; compulsory social security has received the maximum inputs from the Chinese air transport sector, which articulates the non-commercial usage of Chinese air transport services in Indonesian air services.

Still Chinese manufacturing and allied services dominate the Indonesian domestic production framework. Manufacture of chemicals and chemical products is making to top the list of inputs that have gone into all the sectors of the Indonesian sectors. Chinese services play a minimal role in providing the inputs to the Indonesian economy. Out of USD 22 Billion[28] of inputs provided by the Chinese sectors, 93% is coming from manufacturing and allied services. Thus, exercising of China-ASEAN

[27]Author's calculation from National Input–Output Table provided by WIOD.

[28]WIOD database author's calculation.

FTA of services becomes crucial at this level from policy implication point of view. Article 8 of China-ASEAN air transport agreement talks about the security and operational framework of aviation industries between China and ASEAN members which could be expedited for expanding trade in air transport services.

8 Conclusion

The aviation sector in Indonesia has an optimistic prospect with great potential. With an estimated population of 255 million people, Indonesia is the world's fourth most populous nation after China, India and the USA. It is also the leading market in Southeast Asia as its population accumulates up to 40% of the 625 million combined population of the ten ASEAN countries. Being an archipelago comprising over 17,000 islands and with poor land-based transport infrastructure, Indonesia naturally necessitates robust air travel network for the mobility of its people and goods, and aviation seems to be the most indispensable sector as far as mobility and trade facilitation are concerned.

In 2017, president of Indonesian agreed to prioritize five sectors which are infrastructure, tourism, maritime, energy and food sectors. The Ministry of Transportation will prioritize infrastructure development programs, especially accessibility that supports the tourism sector, including developing airports close to the leading tourist destinations.

Looking at the analysis, it was observed that the Chinese airlines are though growing, yet they have not made enough inroads into the Indonesian market as the central government in China consciously focuses on the manufacturing aspects of aviation and auxiliary services, instead of directly looking at the growth of the commercial air passenger services. Chinese air services currently circumvented with domestic meeting demand.

To avail these growing opportunities in Indonesian market, Indian government needs to put it negotiation on a fast track assuming ASEAN countries' engagement with India will move forward as their 25 years of cooperation promises deeper engagement in 2017.

Overall looking at the prospects of India's entry into Indonesian air services market, it is found that India has relative strength in some of the air services which can be extended to Indonesian market. India has relative advantage in terms of pricing which can be replicated in Indonesian market if Indian domestic players like Air India, Indigo, Spice Jet, Jet airways are allowed to operate either through modes 3 or mode 2 or through both (once air transport services are revisited by GATS for inclusion). This is possible because these are considered as low-cost airlines. Besides, Indian domestic players have already ventured into foreign territories[29] by providing competitive, just in time and safe services which provides an edge to these airlines to

[29]Jet Airways everyday flight from Delhi to London and return. Similarly, Indigo Airlines is providing air services to UAE, Middle East, Dubai, etc. What we intend to portray is after GATS

operate in the domestic Indonesian market and can provide other destination services to other countries of ASEAN. Service delivery through mode 3 and mode 2 is doable for Indian domestic airlines. With the proven capability and services facilities of these Indian domestic airlines such as Air India, Indigo, Jet airways, and Spice Jet, India can deliver such services at competitive rate. Hence, Indian government needs to act bilaterally with Indonesian government to push its air services sector through mode 3 and mode 2.

As there is a requirement for building airports in Indonesia, Indian companies such as GMR[30] can build such airports as they have already done it in Philippines which is a neighbor country of Indonesia and also a part of ASEAN region. This can promote India's overseas foreign direct investment as well as establish brand image and technological capability of Indian companies in the region and in Indonesia in particular. India seems to be having some advantage where it can provide value-added services especially in the auxiliary services sector of air services.

There is a scope for India's air services to be noticed and marketed abroad. Indian government should provide adequate support and cooperation to Indian domestic airlines to be an active player in this global airline services industry.

In relation to services restrictiveness index, it was realized that though Indonesia is not the most restrictive country in air transport services, yet it is fairly restrictive. But looking at the current governmental initiatives and individual STRI measures, it is observed that it is slowly opening up.

---

revisit to air transport services for commercial traffic services, Indigo can provide flights from Denpasar (Bali) to Jakarta (in a domestic framework).

[30]GMR Group is also the only Indian airport developer to have developed and operated airports outside India. GMR Infrastructure in partnership with Megawide Construction Corporation of Philippines is operating and developing Mactan Cebu International Airport.

Annexure 1: Input–Output Model

Basic Input Output Model: Leontief Inverse

A two-country IIO table			Intermediate use		Final Use		Total use
			Country 1	Country 2	Country 1	Country 2	
			1···N		1···N		
Supply	Country 1	1:N	1's use of its own inputs	2's use of inputs from 1	1's use of its own final goods	2's use of final goods from 1	1's total output
	Country 2	1:N	1's use of inputs from 2	2's use of its own inputs	1's use of final goods from 2	2's use of its own final goods	2's total output
Value added			1's value added	2's value added			
Total supply			1's total output	2's total output			

As indicated in figure, all output must be used as an intermediate or final good at home or abroad.

World Input Output Database (WIOD) latest table provides data of 43 countries across 56 sectors.

$$X = AX + F,$$

where X is the $GN \times 1$ vector of gross output, consisting of stacked vectors of gross output for each country. The $N \times 1$ vector X_i denotes gross output of country i in each sector:

$$X = \begin{bmatrix} X1 \cdots & & \\ \vdots & \ddots & \vdots \\ & & \cdots XG \end{bmatrix}$$

The $GN \times GN$ matrix A provides the direct intermediate input–output coefficients, where A_{ij} denotes the $N \times N$ matrix giving direct use of inputs supplied by each sector of country i in each sector of country j.

$$A = \begin{bmatrix} A11 & \cdots & A1G \\ \vdots & \ddots & \vdots \\ AG1 & \cdots & AGG \end{bmatrix}$$

Final demand is given by the $GN \times 1$ matrix F, which gives world demand for final goods. The $N \times 1$ vector F_i denotes the value of final goods produced in country i.

$$= \begin{matrix} F1 \\ \vdots \\ FG \end{matrix}$$

where $F_i = \sum_i F_{ij}$ and $F_{ij} = D_{ij} + E_{ij}$

$$\begin{bmatrix} F11 & \cdots & F1G \\ \vdots & \ddots & \vdots \\ FG1 & \cdots & FGG \end{bmatrix} = \begin{bmatrix} D11 & \cdots & 0 \\ \vdots & \ddots & \vdots \\ 0 & \cdots & DGG \end{bmatrix} + \begin{bmatrix} 0 & \cdots & E1G \\ \vdots & \ddots & \vdots \\ EG1 & \cdots & 0 \end{bmatrix}$$

where D_{ij} is the $N \times 1$ vector of final goods and services produced and consumed domestically, and E_{ij} denotes the $N \times 1$ vector of final goods and services produced in i and exported to (and consumed in) country j.

$$X = (I - A)^{-1} F = BF$$

where B is the $GN \times GN$ "Leontief inverse" matrix. Elements of this matrix express the total output, used both directly and indirectly, required to produce \$1 of final goods and services. As with the direct coefficient matrix A, the Leontief inverse matrix B is composed of $N \times N$ submatrices B_{ij} that denote the value of output used in each sector of country i to produce final goods in each sector of country j.

All gross output produced by country r must be used as an intermediate good or a final good at home or abroad, which can be expressed using the equation:

$$X_{rr} = A_{rr} X_r + A_{rs} X_S + Y_{rs} + Y_{rr}$$

where X_r is the $N \times 1$ gross output vector of country r, Y_{rs} is the $N \times 1$ final demand vector that gives demand in country s for final goods produced in r, and A_{rs} is the $N \times N$ IO coefficient matrix, giving intermediate use in s of goods produced in r.

References

ADB. (1997). Report and recommendation of the president to the board of directors on a proposed loan and technical assistance grant to the republic of Indonesia For the Eastern Islands air transport development project.

Air Transport Services notes by WTO accessed through https://www.wto.org/english/tratop_e/serv_e/transport_e/transport_air_e.htm.

Air Transport Annual Report, World Bank. (2016).

APEC. (2017). Indonesia: Structural reform in air transport service. APEC Policy Support Unit.

Balassa, B. (1965). Trade liberalization and "revealed comparative advantage". *Manchester School of Economic and Social Studies, 33*, 99–123.

Batra, A., & Khan, Z. (2005). Revealed comparative advantage: An analysis for India and China, Working Paper no.168. Indian Council for Research on International Economic Relation (ICRIER), New Delhi, pp. 1–53.

Cristea, A., Hillberry, R., & Mattoo, A. (2014). Open skies over the middle east policy research working paper; no. WPS 6937. Washington, DC: World Bank Group. https://documents.worldbank.org/curated/en/2014/06/19705719/open-skiesovermiddle-east.

Dalum, B., Laursen, K., & Villumsen, G. (1998). Structural change in OECD export specialisation patterns: de-specialisation and 'stickiness'. *International Review of Applied Economics, 12*(3), 423–443.

Damuri, Y. R., & Anas, T. (2005). Strategic directions for ASEAN airlines in a globalizing world: The emergence of low cost carriers in South East Asia. REPSF Project, (04/008).

Hao, L. (2016). How to improve competitiveness of Chines airlines in the world's cargo market? In *Advances in economics, Business and Management research* (Vol. 16).

Kapoor. R. (2014). Creating jobs in India's organized manufacturing sector. *Working Paper of Indian Council for Research on International Economic Relations,* 286.

Kashiramka, S., Banerjee, R., Kumar, A., & Jain, P. K. (2016). Efficiency analysis of airports in India in a changing environment: A data envelopment analysis approach. *Journal of Transport Economics and Policy, 50*(4), 384–403.

Kumar, A., Dash, M. K., & Sahu, R. (2018). Performance efficiency measurement of airports: A comparative analysis of airports authority of India and public private partnership. *International Journal of Strategic Decision Sciences, 9*(2), 19–37.

Laursen, K. (1998). Revealed comparative advantage and the alternatives as measures of international specialization. DRUID Working Paper, No. 98–30. Danish Research Unit for Industrial Dynamics (DRUID).

Nayyar, D. (2019). *Regional Asia: Diversity in development*. New Delhi, India: Oxford University Press.

Qiang, G., Wang, K., Fan, X. L., & Fu, X. W. (2014). Why Chinese airlines haven't become leading cargo carriers-analyzing air freight network and international trade drivers for mainland China. *Journal of Economic Development, 10,* 1–26.

State of Air transport, ICAO (2013).

Wang, Z. et al. (2017). Measures of participation in global value chains and global business cycles. NBER Working Paper Series, 23222.

Vollrath, T. L. (1991). A theoretical evaluation of alternative trade intensity measures of revealed comparative advantage. *Weltwirtschaftliches Archive, 127*, 265–279; *Review of World Economics, 127*, 265–280.

The manufacturer's authorised representative in the EU is Springer Nature Customer Service Centre GmbH, Europaplatz 3, 69115 Heidelberg, Germany. If you have any concerns regarding our products, please contact ProductSafety@springernature.com

Printed and bound by CPI Group (UK) Ltd, Croydon, CR0 4YY
30/09/2026
02225295-0013